ZINN & THE ART OF MOUNTAIN BIKE MAINTENANCE

4th Edition

LENNARD ZINN

Illustrated by Todd Telander

VELO press

BOULDER, COLORADO

Zinn & the Art of Mountain Bike Maintenance, 4th Edition

Printed in the United States of America

10 9

Distributed in the United States and Canada by Publishers Group West

Library of Congress Cataloging-in-Publication Data
Zinn, Lennard.
Zinn & the art of mountain bike maintenance / Lennard Zinn ; illustrated by Todd Telander. — 4th ed.
p. cm.
Rev. ed of Zinn and the art of mountain bike maintenance. c1997.
Includes bibliographical references and index.
ISBN 978-1-931382-59-5 (paper)
1. All terrain bicycles—Maintenance and repair. I. Title: Zinn & the art of mountain bike maintenance. II. Zinn, Lennard. Zinn & the art of mountain bike maintenance. III. Title.

TL430.Z56 2001
629.28'772—dc21 2001035854

VeloPress®, a division of Inside Communications, Inc.
1830 N. 55th Street
Boulder, Colorado 80301–2700 USA
303/440-0601; Fax 303/444-6788; E-mail velopress@insideinc.com

To purchase additional copies of this book or other VeloPress books, call 800/234-8356 or visit us on the web at www.velopress.com.

Cover design by Kristina Kachele
Interior design and composition by Erin Johnson
Cover photo by Don Karle, bike built by Lennard Zinn.

ZINN & THE ART OF MOUNTAIN BIKE MAINTENANCE

To Sonny, my wife,
without whose support this book
could not have been written;
or at least a few more decades
would have passed before
it got done.

TABLE OF CONTENTS

Introduction . . . 1

CHAPTERS

1 Tools . . . 11
2 Basic stuff: Preride inspection, wheel removal, and general cleaning . . . 23
3 Emergency repairs: How to get home when something big breaks or you get hurt . . . 37
4 Chains . . . 53
5 Transmission: Front and rear derailleurs, cables, and shifters . . . 67
6 Wheels: Tires, rims and spokes, hubs, cassettes, and freewheels . . . 103
7 Brakes: Cables, levers, and calipers . . . 135
8 Cranks and bottom brackets . . . 183
9 Pedals . . . 203
10 Saddles and seatposts . . . 221
11 Handlebars, stems, and headsets . . . 233
12 Wheel building . . . 267
13 Forks . . . 287
14 Frames . . . 323
15 Cycling computers . . . 345

APPENDIXES

A Troubleshooting index . . . 351
B Gear development . . . 359
C Mountain bike fitting . . . 363
D Torque table . . . 373
E Pedal and cleat compatibility . . . 391

Glossary . . . 395
Bibliography . . . 403
Illustration index . . . 405
Index . . . 409
About the author . . . 421

A TIP OF THE HELMET TO ...

My heartfelt thanks go out to Todd Telander, whose illustrations made the procedures more intelligible and beautiful; to my editors and in-house support system, Charles Pelkey and Mark Saunders, for separating the wheat from the chaff and adding more wheat when necessary; to Terry Rosen, for bugging me to write this book for so many years; to Mike Sitrin, formerly of VeloPress, for doing the same and promising to publish the first edition when I did; to Felix Magowan and John Wilcockson of Inside Communications for their vision, financial support and encouragement; to John Muir and Robert Pirsig, for writing such great books to encourage this effort. Special thanks to Erin Johnson for making it look beautiful, and to VeloPress for the countless efforts to improve it.

For technical assistance with the details, thanks to Wayne Stetina, Steve Hed, Ken Beach, and to Scott, John, and Rusty at Louisville Cyclery (Louisville, Colorado), as well as to folks at Shimano, RockShox, Manitou, Cane Creek, Hayes, Avid, ITM, 3T, Cinelli, Deda, Easton, Salsa, Mavic, Selle San Marco, Cannondale and Ritchey. Thanks go especially to Portia Masterson of Self Propulsion in Golden, Colorado, for her suggestions for the second edition and to Charlie Hancock, Sander Rigney, Doug Bradbury and Chris DiStefano for assistance with the third edition.

I also want to thank my entire family for all of their support and inspiration: Emily and Sarah, my daughters, for showing me that books can be written, completed, and published at a prolific rate; Dad and Mom, for encouraging me my whole life; Rex and Steve, for their suggestions; Kai, Ron, and Dad, for being authors themselves and an inspiration to me; and Marlies, for taking the kids when I needed it. Thanks, Sarah, for proving Groucho Marx right.

INTRODUCTION

Peace of mind isn't at all superficial, really. It's the whole thing. That which produces it is good maintenance; that which disturbs it is poor maintenance. What we call workability of the machine is just an objectification of this peace of mind. The ultimate test's always your own serenity. If you don't have this when you start and maintain it while you're working, you're likely to build your personal problems right into the machine itself.

—Robert M. Pirsig, *Zen and the Art of Motorcycle Maintenance*

ABOUT THIS BOOK

This book is intended for those with an interest in maintaining their own mountain bikes. This book has been written for mountain bike owners who do not think they're capable of maintaining their own bikes. In *Zen and the Art of Motorcycle Maintenance*, Robert Pirsig explores the dichotomy between the purely classical and purely romantic views of the world, a dichotomy that also applies to mountain biking. Riding a mountain bike is generally a romantic experience of emotion, inspiration, and intuition, even when solving the complex physics of how to negotiate a technical section of trail without putting your foot down. Mountain bike mechanics, however, is a purely classical structure of underlying form dominated by reason and physical laws. The two practices—bike riding and bike maintaining—fit eloquently together. Each is designed to function in a particular way, and one without the other would be missing out on half the fun.

The romantic can appreciate how success at bike mechanics requires that the procedures be done with love, without which the care you imagined putting into your mountain bike will be lost. And even the pure romantic can follow the simple step-by-step procedures and "exploded" diagrams (of which Fig. i.1 is an extreme example and is the *only* one in the book not intended to be simple and clear!) in this book and discover a passion for spreading new grease on old parts.

Zinn & the Art of Mountain Bike Maintenance is organized in such a way that you can pick maintenance tasks appropriate for you. The repairs illustrated on these pages require no special skills to perform; anyone can do them. It takes only a willingness to learn.

Mountain bikes are notoriously resilient creatures. You can keep one running a really long time just by changing the tires and occasionally lubricating the chain. Chapter 2 is about the most minimal

i.1 **Believe it or not, you will be able to put all of this back together!**

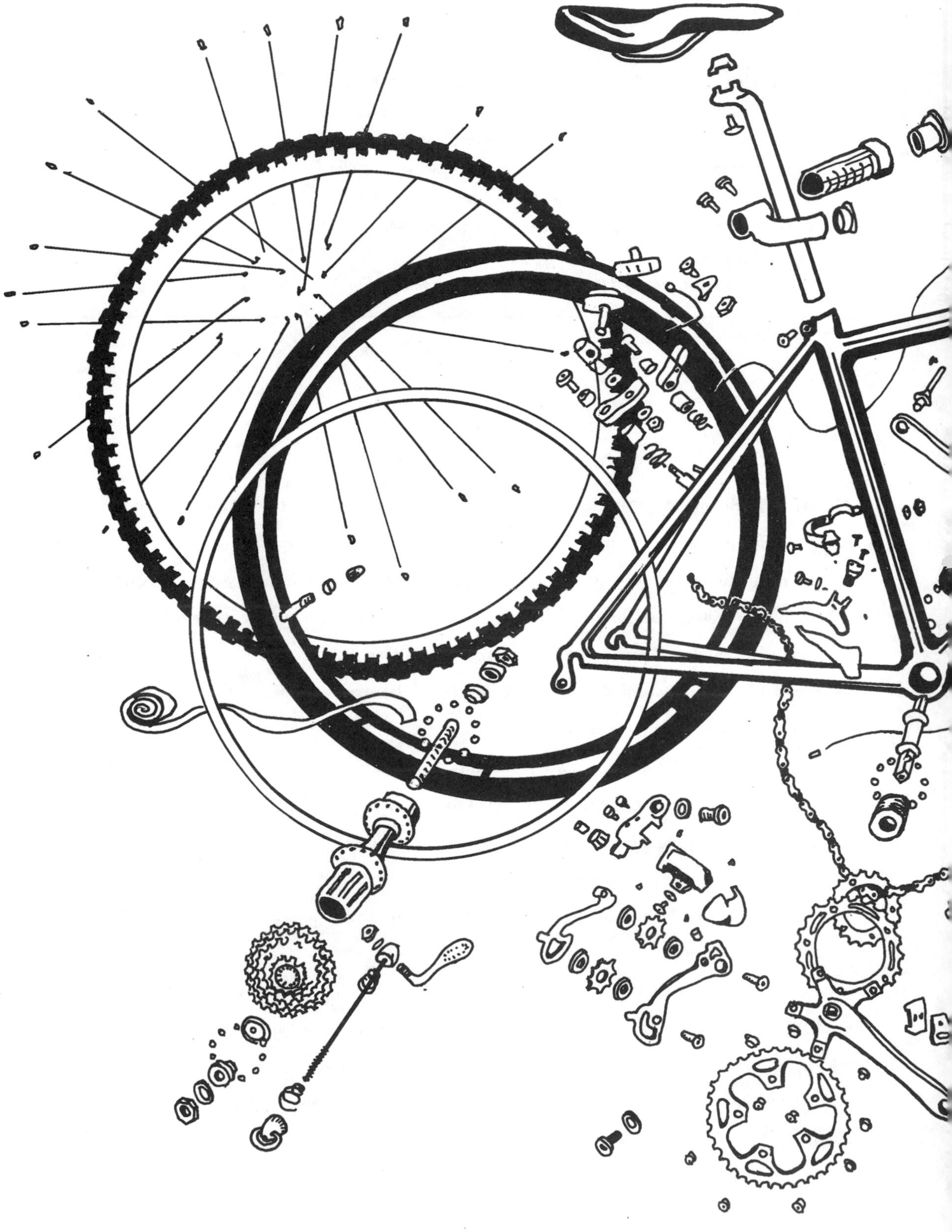

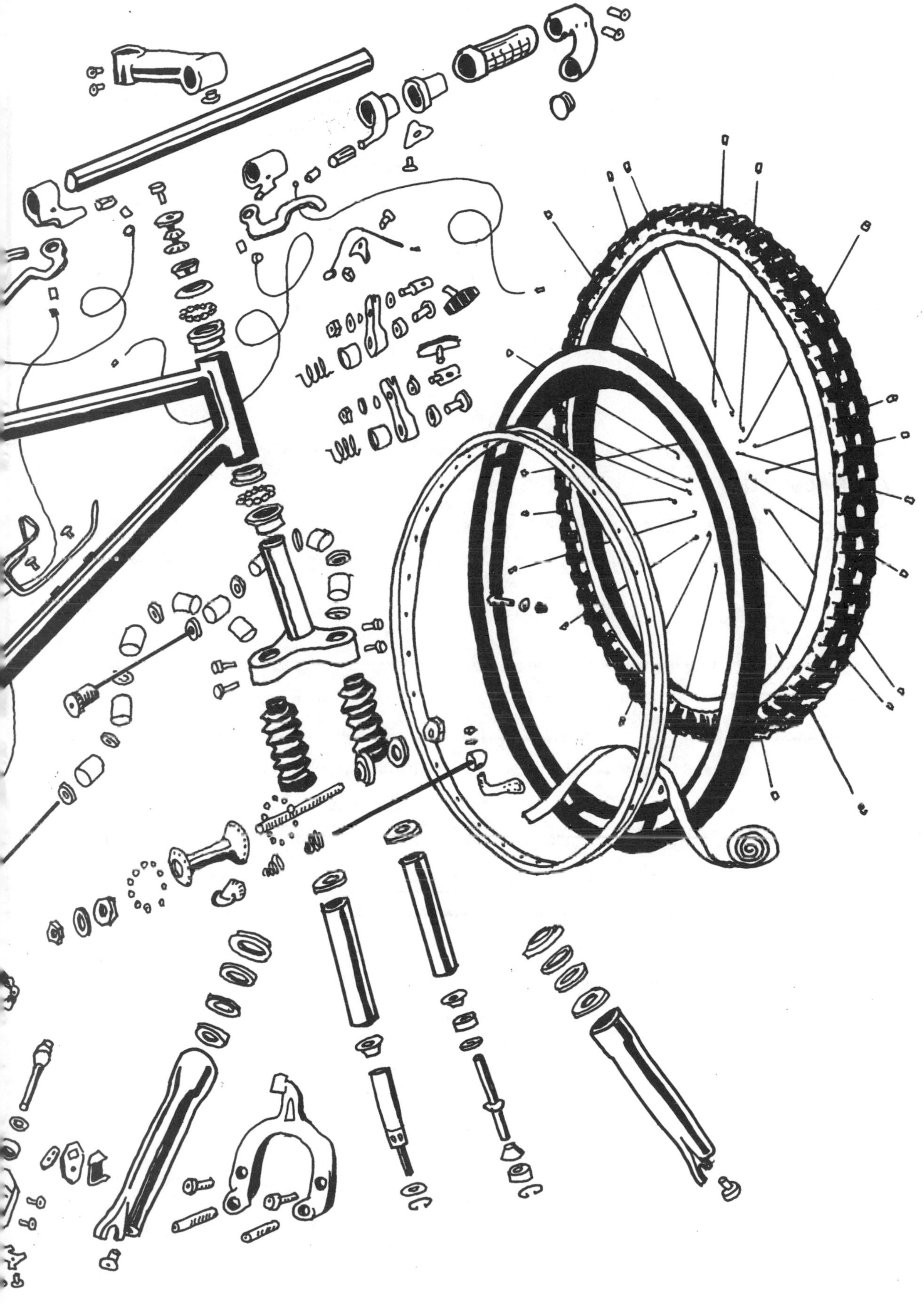

maintenance your bike requires. Even if that is the only part of this book you end up using, you'll have gotten your money's worth by avoiding some unpleasant experiences out on the trail.

This book was originally intended for home enthusiasts, not shop mechanics. For that reason, I have not included the long and precise lists of parts specifications that a shop mechanic might need. Nonetheless, when combined with a specification manual, this book can be a useful, easy-to-follow reference for shop mechanics too.

WHY DO IT YOURSELF?

There are a number of reasons why you would want to maintain your own mountain bike. Obviously, if done right, it is a lot cheaper to do it yourself than to pay someone else to do it. This is certainly an important factor for those riders who live to ride and have no visible means of support. Self-maintenance is a necessity for that crew.

As your income goes up and the time available to maintain your bike goes down, this becomes less and less true. If you're a well-paid professional with limited free time, it probably does not make as much economic sense to maintain your own bike. Yet you may find that you enjoy working on your bike for reasons other than just saving money. Unless you have a mechanic whom you trust and to whom you take your bike regularly, you are not likely to find anyone else who cares as much about your bicycle's smooth operation and cleanliness as you do. Furthermore, if you love to ride but have limited time to ride, you frankly need to be able to fix mechanical breakdowns that occur on the trail.

It is a given: Breakdowns will happen, even if you have the world's best mechanic working on your bike. For this reason, it takes away from my enjoyment of a ride if I have something on my bike that I do not understand well enough to know whether it is likely to last the ride or how to fix it if it does not.

There is an aspect of bicycle mechanics that can be extremely enjoyable in and of itself, almost independent of riding the bike. Bicycles are the epitome of elegant simplicity. Bicycle parts, particularly high-end components, are meant to work well and last a long time. With the proper attention, they can shine both in appearance and in performance for years to come. There is real satisfaction in dismantling a filthy part that is not functioning well, cleaning it up, lubricating it with fresh grease, and reassembling it so that it works like new again. Knowing that I made those parts work so smoothly—and that I can do it again when they get dirty or worn—is rewarding. I am eager to ride hard to see how they hold up rather than being reluctant to ride for fear of breaking something.

Also, if you share my stubborn unwillingness to throw something out and buy a new one simply because it has quit working—be it a leaky Waterpik; a torn tent; a bag with a broken zipper; or an old car, dishwasher, clock, or chainsaw that are no longer running well—then this book is for you. It is satisfying to keep an old piece of equipment running long past its time, and it's a great learning experience!

There is also something very liberating about going on a long ride and knowing that you can fix just about anything that might go wrong with your bike out on the trail. Armed with this knowledge (which begins with learning to identify the parts of a mountain bike, shown in Fig. i.2), and the tools to put it into action, you will have more confidence to explore new areas and go farther than you might otherwise.

To illustrate, an experience from way back in 1995 comes to mind, when I took a day to ride the entire 110-mile White Rim Trail loop in Utah's Canyonlands National Park. It is as desolate as you can imagine out there, and I was completely alone with the sky, the sun, and the rocks for long stretches. I had a good mileage base in my legs, so I knew I was physically capable of doing the ride during the limited daylight hours of late October. I had checked, replaced, or adjusted practically every part of my bike in the days before the ride. I had also tried out the bike on long rides close to town. Finally, I added to my saddlebag tool kit a few tools that I do not ordinarily carry.

I knew that there was very little chance of anything going wrong with my bike, and with the tools I had, I could fix almost anything short of a broken frame on the trail. Armed with this knowledge and experience, I really enjoyed the ride! I stopped and gawked at almost every breathtaking vista, vertical box canyon, colorful balanced rock, or arch. I took scenic detours. I knew that I had a good cushion of safety, so I could totally immerse myself in the pleasure of the ride. I had no nagging fear of something going wrong to dilute the experience.

Confidence in your mechanical ability allows you to be more courageous about what you will try. And armed with this confidence you'll be more willing to share your love of the sport with less-experienced riders. Bringing new people along on rides is a lot more fun if you know that you can fix their bikes and they won't be stranded with an old junker that won't roll.

HOW TO USE THIS BOOK

Skim through the entire book. Skip the detailed steps, but look at the exploded diagrams and get the general flavor of the book and what's inside. When it is time to perform a particular task, you'll know where to find it, and you'll have a general idea of how to approach it.

Illustrator Todd Telander and I have done our best to make these pages as understandable as possible. Exploded diagrams are purposefully used instead of photographs to show more clearly how each part goes together. The first time you go through a procedure, you may find it easier to have a friend read the instructions out loud as you perform the steps.

Obviously, some maintenance tasks are more complicated than others. I am convinced that anyone with an opposable thumb can perform virtually any repair on a bike. Still, it pays to spend some time getting familiar with the really simple tasks, such as fixing a flat, before throwing yourself into complex jobs, such as building a wheel.

Tasks and tools required are divided into three levels indicating their complexity or your proficiency. Level 1 tasks need level 1 tools and require of you only an eagerness to learn. Level 2 and level 3 tasks also have corresponding tool sets and are progressively more difficult. All repairs mentioned in this book are classified as level 1 unless otherwise indicated. Tools are shown in Chapter 1. The section at the end of Chapter 2, A General Guide to Performing Mechanical Work (§ii-17), is a must-read; it states general policies and approaches that apply to all mechanical work.

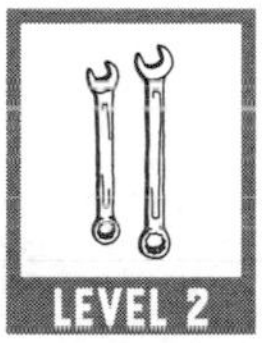

Each chapter starts with a list of required tools in the margin. If a section involves a higher level of work, there will be an icon designating the level and tools necessary to perform the tasks in that section. Tasks and illustrations are numbered for easy reference.

i.2 **See? There it is all back together!**

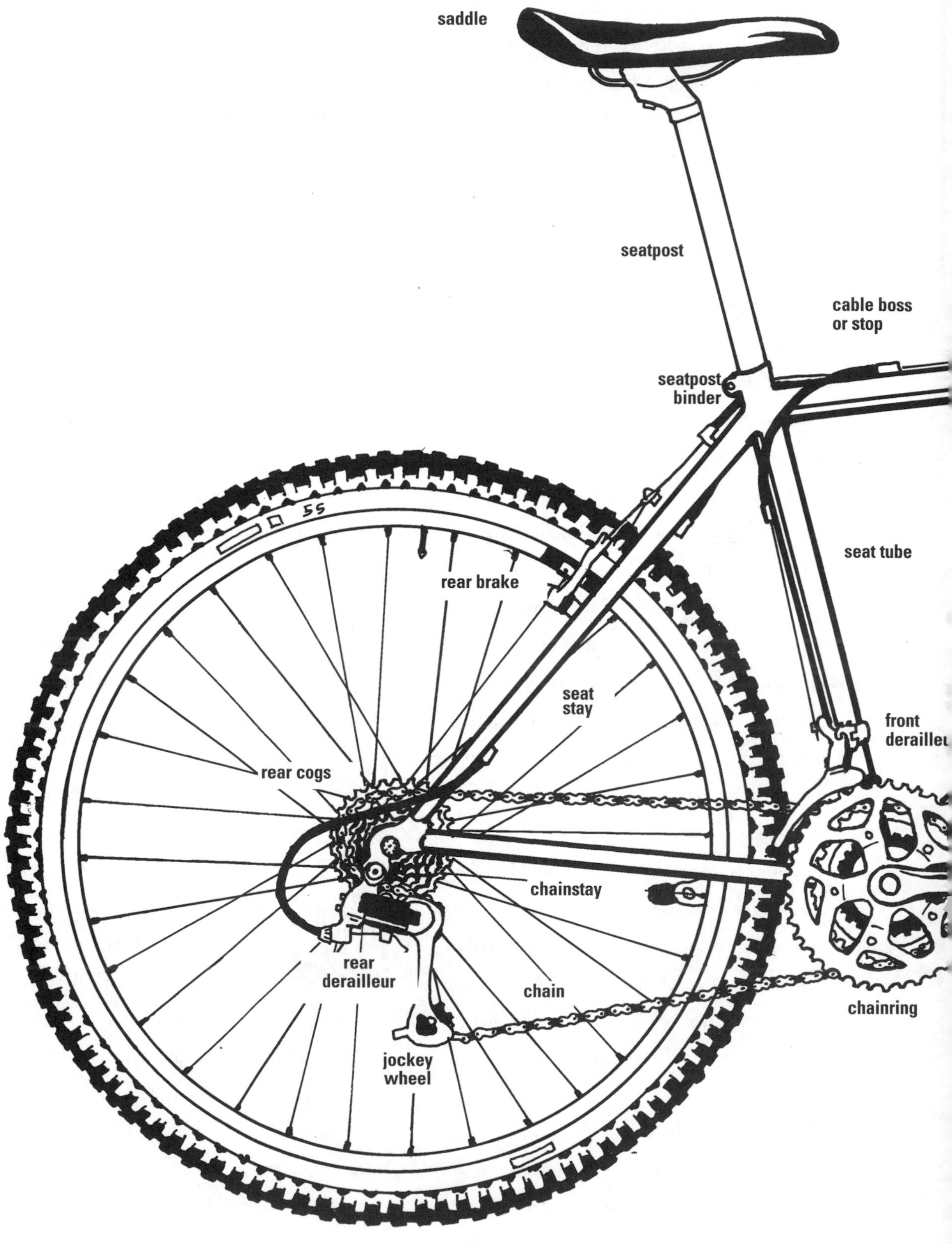

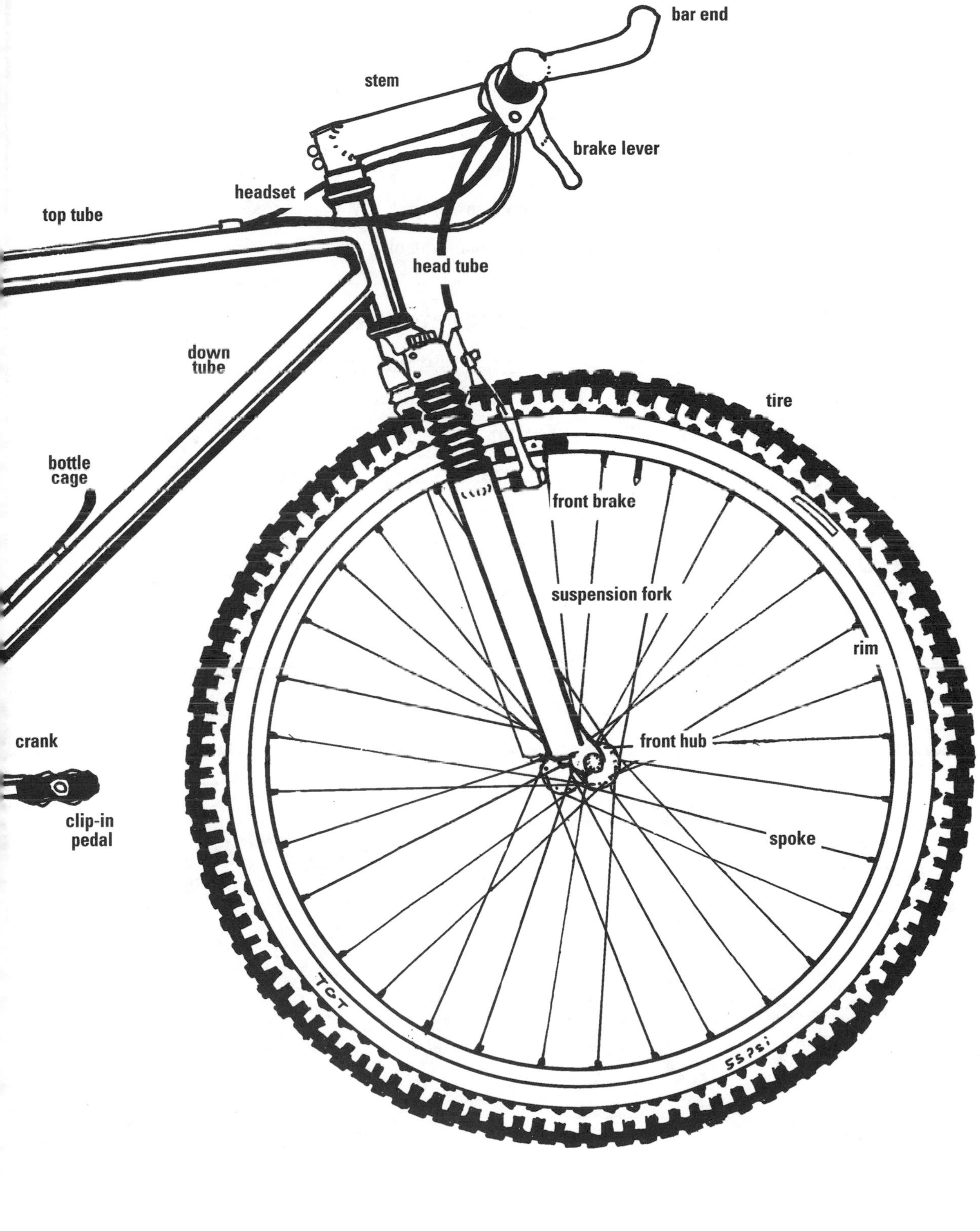
bar end
stem
brake lever
headset
top tube
head tube
down tube
tire
bottle cage
front brake
suspension fork
rim
crank
front hub
clip-in pedal
spoke

Section references use the symbol "§." For instance, "§iii-6" means "see Section iii-6." Illustrations are referred to as "Figures," for instance, "Figure 3.3."

At the end of some chapters there is a troubleshooting section. This is the place to go to identify the source of a certain noise or particular malfunction in the bike. There is also a comprehensive troubleshooting guide in Appendix A.

There is a wealth of other valuable information in the appendixes. Get used to using the appendixes; many tasks will be simplified.

Appendix B is a complete gear chart and includes instructions on how to calculate your gear with nonstandard size wheels. Appendix C is an extensive section on selecting the properly sized bike and positioning it to fit you. Appendix D lists the tightening specifications of almost every bolt on the bike. As bike parts become ever lighter and made out of ever more exotic materials, tightening them to the recommended torque spec becomes ever more important. Appendix E reveals which clip-in pedals work with which cleats and vice versa; knowing which pedals your cleats work in can save you lots of time switching pedals when trading bikes around with friends or trying demo bikes. The glossary is a comprehensive dictionary of mountain bike technical terms. There is a separate index listing the illustrations in the book, if you want to quickly check and see what something looks like.

THE MOUNTAIN BIKE

This is the creature to which this book is devoted (Fig. i.2). All of its major parts are illustrated and labeled here. Take a minute to familiarize yourself

i.3 Fully rigid

i.4 **Fully suspended**

i.5 **Hybrid**

with these parts now, and refer back to this diagram whenever necessary.

The mountain bike comes in a variety of forms, from models with rigid frames and forks (Fig. i.3), to hardtails (front suspension only—Fig. i.2), to models with front- and rear-suspension systems (Fig. i.4). A mountain bike generally comes with knobby tires in a 26-inch diameter, although larger 29-inch tires and wheels are gaining favor, particularly for tall riders, and 24-inch and smaller wheels and tires are found on tiny mountain bikes. Tire widths and shapes vary and include everything from studded snow tires to smooth street tires. This book also covers "hybrid" bikes (Fig. i.5), which are a cross between road bikes and mountain bikes.

However a mountain bike is configured, I think that by clearly spelling out the steps necessary to properly maintain and repair it, even those who see themselves as having no mechanical skills will be able to tackle problems as they arise. With a little bit of practice and a willingness to learn, your bike will suddenly transform itself from a mysterious contraption seemingly too complicated to tamper with, to a simple, very understandable machine that can be a genuine delight to work on. Just allow yourself the opportunity and the dignity to follow along, rather than deciding in advance that you will never be able to do this. All you have to do is follow the instructions and trust yourself.

So, set aside your self-image as someone who is "not mechanically oriented" (and any other factors that may stand in the way of your making your mountain bike ride like a dream), and let's start playing with your bike!

CHAPTER 1

TOOLS

Behold, we lay a tool here and on the morrow it is gone.
—The Book of Mormon

You can't do much work on a bike without tools. Still, it's not always clear exactly which tools to buy. This chapter will clarify what tools you should consider owning on the basis of your level of mechanical experience and interest.

As I mentioned in the introduction, the maintenance and repair procedures in this book are classified by their degree of difficulty. All repairs mentioned are classified as level 1, unless otherwise indicated. The tools for levels 1, 2, and 3 are pictured and described on the following pages. Lists of the tools needed in each chapter are shown in the margin at the beginning of each chapter.

For the uninitiated, there is no need to rush out and buy a large number of bike-specific tools. With only a few exceptions, the Level 1 Tool Kit (Fig. 1.1A) consists of standard metric tools. This is the same collection of tools I recommend later in this chapter for carrying with you on rides, though in a more compact and lightweight form (Figs. 1.5 and 1.6). The Level 2 Tool Kit (Fig. 1.2) contains several bike-specific tools, allowing you to do more complex work on the bike. Level 3 tools (Fig. 1.3) are extensive (and expensive), and they ensure that your riding buddies will show up not only to ask your sage advice, but to borrow your tools as well.

And if you really want to go all out and be set up like a pro (and even have mechanics wanting to borrow your tools), you can splurge on the set shown in Figure 1.4. If you are one to loan tools, you might consider marking your collection so as to help recover those items that might otherwise take a long time finding their way back to your workshop. It wouldn't hurt writing down the details about what tool you lent to whom and on what date. You would be surprised how easy it is to forget who has one of your seldom-used tools such as snapring pliers or a metric tap.

i-1 LEVEL 1 TOOL KIT

Level 1 repairs are the simplest and do not require a workshop, although it is nice to have a good space to work. You will need the following tools (Fig. 1.1A):

- **Tire pump** with a gauge and a valve head to match your tubes (either Presta or Schrader valves; see Fig. 1.1B). **Standard screwdrivers:** small, medium, and large (one of each).
- **Phillips-head screwdrivers**: one small and one medium.
- Set of three plastic **tire levers**.
- At least two **spare tubes** of the same size and valve type as those on your bike.
- Container of regular **talcum powder.** It works well for coating tubes and the inner casings of tires. Do not inhale this stuff; it's bad for the lungs.
- **Patch kit.** Choose one that comes with sandpaper instead of a metal scratcher. At least every 18 months, check that the glue has not dried up, whether open or not.
- One 6-inch **adjustable wrench** (a.k.a. "crescent wrench").
- **Pliers:** regular and needle-nose.
- Set of **metric Allen wrenches** (a.k.a. "hex keys") that includes 2.5mm, 3mm, 4mm, 5mm, 6mm, and 8mm sizes. Folding sets are available and work nicely to keep your wrenches organized. I also recommend buying extras of the 4mm, 5mm, 6mm, and 8mm sizes.

LEVEL 1 TOOL KIT

- Set of **metric open-end wrenches** that includes 7mm, 8mm, 9mm, 10mm, 13mm, 14mm, 15mm, and 17mm sizes.
- 15mm **pedal wrench**. This is thinner and longer than a standard 15mm wrench and thicker than a cone wrench.
- **Chain tool** for breaking and reassembling chains.
- **Spoke wrench** to match the size of nipples used on your wheels.
- Tube or jar of **grease.** I recommend using grease designed specifically for bicycles; however, standard automotive grease is okay, except in suspension forks and twist shifters.
- Drip bottle or can of **chain lubricant.** Please choose a nonaerosol; it is easier to control, uses

1.1A Level 1 tool kit

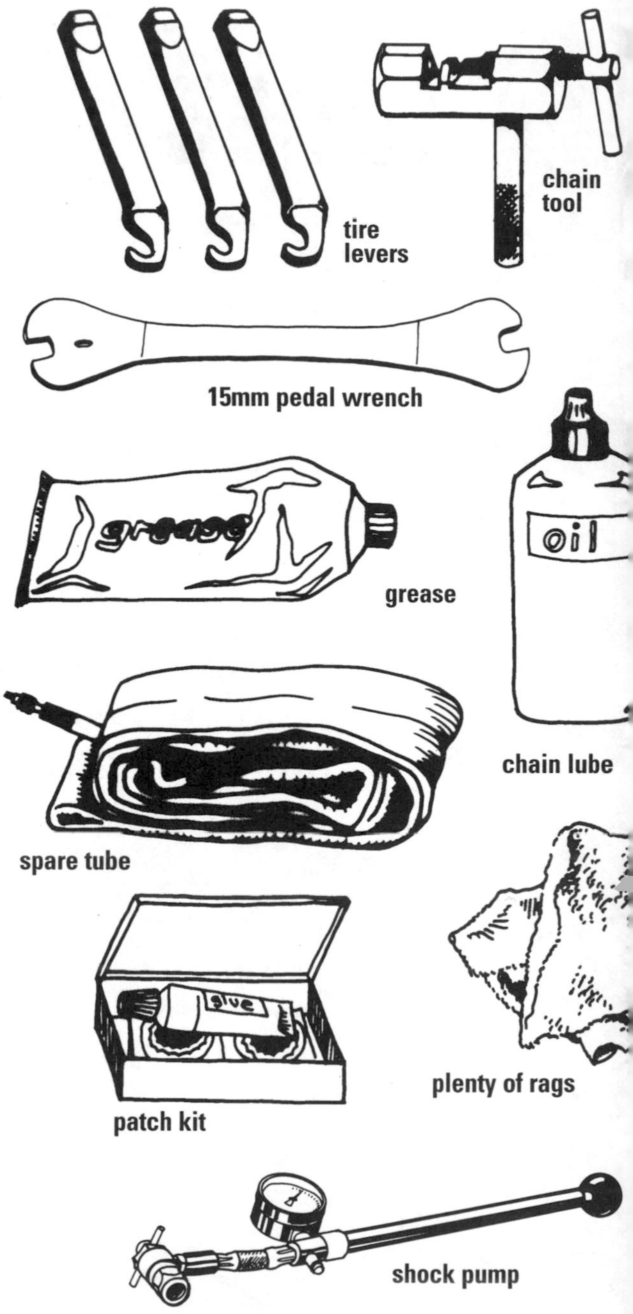

TOOLS

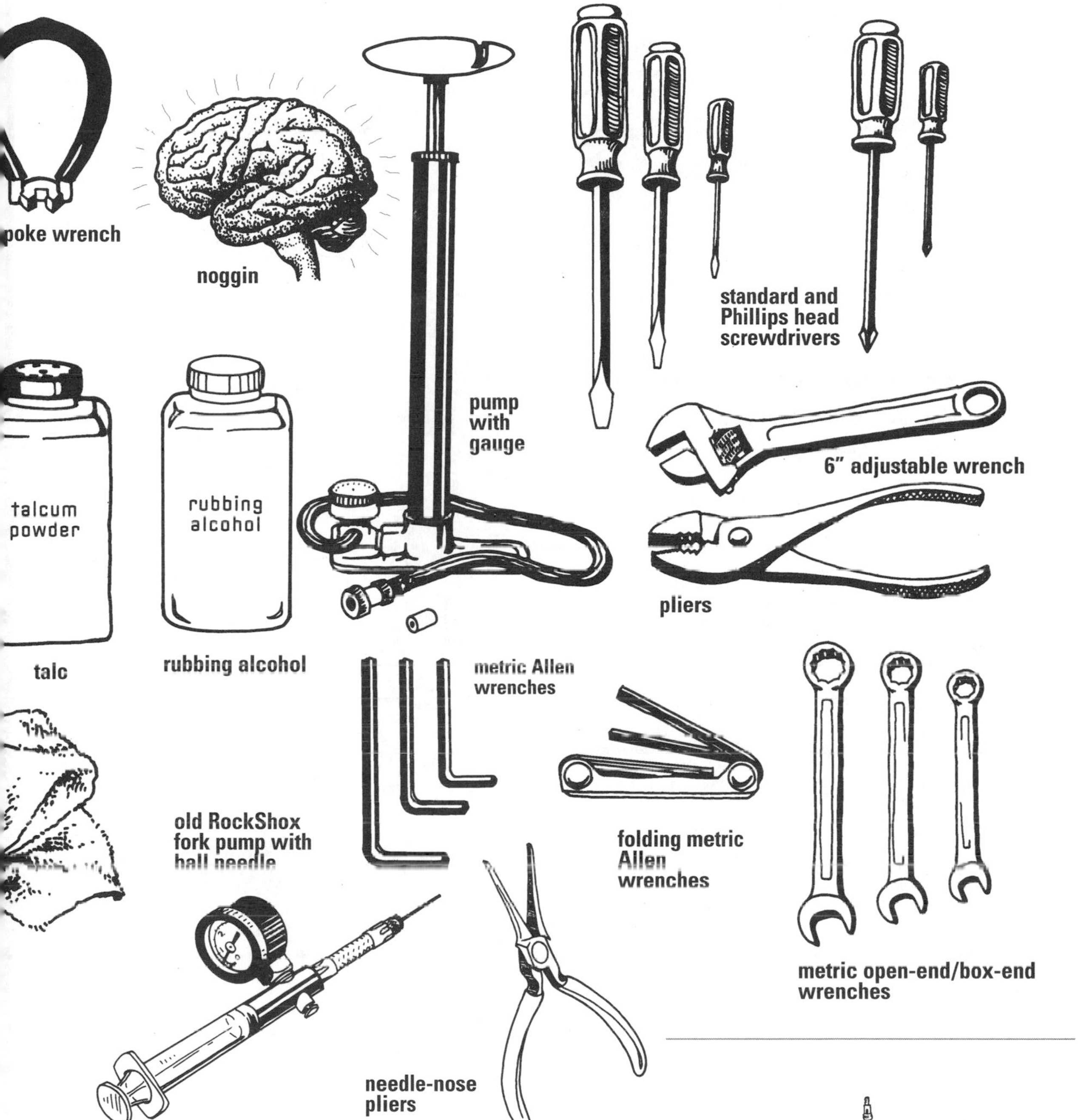

LEVEL 1 TOOL KIT

1.1B **Valve types**

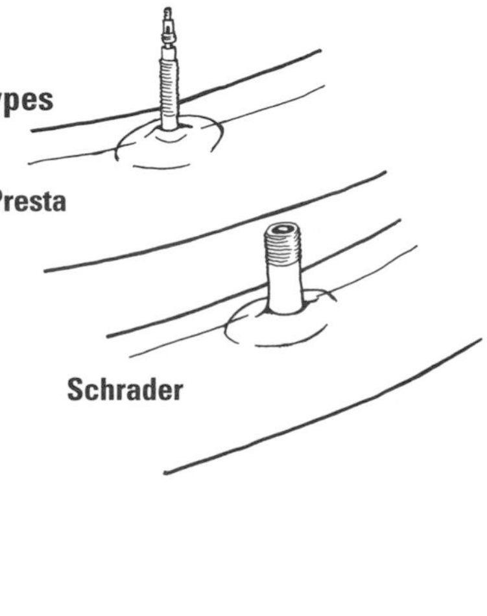

less packaging, and wastes less in overspray.

- **Rubbing alcohol** for removing and installing handlebar grips and for cleaning disc-brake pads, rotors, and internal parts.
- A lot of **rags!**

Other

- If you have an air-sprung suspension fork or rear shock, you need a **shock pump.** Get one with a no-leak head if your front or rear shock has standard Schrader valves, and get the adapter you need if your fork requires either a ball needle or a special adapter to insert down inside a deep Schrader valve.
- You'll also want stuff like **tape, zip-ties, safety glasses,** and rubber dish **gloves** or a box of cheap latex gloves. A **bucket,** large **brushes** and **sponges,** and **dish soap** also will serve you well for cleaning a dirty machine rapidly.

i-2 LEVEL 2 TOOL KIT

Level 2 repairs are a bit more complex, and I recommend that you use a well-organized workspace with a shop bench. Keeping your workspace well organized is probably the best way to make maintenance and repair easy and quick. You will need the entire Level 1 Tool Kit (Fig. 1.1A) plus the following tools (Fig. 1.2):

- **Portable bike stand.** Be sure that the stand is sturdy enough to remain stable when you're really cranking on the wrenches.
- **Shop apron** (this is to keep your nice duds nice).
- **Hacksaw** with a fine-toothed blade.
- Set of **razor blades** or a sharp **shop knife.**
- **Files:** one round and one flat.
- **Cable cutter** for cutting brake and shifter cables without fraying the ends.
- **Cable-housing cutter** for cutting coaxial-indexed cable housing. If you purchase a Shimano, Park, or Wrench Force housing cutter, you won't need to buy a separate cable cutter, because either of these cleanly cuts both cables and housings.

1.2 **Level 2 tool kit**

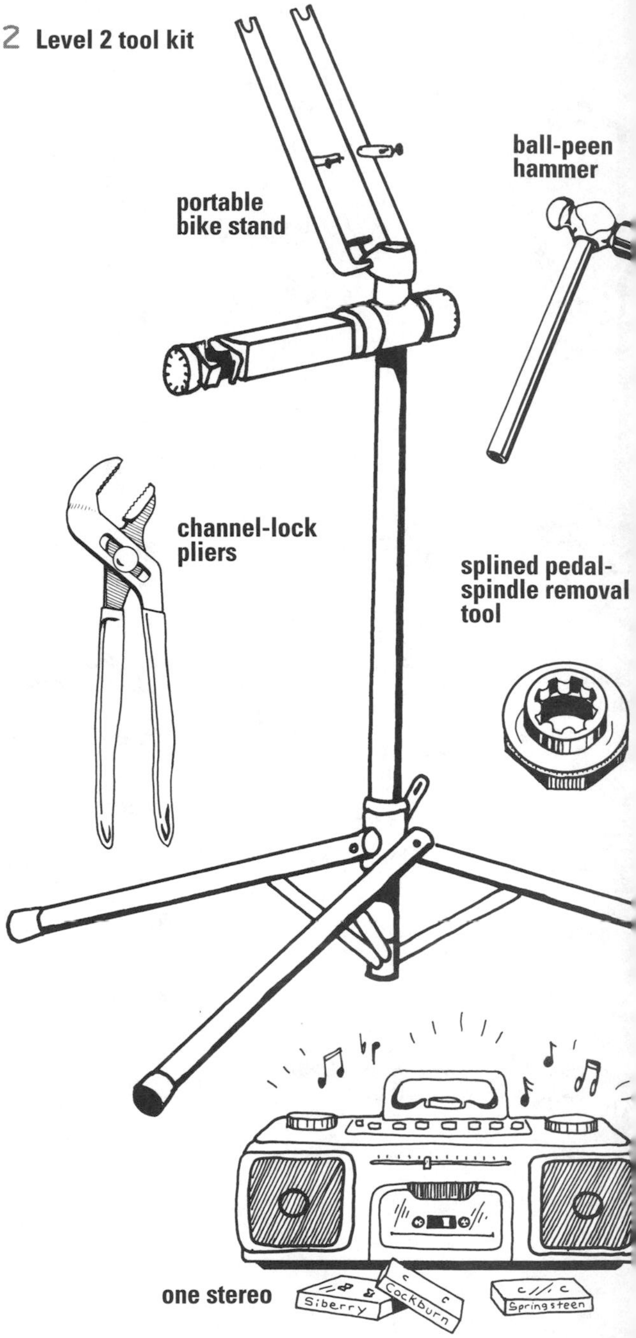

- Set of **metric socket wrenches** that includes 7mm, 8mm, 9mm, 10mm, 13mm, 14mm, and 15mm sizes.
- **Crank puller** for removing crankarms. Its push rod is sized for either square-taper crankarms or for ISIS or Octalink crankarms, so get the right one for your crankset.

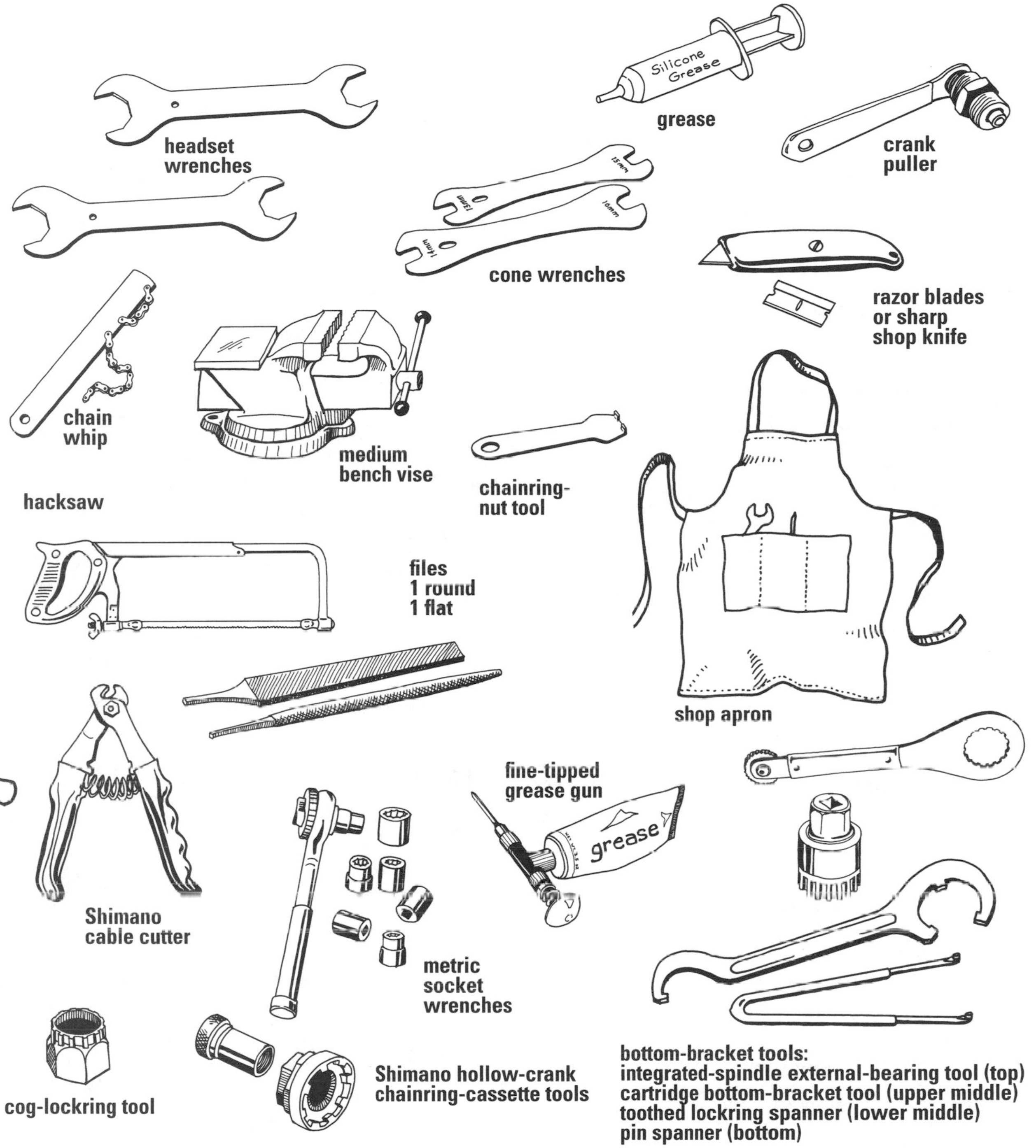

- **Chainring-nut tool** for holding the nut while you tighten or loosen a chainring bolt.
- **Chainring-cassette removal tools** for Shimano Octalink–style hollow cranks.
- **Bottom-bracket tools.** For Shimano cartridge bottom brackets and clones of them, you'll need the splined tool specifically made for this type of bottom bracket. Note that if you have an ISIS or Octalink splined-spindle bottom bracket, you need a tool with a bore large enough to swallow the fatter spindle. For recent integrated-spindle cranks, you'll need yet another oversized splined

wrench to remove the cups, which are larger and sit outboard of the bottom-bracket shell, and a little splined tool to tighten the left crank's adjustment cap. For cup-and-cone bottom brackets, you'll need a lockring spanner and a pin spanner to fit your bottom bracket.

- **Cone wrenches,** if you have loose-bearing hubs. The standard sizes are 13mm, 14mm, 15mm, and 16mm, but check what size you need before buying.
- Medium **ball-peen hammer.**
- Two **headset wrenches.** Be sure to check the size of your headset before buying these. This purchase is unnecessary if you have a threadless headset and plan to work only on your own bike. Some suspension forks have crown nuts requiring headset wrenches.
- Medium **bench vise.**
- **Cog lockring tool** for removing cogs from the rear hub.
- **Chain whip** for holding cogs while loosening the cassette lockring.
- **Channel-lock pliers.**
- **Splined pedal-spindle removal tool.**
- Fine-tipped **grease gun.**
- Tube of **silicone-based grease** if you have Grip Shift.
- Tube of **nonlithium grease** for suspension forks.
- One **stereo** with **good tunes**. This is especially important if you plan on spending a lot of time working on your bike.

LEVEL 3 TOOL KIT

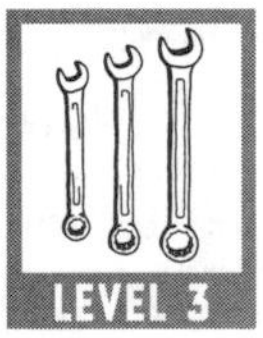

i-3 LEVEL 3 TOOL KIT

If you are an accomplished level 3 mechanic, you can even build up brand-new frames. That is assuming, of course, that these tools (Fig. 1.3) are neatly organized in your shop.

1.3 **Level 3 tool kit**

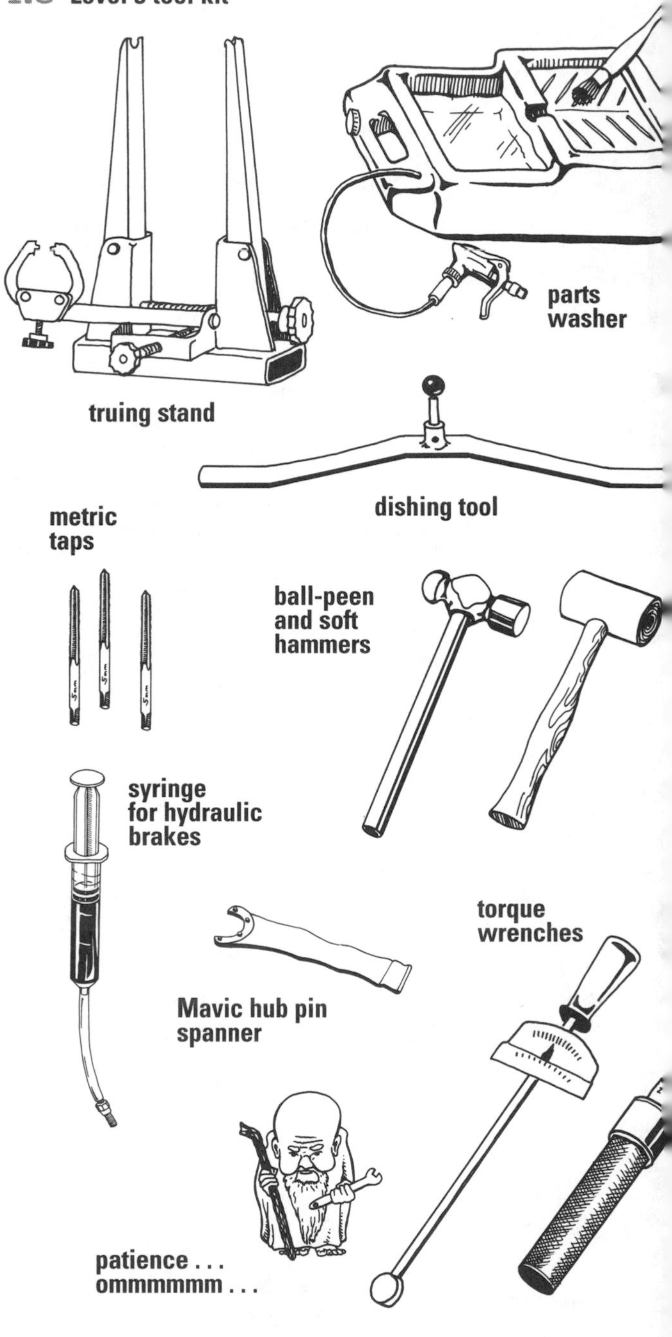

- **Parts-washing tank.** Please use an environmentally safe degreaser. Dispose of used solvent responsibly; check with your local environmental safety office.
- Fixed **bike stand** with a clamp.
- Large bench-mounted **vise** to free stuck parts.

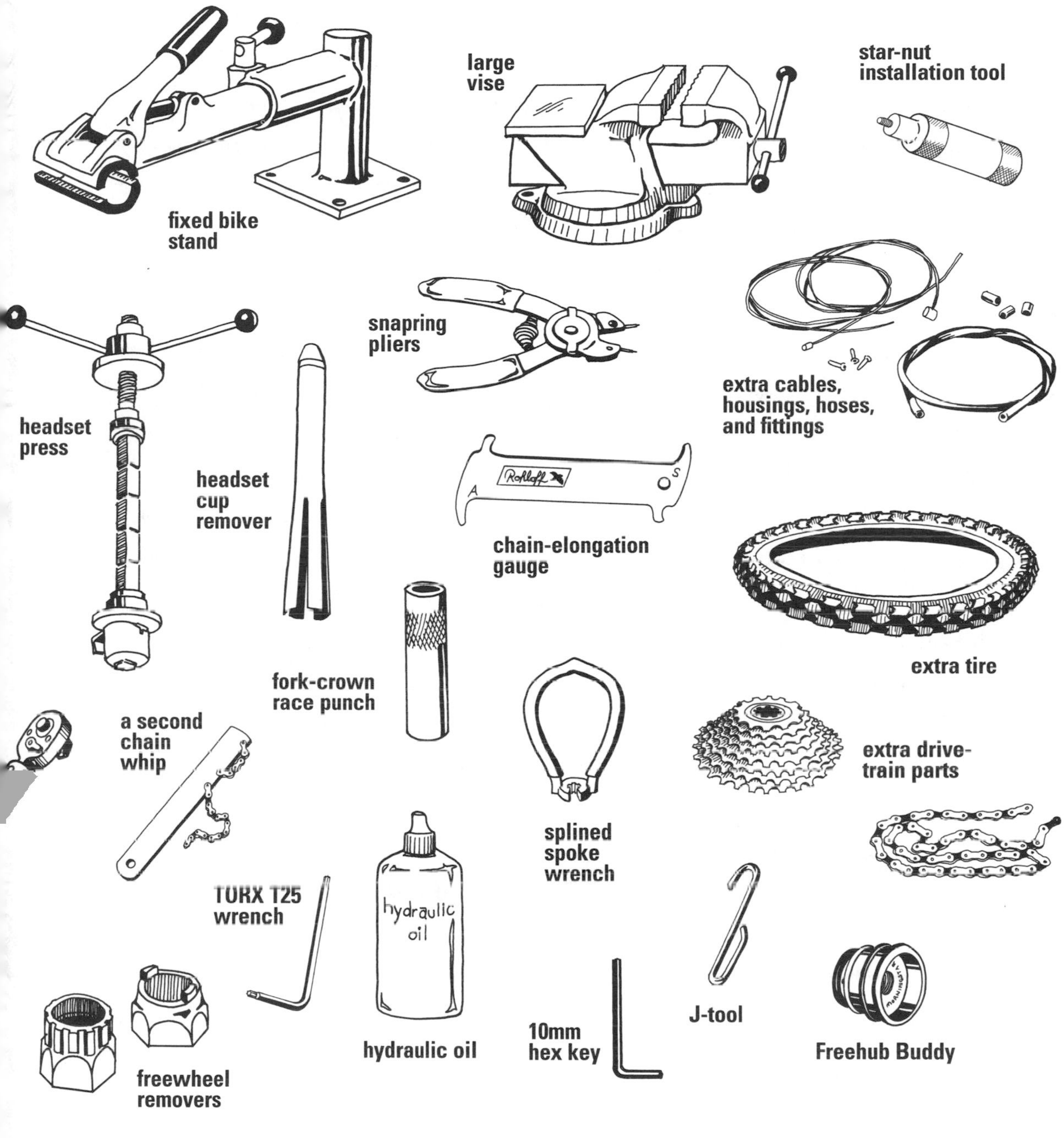

- **Headset press** used to install headset bearing cups. The press should fit all cup sizes and may require adapters for internal cups or for cups with pressed-in bearings.
- **Fork-crown race punch** (a.k.a. "slide hammer") for installing the fork-crown race of the headset.
- **Headset cup remover**.
- **Star-nut installation tool** for threadless headsets.
- An **extra chain whip** for disassembling freewheels or old-style cassettes.
- **Freewheel removers** for Shimano, Sachs, and Suntour freewheels.

- Large **ball-peen hammer.**
- **Soft hammer.** Choose a rubber, plastic, or wooden mallet to prevent damage to parts.
- **Torque wrenches.** Torque wrenches are great for checking proper bolt tightness. Following manufacturer-specified torque settings dissuades parts from stripping, breaking, creaking, or falling off while you are riding. Ideally, you want a small wrench and a big, long wrench, one for small bolts, and one for large bolts.
- Set of **metric taps** that includes 5mm by 0.8mm, 6mm by 1mm, and 10mm by 1mm for fixing mangled frame threads.
- Pair of **snapring pliers** for removing snaprings from suspension forks, pedals, derailleurs, and other parts.
- **Chain-elongation gauge** to determine whether a chain needs replacing. An accurate 12-inch ruler will substitute adequately.
- **Truing stand** for truing and building wheels.
- **Dishing tool** for checking that the wheel you just finished building is properly centered.
- **Spoke wrenches** of all sizes.
- **Splined spoke wrench** for Mavic.
- **Pin spanner** for adjusting Mavic hubs.
- **Morningstar Freehub Buddy** for flushing and lubricating freehubs.
- **Morningstar J-tool** for removing freehub dust covers.
- **Hydraulic fluids** of different types and viscosities for different hydraulic brakes, suspension forks, and rear shocks.
- **Syringe** for bleeding hydraulic brakes—the type varies with brake brand. All require some sort of a tube at least, and may only require a squeeze bottle of fluid rather than a syringe.
- **TORX wrenches.** These have star-shaped tips and fit some disc-brake-rotor bolts. TORX T25 is the size for disc-brake rotors.
- 10mm **hex keys,** for some suspension pivots.
- One healthy dose of **patience** and an equal willingness to work and rework jobs until they have been properly finished.

Other

- **Spare parts** to save you from last-minute runs to the bike shop, such as several sizes of ball bearings, spare cables, cable housing, and a lifetime supply of those little cable-end caps. Keep on hand spare tires, tubes, chains, and cogsets. If you expect to be working on suspension forks, rear shocks, and hydraulic brakes, be sure to have spare springs, hoses, seals, and fittings.
- **Various fluids.** Special suspension oils and greases, threadlock fluid, titanium antiseize compound, outboard-motor gear oil, or specialty freehub lubricants are required for some jobs.

i-4 NOW, IF YOU REALLY WANT A WELL-STOCKED SHOP

The following tools (Fig. 1.4) are not even part of the Level 3 Tool Kit and are not often needed for bike repairs. That said, they sure do come in handy when you need them.

- Morningstar Rotors on Center (ROC) and Drumstix **alignment tools for disc-brake rotors** for straightening out-of-true rotors and getting rid of that annoying brake rub noise.
- **Park universal fork-crown race remover.** This manly tool allows you to remove headset fork-crown races from any fork without pounding at them with a hammer and screwdriver and mar-

1.4 Tools for the well-stocked shop

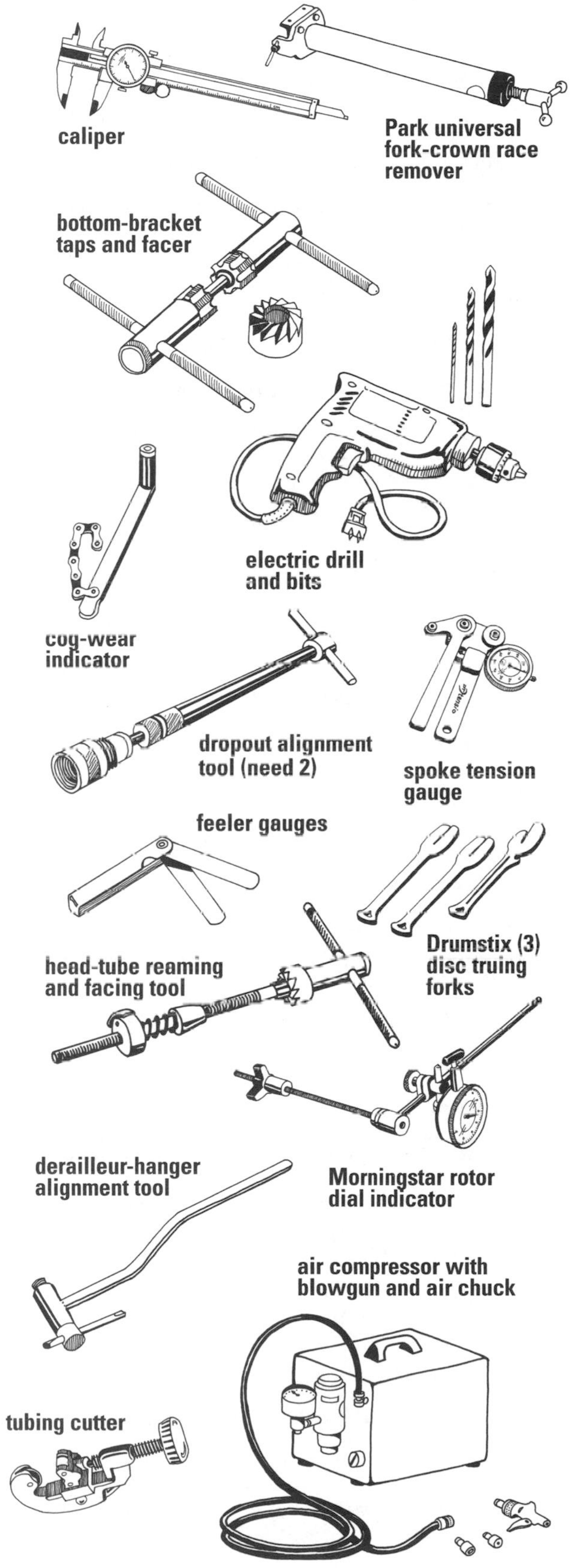

ring the fork crown.

- **Measuring calipers** with vernier, dial, or digital measurement for measuring parts in order to optimize function.
- **Tubing cutter** for cutting handlebars off straight without getting out the hacksaw. Forget about it for cutting off carbon handlebars, though.
- **Hydraulic brake-hose cutter** in order to get an optimal square cut and to reduce the likelihood of fluid leaks.
- **English-threaded** bottom-bracket **tap set.** This cuts threads in both ends of the bottom-bracket shell while keeping the threads in proper alignment.
- Bottom-bracket **shell facer.** Like a bottom-bracket tap, this tool cuts the faces of the bottom-bracket shell so they are parallel to each other.
- **Head-tube reamer and facer.** This tool keeps both ends of the head tube perfectly parallel and of the proper inside diameter for the headset cups.
- **Electric drill** with drill bit set.
- **Dropout-alignment tools** (a.k.a. "tip adjusters"). You need two—one for each dropout.
- **Derailleur-hanger alignment tool** to straighten the hanger after you shift it into the spokes or crash on it.
- **Cog-wear indicator gauge** to determine if cogs are worn out.
- **Feeler gauges** for precise adjustment of some disc brakes.
- **Air compressor** with blowgun and air chuck. Useful for lots of things, including overhauling disc brakes and seating tubeless tires.
- **Spoke-tension gauge** to check for proper spoke tension and thus ensure long wheel life.

1.5 **Tools to take on all rides**

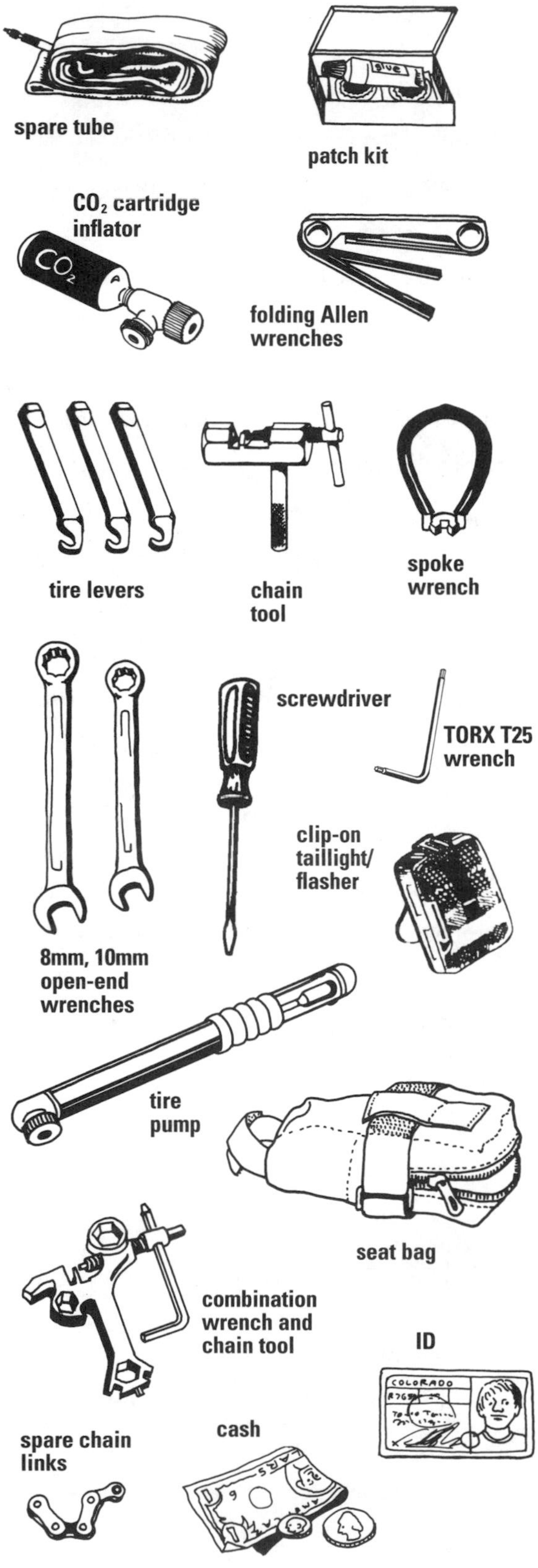

i-5 SETTING UP YOUR HOME SHOP

I recommend keeping this area clean and very well organized. Lame as it sounds, remember that a "clean shop is a happy shop!" Make it comfortable to work in and easy to find the tools you need. Hanging tools on pegboard or slatboard or placing them in bins or trays are all effective ways to maintain an organized work area. Being able to find the tools that you need will increase the enjoyment of working on a bike immensely. It is harder to do a job with love if you're frustrated about not being able to find the cable cutter. Placing small parts in one of those bench-top organizers with several rows of little drawers is another good way to keep chaos from taking over.

i-6 TOOLS TO CARRY WITH YOU WHILE RIDING

a. For most riding

Keep all of the following stuff (see Fig. 1.5) in a bag under your seat or somehow attached to your bike. Some people may prefer to keep it in a hydration (a.k.a. CamelBak) pack or a fanny pack. The operative words here are "light" and "serviceable." Many of these tools are combined in some of the popular "multitools." Make sure you try all tools at home before depending on them on the trail.

- **Spare tube.** This is a no-brainer. Make sure the valve matches the ones on your bike and pump and check that the Presta valve nut is loose enough to unscrew by hand out on the trail. Keep the tube in a plastic bag to prevent deterioration and to protect it from the sharp tools in your bag.
- **Tire pump** and/or **CO_2 cartridge inflator** with a spare cartridge. Larger pumps are faster than itty-bitty mini-pumps. Make sure the pump or cartridge is set up for your type of valves.

- **Patch kit.** You'll need something after you've used your spare tube. Check it at least every one and a half years to make sure the glue is not dried up.
- At least two **plastic tire levers,** preferably three.
- **Chain tool** that works.
- 8mm and 10mm **open-end wrenches.**
- **Spoke wrench** sized to your spokes.
- **Small screwdriver** for adjusting derailleurs and other parts.
- Compact set of **Allen wrenches** that includes 2.5mm, 3mm, 4mm, 5mm, and 6mm sizes. (Some of you might need to bring along an 8mm, too.)
- A good **multitool** to replace some or all of the above six items with less weight and bulk.
- **TORX T25 wrench** if you have disc-brake rotors with TORX screws.
- **Spare chain links** from your chain. If you're using a Shimano chain, bring at least two "subpin" rivets. If you use SRAM, Wippermann, or Sachs chains, bring along an extra "master link." Like the Shimano subpin, you'll never need one … unless, of course, you forget to bring one.
- **Identification.**
- **Cash,** for obvious reasons, *and* to boot (i.e., temporarily patch) sidewall cuts in tires.
- **Taillight** that you can clip on, or better yet, that you can leave mounted onto your bike in case you stay out after dark.
- **Wet wipes** or latex gloves to keep your hands clean.

b. For long or multiday trips

The items in Figure 1.6 are, of course, in addition to proper amounts of food, water, and extra clothes, as well as in addition to the tools shown in Figure 1.5.

- **Spare spokes.** Innovations in Cycling sells a really cool folding spoke made from Kevlar. It's worth

1.6 Tools for extended backcountry riding

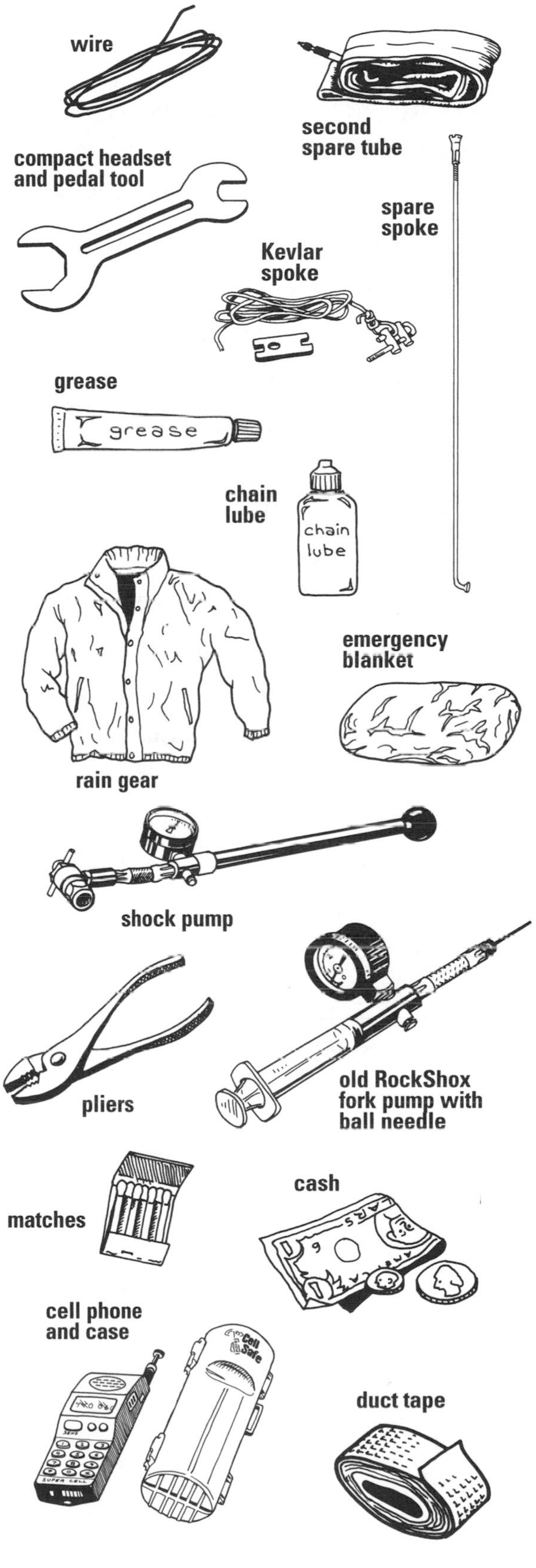

TOOLS TO CARRY WITH YOU

getting one or two for emergency repairs on a long ride.

- Another **spare tube.**
- Small plastic bottle of **chain lube.**
- Small tube of **grease.**
- Compact 15mm **pedal wrench.** One with a headset wrench on the other end can be particularly handy if you or your buddy has a threaded headset.
- **Pliers.** Useful for innumerable purposes.
- **Shock pump** for your front and/or rear shock. If your fork requires a pump adapter, make sure that you bring one.
- **Wire** and/or a small **bungee cord** can be very handy for all kinds of things.
- **Duct tape.** It's like The Force. It has a light side and a dark side, and it holds the universe (and sometimes your bike or your shoes) together.
- **Money,** or its **plastic equivalent,** which can get you out of lots of scrapes.
- **Matches,** because you never know when you can be stranded overnight.
- A lightweight, aluminized, folding **emergency blanket.**
- **Rain gear.**
- **Cell phone** with protective case.
- **Headlight.** This can be a lightweight unit to clip onto the handlebar or a headlamp with a strap that will fit over your helmet. An extra battery for it is a good idea, too.
- Small **flashlight.** This can be a little LED type or a small Maglight—just something to give you some illumination to find things in the dark, especially if your headlight dies.

NOTE: *Read Chapter 3 on emergency repairs before embarking on a lengthy trip. And, if you are planning a bike-centered vacation, be sure to bring along a Level 1 Tool Kit in the car, some headset wrenches, and incidentals such as duct tape and sandpaper.*

CHAPTER 2

BASIC STUFF

Preride inspection, wheel removal, and general cleaning

Everything should be made as simple as possible, but not simpler.
—Albert Einstein

Making sure your bike is safe is essential. It's a good idea to get into the habit of checking your bike before heading out on a ride. Performing the preride inspection regularly could help you avoid delays due to parts failure. I won't even mention the injury risks you face by riding a poorly maintained bike.

After that, unless you always have a mechanic with you, you need to know how to take your wheels on and off, or you won't be able to effectively deal with minor annoyances like flat tires or jammed chains. And if you do absolutely nothing else to your bike, keeping your chain and a few other parts clean will enhance the enjoyment of the ride. This chapter's three very basic cleaning and maintenance procedures are fundamental to keeping your bike running smoothly.

All home mechanics in particular should read A General Guide to Performing Mechanical Work, which is the last section in this chapter.

ii-1 PRERIDE INSPECTION

1. Check to be sure that the quick-release levers or axle nuts (the ones that secure the hub axle to the dropouts) are tight.
2. Check the brake pads for excessive or uneven wear.
3. Grab and twist the brake pads and brake arms to make sure the bolts are tight.
4. Squeeze the brake levers. This should bring the pads flat against the rims (or slightly toed-in), without hitting the tires, or in the case of disc brakes, should bring the pads against the rotor. Make certain that you cannot squeeze the levers all of the way to the handlebar (see Chapter 7, §vii-3 and §vii-4, for brake-cable tension adjustment or §vii-15 for hydraulic disc-brake bleeding, after first making sure that your disc-brake pads are in place and in good condition).
5. Spin the wheels. Check for wobbles while sighting on the rims, not the tires. (If a tire wobbles

excessively on a straight rim, it may not be fully seated in the rim; check it all of the way around on both sides.) Make sure that the rims do not rub on the brake pads.

6. Check the tire pressure. On most mountain bike tires the proper pressure is between 30 and 60 pounds per square inch (psi). Look to see that there are no foreign objects sticking in the tire. If there are, you may have to pull the tube out and repair or replace it. For some, it might be worth your time to look at the section on tire sealants (i.e., the goop inside the tube that fills any small holes you may get) in Chapter 6, §vi-10.
7. Check the tires for excessive wear, cracking, or gashes.
8. Be certain that the handlebar and stem are tight and that the stem is lined up with the front tire.
9. Check that the gears shift smoothly, and the chain does not skip or shift by itself. Make sure that indexed (or "click") shifting moves the chain one cog, starting with the first click. Make sure that the chain does not overshift the smallest or biggest rear cog or the smallest or biggest front chainring.
10. Check the chain for rust, dirt, stiff links, or noticeable signs of wear. It should be clean and lubricated. (Be cautious about overdoing it, though. With some lubricants, overlubricated, gooey chains pick up lots of dirt, particularly in dry climates.) The chain should be replaced on a mountain bike about every 500 to 1,000 miles of off-road riding or every 2,000 miles of paved riding.
11. Apply the front brake and push the bike forward and back. The headset should be tight and not make clunking noises or allow the fork any fore-and-aft play.

If all these things check out, go ride your bike! If not, check the table of contents or Appendix A, go to the appropriate chapter, and fix the problems before you go out and ride.

ii-2 REMOVING THE FRONT WHEEL

You can't transport your mountain bike easily if you can't remove the front wheel, because removing the front wheel is required for most roof racks and for jamming a mountain bike inside your car. As outlined in the following sections, wheel removal involves releasing the brake and opening the hub quick-release, or bolt-on skewer, or through-axle mechanism, or the axle nuts on the low-end models.

If you have a single-leg fork (i.e., a Cannondale Lefty) or a 20mm through-axle front hub, the wheel removal is different. See the note at the end of §ii-5 for a Cannondale Lefty and §ii-10 for a through-axle.

ii-3 RELEASING THE BRAKE

Most brakes have a mechanism to release the brake arms so that they spring away from the rim (Figs. 2.1 and 2.2), allowing the tire to pass between the pads. If yours does not, you will have to deflate the tire. V-brakes (a.k.a. "sidepull cantilevers"—Fig. 2.1) are released by pulling the end of the curved cable-guide tube (a.k.a. the "noodle") out of the horizontal link atop one of the brake arms while either holding the link or squeezing the pads against the rim with the other hand (Fig. 2.1). Most cantilever brakes (Fig. 2.2) and U-brakes (Fig. 7.49) are released by pulling the enlarged head of the straddle cable out of a notch in the top of the brake arm while holding the pads against the rim with the other hand (Fig. 2.2).

Most disc brakes (Figs. 7.19 and 7.20) allow the disc to fall away without releasing the pads, as the

2.1 Releasing the noodle from the link on a V-brake

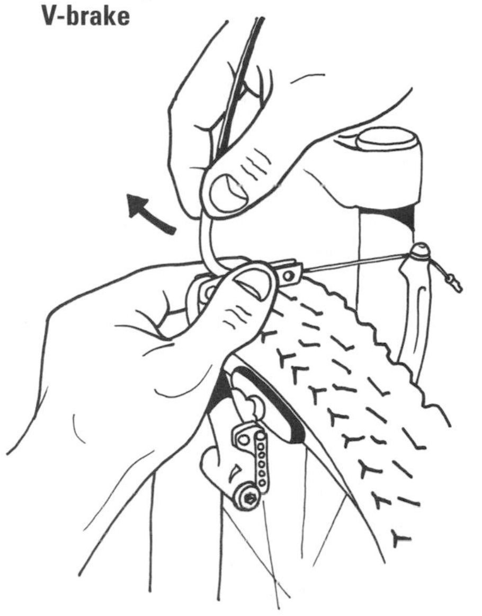

2.2 Releasing a cantilever brake

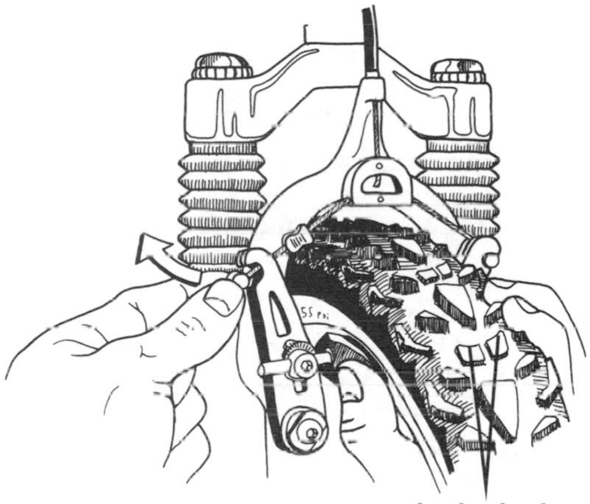

2.3 Opening a quick-release skewer

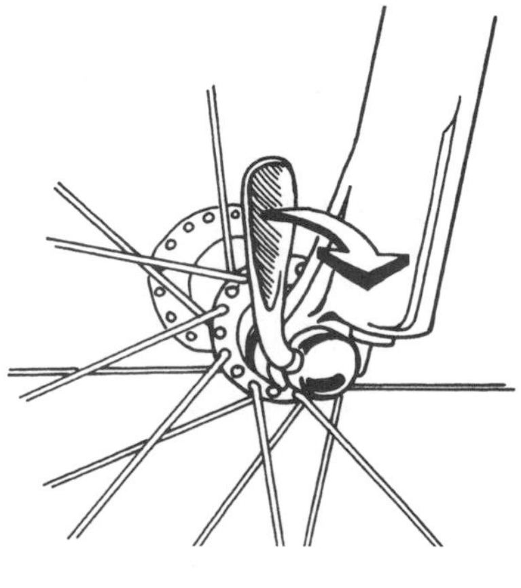

caliper is bolted to the fork and the disc slips in and out of it easily. However, models manufactured before the advent of disc-brake mounting tabs on the forks make wheel removal much harder. Releasing the old (mid-1990s) Dia-Compe cable-actuated hydraulic disc brakes requires opening a latch (under the caliper) that secures the caliper to the fork. The entire caliper can then be swung up and forward, allowing the wheel to come out. Do not squeeze the lever of a hydraulic disc brake when there is neither a disc nor a travel spacer between the pads, or else the pistons can pop out too far, and you won't be able to get your rotor back in between the pads without some extra work to push the pistons back in.

Roller-cam brakes (Fig. 7.50) are released by pulling the cam down and out from between the two rollers while holding the pads against the rim. Many linkage brakes (Fig. 7.48) are released in the same way as V-brakes or cantilever brakes. Releasing hydraulic rim brakes (Fig. 7.43) usually requires detaching the U-shaped brake booster connecting the piston cylinders together, if installed, followed by unscrewing or quick-releasing one wheel cylinder.

ii-4 DETACHING A WHEEL WITH A QUICK-RELEASE SKEWER

This is easy, and you don't need a tool.

1. Pull outward on the lever to open it (Fig. 2.3).
2. After opening the quick-release lever, unscrew the nut on the opposite end of the quick-release skewer's shaft until both the nut and the head of the skewer clear the fork's wheel-retention tabs.
3. Pull the wheel off.

NOTE: *Some bikes have non-quick-release superlight titanium bolt-on skewers (Fig. 2.4). The wheel is removed by unscrewing the skewer with a 5mm Allen wrench*

2.4 Bolt-on skewer

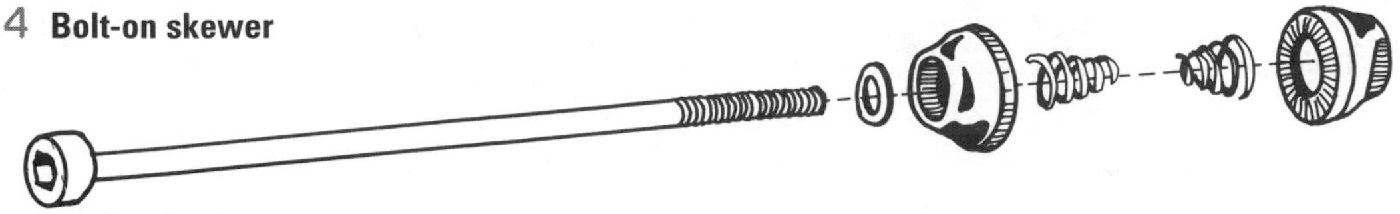

2.5 Loosening an axle nut

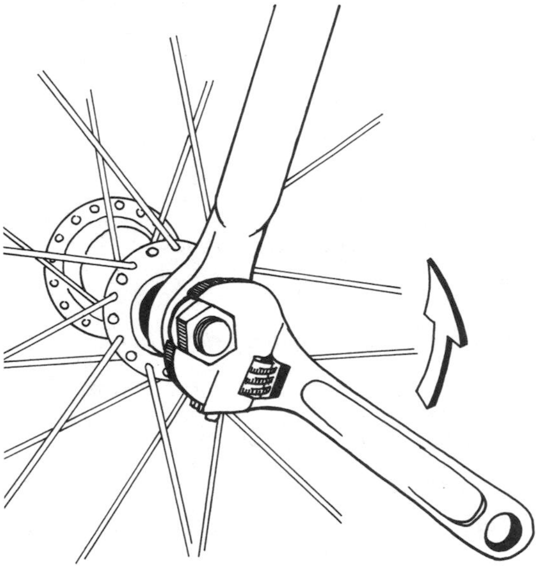

until the head and the nut clear the wheel-retention tabs on the fork ends.

DETACHING WHEELS — INSTALLING FRONT WHEEL — TIGHTENING THE QUICK-RELEASE SKEWER

ii-5 DETACHING A WHEEL WITH AXLE NUTS

1. Unscrew the nuts on the axle ends (usually with a 15mm wrench) until they allow the wheel to fall out (Fig. 2.5).
2. Most mountain bikes have some type of wheel-retention system consisting of nubs or bent tabs on the fork ends (also known as "dropouts") or an axle washer with a bent tooth hooked into a hole in the fork end. These systems prevent the wheel from falling out if the axle nuts loosen. Loosen the nuts enough to clear the retention tabs on the fork ends.
3. Pull the wheel out.

NOTE: *For Cannondale Lefty forks, first remove the disc brake with a 5mm hex key, and then unscrew the axle bolt (usually with a 5mm hex key as well). This procedure pulls the wheel right off without any further encouragement from you. On reinstallation, grease the bearing seats on the axle (the thing sticking out from the fork). Slide the hub back on, line it up, and tighten the bolt. Mount the brake again, assuring that you keep the same spacers between it and the mounting tabs on the fork.*

ii-6 INSTALLING THE FRONT WHEEL

With rim brakes, leave the brake open and lower the fork onto the wheel so that the bike's weight pushes the dropouts down onto the hub axle. This action will seat the axle fully into the fork and center the rim between the brake pads. If your fork or wheel is misaligned, you'll need to hold the rim centered between the brake pads when securing the hub.

With a disc brake, drop the slot in the caliper (the part attached to the fork) over the rotor (the big disc attached to the wheel). Make sure that the rotor does not dislodge either pad.

Continue with the appropriate hub-securing step.

ii-7 TIGHTENING THE QUICK-RELEASE SKEWER

The quick-release skewer is not a glorified wing nut and should not be treated as such.

1. Hold the quick-release lever in the "open" position.
2. Finger tighten the opposite-end nut until it snugs up against the face of the dropout.

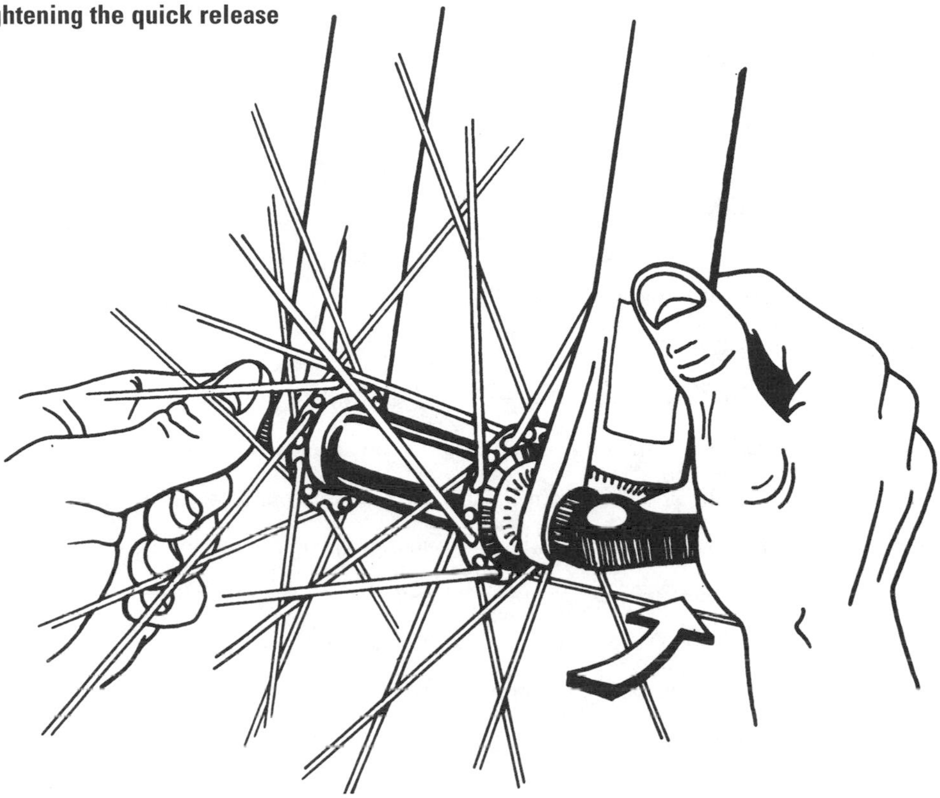

2.6 **Tightening the quick release**

3. Push the lever over (Fig. 2.6) to the "closed" position (it should now be at a 90-degree angle to the axle). If done right, it should have taken a good amount of hand pressure to close the quick-release lever properly; the lever should have left its imprint on your palm for a few seconds.
4. If the quick-release lever does not close tightly enough, open the lever again, tighten the end nut one-quarter turn, and close the lever again. Repeat until tight.
5. If, however, the lever cannot be pushed down perpendicular to the axle, then the nut is too tight. Open the quick-release lever, unscrew the end nut one-quarter turn or so, and try closing the lever again. Repeat this procedure until the quick-release lever is fully closed and snug. When you are done, it is important to have the lever pointing straight up or toward the back of the bike so that it cannot hook on obstacles and be accidentally opened.
6. Double-check that the axle is tightened into the fork by trying to pull the wheel out.

II-8 TIGHTENING BOLT-ON SKEWERS

Hold the end nut with one hand and tighten the skewer with a 5mm Allen wrench. Control Tech, a company that used to make lots of these skewers, recommended 65 inch-pounds (in-lbs) of tightening torque for steel bolt-on skewers and 85 in-lbs for titanium versions. You can come close to the right amount of torque by using a short Allen wrench and tightening as tightly as you can with your fingers. It is easy to overtighten these skewers, so try to avoid that by approximating the pressure a quick-release skewer applies and do not go higher than that.

ii-9 TIGHTENING AXLE NUTS (MASS-MERCHANT BIKES)

Snug up the nuts clockwise (opposite direction of Fig. 2.5) with a wrench (usually 15mm). Use the wrench a little on each side until the nuts are quite tight.

ii-10 REMOVING AND INSTALLING FRONT WHEELS WITH THROUGH-AXLES

In this context of the front wheel, through-axles (a.k.a., 20mm through-axles) are extra-long, removable front-wheel axles, generally 20mm in diameter, that pass through the hub cartridge bearings (which have a 20mm inside diameter) and are clamped directly into the fork ends. Intended to stiffen the fork against lateral and twisting flex, they are no longer only confined to downhill bikes. Any bike with a long-travel fork used under extreme conditions, such as a bike used for jumping or free-riding (extreme, fast and rough, generally noncompetition downhill riding), would offer improved tracking and steering as well as smoother up-and-down action with a through-axle. This is particularly true for an "upside-down" fork, in which the lower legs are the fork's inner legs, motorcycle style, rather than standard (and bigger diameter) outer legs. Because the wheel moves up and down with the inner legs, which slide up and down in the fixed upper outer legs, it is not possible to equip them with a brace (which adds considerable lateral and torsional stiffness to a standard telescoping suspension fork) between the lower legs.

There are a number of different through-axle systems, but they share some common traits. Through-axles generally resemble a long bolt with a head on the bike's drive side. The head is too large to pass through the hub bearings and the dropouts; it snugs up against the drive-side fork dropout. On the other end, the disc-brake-rotor end, the through-axle usually has some sort of a bolt system to draw the ends toward each other to remove any lateral movement of the front wheel.

To remove most through-axles, you loosen whatever clamp bolts are securing the axle on the drive end of the "casting" (another word for the cast magnesium outer fork legs) or, in the case of an upside-down fork, the ends of the inner legs. You then loosen the draw bolt in the axle end on the rotor side to free the opposite shoulder from the casting, loosen the pinch bolts on the rotor-side casting, and pull the axle out to the drive side.

To install most through-axles, you stick the wheel in (*sans* axle) with the rotor between the pads of the disc-brake caliper. You then push the axle through from the drive side and tighten the draw bolt in the axle end on the rotor side (gently—you're not tightening the axle in—you're just removing the lateral slop in the wheel and seating the axle head into or against the drive-side casting). You first snug up the clamping bolts on the rotor side dropout a bit so the axle does not spin when you tighten the draw bolt. Tighten whatever clamping bolts are on the dropouts.

That said, there are lots of through-axle variations. It should be understood that the axle is part of the fork, not part of the wheel, so it varies according to the fork, not the wheel; all 20mm through-axle hubs have the same (20mm) internal diameter of the bearings, the same overall width of the hub, and the same position of the rotor.

The RockShox Boxxer and Fox through-axles are pretty much as described above, with two pinch bolts on each end of the casting to hold the axle in place. Manitou Dorado upside-down forks, in order

TIGHTENING AXLE NUTS — REMOVING & INSTALLING FRONT WHEELS WITH THROUGH-AXLES to prevent rotation of the axle and keep the lower inner legs stiffer, have a big hex-shaped drive-side end of the axle and a smaller hex that will pass through the hub on the rotor end. The hex ends seat into female hex seats in the ends of the inner legs, and, as above, you draw the drive end of the axle into its seat by tightening the bolt on the rotor end. Two pinch bolts on each leg lock it down.

The 2005 Marzocchi through-axle forks have either one or two pinch bolts on each end of the casting. The 2004 Marzocchi downhill forks have a standard through-axle, and the QR20s have a little quick-release lever on the end of each leg to clamp onto the axle ends. The Maverick upside-down fork also has quick releases. Older Marzocchis have a single pinch bolt securing a curved clamp that slides in and out from the side of the end of the casting on a tongue and groove.

The 2005 RockShox Maxle is a through-axle with a quick-release lever on the drive side that is faster to install and remove than a standard quick-release skewer. You push the Maxle in through the hub and the casting from the drive side. Using the quick-release lever as a handle, tighten the axle into the rotor-end casting 1.5 turns, then flip the quick-release lever over, and you are done! There are no pinch bolts on either fork end; the Maxle tightens up by means of internal wedges in each end. Removal requires only flipping open the Maxle quick-release lever, unscrewing the axle 1.5 turns, and pulling it out. This is definitely quicker than a standard hub with a quick-release, when you include tightening and loosening the skewer enough to clear the fork-end "lawyer tabs" (i.e., wheel-retention devices).

Roof racks present a challenge for a through-axle fork. If the rack clamps the fork ends, you must first install a through-axle adapter like the Hurricane Components Fork Up, which clamps onto the fork mount like a standard fork and has a 20mm internal-diameter tube 100mm long (welded above the adapter's dropouts) through which you then run the axle.

ii-11 CLOSING THE BRAKES

1. The steps required to close the brakes are the reverse of what you did to release them. With a V-brake (sidepull cantilever), hold the link in one hand, pull the noodle back, push the cable coming out of the noodle into the slot in the end of the link, and pop the end of the noodle back into the slotted hole (Fig. 2.1 in reverse). With a cantilever or U-brake, hold the brake pads against the rim with one hand and hook the enlarged end of the straddle cable back into the end of the brake arm with your other hand (Fig. 2.2 in reverse). With most disc brakes, the brake is ready to apply as soon as the wheel is installed. Do the reverse of §ii-3 to reconnect the more rare types of brakes, or find the brake type at the beginning of Chapter 7 and read up on it.
2. Check that the brake cables are connected securely by squeezing the levers. Lift the front end of the bike and spin the front wheel, gently applying the brakes several times. Check that the pads are not dragging, and recenter the wheel (or adjust the brakes as described in Chapter 7, for your type of brake). If everything is reconnected and centered properly, you're done. Go ride your bike.

ii-12 REMOVING THE REAR WHEEL

Removing the rear wheel is done in the same way as removing the front (§ii-2 to §ii-5), with the added complication of the chain and cogs.

2.7 **Removal and installation of the rear wheel**

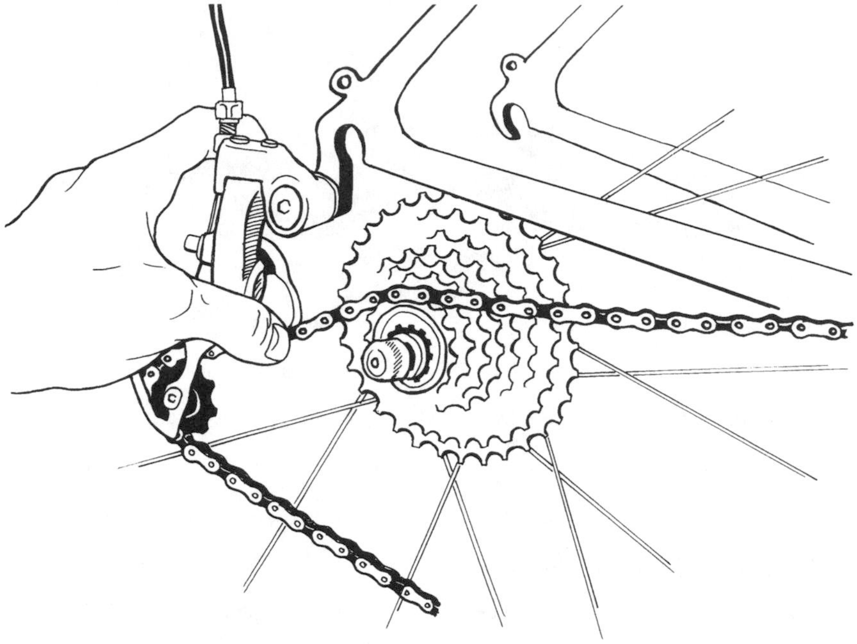

1. Shift the chain onto the smallest cog by lifting the rear wheel off of the ground and shifting while turning the cranks.
2. To release the wheel from the rear dropouts and the brakes, follow the same procedure as with the front wheel. When you push the wheel out, you'll need to move the chain out of the way. This is usually a matter of grabbing the rear derailleur and pulling it back so the jockey wheels (pulley wheels) move out of the way, while pushing forward on the quick-release or axle nuts with your thumbs and letting the wheel fall as you hold the bike up (Fig. 2.7). If the bottom half of the chain catches the wheel as it falls, jiggle the wheel while lifting it to free the cogs from the chain.

INSTALLING THE REAR WHEEL

ii-13 INSTALLING THE REAR WHEEL

1. Check to make sure that the rear derailleur is shifted to its outermost position (under the smallest cog [Fig. 5.4]).
2. Slip the wheel up between the seat stays and maneuver the upper section of chain onto the smallest cog (Fig. 2.7).
3. Set the bike down on the rear wheel, and as you let the bike drop down, pull the rear derailleur back with your right hand and pull the axle ends back into the dropouts with your index fingers. Your thumbs push forward on the rear dropouts, which should now slide over the axle ends. (If the axle does not slip into the dropouts, you may need to spread the dropouts apart or squeeze them toward each other to get them to fall between the quick-release ends and the axle ends.) If you have a rear disc brake, guide the rotor in between the brake pads.
4. Check that the axle is fully seated in the dropouts, which should center the wheel between the brake pads. If the rim rubs on one brake pad, hold the rim in a centered position as you secure the axle.
5. Tighten the quick-release skewer, bolt-on skewer,

2.8 **Wiping down chain**

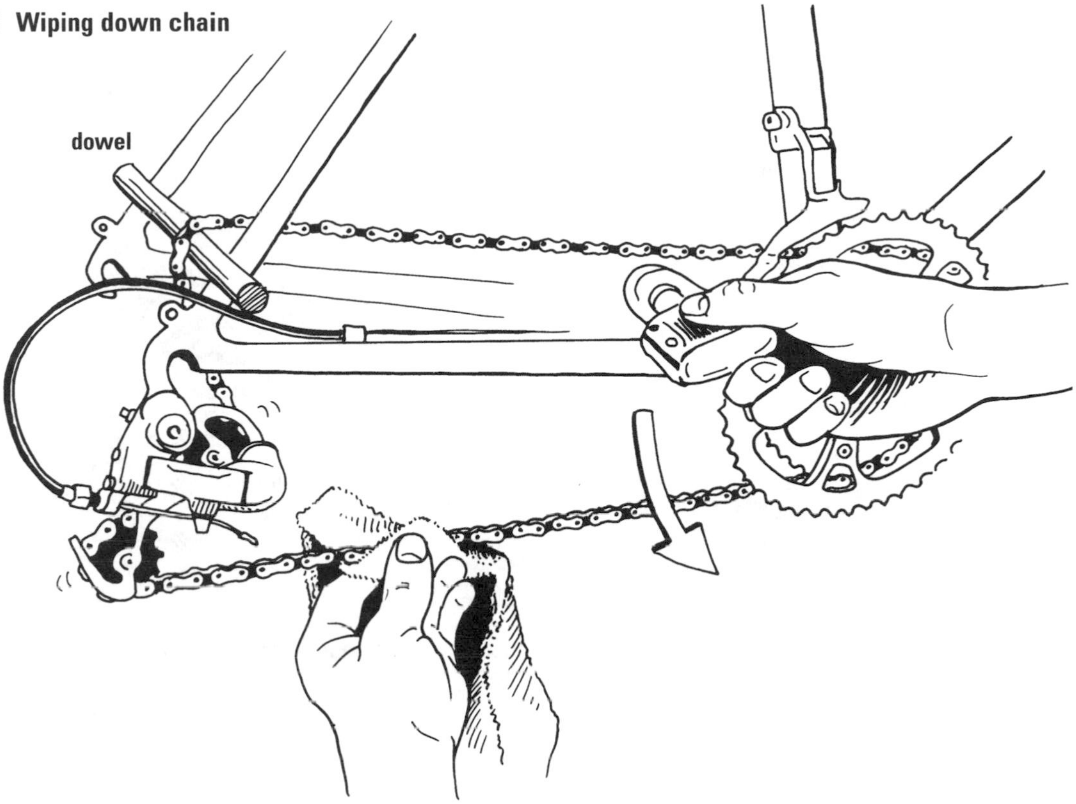

or axle nuts in the same way as explained for the front wheel.

6. Reconnect the rear brake the same way as you did on the front wheel.

You're done. Go ride your bike.

ii-14 CLEANING THE BICYCLE

Most cleaning can be done with soap, water, and a brush. Soap and water are easier on you and on the earth than stronger solvents, which are generally only needed for the drivetrain, if at all. Avoid using the high-pressure sprayers you find at pay car washes to clean your bike. The soaps are corrosive, and the high pressure forces them into bearings, pivots, and frame tubes, causing extensive damage over time.

Using a bike stand is highly recommended when scrubbing the bike. In the absence of a bike stand, the bike can be hung from a garage ceiling with rope, or stood upside down on the saddle and handlebar, or balanced on the front of the fork and the handlebar with the front wheel removed.

1. The wheels can be cleaned easily while they are on the bike. Remove the wheels to clean the frame, fork, and components.
2. If the bike has a chain hanger (a little nub attached to the inner side of the right seat stay, a few centimeters above the dropout), hook the chain over it. If not, pull the chain back over a dowel stick (Fig. 2.8) or an old rear hub secured into the dropouts.
3. Fill a bucket with hot water and dish soap. Scrub the entire bike and wheels with a stiff nylon-bristle brush. Leave the chain, cogs, chainrings, and derailleurs for last.
4. Rinse the bike with water (low pressure!), either by hosing it off or by wiping it with a wet rag.

Avoid getting water in the bearings of the bottom bracket, headset, pedals, or hubs. Also avoid getting water into the lip seals of suspension forks, as well as any pivots or shock seals on rear-suspension systems. In addition, most metal frames and rigid forks have vent holes in the tubes to allow expanding hot gases to escape during welding. The holes are often open to the outside on the seat stays, fork legs, chainstays, and seat stay and chainstay bridges. Avoid getting water in these holes, especially if you have to use a high-pressure car wash. Taping over the vent holes, even when riding, is a good idea.

ii-15 CLEANING THE DRIVETRAIN

The drivetrain consists of an oil-covered chain running over the gears and derailleurs. It is totally exposed to the elements, so it picks up lots of dirt. Because the drivetrain is what transfers your energy into the bike's forward motion, it should move freely. Frequent cleaning and lubrication keep it rolling well and extend the life of your bike.

The drivetrain can often be cleaned sufficiently by using a rag and wiping down the chain, derailleur jockey wheels, and chainrings. You might want to wear rubber gloves for this. If you keep the gloves, rag, and lube near where you store your bike, you will tend to clean it before or after almost every ride without dirtying your hands. And the drivetrain will last longer and perform better.

1. To wipe the chain, turn the cranks while holding a rag in your hand and grabbing the chain (Fig. 2.8).
2. Holding a rag, squeeze the teeth of the jockey wheels in between your index finger and thumb as you turn the cranks (Fig. 2.9). This simple procedure will remove almost any buildup on the jockey wheels.

2.9 Cleaning jockey wheels

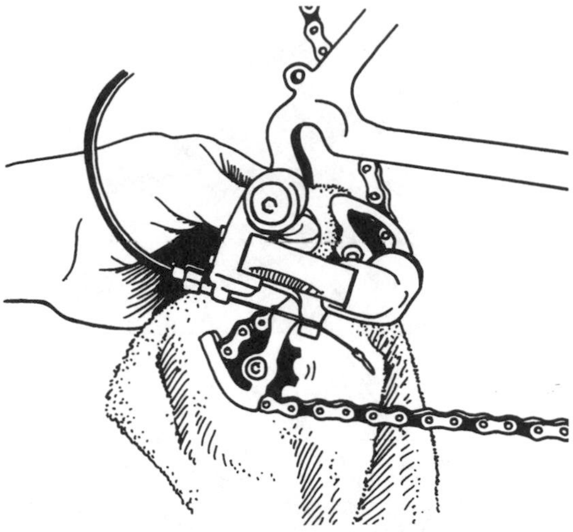

2.10 Cogset cleaning

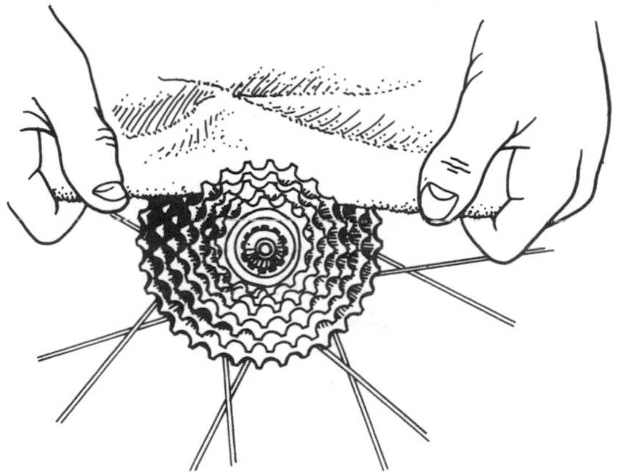

3. Slip a rag between cogs of the freewheel and work it back and forth to clean each cog (Fig. 2.10).
4. Last, thoroughly wipe down the derailleurs and the front chainrings with the rag.

Your chain will last much longer if you perform this sort of quick cleaning regularly, followed by dripping chain lube on the chain and another light wipe down. You'll also be able to skip those heavy-duty solvent cleanings that are necessary when a chain gets really grungy. You can get it just as clean as with a solvent if you wipe the chain down thor-

2.11 **Using a solvent-bath chain cleaner**

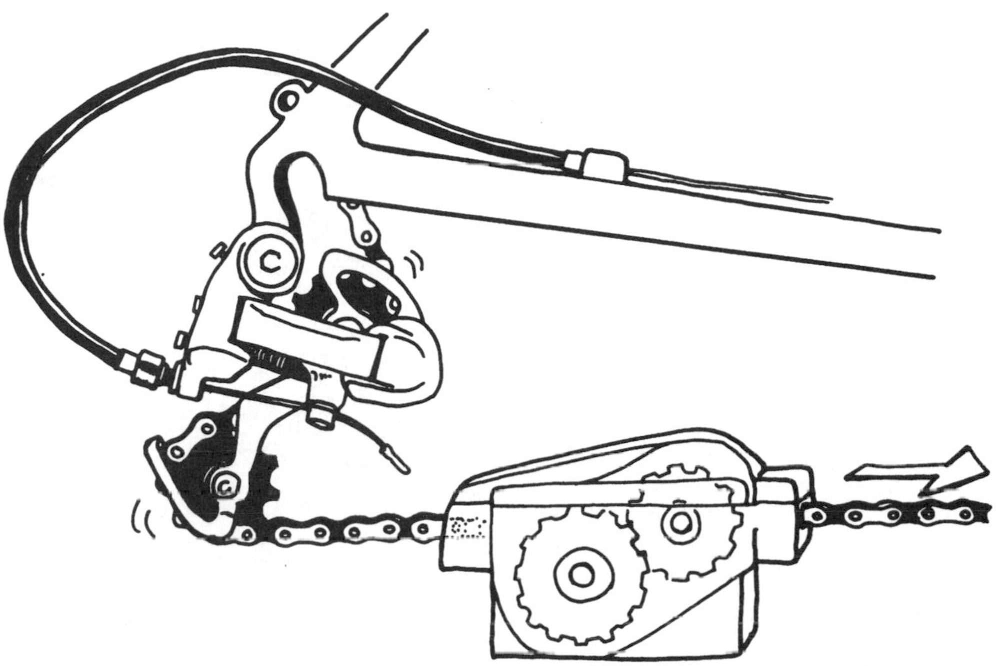

oughly after lubricating it and clean in between all of the outer link plates with cotton swabs (they won't fit in between the inner link plates, but the roller will spin with them).

You can also remove mud packed into derailleurs and cogs with the soapy water and scrub brush. The soap will not dissolve the dirty lubricant that is all over the drivetrain, but the brush will smear it all over the bike if you're not careful. Use a different brush than the one you use for cleaning the frame, since the bristles of this brush will become black and oily. Follow the brushing with a cloth wipe down.

ii-16 SOLVENT CLEANING OF THE CHAIN

If you frequently wipe your chain down and then lubricate it sparingly by putting lube only on the chain rollers where it is needed (Fig. 4.1), rather than all over the chain, you can minimize the need for solvent cleaning with its associated disposal and toxicity problems. If you determine that using a solvent is necessary, work in a well-ventilated area, use as little solvent as necessary, and pick an environmentally friendly one. Using one of the many citrus solvents on the market will minimize the danger of breathing the stuff, or getting it onto and into your skin, and will reduce a major disposal problem. If you are using a lot of solvents, organic ones such as diesel fuel can be recycled and therefore may be preferable to using citrus solvents, as long as you protect yourself from the fumes with a respirator, and dispose of the solvent properly if not recycling it.

Because all solvents suck the oils out of your skin, I recommend using rubber gloves, even with "green" solvents. A self-contained chain cleaner with internal brushes and a solvent bath is a quick and convenient way to clean a chain (Fig. 2.11), and it can be done without risk of later chain breakage caused by opening and closing the chain. A nylon brush or an old toothbrush dipped in a solvent is good for cleaning cogs, pulleys, and chainrings, and it can be used for a quick clean of the chain as well.

A way to thoroughly clean the chain is to remove it and put it in a solvent bath, but I don't recommend this approach unless you have a chain with a master link. Opening a standard chain by pushing rivets in and out with a chain tool is hard on the chain and can lead to breakage while riding. Because a nine-speed chain must be narrow so that it will fit in the tight space between cogs, only a very small length of each rivet protrudes from the chain plates. Even if you use one of Shimano's special link pins every time you open the (Shimano) chain, you are still weakening the chain and can bring on breakage under shifting load.

1. Follow the directions in Chapter 4, §iv-7, for removing the chain, or, ideally, those in §iv-11 for using a master link.
2. Put the chain in an old water bottle that is about one-fourth full of a solvent.
3. Shake the bottle vigorously to clean the chain. Do this close to the ground, in case the water bottle leaks.
4. Hang the chain up to dry completely, especially inside the rollers.
5. Install the chain on the bike, following the directions in Chapter 4, §iv-8 to §iv-10, or better yet, get a master link and use it to put the chain together (§iv-11).
6. Drip chain lubricant into each of the chain's links and rollers.
7. Lightly wipe down the chain with a rag.

You can reuse much of the solvent by allowing it to settle in a clear container over a period of days or weeks. Decant and save the clear stuff and dispose of the sludge.

A clean bike invites you to jump on it, and it will feel faster. Corrosion problems are minimized, and you can see other problems as they arise. A clean bike is a happy bike.

ii-17 A GENERAL GUIDE TO PERFORMING MECHANICAL WORK

a. Threaded parts

All threads must be prepped before tightening

Depending on the bolt in question, prep with lubricant, threadlock compound, or an antiseize compound. Clean off excess thread-prepping compound to minimize dirt attraction.

1. Lubricated threads: Most threads should be lubricated with grease or oil. If a bolt is already installed, you can back it out and drip a little chain lube on it, and tighten it back down. Lube items such as crank bolts, pedal axles, cleat bolts on shoes, derailleur and brake-cable anchor bolts, and control-lever mounting bolts.
2. Locked threads: Some threads need to be locked to prevent the bolts they are on from vibrating loose. These are bolts that need to stay in place but are not supposed to be tightened down fully for some reason or other, usually to avoid seizing a moving part, throwing a part out of adjustment, or stripping threads in a soft material. Examples of bolts of this type are derailleur limit screws, jockey-wheel center bolts, brake mounting bolts (for rim brakes), and spokes. Use Loctite, Finish Line Threadlock, or the equivalent; use Wheelsmith Spoke-Prep or the equivalent on spokes. If the wheel has extremely high spoke tension on both sides the spokes will stay in adjustment when using grease on the threads instead of Spoke-Prep or the equivalent. Some

DT spoke nipples come with threadlock compound already inside them.

3. Antiseize threads: Some threads have a tendency to bind up and gall, making full tightening as well as extraction problematic. They need an antiseize compound on them to prevent galling. Examples of this kind of thread are any steel or aluminum bolt threaded into a titanium part—including any parts mounted to titanium frames, such as bottom-bracket cups—and any titanium bolt threaded into a steel or aluminum part. Use Finish Line Ti-Prep or an equivalent antiseize formulation.

IMPORTANT: *Never thread a titanium bolt into a titanium part. Even with an antiseize compound, a titanium bolt will almost certainly gall and rip the titanium part when you try to remove the bolt.*

Wrenches (Fig. 2.12) must be fully engaged before tightening or loosening

1. Allen wrenches (hex keys) and TORX wrenches must be fully inserted into the bolt head, or the wrench and/or the bolt hole will round off. A good example is a shoe-cleat bolt; clean dirt and rocks out of shoe-cleat bolts before tapping the hex key in fully with a hammer so it engages maximally.
2. Open-end, box-end, and socket wrenches must be properly seated around a hex bolt, or the bolt head will round off. A good example is an aluminum headset nut.
3. Splined wrenches must be fully engaged. If they are not, the splines will be damaged, or the tool will snap. If you strip the splines in a cassette lockring, you will not be able to get it off.
4. Toothed-lockring spanners need to stay lined up on the lockring; if they slide off, they will not

2.12 Wrenches

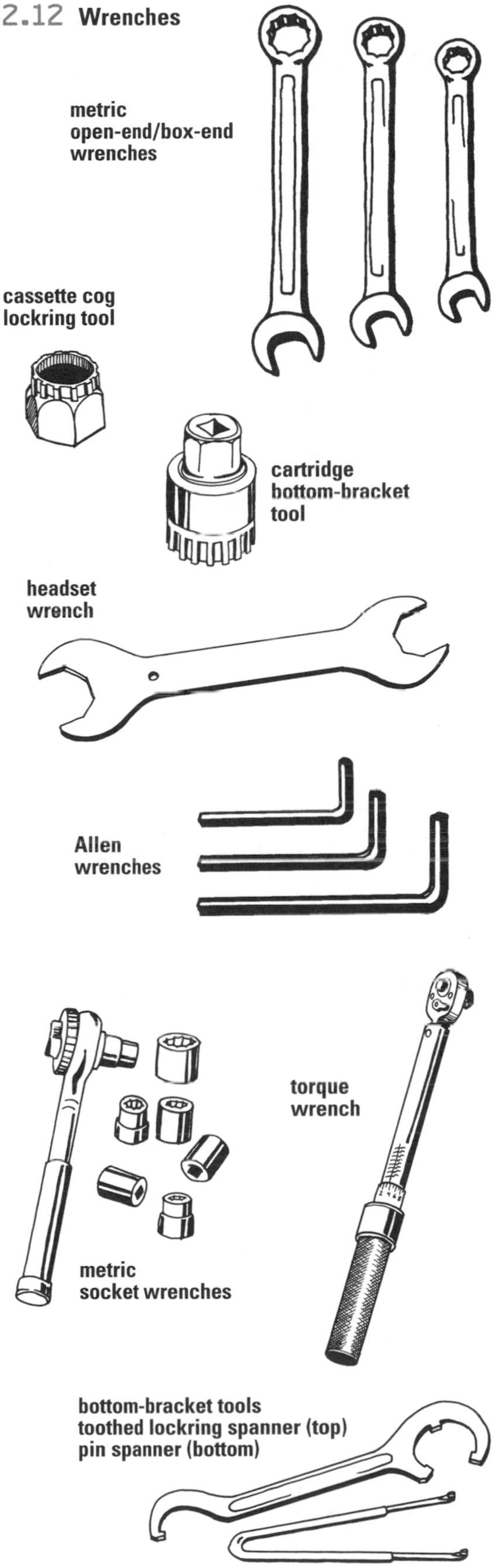

only tear up the lockring, they will also damage the frame paint. Such a lockring can be found on a bottom-bracket adjustable cup.

5. Pin spanners need to be fully seated in the pinholes in the part being turned in order to prevent slipping out and damaging the holes in the part. You can find pinholes in some bottom-bracket adjustable cups, crank-bolt collars, and cartridge-bearing hubs.

Tightening torque

A full list of specific tightening torques can be found in Appendix D. To best understand them it helps to know a little about metric bolt sizes, particularly as they are used on bikes.

The designation M in front of the bolt size number means millimeters and refers to the bolt shaft, not to the hex key that turns it: An M5 bolt is 5mm in diameter, an M6 is 6mm, and so on, but the designation may not have any relationship to the wrench size. For instance, an M5 bolt usually takes a 4mm hex key (or in the case of a hex-head style, an 8mm box-end or socket wrench). However, M5 bolts on bicycles often accept different wrench sizes than normally found on M5 bolts. Bolts that attach bottle cages to the frame are M5, and although some accept the normal 4mm hex key, many have a rounded "cap" head and take a 3mm hex key. The bolts that clamp a front derailleur around the seat tube, or that anchor the cable on a front or rear derailleur, are also M5, but they instead take a bigger than standard hex key size, namely a 5mm. And when you get to the big, single bolts found on old stems and some seatposts, you find lots of different bolt sizes (M6, M7, and even M8), but usually only one wrench size (6mm hex key).

Generally, tightness can be classified in four levels:

1. Snug (10–30 in-lbs, or 1–3 N·m [newton-meters in SI units]): Small setscrews (such as Grip Shift mounting screw), bearing-preload bolts (as on threadless-headset top caps), and screws going into plastic parts need to be merely snug.
2. Firmly tightened (30–80 in-lbs, or 3–9 N·m): Small bolts—often M5 size—such as shoe-cleat bolts, cable anchor bolts on brakes and derailleurs, small stem bolts, brake-lever-clamp bolts, and some disc-brake-caliper mounting bolts need to be firmly tightened.
3. Tight (80–240 in-lbs, or 9–27 N·m): Wheel axles, old-style single-bolt stem bolts (M6, M7, or M8), most M6 disc-brake-caliper mounting bolts, seatpost binder bolts, and seatpost saddle-clamp bolts need to be tight.
4. Really tight (280–600 in-lbs, or 31–68 N·m): Crankarm bolts, pedal axles, cassette lockring bolts, and bottom-bracket cups are large parts that need to be really tight.

b. Cleanliness

1. Do not expect parts to work by just squirting or slathering lubricant on them (meanwhile patting yourself on the back for maintaining your bike). The lube will pick up lots of dirt and get very gunky.
2. Do not expect parts to work by washing them and then not lubricating them. They will get dry and squeaky.

c. Test Riding

Always test ride the bike after adjusting it in the bike stand. Parts behave differently under load.

CHAPTER 3

EMERGENCY REPAIRS

How to get home when something big breaks or you get lost or hurt

Always carry a flagon of whiskey in case of a snakebite, and furthermore, always carry a small snake.
—W. C. Fields

TOOLS

carry-along tools (Fig. 1.5)

extended-trip carry-along tools (Fig. 1.6)

This chapter is included so you do not face disaster if you have a mechanical problem on the trail. If you ride your bike out in the boonies, sooner or later you will encounter a mechanical problem that has the potential to turn into an emergency. The best way to avoid such an emergency is to plan ahead and be prepared before it happens. Proper planning involves steps as simple as bringing along a few tools, spare tubes, and a little knowledge.

On the trail if something breaks, the procedures in this chapter will help you to deal with it, whether or not you have all of the tools that you need. You always have the option of walking, but this chapter is designed to get you home pedaling.

Finally, you may find yourself with a perfectly functioning bicycle and still be in dire straits because you're either lost, bonking (i.e., your body has run out of fuel), or injured on the trail. Carefully read the final part of this chapter for pointers on how to avoid getting lost or injured and what to do if the worst does happen.

If this chapter does nothing other than alert you to some of the dangers facing you out in the backcountry, then with luck you'll prepare for them and this chapter will have accomplished its purpose.

iii-1 RECOMMENDED TOOLS

The take-along tool kit for your seat bag is described in Chapter 1, §i-6 (Fig. 1.5). If you're going to be a long way from civilization, take along the extra tools recommended for longer trips (Fig. 1.6).

iii-2 FLAT TIRE PREVENTION

The potential for flat tires can be greatly reduced with the use of some tire sealants, by using tubeless tires, or, best yet, by using both together. "Slime" is one sealant that works well and is widely available. The stuff is a viscous liquid with chopped fibers in it that plug holes in the tube as they happen (use of Slime is covered in Chapter 6, §vi-10); it can be injected into your tube, or you can purchase tubes with a sealant already inside. Tubeless tires are discussed in Chapter 6, §vi-2 and §vi-7.

If you have Slime or another tire sealant in your tube or tubeless tire and your tire gets low owing to a small hole through the tread (this is most likely to happen when you stop riding for a while), put more air in and spin the wheel or ride for a couple of miles to get the sealant to flow out to the hole. A large hole will not be filled, although amazingly big holes can be plugged enough to get you home if you locate where the sealant is squirting out through the tire. Rotate the wheel so that the puncture is at the bottom and wait. The sealant may pool enough there to plug the hole. Add more air and continue riding. If the hole is on the rim side the sealant will not flow to it.

I recommend against the older, plastic tire liners placed between the tire and tube. They are so stiff that they decrease traction and cornering ability, and they can slip sideways and cut into the tube.

There is, however, a new generation of liners made of Kevlar. These liners are considerably lighter than their stiff plastic counterparts. They are fairly expensive, though. A pair of "Spin Skins" for mountain bike tires can run around $33.

iii-3 FIXING FLAT TIRES

a. If you have a spare or a patch kit

Simple flat tires are easy to deal with. The first flat you get on a ride, whether in a standard inner tube and tire or in a tubeless tire, is most easily fixed by installing your spare tube (Chapter 6, §vi-6, describes how).

Check your spare tube before leaving home to make sure that it holds air and that you can loosen the valve nut by hand out on the trail (assuming it has a Presta valve; see Fig. 1.1B—in Chapter 1, or Figs. 6.2 and 6.3—in Chapter 6). If you have tubeless tires, take the additional step of making sure that the knurled retainer nut that holds your valve stem into the rim can also be loosened by hand out on the trail, in case you have to install a spare tube.

Before installing the new tube, make sure you remove all thorns from the tire and feel around the inside of the tire for any other sharp objects and remove them as well. Check the rim to see that your flat wasn't caused by a protruding spoke or nipple, a metal shard from the rim, or the edge of a spoke hole protruding through a worn rim strip. Many rim strips are totally inadequate, being either too narrow or prone to cracking or tearing. Also, metal hunks left from the drilling of rims during manufacture can work their way out into the tube. Endeavor to eliminate these problems before leaving on a backcountry ride by shaking out any metal fragments and using good rim strips or a couple of layers of fiberglass packing tape (with lengthwise superstrong fibers) as rim strips. If the hole in the tube is on the rim side, tire sealant will not fill the hole because the liquid will be thrown to the outside toward the tread when the wheel turns.

After you run out of spare tubes, additional flats must be patched (also covered in Chapter 6, §vi-3 to §vi-5).

b. Torn sidewall

Rocks and glass can cut tire sidewalls. The likelihood of sidewall problems is reduced if you do not venture into the backcountry on old tires with rotten and weakened sidewall cords. If your tire's sidewall is torn or cut, the tube will stick out, and on a tubeless tire, no amount of sealant will close the leak. Just patching the tube or installing a new one isn't going to solve the problem. Without reinforcement, your tube will blow out through the sidewall gash very soon.

First, you have to look for something to reinforce the sidewall (Fig. 3.1). Dollar bills work surprisingly well as tire boots (i.e., temporary internal casing reinforcements). The paper is pretty tough and should hold for the rest of the ride if you are careful. (I told you that cash would get you out of bad situations. Just don't try putting a credit card in there; tire cuts don't take American Express or Visa!) Business cards are a bit small but work better than nothing. You might even try an energy bar wrapper. A small piece of a tire liner cut into an oval, or duct tape, might be a good addition to your patch kit for this purpose. A piece of a plastic soda bottle can also work. You get the idea.

1. Lay the cash or other reinforcement inside the tire over the gash (Fig. 3.1), or wrap it around the tube at that spot. Place several layers between the tire and tube to support the tube and prevent it from bulging out through the hole in the sidewall.
2. Put a little air in the tube to hold the makeshift reinforcement in place.
3. Mount the tire bead (the edge of the tire, which has steel or Kevlar strands fixing its diameter—see Fig. 6.7) on the rim. You may need to let a little air out of the tube to do so.
4. After making sure that the tire is seated and the boot is still in place, inflate the tube to about 40 psi, if you are good at estimating without a gauge. Much less than 40 psi will allow the boot to move around and may also lead to a pinch flat if you're riding on rocky terrain. In any case, this type of fix is not a perfect solution, so you will need to check the boot periodically to make certain that the tube is not bulging out again.

3.1 **Temporary fix for a torn tire casing**

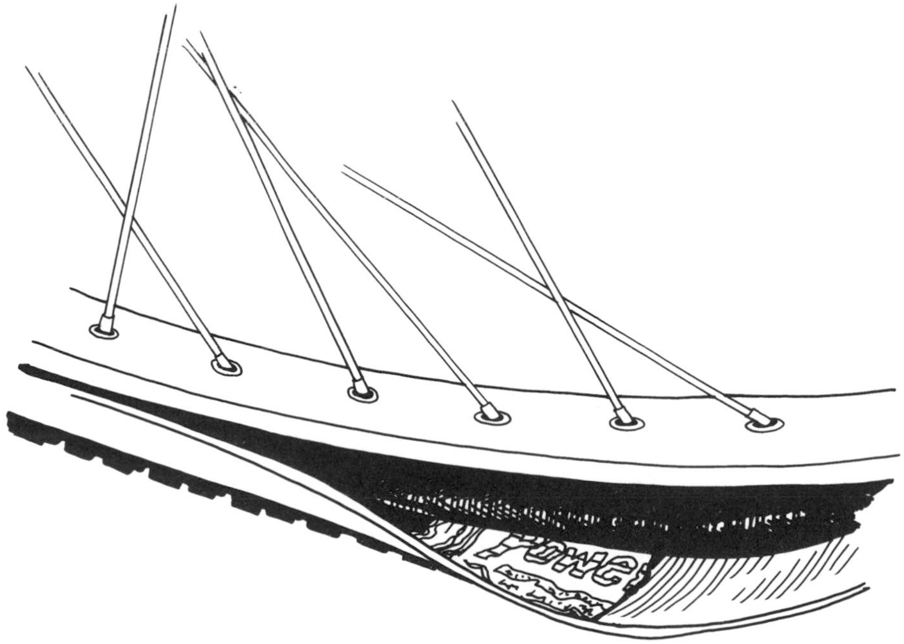

JAMMED CHAIN — BROKEN CHAIN

c. No more spare tubes or patches

Now comes the frustrating part: You have run out of spare tubes and have used up all of your patches (or your CO_2 cartridge is empty and you don't have a pump) and still you have a flat tire. The solution is obvious. You are going to have to walk or ride home without air in your tire. Riding a flat for a long way will trash your tire and will probably damage your rim, yet there are ways to minimize that damage. Try filling the space in the tire with grass, leaves, or similar material. Pack it in tightly and then remount the tire on the rim. This procedure should make the ride a little less dangerous by minimizing the flat tire's tendency to slide sideways out from under the bike during a turn.

iii-4 CHAIN JAMMED BETWEEN THE CHAINRING AND THE CHAINSTAY

If your chain gets jammed between the chainring and the chainstay, it may be hard to get it out if the clearance is tight. You may find that you tug and tug on the chain, and it won't come out. Well, chainrings flex, and if you apply some mechanical advantage, the chain will come free quite easily. Just insert a screwdriver or similar thin lever between the chainring and the chainstay, and pry the space open while pulling the chain out (Fig. 3.2). You will probably be amazed at how easy this is, especially in light of how much hard tugging would not free the chain.

If you still cannot free the chain, disassemble the chain with a chain tool (Chapter 4, §iv-7 or §iv-11), pull it out, and put it back together (§iv-9 to §iv-11).

3.2 Freeing a jammed chain

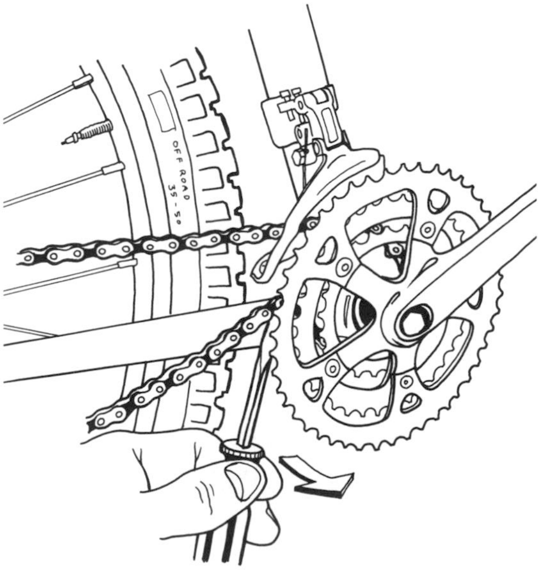

iii-5 BROKEN CHAIN

Chains can break when you are mountain bike riding, usually while shifting the front derailleur under load. The side force of the derailleur cage plate pushing laterally against the chain coupled with the high tension can pop a chain plate off the end of a rivet. As the chain rips apart, it can cause collateral damage to other parts. The open chain plate can snag the front-derailleur cage, bending it or tearing it off, or it can jam into the rear dropout. When a chain breaks, the end link is certainly shot, and some others in the area may be as well.

1. Remove the damaged links with the chain tool. (You or your riding partner did remember to bring a chain tool, right?) Again, the procedures for removing the damaged links and reinstalling the chain are covered in Chapter 4, §iv-7 to §iv-11.
2. If you have brought along extra chain links, replace the same number you remove. If not, you'll need to use the chain in its shortened state—it will still work, but be careful to avoid shifting into the big chainring–largest cog combination. Otherwise, you can rip up your rear derailleur if the chain is not long enough to encompass this span with a little slack left.

3.3 **Fixing broken chain**

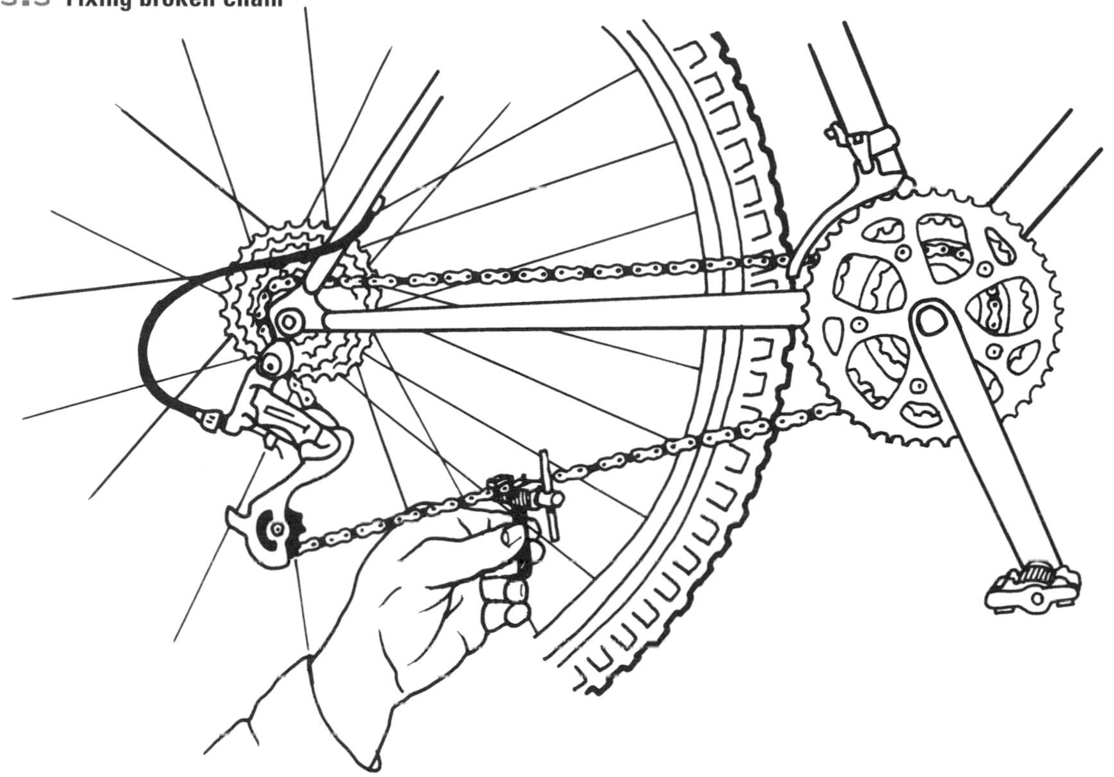

3. Join the ends and connect the chain (Fig. 3.3); the procedure is in Chapter 4, §iv-9 and §iv-10. Some lightweight chain tools and multitools are more difficult to use than a shop chain tool. Some flex so badly that it is hard to keep the push rod lined up with the rivet. Others pinch the plates so tightly that the chain link binds up. It's a good idea to find these things out before you need to perform repairs on the trail. Try the tool out at home or at your local bike shop. This way you'll know what you're getting into before you reach the trailhead.

iii-6 BENT WHEEL

If the rim is banging against the brake pads, or worse yet, the frame or fork, pedaling becomes very difficult. It can happen because of a loose or broken spoke or a badly bent, or even broken, rim. Below are four ways to deal with this problem.

iii-7 LOOSE SPOKES

If you have a loose spoke or two, the rim will wobble all over the place.

1. Find the loose spoke (or spokes) by feeling all of them. The really loose ones, which would cause a wobble of large magnitude, will be obvious. If you find a broken spoke, skip to the next section (§iii-8). If you discover no loose or broken spokes, skip ahead to §iii-10.
2. Get out the spoke wrench that you carry for such an eventuality. (If you don't have one, skip to §iii-9 below.)
3. Mark the loose spokes by tying blades of grass, sandwich bag twist-ties, tape, or the like around them.

3.4 **Tightening and loosening spokes**

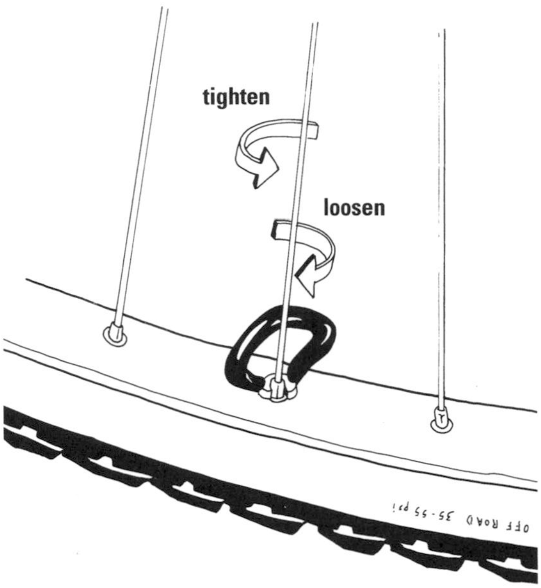

3.5 **Wrapping broken spoke**

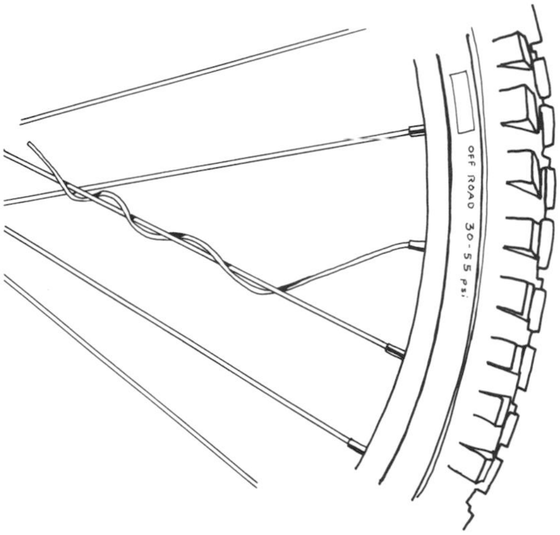

4. Tighten the loose spokes (Fig. 3.4), and true the wheel, following the procedures in §vi-11.

iii-8 BROKEN SPOKES

BROKEN SPOKES

If you break a spoke, the wheel will wobble wildly.

1. Locate the broken spoke.
2. Remove the remainder of the spoke, both the piece going through the hub and the piece threaded into the nipple. If the broken spoke is on the drive side of the rear wheel, you may not be able to remove it from the hub, because it will be behind the cogs. If so, skip to step 6 after wrapping it around neighboring spokes (Fig. 3.5) to prevent it from slapping around.
3. Get out your spoke wrench. (If you have no spoke wrench, skip to §iii-9 below.)
4. If you brought a spare spoke of the right length or the Kevlar replacement spoke mentioned in Chapter 1, §i-6b, you're in business. (If not, skip to step 6.) Put the new spoke through the hub hole, weave it through the other spokes the same way the old one was, and thread it into the spoke nipple that is still sticking out of the rim. If it looks just like the other spokes, mark it with a pen or by tying blades of grass, sandwich bag twist-ties, tape, or the like around it. If you are using a Kevlar replacement spoke, thread it through the hub hole, attach the ends to the enclosed stub of spoke, adjust the ends to length, tie them off, and tighten the spoke nipple.
5. Tighten the nipple on the new spoke with a spoke wrench (Fig. 3.4), checking the rim clearance with the brake pad as you go. Stop when the rim is centered between the pads at that point, and finish your ride.
6. If you can't replace the spoke but you do have a spoke wrench, bring the wheel into rideable trueness by loosening the spoke on either side of the broken one. These two spokes come from the

3.6 **Brake-lever adjusting barrel**

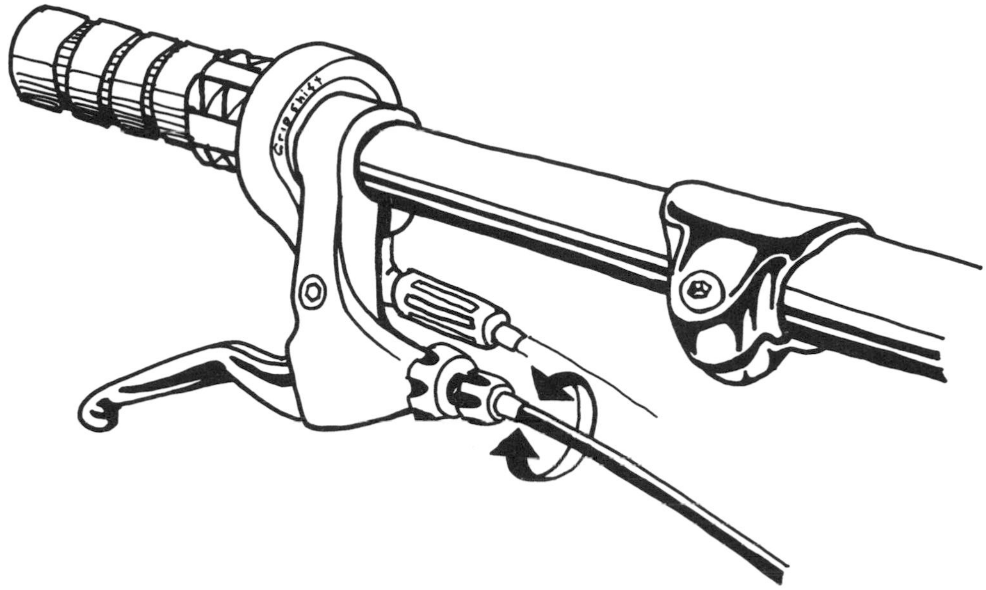

opposite side of the hub and will let the rim move toward the side with the broken spoke as they are loosened. A spoke nipple loosens counterclockwise when viewed from its top (i.e., from the tire side—see Fig. 3.4). Ride home, conservatively, as this wheel will rapidly get worse.

7. Once at home, replace the spoke, following the procedure in Chapter 6, §vi-12, or take it to a bike shop for repair. After you have had a broken spoke more than once on a wheel, all of the spokes on the wheel should be replaced, and the rim may need replacement as well.

iii-9 NO SPOKE WRENCH

If the rim is banging the brake pads, but the tire is not hitting the chainstays or fork legs, just open the brake so that you can get home.

1. Loosen the brake-cable tension by screwing in (clockwise) the barrel adjuster on the brake lever (Fig. 3.6). Remember that braking on that wheel is greatly reduced or nonexistent, so ride slowly and carefully.
2. If the rim is still banging the brakes, and you have a wrench to loosen the brake cable (usually a 5mm Allen), do so, and then clamp the cable back down. You can also unhook the cable as you would when removing the wheel (§ii-3, Figs. 2.1 and 2.2), but the brake arm on some brakes can flip around into the spokes as you ride, so I don't recommend it. You now have no brake on this wheel; ride carefully and walk the bike through difficult sections.
3. If the bent wheel still will not turn, you can remove both brake arms from the cantilever posts, put them in your pocket, and pedal home slowly. You will usually need a 5mm Allen wrench for this. Do not attempt to ride a bike with brakes still attached to the frame or fork but disconnected from the cable. The brake arms will flap around as you ride and may get caught in the

3.7 **Fixing a bent rim**

spokes, which could crack your seat stay or fork, not to mention your head, in a heartbeat.

If you want to straighten the wheel without using a spoke wrench, follow the procedures for dealing with a bent rim in the next section, §iii-10. Recognize that if you bend the rim by smacking it on the ground to correct for a loose or broken spoke, you will permanently deform the rim. Try to get home without resorting to this, because you will have to replace the rim.

BENT RIM

iii-10 BENT RIM

LEVEL 2

If your rim is only mildly out of true, and you brought your spoke wrench, you can fix it. The procedure for truing a wheel is explained in §vi-11.

If the wheel is really whacked out, spoke truing won't do much. To get the rim to clear the brakes so that you can pedal home, follow the steps in §iii-9: No Spoke Wrench.

If the wheel is bent to the point that it won't turn, even when the brake is removed, you can beat it straight as long as the rim is not broken.

1. Find the area that is bent outward the most and mark it on the outward side.
2. Leaving the tire on and inflated, hold the wheel by its sides with the bent part at the top with the mark facing away from you.
3. Smack the bent section of the rim against the flat ground (Fig. 3.7). (It usually works fine to leave the tire on and inflated.)
4. Put the wheel back in the frame or fork, and see if anything has changed.
5. Repeat the process until the wheel is rideable. You may be surprised how straight you can get a wheel this way. Of course, you can also

3.8 **Opening front derailleur cage**

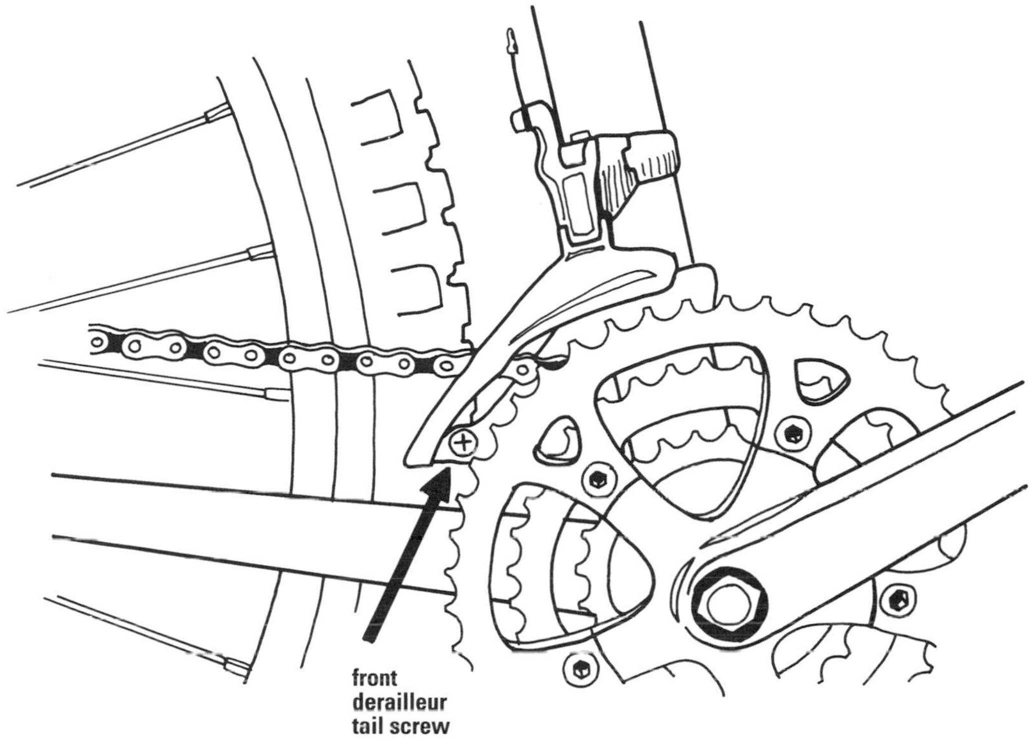

make it a lot worse if you hit it too hard or at the wrong spot.

iii-11 DAMAGED FRONT DERAILLEUR

If the front derailleur is mildly bent, straighten it with your hands or leave it until you get home. If it has simply rotated around the seat tube (the chain, your foot, or a pants leg can catch it and turn it), reposition it so the cage is just above and parallel to the chainrings, and then tighten the derailleur in place with a 5mm Allen wrench. If the derailleur is broken or so bent that you can't ride, you will need to remove it or route the chain around it as described below.

a. With only a screwdriver

1. Get the chain out of the derailleur cage. To do this, open the derailleur cage by removing the screw at its tail (Fig. 3.8).
2. Bypass the derailleur by putting the chain on a chainring that does not interfere with it (either shift the derailleur to the inside and put the chain on the big chainring or vice versa).

b. With Allen wrenches and a screwdriver (or a chain tool)

1. Remove the derailleur from the seat tube, usually with a 5mm Allen wrench.
2. Remove the screw at the tail of the derailleur cage with a screwdriver (Fig. 3.8).
3. Pry open the cage, and separate it from the chain. You could also disassemble the chain, pull it out of the derailleur, and reconnect it (Chapter 4, §iv-7 to §iv-11), but you will shorten the chain's life in the process.
4. Manually put the chain on whichever chainring is most appropriate for the ride home. If in

3.9 **Bypassing a damaged rear derailleur**

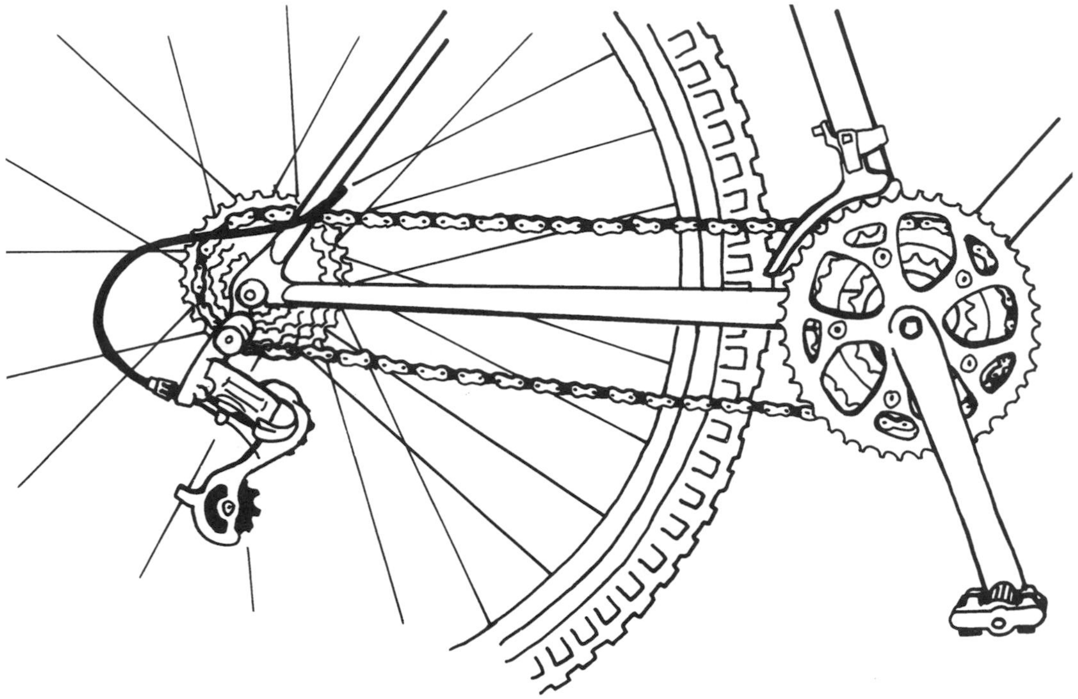

doubt, put it on the middle one.

5. Tie the cable up so it won't catch in your wheel.
6. Stuff the derailleur in your pocket and ride home.

iii-12 DAMAGED REAR DERAILLEUR

DAMAGED REAR DERAILLEUR

If the rear derailleur gets bent just a bit, you can probably straighten it enough to get home. If only a jockey wheel fell out, you may be able to fix that as described in §iii-13. Or if the return spring breaks and the chain hangs slack, you can try the fix in §iii-14. But if the rear derailleur gets really bent or broken, then you will not be able to continue to pedal with the chain routed through it.

If you only need to descend back to your home or car, it's your lucky day. Tie up your chain to the chainstay with tape, wire, or string, and coast back down.

To pedal home, you can also route the chain around the derailleur, effectively turning your bike into a single-speed for the duration of your ride (Fig. 3.9). However, the only rear-suspension bikes that can be set up as a single-speed bike are "unified-rear-triangle" bikes, where the dropouts are rigidly attached to the bottom-bracket shell, or bikes whose pivot is centered on the bottom bracket (like the bike on the cover). Other rear-suspension systems will alternately yank on and slacken the chain as they move. Taking the derailleur out of the equation means that there is nothing to take in or let out the slack. If you have a lockout on the rear shock, you can use that and continue with the following instructions. Otherwise, you must try another way to repair the derailleur (such as the repair in §iii-13), or you will be walking home.

1. Open the chain with a chain tool (Chapter 4, §iv-7), or by hand if you have a master link (Chapter 4, §iv-11), and pull it out of the derailleur.
2. Pick the gear combination in which you think you can make it home most effectively, and set

the front derailleur over the chainring you have picked. Be aware that the chain line must be straight (i.e., the chain must parallel the frame), or the chain will fall off of the cog and the chainring and frustrate any attempts to pedal.

3. Wrap the chain over the chainring and the rear cog you have chosen, bypassing the rear derailleur entirely.
4. Remove any overlapping chain, making the chain as short as you can and still be able to connect the ends together. Push the wheel a bit forward in the dropouts to get a bit more slack.
5. Connect the chain with the chain tool as described in Chapter 4, §iv-9. Pull the wheel back in the dropouts as far as you can to tension the chain.
6. Ride home.

iii-13 REAR-DERAILLEUR JOCKEY WHEEL FELL OUT

If you can find the jockey wheel and the bolt, just reassemble the parts onto the derailleur (see Chapter 5, §v-29).

If you find the jockey wheel but not the bolt, you can reattach the wheel with one of the bolts holding a water-bottle cage on (provided you did not try to save weight by using short bottle-boss bolts!). The thread should be the same, although if the bolt is too long, you will need to be careful you don't shift the derailleur inward far enough to catch it on the spokes as you ride.

If you cannot find the jockey wheel, you can still rig up the derailleur to work, or at least to pedal without shifting. If you lost the upper jockey pulley and your derailleur is a type with the same bolts top and bottom, then put the lower pulley on top first. Now, if you found the bolt for the lost pulley, just tighten it back in where it was, making sure the chain is routed over it in the normal fashion as if the pulley were still on it. If the bolt is also missing, you can still rig it up to work. Collect three threaded collars from the Presta valves on both of your wheels and from your spare tube. String them up between the cage plates with a twist-tie, wire, or zip-tie.

iii-14 BROKEN REAR-DERAILLEUR RETURN KNUCKLE SPRING

If the spring in the rear derailleur's lower knuckle breaks, or gets dislodged, it will not twist the jockey-wheel cage and pull tension on the chain. If you have a bungee cord, you can hook it to the derailleur's jockey-wheel cage and loop it around the end of the quick-release skewer. Reverse the skewer so that the lever is on the drive side pointed back. Hook the other end of the bungee to wherever you can to maintain good tension, such as a water-bottle cage or the seat tube.

iii-15 BROKEN FRONT-DERAILLEUR CABLE

Your chain will be on the inner chainring, and you will still be able to use all of your rear cogs. You have three options, depending on which chainring you want for your return ride:

1. Leave it on the inner ring and ride home.
2. Tighten the inner derailleur stop screw until the derailleur sits over the middle chainring (Fig. 3.10). Leave the chain on the middle ring and ride home.
3. Bypass the front derailleur by removing the chain from the derailleur and putting it on the big chainring. You can do this either by opening the derailleur cage with a screwdriver (Fig. 3.8) or by disconnecting and reconnecting the chain with a chain tool (Chapter 4, §iv-7 and iv-9 to §iv-11).

3.10 **Tightening the inner front-derailleur stop screw**

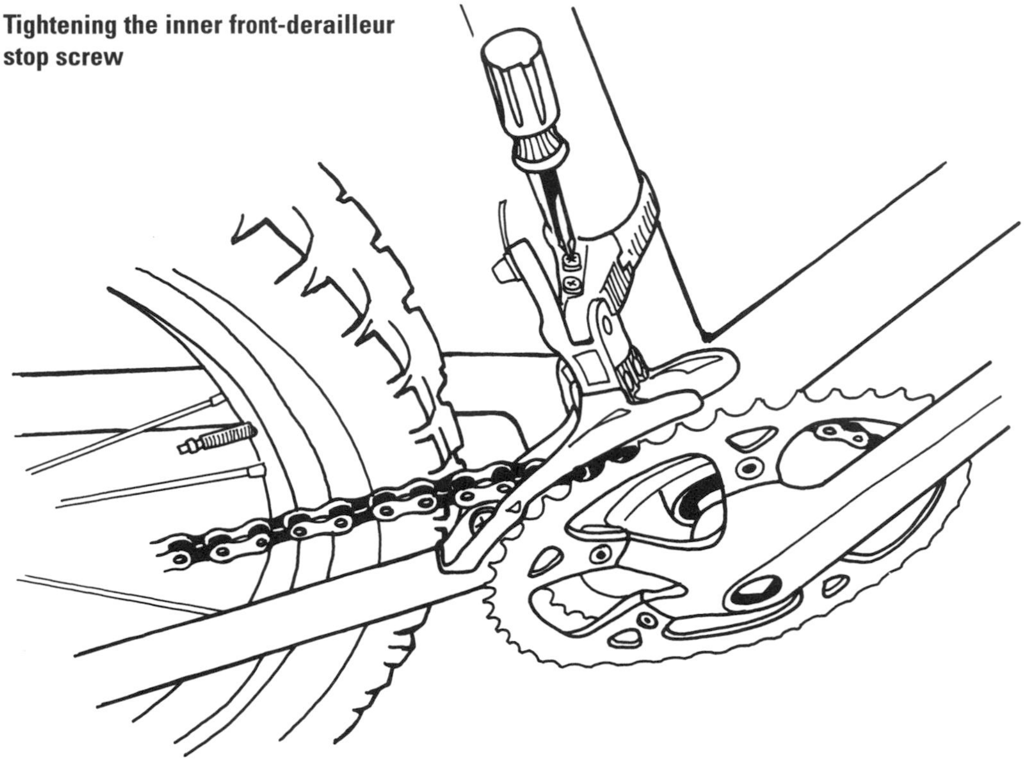

NOTE: *You have probably noticed by now that a chain tool is one of the handiest items you can take along. As the ad says: "Don't leave home without it."*

iii-16 BROKEN REAR-DERAILLEUR CABLE

BROKEN REAR-DERAILLEUR CABLE

Your chain will be on the smallest or largest rear cog, depending on which type of derailleur you have, and you will still be able to use all three front chainrings. Most derailleurs use spring tension to move the chain to the small cog, so that is where the chain most likely will be. Shimano Low Normal (current) or Rapid Rise (late 1990s) rear derailleurs use spring tension to move the chain to the largest cog, so a broken cable will leave it stuck there. You have three options:

1. Leave the chain on the cog it's on and ride home.
2. With a standard rear derailleur, move the chain to a larger cog, push inward on the derailleur with your hand, and tighten the high-gear limit screw on the rear derailleur (usually the upper one of the two screws) until it lines up with a larger cog (see Fig. 3.11). Move the chain to that cog and ride home. With a Shimano Low Normal or Rapid Rise rear derailleur, move the chain to a smaller cog, push outward on the derailleur with your hand, and tighten the low-gear limit screw on the rear derailleur (usually the lower one of the two screws) until it lines up with a smaller cog. Move the chain to that cog and ride home. You may have to fine-tune the adjustment of the derailleur limit screw to get it to run quietly without skipping.
3. If you do not have a screwdriver, you can push inward on a standard rear derailleur while turning the crank with the rear wheel off of the ground to shift to a larger cog. Jam a stick in between the derailleur-cage plates to prevent the derailleur from moving back down to the small cog (Fig. 3.12). Don't try this with a Shimano Low

3.11 **Broken rear-derailleur cable—option 2**

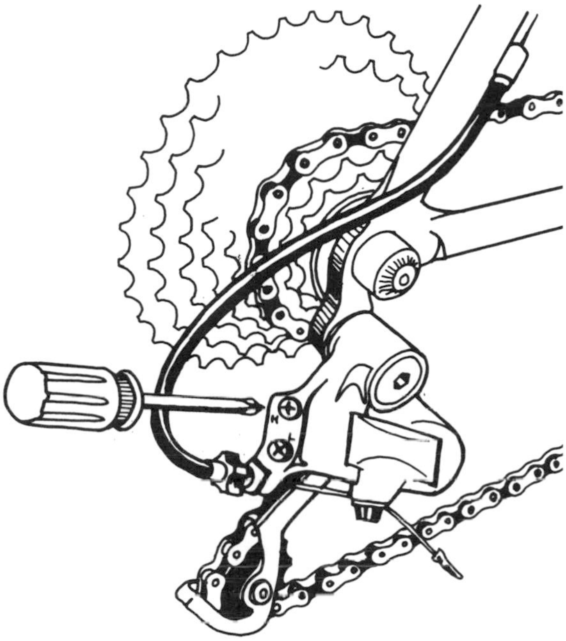

3.12 **Broken rear-derailleur cable—option 3**

Normal or Rapid Rise rear derailleur, because the stick will be too close to the spokes for comfort.

iii-17 BROKEN BRAKE CABLE OR BLOWN HYDRAULIC BRAKE HOSE

Walk home, or ride slowly and carefully home if the trail is not dangerous.

iii-18 FLAT SUSPENSION FORK

Not much you can do here. If you have a blown or leaking air-spring fork and can't pump it, you will just have to ride back with it bottoming out the whole way. Go slowly and keep your weight back.

iii-19 BROKEN SEAT RAILS OR SEATPOST CLAMP

If you can't tape or tie the saddle back on, try wrapping your gloves or some clothing over the top of the seatpost to pad it. Sticking an inverted water bottle over the top of the post also might make it rideable. Otherwise, remove the seatpost and ride home without it.

iii-20 BROKEN SEATPOST

If the seatpost shaft breaks, you can splint it internally with a stick, tape it up, and ride very carefully. Failing that, remove the seatpost and ride home standing up.

If the elastomer breaks or falls out of a suspension seatpost, you may be able to replace the elastomer with a piece of wood, provided that you have a screwdriver to tighten the preload screw in the bottom of the shaft.

iii-21 BROKEN HANDLEBAR

It's probably best to walk home. You could splint it by jamming a stick inside and wrapping it with duct tape. If the break is right next to the stem clamp, you could also loosen the clamp, move the handlebar over so the break is inside the clamp, and retighten it. In either case, you must ride very carefully. The stick could easily break or the clamp could let go of the broken handlebar, leaving you with no way to control the bike. A sudden collision of your face with the ground would follow. From what I've heard, that can be a painful experience. In fact, now that I think of it, you might want to consider just walking your bike home.

iii-22 BROKEN LINKAGE BOLT ON REAR SUSPENSION

Try sticking a hex key in where the bolt was and tape it in place.

iii-23 SEIZED FREEHUB OR FREEWHEEL

If your rear cogs will not freewheel, you cannot coast. If you do stop pedaling, the forward-turning cogs will pull the slack chain around and rip up the rear derailleur. Try squirting some chain lube into the front and back of the freewheel mechanism. No chain lube and the temperature is above freezing? Try squirting water in to get it to turn. If the temperature is below freezing, think it or not, you can sometimes free a frozen freehub by peeing on it. Hey, don't laugh. It's warm!

No matter what liquid you lubricate it with, you may need to hit the freehub with a stick to get it to turn.

iii-24 TRAIL SAFETY: AVOIDING GETTING LOST OR HURT, AND DEALING WITH IT IF YOU DO

Mountain biking in the backcountry can be dangerous. You need to prepare properly and to take personal responsibility for your own and others' safety when riding in deserted country. Two deaths near Moab, Utah, in the summer of 1995 highlight the risks facing anyone who rides off into the backcountry.

The two who died in Moab were riding the popular Porcupine Rim Trail. The account of these riders pinpoints a number of details that cost them their lives. The pair got lost on the descent off Porcupine Rim, missed the turn into Jackass Canyon, and then headed instead into Negro Bill Canyon—which divides the Porcupine Rim Trail from Moab's most famous ride, the Slickrock Trail. It may come as a surprise that people could die and go undiscovered for 17 days so close to a main highway into town (which was right below them) and to two heavily traveled trails. But apparently they hadn't told anyone of their plans, so no one in town noticed when they did not return.

Their parents, not hearing from them for a few days, called the sheriff, and a search was mounted.

Once lost, they abandoned their bikes and tried to walk down to the road, instead of riding back the way they had come. That road and the Colorado River are very close as the crow flies and are visible at a number of points, but, owing to the numerous cliffs, are quite difficult to reach. The two climbed, fell, or slid down to a ledge from which they apparently were unable to climb either up or down, and there they slowly perished from exposure.

They died on this ledge, in such a way that they were very difficult to spot from the air. They had placed no items to indicate their positions to airborne spotters. Had searchers found their bikes, they could have concentrated the search on a small area. Regrettably, their bikes and helmets were picked up by thieves who then did not leave word with the authorities.

Eventually, a helicopter searcher saw the bodies on the ledge, and a Forest Service ranger rappelled 160 feet down to them. He was able to then walk out unaided, indicating that perhaps the riders were so injured, exhausted, delirious, or hypothermic that they had been unable to take the same route out.

Cliffs, steep hills, and an array of other natural features can also pose a risk. In the fall of 1995, another Moab rider barely managed to jump off his bike before it went hurtling over the edge of a cliff and dropped some 400 feet. Anyone who has ridden much in the canyon country of the Southwest can tell you that there are countless other trails near cliff edges that present a similar threat.

Even in seemingly safe areas, the risks can be high. Pro rider Paul Willerton came close to meeting his end on a relatively standard, cliffless, but isolated trail near Winter Park, Colorado. Unable to walk after crashing and breaking his leg, Willerton had to drag himself many miles by using only his arms.

We all tend to think that nothing like these events will ever happen to us. But things like these can happen, far too easily. That shouldn't discourage you from riding in the backcountry, but it should encourage you to think and utilize the following 12 basic backcountry survival skills—they could make the difference between life and death.

1. Always take plenty of water. You can survive a long time without food but not without water.
2. Tell someone where you are going and when you expect to return. If you know of someone who is missing, call the police or sheriff.
3. If you find personal effects on the ground, assume it could indicate that someone is lost or in trouble. Report the find and mark the location.
4. If you get lost, backtrack. Even if going back is longer, it is better than getting stranded.
5. Don't go down something you can't get back up or up something you can't get back down.
6. Bring matches, extra clothing and food, a flashlight, and perhaps an aluminized emergency blanket, in case you have to spend the night out or need to signal searchers.
7. If the area is new to you, go with someone who is familiar with it, or take a map and compass—and know how to use them.
8. Wear a helmet. It's hard to ride home with a cracked skull.
9. Bring basic first aid stuff and bike tools, and know how to use them well enough to keep yourself and your bike going.
10. Walk your bike when it's appropriate. Falling off a cliff is a poor alternative to taking a few extra seconds or displaying less bravado. Try riding on difficult sections of trail to improve your bike handling, but if the risk of falling off a cliff is great or a mistake could leave you injured a long way from help, find another place to practice those moves.
11. Don't ride beyond your limits if you are a long way out. Take a break. Get out of the hot sun. Avoid dehydration and bonking by drinking and eating enough.
12. Teach your friends all these things.

The above 12 rules are in addition to the International Mountain Bike Association (IMBA) Rules of the Trail (below), which we would all do well to adhere to.

1. Plan ahead.
2. Always yield trail.
3. Never scare animals.
4. Ride on open trails only.
5. Control your bicycle.
6. Leave no trace.

Keep in mind that your decisions affect not only you, but they also could affect your riding partners, your families, and countless others. It is important to understand that endangering yourself can also endanger the person trying to rescue you. Search and rescue parties are usually made up of helpful people who will gladly come and try to save you, but no one appreciates being put in harm's way unnecessarily.

In summary, make appropriate decisions when cycling the backcountry. Learn survival skills, and prepare well. Recognize that even though you have a $4,000 bike and are riding on popular trails, you are not immune to danger. When ignorance makes us oblivious to danger, it sadly becomes the danger itself.

CHAPTER 4

CHAINS

A chain is only as strong as its weakest link.
—Anonymous

A sausage is only as good as its last link.
—Bluto

TOOLS

chain lubricant
12-inch ruler
chain tool
lots of rags

OPTIONAL TOOLS

solvent (citrus-based)
chain-cleaning tool
old water bottle or jar
caliper
pliers
solvent tank
chain-elongation indicator
Rohloff cog-wear indicator

A bike chain is a simple series of links connected by rivets. Rollers surround each rivet between the link plates and engage the teeth of the cogs and chainrings. It is an extremely efficient method of transmitting mechanical energy from your pedals to your rear wheel. In terms of weight, cost, and efficiency, the bicycle chain has no equal, and—believe me—people are still trying to improve on it.

To keep your bike running smoothly, you do have to pay at least some attention to your chain. It needs to be kept clean and well lubricated in order to transmit your energy most efficiently, shift smoothly, and maximize chain life. Chains need to be replaced frequently to prolong the working life of other, more expensive, drivetrain components because a chain gets longer as its internal parts wear, thus contacting the gear teeth differently than intended.

CHAIN SERVICE AND ASSEMBLY

iv-1 LUBRICATION

When lubricating the chain, use a lubricant intended for bicycle chains. If you want to get fancy about it, you can assess the type of conditions in which you ride and choose a lubricant intended for those conditions. Some lubricants are dry and pick up less dirt in dry conditions; some are sticky and therefore less prone to washing off in wet conditions.

1. Drip a small amount of lubricant across each roller (Fig. 4.1), periodically moving the chain to give easy access to the links you are working on. If you are in a hurry, you can turn the crank slowly while dripping lubricant onto the chain as it goes by. This is better than not lubricating the chain, but it will cause you to apply too much lubricant. That, in turn, will cause the chain to

4.1 **Lubing chain**

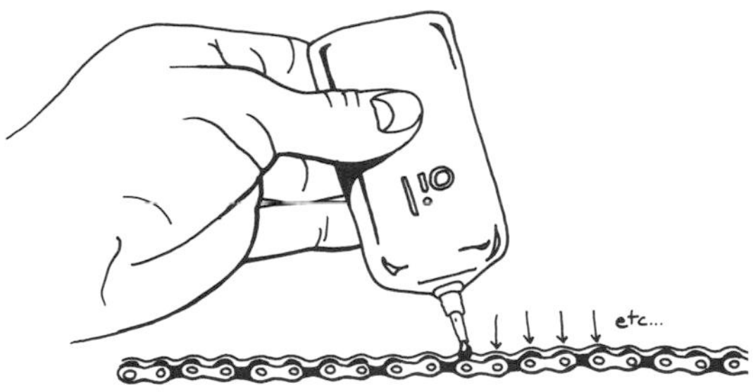

4.2 **Wiping chain with rag**

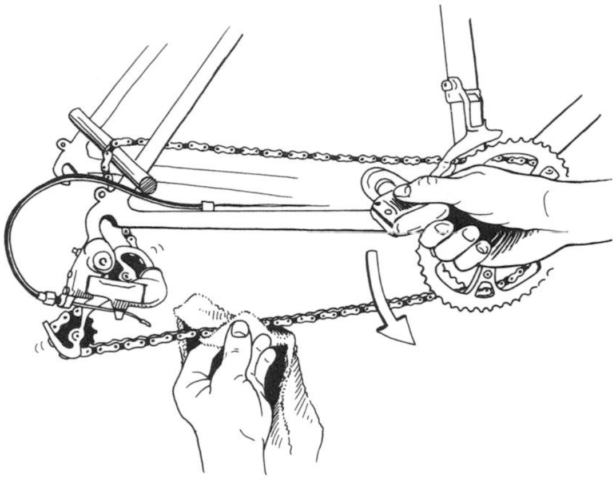

pick up dirt faster, and you'll then wear out your chain sooner.

2. Wipe the chain off lightly with a rag. In wet conditions, expect to use more lubricant (after every ride, or even several times during a long, rainy ride). The lubricant for wet conditions needs to adhere well to the chain and not be easily washed off; this usually means a thick and sticky lubricant—even grease. For dry conditions, less quantity of a dry lubricant that does not pick up dirt is preferable.

iv-2 CLEANING BY FREQUENT WIPING AND LUBRICATION

Cleaning the chain can be accomplished in a number of ways. The simplest method to maintain a chain is to wipe it down frequently and then lubricate it. If this procedure is done before every ride, you will never need to clean your chain with a solvent. The lubricant softens the old sludge buildup, which is driven out of the chain when you ride. The problem is that the lubricant also picks up new dirt and grime. If new dirt and grime is wiped off before it's driven deep into the chain, and the chain is relubricated frequently, it will stay clean and supple. Chain cleaning can be performed with the bike standing on the ground or in a bike stand.

1. With a rag in your hand, grasp the lower length of the chain (between the bottom of the chainring and the rear-derailleur lower jockey wheel).
2. Turn the crank backward a number of revolutions, pulling the chain through the rag (Fig. 4.2). Periodically rotate the rag to present a cleaner section of it to the chain.
3. Lubricate each chain roller as above.

To simplify this, I recommend leaving a pair of rubber gloves, a rag, and some chain lube next to your bike. Then whenever you return from a ride, put on the gloves, wipe and lube the chain, and put your bike away. It takes maybe a minute, your hands stay clean, and your bike is ready for the next ride.

iv-3 CHAIN-CLEANING UNITS

Several companies make chain-cleaning units that scrub the chain with a solvent while it is still on the bike. These types of chain cleaners are generally made of clear plastic and have two or three rotating brushes that scrub the chain as it moves through the

4.3 **Using a solvent-bath chain cleaner**

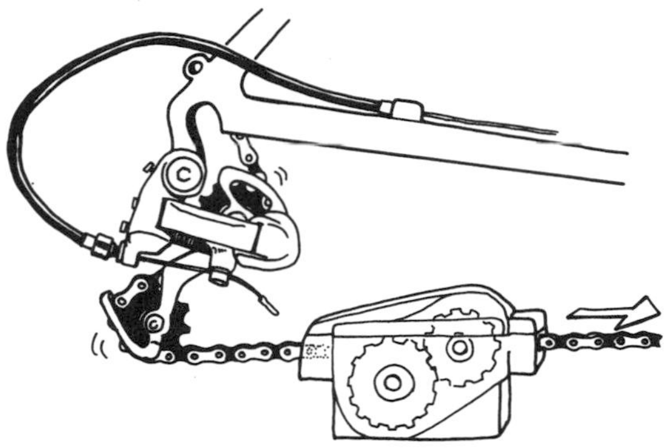

solvent bath (Fig. 4.3). These units offer the advantage of letting you clean your chain without removing it from the bike. Regularly removing your chain is a pain, and it shortens chain life.

Most chain-cleaning units come with a nontoxic, citrus-based solvent. For your safety, and other environmental reasons, I strongly recommend that you purchase nontoxic citrus solvents for your chain cleaner, even if the unit already comes with a petroleum-based solvent. If you recycle used petroleum solvents, then go ahead and use them. In either case, wear gloves and glasses when using any sort of solvent, citrus or petroleum based.

Citrus chain solvents often contain some lubricants, so they won't dry the chain out. The effective combination of lubricant and solvent is why diesel fuel used to have such a following as a chain cleaner. A really strong solvent without lubricant (acetone, for example) will displace the oil from inside the rollers. It will later evaporate, leaving a dry, squeaking chain that is hard to rehabilitate. The same can happen with a citrus-based solvent that does not include a lubricant if no lubricant is separately applied, especially if the chain is not allowed to dry long enough. The procedure for using a chain-cleaning unit is straightforward:

1. Remove the top and pour in the solvent up to the fill line.
2. Place the chain-cleaning unit up against the bottom of the chain, and reinstall the top so that the chain runs through it.
3. Turn the bike's crank backward (Fig. 4.3).
4. Lubricate as above (§iv-1).

iv-4 REMOVAL AND CLEANING

You can also clean the chain by removing it from the bicycle and cleaning it in a solvent. I recommend against this procedure unless your chain has a master link, because repeated disassembly by pushing rivets in and out weakens the chain.

On a road bike, chain breakage is now an issue because of super-narrow 10-speed chains, but mountain bike chains are prone to breakage because of the conditions in which they are used. A chain that breaks while riding generally does it during shifting of the front derailleur while pedaling hard. This technique can pry a link plate open so that the head of a rivet pops out of the plate, tearing the chain apart. Chain disassembly and reassembly expands the size of the rivet hole where you put it together, allowing the rivet to pop out more easily. Shimano supplies special "subpins" for reassembly of its chains that are meant to prevent this problem, but the chain is still not as strong there as if you had left the original pin in place.

A hand-opened master link can avoid the chain weakening of pushing pins out. Master links are standard on Wippermann and Taya chains, on many KMC chains, and on SRAM and Sachs chains of 1998 and later. Lickton Cycle's aftermarket Super Link can also be installed into many chains.

If you do disassemble the chain (see §iv-7 or §iv-11 for instructions), you can clean it well, even without a solvent tank. Just drop your chain into an old jar or water bottle half filled with solvent. Using an old water bottle or jar allows you to clean the chain without touching or breathing the solvent—something to be avoided even when you are using citrus solvents.

The procedure for cleaning the chain without using a chain-cleaning unit could not be simpler:

1. Remove the chain from the bike (§iv-7 or §iv-11 below).
2. Drop it in a water bottle or jar.
3. Pour in enough solvent to cover the chain.
4. Shake the bottle vigorously (low to the ground, in case the top pops off).
5. Hang the chain to air dry.
6. Reassemble it on the bike (see §iv-8 to §iv-11 below).
7. Lubricate it as above (§iv-1).

Allow the solvent in the bottle or jar to settle for a few days so you can decant the clear stuff and use it again. I'll say it throughout the book—it is important to use a citrus-based solvent. It is not only safer for the environment, it is gentler on your skin and less harmful to breathe. Wear rubber gloves when working with any solvent, and use a respirator meant for volatile organic compounds if you are not using a citrus-based solvent. There is no sense in fixing your bike so it goes faster if you end up becoming a slower, sickly bike rider.

iv-5 CHAIN REPLACEMENT

As the rollers, pins, and plates wear out, the chain lengthens. That, in turn, hastens the wear and tear on other drivetrain parts. An elongated chain concentrates the load on each individual gear tooth, rather than distributing it over all of the teeth that the chain contacts, and causes the gear teeth to become hook-shaped and the tooth valleys to become wider. If such wear has already occurred, a new chain will not solve the problem. A new chain will not mesh with deformed teeth, and it is likely to skip whenever you pedal hard. So before all of that extra wear and tear takes place, get in the habit of replacing your chain on a regular basis.

How long it takes for the chain to wear out will vary, depending on chain type, maintenance, riding conditions, and strength and weight of the rider. Figure on replacing your chain every 500 to 1,000 miles, especially for bikes ridden in dirty conditions by a large rider. Lighter riders riding mostly on paved roads can often extend replacement time to over 2,000 miles.

iv-6 CHECKING FOR CHAIN ELONGATION

The simplest method is to use a chain-elongation gauge; one example is the model made by Rohloff (Fig. 4.4). The gauge falls completely into the chain if the chain is worn out. If the chain is still in good shape, the gauge's tooth will not go all of the way in. Park, Wippermann, and others offer similar chain-elongation gauges as well.

Another way to measure chain wear is with an accurate ruler. Chains are measured on an inch standard and should measure a half-inch between adjacent rivets. There should be exactly an integral number of links in 1 foot—12 links, to be exact, where each complete link consists of an inner and outer pair of plates (Fig. 4.5).

1. Set one end of the ruler on a rivet edge, and measure to the rivet edge at the other end of the ruler, 12 links away.

4.4 **Checking chain wear . . . If the curved tooth with the S (indicating steel cogs) falls completely into the chain, replace it. (The A side is for aluminum cogs.)**

2. The distance between these rivets should be 12 inches exactly. If it is 12⅛ inches or greater, replace the chain; if it is 12$\frac{1}{16}$ inches or more, it is a good idea to replace it (but necessary to do so if you have any titanium or alloy cogs or an 11-tooth small cog). Some chain manufacturers recommend replacement if elongation is 1 percent, or ½ inch in 50 complete link pairs (50 inches), which is a little less than ⅛ inch over 12 link pairs (1 foot). If the chain is off of the bike, you can hang it next to a new chain for comparison; if the used one is more than a half-inch longer for the same number of links, replace it.

iv-7 CHAIN REMOVAL

The following procedure applies to all standard derailleur chains except those with a master link. Master-link–equipped chains include all Wippermann and Taya chains, chains with Lickton's Super Link, Power Link–equipped SRAM or Sachs chains, and many KMC chains. All of these chains snap open by hand at the master link (see §iv-11), although if need be, they can also be opened at any other link by using a chain tool as described below.

1. Place any link over the back teeth on a chain tool (Fig. 4.6).
2. Tighten the chain-tool handle clockwise to push the link rivet out. Unless you have a Shimano

4.5 **One complete chain link**

4.6 **Removing a chain rivet**

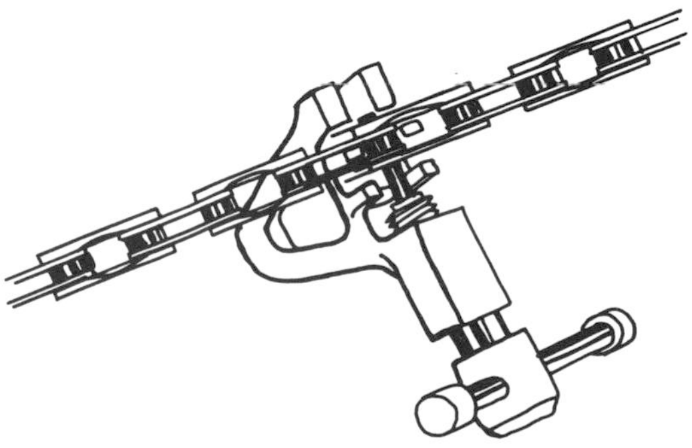

4.7 **Determining chain length**

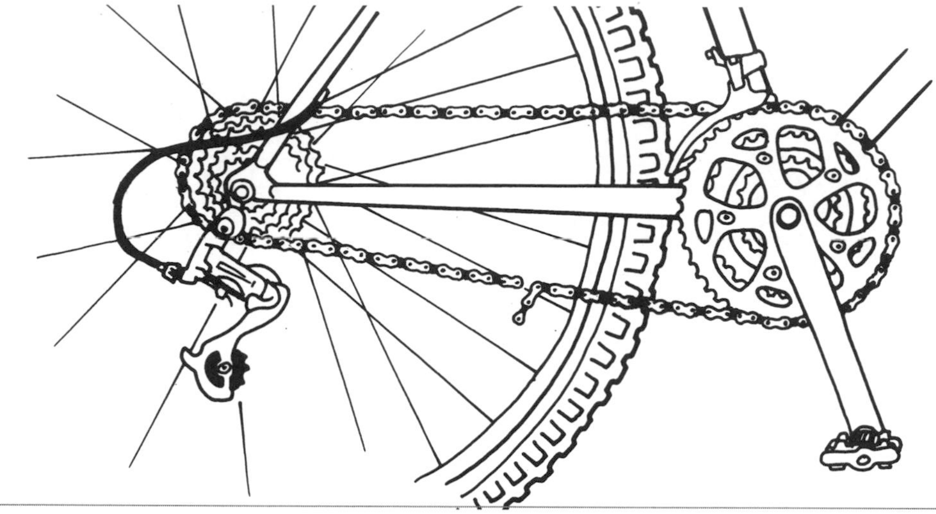

4.8 **Chain assembly**

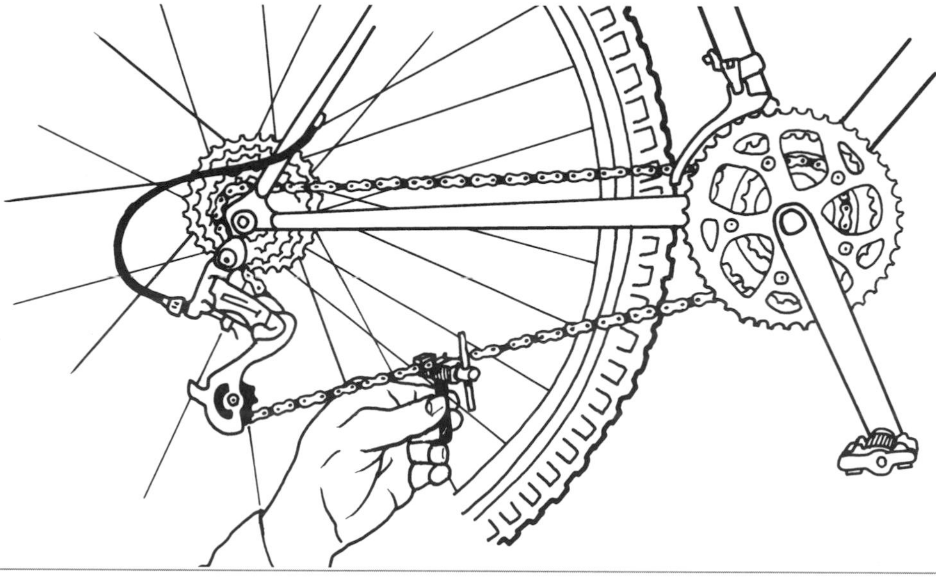

chain and a new subpin for it, be careful to leave 1mm or so of rivet protruding inward from the chain plate to hook the chain back together when reassembling.

iv-8 CHAIN INSTALLATION

Installing a new chain is a fairly easy process, but read the caution in step 3 below before you start.

1. Start by determining the chain length. If you are putting on a new chain, determine how many links you'll need in one of two ways: (a) Under the assumption that your old chain was the correct length, compare it with the new one and use the same number of links. (b) If you have a standard long-cage mountain bike rear derailleur on your bike, wrap the chain around the big chainring and the biggest cog without going through either derailleur. Bring the two ends together until the ends overlap; one full link (Fig. 4.5—a complete link pair) should be the amount of

overlap (Fig. 4.7). Remove the remaining links and save them in your spare-tire bag so you have spares in case of chain breakage on the trail.

2. Routing the chain properly is the next step. Shift the derailleurs so that the chain will rest on the smallest cog in the rear and on the smallest chainring up front. Starting with the rear-derailleur pulley that is farthest from the derailleur body (this will be the bottom pulley once the chain is taut), guide the chain up through the rear derailleur, going around the two jockey pulleys. Make sure the chain passes inside of the prongs on the rear-derailleur cage. Guide the chain over the smallest rear cog. Guide the chain through the front-derailleur cage. Wrap the chain around the smallest front chainring. Bring the chain ends together so they meet.
3. Finally, connect the chain by using a master link, a Shimano subpin, or the existing pin you pushed out. Connecting a chain without a master link or a Shimano subpin is much easier if the link rivet that was partially removed when the chain was taken apart is sticking out toward you. Positioning the link rivet this way allows you to use the chain tool (Fig. 4.8) in a much more comfortable manner (driving the rivet toward the bike, instead of back at you).

iv-9 CONNECTING A STANDARD CHAIN

A "standard" chain—i.e., a non-Shimano chain without a master link—is a disappearing breed, as mountain bikes have more rear cogs and correspondingly narrow chains.

1. Push the ends together, snapping the end link over the little stub of pin you left sticking out to the inside between the opposite end plates. You will need to flex those end plates wider apart as you push the same link in to get the pin to snap into the hole.
2. Push the rivet through with the chain tool (Fig. 4.9) until the same amount protrudes on either end.
3. The link will likely be stiff because of the outer plates' being pushed closer together than they were meant to be. If this link does not fold as easily as the surrounding links, continue on with step 4. If it folds freely, you're done.
4. Put the link over the set of teeth on the tool closest to the screw handle (Fig. 4.10). (If your chain tool only has one set of teeth you will need to free the stiff link by following the procedure in §iv-14a instead.)
5. Push the pin a fraction of a turn to spread the plates apart.

4.9 Replacing a chain rivet

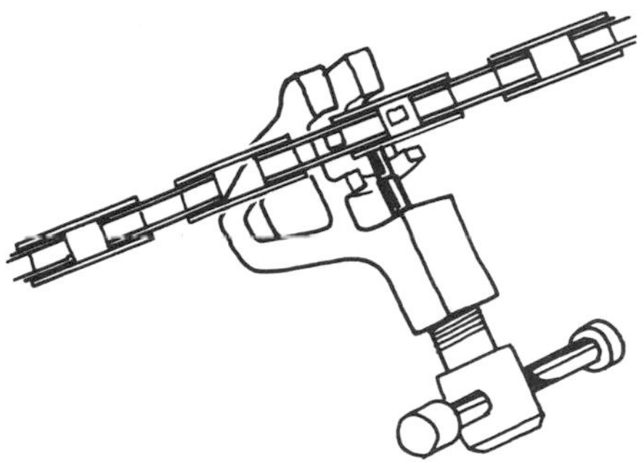

4.10 Loosening a stiff link

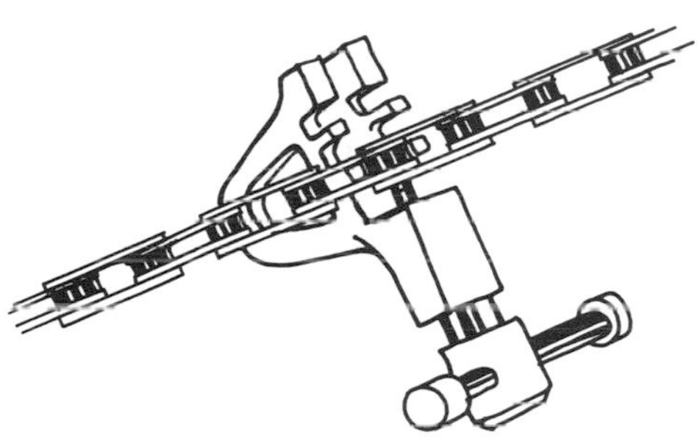

4.11 **Snapping the end off of a Shimano subpin**

4.12 **SRAM Power Link (also Sachs Power Link and Lickton's Super Link)**

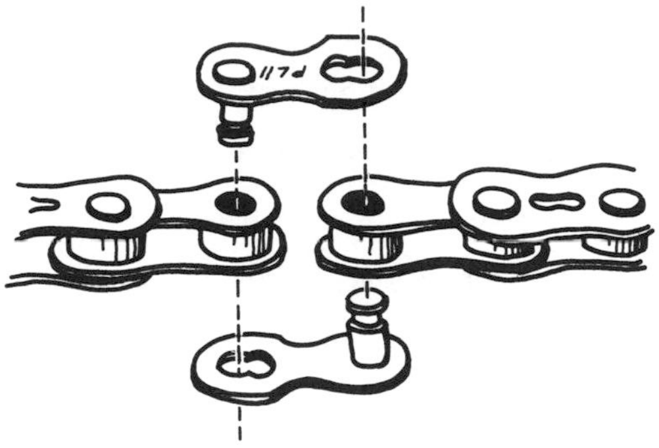

iv-10 CONNECTING A SHIMANO CHAIN

Shimano chains have a special connecting pin (subpin in Shimano-speak) to ensure a stronger chain connection. On a new chain insert the subpin through the outer plate holes Shimano left open (Campagnolo calls this the "virgin hole"), rather than through an outer plate from which you have removed a rivet. This will make for the strongest possible connection.

1. Make sure you have a Shimano subpin, which looks like a silver (for nine-speed) or black (for eight-speed) rivet with a second segment ending in a pointed tip. It is twice as long as a standard rivet and has a breakage groove at the middle of its length. Two subpins come with a new Shimano chain. If you are reinstalling an old Shimano chain, get a new subpin at a bike shop. If you don't have a subpin and are going to connect it anyway, follow the procedure above in §iv-9, but be aware that the chain is now more likely to break than if it had been assembled with the proper subpin.
2. Remove any extra links, pushing the appropriate rivet completely out. As I explained in the paragraph above step 1, remove extra lengths at the end of the chain without a pair of open outer link plates (the right-hand end in Fig. 4.7).
3. Line up the chain ends.
4. Push the subpin in with your fingers, pointed end first. It will go in about halfway.
5. With the chain tool, push the subpin through (Fig. 4.9) until there is only as much left protruding at the tail end as the other rivets in the chain.
6. Break off the leading half of the subpin with a pair of pliers (Fig. 4.11).
7. The chain should move freely. If it does not, flex it back and forth at this rivet as described in §iv-14a.

CONNECTING A SHIMANO CHAIN — MASTER LINKS

iv-11 CONNECTING AND DISCONNECTING A MASTER LINK

a. Lickton's Super Link and SRAM (Sachs) Power Link (Fig. 4.12)

These links are the same; SRAM (which purchased Sachs) licensed Lickton's design. The master link is made up of two symmetrical link halves, each of which has a single pin sticking out of it. There is a round keyhole in the center of each plate that tapers into a slot on the end opposite the pin.

Connecting

1. Put the pin of each half of the link through the hole in each end of the chain; one pin will go down and one up (Fig. 4.12).

4.13 **Wippermann ConneX link—note its orientation with the link's high bump away from the chainring**

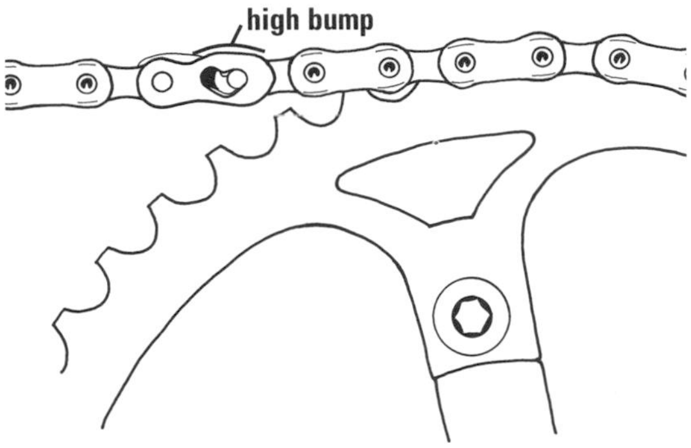

4.14 **Taya chain master link**

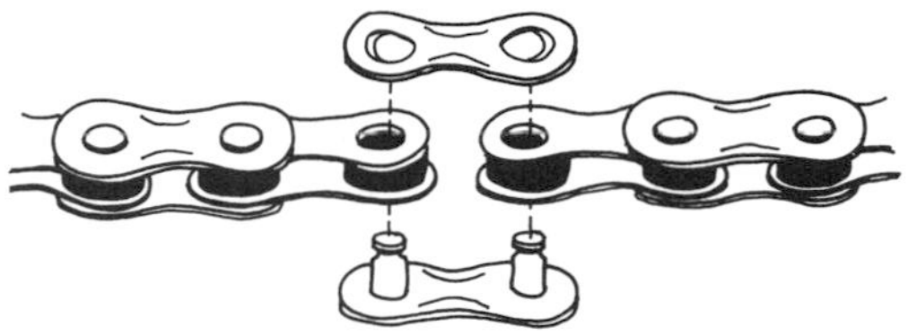

2. Pull the links close together so that each pin goes through the keyhole in the opposite plate.
3. Pull the chain ends apart so that the groove at the top of each pin slides to the end of the slot in each plate.

Disconnecting

1. While squeezing the master link plates together to free the pins, push the chain ends toward each other so that the pins slide out of the slot to the keyhole in each plate.
2. Pull the two halves of the master link apart.

NOTE: *In practice, this is often hard to do with an old chain. Try squeezing the link plates toward each other with a clothespin or a pair of VISE-GRIP pliers set on very low pressure to disengage the link plate slots from the pin grooves while you push the ends toward each other. In desperation, you may have to just open the chain somewhere else (§iv-7) and reassemble it as described in §iv-9 or use a second master link.*

b. Wippermann ConneX Link (Fig. 4.13)

The Wippermann link works much the same way as the SRAM Power Link mentioned above, but unlike other master links, the edges of the link plates are not symmetrical. This means that there is a definite orientation for the link, and you want to make sure you don't install it upside down.

Orient the chain so that the taller convex edge is away from the chainring or cog (Fig. 4.13). The link plate is bowl-shaped, and if you have the convex bottom of the bowl toward the cog or chainring, then when it is on an 11- or 12- or maybe even a 13-tooth cog, the convex edge will ride up on the spacer between cogs, lifting the rollers out of the tooth valleys and causing the chain to skip under load.

So, install the ConneX link the same way as the SRAM Power Link in §iv-11a above, but make sure the convex link edge is facing outward from the chain loop (Fig. 4.13), so that the long concave edge can run over the cog spacers on the smallest cogs without lifting the chain.

c. Taya Master Link (Fig. 4.14)

1. Connect the two ends of the chain together with the master link that has two rivets sticking out of it (Fig. 4.14).
2. Snap the outer master link plate over the rivets and into their grooves. To facilitate hooking each keyhole-shaped hole over its corresponding

rivet, flex the plate with the protruding rivets so that the ends of the rivets are closer together.

Disconnecting

1. Flex the master link so that the pins come closer together.
2. Pull the plate with the oval holes off of the rivets.

TROUBLESHOOTING CHAINS

iv-12 CHAIN SUCK

Chain suck occurs when the chain does not release from the bottom of the chainring and pulls up rather than running straight to the lower rear-derailleur jockey wheel. The chain will come around and get "sucked" up by the inner or middle chainring until it hits the chainstay (Fig. 4.15). Sometimes the chain becomes wedged between the chainstay and the chainring.

A number of things can cause chain suck. To eliminate it, try the simplest methods first.

1. Clean and lube the chain and clean the chainrings to see if it improves; a rusty chain will take longer to slide off of the chainring than will a clean, well-lubed chain.
2. Check for tight (or stiff) links (Fig. 4.16) by watching the chain move through the derailleur jockey wheels as you slowly turn the crank backward. Loosen stiff links by flexing them side to side with your thumbs and fingers (Fig. 4.17).
3. If chain suck persists, check that there are no bent or torn teeth on the chainring. Try straightening any broken or torn teeth you find with pliers or filing away rough, bent-over edges.
4. If your chain still sucks, try another chain with wider spacing between link plates (if it is too

4.15 **Chain suck**

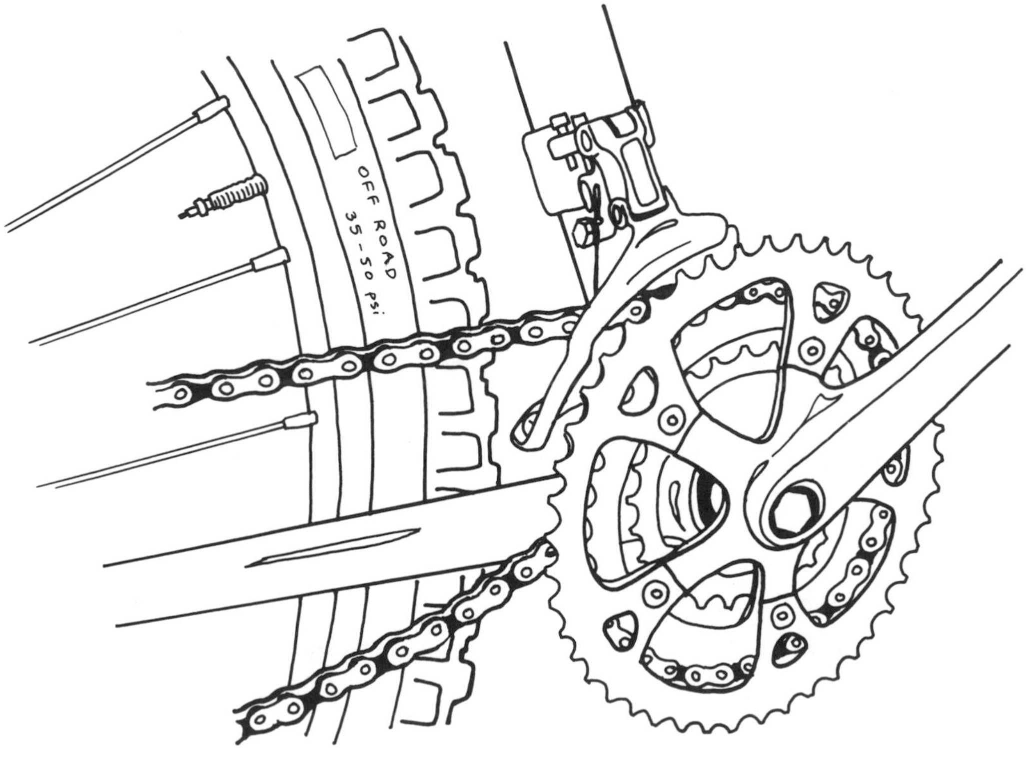

4.16 **Stiff link**

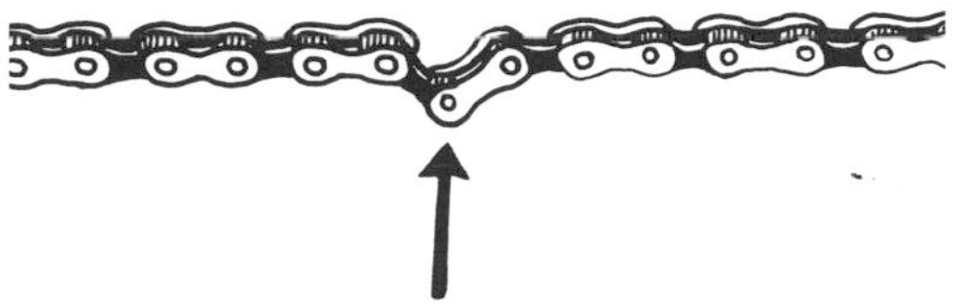

4.17 **Loosening stiff link(s)**

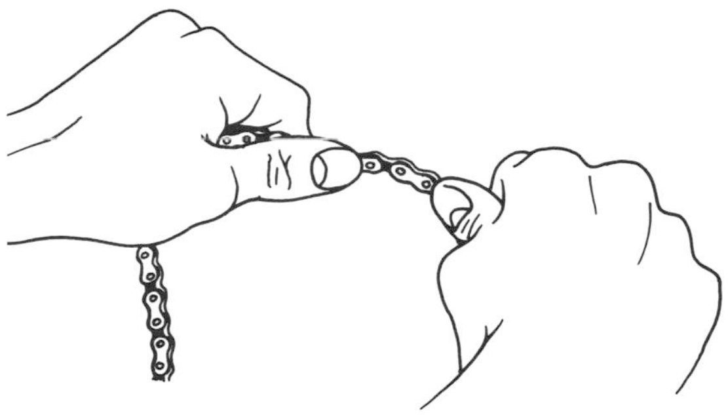

narrow, it can pinch the chainring). You can use a measuring caliper to compare link spacing of various chains (Fig. 1.4).

5. Another approach is to replace the inner (and perhaps middle) chainring with a thin stainless steel (or shiny chromed) chainring. The thin, slick rings will release the chain more easily.
6. Increase the rear derailleur's pivot-spring (p-spring) tension (see Chapter 5, §v-2g) so it will increase the tension on the lower run of the chain as it comes off of the bottom of the chainring.
7. If the problem still persists, a new chainring or an anti–chain suck device that attaches under the chainstays may help. Ask at your bike shop about what is available.

iv-13 SQUEAKING CHAIN

Squeaking is caused by dry or rusted surfaces inside the chain rubbing on each other.

1. Wipe down and lubricate the chain (§iv-1 and §iv-2).
2. If the squeak does not go away after a single ride with fresh lubricant, replace the chain. (If the initial remedy does not work, the chain is too dry inside and probably rusted as well. Chains seldom heal from this condition. Life is too short, and bike riding is too joyful, to put up with the sound of a squeaking chain.)

iv-14 SKIPPING CHAIN

There can be a number of causes for a chain to skip and jump as you pedal.

a. Stiff links

1. Turn the crank backward slowly to see if a stiff chain link (Fig. 4.16) exists; a stiff link will be visible because it will be unable to bend properly as it goes through the rear derailleur jockey wheels. It will deflect the jockey wheels when passing through.
2. Loosen stiff links by flexing them from side to side between the index finger and thumb of both hands (Fig. 4.17) or by using the second set of teeth on a chain tool (§iv-9, Fig. 4.10). Set the stiff link over the teeth closest to the screw handle, and push the pin a fraction of a turn to spread the link.
3. Wipe down and lubricate the chain.

b. Rusted chain

A rusted chain will squeak. If you watch it move through the rear derailleur, it will look as though many links are tight; they will not bend easily and will cause the jockey wheels to jump back and forth.

1. Lubricate the chain.
2. If the lubrication does not fix the problem after a few miles of riding, replace the chain.

c. Worn-out chain

If the chain is worn out, it will be elongated and will skip because it does not mesh well with the cogs. A new chain will fix the problem, unless the worn chain was used long enough to ruin some cogs.

1. Check for chain elongation as described above in §iv-6.
2. If the chain is elongated beyond the specifications discussed in §iv-6, replace it.
3. If replacing the chain does not help or makes matters worse, see the next section.

d. Worn cogs

If you just replaced the chain, and now it is skipping, probably at least one of the cogs is worn out. If this is the case, the chain will probably skip on the cogs you use most frequently and not on others. However, if it only skips on the smallest cog or two and you have a Wippermann chain, check that you have not installed the ConneX link upside down (see §iv-11b).

SKIPPING CHAIN

1. Check each cog visually for wear. If its teeth are hook-shaped, the cog is shot and should be replaced. Rohloff makes a simple tool that checks for cog wear by putting tension on a length of chain wrapped around the cog (see Fig. 1.4 in Chapter 1). If chain links on the Rohloff cog wear indicator tool can be lifted off of the cog while under tension, the cog is worn out.
2. Replace the offending cogs, or the entire cassette, or the freewheel. See cog change in Chapter 6, §vi-19.
3. Replace the chain as well, if you have not just done so. An old chain will wear out your new cogs rapidly.

e. Misadjusted rear derailleur

If the rear derailleur is poorly adjusted or bent, it can cause the chain to skip by lining up the chain between gears.

1. Check that the rear derailleur shifts equally well in both directions and that the chain can be pedaled backward without catching.
2. Adjust the rear derailleur by following the procedure described in Chapter 5 (§v-6 to §v-14).

f. Sticky shift cable

If the shift cable does not move freely enough to let the derailleur's spring return the chain to be lined up under the cog, it will jump off under load. Frayed, rough, rusted, or worn cables or housings will cause the problem, as will overly thick cables, or kinked or sharply bent housings. Replacing the shift cables and housings (Chapter 5, §v-6 to §v-14) should eliminate the problem.

g. Loose rear-derailleur jockey wheel(s)

A loose jockey wheel on the rear derailleur can cause the chain to skip by letting it move too far laterally.

1. Check that the bolts holding the jockey wheel to the cage are tight by using an appropriately sized (usually 3mm) Allen wrench.
2. Tighten the jockey-wheel bolts if necessary. Hold the Allen wrench close to its bend so that

you don't have enough leverage to overtighten the bolts. If the jockey-wheel bolts loosen regularly, put Loctite on their threads.

h. Bent rear derailleur or rear-derailleur hanger

If the derailleur or derailleur hanger is bent, adjustments won't work. You will probably know when it happened, too. It was either when you shifted your derailleur into your spokes, when you crashed onto the derailleur, or when you pedaled a stick or a tumbleweed through the derailleur.

1. Unless you have a derailleur-hanger alignment tool and know how to use it (Chapter 14, Fig. 14.3), take the bike to a shop and have it checked, and have the dropout hanger alignment corrected. Some bikes, especially those made out of carbon or aluminum, have a replaceable (bolt-on) right rear dropout and derailleur hanger, which you can purchase and bolt on yourself.
2. If a straight derailleur hanger does not correct the misalignment, your rear derailleur is bent. This is generally cause for replacement of the entire derailleur. (See Chapter 5, §v-1.) With some derailleurs, you can just replace the jockey-wheel cage, which is usually what is bent. If you know what you are doing, and are careful, you can sometimes bend a bent derailleur cage back with your hands. It seldom works well, but it's worth a try if your only other alternative is to replace the entire rear derailleur. Just make sure you don't bend the derailleur hanger in the process.

i. Worn derailleur pivots

If the derailleur pivots are worn, the derailleur will be loose and will move around under the cogs, causing the chain to skip. Replacing the derailleur is the solution.

j. Bent rear-derailleur mounting bolt

If the mounting bolt is bent, the derailleur will not line up straight. To fix the derailleur, get a new bolt and install it following the instructions in Chapter 5, §v-34, Upper Pivot Overhaul. Be sure to observe how the spring-loaded assembly goes together during disassembly to ease reassembly.

k. Missing chain rollers

You can have a chain that passes the elongation tests mentioned in §iv-6 yet will skip because every here and there, one of the cylindrical rollers has broken and fallen off of its rivet or is so worn that it is spool-shaped. If you don't happen to check that particular link with the chain-elongation gauge, you'll likely miss broken rollers. The width of the gauge is the same as between the inner plates, so it won't catch spool-shaped rollers, either, because it will ride up on the edges of the rollers and not fall down into the center of the narrower waist of the worn roller. You might never know the chain is shot without inspecting every link.

l. Inverted ConneX link

If you have a Wippermann chain and have the ConneX master link upside down (described in §iv-11b), the taller link edge will ride up on the spacers between the smallest cogs, lift the rollers off of the cog, and cause the chain to skip. Remove, invert, and reinstall the ConneX master link as described in §iv-11b.

CHAPTER 5

TRANSMISSION

Front and rear derailleurs, cables, and shifters

Most Americans want to be somewhere else, but when they get there, they want to go home.
—Henry Ford

TOOLS

- **3mm, 4mm, 5mm, and 6mm Allen wrenches**
- **flat-blade and Phillips screwdrivers (small and medium)**
- **cable cutter**
- **indexed housing cutter**
- **pliers**
- **grease**
- **chain lubricant**
- **rubbing alcohol**

There is nothing like having your derailleurs working smoothly, predictably, and quietly under all conditions. Knowing that you can shift whenever you need to inspires confidence when riding on difficult singletrack sections of trail. It really is a lot more pleasant to ride through beautiful terrain without the grinding and clunking noises of an out-of-whack derailleur.

Improperly adjusted rear derailleurs are a pretty common problem, which is surprising because derailleur adjustments are easy, provided the equipment is clean and in good working order. A few simple adjustments to the limit screws and the cable tension and you're on your way. Once you see how easy it is, you will probably keep yours in adjustment all of the time.

THE REAR DERAILLEUR

The rear derailleur is one of the more complex parts on a bike (Fig. 5.1). It moves the chain from one rear cog to another, and it also takes up chain slack when the bike bounces or the front derailleur is shifted.

The rear-derailleur bolts to a hanger on the rear dropout (Fig. 5.2). Two jockey wheels (pulley wheels) hold the chain tight and help guide the chain as the derailleur shifts. Depending on the model, a rear derailleur has one or two springs in the lower, or both upper and lower, knuckles that pull the jockey wheels tightly against the chain, creating a desirable amount of chain tension.

Except on Shimano's reverse-action Low Normal or (older) Rapid Rise derailleurs, increasing the tension on the rear-derailleur cable moves the derailleur inward toward the larger cogs. When the cable tension is released, a return spring between the derailleur's two parallelogram plates pulls the chain back toward the smallest cogs. By connecting the return spring to the other pair of corners of the rear derailleur's parallelogram linkage, Low Normal and Rapid Rise derailleurs work in exactly the opposite

5.1 Rear derailleur exploded

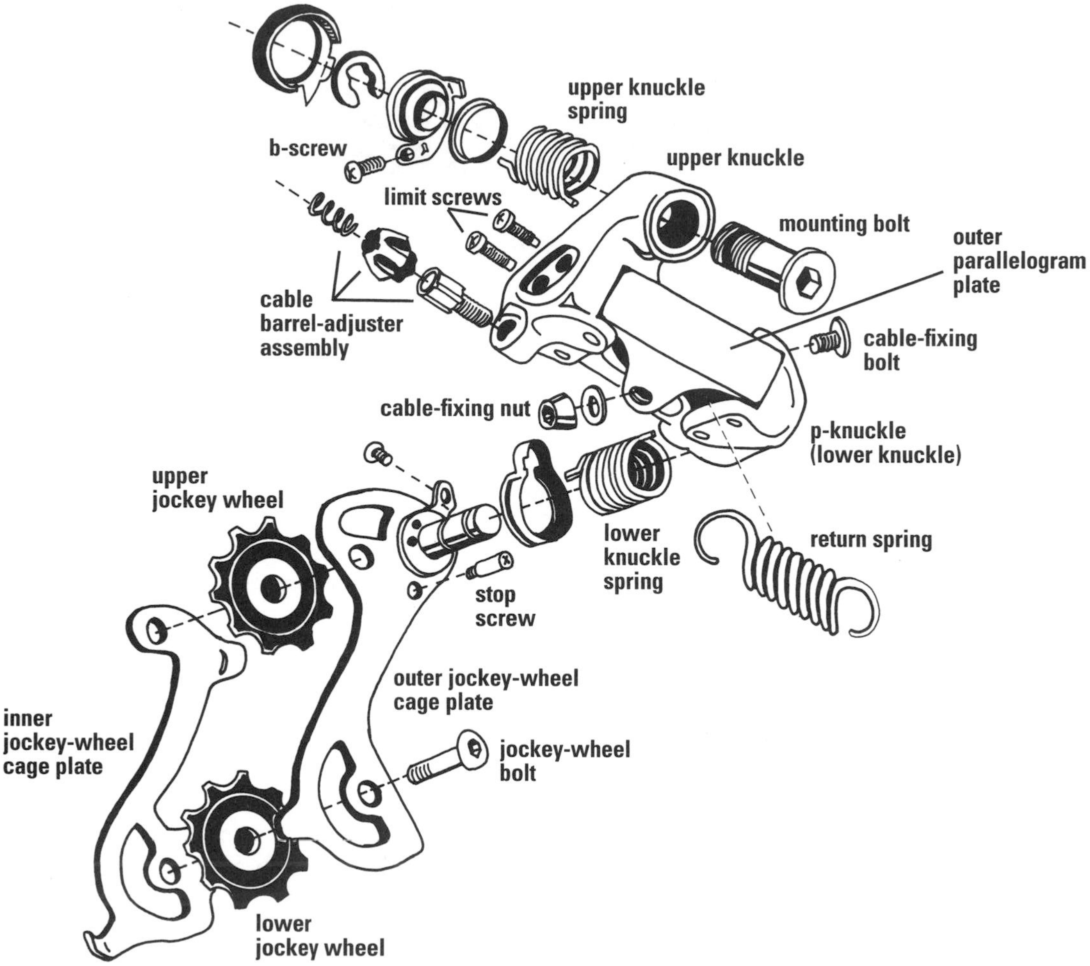

fashion. In fact, Low Normal refers to exactly this phenomenon—i.e., the derailleur's "normal" position, when the cable tension is removed, is in the low-gear position (large cog) rather than in the high-gear position found in traditional rear derailleurs.

The chain length, the balance between the springs in the upper and lower knuckle pivots, and the b-screw (Fig. 5.2) adjustment determine how closely the derailleur tracks to the cogs during its lateral movement and how well it keeps the chain from bouncing off of the front chainrings when the bike hits bumps. The two limit screws on the rear derailleur (Fig. 5.3) prevent the derailleur from moving the chain too far to the inside (into the spokes) or to the outside (into the dropout). In addition to limit screws, most rear derailleurs have a cable-tensioning barrel adjuster located at the back of the derailleur, where the cable enters it (Fig. 5.3). This barrel adjuster can be used to fine-tune the shifting adjustment to land the chain precisely on each cog with each click of the shifter. Rear derailleurs also often have a tensioning screw (the b-screw) at the back of the derailleur (Fig. 5.2) that rotates it around its mounting point to control the space between the bottom of the cogs and the upper jockey wheel.

5.2 **Right rear dropout**

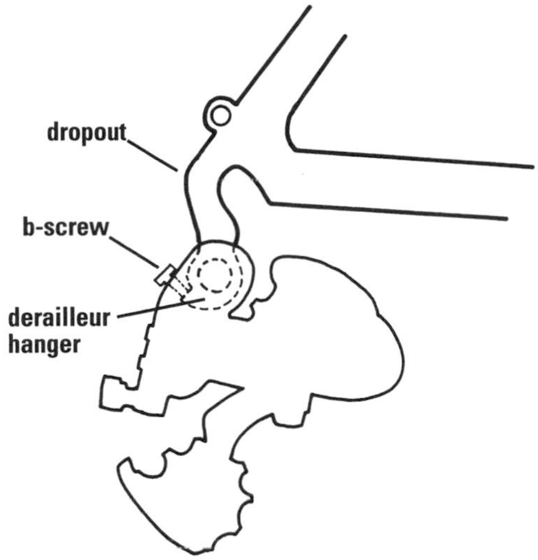

V-1 REAR-DERAILLEUR INSTALLATION

1. Apply a small amount of grease to the derailleur's mounting bolt and then thread the bolt a few turns into the large hole on the right rear dropout.
2. Pull the derailleur back so that the b-screw on the derailleur ends up behind the flat on the back of the derailleur hanger on the dropout (Fig. 5.2). Cheap derailleurs sometimes do not have a b-screw adjustment; instead, they just have a nonadjustable tab extending inward where the b-screw would have been. Make sure this tab is behind the flat on the derailleur hanger.
3. Tighten the mounting bolt until the derailleur fits snugly against the hanger.

NOTE: *Shimano Saint rear derailleurs do not mount to the dropout derailleur hanger. Rather, they mount onto the axle of the rear hub. To install one, install the rear wheel into the dropouts and push the axle through it from the nondrive side. Making sure the axle is seated fully into the dropouts, install the rear derailleur onto the greased, threaded, drive-side end of the axle; there is a hub-axle fixing nut built into its upper knuckle. Make sure that the derailleur's end stopper is in the dropout slot adjacent to the hub axle and that the b-screw is behind the dropout-hanger tab (same as shown in Fig. 5.2). Tighten the hub axle with a 6mm hex key from the nondrive side.*

After performing all of the standard rear-derailleur adjustments described below in steps 4 through 7, come back to this section, because you have one additional adjustment for a Shimano Saint derailleur. With a 2mm hex key, turn the bump stopper screw on the front of the upper knuckle (it is on the opposite side of the knuckle from the b-screw) to stop the derailleur so the lower pivot cannot hit the chainstay. Pull up on the lower jockey wheel to swing the derailleur up as high as it will go, and turn the bump stopper screw to stop it when the lower derailleur-pivot body is 5–10mm below the chainstay.

4. Route the chain through the jockey wheels and connect it back together, making sure that it is the correct length (see Chapter 4, §iv-8 to §iv-11).
5. Install the cables and housings (see §v-6 to §v-14 below).
6. Pull the cable tight with a pair of pliers, and tighten the cable anchor bolt.
7. Follow the adjustment procedure described in the next section.

V-2 ADJUSTMENT OF REAR DERAILLEUR AND RIGHT-HAND SHIFTER

Perform all of the following derailleur adjustments with the bike held in a stand or hung from the ceiling. That way, you can turn the crank and shift gears while you put the derailleur through its paces. After adjusting it off of the ground, test the shifting while riding. Derailleurs often perform differently under load than in a bike stand.

5.3 Rear-derailleur adjustments

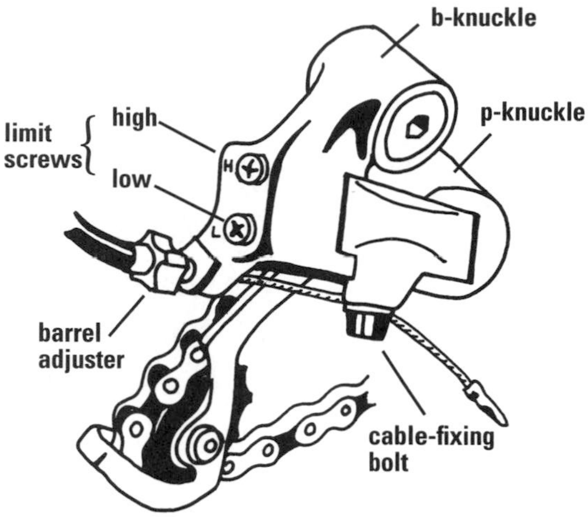

Before starting, lubricate or replace the chain (see Chapter 4) so that the whole drivetrain runs smoothly.

a. Limit-screw adjustments

The first, and most important, rear-derailleur adjustment is setting the limit screws. Properly set, these screws (Fig. 5.3) should make certain that you will not ruin your frame, wheel, or derailleur by shifting into the spokes or by jamming the chain between the dropout and the smallest cog. It is never pleasant to see your expensive equipment turned into shredded metal. All it takes is a small screwdriver to turn these limit screws. Remember, it's "lefty loosey, righty tighty" for turning these screws.

b. High-gear limit-screw adjustment

This screw limits the outward movement of the rear derailleur. You will tighten or loosen this screw until the derailleur shifts the chain to the smallest cog quickly but does not overshift.

How do you determine which limit screw works on the high gear? Often, it will be labeled with an "H," and it is usually the upper of the two screws (Fig. 5.3). If you are not certain, just try both screws. Whichever screw, when tightened, moves the derailleur inward when the chain is on the smallest cog is the one you are looking for. On most derailleurs, you can also see which screw to adjust by looking in between the derailleur's parallelogram side plates. You will see one tab on the back end of each plate. Each tab is designed to hit a limit screw at one end of the movement. Shift into your highest gear, and notice which screw is touching one of the tabs; that is the high-gear limit screw. The procedure for the limit-screw adjustment is as follows:

1. Shift the chain to the large front chainring.
2. While slowly turning the crank, shift the rear derailleur to the smallest rear cog (highest gear) (Fig. 5.4).
3. If there is hesitation in the chain's shifting movement, try adjusting the cable tension first, before attending to the limit screws.
   (a) With a traditional rear derailleur, loosen the cable a little to see if it is stopping the derailleur from moving out far enough. Do this by turning the barrel adjuster on the derailleur or shift lever clockwise (when viewed from the end of the barrel adjuster, as if it were a screw viewed from the top) or by loosening the cable anchor bolt, letting out some slack in the cable, and retightening the bolt.
   (b) With a Low Normal or Rapid Rise rear derailleur, tighten the cable a little to see whether it is not pulling the derailleur outward far enough. Do this by turning the barrel adjuster on the derailleur or shift lever counterclockwise (when viewed from the end of the barrel adjuster, as if it were a screw viewed from the top).

5.4 **High gear**

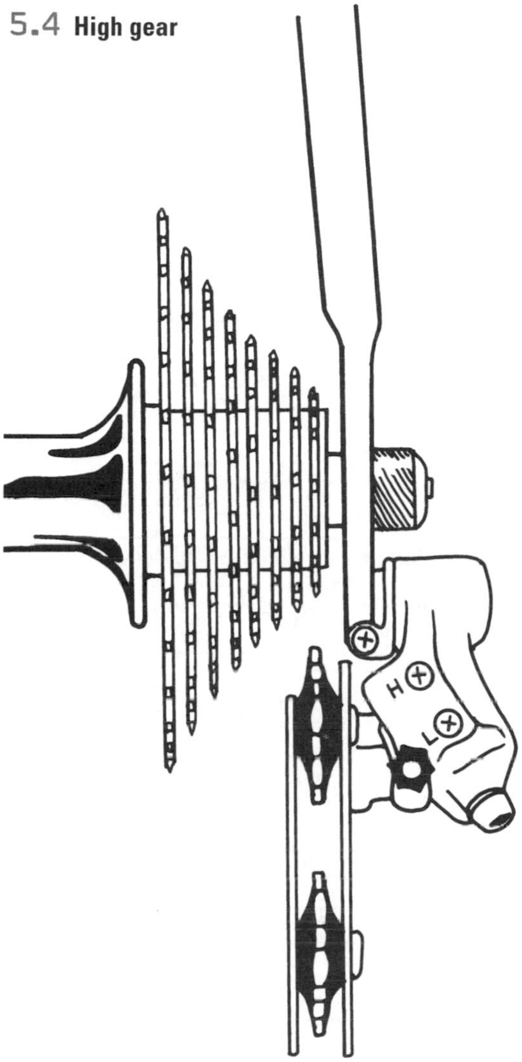

5.5 **Low gear**

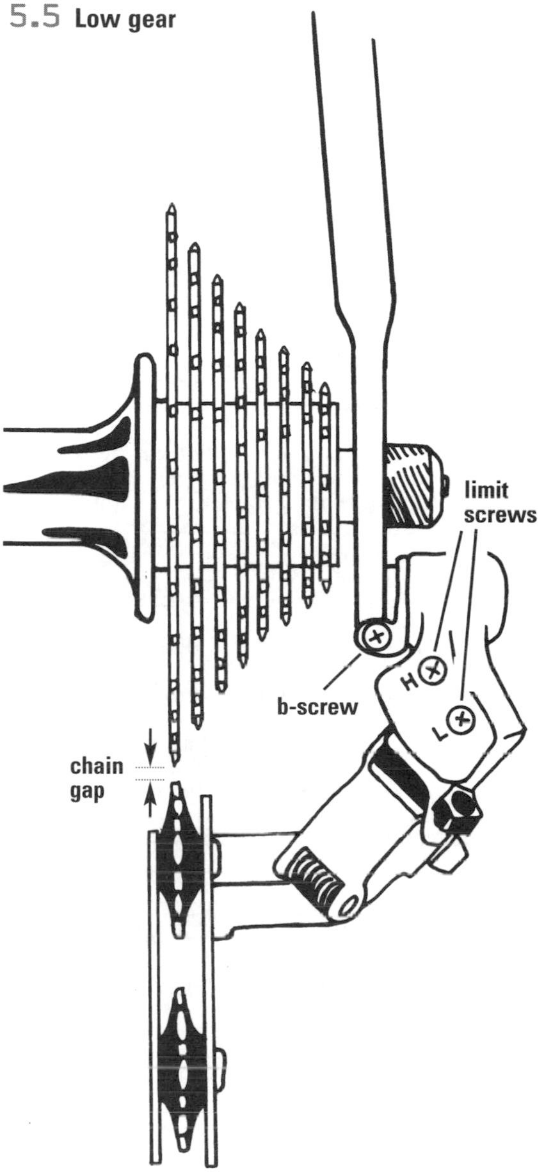

4. If the chain still won't drop smoothly and without hesitation to the smallest cog, loosen the high-gear limit screw one-quarter turn at a time, continuously repeating the shift, until the chain repeatedly drops quickly and easily.
5. If the derailleur tries to go past the smallest cog (or it succeeds in doing so and thereby throws the chain into the dropout), tighten the high-gear limit screw one-quarter turn and redo the shift. Repeat until the derailleur shifts the chain quickly and easily into the highest gear without throwing the chain into the dropout.

c. Low-gear limit-screw adjustment

This screw stops the inward movement of the rear derailleur, preventing it from going into the spokes. This screw is usually labeled "L," and it is usually the bottom screw (Fig. 5.3). You can check which one it is by shifting to the largest cog, maintaining pressure on the shifter, and turning the screw to see if it changes the position of the derailleur.

1. Shift the chain to the inner chainring on the front. Shift the rear derailleur to the lowest gear (largest cog) (Fig. 5.5). Do it gently, in case the limit screw does not stop the derailleur from going into the spokes.
2. If the derailleur touches the spokes or shoves the chain over the largest cog, tighten the low-gear limit screw until the derailleur does not.
3. If the derailleur cannot bring the chain onto the largest cog, loosen the screw one-quarter turn. On a Low Normal or Rapid Rise rear derailleur, you must first check that the cable tension is not so high that it prevents the chain from getting to the large cog. Loosen the cable by turning the barrel adjuster on the derailleur or shift lever clockwise (when viewed from the end of the barrel adjuster, as if it were a screw viewed from the top), or by loosening the cable anchor bolt, letting out some slack in the cable and retightening the bolt.
4. Once the cable tension is right, keep loosening the low-gear limit screw one-quarter turn at a time until the chain shifts easily up to the cog but does not brush the spokes.

d. Cable-tension adjustment: indexed rear shifters

With an indexed shifting system (one that "clicks" into each gear), it is the cable tension that determines whether the derailleur moves to the proper gear with each click.

1. With the chain on the large chainring in the front, shift the rear derailleur to the smallest cog. Keep clicking the shifter until you are sure it will not let any more cable out (or it will not pull any more cable, if you have a Low Normal or Rapid Rise rear derailleur).
2. Shift one click in the other direction; this should move the chain smoothly to the second cog.
3. If the chain does not climb to the second cog, or if it does so slowly, the cable tension is off. On a traditional rear derailleur, increase the tension in the cable by turning either the derailleur-cable barrel adjuster (Fig. 5.3) or the shifter barrel

5.6 Shifter barrel adjuster

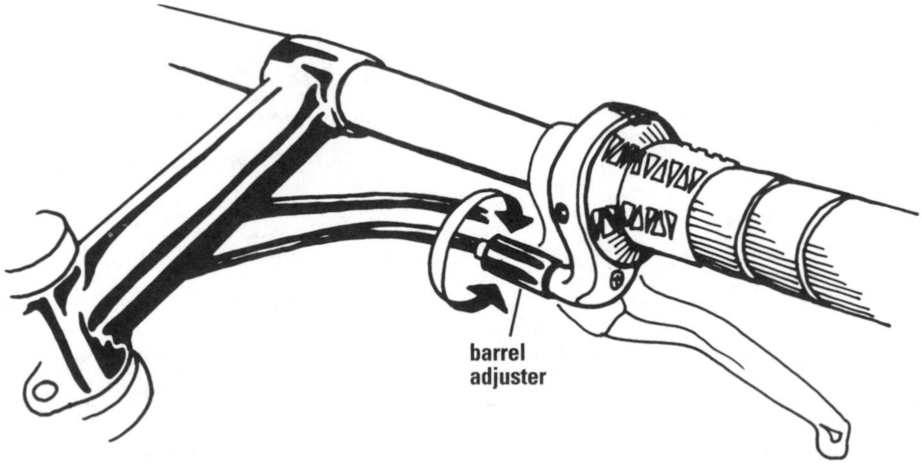

ADJUSTING
RIGHT-HAND
SHIFTER

adjuster (Fig. 5.6) counterclockwise (when viewed from the end of the barrel adjuster, where the cable housing inserts into it, as if it were a screw viewed from the top). Turn the opposite way for a Low Normal or Rapid Rise derailleur.

If you run out of barrel-adjustment range and the cable is still not tight enough, retighten both adjusters clockwise, to one turn from where they stop, loosen the cable anchor bolt, and pull some of the slack out of the cable. Tighten the anchor bolt and repeat the adjustment. Note that Shimano Rapid Rise, some Shimano Low Normal, SRAM, and Sachs DiRT derailleurs have no barrel adjuster—use the barrel adjuster on the shifter alone.

4. If the chain overshifts the second cog, or comes close to overshifting, decrease the cable tension by turning one of the barrel adjusters clockwise (or with a Low Normal or Rapid Rise derailleur, increase the tension by turning one of the barrel adjusters counterclockwise). Again, always determine clockwise and counterclockwise from the position of the end of the barrel adjuster where the cable housing inserts into it.
5. Keep adjusting the cable tension in small increments while shifting back and forth between the two smallest cogs until the chain moves easily in both directions.
6. Shift to the middle chainring in the front and onto one of the middle rear cogs. Shift the rear derailleur back and forth a few cogs, again checking for precise and quick movement of the chain from cog to cog. Fine-tune the shifting by making small adjustments to the cable-tensioning barrel adjuster on the shifter or rear derailleur.
7. Shift to the inner ring in the front and to the largest cog in the rear. Shift up and down one click in the rear, again checking for symmetry and precision of chain movement in either direction between the two largest cogs. Fine-tune the barrel adjuster until you get it just right.
8. Go back through the gears. With the chain in the middle chainring in front, the rear derailleur should shift smoothly back and forth between any pair of cogs. With the chain on the big chainring, the rear derailleur should shift easily on all but perhaps the largest one or two cogs in the rear. With the chain on the inner chainring, the rear derailleur should shift easily on all but perhaps the two smallest cogs.
9. Skip to step f.

NOTE: *If the shifter barrel adjuster does not hold its adjustment, your derailleur performance will steadily worsen as you ride. This problem has occurred in early XTR shifters, which have no springs or notches to hold the adjuster in place, as most barrel adjusters have. If you have this problem, there are a couple of things you can do, besides getting a new shifter. One is to put Finish Line Ti-Prep on the threads to create a bit more friction; I have found this to be a temporary fix only. Applying Loctite or scoring the threads crosswise may also help, although I have not tried either method. One foolproof solution, though a bit of a hassle, is to keep the shifter barrel adjuster turned all of the way in and make all cable-tension adjustments with the barrel adjuster on the rear derailleur. This fix will not work with barrel-adjuster-free rear derailleurs, though.*

ANOTHER NOTE: *If the cable tension is okay in the mid-sized cogs, too high in the large cogs, and too low in the small cogs (or the opposite with a Low Normal or Rapid Rise rear derailleur), then the rear derailleur is moving more than one cog spacing with each click of the shifter. The problem could be that you are using an eight-speed shifter with a nine-speed cogset or another mismatched combination.*

If the shifter and cogs are both for the same number of gears, the problem could be that some of the spacers between cogs are too thin, making the entire stack of cogs narrower than it should be. This is a rare, albeit not unprecedented, situation when using components from a single company all designed to work together, but it is not uncommon when mixing components from different manufacturers.

You can actually remedy this spacing problem without going out and buying a new cogset, however. Remove the cassette lockring (see §vi-19) and pull apart those cogs that are separable from each other. Trace around one of the spacers on a piece of aluminum you have cut from a beer or pop can. Follow the tracing with a box-cutter knife or similar implement in order to cut out a "beer-can" spacer shim. Fine-tune its shape until it will slip over the freehub body. Reassemble the cogset onto the freehub, placing the shim between a spacer and a cog where it seems that the shifting starts to get thrown off. If this improves shifting but does not completely fix the problem, try adding another beer-can shim. A beer-can shim is approximately 0.1mm thick, and I have seen 0.3mm variation between the total stack height of a SRAM and a Shimano 11-34 nine-speed cogset, for example. Experiment with various positions for the shim(s) within the cogset until you have optimized your shifting performance.

ADJUSTING RIGHT-HAND SHIFTER

e. Cable-tension adjustment: Nonindexed rear shifters

If you do not have indexed shifting, adjustment is complete after you remove the slack in the cable. With proper cable tension, when the chain is on the smallest cog, the derailleur should move as soon as the shift lever does. If there is free play in the lever, tighten the cable by turning the cable barrel adjuster on the derailleur or shifter counterclockwise. If your rear derailleur and shifter don't have barrel adjusters, loosen the cable anchor bolt, pull some slack out of the cable with pliers, and retighten the clamp bolt.

Fine details of rear-derailleur adjustment

In most cases, you can stop after adjusting the limit screws and cable tension, but there is more you can do if you are a stickler for optimum performance. If you are still having shifting trouble, you would be well advised to proceed to at least step f, and maybe to step g and its following note as well. And if you have a problem with your chain bouncing off, attend to step g.

f. Chain gap: The "b-screw" adjustment

You can get a bit more shifting precision by adjusting the small screw (b-screw—see Fig. 5.2) that changes the derailleur's position against the derailleur-hanger tab on the right rear dropout. Viewing from behind with the chain on the inner chainring and largest cog (Fig. 5.5), adjust the screw so that the upper jockey wheel is close to the cog, but not pinching the chain against the cog. Repeat on the smallest cog (Fig. 5.4). You'll know that you've moved the jockey wheel in too closely when it starts making noise.

SRAM (maker of Grip Shift) suggests setting the b-screw on its early ESP derailleurs with the chain on the middle chainring and largest cog. Viewing from the drive side, turn the screw so that the length of chain across the "chain gap" (from where the chain leaves the bottom of the cog to its first contact

5.7 **Chain-gap adjustment of an early SRAM derailleur**

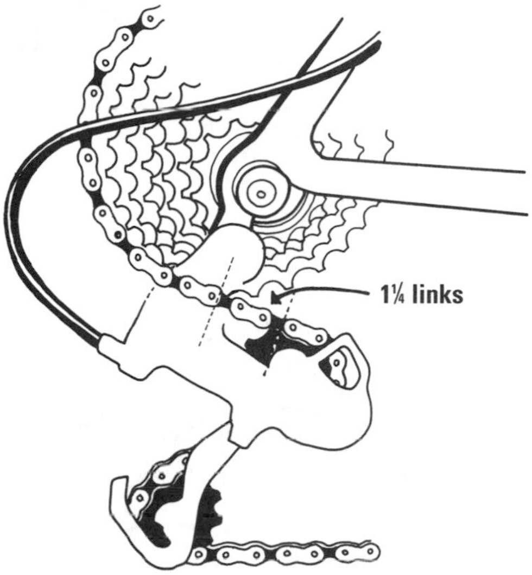

5.8 **Removing the p-knuckle screw with a 2mm hex key**

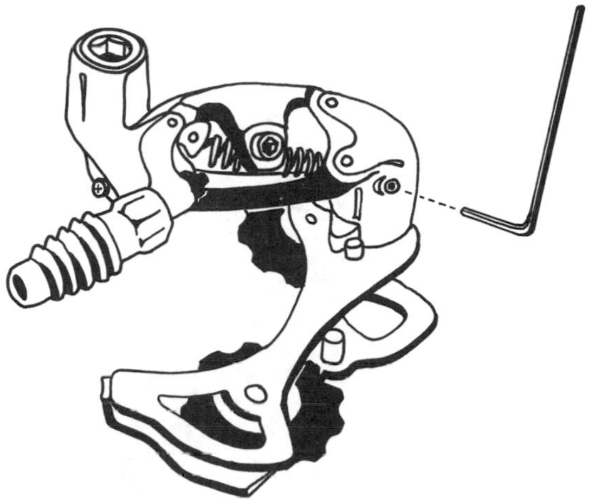

at the top of the upper jockey wheel) is one to one-and-one-quarter links (Fig. 5.7), where one link is a complete male-female link pair (Fig. 4.5). SRAM derailleurs from 2000 and later specify a 6mm vertical distance from the top of the upper jockey wheel to the bottom of the large cog (the chain gap depicted in Fig. 5.5), when in the small-chainring, large-cog combination.

g. Lower-knuckle pivot-spring ("p-spring") tension adjustment

LEVEL 2

The lower pivot spring twists the derailleur forward and puts pressure on the chain through the jockey wheels. By increasing the lower-knuckle pivot-spring tension, you can bring the upper jockey wheel closer to the cogs and increase tension in the lower run of the chain. This procedure will keep the chain from bouncing as much over rough terrain. It does put more drag (i.e., friction) on the chain, so I wouldn't do it on a cross-country bike unless I had to. But increasing the p-spring tension can be well worth doing for downhill racing and other gravity-driven riding.

This is definitely a complex adjustment requiring disassembly of the derailleur pivot, so be sure it is justified. Also, if you were thinking about replacing your steel pivot bolt with a lightweight aluminum one, now is the time to do it.

On post-1997 Shimano XT, LX, and STX rear derailleurs, and a year or two later with other models, there is a setscrew on the side of the lower pivot (Fig. 5.8) that makes it possible to disassemble the pivot without disconnecting the derailleur from the cable and the chain. Nevertheless, I recommend removing the derailleur first. You would have to unscrew the mounting bolt anyway, and the derailleur will get so twisted around that it will be hard to tell which way is up with the cable and chain connected. You could end up turning the jockey cage the wrong direction and deforming the spring so it would not fit back in the knuckle.

5.9 Increasing the p-spring tension by putting the spring end in another hole

5.10 Removing the stop screw that prevents the jockey cage from twisting all of the way around

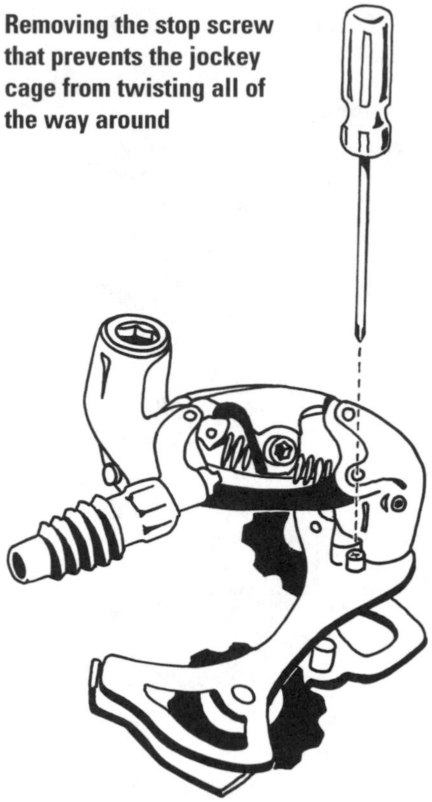

5.11 Unscrewing the pivot bolt with a 5mm hex key to pull the derailleur cage off of the p-spring

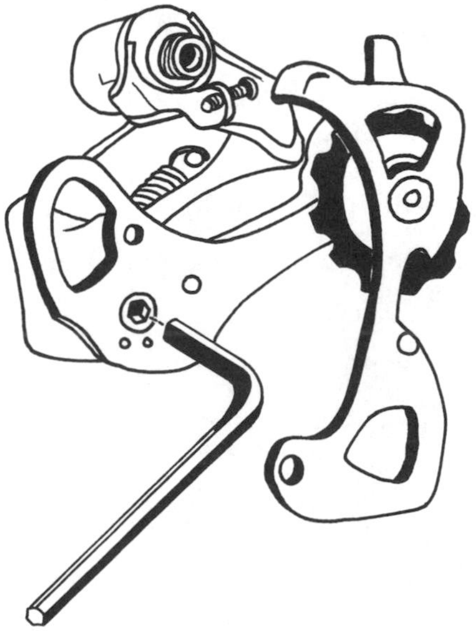

The setscrew on the lower pivot engages a groove in the pivot shaft to keep it from pulling apart. Remove the screw with a 2mm hex key (Fig. 5.8), and pull the jockey cage away from the spring. Put the spring in the next spring hole to increase its tension (Fig. 5.9), push the pivot assembly back together, and replace the setscrew. Shimano derailleurs come with the p-spring in the low-tension hole.

Increasing p-spring tension on older Shimano derailleurs is more complicated because there is no setscrew on the lower-knuckle housing. After removing the derailleur from the bike, remove the tall stop screw that prevents the jockey cage from twisting all of the way around (Fig. 5.10). Remove the upper jockey wheel and unscrew the pivot bolt from the back with a 5mm hex key (Fig. 5.11). Pull the derailleur cage off the end of the spring and move the end of the spring into the other spring hole. Wind the jockey-wheel cage

5.12 **Front derailleur**

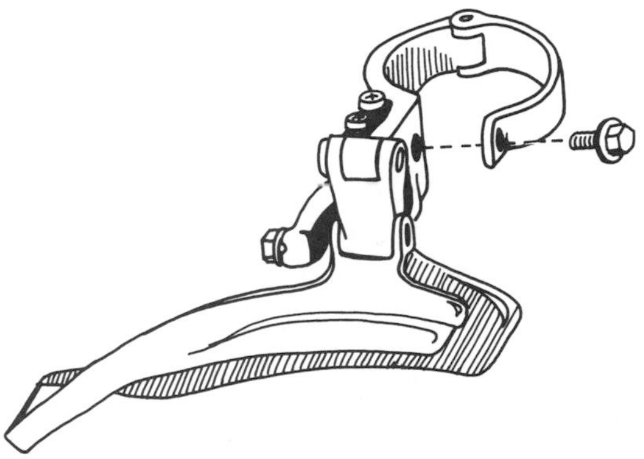

5.13 **XTR bottom-bracket-mount (E-type) front derailleur and band-clamp adapter (below)**

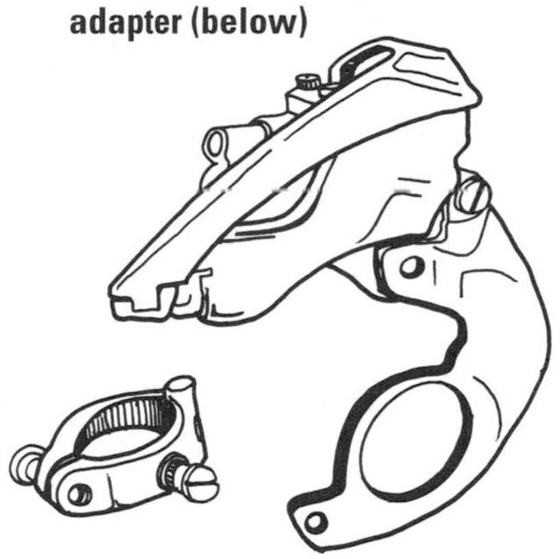

back around, screw it all back together with the pivot bolt, and replace the stop screw.

NOTE: *If you cannot get the rear derailleur to shift well, or it makes noise in even mild cross-gears no matter what you do, or it throws the chain off despite your best efforts, refer to the chain-line discussion under the troubleshooting section at the end of this chapter after ensuring that neither the derailleur nor the derailleur hanger on the frame dropout is bent.*

THE FRONT DERAILLEUR

The front derailleur moves the chain between the chainrings. The working parts consist of a cage to enclose the chain, a linkage, and an arm attached to the shifter cable. The front derailleur is attached to the frame, usually by a clamp surrounding the seat tube (Fig. 5.12). Some Shimano models attach to the face of the bottom-bracket shell. These are called "E-type" front derailleurs. Some Shimano E-type front derailleurs mount both to the face of the bottom bracket and to a braze-on boss (or band clamp adapter) on the seat tube (Fig. 5.13).

Standard seat-tube band clamps also vary. A "top swing" front derailleur has a band clamp that is lower than the height of the top of the front derailleur's cage (see Figs. 5.30A, 5.30B). The front derailleur's activation linkage and pivots are behind the cage, similar to those shown in Figure 5.13 on an E-type derailleur. A "traditional" mount has a band clamp well above the cage, and the large outer linkage plate and cage pivot are above the cage (see Fig. 5.14). Which style to choose depends largely on the bike's frame, as often a pivot or shock mount on the frame will preclude the use of one clamp style or another.

The direction that the cable pulls also distinguishes front derailleurs from each other. A "bottom pull" front derailleur requires the cable to come from below, generally by wrapping around underneath the bottom-bracket shell. A "top pull" front derailleur is activated by a cable pulling on it from above, generally after it runs along the top tube and the cable housing terminates at a cable stop on the back of the seat tube. Many modern front derailleurs have a dual cable-pull option; the cable can come either from below or above—either straight to the cable anchor bolt from above or over the top of a rocker-arm assembly, wrapping down again to attach at the bolt (see Figs. 5.30A, 5.30B).

5.14 **Proper clearance**

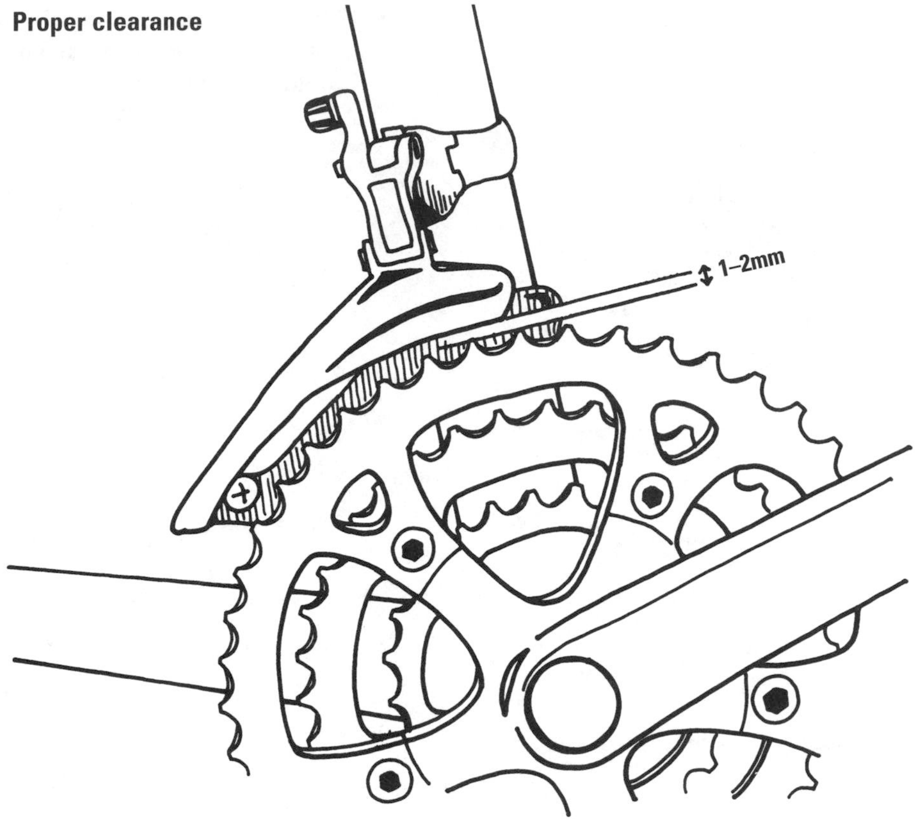

v-3 FRONT-DERAILLEUR INSTALLATION: BAND TYPE

1. Clamp the front derailleur around the seat tube. Older front derailleurs must have a band-clamp diameter matching that of the seat tube, but modern Shimano and SRAM front derailleurs work on more than one seat-tube diameter. They have a band clamp for a 35mm (1⅜ inch) diameter seat tube, but they come with shims for either 31.8mm (1¼ inch) or 28.6mm (1⅛ inch) seat tubes. In the case of Shimano front derailleurs, C-shaped aluminum shims are held in place by C-shaped plastic brackets that clip within the circle of the front-derailleur band clamp.
2. Adjust the height and rotation as described in §v-5a.
3. Tighten the clamp bolt (Fig. 5.12).

v-4 FRONT-DERAILLEUR INSTALLATION: E-TYPE BRACKET (I.E., BOTTOM-BRACKET FACE-MOUNTING TYPE)

1. Remove the bottom bracket (see Chapter 8, §viii-11 and §viii-12).
2. Slip the (E-type) derailleur bracket over the right-hand bottom-bracket cup, and start the cup into the bottom-bracket shell a few threads.
3. With less expensive models, place its C-shaped stabilizer around the seat tube to fix the rotational adjustment. With a high-end E-type front derailleur (Fig. 5.13), loosely screw the mounting bolt into the frame's special braze-on boss designed for it. (If the frame does not have the braze-on boss, a separate seat-tube band clamp with a threaded hole in the side is used [see Fig.

5.13]. The circular band will need to be bent to fit if you have an oval-shaped seat tube.)

4. Tighten the right-hand bottom-bracket cup against the bottom-bracket face.
5. If applicable, tighten the mounting bolt into the braze-on boss (or band-clamp hole).
6. Complete the bottom-bracket installation (see Chapter 8, §viii-7 to §viii-10).

NOTE: *There are no (or limited) height and rotational adjustments on these derailleurs, and they must be used with the chainring size for which they were intended. They can be turned only slightly to line up better with the chain.*

Some E-type front derailleurs have two mounting-bolt holes for two possible outer chainring sizes. The derailleur's rotational adjustment can be fine tuned without the braze-on boss, because the band clamp can be twisted around the seat tube a few degrees.

v-5 ADJUSTMENTS OF FRONT DERAILLEUR AND LEFT-HAND SHIFTER

a. Position adjustments

With a seat-tube-clamp front derailleur, the position is adjusted with a 5mm Allen (or an 8mm box) wrench on the band-clamp bolt. E-type front derailleurs have little or no vertical or rotational (twist about the seat tube) adjustments.

1. Position the height of the front derailleur so that the outer cage passes about 1–2mm (1/16–1/8 inches) above the highest point of the outer chainring (Fig. 5.14). Out of the box, new Shimano front derailleurs have a piece of clear tape on the cage illustrating the proper gap, with teeth drawn onto it to line up with the chainring teeth. They also have a plastic block called a "Pro-set alignment block" installed that forces the derailleur out to the high-gear position. Leave that block in place for this step, and remove it for the second part of step 2 (and from then on!).
2. Position the outer plate of the derailleur cage parallel to the chainrings (or to the chain in the lowest and highest gears) when viewed from above. Check this by shifting to the big chainring and smallest cog and sighting from the top (Fig. 5.15). Many derailleurs (Sachs, most Shimano, Suntour) need the outer face of the cage to be exactly parallel to the chainring; check this by measuring the space between the cage and the inner side of the crankarm as it passes by. The cage of some derailleurs flares wider at the tail (Shimano XTR is one example). The outer tail of the derailleur cage on these models needs to be out a bit from parallel to the plane of the frame in order to parallel the chain. Similarly, when on the inner chainring (Fig. 5.16) and largest cog, the inner cage plate should parallel the chain,

5.15–5.16 Proper cage alignment

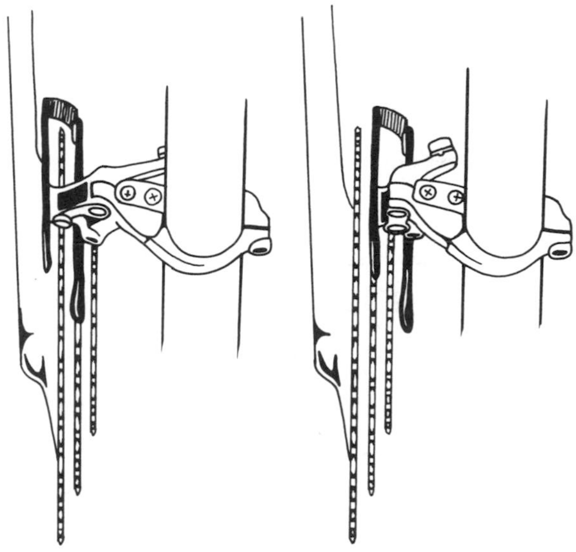

ADJUSTING FRONT DERAILLEUR

making the tail a bit in from parallel with the plane of the frame.

NOTE: *Height and rotational adjustments of the seat-tube-clamp version of Shimano's differential-plate XTR front derailleur are set in the same manner as standard front derailleurs.*

b. Limit-screw adjustments

The front derailleur has two limit screws that stop the derailleur from throwing the chain to the inside or outside of the chainrings. These are usually labeled "L" for low gear (small chainring) and "H" for high gear (large chainring) (Fig. 5.17). On most derailleurs, the low-gear screw is closer to the frame; however, Shimano XTR differential-plate derailleurs, among others, have the limit-screw positions reversed, but their adjustment is the same.

If in doubt, you can determine which limit screw controls which function by the same trial-and-error method outlined above for the rear derailleur. Shift the chain to the inner ring, then tighten one of the limit screws. If tightening that screw moves the front derailleur outward, then it is the low-gear limit screw. If turning that screw does not move the front derailleur, then the other screw is the low-gear limit screw.

c. Low-gear limit-screw adjustment

1. Shift back and forth between the middle and inner chainrings.
2. If the chain drops off of the little ring to the inside, tighten the low-gear limit screw (clockwise) one-quarter turn and try shifting again.
3. If the chain does not drop easily onto the inner chainring when shifted, loosen the low-gear limit screw one-quarter turn and repeat the shift.

5.17 **Limit screws**

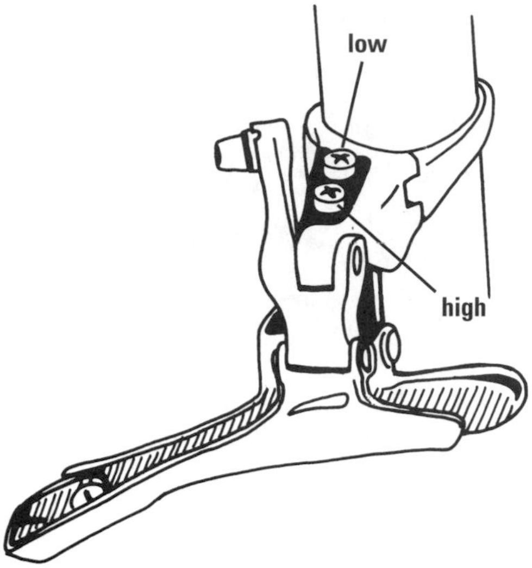

Make sure that overly high cable tension is not preventing the derailleur from reaching the inner limit screw; if it is, back off on the cable tension by turning the shifter barrel adjuster clockwise.

d. High-gear limit-screw adjustment

1. Shift the chain back and forth between the middle and outer chainring.
2. If the chain jumps over the big chainring, tighten the high-gear limit screw one-quarter turn and repeat the shift.
3. If the chain is sluggish going up to the big chainring or does not go up at all, loosen the high-gear limit screw one-quarter turn and try the shift again.

e. Cable-tension adjustment

1. With the chain on the inner chainring, remove any excess cable slack by turning the barrel adjuster on the shifter (as shown in Fig. 5.6, except on the left shifter) counterclockwise (again, determine rotation direction by looking

5.18 **Cable-housing types and end caps**

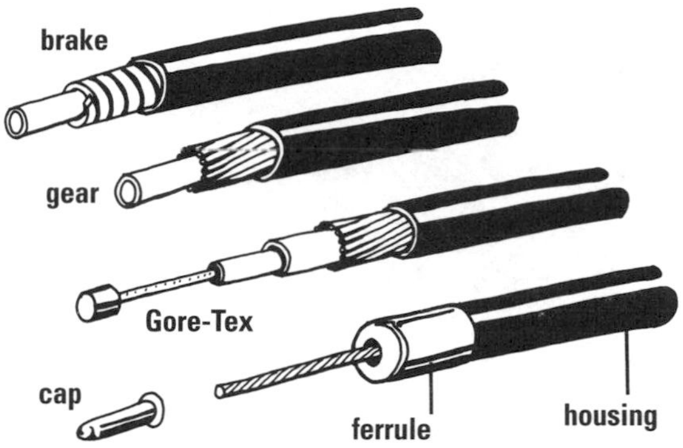

at the adjuster from the end from which the cable housing emerges, as if you were looking at the top of a bolt). (Or, tighten the cable without the barrel adjuster: loosen the cable anchor bolt, pull the cable tight with pliers, and tighten the bolt.)

2. Check that the cable is loose enough to allow the chain to shift smoothly and repeatedly from the middle to the inner chainring.
3. Check that the cable is tight enough so that the derailleur starts to move as soon as you move the shifter.

NOTE: *This tension adjustment should work for indexed as well as friction shifters. With indexed front shifting, you may want to fine-tune the barrel adjuster to avoid noise from the chain dragging on the derailleur in some cross-gears, or to get more precise shifting.*

ANOTHER NOTE: *Some front derailleurs have a cam screw at the end of the spring to adjust spring tension. For quicker shifting to the smaller rings, increase the spring tension by turning the screw clockwise.*

NOTE ON SHIFTING TROUBLE: *If you cannot get the front derailleur to shift well, or it rubs in cross-gears no matter what you do, or it throws the chain off despite your best efforts, refer to the chainline discussion under the troubleshooting section at the end of this chapter.*

REPLACING AND LUBRICATING SHIFT CABLES AND HOUSINGS

In order for your derailleurs to function properly, you need to have clean, smooth-running cables (also called "inner wires"). Because of all the muck that you encounter on a mountain bike, you need to regularly replace those cables. As with replacing a chain, replacing cables is a maintenance operation, not a repair operation. Do not wait until cables break to replace them. Replace any cables that have broken strands, kinks, or fraying between the shifter and the derailleur. You should also replace housings (also called "outer wires") if they are bent, mashed, or just plain gritty or if the color clashes with your bike (this is really important).

v-6 BUYING CABLES

1. Buy new cables and housing with at least as much length as the ones you are replacing.
2. Make sure that the cables and housing are for indexed systems. These cables will stretch minimally, and the housings will not compress in length. Under its external plastic sheath, indexed housing is not made of steel coil like brake housings; it is made of parallel (coaxial) steel strands of thin wire. If you look at the end, you will see numerous wire ends sticking out surrounding a central Teflon tube (make sure it has this Teflon liner, too) (Fig. 5.18). Gore-Tex cable is discussed in §v-16.
3. For each end of every housing section, buy two cable-crimp caps (Fig. 5.18) to prevent fraying and a tubular cable-housing end ferrule. These

ferrules will prevent kinking at the cable entry points, cable stops, shifters, and derailleurs. You might also consider getting ferrules that have a long nose on them that sticks out through the slot in a cable stop on the frame. A tubular rubber dust shield comes with them and slips onto the long nose from the opposite side of the cable stop to prevent entry of dirt and water into the housing. While you're at it, buying rubber cable donuts (Fig. 5.32) or sheathing for bare-cable runs is worthwhile to protect your frame.

4. It is a good idea to buy a bunch of cables, cable caps, and ferrules (Fig. 5.18) to keep on hand in your work area. They're cheap, and you should be changing cables regularly without having to make a special trip to the bike shop every time you need a little cable-end cap.

5.19–5.20 **Housing length**

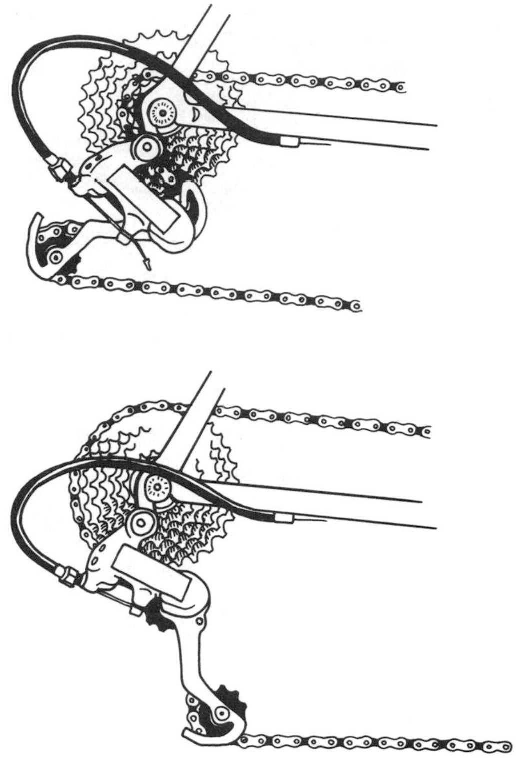

5.21 **Thumb shifter**

5.22 **Rapidfire shifter**

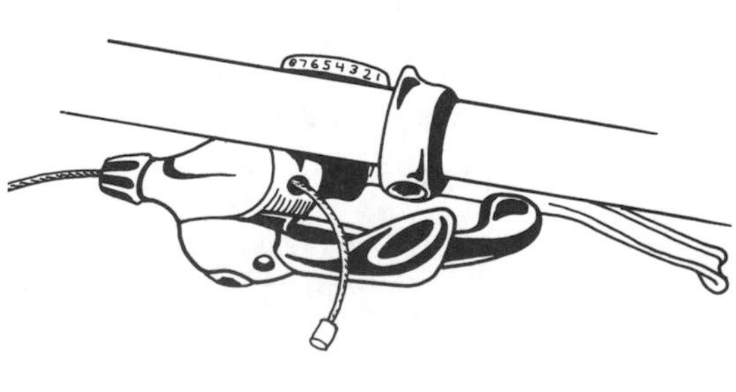

V-7 CUTTING THE HOUSING TO LENGTH

CUTTING THE HOUSING TO LENGTH

1. Use a special cable-housing cutter such as those from Park, Shimano, or Wrench Force (see Chapter 1, §i-2). Standard side cutters for cutting wire will not cut index-shift housing, and they won't do a good job on cables, either.
2. Cut the housing to the same lengths as your old ones. If you have no old housings to compare with, cut them so that the housing sections curve smoothly from cable stop to cable stop, and turning the handlebar does not pull or kink them. Allow for enough length at the rear derailleur so that the derailleur can freely swing back (Fig. 5.19) and forth (Fig. 5.20 for chainstay cable; Fig. 5.28 for seat-stay cable). Current SRAM and old Sachs DiRT rear derailleurs (SRAM now owns Sachs) use a short housing section without a cable loop (the bare cable runs over a pulley), and they are

5.23 **Replacing the cable in a left Shimano XT Dual Control shifter/hydraulic brake lever**

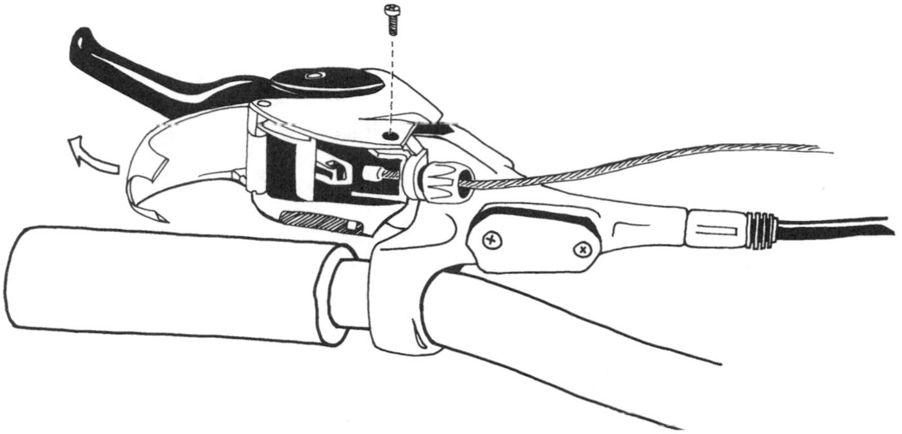

particularly sensitive to housing length. The housing should curve gently into its receptacle without being so short that it limits derailleur movement or so long that it has a sharp bend; the latter is particularly important to watch for with a seat-stay cable as the derailleur swings backward.

3. With a nail or toothpick, open each Teflon sleeve-end that has been smashed shut by the cutter.
4. Place a ferrule (Fig. 5.18) over each housing end.

V-8 REPLACING CABLE IN THUMB SHIFTERS, SHIMANO RAPIDFIRE LEVERS, OR SRAM TRIGGER LEVERS

1. Disconnect the cable at the derailleur and clip off the end cap.
2. Shift the lever (on Rapidfire or SRAM, the upper, chain-dump lever) to the gear setting that lets the most cable out. On most systems, this will be the highest gear position for the rear shift lever (small cog), and the lowest for the front (small chainring). On Low Normal or Rapid Rise systems, however, it will be the low gear position front and rear.
3. If installed, unscrew the large plastic plug that covers the cable-access hole on many Shimano Rapidfire levers. On SRAM trigger levers, open the rubber cable-change flap. Push out the old cable and recycle it.
4. The recessed hole into which the cable head seats should be visible right up against the barrel adjuster. Thread the new cable through the hole and out through the barrel adjuster (Figs. 5.21 and 5.22).
5. Guide the cable through each housing segment and cable stop. Slotted cable stops on your frame allow you to slip the cable and housing in and out from the side. Replace the plastic plug or rubber flap over the cable-access hole in the shifter.

V-9 REPLACING SHIFT CABLE IN SHIMANO "DUAL CONTROL" INTEGRATED SHIFTERS AND HYDRAULIC DISC-BRAKE LEVERS

These models are 2003 (and later) XTR, 2004 (and later) XT, and 2005 (and later) LX, and any one may be used with the Saint group. Note that cable change is different (and more complicated) for the front shifter than for the rear one.

The brake lever on these units (Fig. 5.23), when moved laterally downward with the palm side of the fingertips, pulls shift cable. When the brake lever is moved laterally upward with the back (fingernail) side of the fingertips, it releases shift cable. (Of course, when the brake lever is pulled straight back toward the handlebar, it pushes on the hydraulic fluid to apply the disc brakes.)

a. Either lever

1. Disconnect the cable at the derailleur and clip off the end cap.
2. With the fingernail-side of the fingers on the brake lever or with the thumb on the auxiliary release lever, if installed, flip the lever repeatedly until the indicator needle reaches the "L" position on the gear-indicator window to release the maximum amount of cable.

b. Rear (right) lever

1. Remove the large plastic Phillips screw plug on the lever end of the large cover with the Shimano logo on it. Push on the cable; the end should pop right out of the hole the screw plug was in. You may need to coax it a bit with a paper clip or thin knife to guide it out of the hole while you push the cable.
2. Slip the new cable straight in through the unplugged hole in the cover and into the recessed receptacle into which the cable head seats. Thread the cable straight out through the barrel adjuster.
3. Guide the cable through each housing segment and cable stop. Slotted cable stops on your frame allow you to slip the cable and housing in and out from the side. Replace the plastic plug in the cable-access hole in the shifter.

c. Front (left) lever

1. Open the cover concealing the cable hook. This is quite ingeniously designed and consequently simple to perform. Remove the Phillips screw on the cover adjacent to the barrel adjuster (Fig. 5.23); it is on the opposite side of the shifter housing from the gear-indicator window. Do not remove the other two, smaller Phillips screws also on the same plastic cover piece. Flip open the shifter-housing cover; it has the Shimano logo on it and hinges from its end opposite the barrel adjuster.
2. While jiggling the cable a bit to free it from the cable hook, pry up on the cable where it exits the cable hook to flip the cable head out of the hook (Fig. 5.23). Pull the old cable out, and snap the head of the new cable into the cable hook.
3. With the palm side of the fingers, shift the brake lever laterally to pull the cable hook over until the gear indicator moves to the "H" position in the indicator window; in other words, activate the lever to pull as much cable as it can. Now slip the other end of the cable out through the barrel adjuster.
4. Close the cover and tighten the screw (gently!).
5. Guide the cable through each housing segment and cable stop. Slotted cable stops on your frame allow you to slip the cable and housing in and out from the side.

1996–2000 XTR RAPIDFIRE CABLE REPLACEMENT

V-10 1996–2000 XTR RAPIDFIRE CABLE REPLACEMENT

The 1996–2000 Shimano XTR shifters have a plastic cover over the wire-end hook (Fig. 5.24) and also have a slotted barrel adjuster and shifter body.

1. Shift the smaller (upper and forward) finger-operated lever until the shifter lets all of the cable out; i.e., the rear shifter is in high-gear (small-cog) position—"H" on the indicator, and the front shifter is in the low-gear (small-chainring) position—"L" on the indicator.

5.24 Replacing the cable in a 1996–2000 Shimano XTR Rapidfire SL shifter

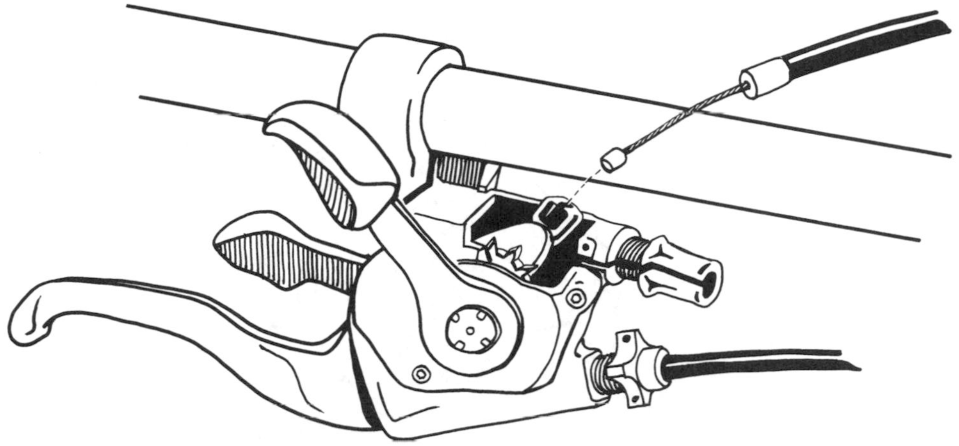

2. Turn the shifter barrel adjuster so its cable slot is lined up with the slot in the shifter body (Fig. 5.24), which is the slot on the opposite side from the gear indicator. Post-1999 XTR barrel adjusters are in a plastic housing that pulls out of the lever body; with this type, pull the entire barrel adjuster straight out.
3. Unscrew the Phillips-head screw on the plastic cover; it will not come completely out (so that you could lose it), being retained in the cover by a plastic ring. Open the cover.
4. Pull the old cable down out of the slot, and then pull the cable head out of the hook.
5. Slip the new cable head into the cable hook (Fig. 5.24), and pull the cable into the slot. Turn the barrel adjuster so the slots no longer line up. Or, with post-1999 XTR, push the barrel adjuster back in.
6. Close the cover and tighten the screw (gently!).
7. Guide the cable through each housing segment and cable stop. Slotted cable stops on your frame allow you to slip the cable and housing in and out from the side.

NOTE: *Replacing the thin cables connected to the XTR "Rapidfire Remote" bar-end-mounted shifters (which only were manufactured for a couple of years) requires buying the thin double-headed cables and housings from Shimano. The small heads simply slip through the holes in both sets of shift levers (on the handlebar and on the bar end) from the back side. You install the remote shifter's little plastic caps onto the metal cable heads to keep them from pulling back through. That's it.*

V-11 REPLACING CABLE IN SRAM (GRIP SHIFT) AND SACHS TWIST SHIFTERS FROM 1998 AND LATER

Changing cables is easy on current Grip Shift and Half Pipe shifters via the cable-hole cover. The high-end twist-shifter models got this feature in 1998, and by 2000, all SRAM shifters had the quick-cable-change system.

1. Disconnect the cable at the derailleur and cut off the end cap.
2. Twist the shifter to let out the maximum amount of cable (shift to "9" with the rear shifter and "1" with the front).

5.25 **SRAM Half Pipe twist shifter**

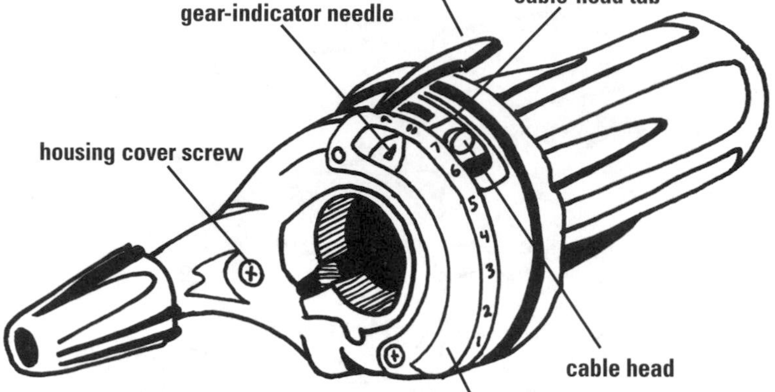

3. Getting at the end of the cable differs with each model. Some, such as Half Pipe shifters, for instance, have a rectangular rubber hatch that you pull open (Fig. 5.25). While pushing back on the cable, you then pry up the plastic tab that obscures half of the cable head. Use a small screwdriver. The cable should pop out from under the hook on the tab. Other high-end SRAM shifters have a plastic hatch that you slide off to the side. Once the hatch is off, you will see the cable head on the front shifter, and on the rear shifter, you will see a small setscrew that you remove with a 2.5mm hex key to reveal the cable head. On low-end shifters, you peel back the corner of the rubber grip cover, and you will see the cable head.
4. Push out the old cable.
5. Slide in the new cable and pull it snug. Replace the setscrew, if present, and carefully screw it in until it contacts the cable head. If it feels as though it has stripped the threads, it hasn't—it just has gone in beyond the threads and is turning freely. No worries.
6. Push the cover that conceals the cable head back into place.

REPLACING CABLE IN PRE-1998 GRIP SHIFT

V-12 REPLACING CABLE IN (AND OVERHAULING) PRE-1998 GRIP SHIFT

Prior to 1998, all Grip Shifts had to be disassembled to replace the cable; 1998–2000 low-end shifters still require disassembly for cable changing.

1. Disconnect the derailleur cable.
2. Move the brake lever inboard to make room for pulling the grip apart. If a bend in the handlebar or other obstruction prevents this, you must roll or slide the handlebar grip away from the Grip Shift to allow room for the shifter to slide apart.
3. With a Phillips screwdriver, remove the triangular plastic cover holding the two main sections together (Figs. 5.26 and 5.27).
4. Pull the outer shifter section away from the main body to separate it from the inner housing. Watch for the spring (Figs. 5.26 and 5.27) to ensure that it does not fall out. It can be nudged back into place if it does.

5.26 **Pre-1998 Grip Shift right shifter**

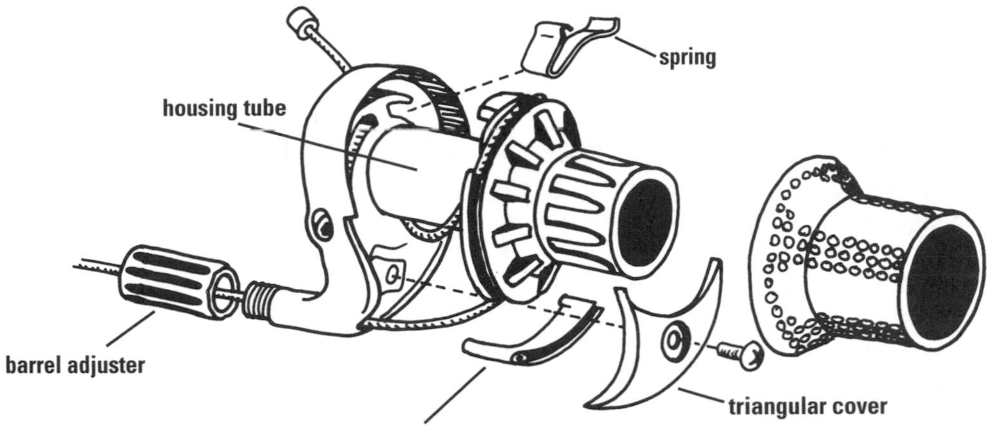

5.27 **Pre-1998 Grip Shift left shifter**

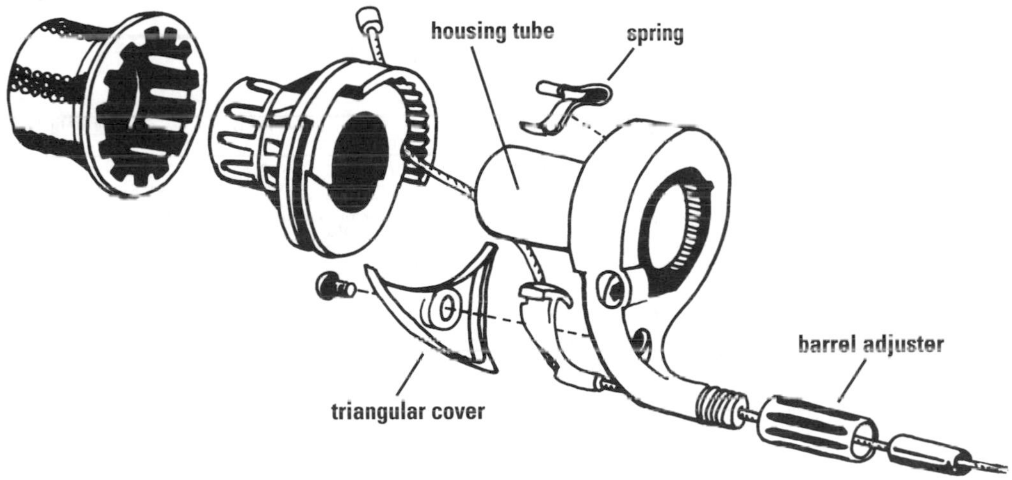

5. Pull the old cable out and recycle it.
6. Clean and dry the two parts if they are dirty; a rag and a cotton swab are usually sufficient. Finish Line offers a cleaning and grease kit specifically designed for Grip Shift shifters. A really gummed-up shifter may require a solvent and compressed air to clean and dry it.
7. Use a nonlithium grease to lubricate the inner housing tube and spring cavity, all cable grooves, and the indexing notches in the twister. Use SRAM Jonnisnot or Finish Line's silicone-based Teflon grease.
8. Thread the cable through the hole, seating the cable end in its little pocket.
9. For the rear shifter, loop the cable once around the housing tube, and exit it through the barrel adjuster (Fig. 5.26). For the front shifter, the cable routes directly into its guide (Fig. 5.27).

5.28 **Attaching a rear-derailleur cable**

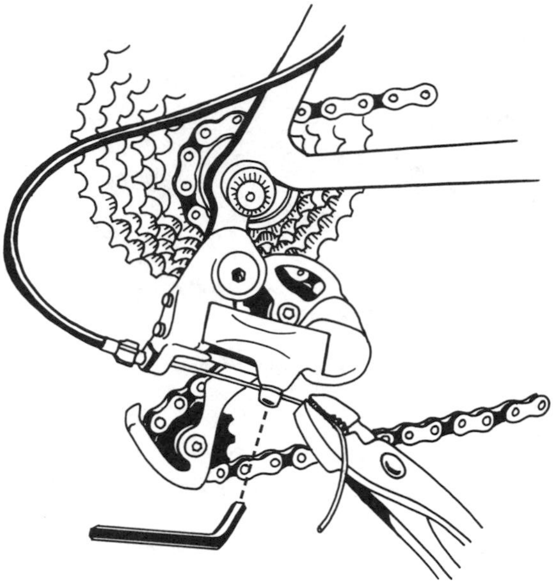

5.29 **Pull the cable tight before tightening with an Allen wrench**

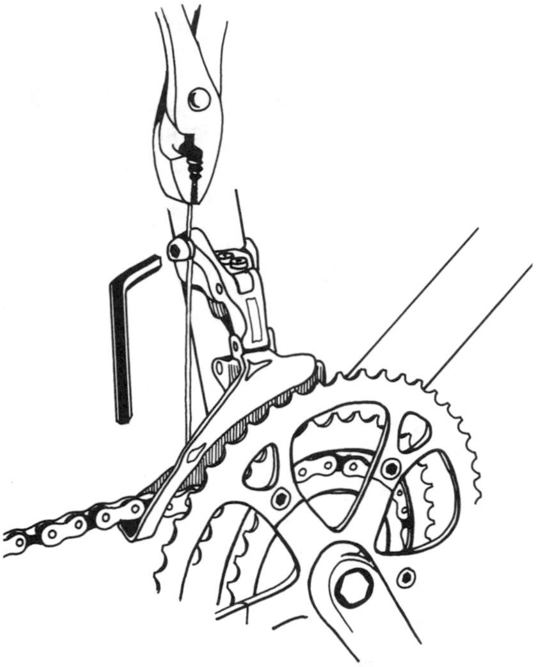

10. Make sure the spring is in its cavity in the housing; hold the spring in with a small amount of grease if need be.
11. Slide the outer (twister) body over the inner tube. Be sure that the shifter is in the position that lets the most cable out (on models with numbers, line up the highest number with the indicator mark on rear shifters, lowest number on front shifters).
12. Lift the cable loop into the groove in the twister (Fig. 5.26), and push straight inward on it as you pull tension on the cable exiting the shifter. The twister should slide in until flush under the housing edge; you may have to jiggle it back and forth slightly while pushing in to get it properly seated.
13. Replace the cover and screw.
14. Check that the shifter clicks properly.
15. Slide the grip back into place.
16. Guide the cable through each housing segment and cable stop. Slotted cable stops on your frame allow you to slip the cable and housing in and out from the side—use them that way to save yourself some effort.

ATTACH CABLE TO REAR DERAILLEUR

V-13 ATTACH CABLE TO REAR DERAILLEUR

1. Put the chain on the smallest cog so the rear derailleur moves to the outside.
2. Run the cable through the barrel adjuster, and route it through each of the housing segments until you reach the cable anchor bolt on the derailleur. Make sure that the rear shifter is on the highest gear setting; this ensures that the maximum amount of cable is available to the derailleur.
3. Pull the cable taut and into its groove under the cable anchor bolt (Fig. 5.28).
4. Tighten the bolt. On most derailleurs this takes a 5mm Allen wrench.

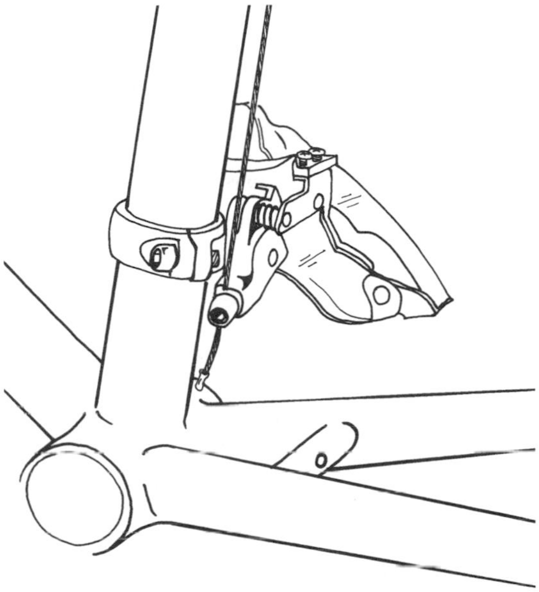

5.30A **Over-the-top-tube (i.e., top-pull) cable routing to a Shimano low-clamp "top swing" front derailleur**

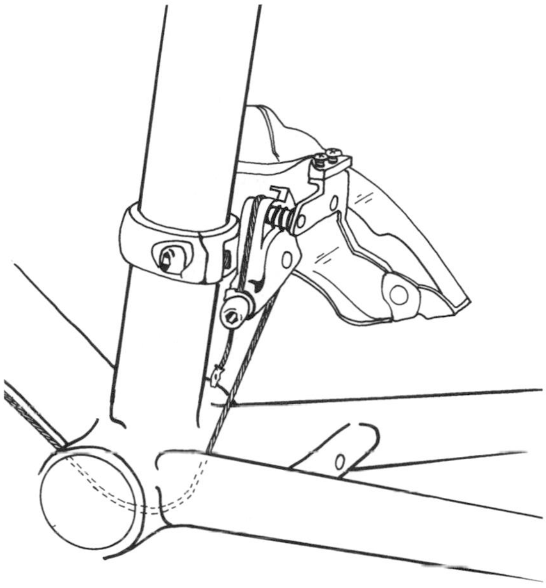

5.30B **Under-the-bottom-bracket (i.e., bottom-pull) cable routing to a Shimano "top swing" front derailleur**

V-14 ATTACH CABLE TO FRONT DERAILLEUR

1. Shift the chain to the inner chainring so that the derailleur moves farthest to the inside. This ensures that the maximum amount of cable is available to the derailleur.
2. Place the cable into its groove under the anchor bolt on the derailleur arm while pulling the cable taut with pliers (Fig. 5.29), and tighten the bolt. Make sure you do not hook up a top-pull-style front derailleur from the bottom, or vice versa.

Many front derailleurs now work both top-pull and bottom-pull style. They are actually top-pull front derailleurs, because you hook up directly to the cable anchor bolt when the cable comes from the top (Fig. 5.30A). But if the frame routes the cable to the front derailleur from the bottom, it is no problem; you simply run the cable up over and around a pivoting rocker arm to the cable anchor bolt located on its outboard end (Fig. 5.30B). Note that some older derailleur models require housing to run the full length of the cable to the front derailleur.

V-15 FINAL CABLE TOUCHES

A high-quality cable assembly includes the cable-housing end ferrules throughout, ideally ones with rubber seals on them to keep contamination out of the housings, and crimped cable caps. Clip cables about 1cm or 2cm past the cable-clamp bolts before crimping the cable caps on (Fig. 5.31). Also, little rubber cable donuts (Fig. 5.32) or pieces of thin cable sheathing can be installed to keep the bare cables from scratching the frame's finish.

V-16 GORE-TEX CABLES

If you are using Gore-Tex cables, follow the instructions on the package, as these require very special treatment in order to work properly. The Gore-Tex needs to be removed from the cable at the last inch

5.31 **Crimp cable ends**

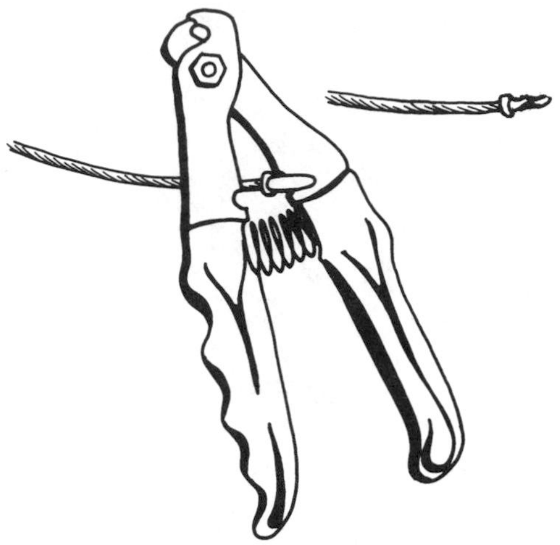

5.32 **Little rubber donuts**

or so before the cable anchor bolt, as well as from all of the cable that is inside the shift lever or Grip Shift. A plastic tube covers the cable (Fig. 5.18) over its entire length from shifter to derailleur. A little rubber accordion-like seal (called a "Grub") at the anchor bolt covers the end of the cable-cover tube and keeps dirt and water out of it.

CABLE LUBRICATION — REDUCING CABLE FRICTION

V-17 CABLE LUBRICATION

New cables and housings with Teflon liners do not need to be lubricated. Used cables and housings can be lubricated with chain lubricant. Grease sometimes slows cable movement, so various manufacturers recommend (and some even supply) their own molybdenum disulfide grease for cables.

1. Pull the housing segments out of their slotted cable stops; there is no reason to disconnect the cable at the derailleur.
2. Coat with lubricant the areas of the cable that will be inside of the cable housing segments.

NOTE: *If you do not have slotted cable stops, you might as well replace the cables and housings because an old cable will have a frayed end and will be hard to put back through the housing after lubrication. That's another reason to keep cables, housing ferrules, and cable ends in stock.*

V-18 EASY STEPS TO REDUCE CABLE FRICTION

Besides replacing your cables and housings with good-quality cables and lined housings, there are other steps you can take to improve shifting efficiency.

1. The most important friction-reducing step is to route the cable so that it makes smooth bends and so that turning the handlebar does not increase the tension on the shift cables.
2. Choose cables that offer particularly low friction. "Die-drawn" cables, which have been mechanically pulled through a small hole in a piece of hard steel called a die, move with lower friction than standard cables. Die-drawing flattens all of the outer strands and smoothes the cable surface. Thinner cables and lined housings with a large inside diameter also reduce friction. Gore-Tex cables are cables coated with Gore-Tex. They offer lower friction and are further sealed end-to-end with a plastic sheath (Fig. 5.18).
3. Shifting when the cable is released (as opposed to pulled) can be quickened by increasing the size of the derailleur-return spring. You can buy an after-market stiffer spring designed specifically for some Shimano derailleurs.

SHIFTERS

Twist shifters (of which Grip Shift by SRAM is the predominant one), Rapidfire levers, thumb shifters, (Figs. 5.33 through 5.35), and Shimano's post-2003 Dual Control brake and shift levers (Fig. 5.23) all move the derailleurs, but they go about it in very different ways.

V-19 BAR-END AND GRIP REPLACEMENT AND INSTALLATION

Replacing shifters requires removing at least grips and often bar ends and brake levers as well. Shifters are generally labeled right and left, but if you're in doubt, you can tell which is which because the right one has a lot more clicks. Obviously, this is not true with friction shifters.

1. Remove bar ends, if installed, usually with a 5mm Allen wrench.
2. Remove grips by rolling them back or lifting them away from the handlebar at either end, squirting water or rubbing alcohol underneath, and twisting back and forth while sliding them off. If you are planning on replacing them, you can cut the grips off.
3. Squirt rubbing alcohol inside when replacing grips, although they will slip for a number of days until the alcohol evaporates. You can also lubricate them with spray adhesive, and they will slide right on and not move once the glue sets. If the grips have closed ends, you can punch a hole in the ends and put the grips on by inflating them with an air compressor. Because of the

5.33 **Grip Shift**

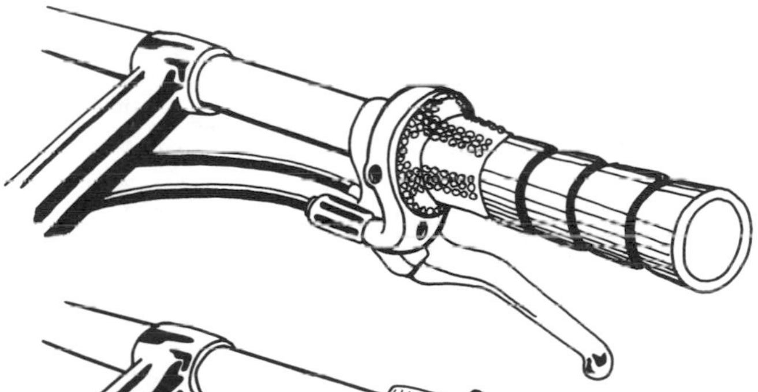

5.34 **Rapidfire shifter**

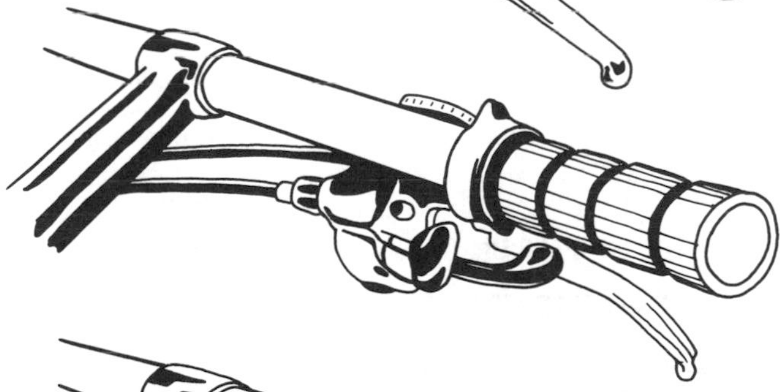

5.35 **Thumb shifter**

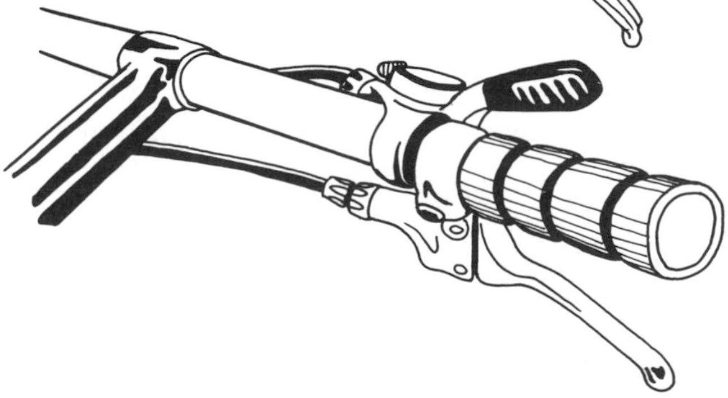

length of the handlebar, it will take two people to span the reach and install the grips. Cover the opposite end of the handlebar (the palm of your helper's hand works well), and push the grip with the little hole in it onto the handlebar (at your end) an inch or so. Press the compressed-air-gun tip against that hole, and the grip will balloon up and slide right on. Then push the fully closed grip an inch or so onto the opposite end of the handlebar, and again press the air-gun tip against the first grip's hole. This will inflate both grips so they can easily be pushed on. Removal can be done the same way, in reverse.

REPLACING SHIFTER UNITS

v-20 REPLACING SHIFTER AND INTEGRATED BRAKE LEVER (FIG. 5.34)

If you are replacing the entire brake lever and shifter unit, proceed as follows:

1. Remove the old brake lever and shifter.
2. Slide the new brake lever and shifter onto the bar, making sure that you put the right shifter on the right side and vice versa.
3. Slide the grip back into position.
4. Mount the bar end, if you have one.
5. Rotate the brake lever to the position you like.
6. Tighten the brake-lever fixing bolt.

v-21 REPLACING THE SHIFTER UNIT ON INTEGRAL BRAKE AND SHIFT LEVERS (I.E., RAPIDFIRE—FIGS. 5.24 AND 5.34)

1. After shifting to the high-gear position to release the maximum amount of cable, unbolt the old shift lever from the brake-lever body.
2. Position the new shifter exactly as the old one was.
3. Replace the bolt and tighten it.
4. Install the cable and tighten it.

NOTE: *For Rapidfire Remote installation, mount the remote lever onto the tip of the bar end by using a 2mm hex key. Hook up the cables as described in §v-10.*

v-22 REPLACING GRIP SHIFT (FIG. 5.33), HALF PIPE (FIG. 5.36), AND OTHER TWIST SHIFTERS

1. Remove the old shifter. Replace the brake lever if you had to remove it to get the old shifter off.
2. Loosen and slide the brake lever inward to allow room for the shifter.
3. Slide the appropriate (right or left) new shifter on with the cable-exit barrel pointing inward.
4. Slide on the plastic washer over the handlebar that separates the grip from the Grip Shift. This step is not necessary with Half Pipes or with 2001 (and later) Shorties, as the plastic washer is integrated within the shifter.
5. Replace the grip (and bar end).
6. Butt the Grip Shift up against the plastic washer or the grip. Rotate the shifter until the cable-exit barrel is oriented so it will not interfere with the brake lever.
7. Tighten the mounting bolt to the handlebar with a 2.5mm or 3mm Allen wrench.
8. Slide and rotate the brake lever to the position you like, and tighten it down.
9. Route the cable to the derailleur and tighten it. If you need to install the cable into the new shifter see §v-11 or §v-12.

v-23 TOP-MOUNTED THUMB SHIFTERS (FIG. 5.35) OR TRIGGER LEVERS NOT INTEGRATED WITH THE BRAKE LEVER

1. Remove the bar end, grip, brake lever, and old shifter.
2. Slide on the replacement shifter.

3. Slide on the brake lever, grip, and bar end.
4. Tighten the bar end and brake lever in the position you want.
5. Tighten the shifter in the position that is comfortable for you and that allows easy access to the cable barrel adjuster and free cable travel.
6. Install the cable and tighten it.

SHIFTER MAINTENANCE

v-24 GRIP SHIFT

A Grip Shift unit (Figs. 5.26 and 5.33) requires periodic cleaning and lubrication, as described below. Clean only with soap and water and lubricate only with nonlithium (preferably silicone-based Teflon) grease, such as Grip Shift Jonnisnot (they pay people to come up with these names, too!).

If shifting has gotten poor on Half Pipes or other Grip Shifts with the quick-cable-change feature, try replacing the cable and housing first before disassembling the shifter for cleaning.

a. Short Grip Shifts

The exploded diagrams in Figures 5.33 and 5.36, and the text in §v-12, detail how to take apart, clean, and grease a short-length Grip Shift (except for the 2001 [and later] Shortie, which follows the same disassembly procedure as Half Pipes, described below). With older models, and some current low-end models, as long as you have the shifter disassembled, you might as well replace the cable (§v-12), because shifter disassembly is required for the task.

b. Long (Half Pipe) twist shifters or recent Shortie shifters

This section also applies to SRAM's Shortie shifters from 2001 and later. First, remove the cable (§v-11) and the fixed grip (§v-19). Note that, unlike the older Grip Shift models, you do not remove the triangular housing cover to get the twist grip off.

1. Twist the shifter away from you to let out all of the cable (turn it to "1" on the front shifter and "9" on the rear).
2. Remove the shifter from the handlebar by using a 3mm hex key on the setscrew.
3. Squeeze the tabs on the end of the shifter housing tube together (you may have to pry inward on them with a screwdriver on each), and remove the plastic retaining washer from the end (Fig. 5.36).
4. Slowly slide the grip outward as you twist the shifter gently away from you in the cable-release direction. If you pull too fast, the long coil spring inside (Fig. 5.37) may pop out. Pull out the long coil spring.
5. Remove the two Phillips screws and pop off the clear plastic window covering the gear-indicator needle (shown in Fig. 5.25).
6. Pull straight out on the gear-indicator needle (shown in Fig. 5.25) and remove it.

5.36 Squeezing the two tabs together to release the Half Pipe retaining washer

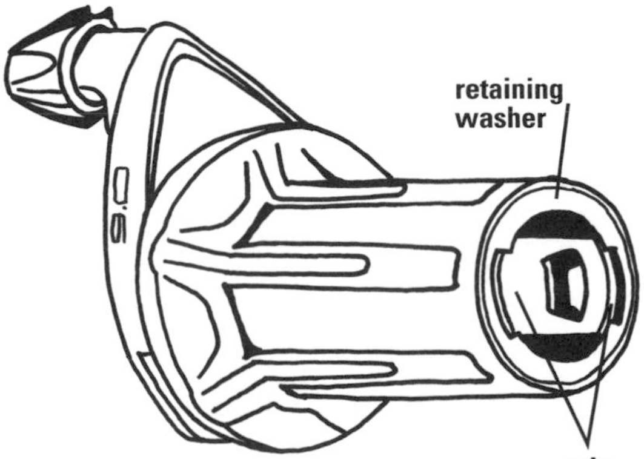

5.37 **Half Pipe springs**

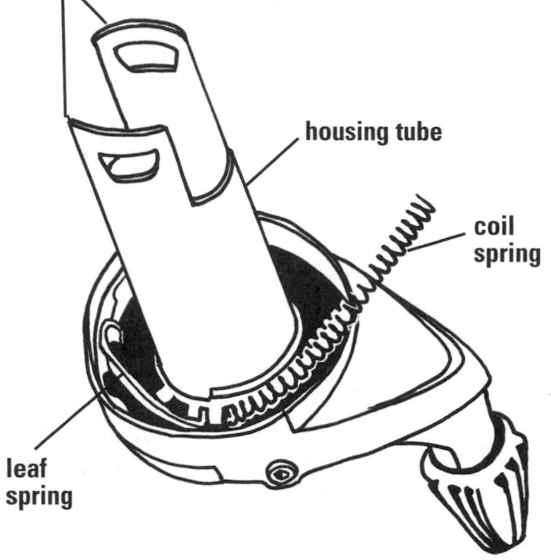

5.38 **Half Pipe disassembled**

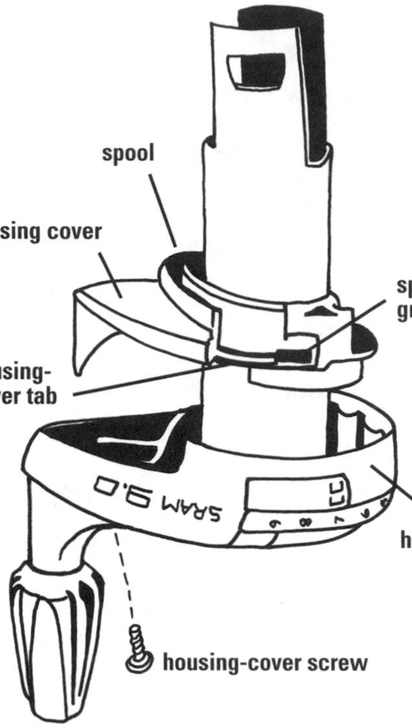

7. After carefully noting the position of the small leaf spring—it looks like a flat bent piece of steel (Fig. 5.37), pull the spring up and out by using needle-nose pliers or tweezers.
8. With a Phillips screwdriver (or, in some cases, a 2.5mm hex key), remove the housing-cover screw (shown in Fig. 5.25).
9. Slide the outer parts (the housing cover and cable spool) away from the housing (Fig. 5.37), being careful not to break the tab on the housing cover. To get the housing cover to come up, you may need to push up on it with the end of a paper clip through the hole for the housing-cover screw.
10. Clean all of the parts with soap, water, and clean rags. Use no solvents.
11. With nonlithium (preferably silicone-based Teflon) grease, lubricate the large tube extending from the housing, the cable track, and all detents for the springs.
12. Slide the housing cover and spool back down onto the housing tube, after having first slipped the cover's tab into the spool's groove (Fig. 5.38). Replace the housing-cover screw.
13. Set the leaf spring in place into the spool in the same position that you remember it was before (Fig. 5.37). Carefully press down on one end of the spring as you work to seat the other end in place.
14. Install one end of the coil spring onto its tab (Fig. 5.37). Slide the outer grip onto the tube, angle the other end of the spring up toward the grip, and pop the other end of the spring onto the tab inside the grip.
15. Rotating the grip slightly away from you to compress the coil spring, slide the grip inward until it engages in the housing.

16. Replace the plastic retaining washer over the tabs on the housing tube (Fig. 5.36).
17. Rotate the shifter away from you to the position that would let out the most cable.
18. Peer into the curved slot that the gear-indicator needle slides in. If you followed step 17, you should see the receptacle for the needle at one end of the slot. Slip the gear-indicator needle (Fig. 5.25) back into its receptacle, replace the plastic window, and install the two screws that hold it on.
19. Install the shifter onto the handlebar using a 3mm hex key. Check that it works.
20. Install a new cable (§v-11), connect it to the derailleur, and go ride your bike.

v-25 RAPIDFIRE SL, RAPIDFIRE PLUS, AND DUAL CONTROL LEVERS

Shimano Rapidfire SL (Fig. 5.24), Shimano Rapidfire Plus (Fig. 5.34), and Shimano Dual Control shifters (Fig. 5.23) are not designed to be disassembled by the consumer. Squirting a little chain lube inside every now and then is a good idea, though. If a Rapidfire lever stops working, it requires purchasing a new shifter unit. On an integrated Rapidfire unit, the brake lever does not need to be replaced; just bolt the new Rapidfire shifter to it (§v-21). If you manage to break a Shimano Dual Control shifter, you will be replacing the entire (expensive!) hydraulic brake master-cylinder and shifter-lever unit. Maybe it was still under warranty. . . .

Sometimes the gear-indicator unit on a Shimano shifter stops working, and it can even jam the lever and stop it from reaching all of the gears. This problem was most common in the 1993 and 1994 models. The indicator can be removed from the shifter with a small screwdriver. The indicator's little link arm needs to be stuck back into the hole from whence it came. Once the indicator jams, you can expect it to happen again; eventually, you will want to replace the lever or dispense with the indicator.

Once you get used to shifting Shimano Dual Control levers solely with the front and back of your fingers, moving the brake-lever blade laterally in either direction, you can remove the optional auxiliary release lever that allows you to shift with your thumb in one direction. There is a little screw holding it on that you simply unscrew from the nut and the circlip. If you still have the rubber cap, you can push it over the sharp metal tab that is now exposed.

v-26 ORIGINAL RAPIDFIRE

Shimano's first attempt at a two-lever mountain shifter did not work very well. If you are having trouble with yours, I recommend throwing it out and getting a new system. You know you have an original Rapidfire if the thumb operates both the down and up shift levers. Newer Rapidfire SL and Rapidfire Plus levers (Figs. 5.24 and 5.34) have a thumb-operated cable-pull lever and a finger-operated cable-release lever.

v-27 THUMB SHIFTERS

Indexed (click) thumb shifters (Fig. 5.35) are not to be disassembled further than removing them from their clamp. Periodic (semiannual or so) lubrication with chain lube is recommended and is best accomplished from the back side once the shifter assembly is removed from its clamp (Fig. 5.39).

Frictional (nonclicking) thumb shifters can be disassembled, cleaned, greased, and reassembled. Put the parts back the way you found them. You can avoid the hassle of disassembly by squirting chain lube in instead.

5.39 Indexed thumb shifter exploded

v-28 DOWNHILL-SPECIFIC DRIVETRAIN ADAPTATIONS

Tension arms, rollers, giant front-derailleur cages (of which an early version is illustrated in Fig. 5.40), and other chain-retention systems have become a part of downhill racing, because of the extraordinary demands the sport places on the drive system. Downhill-specific products are outside of the scope of this book, but, at least once assembled on the bike, many of these drivetrain items are fairly obvious in their function and maintenance.

DERAILLEUR MAINTENANCE

v-29 JOCKEY-WHEEL MAINTENANCE

The jockey wheels (a.k.a. "guide pulleys"—Fig. 5.41) on a derailleur will wear out over time. For best performance, standard jockey wheels should be overhauled every 200–500 miles. That should take care of the gunk that the chain and the trail regularly deliver to them. The mounting bolts on jockey wheels also need to be checked regularly. If a loose jockey-wheel bolt falls off while you are riding, you'll need to follow the procedure for a broken rear derailleur on the trail described in Chapter 3.

Some expensive guide pulleys have cartridge bearings (Fig. 5.41), whereas standard ones have a center bushing sleeve made of either steel or ceramic (SRAM upper jockey wheels have an oversized steel center bushing). A washer with a curved rim facing inward is usually installed on both sides of a standard jockey wheel. Some guide pulleys also have rubber seals around the edges of these washers.

5.40 This sucka ain't goin' nowhere

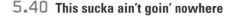

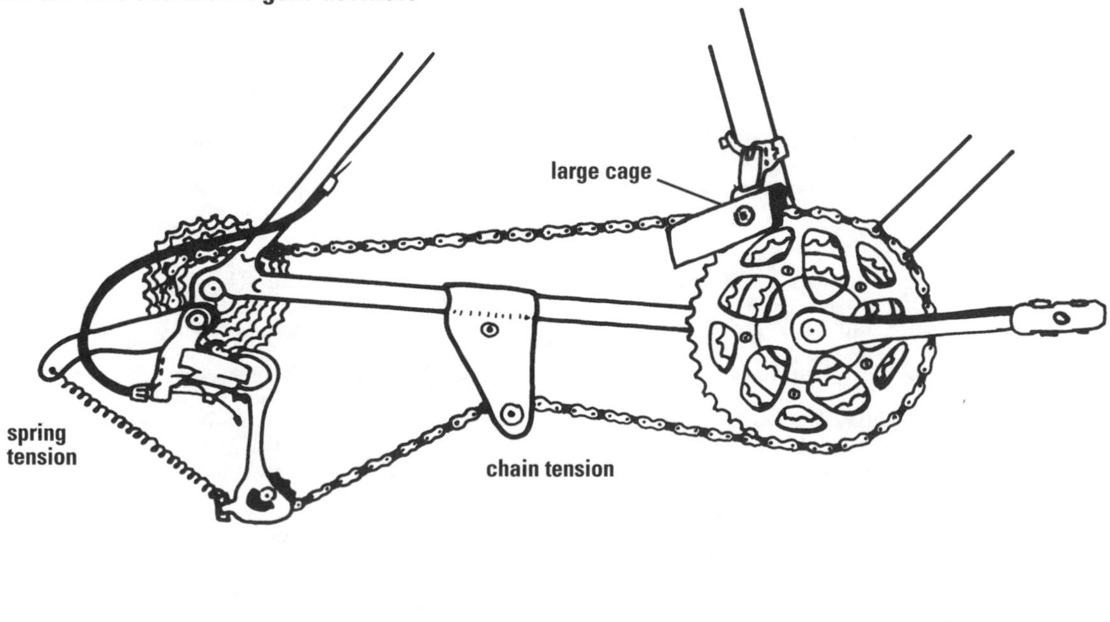

5.41 Jockey wheels exploded

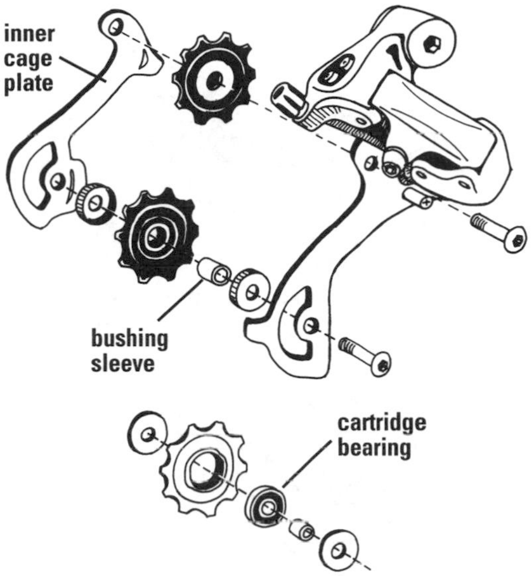

V-30 OVERHAULING STANDARD JOCKEY WHEELS

1. Remove the jockey wheels by undoing the bolts that hold them to the derailleur (Fig. 5.41). This usually takes a 2.5mm or 3mm Allen wrench.
2. Wipe all parts clean with a rag. A solvent is usually not necessary but can be used.
3. If the teeth on the jockey wheels are broken or worn off, replace the wheels.
4. Smear grease over each bolt and sleeve and inside each jockey wheel.
5. Reassemble the jockey wheels on the derailleur. Be sure to orient the inner cage plate properly (the larger part of the cage plate should be at the bottom jockey wheel).

V-31 CARTRIDGE-BEARING JOCKEY-WHEEL OVERHAUL

If the cartridge bearings (bottom, Fig. 5.41) in high-end jockey wheels do not turn freely, they can usually be overhauled.

1. With a single-edge razor blade, pry the plastic cover off one or, preferably, both sides of the bearing (Fig. 6.26 in Chapter 6).
2. With a toothbrush and solvent, clean the bearing. Use a citrus-based solvent, and wear gloves and glasses to protect skin and eyes.
3. Blow the solvent out with compressed air or your tire pump, and allow the parts to dry.
4. Squeeze new grease into the bearing and replace the covers.

V-32 REAR-DERAILLEUR OVERHAUL

Except for the jockey wheels and upper and lower main pivots, most rear derailleurs are not designed to be disassembled. If the pivot springs seem to be operating effectively, all you need to do is overhaul the jockey wheels (see above), and clean and lubricate the parallelogram and spring as follows.

V-33 MINOR WIPE AND LUBE

1. Clean the derailleur as well as you can with a rag, including between the parallelogram plates.
2. Drip chain lube on both ends of every pivot pin.
3. If you have the clothespin-type spring in the parallelogram (as opposed to the full coil spring running diagonally from one corner of the parallelogram to the other), put a dab of grease where the spring end slides along the underside of the outer parallelogram plate.

V-34 UPPER PIVOT OVERHAUL

LEVEL 2

CAUTION: *Don't do this job unless you absolutely have to in order to rehabilitate a poorly functioning rear derailleur. The strong spring resists your best intentions at reassembly, and you may not be able to get it back together properly, even with a second set of hands.*

1. Remove the rear derailleur; it usually takes a 5mm Allen wrench to unscrew it from the frame and to disconnect the cable.
2. With a screwdriver, pry the circlip (Fig. 5.42) off of the threaded end of the mounting bolt. Don't lose it; it will tend to fly when it comes off.
3. Pull the mounting bolt and the upper pivot spring out of the derailleur.
4. Clean and dry the parts with or without the use of a solvent.
5. Grease liberally, and replace the parts.
6. Each end of the spring has a hole that it needs to go into. If there are several holes, and you don't know which one it was in before, try the middle one. (If the derailleur does not keep tension on the chain well enough, you can later try another hole that increases the spring tension.)
7. Push it all together, and replace the circlip with pliers.

V-35 LOWER PIVOT OVERHAUL

1. Remove the derailleur from the bike.
2. Shimano derailleurs can be divided into two types: ones that have a setscrew on the side of the lower pivot, and ones that do not. If yours has a setscrew (Fig. 5.8), remove it using a 2mm hex key and pull the jockey cage away from the derailleur.

   If your derailleur has no setscrew, find and unscrew the tall cage-stop screw on the derailleur cage (Fig. 5.10); it is located near the upper jockey wheel. It is designed to maintain tension on the lower pivot spring and prevent the cage from springing all of the way around. Once the screw is removed, slowly guide the cage around until the spring tension is relieved. Remove the upper jockey wheel and unscrew the pivot bolt from the back with a 5mm (sometimes 6mm) hex key (Fig. 5.11). Be sure to hold the jockey-wheel cage to keep it from twisting.
3. Determine in which hole the spring end has been placed, then remove the spring.
4. Clean and dry the bolt and the spring with a rag. A solvent may be used if necessary.
5. Grease all parts liberally.
6. Replace the spring ends in their holes in the derailleur body and jockey-wheel cage (Fig. 5.9). Put the spring in the adjacent hole if you want to increase its tension (see §v-2g).
7. If your derailleur has a setscrew, push the assembly together, wind the spring, and replace the setscrew. If your derailleur does not take a setscrew, wind the jockey-wheel cage back around, screw it all back together with the pivot bolt, and replace the stop screw.

5.42 Rear-derailleur pivots

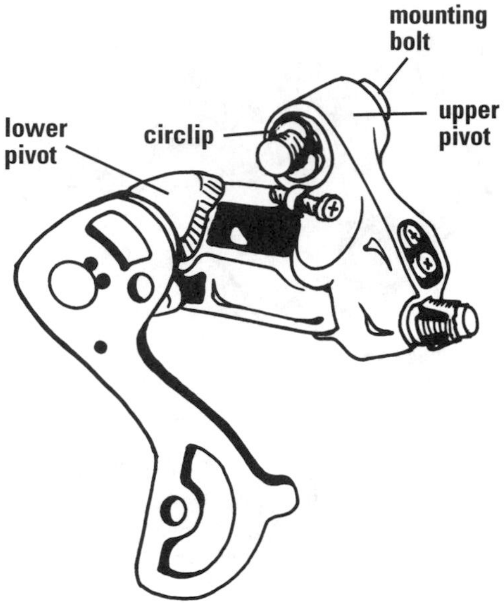

v-36 PARALLELOGRAM OVERHAUL

Very few derailleurs can be completely disassembled. Those that can (Mavic, first-generation SRAM, and 2002 high-end SRAM) have removable pins holding them together. The pins have circlips on the ends that can be popped off with a screwdriver, after which you can pull out the pins. Disassemble the derailleur carefully in a box so the circlips do not fly away and make note of where each part belongs so that you can get it back together again. Clean all parts, grease them, and reassemble.

v-37 REPLACING STOCK BOLTS WITH LIGHTWEIGHT VERSIONS

Lightweight aluminum and titanium derailleur bolts are available as replacement items for many derailleurs. Removing and replacing jockey-wheel bolts is simple, as long as you keep all of the jockey-wheel parts together and put the inner cage plate back on the way it was. Upper and lower pivot bolts are replaced following the instructions in §v-34 and §v-35.

TROUBLESHOOTING REAR-DERAILLEUR AND RIGHT-HAND SHIFTER PROBLEMS

Once you have made the adjustments outlined above, your drivetrain should be quiet and should stay in gear, even if you turn the crank backward. If you cannot fine-tune the adjustment so that each click with the right shifter results in a clean, quick shift, you need to check some of the following possibilities. For skipping- and jumping-chain problems, see also the troubleshooting section at the end of Chapter 4.

v-38 SHIFTER COMPATIBILITY

Check to see whether your shifter is compatible with your derailleur and your cogs. This is especially important if any of these parts are not original equipment on your bike. It should be obvious that a seven-speed shifter will not work on an eight- or nine-speed cassette, but components of different brands for the same number of speeds often will not work together either. If the shifter is a different brand from your derailleur, be certain that they are nonetheless designed to work together. The most common example of this is SRAM's Grip Shift, some models of which are specifically designed to work with a Shimano rear derailleur. SRAM ESP derailleurs work only with a longer-pull SRAM ESP twist shifter.

If your shifter and derailleur are incompatible, you will need to change one of them. Quality being equal, I suggest replacing the less costly item (generally the shifter, except in the case of Shimano Dual Control levers for hydraulic disc brakes).

v-39 STICKY CABLES

Check your derailleur cables to confirm that they run smoothly through the housing. Sticky cable movement will cause sluggish shifting. Lubricate the cable by smearing it with chain lube or a specific lubricant that came with your shifters (§v-17).

If lubricating the cable does not help, replace the cable and housing (see §v-6 to §v-16).

v-40 BENT REAR-DERAILLEUR HANGER

A bent hanger will hold the derailleur crooked and bedevil shifting. Instructions for straightening the hanger are in Chapter 14 (§xiv-5).

V-41 BENT REAR-DERAILLEUR CAGE

A bent derailleur cage will line the jockey wheels up at an angle. Mild bending can be straightened by hand, eyeballing the crank for reference.

V-42 LOOSE PIVOTS (WORN-OUT REAR DERAILLEUR)

A loose and floppy rear derailleur will not shift well. Replace it.

TROUBLESHOOTING FRONT-DERAILLEUR AND LEFT-HAND SHIFTER PROBLEMS

V-43 CHAIN SUCK

For chain suck problems (Fig. 4.15), you should refer to the troubleshooting section at the end of Chapter 4.

V-44 CHAIN LINE

You probably have chain-line problems if (1) your chain falls off to the inside no matter how much you adjust the low-gear limit screw, cable tension, and derailleur position; (2) you have chain rub, noise, or auto-shift problems in mild cross-gears that are not corrected with derailleur adjustments; or (3) your front derailleur cannot move your chain onto the large chainring, even if the outer limit screw is backed all of the way out.

NOTE: *If problem 2 occurs only sometimes on your full-suspension bike (for example, when sitting, but not when standing) it could be that, as the rear suspension compresses, the chain is no longer running in the groove formed for it in the front-derailleur cage. Instead, the chain is hitting the forward ridge above the groove. You may have to put up with it because your alternatives are to tighten the suspension (i.e., increase the spring rate) so that it does not move as much or to get a derailleur without the internal cage shaping (which won't shift as fast).*

Chain line is the relative alignment of the front chainrings with the rear cogs; it is the imaginary line connecting the center of the middle chainring with the middle of the cogset (Fig. 5.43). This line should in theory be straight and parallel with the vertical plane of the bicycle. Even owners of new bikes may find they have poor chain lines, owing to mismatched cranks and bottom brackets.

The chain line is adjusted by moving or replacing the bottom bracket to move the cranks left or right. You can roughly check the chain line by placing a long straight edge against the middle chainring and back to the rear cogs; it ideally would come out in the center of the rear cogs, but the tire-clearance issues of most mountain bikes, particularly on full-suspension models with large tires, make this unreasonable to expect; the chainrings have simply got to be further out than the cogs or the bike designer cannot fit everything in.

Continue to the next section for a precise chain-line measurement method, if you want your shifting to be as good as possible.

LEVEL 2

V-45 PRECISE CHAIN-LINE MEASUREMENT

You will need a measuring caliper (Fig. 1.4). The position of the middle chainring, as measured from the center of the seat tube to the center of the middle chainring, is often called the chain line, although this is only the front endpoint of the line.

1. Find the middle chainring position, or front endpoint of the chain line (CL_F in Fig. 5.43), as follows:

(a) Measure from the left side of the down tube to the outside of the large chainring (d_1 in Fig. 5.43). (Do not measure from the seat tube, as it may be oval where it meets the bottom-bracket shell. The frame tubes are labeled in Figure 14.1.)

(b) Measure the distance from the right side of the down tube to the inside of the inner chainring (d_2 in Fig. 5.43).

(c) Add these two measurements and divide the sum by two:

$$CL_F = (d_1 + d_2) \div 2.$$

5.43 **Measuring chain line**

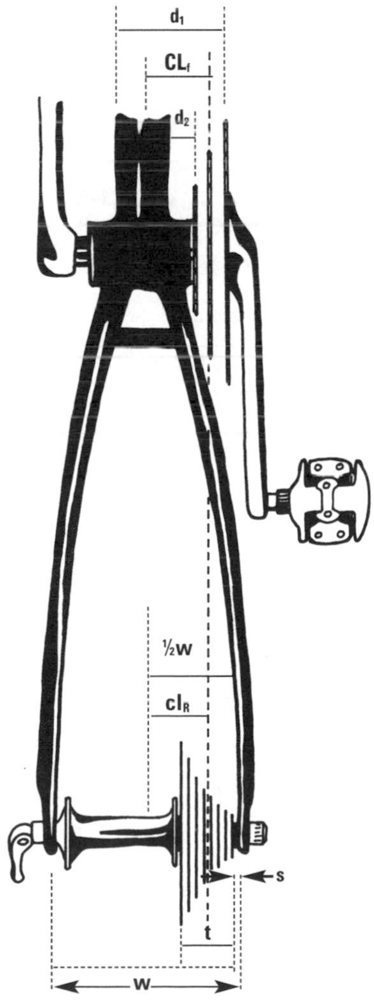

2. Find the rear endpoint of the chain line (CL_R in Fig. 5.43), which is the distance from the center of the plane of the bicycle to the center of the cogset, as follows:

(a) Measure the thickness of the cog stack, end to end (t in Fig. 5.43).

(b) Measure the space between the face of the smallest cog and the inside face of the dropout (s in Fig. 5.43).

(c) Measure the length of the axle from dropout to dropout (w in Fig. 5.43); this dimension is also called the "axle overlock dimension," referring to the distance from locknut face to locknut face on either end. Generally, on any mountain bike since 1989 or so, this will be 135mm.

(d) Subtract one-half of the thickness of the cog stack and the distance from the inside face of the right rear dropout from one-half of the rear-axle length:

$$CL_R = w/2 - t/2 - s.$$

3. If $CL_F = CL_R$, your chain line is perfect. This, however, almost never occurs on a mountain bike, because of considerations about chainstay clearance of the tire and the chainrings, prevention of chain rub on large chainrings in cross-gears, and inward movement range of the front derailleur. Shimano specifies a "chain line" (meaning CL_F, the front endpoint of the chain line) as 47.5mm for bikes with a 68mm-wide bottom-bracket shell and 50mm for 73mm-wide shells (both of these specified dimensions are plus or minus 1mm). CL_R, the rear endpoint of the chain line, on the other hand, usually comes out around 44.5mm. Shimano's specifications, then, are primarily intended to avoid chainring rub on chainstays,

not to promote ideal shifting. I recommend having the chainrings in toward the frame as far as you can, without rubbing the frame or losing front-derailleur shifting performance because of bottoming out on the seat tube. Your bike will shift best and run quietest if you get the chain line at around 45mm, but you may have some problems there, such as the following:

(a) Your inner and middle chainrings might rub the chainstay;

(b) your front derailleur may bottom out on the seat tube before moving inward enough to shift to the inner chainring (this is particularly a problem with bikes with oversized seat tubes); and

(c) when crossing to the smallest cog from the inner and even middle chainring, the chain may rub on the next larger chainring (this is not a problem if you simply avoid those cross-gears).

4. To improve the chain line, move the chainrings, because there is little or nothing you can do with the rear cog position. The chainrings are moved by using a different bottom bracket, by exchanging bottom-bracket spindles for a longer or shorter one, or by moving the bottom bracket right or left (bottom-bracket installation and overhauling is covered in Chapter 8).

FRONT-DERAILLEUR & SHIFTER PROBLEMS

NOTE: *Some brand-new bikes have terrible chain lines that can only be corrected by buying a new bottom bracket. This problem usually has to do with a conceptually impaired bean-counting product manager selecting the parts for a given bike model. Product managers know that customers often pay attention to the quality and brand of the cranks on the bike and pay little heed to the quality of the bottom bracket—the unseen part of the mix. With a cheap bottom bracket with an overly long spindle, the cranks may sit way too far out, and the chain line will stink. You will end up having to replace the longer bottom bracket with a shorter one if you want the bike to shift decently. In such a case, good shops will replace the bottom bracket before selling the bike to you.*

ANOTHER NOTE: *The chain line can also be off if the frame is out of alignment (Chapter 14, §xiv-6). If that's the case, it is probably not something you can fix yourself.*

5. If improving the chain line does not fix your problem, or if you don't want to mess with the chain line, buy and install a Third Eye Chain Watcher (Fig. 5.44), a Jump Stop, or a Deda Elementi Dog Fang. All three are inexpensive plastic gizmos that clamp around the seat tube next to the inner chainring (the Jump Stop has a metal plate). Clamp one on and adjust the position so that the prong, plate, or "fang" nudges the chain back on when it tries to fall off to the inside.

5.44 Third Eye Chain Watcher

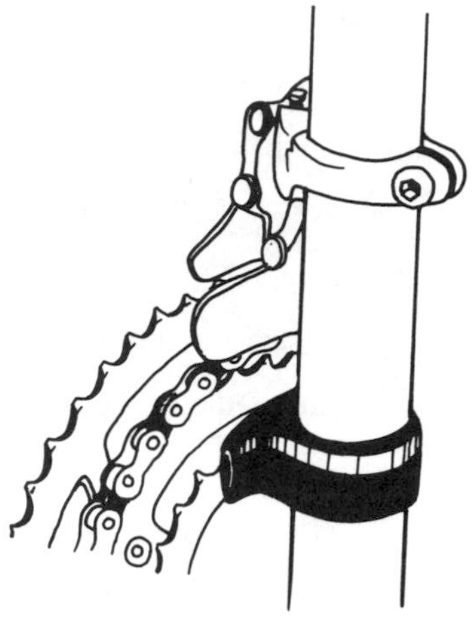

CHAPTER 6

WHEELS

Tires, rims and spokes, hubs, cassettes, and freewheels

I'm just sitting here watching the wheels go round and round. I really love to watch them roll.
—John Lennon

Early bicycles may have existed without pedals and steering systems, but they always had wheels. After all, without wheels, it ain't a bike!

With the exception of molded composite versions, wheels on mountain bikes are strung together with spokes. The hub is at the center, and its bearings allow the wheel to turn freely around an axle. The rim is supported and aligned by the tension on the spokes. On most bikes, the rim serves as both support for the tire and as a braking surface.

On the rear wheel, a freewheel or cassette freehub (rear hub with a built-in freewheel) allows the wheel to spin while coasting and engages when forward force is applied to the pedals (Fig. 6.1).

The tires provide grip and traction for propulsion and steering. The air pressure in the tire is your first line of suspension. On most mountain bikes, inner tubes keep the air inside the tires, but tubeless tires are making huge inroads into this dominance, particularly at the high-cost end.

This chapter addresses how to fix a flat, replace a tire or tube, true a wheel, fix a broken spoke or bent rim, overhaul hubs, change rear cogs, and lubricate cassettes and freewheels. Have at it.

REPLACING OR REPAIRING TIRES AND INNER TUBES

vi-1 REMOVING A STANDARD TIRE AND TUBE

NOTE: *If you have tubeless tires, skip to §vi-2.*

1. Remove the wheel (see Chapter 2, §ii-2 and §ii-12). If the wheel is on a Cannondale "Lefty" one-legged fork, you can skip this step, because you can change the tire while the wheel is on the bike!
2. If your tire is not already flat, deflate it.
   (a) To deflate a Schrader valve (the kind of valve you would find on your car's tire), push down on the valve pin with something thin enough to fit in that won't break off, such as a pen cap or a paper clip (Fig. 6.2).
   (b) Presta valves are thinner and have a small

TOOLS

- spoke wrench
- 13mm, 14mm, 15mm, and 16mm cone wrenches
- 17mm open-end wrench (or an adjustable wrench)
- screwdriver
- 5mm, 6mm, and 10mm Allen wrenches
- grease
- oil
- chain whip
- cassette-lockring remover
- large adjustable wrench
- freewheel remover (if your bike does not have a cassette)
- pump
- tire levers
- tube patch kit

OPTIONAL TOOLS

- truing stand
- wheel-dishing tool
- linseed oil
- tweezers
- cog-wear indicator
- Morningstar Freehub Buddy

6.1 **The whole thing**

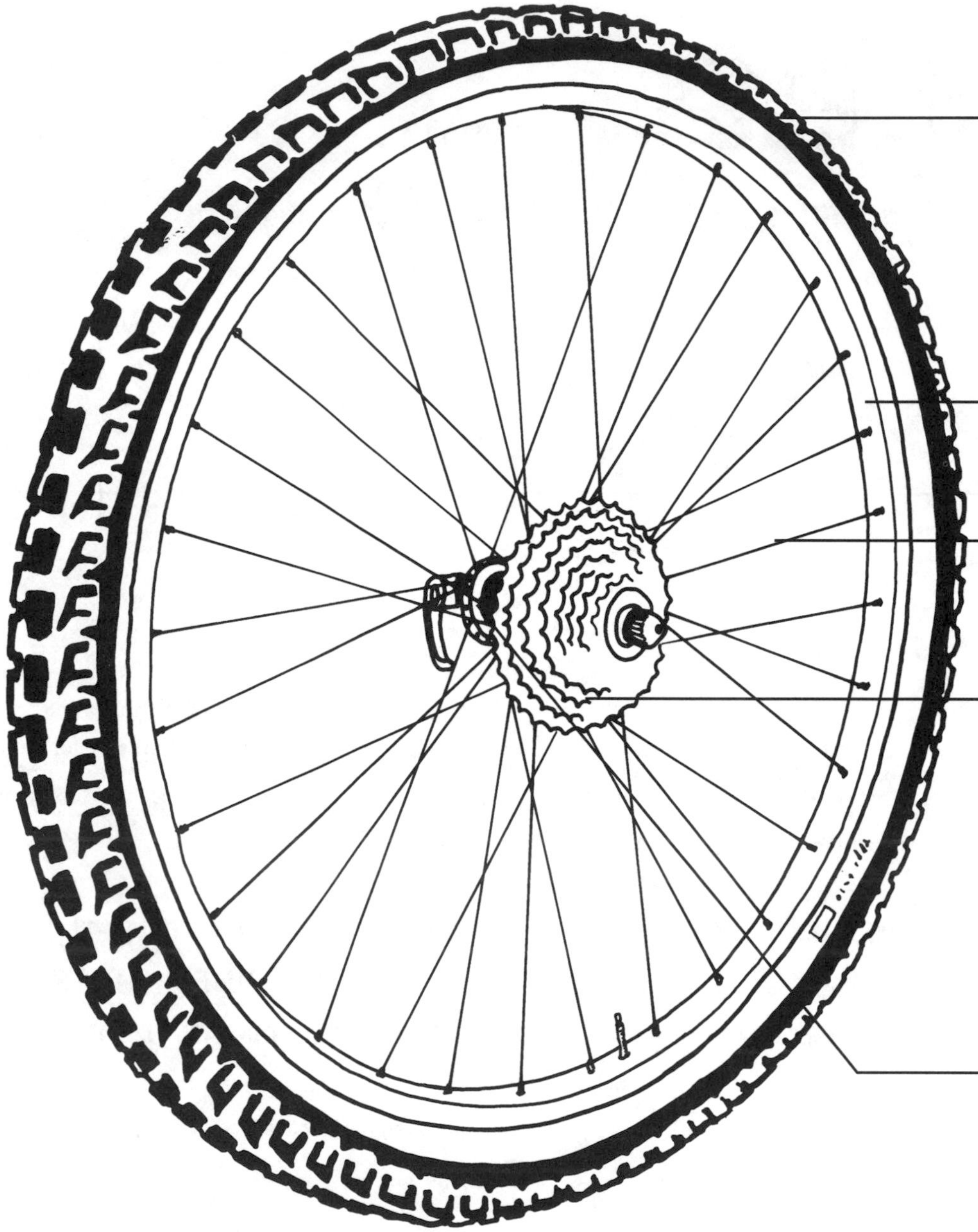

threaded rod with a tiny nut on the end. To let air out, unscrew the little nut a few turns, and push down on the thin rod (Fig. 6.3). To seal, tighten the little nut down again (with your fingers only!); leave it tightened down for riding.

NOTE: *If you have deep-section rims (i.e., Spinergy, Zipp, or Hed), you will probably have "valve extenders"—thin, threaded tubes that screw onto the Presta valve stems. To deflate most of them, you need to insert a thin rod (a spoke is perfect) down into the valve extender to release the air. To install valve extenders so they seal*

6.2 **Schrader valve**

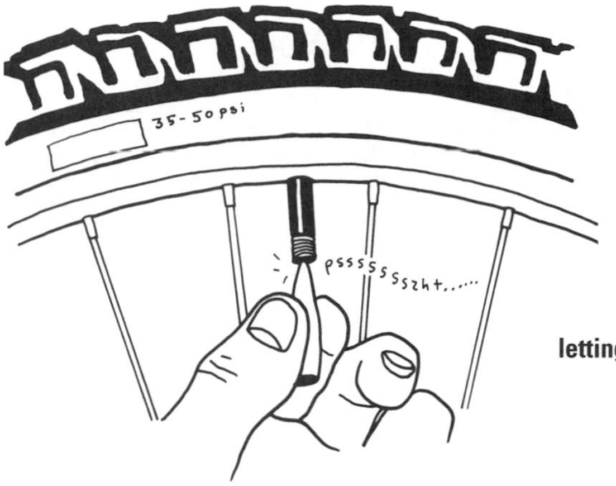

6.3 **Presta valve**

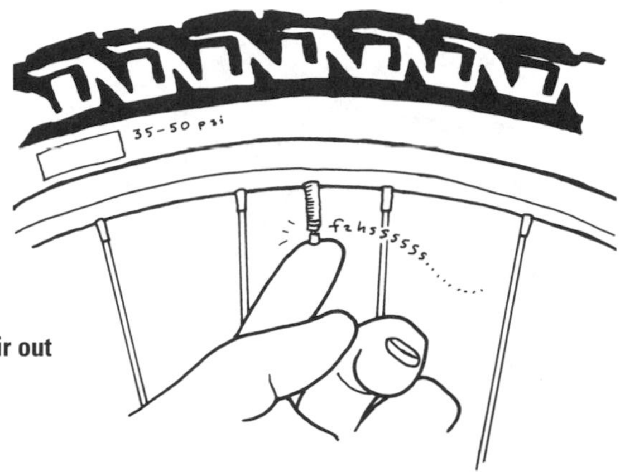

letting air out

properly and allow easy inflation, you need to unscrew the little nut on the Presta valve against the mashed threads at the top of the valve shaft (they are mashed to keep the nut from unscrewing completely off). Back the nut firmly into these mashed threads with a pair of pliers so it stays unscrewed and does not tighten back down against the valve stem from the vibration of riding, thereby preventing air from going in when you pump it into the valve. Spinergy extenders also extend the valve nut and thus do not require this additional procedure; they actually allow you to tighten and loosen the valve nut with the extender in place.

You also should wrap a turn or two of Teflon pipe thread tape around the top threads on the valve stem before screwing on the valve extender to seal it; if you do not, air will leak out when pumping, and your pressure gauge on your pump will not give an accurate reading of the pressure in the tire. Tighten the valve extender onto the valve stem with a pair of pliers.

3. If you can push the tire bead off of the rim with your thumbs without using tire levers, by all means do it, for there is less chance of damaging either the tube or the tire. It is easiest to start just one side or the other of the valve stem.

PRO TIP

Tire Removal

Removal of the tire is most easily accomplished by starting near the valve stem. That way, the beads of the deflated tire can have fallen into the dropped center of the rim on the opposite side of the wheel, making it effectively a smaller-circumference rim off of which you are pushing the tire bead. If, instead, you try to push the tire bead off of (or onto) the rim on the side opposite the valve stem, the circumference on which the bead is resting is larger, because the valve stem is forcing the beads to stay up on their seating ledges opposite the side where you are working. (Figure 6.7 illustrates a tubeless tire, but it does show the tire beads, rim ledges, and valley that I am talking about.)

4. If you can't get the tire off with your hands alone, insert a tire lever, scoop side up, between the rim sidewall and the tire until you catch the edge of the tire bead. Again, this is most easily done adjacent to the valve stem.

6.4–6.5 **Removing tires with levers**

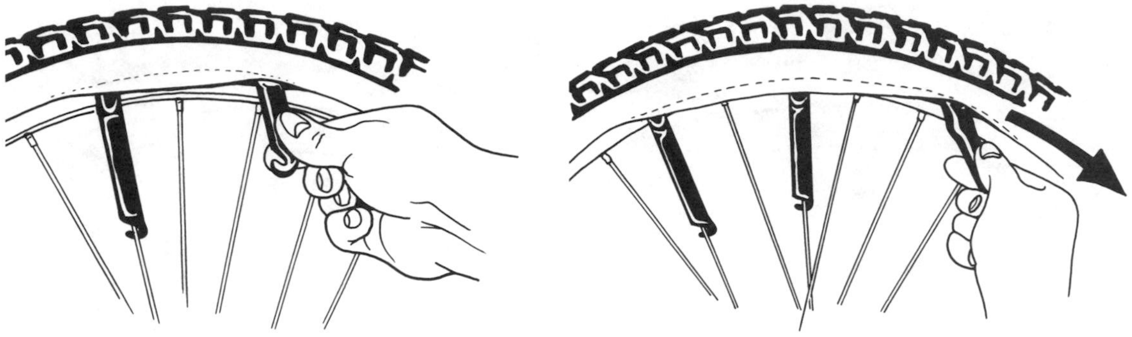

5. Pry down on the lever until the tire bead is pulled out over the rim (Fig. 6.4). If the lever has a hook on the other end, hook it onto the nearest spoke. Otherwise, keep holding it down.
6. Place the next lever a few inches away, and do the same thing with it (Fig. 6.4).
7. If needed, place a third lever a few inches farther on, pry it out, and continue sliding this lever around the tire, pulling the bead out as you go (Fig. 6.5). Some people slide their fingers around under the bead, but beware of cutting your fingers on sharp tire beads.

NOTE: *There are various "quick" tire levers on the market that only require using the one lever. But if the tire is really stubborn, the tried-and-true three-lever method outlined above may be the only way you can get the tire off.*

8. Once the bead is off on one side, pull the tube out (Fig. 6.6). If you are patching or replacing the tube, you do not need to remove the other side of the tire from the rim. If you are replacing the tire, the other bead should come off easily with your fingers. If it does not, use the tire levers as outlined above.

REMOVING A TUBELESS TIRE

vi-2 REMOVING A TUBELESS TIRE

If you have tubeless tires, do all tire removal and installation with your hands only, as tire levers can damage the sealing flap extending beyond the tire bead (Fig. 6.7), and then your tire will not seal. If you are planning on patching the tire, you must find the leak before removing it from the rim (§vi-3).

Because the "UST" tubeless system—originated by Mavic, Michelin, and Hutchinson and since adopted by Shimano and other wheel makers as well as most tire manufacturers—is the only one in wide use, this section specifically addresses that system.

1. Remove the wheel (see Chapter 2, §ii-2 and §ii-12). If the wheel is on a Cannondale "Lefty" one-legged fork, you need not remove the wheel!
2. If your tire is not already flat, deflate it at the valve.
   (a) Tubeless tire valves just screw into the rim with rubber seals around them. They can be either Schrader valves (the kind of valve you would find on your car's tire), Presta valves (Fig. 1.1B), or both. Mavic UST valves are both; unscrew and remove the outer, Schrader-size externally threaded tube to make it a Presta valve. To use it as a Schrader valve, screw on the

6.6 **Removing the inner tube**

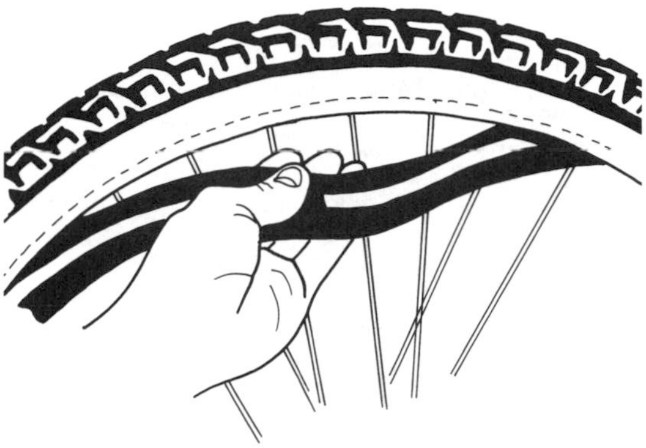

6.7 **Cross section of UST tubeless tire and rim**

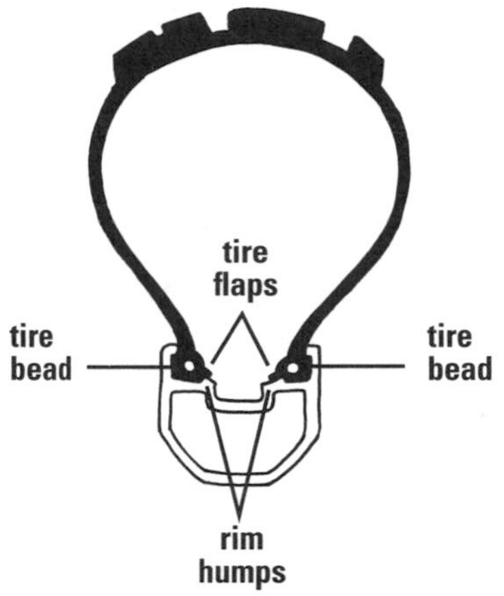

Schrader tube after unscrewing the little nut on the end of the inner Presta valve.

(b) To deflate a Schrader valve, push down on the valve pin with something thin enough to fit in that won't break off, such as a pen cap or a paper clip (Fig. 6.2).

(c) To let air out of a Presta valve, unscrew the little nut a few turns, and push down on the thin rod (Fig. 6.3). To seal, tighten the little nut down again (with your fingers only!). Leave it tightened down for riding.

3. Push inward on the tire beads all of the way around with your thumbs to get them to pop off of the "hump" (Fig. 6.7) and fall into the dropped center of the rim.
4. Starting adjacent to the valve stem, push the tire off of the rim with your thumbs. See the Pro Tip in §vi-1 for the reason to start at the valve stem.

vi-3 FINDING LEAKS

Keep in mind that you can only patch small holes. If the hole is bigger than the eraser end of a pencil, a round patch is not likely to work. A slit of up to an inch or so can be repaired with a long oval patch.

1. If the leak location is not obvious, put some air in the tube to inflate it until it is two to three times larger than its deflated size. Be careful. You can explode it if you put too much air in, especially with latex or urethane tubes.

NOTE: *For tubeless tires, leave the tire on the rim and inflate it to 25–50 psi, then continue with steps 2 and 3.*

2. Listen and/or feel for air coming out, and mark the leak(s).
3. If you cannot find the leak by listening and/or feeling, submerge the tube (or tubeless tire mounted on the rim) in water. Look for air bubbling out (Fig. 6.8), and mark the spot(s).

6.8 **Checking for puncture**

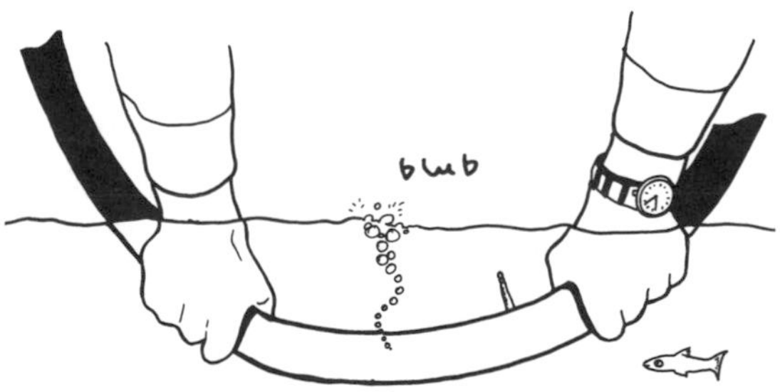

NOTE ON PATCHING TUBELESS TIRES: *The following instructions apply to patching a tube, but the procedure is the same for patching a tubeless tire, except that you patch the inside of the tire versus the outside of a tube. Also, you can always stick a tube inside a tubeless tire if you don't want to deal with patching the tire. And as for using a tubeless tire where there are a lot of cacti or thorns, it is arduous and next to impossible to find and patch all of the holes. Rather than throw the (expensive) tire out, fill it with Slime (§vi-10).*

vi-4 USING STANDARD PATCHES

1. Dry the tube thoroughly near the hole.
2. Rough up and clean the surface within about a 1-inch radius around the hole with a small piece of sandpaper (usually supplied with the patch kit). Do not touch the sanded area, and don't rough up the tube with one of those little metal "cheese graters" that come with some patch kits. They tend to do to your tube what they do to cheese.
3. Use a patch kit designed for bicycle tires that has thin, usually orange, gummy edges surrounding the black patches. Rema and Delta are common brands.
4. Apply patch cement in a thin, smooth layer all over an area centered on the hole (Fig. 6.9). Cover an area that is bigger than the size of the patch.
5. Let the glue dry until there are no more shiny, wet spots (5–10 minutes).
6. Oftentimes, the cellophane atop the patch is scored. If you fold the patch now, then this cellophane will split at the scored cuts and be easy to remove after the patch is well stuck down. Remove the foil backing from the gummy underside of the patch (but not the cellophane top cover).
7. Stick the patch over the hole, and push it down in place, making sure that all of the gummy edges are stuck down. You are done, unless you want the cellophane cover off.
8. Although there is no need to do so, the standard procedure is to remove the cellophane top covering. Be careful not to peel off the edges of the patch (Fig. 6.10) when removing the cellophane. If the cellophane atop the patch was scored and you folded it before sticking down the patch, then the cellophane will split at the scored cuts, allowing you to peel outward and avoid pulling the newly adhered patch away from the tube.

6.9 Smearing patch glue

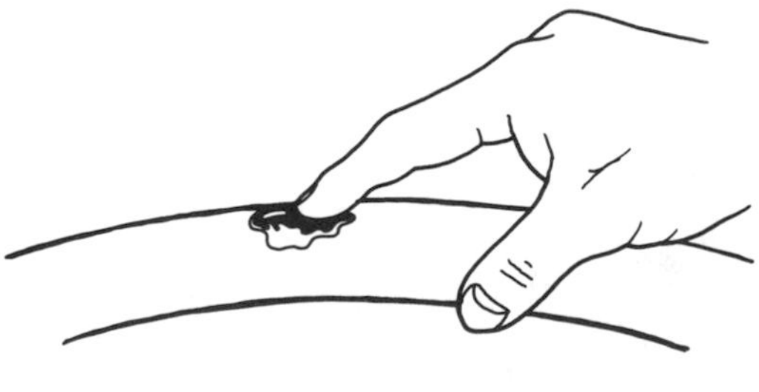

6.10 Removing the cellophane backing

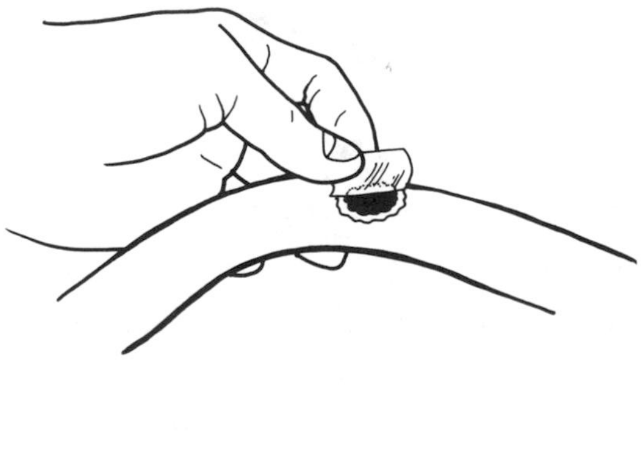

vi-5 USING GLUELESS PATCHES

There are a number of adhesive-backed patches on the market that do not require cement to stick them on. Most often, you simply need to clean the area around the hole with the little alcohol pad supplied with the patch. Let the alcohol dry, peel the backing off, and stick on the patch. The advantage of glueless patches is that they are very fast to use, take little room in a pack, and you never open your patch kit to discover that your glue tube is dried up. On the downside, I have not found any that stick nearly as well as the standard type. With a standard patch installed on a tube, you can inflate the tube to look for more leaks without having it in the tire. If you do that with a glueless patch, it usually lifts the patch enough to start it leaking. You must install it in the tire and on the rim before putting air in it after patching. And don't expect the glueless patch to be a permanent fix, as you can with a glued-on Rema-style patch.

vi-6 INSTALLING A TUBE AND TIRE

Feel around the inside of the tire to see if there is anything sticking through that can puncture the tube. This is best done by sliding a rag all the way around the inside of the tire. The rag will catch on anything sharp and saves your fingers from being cut by anything that is stuck in the tire.

1. Replace any tire that has worn-out areas (inside or out) where the tread-casing fibers appear to be cut or frayed.
2. Examine the rim to be certain that the rim tape is in place and that there are no spokes or anything else sticking up that can puncture the tube. Replace the rim tape if necessary. With an asymmetrically drilled rim, make sure the adhesive and/or the fit of the rim tape is very good. The rim tape only needs to slide over a little bit to expose the edge of one of the offset holes and puncture your tube.
3. By hand, push one side bead of the tire onto the rim. Ideally, you first want to check the direction of the tire rotation and orient the tire label so it is next to the valve stem for ease of finding both.

> **PRO TIP**
>
> ### Tire Direction
>
> Tire direction makes a difference for technical riding. On the front, you want the concave or v-shaped scooping edges of the tread blocks forward for braking (Fig. 2.2), whereas on the rear, you want the scooping edges oriented backward for propulsion traction. Some tires have an arrow indicating rotation direction for use either on the front or the rear. If not, hold the tire up above your head and look at the tread as the ground sees it. Consider which way the wheel is rotating and what happens during braking and driving. The best way to orient the tread will then be apparent.

4. Optional: Smear talcum powder around the inside of the tire and on the outside of the tube, so the two do not adhere to each other. Don't inhale the stuff.
5. Put just enough air in the tube to give it shape. Close the valve, if a Presta.
6. Push the valve through the valve hole in the rim.
7. Push the tube up inside the tire all of the way around.

6.11–6.12 **Installing a tire by hand**

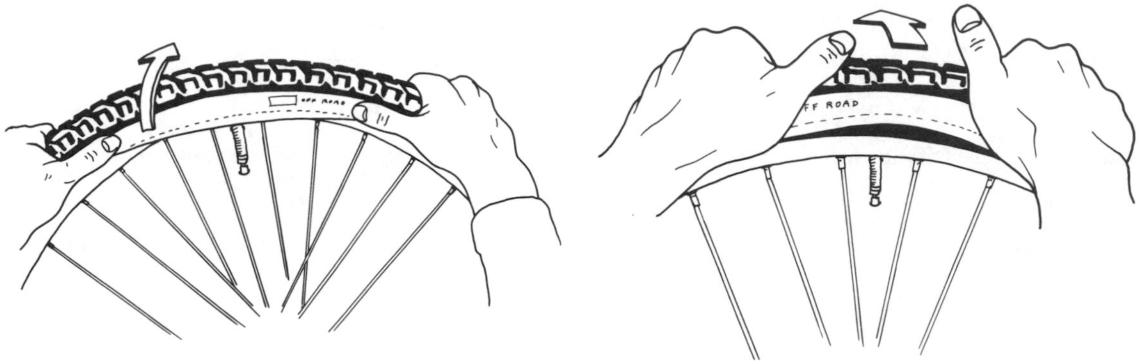

8. Starting at the side opposite the valve stem (see Pro Tip in §vi-1 for the reason why), push the tire bead onto the rim with your thumbs. Be sure that the tube doesn't get pinched between the tire bead and the rim.
9. Work around the rim in both directions with your thumbs, pushing the tire onto the rim (Fig. 6.11). Finish from both sides at the valve (Fig. 6.12). You can usually install a mountain bike tire without tools. If you cannot, first try deflating the tube when you have gotten as far around as you can with your hands. You should now be able to push the tire on the last bit, as deflating the tube will allow the beads on the far side, opposite the valve stem, to drop into the lower center of the rim. If this does not allow you to complete the mounting by hand, use tire levers to pry the tire bead on, but make sure you don't catch any of the tube under the edge of the bead. Finish the same way, at the valve.
10. Reseat the valve stem and draw up any nearby folds of the tube stuck under the tire bead by pushing up on the valve after you have pushed the last bit of bead onto the rim (Fig. 6.13). You may have to manipulate the tire so that all the tube is tucked under the tire bead.
11. Go around the rim and inspect for any part of the tube that might be protruding out from under the edge of the tire bead. If you have a fold of the tube under the edge of the bead, it can blow the tire off the rim either when you inflate it or while you are riding. It will sound as though a gun went off next to you and will leave you with an unpatchable tube.
12. Pump the tire up. Generally, 35–45 psi is a good amount. Much more, and the ride gets harsh. Much less, and you run the risk of a pinch flat, or "snake bite."

PRO TIP

Low Tire Pressure

If you have an anti-pinch-flat tube, like Hutchinson's thick green tube, you can get a smoother ride, better traction on side hills, and lower rolling resistance on rough terrain by running on lower tire pressure (under 30 psi).

vi-7 INSTALLING A UST TUBELESS TIRE

Again, these instructions apply to the UST tubeless system. To prevent damage to the seal, tire levers are not to be used for this procedure.

6.13 **Seating the tube by pushing up on the valve**

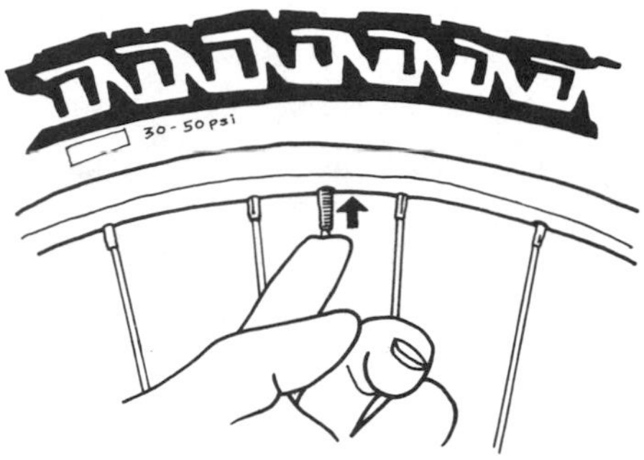

6.14 **Putting Slime tire sealant in a tubeless tire**

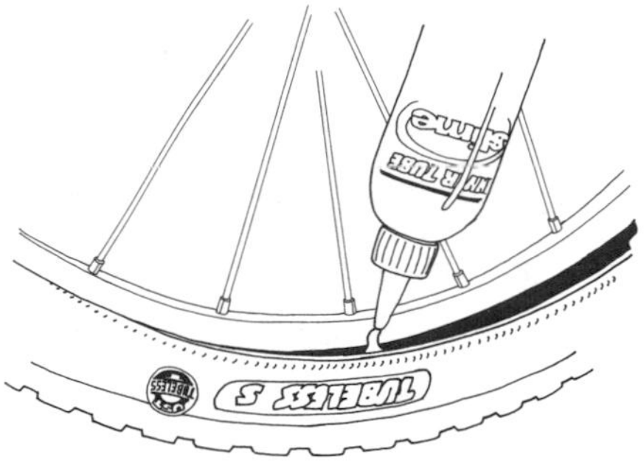

1. Examine the rim to be sure that the tire will seal to it. First of all, it must be a UST rim (and tire)—only a rim without spoke holes on the inside, and with the "hump" along the edge of each bead ledge, will seal with the tire (Fig. 6.7). Furthermore, the rim edges and the hump must not be dented or gouged, or air will escape at those spots.
2. Wet the edges of the tire (with dish soap and water or just water) to facilitate sealing it on initial inflation.
3. Determine rotation direction (see first Pro Tip under §vi-6), and locate the label at the valve stem. Starting opposite the valve, push one bead of the tire onto the rim with your thumbs and fingers only, finishing at the valve.
4. Push the other bead onto the rim by hand, again starting on the side of the rim opposite the valve stem (see first Pro Tip in §vi-1) and finishing at the valve stem. If you instead start at the valve stem, you will have to work harder, because the valve holds the tire bead up on the ledge and forces the rim to stretch around a larger circle. Consider adding tire sealant just before you push the last of the bead on to close off any slow leaks (see §vi-10 and Fig. 6.14).
5. Pump the tire up with a floor pump, initially putting air in as fast as possible until you hear the tire seat. Just as with a tubeless car tire, seating the bead is a lot more effective with an air compressor (Fig. 1.4), but it can be done with a manual pump. Sometimes, a UST tire can even be seated using a hand pump, but be aware that you have to get a lot of air into the tire in a hurry to force the beads to pop up over the humps and then onto the ledges.
6. Pump up (or deflate) to your desired riding pressure.

PRO TIP

Low Tire Pressure

You can get a smoother ride, better traction on side hills, and lower rolling resistance on rough terrain by running on lower tire pressure (under 30 psi). You can't pinch-flat a tubeless tire (there is no tube to pinch!), although you can dent your rim. Begin by experimenting with tire pressures, and don't be afraid to even try less than 20 psi with tubeless tires—you might discover that you like it!

vi-8 INSTALLING A STANDARD TIRE AS A TUBELESS TIRE

With "Stan's No Tubes" tubeless systems, you can use a standard rim and tire and even make a 29-inch tire become tubeless. Stan's system includes liquid-latex–based sealant, ½-inch strapping tape, and a rubber rim strip with thick edges to seal the tire beads. The rim strips are available for three different 26-inch rim widths, as well as for 29-inch wheels. You can also forgo the rim strip and just tape over the rim holes with both strapping tape and electrical tape and use Stan's sealant (this was the original way Stan offered the system).

Do this only on wheels that you use frequently, because standard tires that you don't ride often are difficult to keep sealed with the sealant solution. If the wheel just sits, rather than being constantly stirred up by riding, the latex in the solution tends to pool up and harden at the bottom of the tire.

INSTALLING A STANDARD TIRE AS A TUBELESS TIRE

1. Unless you are using a UST rim (Fig. 6.7), use a drill to enlarge the inside valve hole to ⅜ inch, and smooth the burred edge. This allows clearance for the rubber sealing section at the base of the valve stem. With a UST rim, skip to the second part of step 3.
2. Wrap two layers of ½-inch-wide fiberglass strapping tape around the rim, completely covering the rim holes. Cut through the tape at the valve hole.
3. Install the rim strip, stretching it evenly around the rim and pushing the edges under the rim hooks; wetting the strip with soapy water makes this easier. If you are using a UST rim (Fig. 6.7), install the valve instead of a rim strip. (If you are using Stan's old system, i.e., using Stan's sealant without the rim strip, wrap a layer of electrical tape over the strapping tape. This method works better if you first smooth the edges of the rim holes with sandpaper and clean the rim bed with rubbing alcohol before applying the strapping tape in step 2. Then install the valve, first dripping a little sealant solution around the rubber base and rubber washer.) Tighten the valve nut down by hand against the rim.
4. Determine rotation direction (see first Pro Tip under §vi-6), and locate the label at the valve stem.
5. Install one bead of the tire on the rim, covering the sidewalls and along the rim beads with a one-to-eight solution of dish soap and water.
6. Shake the sealant bottle well, and turn it upside down when pouring it to keep the particles in solution. Put 60g (1.5 scoops—or 2 to 2.5 scoops for large tires or more sealing protection) of the sealant solution into the tire. Install the other tire bead, as described in step 4 for installing UST tires. If you have Stan's 2 oz. refill bottle, you can install both beads of the tire first. You then unscrew the valve core and squirt in the sealant through the valve stem.
7. Inflate the tire to a maximum of 40 psi, preferably with an air compressor. Wear safety glasses. To check if you got the rim strip on correctly, it is a good idea to inflate the tire first with just soapy water covering it and the rim edge before adding the sealant.
8. Wherever you see soap bubbles, which indicate escaping air, tip the wheel so the latex solution flows to the area and fills the holes. Continue doing this, repeatedly reinflating the tire to 40 psi, until the tire seals completely.

When riding, the latex splashing around inside will not seal the tire beads or sidewalls if you did not seal them completely before. If you have leaks, redo step 8.

Tire sealants are blurring the lines between "standard" 26-inch mountain bike tires and UST tires. For 2005, Geax, for instance, has a T.N.T. (Tube No Tube) tire, which is essentially a beefed up standard tire or a superlight UST tire, that comes with sealant. Run it with a tube on a standard rim, and it provides better sidewall cut resistance. Run it on a UST rim with the sealant, and you have a superlight and reliable tubeless tire.

vi-9 PATCHING TIRE CASING (SIDEWALL) WITH A STANDARD TIRE AND TUBE

Unless it is an emergency, don't do it! If your casing is cut, it's best to get a new tire because patching the tire casing is dangerous. No matter what you use as a patch, the tube will find a way to bulge out of the patched hole, and when it does, your tire will go flat immediately. Imagine coming down a steep descent and suddenly your front tire goes completely flat—you get the picture. In emergency situations, you can put layers of nonstretchable material, such as a dollar bill, an empty energy bar wrapper (or two), even a short section of the exploded tube (double thickness is better) between the tube and tire (see Chapter 3, §iii-3b and Fig. 3.1).

vi-10 TIRE SEALANTS

Slime is green goo with chopped fibers in it; when it sloshes around in an inner tube (or inside a tubeless tire), it flows to punctures and seals them. There are other brands of tire sealants besides Slime (including Stan's No Tubes sealant mentioned in §vi-8 above); these instructions generally apply to them as well. Although they are messy (though washable with water) and add weight to your wheels, tire sealants can virtually eliminate flat tires due to simple punctures.

If installing sealant in a tube (rather than in a tubeless tire), only use it in a tube without cuts in it and with a Schrader valve (Fig. 6.2) in good condition. You can put Slime in a tube with a slow leak; simply inject it as described below, pump the tube up, and spin the wheel for about five minutes. Be forewarned that after about a year, the stuff dries up and doesn't work well anymore.

a. Putting tire sealant in a tubeless tire

Simply pop the tire off of one side of the rim (§vi-2), shake the bottle, and squirt 2–4 oz. or so of sealant into the tire (Fig. 6.14). You can also use one scoop—about 40 g—of Stan's No Tubes sealant). Push the tire bead back onto the rim (§vi-7) and inflate. This can eliminate the aggravating air loss common with many UST tubeless tires.

b. Slime installation into a tube that's already installed in a tire

NOTE: *The tube must be of proper size. If it is too small (for instance, a 26-by-1.325–1.5-inch tube inside of a 26-by-2.0-inch tire) and stretches when inflated in the tire, any holes will stretch open and won't seal.*

1. Shake Slime bottle.
2. Remove Schrader valve core by using valve cap and core remover packaged with the Slime.
3. Rotate the wheel so the valve stem is at the 4 o'clock position.
4. Cut off the bottle spout, and connect the bottle spout and valve stem with the supplied surgical tubing.
5. Squeeze the bottle slowly to inject the Slime.
6. Stop squeezing after injecting 4 oz.; wait several minutes to clear the stem.
7. Remove the surgical tube.

8. Screw the valve core firmly back into the valve stem in a clockwise direction.
9. Inflate the tube.

If the tube has a leak, spin the wheel for 5 minutes to spread the Slime around in the tube.

NOTE: *If you have Presta valves (Figs. 1.1B and 6.3) and you want to use tire sealant, you can purchase tubes with it already installed.*

c. Maintaining tire-sealant–filled tubes

When pumping in air, always have the stem at 4 o'clock and wait a minute before you connect the pump for Slime to drain away; if you don't, Slime will leak out, eventually clogging the valve.

Sealing punctures:

1. If you find your tire flat, pump it up and ride it a bit to see if it seals.
2. If you get numerous punctures, you may need to pump repeatedly and ride the bike a bit until the tube seals up.
3. Pinch flats, caused by pinching the tube between the tire and rim, are hard to seal because the two "snake-bite" holes are on the side. Try laying the bike on the same side as the holes. Chances of sealing are not good.
4. Embedded nails and other foreign objects can be removed; spin the wheel to seal the hole.
5. Punctures on the rim side of the tube will not seal because the Slime is thrown to the outside.
6. Sidewall gashes in the tube need to be patched, but sidewall gashes in the tire cannot be patched so a new tire is required.
7. Replace the tube after a year or so. The sealant will have become too viscous to work properly anymore.

RIMS AND SPOKES

vi-11 TRUING A WHEEL

LEVEL 2

For more information on truing wheels, see Chapter 12, §xii-4, on wheel building.

If your wheel has a wobble in it, you can fix it by adjusting the tension on the spokes. An extreme bend in the rim cannot be fixed by spoke truing alone, because the spoke tension on the two sides of the wheel will be so uneven that the wheel will rapidly fall apart.

Get a spoke wrench of the right size for your spoke nipples—they come in different sizes (as well as square or splined shapes), and you will wreck your nipples if you use a spoke wrench that is too large.

1. Check that there are no broken spokes in the wheel, or any spokes that are so loose that they flop around. If there is a broken spoke, follow the replacement procedure in the following section, vi-12. If there is a single loose spoke, check to see that the rim is not dented or cracked in that area. I recommend replacing the rim if it is. If the rim looks okay, mark the loose spoke with a piece of tape, and tighten it up with the spoke wrench until it seems to be at the same tension as adjacent spokes on the same side of the wheel (pluck the spoke and listen to the tone). Then follow the truing procedure below.
2. Grab the rim while the wheel is on the bike, and flex it side to side to check the hub-bearing adjustment. If the bearings are loose, the wheel will clunk side to side. The hub will need to be tightened before you true the wheel, or else the wheel will behave erratically. Follow the hub-adjustment procedure, §vi-15d, steps 28–31.

6.15–6.16 **Lateral truing**

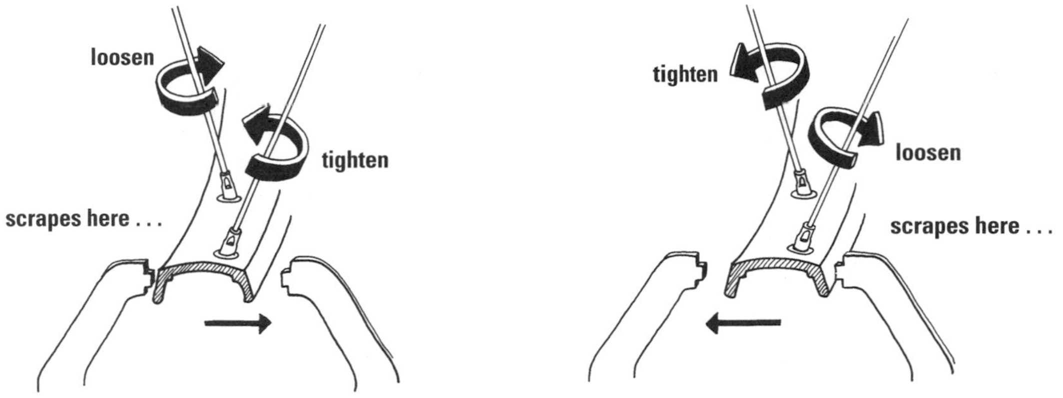

3. Put the wheel in a truing stand, if you have one. Otherwise, leave it on the bike. Suspend the bike in a bike stand or from the ceiling, or turn it upside down on the handlebar and saddle.
4. Adjust the truing stand feeler, or hold one of your brake pads so that it scrapes the rim at the biggest wobble.
5. Where the rim scrapes, tighten the spoke or spokes that come to the rim from the opposite side of the hub, and loosen the spoke or spokes that come from the same side of the hub as the rim scrapes (Figs. 6.15–6.16). This approach will pull the rim away from the feeler or brake pad. When correcting a wheel that is laterally out of true (wobbles side to side), always adjust spokes in pairs: one spoke coming from one side of the wheel, the other from the opposite side.

NOTE: *Tightening spokes is similar to opening a jar upside down. With the jar right side up, turning the lid to the left opens the jar, but this reverses when you turn the jar upside down (try it and see). Spoke nipples are just like the lid on that upside-down jar. In other words, when the nipples are at the bottom of the rim, counterclockwise tightens, and clockwise loosens (Figs. 6.15–6.16). The opposite is true when the nipples you are turning are at the top of the wheel. It may take you a few attempts before you catch on, but you will eventually get it. If you temporarily make the wheel worse, simply reverse what you have done and start over.*

It is best to tighten and loosen by small amounts (about one-quarter turn at a time), decreasing the amount you turn the spoke nipples as you move away from the spot where the rim scrapes the hardest. If the wobble gets worse, then you are turning the spokes the wrong direction.

Some wheels (Shimano's complete wheels, for instance) have the spoke nipples at the hub and not at the rim. You need a special spoke wrench (it should come with the wheels) to get in there at them. You must be particularly careful about the rotation direction (note the discussion above about jar lids) to make sure you are tightening or loosening as you intend.

6. As the rim moves more toward center, readjust the truing-stand feeler or the brake pad so that it again finds the most out-of-true spot on the wheel.

7. Check the wobble first on one side of the wheel and then the other, adjusting spokes accordingly, so that you don't end up pulling the whole wheel off-center by chasing wobbles only on one side. As the wheel gets closer to true, you will need to decrease the amount you turn the spokes to avoid overcorrecting.
8. Accept a certain amount of wobble, especially if truing in a bike, for the in-the-bike method of wheel truing is not very accurate and is not at all suited for making a wheel absolutely true. If you have access to a wheel-dishing tool, check to make sure that the wheel is centered (Chapter 12, §xii-5).

vi-12 REPLACING A BROKEN SPOKE

LEVEL 2

Go to the bike store and get a new spoke of the same length.

REMEMBER: *The spokes on the front wheel are usually not the same length as the spokes on the rear. Also, the spokes on the drive side of the rear wheel are almost always shorter than those on the other side. Same goes for a disc-brake side of a front wheel.*

1. Make sure you are using the proper thickness and length of spoke.
2. Thread the spoke through the spoke hole in the hub flange. If the broken spoke is on the drive side of the rear wheel, you will need to remove the cassette cogs or the freewheel to get at the hub flange (§vi-19 and §vi-20). If the spoke is adjacent to the disc-brake rotor, remove the rotor (§vii-14a).
3. Weave the new spoke in with the other spokes just as it was before (Fig. 6.17). It may take some bending to get it in place.

6.17 Weaving in a new spoke

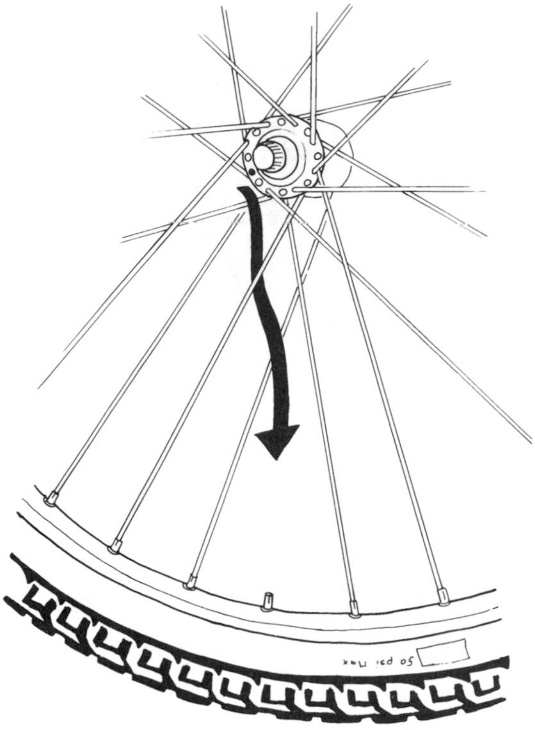

4. Thread it into the same nipple, if the nipple is in good shape. Otherwise, use a new nipple; you'll need to remove the tire, tube, and rim strip to install one.
5. Mark the new spoke with a piece of tape, and tighten it up about as snugly as the neighboring spokes on that side of the wheel are tightened.
6. Follow the steps for truing a wheel as outlined above, in §vi-11.

HUBS

vi-13 OVERHAULING HUBS

LEVEL 2

Hubs should turn smoothly and noiselessly. If they are regularly maintained (and of decent quality to start with), you can expect them to still be running smoothly when you are ready to give up on the rest of your bike.

6.18 **Front hub with cartridge bearing**

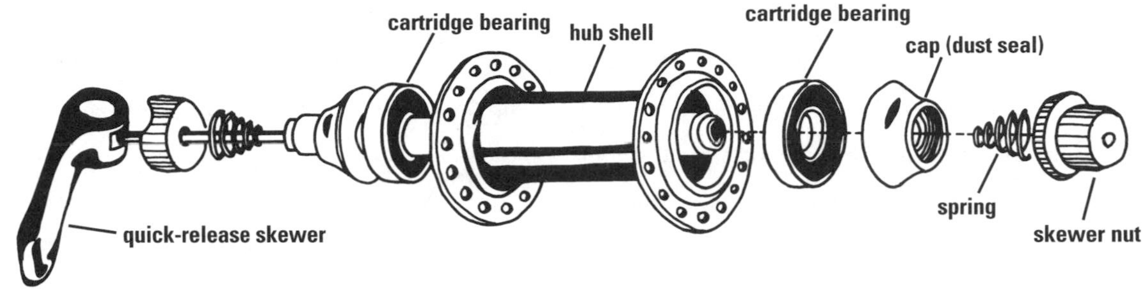

6.19 **Front hub with standard ball bearings**

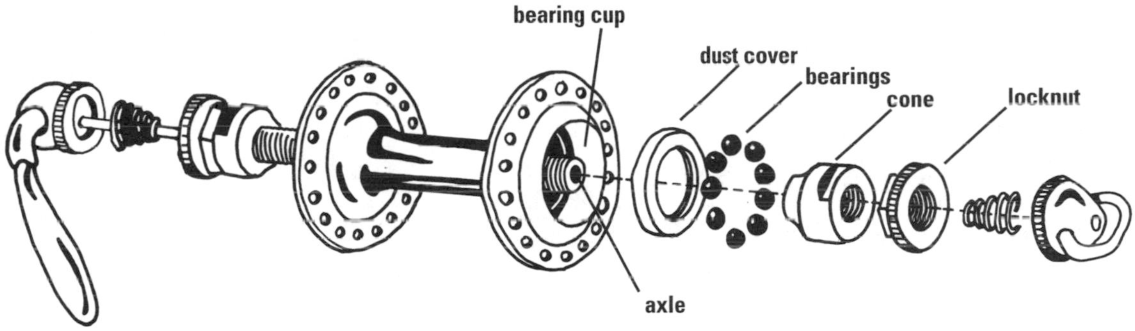

There are two general types of hubs: the "sealed-bearing" (or "cartridge-bearing") type (Fig. 6.18) and the standard "cup-and-cone" type (Fig. 6.19). All hubs have a "hub shell" that contains the axle and bearings and is connected to the rim with spokes.

Standard cup-and-cone hubs have loose ball bearings that roll along very smooth bearing surfaces called the "bearing races," with an axle going through the center of the hub. These hubs also have a pair of conical-shaped nuts threaded onto the axle called "cones" (Fig. 6.19). On each side of the hub, a cone presses the bearings gently inside the bearing cup and guides the bearings as they travel along the bearing race. In high-quality hubs, the bearing race surface on the cone and cup that comes in contact with the bearings has been machined to minimize friction. The operation of the hub depends on the smoothness and lubrication of the cones, ball bearings, and cups. Outboard of the cones are one or more spacers (or washers) followed by threaded locknuts that tighten down against the cones and spacers to keep the hub in proper adjustment. The rear hub will have more spacers on both sides, especially on the drive side (Fig. 6.28).

The term "sealed-bearing" hub is a bit of a misnomer, because many cup-and-cone hubs offer better protection against dirt and water than some sealed-bearing hubs. The phrase "cartridge-bearing hub" is more accurate, because the distinguishing feature of these hubs is that the bearings, races, and cones are all assembled as a complete cartridge unit at the factory and then plugged into a hub shell that is machined to accept the cartridge bearing. Cartridge-bearing front hubs have two bearings, one on either end of the hub shell (Fig. 6.18). Rear hubs (Fig. 6.27) have at least that and come with additional bearing cartridges to stabilize the rear freehub body (the part onto which the rear cogs are attached), assuming it is not a hub for a thread-on freewheel as shown in Figure 6.28.

Cartridge-bearing hubs can have any number of axle-assembly types. Some have a threaded axle with locknuts quite similar to a cup-and-cone hub. Much more common on mountain bikes are aluminum axles, often very large in diameter with correspondingly large bearings. Their end caps usually snap on, screw on, or are held on with setscrews or circlips. The large-diameter axles and bearings are meant to prevent independent movement of the legs of suspension forks or rear-suspension assemblies. Some have super-oversized, perhaps 20mm-diameter, "through-axles" (rather than quick-release axles) for very high stiffness (see §ii-10). On these, the fork ends—and sometimes the frame's rear dropouts—clamp around the ends of the axle.

vi-14 ALL HUBS

1. Remove the wheel from the bike (Chapter 2, §ii-2 to §ii-5, §ii-10, and §ii-12).
2. Remove the quick-release skewer or the nuts and washers that are there to hold the wheel onto the bike.

vi-15 OVERHAULING STANDARD CUP-AND-CONE HUB, FRONT OR REAR

Take some time to evaluate the hub's condition before disassembling it. That will help you to isolate problems. Spin the hub while holding the axle, and turn the axle while holding the hub. Does it turn roughly? Is the axle bent or broken? Wobble the axle side to side. Is the bearing adjustment loose?

NOTE: *Some hubs that have large rubber seals covering the axle nuts (Shimano STX comes to mind) can squeal hideously, even though the inside workings of the hub are in good shape. The squeal can be caused by dust in the seal or its misseating against the hub face. The seal can be pulled off by squeezing and yanking it. Brush it off, put it back into its mating grooves on the hub, and it will probably be silent for a while.*

a. Disassembly

1. Set the wheel flat on a table or workbench. Slip a cone wrench of the appropriate size (usually 13mm, 14mm, or 15mm) onto the wrench flats on one of the cones. On a rear wheel, work on the nondrive side.
2. Put an appropriately sized wrench or adjustable wrench on the locknut on the same side.
3. While holding the cone with the cone wrench, loosen the locknut (Fig. 6.20). This procedure may take considerable force, as these are often fastened together very tightly to maintain the hub's adjustment. Make sure that you are unscrewing the locknut counterclockwise ("lefty loosey, righty tighty," as shown in Fig. 6.20).
4. As soon as the locknut loosens, move the cone wrench from the cone on top to the cone on the opposite end of the axle, in order to hold the axle in place as you unscrew the locknut. The locknut will generally unscrew with your fingers; use a wrench on it if necessary to get past any damaged threads.
5. Slide any spacers off. If they will not slide off, the cone will push them off when you unscrew it. Please note that some spacers have a small tooth or "key" that corresponds to a groove along the axle; make sure it's lined up before unscrewing the cone, or you'll damage the threads.

6.20 **Loosening and tightening a locknut**

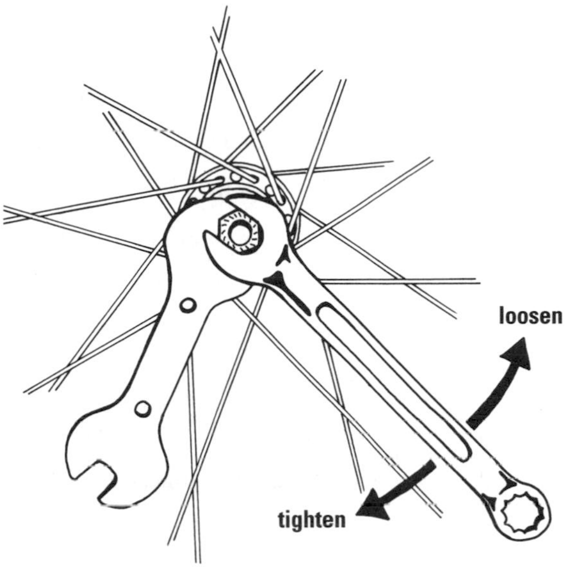

6.21 **Removing a dustcap**

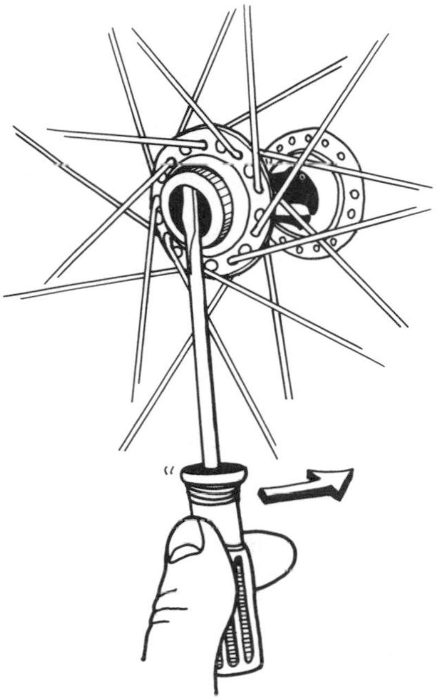

6. Unscrew the cone off of the axle. Again, you may need to hold the opposite cone with a wrench and use a wrench on this cone. An easy way to keep track of the various nuts, spacers, and cones is to lay them down on your workbench in the order in which they were removed (Fig. 6.19), or you can slide a twist-tie through all the parts in the correct order and orientation. Either method serves as an easy guide when reassembling the hub.
7. Put your hand over the end of the hub from which you removed the nuts and spacers (to catch any bearings that might fall out), and flip the wheel over. Have a rag underneath the wheel to catch stray bearings.
8. Pull the axle up and out, being careful not to lose any bearings that might fall out of the hub or that might be stuck to the axle. Leave the cone, spacers, and locknut all tightened together on the opposite end of the axle from the one you disassembled. If you are replacing a bent or broken axle, measure the amount of axle sticking out beyond the locknut. Put the cone, spacers, and locknut on the new axle identically.
9. Remove all of the ball bearings from both sides of the hub. They may stick to a screwdriver with a coating of grease on the tip, or you can push them down through the center of the hub and out the other side with the screwdriver. Tweezers or a small magnet might also be useful for removing bearings. Put the bearings in a cup, a jar lid, or the like. Count the bearings, and make sure you have the same number from each side.
10. With a screwdriver, gently pop off the seals that are pressed into either end of the hub shell (Fig. 6.21). Be careful not to deform them; leave them in if you can't pop them out without damage. If they are not removed, it is tedious, but not impossible, to clean the dirty grease out of their concave inside with a rag and a thin screwdriver.

b. Cleaning

11. Wipe the hub shell out with a rag. Remove all dirt and grease from the bearing surfaces. Using a screwdriver, push a rag through the axle hole in the hub and spin the wheel around it to clean out any grease or dirt. Wipe off the outer faces of the shell. Finish with a very clean rag on the bearing surfaces. They should shine and be completely free of dirt or grease. If you let your hub go too long between overhauls, the grease may have solidified and glazed over so completely that you will need a solvent to remove it. If you are working on a rear cassette hub, take this opportunity to lubricate the cassette. (See Lubricating Freehub Mechanisms, §vi-21.)

12. Wipe the axle, nuts, and cones with a rag. Clean the cones particularly well with a clean rag. Again, a solvent may be required if the grease has solidified. Get any dirt out of the threads on the disassembled axle end, as the cone will then push any dirt into the hub upon reassembly.

13. Wipe the grease and dirt off of the seals. A rag over the end of a screwdriver is sometimes useful to get inside. Again, glaze-hard grease may have to be removed with a solvent. Keep the solvent out of the freehub body.

14. Wipe the bearings off by rubbing all of them together between two rags. This may be sufficient to clean them completely, but small specks of dirt can still adhere to them, so I prefer to take the next step as well.

15. If you are overhauling low-quality hubs, skip to step 16. Super clean and polish the bearings. I prefer to wash them in a plugged sink with an abrasive soap such as Lava, rubbing them between my hands as if I were washing my palms. This really gets them shining, unless they are caked with glaze-hard grease. Make sure you have plugged the sink drain! This method has the added advantage of getting my hands super clean for the assembly step. It is silly to contaminate your super-clean parts with dirty hands. If there is hardened glaze on the bearings, soak them in a solvent. If that does not remove it, go buy new bearings at the bike shop. Take a few of the old bearings along so you are sure to buy the right size.

16. Dry all bearings and any other wet parts. Inspect the bearings and bearing surfaces carefully. If any of the bearings have pits or gouges in them, replace all of them. The same goes for the cones. A lack of sheen or a patina on either balls or cones indicates wear and is cause for replacement. Most bike shops stock replacement cones. If the bearing cups in the hub shell are pitted, the only thing you can do is buy new hubs. Regular maintenance and proper adjustment can prevent pitted bearing races in the hubs.

NOTE: *Using new ball bearings when overhauling standard cup-and-cone hubs ensures round, smooth bearings; however, do not avoid performing an overhaul just because you don't have any new ball bearings. Inspect the ball bearings carefully. If there is even the slightest hint of uneven wear or pitting on the balls, cups, or cones, throw the bearings out and complete the overhaul with new bearings. Err on the side of caution.*

c. Assembly and lubrication

17. Press the seals or dust covers in on both ends of the hub shell.

18. Smear grease with your clean finger into the bearing race on one end of the hub shell. I like using light-colored or clear grease so that I can see if it

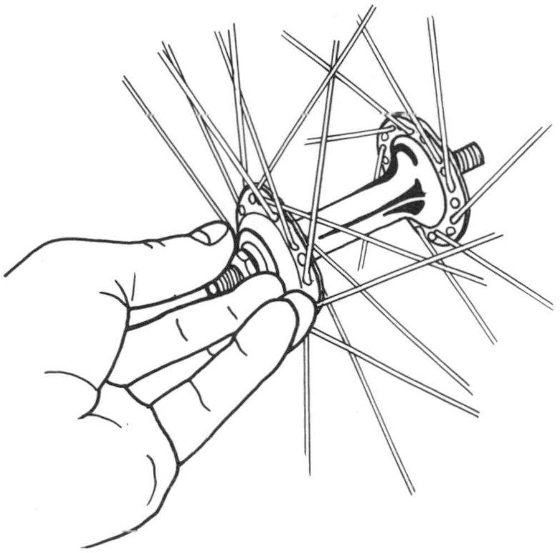

6.22 **Push inward on the axle and flip the wheel over**

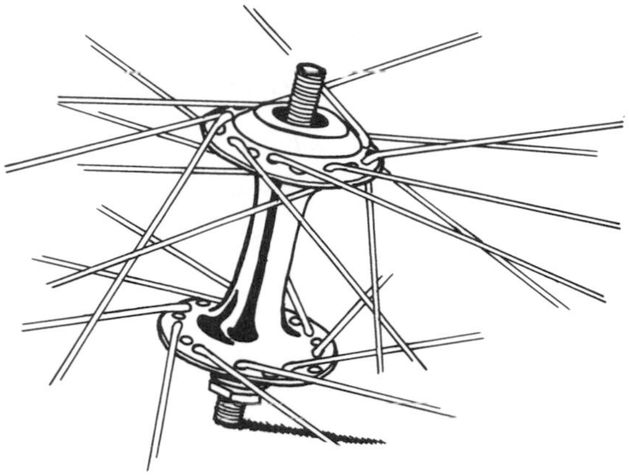

6.23 **Setting the axle on the floor to keep the cone in contact with the bearings**

gets dirty, but any bike grease will do. Grease not only lubricates the bearings, it also forms a barrier to dirt and water. Use enough grease to cover the balls halfway. Too much grease will slow the hub by packing around the axle.

19. Stick half of the ball bearings into the grease, making sure you put in the same number of bearings that came out. Distribute them uniformly around in the bearing race.
20. Smear grease on the cone that is still attached to the axle, and slide the axle into the hub shell. Lift the wheel up a bit (30-degree angle), so that you can push the axle in until the cone slides into position and keeps all the bearings in place. On rear hubs it is important to replace the axle and cone assembly into the same side of the hub from which it was removed because of the spacing for cogs.
21. Holding the axle pushed inward with one hand to secure the bearings, turn the wheel over (Fig. 6.22).
22. Smear grease into the bearing race that is now facing up. Lift the wheel and allow the axle to slide down just enough so that it is not sticking up past the bearing race. Make sure no bearings fall out of the bottom. If the race and bearings are properly greased and the axle remains in the hub shell, they are not likely to fall out.
23. While the top end of the axle is still below the bearing race, place the remaining bearings uniformly around in the grease. Make sure you have inserted the correct number of bearings.
24. Slide the axle back up into place by setting the wheel down on the table, so that the wheel rests on the lower axle end, seating the cone up into the bearings (Fig. 6.23).
25. With your fingers, screw the top cone down into place, seating it snugly onto the bearings. Covering the top cone with a film of grease is also a good idea.
26. In correct order, slide on the washer and any spacers. Watch for those washers with the little tooth or "key" that fits into the lengthwise groove in the axle.
27. Use your fingers to screw on the locknut. Note that the two sides of the locknut are not the same.

If you are unsure about which way the locknut goes back on, check the orientation of the locknut that is on the opposite end of the axle (this locknut was not removed during this overhaul and is assumed to be in the correct orientation). As a general rule, the rough surface of the locknut faces out so that it can get a better bite into the dropout.

d. Hub adjustment

28. Tighten the cone until it lightly contacts the bearings. The axle should turn smoothly without any roughness or grinding, and there should be a small amount of lateral play. Tighten the locknut until it is snug against the cone. The slight looseness in the hub (called axle-end play) will be taken out when the quick-release skewer is tightened down with the wheel in the frame. If the hub is a bolt-on type without a quick-release skewer, you want to adjust it without any play in it.
29. Place the cone wrench into the flats of the hub cone. Tighten the locknut with another wrench (Fig. 6.24). Tighten it about as tightly as you can against the cone and spacers, in order to hold the adjustment. Be aware that you can ruin the hub if you accidentally tighten the cone down against the bearings instead of against the locknut.
30. If the adjustment is off, loosen the locknut while holding the cone with the cone wrench. If the hub is too tight, unscrew the cone a bit. If the hub is too loose, screw the cone in a bit.
31. Repeat steps 28–30 until the hub adjustment feels right. It should have a slight amount of end play so that the pressure of the quick-release skewer will compress it to a perfect adjustment. Tighten the locknut firmly against the cone to hold the adjustment.

6.24 Tightening and loosening a locknut

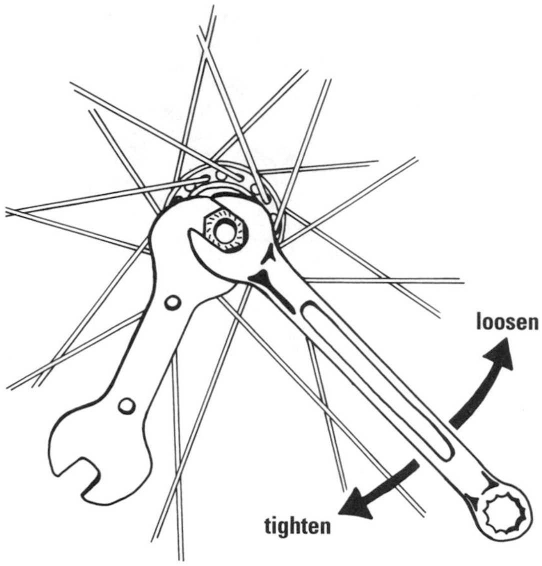

NOTE: *You may find that tightening the locknut against the cone suddenly turns your "Mona Lisa" perfect hub adjustment into something slightly less beautiful. If it is too tight, back off both cones (by using a cone wrench on either side of the hub, each on one cone) a fraction of a turn. If too loose, tighten both locknuts a bit. If still off, you might have to loosen one side and go back to step 29. It's rare that I get a hub adjustment perfectly "dialed-in" on the first try, so expect that you might have to tinker with the adjustment a bit before it's right.*

32. Put the skewer back into the hub. Make sure that the conical springs have their narrow ends to the inside (see Fig. 6.19).
33. Install the wheel in the bike, tightening the skewer. Check that the wheel spins well without any side play at the rim. If it needs readjustment, go back to step 31.
34. Congratulate yourself on a job well done! Hub overhaul is a delicate job, and it makes a difference in the longevity and performance of your bike.

WHEELS

6.25 **Tapping out a cartridge bearing**

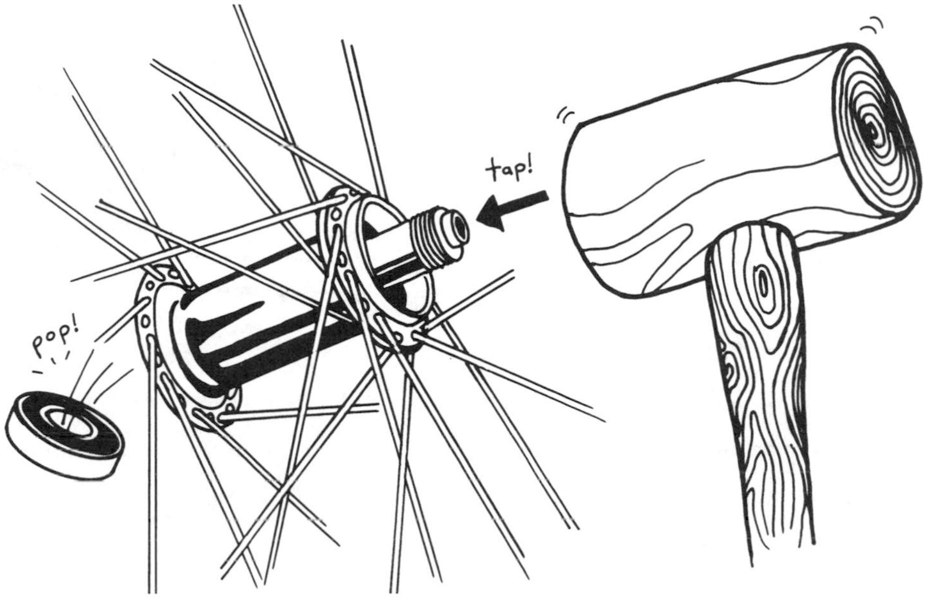

vi-16 OVERHAUL CARTRIDGE-BEARING HUB

Cartridge-bearing hubs (Figs. 6.18 and 6.27) generally do not need much maintenance; however, if you ride through water above your hubs, you can expect water and dirt to get through any kind of seal. If the ball bearings inside the cartridges get wet or they start making noise, they should be overhauled or replaced.

There are many types of cartridge-bearing hubs, and it is outside the scope of this book to explain how to disassemble every one of them. Some have a threaded axle with locknuts similar to loose-ball hubs. Others have an end cap (Fig. 6.18) that can be removed by just pulling it off, by loosening a set screw on the cap, or by unscrewing the axle from either end with two 5mm Allen wrenches; the ends of the axle on this latter type will have a 5mm hex cut inside either end. Older Mavic hubs have cup-shaped end flanges held on with snaprings. Current Mavic hubs have one end cap with a 5mm hex hole, whereas the other end cap pulls off. To get the axle out, you have to unscrew and remove either the end cap with the hex hole or the threaded collar on the other end. You can hold the collar with a pin tool that comes with the hubs while fixing the other end of the axle with a 5mm hex key. Alternatively, if you have a 10mm hex key, you can insert it into the collar end of the axle after you pull off the end cap on that end. Hold the axle with the 10mm hex key while you unscrew the 5mm end cap from the other end.

If your hub has dust covers concealing the bearings, pry them off after the axle-end caps have been removed.

Once the end cap and dust covers have been removed, you can usually smack the end of the axle with a soft hammer or on a table, and it will either pop the axle out, or it will push the opposite bearing out (Fig. 6.25). The axle may have a shoulder on either side, internal to the bearings, that can be used to force the bearings out, or you will push the axle end into the center of the hub, behind the bearing, and use the end of the axle (or a large drift punch) to push the bearing out. A tap with a soft hammer,

OVERHAUL A CARTRIDGE-BEARING HUB

and the axle shoulder, the axle end, or the drift punch should force the bearing out of the hub. Pop the other bearing out the same way.

If the axle has no shoulder to push out the bearing (i.e., Mavic), you need to tap the bearings out with another tool. If you have a bearing puller for your hub, then great, use it. Otherwise, you can often use the tip of a large screwdriver placed through the bore of the hub shell against the bearing. Move the tip of the screwdriver against different points around the inner bearing as you tap on it with a hammer. Make sure that the screwdriver tip is contacting the inner bearing bore—you don't want to be pounding it into the bearing's side seal!

If the bearings don't want to come out without undue force, you can leave them in the hub shell and pop off the outer bearing seal on each with the tip of a knife blade (Fig. 6.26). If the grease inside is pretty clean, you can just wipe it out and pack new grease in from the outside. That may be all that is necessary.

Cartridge bearings are vulnerable to lateral stress; if you have to use a lot of force to pound them out, they will need to be replaced. Once the cartridge bearings are out, you can sometimes overhaul them (otherwise you'll need to buy new ones):

OVERHAUL A CARTRIDGE-BEARING HUB

1. Gently pop the bearing covers off with a single-edge razor blade (Fig. 6.26).
2. Squirt a citrus-based solvent into the bearing under pressure (wear rubber gloves and protective glasses) to wash out the grease, water, and dirt. Scrub with a clean toothbrush. Brush your teeth later with a different toothbrush.
3. Blow out the bearing with compressed air to dry it.
4. Pack it with grease and snap the bearing covers back on. Replace the bearing if it doesn't turn smoothly.
5. Reassemble the hub the opposite way it came apart.

6.26 Removing a seal from a cartridge bearing

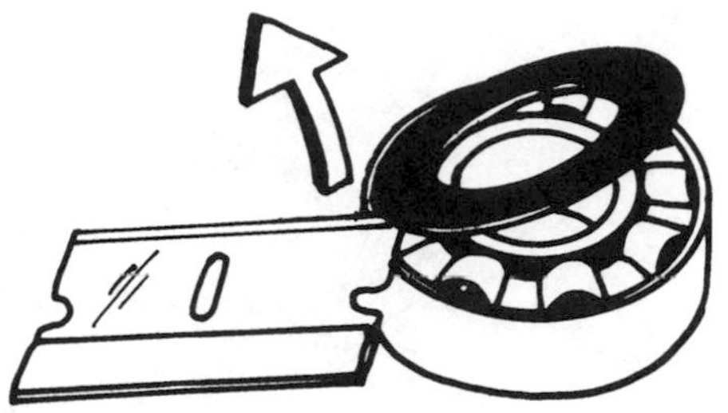

NOTE: *Reinstalling the bearings in most new cartridge-bearing hubs is relatively easy: Simply press the bearings in with your hand, or use the shoulder on the axle as a punch to press the bearings into place. In most cases, even a soft hammer is not necessary; however, with older cartridge-bearing hubs (Suntour, Sanshin, early Specialized, and others), it isn't so easy. The tolerance between the hub cups and the outer surface of the bearing is so tight that these bearings must be pressed in or pounded in with a hammer. A direct blow from a hammer would ruin the bearing, so with these types of hubs, it is best to use either an old cartridge bearing or a similar-sized piece of metal (such as a wrench socket the same size as the outer diameter of the bearing) to tap the bearings into the hub.*

6. Sometimes the bearings will be slightly out of alignment after installation, making the hub noticeably hard to turn. A light tap on either end of the axle with a soft hammer will often free them. With Mavic hubs, once the wheel is mounted in the frame or fork with the skewer tightened, turn the threaded ring on one face of the hub (the side opposite the cogs on the rear) with the Mavic pin tool. Screw it in to remove side play, unscrew it to eliminate hub binding. A little Loctite on the adjuster threads is a good idea if it doesn't hold its adjustment.

6.27 **Rear freehub with cartridge bearings and a cassette cogset**

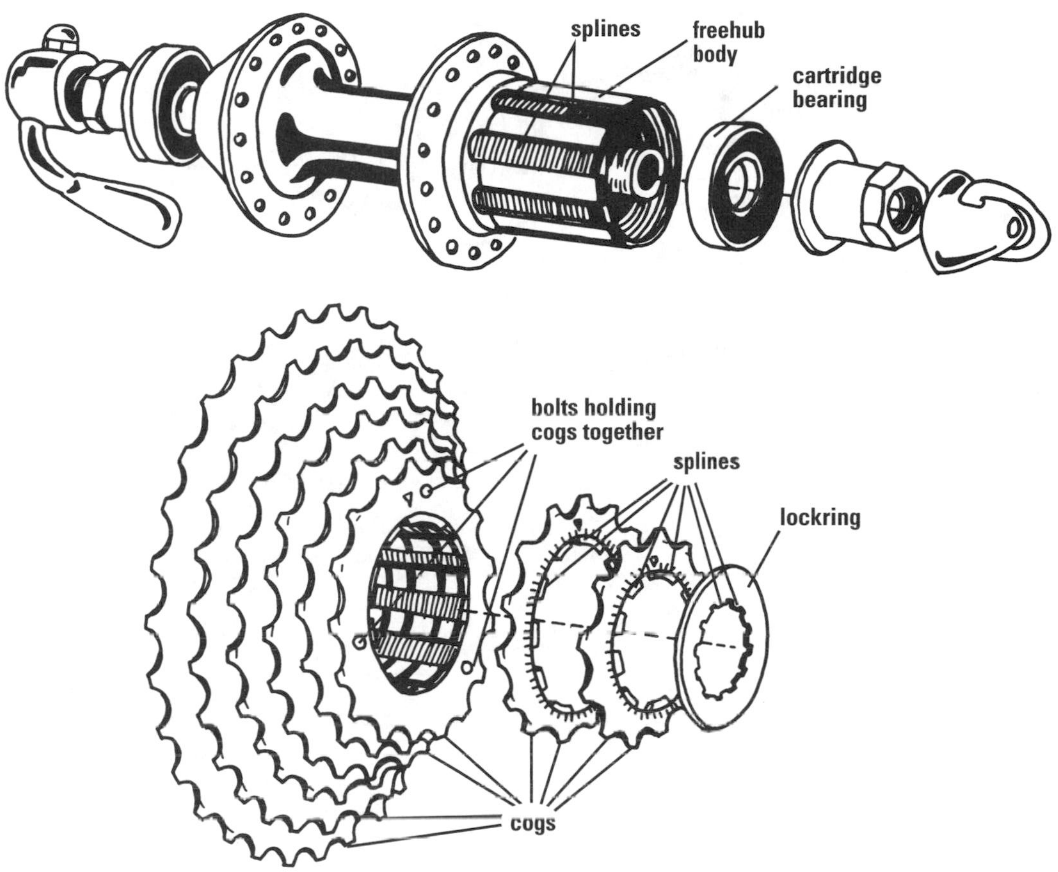

vi-17 GREASE GUARD HUBS

Wilderness Trail Bikes, Suntour, and others have made high-end hubs, some labeled Grease Guard, that have small grease ports on them that accept a small-tipped grease gun. The tip in this type of grease gun is about the size of the tip of a pencil. Injecting grease into these grease ports forces grease through the bearings from the inside out, squeezing the old grease out of the outer end. Grease injection systems do not eliminate the need for overhauling your hubs. Grease injection merely extends the amount of time between overhauls; furthermore, these systems are only as good as you are about using them.

FREEHUBS, FREEWHEELS, AND COGS

Both freehubs and freewheels are freewheeling mechanisms, meaning that they allow the rear wheel to turn forward freely while the pedals are not turning.

A freehub is an integral part of the rear hub. The cogs slide onto the freehub body, engaging longitudinal grooves, or "splines" (Fig. 6.27). A freehub can also be called a "cassette hub," the group of cogs being called the "cassette."

A freewheel is a separate unit with the cogs attached to it. The entire freewheel threads onto the drive side of the rear hub (Fig. 6.28). Thread-on

6.28 **Threaded rear hub with standard ball bearings and a freewheel**

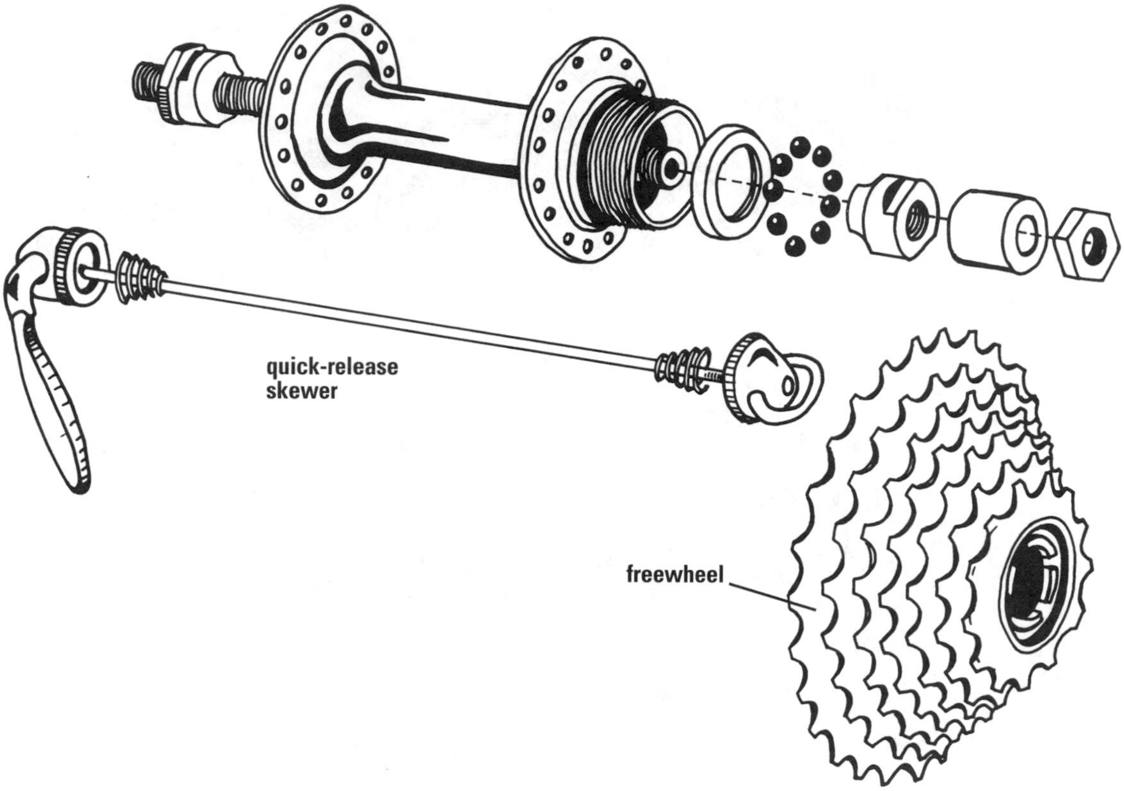

freewheels have fallen out of fashion relative to freehubs; interchanging cogs on a freewheel is more difficult, and a freewheel does not support the drive side of the hub axle. Freewheels can be removed by using a freewheel tool made to fit the specific freewheel. Entire freewheels with different gear combinations can be changed in this way.

Freehubs and freewheels usually rely on a series of spring-loaded pawls that engage internal teeth when pressure is applied to the pedals but allow the bike to freewheel when the rider is coasting. The pawls riding over the teeth as they rotate past makes the familiar clicking noise when coasting.

Many freehubs can be lubricated without removing them from the hub. Changing gear combinations is accomplished by removing the cogs from the freehub body and putting on different ones.

vi-18 CLEANING REAR COGS

The quickest, though perfunctory, way to clean the rear cogs is to slide a rag back and forth between each pair of cogs (Fig. 6.29). The other way is to remove them (see §vi-19 below) and wipe them off with a rag or immerse them in solvent.

vi-19 CHANGING CASSETTE COGS

1. Get out a chain whip, a cassette-lockring remover, a wrench (adjustable or open) to fit the remover, and the cog(s) you want to install. (Note that some very old cassettes from the early

6.29 Cleaning cogs

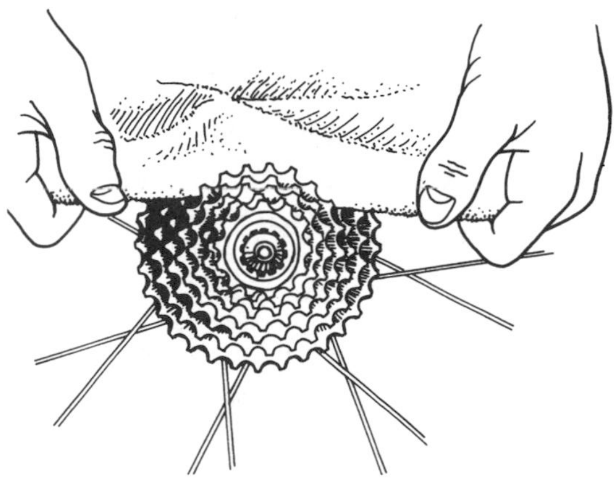

6.30 Removing a freewheel lockring

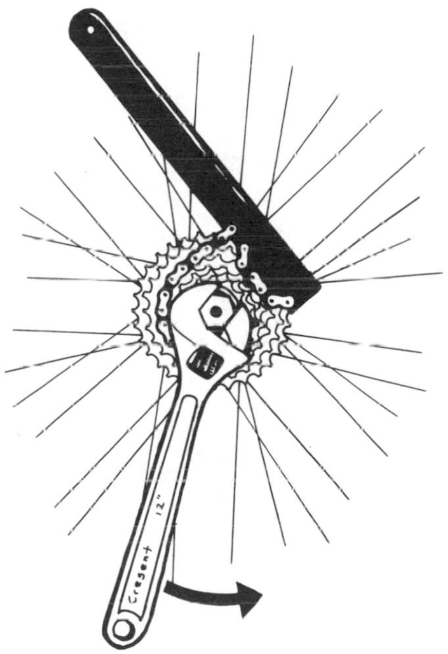

1980s have a threaded smallest cog instead of a lockring. These require two chain whips and no lockring remover.)

2. Remove the quick-release skewer from the hub axle.
3. Wrap the chain whip around a cog at least two up from the smallest cog, wrapped in the drive direction to hold the cassette in place. In place of the chain whip, you can substitute a special tool that has two pins to hold the first cog; it will be labeled 11T on one side and 12T on the other side, because the pins will be located differently depending on the size of the first cog (11- or 12-tooth).
4. Insert the splined lockring remover into the lockring—the metallic ring with a splined hole holding the smallest cog in place. Unscrew the lockring in a counterclockwise direction while holding the chain whip to keep the cassette from turning (Fig. 6.30). If the lockring is so tight that the tool pops out and damages it, put the quick-release skewer without its springs through the hub and tool and tighten it. Loosen the lockring a fraction of a turn, remove the skewer, and unscrew the lockring the rest of the way.
5. Pull the cogs straight off. Some cassette cogsets are all single cogs separated by loose spacers, some cogsets are bolted together, and some cogsets are a combination of both.
6. Clean the cogs with a rag or a toothbrush—use a solvent if necessary, and don't put the toothbrush back by the bathroom sink!
7. Inspect the cogs for wear. If the teeth are hook-shaped or the chain can be lifted off of them when it is wrapped around the cog under tension, they may be ripe for replacement. Rohloff also makes a cog-wear-indicator tool (Fig. 1.4). If you have access to one, use it according to its supplied instructions.
8. Replace the cogs.
   - (a) If you are replacing the entire cogset, just slide the new one on. Usually, one spline is wider than the others to ensure proper alignment (Fig. 6.31).
   - (b) If you are installing a nine-speed cassette, see the notes under step 9.

6.31 **Spline vs. spleen**

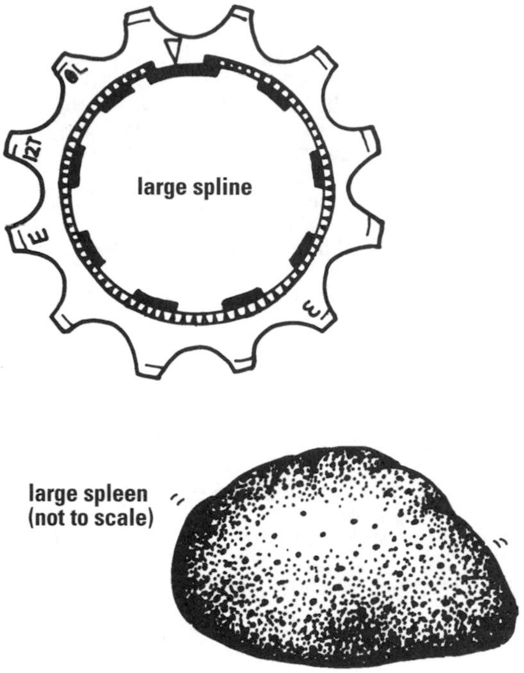

(c) If you are replacing some individual cogs within your cogset, be certain that they are of the same type and model. For example, not all 16-tooth Shimano cogs are alike. Most cogs have shifting ramps, differentially shaped teeth, and other asymmetries. They differ with model as well as with sizes of the adjacent cogs, so you need to buy one for the exact location and model. Install them in decreasing numerical sequence with the numbers facing out.

NOTE: *Some bolt-together cogsets are held together by three long bolts (Fig. 6.27) and can be disassembled for cleaning and then reinstalled onto the freehub as separate cogs to facilitate future cog changes and cleaning. But high-end cogsets usually have light-weight splined aluminum carriers onto which the cogs are mounted. These cannot be disassembled, and you replace the entire carrier with cogs assembled onto it.*

CHANGING CASSETTE COGS

9. When all the cogs are on, tighten the lockring with the lockring remover and wrench. (If you have the old freehub type with the thread-on first cog, tighten that on with a chain whip instead.) Make sure that all of the cogs are seated and can't wobble side to side, which would indicate that the first or second cog is sitting against the ends of the splines. If the cogs are loose after tightening the lockring, loosen the lockring, line up the first and second cog until they fall in place, and tighten the lockring again. Make sure that the lockring is compatible with both the freehub and the cogset; these can vary depending on manufacturer and size of the first cog.

NOTE ON COMPATIBILITY: *The above instructions for removing and replacing cogs apply for nine- eight-, seven-, and six-speed cogsets. But the freehub bodies vary, so make sure you only use, for example, an eight-speed cogset on a freehub body designed for eight cogs.*

NOTE ON 11-TOOTH COGS: *Some eight- and nine-speed freehub bodies will not accept 11-tooth cogs (for example, 1992–1994 XTR freehub bodies will not accept 11-28 or 11-30 cogsets). To accept the small 11-tooth cog, the splines of current freehub bodies stop about 2mm before the outer end of the freehub body. If you are motivated to do so, you can grind the last 2mm of splines off of an old-style eight-speed freehub so it will accept an 11-tooth cog. But be aware that the steel is very hard, and you may need a rotary grindstone to do the job!*

NOTE ON NINE-SPEED CONVERSION FROM EIGHT-SPEED CASSETTES: *Ritchey's 2-by-9 system (front double, rear nine) features a nine-speed cassette that fits on an eight-speed freehub by using an eight-speed cogset. The ninth cog is large (33 teeth or more) and bowl-shaped. It takes advantage of some unused space on the inboard end of the freehub body and spaces the teeth the same distance from the next cog as the spacing throughout the cassette. It requires a special shifter made for it; neither standard eight-speed nor nine-speed shifters will work.*

NOTE ON INSTALLING A RITCHEY NINE-SPEED CONVERSION CASSETTE: *Many eight-speed freehubs from Shimano (as well as other companies) have a steel ring against the inboard end of the cassette body. You should remove this ring (it pulls straight off), and then put on the Ritchey ninth cog in its place. Some XT and XTR eight-speed freehubs have a thicker aluminum ring inboard; replace this thick ring with the thinner steel ring supplied with the Ritchey ninth cog, and put on the Ritchey ninth cog. Slide on the eight-speed cassette and tighten it down with the lockring as described in step 9.*

CAUTION ON RITCHEY NINE-SPEED CONVERSION SYSTEM: *To avoid the derailleur's hitting the spokes when on the bowl-shaped Ritchey cog, you must use an "OCR" ("Off-Center Rear") rim; Ritchey, Bontrager, and others supply them. The spoke holes on these rims are offset to the nondrive side and angle the drive-side spokes farther away from the cogs.*

vi-20 CHANGING FREEWHEELS

If you have a freewheel (Fig. 6.28) and want to switch it with another one, follow this procedure. Replacing individual cogs on an existing freewheel is beyond the scope of this book and is rarely done these days because of the unavailability of spare parts.

1. Get out the appropriate freewheel remover for your freewheel, a big adjustable wrench to fit it, and the freewheel you are replacing it with.
2. Remove the quick-release skewer, and take the springs off of it.
3. Slide the skewer back in from the nondrive side, place the freewheel remover into the end of the freewheel so that the notches or splines engage, and thread the skewer nut back on, tightening it against the freewheel remover to keep it from popping out of its notches.
4. Put the big adjustable wrench onto the flats of the freewheel remover, and loosen it (counterclockwise). It may take considerable force to free it, and you may even need to put a large pipe on the end of the wrench for more leverage. Have the tire on the ground for traction as you do it. Once the freewheel pops loose, be careful to not keep unscrewing it without loosening the skewer nut, as this could snap the skewer in two.
5. Loosen the skewer nut a bit, unscrew the freewheel a bit more, etc., until it spins off freely, and there is no longer any danger of having the freewheel remover pop out of the notches it engages.
6. Remove the skewer and spin off the freewheel.
7. Grease the threads on the hub and on the new freewheel.
8. Thread on the new freewheel by hand. Tighten it with a chain whip, with the freewheel remover and a wrench, or by putting it on the bike and pedaling.
9. Replace the skewer with the narrow ends of its conical springs facing inward.

vi-21 LUBRICATING FREEHUB MECHANISMS

Most people ignore their freehubs, even though they may maintain the rest of their bicycle very well. And, the simple method employed in some bike shops of dunking freehubs in a tub of solvent has a net negative effect because it pulls contaminants deep within the freehub, which then lets solvent seep out when riding, thereby contaminating lubricants added in the freehub and wheel bearings. This could explain why replacement freehubs are one of the most oft-purchased replacement parts in bike shops. But a little simple lubrication on a regular basis can prevent their demise.

Many freehubs can be adequately cleaned and lubricated simply by dripping chain lube into them, once the axle assembly is out (step a explains how). But you can only drip in a thin lubricant this way, which will not protect or hold up as long as a thicker formulation. Also, a thin lubricant will get into the wheel bearings, contaminating and thinning the grease on them. See step b for instructions on how to inject cleaning solvents as well as thicker, more protective lubricants into a Shimano freehub.

Some high-end freehubs have grease-injection holes on the freehub body that accept a fine-tip grease gun. With these, you remove the cogs to get at the hole, and you want that hole clean before inserting the grease gun tip or you will push a plug of dirt right into the freehub mechanism. Rather than using bearing grease in the grease gun, inject a thinner lube into them, such as Manitou Microlube (for forks), outboard-motor gear oil, or a special freehub formulation, such as Morningstar's Freehub Soup. Using one of these will avoid grease thickening up inside and sticking the pawls in cold temperatures, preventing engagement of the freehub. In most freehubs (but not DT freehubs and the like), the springs are very light, and it does not take much in the way of sticky or cold-thickened lube to stop them from pushing the pawls radially outward. Believe me, it's a good way to end up on your nose, when you apply power to the pedal and the freehub slips.

LUBRICATING FREEHUB MECHANISMS

If the freehub has teeth on the faces of the hub shell and freehub (DT-Hügi or old Mavic freehubs have these radial teeth), you can just drip oil into the crease between the freehub and the hub shell as you turn the freehub counterclockwise. Recent DT-Hügi hubs pull apart easily for lubrication; follow the instructions in part d.

a. Oiling a standard freehub

LEVEL 2

1. "Standard" freehubs are Shimano or of similar construction, and the best method to lubricate them is described in the next section, using a Freehub Buddy tool. But if you do not have the tool, some lubrication is way better than nothing, so at least do it this way. Disassemble the hub-axle assembly (see §vi-13 to §vi-16).
2. Wipe the inside of the drive-side bearing surface clean.
3. With the wheel lying flat and the freehub pointed up toward you, drip in chain lube between the bearing surface and the freehub body as you spin the freehub counterclockwise. You will hear the clicking noise of the freehub pawls smoothing out as lubricant reaches them. Keep it flowing until old black oil flows out of the other end of the freehub.
4. Wipe off the excess lube, and continue with the hub overhaul.

b. Thorough Shimano freehub lubrication

LEVEL 2

By far the best way to lubricate a Shimano freehub is to inject lubricant under pressure into it using a Morningstar Freehub Buddy tool (Fig. 6.32). Once the hub is apart, most of the work

6.32 **Morningstar Freehub Buddy**

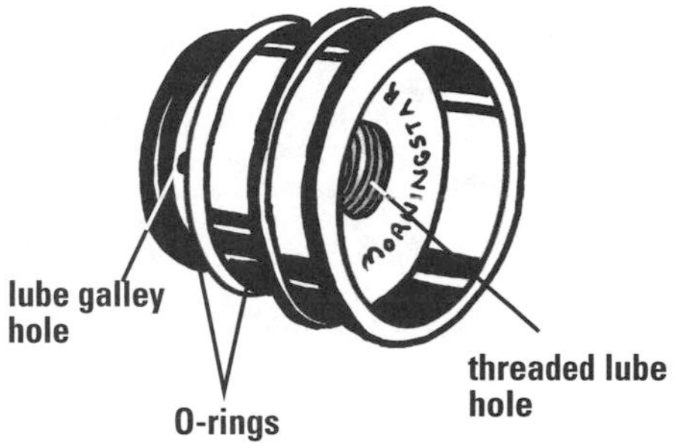

6.33 **Prying out a Shimano freehub dust cover with a J-tool**

is done. This tool is easy to use, but first you may want to order a reusable dust cap from Morningstar (see the note after step 4).

1. To use this tool, you must first disassemble the hub-axle assembly as described in §vi-15.
2. Pry out the freehub dust cover—ideally with the Morningstar J-tool (Fig. 6.33)—to expose the hub bearing race. On newer, deeper freehubs for nine-speeds, you can only start moving the dust cap by prying against the freehub fixing bolt. Then you drop a 6mm bolt down into the anchor bolt and use it as a fulcrum for the J-tool to pry against for the rest of the way.
3. Once the dust cover is off, push the Freehub Buddy into the bearing race (Fig. 6.34).
4. If the freehub has a crunchy feel to it, first inject diesel fuel (as a cleaning solvent) followed by a lubricant into the threaded hole (or the smaller tapered section below the threads) in the center of the Freehub Buddy; it will exit through the lube galley hole in the side of the tool between the two rubber O-rings (Fig. 6.32). The smaller O-ring at the closed end of the Freehub Buddy seals off the center of the hub to prevent lubricant from going in there, and the larger O-ring prevents lube from squirting back out the front of the freehub.

I recommend force-threading the tip of a turkey baster filled with bio-degreaser or diesel fuel into the threaded hole in the center of the Freehub Buddy and squirting it in as you slowly turn the freehub. Tilt the wheel with a bucket below to catch the dirty solvent. Then force-thread the tip of a tube of outboard-motor gear oil or Morningstar's Freehub Soup syringe into the Freehub Buddy's threaded hole (Fig. 6.32) and squeeze the gear oil in. Outboard-motor gear oil works great—it's the perfect weight for a freehub, and it comes in a huge tube whose end fits

6.34 **Freehub Buddy tool installed in the end of a Shimano freehub body**

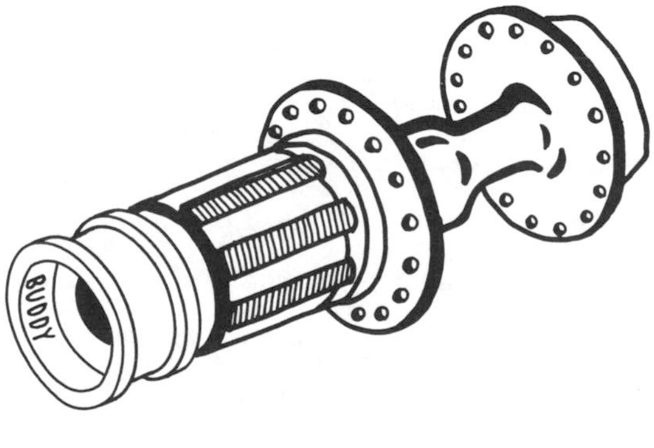

nicely into the center hole of the tool. You can also force-thread a tube of grease, or, better yet, the tip of a glue syringe or turkey baster filled with oil or your own custom mixture of compatible (i.e., synthetic with synthetic or petroleum with petroleum) oil and grease into the Freehub Buddy. Aerosol chain lube can also be squirted into the Freehub Buddy via an included plastic adapter that screws into the threaded hole and accepts the long, thin tube that comes with the spray lube.

Whatever lubricant you use, squeeze it into the Freehub Buddy until all the old dirty lubricant squeezes through the freehub and out the back end of it. Keep going until clean lube oozes out.

Other than by disassembling the entire freehub, the Freehub Buddy is the only way you can get a lubricant thicker than thin chain lube into your freehub, and a thicker lubricant protects better. Be certain that it's not too thick, however. Filling a freehub with thick grease in cold weather may cause the pawls to stick and not spring back into the freehub teeth to lock it up when you want to pedal forward. You could end up freewheeling in both directions! Always spin the freehub by hand, and, if it does not engage well, purge again with lighter oil that is compatible with the grease you put inside.

NOTE: *Many freehub dust caps will be ruined upon removal; they are usually made of stamped sheet metal. Shimano does not sell them separately, which complicates freehub service considerably. Morningstar sells machined, removable dust caps with an O-ring seal as well as freehub tools and lubricants. Contact Morningstar Tooling at P.O. Box 213, Bodfish, CA 93205-0213; e-mail: fhb@qnet.com.*

5. Once the freehub is done, overhaul the hub and replace the axle assembly.

NOTE: *You can also disassemble a Shimano freehub by unscrewing (clockwise—it's left-hand threaded) the hub bearing cup. Morningstar sells a tool that fits into the cup's two notches. I won't go into the details here, but I do illustrate it in my Mountain Bike Performance Handbook.*

A second way to clean and lubricate a Shimano freehub is to remove the freehub body with a 10mm hex wrench and completely flush it out. With a rubber stopper from a hardware store, close off the bottom of the freehub body. Pour solvent into the outer opening, spinning the mechanism, letting contaminants run out. If there is a rubber seal, remove it. Repeat until clean. Squirt in a quantity of outboard gear lube, then park the body on a paper towel and let the excess drain off. With this method, you do not need to remove the freehub body dust seal.

c. Mavic freehub lubrication

To clean and lubricate the freehub body on a current Mavic freehub, for instance, a CrossMax, you will need 5mm and 10mm hex keys and some lightweight oil (Mavic sells its M40122 mineral oil for this purpose).

1. Remove the axle-end cap on the nondrive side by pulling it out. You may need the assistance of some pliers.
2. Insert the 10mm hex key in the nondrive side of the axle and the 5mm hex key in the drive side. Unscrew in a counterclockwise direction and remove the axle.
3. Lay the wheel on its side, cog side up.
4. Carefully, while watching for flying pawl springs (clear the area so you can find them if they do take

flight), rotate the freehub body counterclockwise and pull up, removing the freehub body.

5. Clean the pawls, springs, and hub shell.
6. Replace the springs and pawls, put 10–20 drops of oil into the freehub, and reassemble. Easy, wasn't it?

d. DT-Hügi freehub lubrication

Recent DT Swiss and DT-Hügi high-end freehubs pull apart easily for cleaning and lubrication.

1. Remove the quick-release skewer.
2. Lay the wheel on its side, cogs up, grasp the cogset, and pull up. The freehub body will come off, bringing the axle-end cap with it.
3. Clean and grease the spring, both star-shaped ratchets, and the teeth that engage on the free-hub body and hub shell.
4. Push the freehub and end cap back on, and replace the skewer. That's it!

vi-22 LUBRICATING FREEWHEELS

1. Wipe dirt off of the face of the fixed part of the freewheel surrounding the axle.
2. With the wheel lying flat, and the cogs facing up toward you, drip lubricant into the crease between the fixed and moving parts of the free-wheel as you spin the cogs in a counterclockwise direction. You will hear the clicking noise inside get smoother as you get lubricant in there. Be sure to keep the lubricant going in until the old, dirty oil flows out the back side around the hub flange.
3. Wipe off the excess oil.

CHAPTER 7

BRAKES

Cables, levers, and calipers

Well, I predict that if you think about it long enough you will find yourself going round and round and round and round until you finally reach only one possible, rational, intelligent conclusion. The law of gravity and gravity itself did not exist before Isaac Newton. No other conclusion makes sense.
—Robert M. Pirsig, *Zen and the Art of Motorcycle Maintenance*

Oh, well. We came after Newton, so we'd better have a good set of brakes.

TOOLS

2.5mm, 3mm, 4mm, 5mm, and 6mm Allen wrenches

9mm and 10mm open-end wrenches

small adjustable wrench

pliers

grease

screwdrivers, flat and Phillips

TORX T25 wrench

cable-housing cutter

sharp knife

OPTIONAL TOOLS

Morningstar Roc-Tech tool

bleed kit for your hydraulic brake

Not that long ago (1996—when we published the first edition of this book), by far the most common brake for mountain bikes was the cable-actuated center-pull cantilever (Figs. 7.27–7.42). But "sidepull cantilevers," otherwise known as "V-brakes" (Fig. 7.12), completely eliminated standard cantilevers in a single season after Shimano introduced them (except on bikes using road-bike brake levers, such as for cyclo-cross and some tandems). And now, disc brakes similar to those found on a car or motorcycle (Figs. 7.19 and 7.20) have become the standard on high-end mountain bikes on all but super-light cross-country bikes.

There is good reason that the use of both brakes has become so widespread. V-brakes offer more flexibility than cantilevers; because they do not require a cable hanger, V-brakes can be used on rear-suspension frames without added complexity, and parallel-push V-brake designs allow use of different rims without pad readjustment. V-brakes are also more powerful than cantilevers because their arms are longer, and the direct cable pull from one arm to the other is more efficient than yanking up on a straddle cable tying the two arms together, the way that cantilevers operate. Adjusting V-brakes is also much quicker and simpler than adjusting cantilevers.

Disc brakes, which squeeze the pads against a hub-mounted disc (or "rotor"), stay much cleaner than rim brakes, as mud and water are thrown away from them by the tires, rather than into them, resulting in no drop off in performance in wet conditions. Additionally, the rim does not heat up during braking with disc brakes, so they can offer consistent performance over a wide range of conditions; on the other hand, braking with rim brakes can burst the tire on a long, hot descent. Like car brakes, disc brakes can also have both high stopping power and good modulation of that power. Even better than a V-brake, a disc brake does not get in the way of movement of a suspension frame, and removal and installation of the wheel require no fiddling with releasing the cable. Disc brakes have become an attractive option with the advent of lighter and simpler brake designs at a lower price, combined with built-in mounts for them on frames and suspension forks.

Still, there are a lot of old-style center-pull cantilever brakes out there; hence, working on them is thoroughly covered in this chapter. They're light and simple, they offer good mud clearance, and, above all, they stop your bike. Like V-brakes, cantilevers pivot on bosses attached to the frame and fork.

There are several other options when it comes to mountain bike brakes as well. For rear-suspension frames, linkage brakes that mount on the cantilever bosses offer the same advantage as V-brakes and disc brakes of operating without a cable stop. They rely on an articulated linkage that pulls both brake arms toward one another. The introduction of the V-brake, however, has pretty much dried up the market for these other linkage designs.

Some hydraulic rim brakes (Fig. 7.43) mount on the cantilever bosses and are also useful on rear-suspension bikes. On these brakes, the pads are driven straight toward the rim by hydraulic pressure. Because of their high stopping power and ability to lock up the wheel, these have long been the choice of observed trials riders.

Roller-cam brakes (Fig. 7.50) and U-brakes (Fig. 7.49) also mount on bosses attached to the frame and fork. You should know that the brazed-on bosses for these brakes are positioned higher than those used for standard cantilevers and V-brakes. Roller-cams and U-brakes peaked in popularity in the late 1980s, but there are still a few around.

vii-1 RELEASING BRAKES TO REMOVE A WHEEL

- **V-brakes (Fig. 7.12):** Hold the brake-arm link while pulling back and up on the cable "noodle" until it comes out of the slotted hole in the link (see Chapter 2, Fig. 2.1). You can also hold the pads against the rim and pull the cable noodle back and up to release it from the link, but this approach requires more force.
- **Disc brakes (Figs. 7.19 and 7.20):** Just drop the wheel right out. The disc falls straight out of the caliper (other than in a couple of old designs for frames and forks without built-in disc-brake mounts).
- **Cantilevers (Fig. 7.33) and U-brakes (Fig. 7.49):** Hold the pads against the rim and pull the head of the straddle cable out of the hook at the end of one brake arm (see Chapter 2, Fig. 2.2).
- **Magura hydraulic rim brakes (Fig. 7.43):** If the brake has a stiffening arch over the wheel (Fig. 7.43), pull its left end off of the bolt head it slips over. If the brake has a quick-release lever on one side, open it and pull the brake bracket off of the brake boss (Fig. 7.44). If there is no quick release, you will have to unscrew the mounting bolt on one side to pull the brake bracket off.
- **Other types:** See the section on the particular brake.

CABLES AND HOUSINGS

Given that cables transfer braking force from the levers to most brakes, proper installation and maintenance of the cables are critical to good brake per-

7.1 **Changing cable tension**

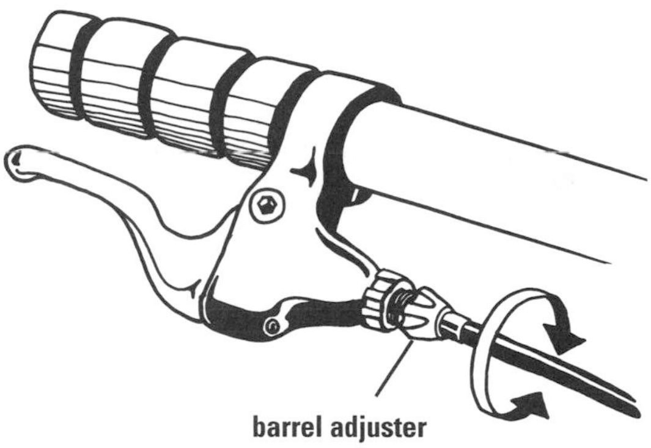

formance. If there is excess friction in the cable system, the brakes will not work properly, no matter how well the brakes, calipers, and levers are adjusted. Each cable should move freely; replace any cable that has any broken strands.

vii-2 CABLE TENSIONING

As brake pads wear and cables stretch, the cable needs to be shortened. The barrel adjuster on the brake lever (Fig. 7.1), through which the cable passes, offers adjustment to mitigate these kinds of changes. The cable should be tight enough that the lever cannot be pulled all the way to the grip, yet loose enough that the brakes (assuming they are centered and the wheels are true) are not dragging on the rims.

vii-3 INCREASING CABLE TENSION

1. Back out the slotted barrel adjuster by turning it counterclockwise (Fig. 7.1) after loosening the similarly slotted locknut (Fig. 7.2). (Determine clockwise versus counterclockwise rotation direction of the barrel adjuster from the perspective of the end where the cable housing enters.) Some barrel adjusters have no locknut (Fig. 7.11); just turn them, and they hold their adjustment by friction.
2. Adjust the cable tension so that the brake lever does not hit the grip when the brake is applied. Lock in the tension by tightening the locknut down against the lever body while holding the barrel adjuster. Again, some levers do not have a locknut on the barrel adjuster and stay in place without it, for example, some Shimano XTR levers (Fig. 7.11).
3. You may find that you need to tighten the cable more than you can by simply fiddling with the barrel adjuster. If you need to take up more slack than the barrel adjuster allows you to, tighten the cable at the brake. First, screw the barrel adjuster most of the way in. This leaves some adjustment in the system for brake setup and cable stretch over time. Loosen the bolt clamping the cable at the brake. Check the cable for wear. If there are any frayed strands, replace it. (See Cable Installation, §vii-6.) Otherwise, pull the cable tight, and retighten the clamping bolt. Tension the cable as needed with the barrel adjuster.

vii-4 REDUCING CABLE TENSION

1. Back out the locknut on the barrel adjuster (Fig. 7.2) a few turns (counterclockwise), unless yours is the type without a locknut. (Determine clockwise versus counterclockwise rotation direction of the barrel adjuster from the perspective of the end where the cable housing enters.)
2. Turn the barrel adjuster clockwise (Fig. 7.1) until your brake pads are properly spaced from the rim.
3. If your lever has a locknut, tighten it clockwise against the lever body to lock in the adjustment.
4. Double-check that the cable is tight enough so that the lever cannot be squeezed all the way to

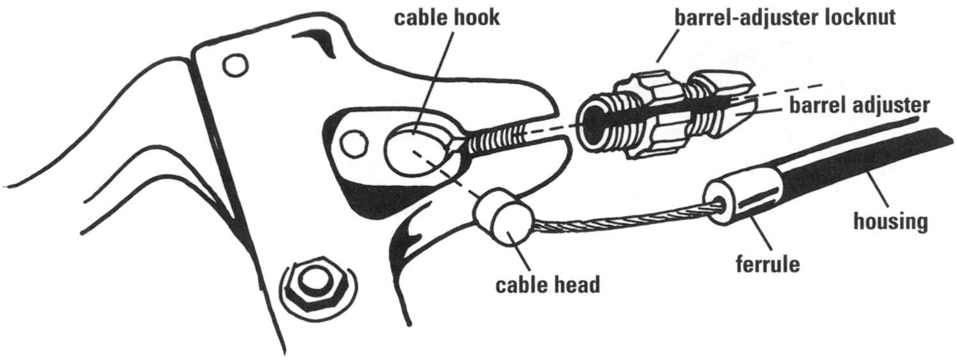

7.2 Cable installation at brake lever—note lined up slots in lever body, barrel adjuster, and locknut

the grip. Check pad alignment with the rim braking surface and adjust as needed (see §vii-10b and §vii-21 for v-brakes and cantilevers respectively).

vii-5 CABLE MAINTENANCE

1. If the cable is frayed or kinked, or has any broken strands, replace it. (See Cable Installation, §vii-6.)
2. If the cable is not sliding well, lubricate it. Use molybdenum disulfide grease if you have it; otherwise, try a chain lubricant. Standard lithium-based greases can eventually gum up cables and restrict movement.
3. To lubricate, open the brake (via the cable quick release as you do when you remove a wheel; see §vii-1).
4. Pull each section of cable housing out of each slotted cable stop. If your bike does not have slotted cable stops, you will have to pull out the entire cable.
5. Slide the housing up the cable, rub lubricant with your fingers on the cable section that was inside the housing, and slide the housing back into place.
6. If the cable still sticks, replace it.

vii-6 CABLE INSTALLATION

As with chains and derailleur cables, brake-cable replacement is a maintenance operation, not a repair operation; don't wait until a cable breaks or seizes up to replace it. Try using die-drawn cables; they have been pulled through a constricting die and will operate with less friction, because the exterior strands have been flattened. Purchase good-quality cables and housings lined with Teflon, or get Gore-Tex–coated cables, which come with their own housings and full-length cable sheaths. Most brake-cable housing is spiral-wrapped to prevent splitting under braking pressure (see Chapter 5, Fig. 5.18). Teflon-lined housing reduces friction and is a must on a mountain bike unless you're using housings with their own separate sheaths, like Nokon (you assemble the housing onto the sheath out of separate snap-together segments) or Gore-Tex. Gore-Tex RideOn cables and housings, when properly installed, can reduce friction significantly and stay that way by virtue of being completely sealed. The Gore-Tex must be peeled off of the cable at the last couple of inches on both ends, where it enters the brake lever and clamps to the brake; if this is not done, the Gore-Tex coating can get completely wadded up and prevent cable movement. A thin plastic tube runs through all of the housing segments and sheaths the cable end-to-end against crud. A rubber accordion-like seal (called the "Grub") covers the end of the plastic tube at each brake and prevents the access of dirt at its one possible entry point.

NOTE: *When installing a new cable, it is a good idea to replace the housings as well, even if you don't think they need to be replaced. Daily riding in particularly dirty conditions means that cables and housings may have to be replaced every couple of months.*

Except in cases in which manufacturers supply lubricants with their cables and housings to be applied during their installation, my opinion is that it is usually best not to use a lubricant on new cables and lined housing. It can gum up inside the housing and attract dirt.

1. Remove the old cable, making sure not to lose any parts of the cable clamps or straddle-cable holders.
2. Cut the housing sections long enough to reach the brakes, and route them so that they do not make any sharp bends. If you are replacing existing housings, look at where they bend before removing them. If the bends are smooth and do not bind when the wheel is turned or the suspension moves, cut the new housings to the same lengths. If you see that binding has been occurring, cut each new segment longer than you think necessary and keep trimming it back until it gives the smoothest path possible for the cable, without the cable tension being affected by turning the handlebar or by movement of the rear swingarm on a full-suspension bike. Use a cutter specifically designed for cutting housings, or a sharp side-cutter.
3. After cutting, make sure the end faces of the housing are flat. If not, flatten them with a file or a clipper.
4. If the end of the Teflon housing liner is mashed shut after cutting, open it up with a sharp object such as a nail or a toothpick, or push a length of cable through from the opposite end to open up the closed-off liner end.
5. Slip a ferrule over each housing end for support (see Chapter 5, Fig. 5.18).
6. Decide which hand you want to control which brake (the standard is that the right hand controls the rear brake).
7. Tighten the adjusting barrel to within one turn of being screwed all of the way in. Rotate the barrel adjuster and locknut so that their slots line up with those on the lever and lever body (Fig. 7.2).
8. Insert the round head of the cable into the lever's cable hook (Figs. 7.2, 7.9, and 7.11).
9. Pull the cable down into the lined-up slots on the barrel and nut. Once the cable is in place, turn the barrel so that the slots are offset to prevent the cable from slipping back out. If you have an old-style lever that is not slotted, you will have to feed the entire length of the cable from the cable hook out through the hole in the lever body.
10. With luck, you have slotted cable stops on your frame. They make cable installation a lot easier. Under the assumption that you have them, slide the rear-wheel brake cable through the housing sections and then route the cable and housing from the brake lever to the brake, snapping the housing and cable into the slot in each stop. If you don't have slotted stops, you will have to feed the cable through the hole in each cable stop.
11. For the front brake, continue at step 12. For the rear brake, skip to step 13.
12. Front-wheel brake: With a V-brake, terminate the housing in the top of the "noodle" guide tube

7.3–7.5 Examples of cable hangers for cantilever brakes

7.3 Stem-clamp cable hanger

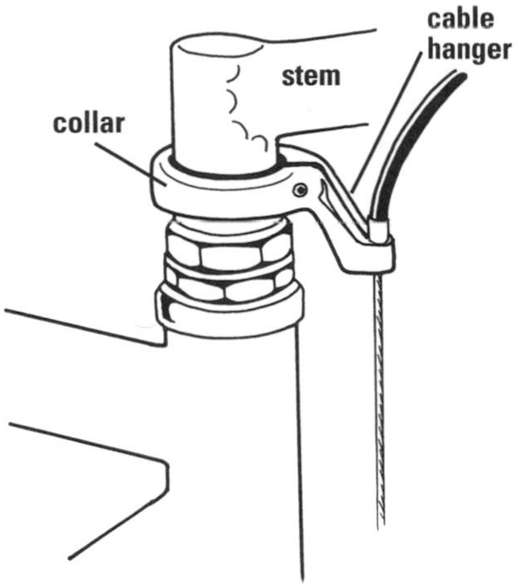

7.4 Headset cable hanger

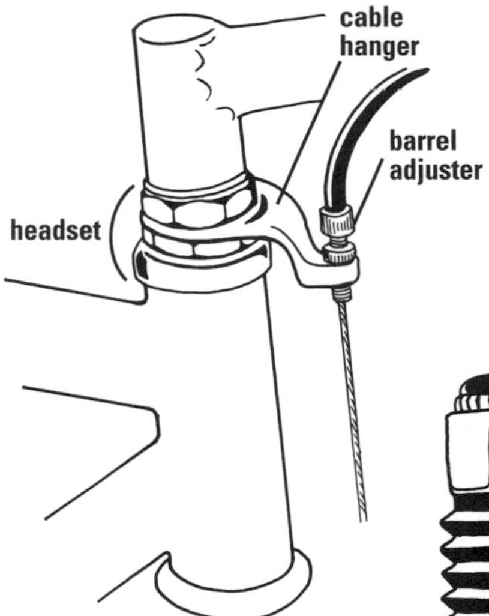

7.5 Suspension-fork cable hanger

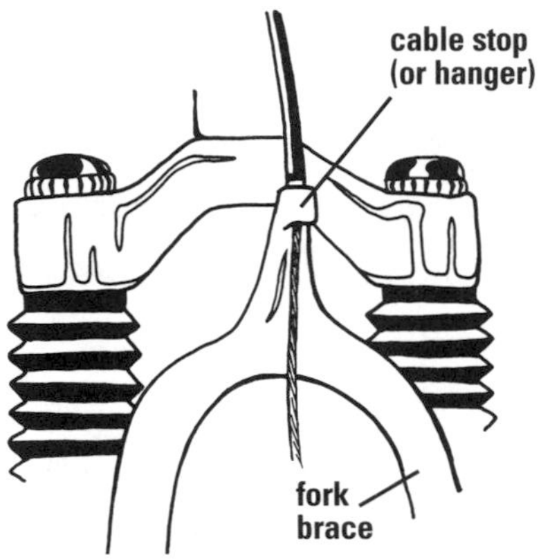

7.6 Tightening cantilever brake cable

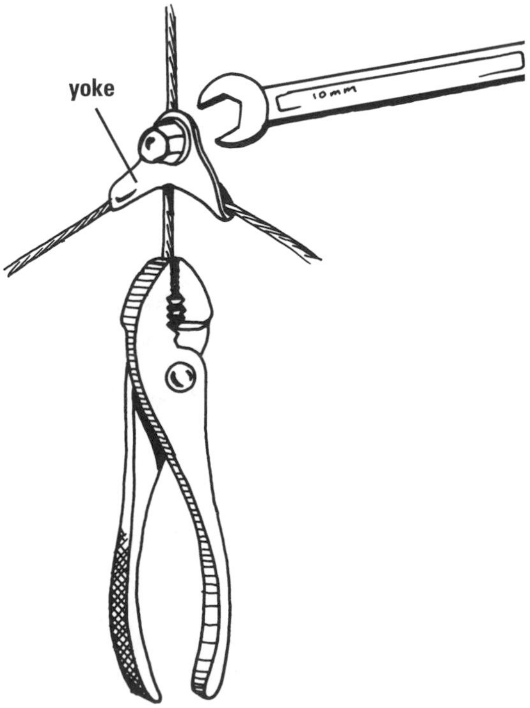

(Fig. 7.12 or 7.13). On a cable-actuated disc brake (Fig. 7.20), the housing usually terminates at a stop on the brake caliper. With a cantilever brake and a suspension fork, terminate the front-brake housing at the stop on the fork brace (Fig. 7.5). For cantilevers without suspension, you may have a cable stop that is integral to the stem or one attached to the headset (Fig. 7.4). If your brake cable passes through an integral cable stop on the stem or a stem through-hole, I recommend bypassing it, as either requires readjustment of the front brake with any change in stem height. Instead, use a cable hanger with a collar that slips around the stem above the headset (Fig. 7.3) or one that slips into the headset stack between locknuts (Fig. 7.4).

13. Attach the cable to the brake. (See the section on your type of brake.) Pull the cable taut and

7.7–7.8 **Brake lever and shifter installation**

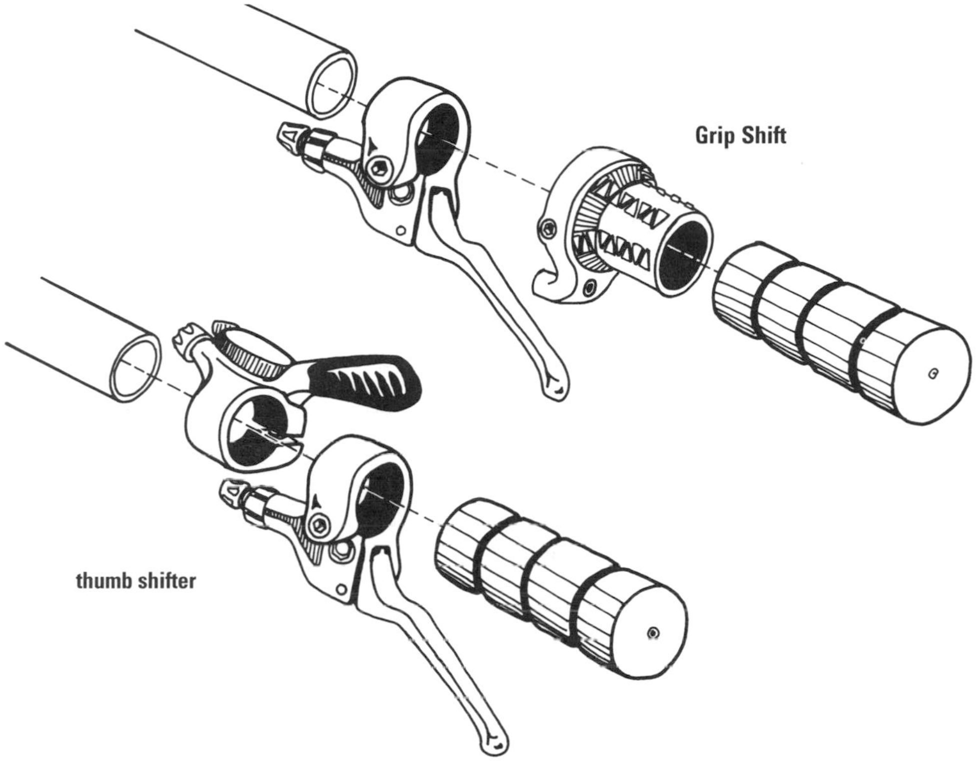

tighten the cable-clamping bolt (Fig. 7.6 for some cantilevers, Figs. 7.37–7.39 for others, and 7.12 or 7.13 for V-brakes). Pull the lever as hard as you can and squeeze it repeatedly for about a minute to stretch the new cable.

14. Adjust cable tension with the lever barrel adjuster (as described in §vii-2 to §vii-4).
15. Cut off cable ends about 2½ inches past the cable anchor bolts. Crimp end caps on all exposed cable ends to prevent fraying (Fig. 5.31 in Chapter 5), and bend the extra to the side. Follow adjustment procedure for your brake, if need be.

NOTE: *Once the cable has been properly installed, the lever should snap back quickly when released. If it does not, recheck the cables and housings for free movement and sharp bends. Release the cable at the brake, and check the levers for free movement. With the cable still loose, check that the brake pads do not drag on the tire as they return to the neutral position; make sure the brake arms rotate freely on their pivot bosses, and check that the brake-arm return springs pull the pads away from the rims.*

BRAKE LEVERS

The levers must operate smoothly and be set up so that you can easily reach them while riding.

vii-7 LEVER LUBRICATION AND SERVICE

1. Lubricate all pivot points in the lever with grease or oil.
2. Check return-spring function for levers that have them.
3. Make sure that the lever or lever body is not bent in a way that hinders movement.
4. Check for stress cracks, and if you find any, replace the lever.

vii-8 LEVER REMOVAL, INSTALLATION, AND POSITIONING

Brake levers mount on the handlebar inboard of the grip and bar end. They are also mounted inboard of twist shifters and usually outboard of thumb shifters (Figs. 7.7 and 7.8). Some integrated systems include both brake lever and shifter in a single unit (Fig. 7.11). Dual-lever trigger shifters on separate band clamps usually mount inboard of the brake lever but can sometimes have that order reversed.

Most brake levers have a wrap-around clamp with a single bolt, so that grips, bar ends, and twist shifters cannot be on the handlebar when removing and installing them, as described below. But some high-end levers mount with two bolts and a separate semi-circular band; these can come off and on the handlebar without removing bar ends, grips, and shifters.

1. If installed, remove the bar end by loosening the mounting bolt and sliding it off.
2. Remove the handlebar grip by lifting the edges on both ends, squirting rubbing alcohol or water underneath, and twisting it until it becomes free and slides off. If you have closed-end grips and an air compressor, you can blow them off by puncturing the end of one grip and blasting air into it with the end of the air blowgun pressed against the hole. Seal the end of the other grip if it also has a hole, and cover the end of the handlebar with your hand once the opposite grip has blown off, in order to blow the one with the blowgun off toward you.
3. If installed, remove the twist shifter by loosening the mounting bolt and sliding it off.
4. Loosen the brake lever's mounting bolt with an Allen wrench and slide the lever off.
5. Slide the new lever on, and replace the other parts in the order in which they were installed. Slide the grips on using rubbing alcohol (it dries quickly) as a lubricant; water works, too, but the grips will twist for a lot more rides. With closed-end grips and an air compressor, you also can inflate each grip so it slides on in a reversal of the removal procedure in step 2.
6. Make certain the levers do not extend beyond the ends of the handlebar. Rotate them and slide them inward to your preferred location. See the Pro Tip in the next section for positioning for high performance.
7. Tighten all mounting bolts on levers, shifters, and bar ends.

NOTE: *If you have a carbon-fiber handlebar, you may need to use lower than normal torque on the mounting bolts to prevent damage to the handlebar. Consult the handlebar or bicycle manufacturer regarding this detail.*

vii-9 REACH AND LEVERAGE ADJUSTMENTS

Some levers have a reach-adjustment set screw; usually it's on the lever body near the barrel adjuster (Figs. 7.9 and 7.10) or under the lever. If you have small hands, you may want to tighten the reach-adjustment set screws so you can reach the levers more easily.

Some brakes also have a leverage adjustment (Figs. 7.9 and 7.11), which moves the cable end in or out relative to the lever pivot. The closer the cable passes by the pivot, the higher the leverage, but the less cable the lever pulls, vice versa. To start with, set the leverage adjustment at the position that offers the weakest leverage (sometimes demarcated with an "L"

7.9 Shimano brake lever for simple V-brakes

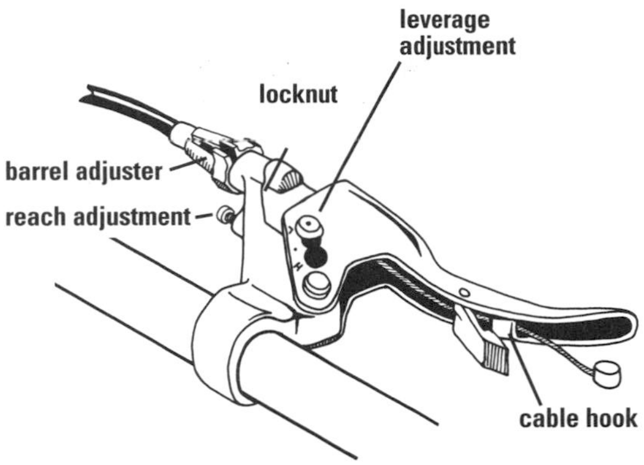

7.10 Brake reach adjustment

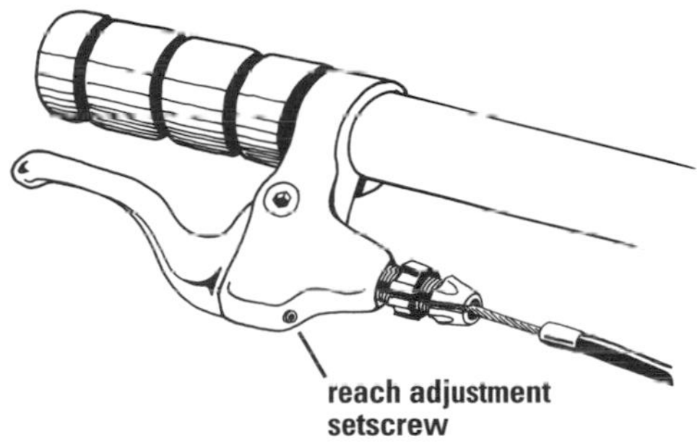

7.11 Rapidfire integrated shift/brake levers (Shimano XTR shown)

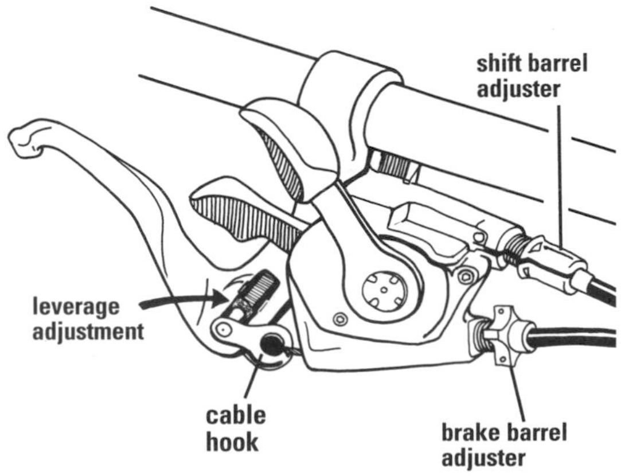

on the lever), where the cable head or cable path is farthest from the pivot. Only increase the leverage if you become very confident in using the brakes.

On Shimano XTR, Avid, and recent SRAM brake levers, a long screw performs the leverage adjustment (Fig. 7.11). On Shimano XT and older SRAM, as well as current low-end SRAM levers, leverage is adjusted by installing, relocating, or removing a series of inserts. On Shimano LX, DX, and M600, leverage is adjusted by loosening a small bolt on the upper face of the lever arm with a 3mm Allen key, sliding the leverage adjuster up and down, and retightening the bolt (Fig. 7.9). The ends of the adjustment range are generally clearly marked with an "L" for lowest leverage—cable path farthest from the lever pivot—and "H" for highest leverage—cable path closest to the lever pivot. These Shimano (LX, DX, and M600) and SRAM levers have a hook to hold the cable end far out along the lever (Fig. 7.9); the cable passes over a trough whose position away from the pivot determines the leverage. On yet some other levers, a rotating notched eccentric disc adjusts the cable-head position relative to the pivot. Again, remember that leverage is increased (and amount of cable pulled is reduced) if the cable head or cable path is closer to the lever pivot, and vice versa.

SAFETY NOTE: *The levers for V-brakes are initially set up with intentionally low leverage (and correspondingly high cable pull), because of the high leverage of the long brake arms. If you use a lever from a cantilever brake with a V-brake, you have more leverage and can end up on your nose. Always start with V-brake levers adjusted to lowest leverage (cable passing farthest from the lever pivot), and increase from that setting if you wish.*

PRO TIP

Maximizing V-Brakes

To get maximum performance out of your V-brakes (sidepull cantilevers) and minimize your effort, you should increase the leverage, but you must also place the lever so that you can only reach it with your forefinger; otherwise you can grab too much brake and do an endo (i.e., go arse over teakettle).

Even though a lot of people want a hard feel to the brakes, the harder the brakes feel, the less power you have. The hard feel indicates that you have less mechanical advantage; it feels hard because you are doing all of the work! A softer feel indicates that you have more leverage. You will do less work and stop the bike more easily.

Set your brake levers up for high leverage, even though you may lose some pad travel. You will be trying to move the cable hook (or the cable path) closer to the lever pivot, usually by turning in a leverage-adjustment screw, by removing some inserts under the cable hook, or by moving the position of an adjuster screw (Figs. 7.9 and 7.11).

Move your levers inboard so that the tip of the lever is under your index finger. The lever will bypass your second finger and let you pull it to the grip, rather than losing some range by hitting your finger(s). Hold the handlebar with three fingers and pull the lever with one. Make sure you pull on the end of the lever, because that is where the leverage is. You will find that you can grip the handlebar better, and your arms will stay more relaxed when braking. In addition, it will be comfortable to simply rest your forefingers on the levers so that you will be ready to brake at any time. I suggest placing the levers of powerful disc brakes in this position, too.

Note that it is easy to move the brake lever inboard far enough with twist shifters and with Shimano Rapidfire or Dual Control integral brake and shift levers, but it may not be easy with Rapidfire or SRAM trigger levers on a separate band clamp. The band clamp usually goes inboard of the brake lever, and it may prevent the lever from moving inward enough for a rider with large hands (and bar ends taking up some handlebar real estate) to get unimpeded one-finger braking. The shifter band clamp can hit the bulge or curve of the handlebar and stop before it has moved inward enough that the brake lever clears the second finger. And even though wider handlebars are back in fashion, the bends in a riser bar can be too far outboard to allow the shifter and the brake lever to move inboard as far as you might wish. Try putting the shifter outboard of the brake lever, and see if you can get the function and finger clearance you desire, especially with SRAM trigger levers.

BRAKE CALIPERS

V-Brakes

V-brakes (a.k.a. "sidepull cantilevers") have tall, cantilever-like arms, a horizontal cable-hook link on top of one arm, and a cable clamp on the top of the other. A curved aluminum guide pipe (noodle) hooks into the horizontal link, taking the cable from the end of the housing out through the link, and directing it toward the cable clamp on the opposite arm (Figs. 7.12 and 7.13). V-brakes usually, although not always, have long, thin brake pads with threaded posts. Some V-brakes, such as Shimano XT and XTR (Fig. 7.12) and

Avid Arch Supreme, have "parallel-push" linkages, which move the brake pads horizontally rather than in an arc around the brake boss the way a cantilever moves. Simple V-brake designs mount the pad directly to the arm so that it moves in a cantilever-like arc (Fig. 7.13).

V-brakes are extremely powerful and can be very grabby if used with a center-pull cantilever brake lever; it is important that you use the levers that were designed for use with V-brakes if those brakes are the type you have (see §vii-9 regarding leverage).

7.12 **Shimano parallel-push V-brake**

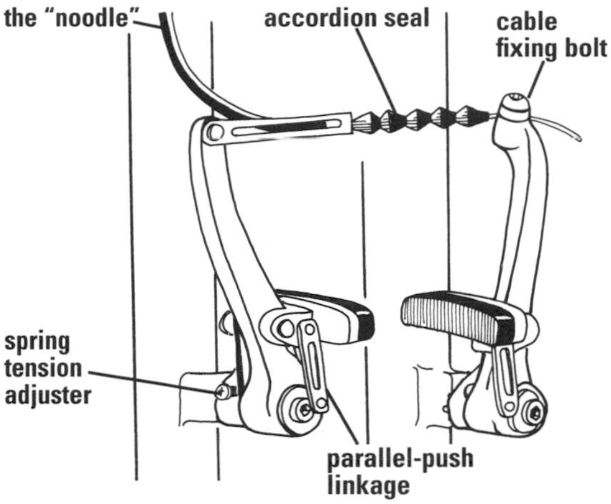

7.13 **Simple V-brake (a.k.a. sidepull cantilever brake)**

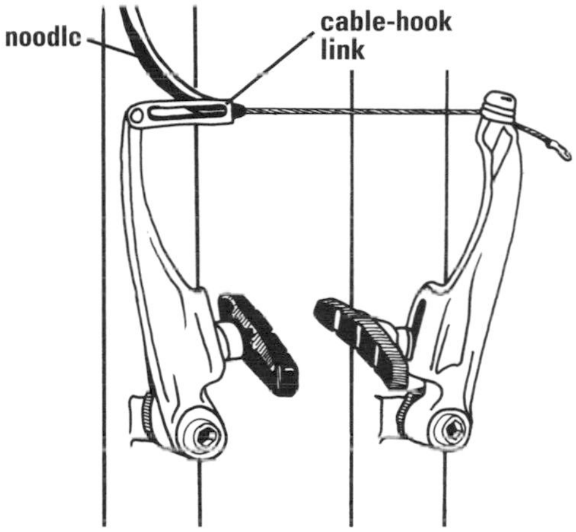

7.14 **Finalizing pad to rim adjustment**

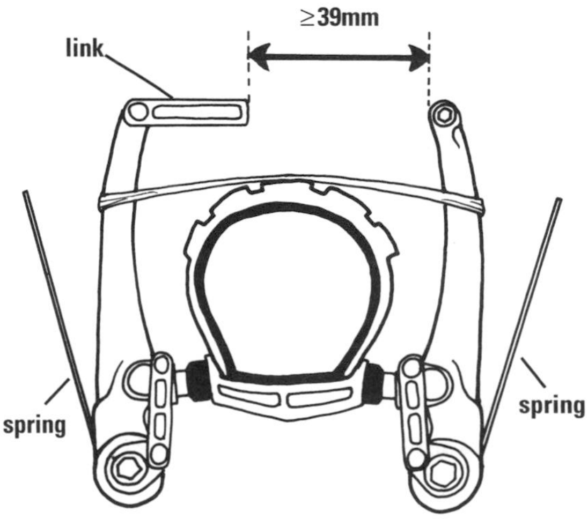

vii-10 V-BRAKE INSTALLATION AND ADJUSTMENT

a. V-brake mounting

1. Grease the brake bosses on your frame or fork.
2. With Shimano, Dia-Compe, and most other V-brakes, slide each brake arm on, inserting the spring pin into the center hole of the boss. You may need to pull outward on the return spring (the tall vertical wire—see Fig. 7.14) to get the pin to line up with the center hole. Tighten the brake bolt with its washer into the boss. You want this bolt to be snug, but if you overtighten it, you can mushroom the end of the brake boss so the brake arm does not pivot freely. See the torque table in Appendix D.

   With Avid Arch Supreme brakes, slide two supplied washers onto each brake boss to prevent binding of the brake-pivot cartridge bearings. Slide the brake on and tighten the bolt. Using the supplied bolts and washers, bolt each end of the pivot arch to the hole in the arm adjacent to each brake pad.

b. V-brake pad adjustment

These instructions apply to threaded pad posts. For V-brakes with unthreaded pad posts (Dia-Compe 747),

7.15 **V-brake pad-holder assembly**

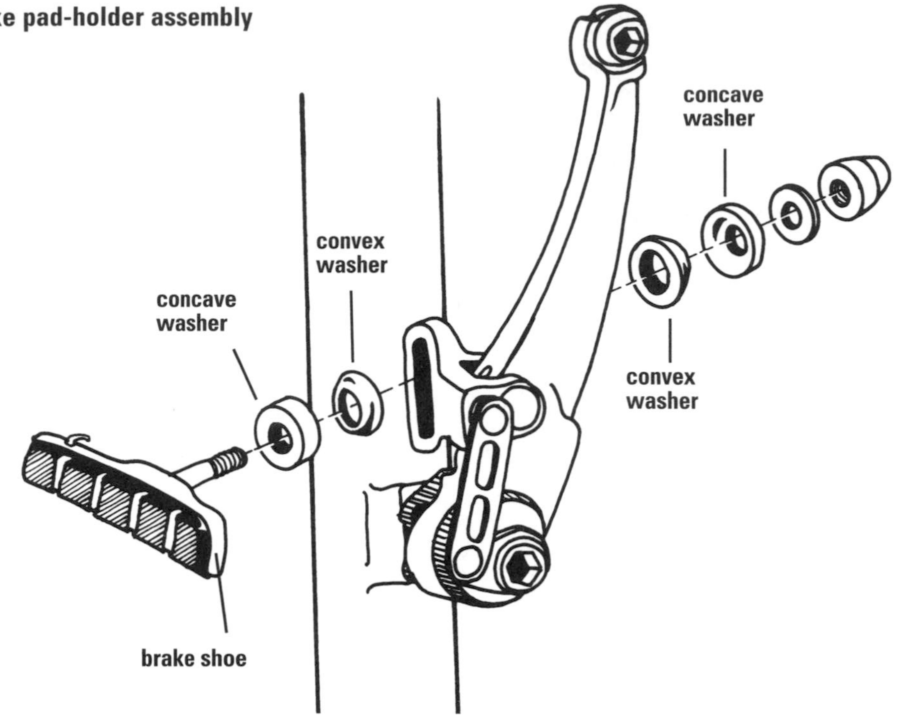

it is best to follow the pad-adjustment procedure for cantilever brakes, in §vii-21, coupled with the pad offset described in step 4 below. (Note that Dia-Compe 747s do not hold the adjustment of their pads well, no matter how much you tighten the eye-bolt nut on the unthreaded pad posts. You may be able to increase the friction between the eye-bolt washers and the curved brake arm by sanding the contacting surfaces on the arms and washers. The brakes will not look as nice, but at least they may work.)

V-BRAKE INSTALLATION & ADJUSTMENT

1. Roughly adjust each pad by loosening the pad nut, pushing the arm toward the rim, and tightening the pad nut with the pad flat against the rim.
2. Determine the proper amount of pad offset from the brake arms: While holding the pads against the rim, measure the space between the end of the link to the inside edge of the opposite brake arm (Fig. 7.14); this length should be at least 39mm. If it is less than 39mm, the end of the noodle can hit the opposite arm when the brake is applied, particularly as the pads wear. Obviously, this placement would prevent the brakes from grabbing the rims, which is not what you have in mind when you apply the brakes; the narrower the rim is, the more this becomes an issue.
3. Set the pad offset (to ensure that the length in Figure 7.14 is ≥39mm) usually by moving stacks of interchangeable pad washers of varying thickness from side to side. Threaded-post pads are offset from the brake arms by concave washers of various thicknesses nesting over convex washers on either side of the mounting tab (Fig. 7.15). By moving the washer stacks from one side of the mounting tab to the other, set the pad offset so that (1) the space between the end of the link and the inside edge of the opposite brake arm (Fig. 7.14) is at least 39mm, and (2) the top of each brake arm is a little outside of vertical relative to the brake mounting bolt when the brake is applied (i.e., the arms are

approximately parallel). On Shimano V-brakes, as they come out of the box, the concave washer on the pad side is 6mm thick, and the one on the nut side is 3mm thick. Avid offers more options, using a 1mm flat washer and 3mm and 5mm concave washers, which can be stacked in combinations.

4. Finalize the pad-to-rim adjustment: On brakes with vertical return springs, such as Shimano and Avid, flip the springs off of their retention pins and connect the tops of the arms together with a rubber band to lightly hold the pads against the rim (Fig. 7.14). Otherwise, hold the pad against the rim or put a rubber band around the brake lever after you have connected the cable.
5. Loosen the pad anchor nut, and then tighten the pad-fixing nut with the pad held flat against the rim. Toe-in (Fig. 7.32), so that the front end of the pad hits the rim before the rear end, is not necessary in many cases, but it is recommended if you have any brake squeal. To get just a bit of toe-in, slip a paper clip between the tail of the brake pad and the rim, and then hold the pad against the rim and tighten it down. The pad's top edge should be about 1mm below the edge of the rim.
6. Rehook the return springs behind the retention pins.

NOTE: *Many high-end V-brakes are "parallel-push," i.e., the linkage attached to the pad-mounting bracket keeps the pad moving horizontally as it contacts and leaves the rim surface (Figs. 7.12 and 7.14–7.16). When interchanging wheels with these brakes, as long as the rims have parallel braking surfaces, there is usually no need to adjust the pads; the only necessary adjustment is to the cable length, if the rim width varies.*

c. Threading the cable to the brake through the curved alloy guide pipe (the "noodle")

For the rear brake, pick the one of the two supplied noodles whose curvature and length best fits your frame for a smooth cable path. Bend the noodle if need be. Hook the head of the noodle into the notch in the horizontal link.

1. Slip the rubber accordion-like dust boot onto the cable, big end first, and over the tip of the noodle (Fig. 7.12). A tight-fitting O-ring ("cable donut"—see Fig. 5.32) on the cable butted up against the narrow end of the boot is a good idea to prevent the boot from falling off of the noodle. If you are using Gore-Tex RideOn cables, you can dispense with the boot and use Gore's little "Grub" seal instead. The Grub seals the end of the Gore plastic sheath, which should be cut to terminate halfway between the guide-pipe tip and the cable anchor bolt.
2. Connect the cable to the anchor bolt on the opposite arm.
3. Set the cable length so that there is 1–1.5mm of space between each pad and the rim. Tighten the cable anchor bolt with the lever barrel adjuster screwed out one turn. Make sure the wheel is centered in the frame or fork.

d. V-brake centering and/or spring-tension adjustment

- Some V-brakes (Shimano) use a vertical return spring (Fig. 7.14) adjusted by a screw at the mounting pivot on each arm (Fig. 7.12); turn the screw clockwise to move the arm farther from the rim, and vice versa. A quick way to increase spring tension or center the brakes on the trail is to bend the vertical springs outward after pulling them off the retention pins on the back of the arms (Fig. 7.14) without fooling with the screws, and rehook them behind the retention pins.

- Dia-Compe 747s use a spring adjuster cam rotated by a 5mm Allen key; turn it toward the imprinted "H" or "L" for more or less spring tension.
- Avid Arch Supremes have an innovative (and very quick) way to set the spring balance. While lightly squeezing the lever so that the pads touch the rim, loosen and retighten the plastic knob at the top of the arch. The W-shaped spring passes through the knob and hooks on the arms; it automatically finds its balance point when the knob is loosened.

If your V-brake springs do not adjust with any of the above three methods, look at spring-tension adjustment for cantilever brakes, §vii-23, because any of the spring configurations used in cantilevers could be built into a V-brake.

IMPORTANT: *Regardless of the type of brake you have, after these adjustments, squeeze the brake lever hard a number of times to stretch the cable and make sure it does not slip at the anchor bolt.*

NOTE: *If a brake arm does not turn freely on the boss, the boss may be damaged. Bulged or mushroomed bosses can be filed and sanded smaller; bent or broken ones must be replaced (with luck they are the bolt-on type; otherwise new ones must be welded on).*

ANOTHER NOTE: *Parallel-push V-brakes, such as high-end Shimano and Avid, often do not hold their pad-centering adjustment, especially when new. You may frequently find that one pad is very close to, or rubbing, the rim after a ride in which they started centered. This is because any bit of grit in any of the numerous pivots will change the return friction on one side relative to the other side, especially as the pivots break in. Brake adjustment is an exercise in symmetry; it can be easily thrown off.*

7.16 Pad replacement on V-brakes

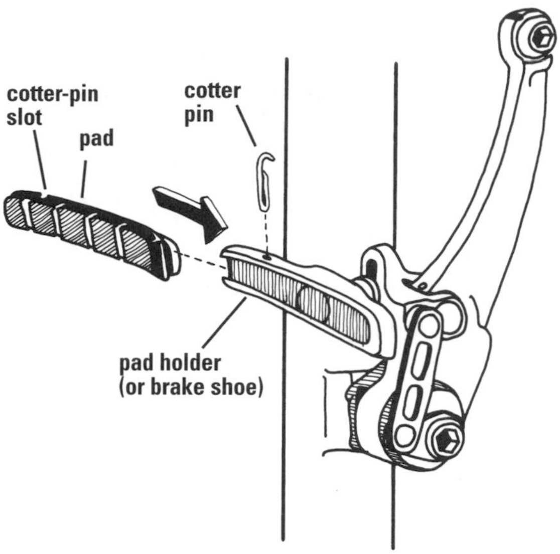

REPLACEMENT OF V-BRAKE PADS IN PAD HOLDERS

vii-11 REPLACEMENT OF V-BRAKE PADS IN PAD HOLDERS

It is only on high-end brakes that you will find removable pads that slide in and out of permanent pad holders.

1. With a pair of pliers, remove the cotter pin from the top of the pad holder (Fig. 7.16).
2. Slide the old pad out of its groove in the pad holder (Fig. 7.16).
3. Slide in the new pad, paying attention to the "R" and "L" markings for right and left and the "Forward" direction arrow, if present. Right and left must be heeded, as these pads only have a slot for the cotter pin on one end. Avid pads have two cotter-pin slots and can be oriented either way.
4. Replace the cotter pin, and check that the pad is secure in the holder.

NOTE: *Avid pads are not interchangeable with most other pad holders, which have a curved groove. Avid pad holders have a straight groove, even though the pad itself is curved. The pads are flexible enough that they can be jammed into each other's holders in a pinch, but the outer curvature of the pad will no longer match that of the rim.*

vii-12 PAD REPLACEMENT ON V-BRAKES WITH ONE-PIECE PAD AND THREADED POST

1. Note how the washers are stacked on the pad post (Fig. 7.15).
2. Unscrew the shoe anchor nut and remove the old pad and post from the arm.
3. After replacing the concave and convex washers as they were, bolt the new pad to the arm. The convex washers are placed on either side of the brake arm with flat sides facing each other (Fig. 7.15). The concave washers are placed adjacent to the convex washers so that the concave and convex surfaces meet and allow angular adjustability of the pad.
4. Follow pad-adjustment procedure, §vii-10b.

vii-13 PAD REPLACEMENT ON V-BRAKES WITH UNTHREADED PAD POSTS

Follow pad replacement and adjustment procedures for cantilever brakes, §vii-20 and §vii-21.

DISC BRAKES

Disc brakes can offer a high "gee-whiz" factor as well as great stopping and modulation, but installing them correctly is a must. Once properly installed, discs require less maintenance than do rim brakes, because the tire is not dragging mud into them. But disc brakes do require more care and cleanliness. There is no need to be intimidated, though. Although being precise, disc brakes are really quite simple.

vii-14 DISC-BRAKE INSTALLATION AND ADJUSTMENT

Once you are used to it, you will find that you can install and adjust many disc brakes quicker than V-brakes or cantilevers! Simply stated, you just bolt the rotor to the hub, tighten the lever onto the handlebar (see §vii-8 for instructions on this), bolt the caliper to the mounts on the frame or fork, and tie down the hose or cable. But the space between the pads and rotor is small, and the speed of accurate mounting depends on you, the brake, and the type of mount the brake accepts.

The two types of mounts built into frames and forks are "International Standard" (IS) mounts (Fig. 7.19) and "post mounts" (Fig. 7.20). IS mounts are drilled transversely (toward the wheel) and are not threaded, whereas post mounts (now found primarily on Manitou forks) are threaded directly into the frame or fork. IS mounts, front or rear, are 51mm apart. Since the 2000 model year, the post mount standard for forks was 74mm, whereas original Hayes and Manitou front post mounts were 68.8mm apart. For a brief time, Hayes and Manitou adopted 70mm front post-mount caliper spacing to mount the various adapter brackets but abandoned it within a season. They switched to 74mm spacing and redesigned all of the brackets to have one caliper that fit all brackets. (Confused yet?) Rear chainstay post mounts are 21.5mm apart; early seat-stay post mounts are also 21.5mm apart, but others are spaced at 74mm.

CAUTION: Unless you want to do a lot of fiddling and chasing of obsolete parts, *do not* buy pre–2000-year disc brakes on eBay or from anywhere else, because chances are they will not work with current forks and hubs. In around 1997, many disc-brake and suspension-fork makers agreed on the IS mount of 51mm front and rear (Manitou, whose engineers strongly think that the radial mounting of the post mount is superior, never agreed to the International Standard), but the agreement did not cover rotor mounting, and manufacturers were all over the map with rotor-mounting systems. So prior to 2000, rotors other than Hayes will generally not fit on current disc-brake hubs. In 2000, fork and disc-brake makers adopted the IS 2000 standard, which also incorporated the six-bolt rotor-mounting pattern that Hayes had established. And although old Hayes rotors will work on current wheels, Hayes's post-mount caliper dimensions, as you saw above, were all over the place until 2000, so you would at a minimum need an obsolete adapter to put a pre-2000 Hayes brake on a current IS fork (and it would not work at all with a current post-mount fork). Also, the Hayes rear chainstay post-mount dimensions, which were incorporated into early Trek, Schwinn, and Gary Fisher frames, among others, have been largely abandoned in favor of rear IS mounts only.

The good news is that since 2000, the forks, frames, brakes, and rotors of the major manufacturers, with the exception of Shimano's Center-Lock rotor mount described below, are completely cross-compatible.

After installing, don't expect to get full brake performance until you have made a number of hard stops (maybe ten) to wear in the pads and rotor.

Avoid touching the rotor's braking surface and getting grease or oil on it. If brake performance ever drops off, try cleaning the rotor and pads with alcohol.

Never squeeze the lever without a disc or another spacer between the pads, as you can push a piston all of the way out. For travel with the wheel out, insert a spacer between the pads—either one that came with the brake or a chunk of corrugated cardboard you cut for the purpose.

a. Rotor mounting and removal

Installation

Up until model year 2000, rotor bolt patterns varied. Starting in 2000, Hayes's six-bolt pattern became the standard, even for Hayes's competitors, such as Shimano, Formula, SRAM, Magura, Grimeca, and Avid. However, Shimano, being the 500-pound gorilla of bicycle components, can dictate standards, and its current brake rotors (starting in 2003 with XTR and in 2004 with XT) have a splined hub attachment, called "Center-Lock." The splined aluminum adapter riveted to the steel rotor slips onto the splines of the hub, and a single lockring holds it in place. Other manufacturers are offering hubs compatible with these rotors. (Incidentally, the rotor should still be positioned in the same place relative

7.17 Bolting rotor onto hub (Shimano XT shown)

to the axle end in either case, so a wheel with a Center-Lock rotor should work fine in a brake set up for a bolt-on rotor of the same diameter.)

Multiple-bolt rotor

1. Loosely bolt the rotor to the hub flange (Fig. 7.17). The logo on the rotor should face outward so that the rotor turns in the proper direction.
2. Gradually snug the bolts, alternately tightening opposing bolts, rather than adjacent bolts. A hex key or a TORX wrench (like a hex key, but with a star-shaped end [see Fig. 1.3]) is required for this; the wrench is usually supplied with brakes with TORX bolts. Torque for rotor bolts ranges from 18 in-lbs (2 N·m) for some manufacturers to 55 in-lbs (6 N·m) for others.
3. Shimano asks you to make one additional step and bend over the corners of small spring-steel plates that should be installed under each pair of bolts (Fig. 7.17). The heads of the bolts are triangular, and bending the plates over them is designed to ensure that they cannot unscrew. Tap a screwdriver with a hammer while its tip is against a plate corner to bend up the plate edges against the screw heads.)

Shimano Center-Lock splined rotor

1. Slip the rotor splines over the hub splines (Fig. 7.18) with the logo on the rotor facing you.
2. Thread the rotor-securing lockring on, and tighten it with the same splined lockring-remover tool you use for holding the rear cogs on. If you have a torque wrench that fits your lockring tool, set it to 40 N·m (350 in-lbs).

Removal

Multiple-bolt rotor

When removing a bolt-on disc rotor, you must loosen all of the screws a fraction of a turn before unscrewing any of them. On braking, the rotor may rotate relative to the hub a bit and lean against one side of each screw. If you remove one screw while the

7.18 Installing Shimano Center Lock splined rotor onto the splines of a Center Lock hub with a cassette lockring tool

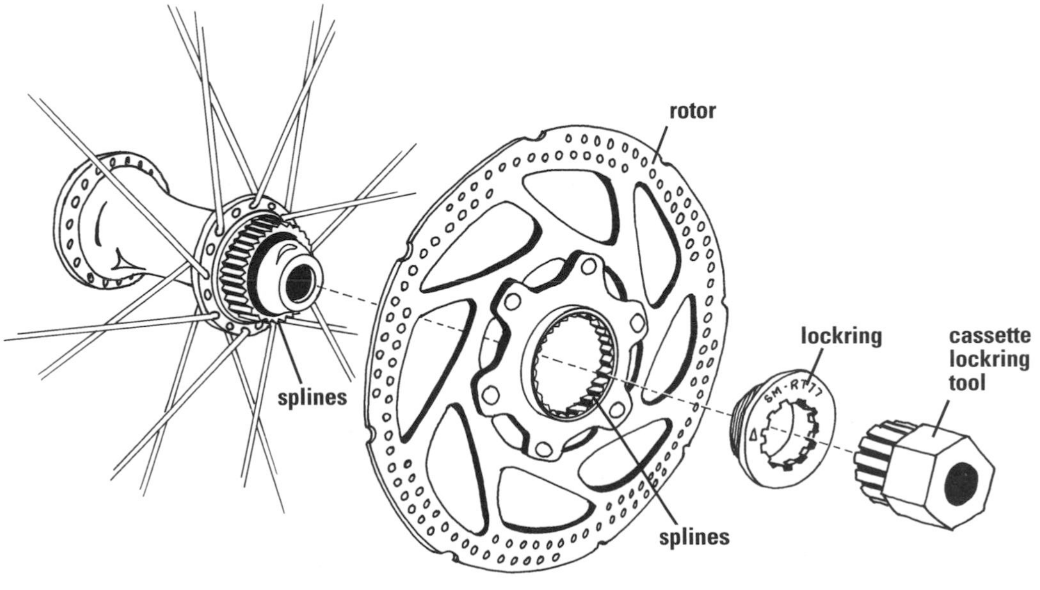

7.19 Mounting a hydraulic Shimano International Standard brake caliper on International Standard fork mounts

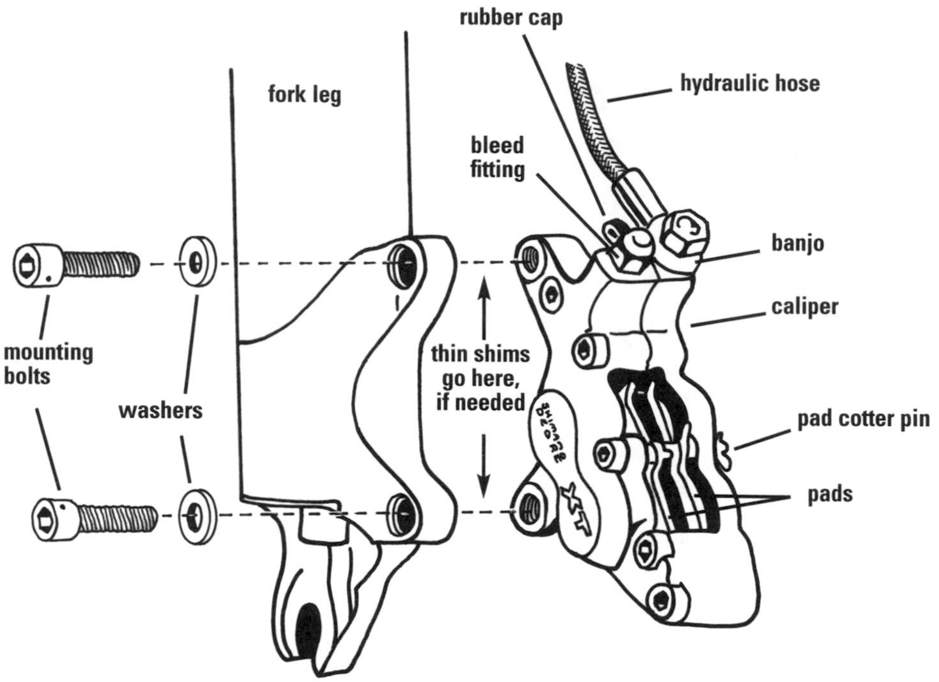

others are still tight, the rotor hole's wall will still be pressed against the side of the screw, and the threads on the screw will be damaged. Then you will wreck the threads in your hub when you put the damaged screw back in.

If you have a Shimano bolt-on rotor with the plates bent up around the triangular bolt heads (Fig. 7.17), bend the plate edges back down before unscrewing the bolts.

NOTE ON HUBS WITH ADAPTERS: *Some disc-brake hubs do not accept a rotor without an adapter. The adapter is attached to the hub, and then the rotor is bolted to the adapter. Some early Mavic disc-brake hubs use bolt-on adapters available in several bolt patterns to match early rotors from various brake brands. If you have one of these hubs and want to use a current brake, the only adapter you can use is the Hayes six-bolt one.*

To attach a rotor to an older SRAM disc-brake hub, you use a splined disc adapter that slides on and is held in place with three set screws and a thread-on collar that is tightened with a standard Shimano splined cassette lockring tool.

Shimano Center-Lock splined rotor

Unscrew the lockring with the splined lockring-removal tool (Fig. 7.18), and pull the rotor off.

b. Installing an International Standard disc-brake caliper onto International Standard mounts

International Standard mounts (Fig. 7.19) are found on most forks and disc-brake compatible frames. International Standard brake calipers have two transverse-drilled threaded bolt holes in them.

NOTE: *If you are using a caliper adapter to mount an Avid, Hayes, Shimano two-piston, or other post-mount brake caliper to an IS fork or frame, first bolt the adapter to the frame or fork mounts, and then follow the directions in section c below for installing a caliper onto post mounts.*

ANOTHER NOTE: *If you are installing a caliper that is not connected to its lever, skip to section e to cut the hose to length; then skip to §vii-15a to fill it with fluid and bleed it; and then come back here and begin with step 1.*

1. First install the wheel on the bike. Slip the caliper over the rotor and up against the frame or fork mounts.
2. Loosely install the mounting bolts (Fig. 7.19) and pull the brake lever to squeeze the pads against the rotor.
3. While squeezing the brake lever, measure the gap between the caliper and the mounting tab at each bolt, and make a stack of that height from the supplied shim washers to put between the caliper and mount for each bolt, as indicated in Figure 7.19. Remove the caliper, and slide each stack of shim washers on its bolt between the caliper and mount tab.
4. Tighten the bolts. Torque varies from 53 to 110 in-lbs, depending on brand.
5. Spin the wheel. The pads should not rub. If they do, add or remove shims until the rubbing has been eliminated.
6. If the rotor is wobbly, you will have to straighten it. See §vii-18 on truing a bent rotor.

NOTE: *Some IS brakes have only one moving pad, and flex the rotor toward the stationary pad. Magura Louise hydraulic disc brakes and most mechanical disc brakes are examples. The stationary inboard pad is adjusted independently so that it just clears the rotor without rubbing. Adjust the inboard pad on a Louise with a 5mm hex key; adjust most mechanical disc brakes with a thumbscrew.*

"FREE-RUNNING DRAG" NOTE: *Some IS brakes use a "floating caliper" in which the entire caliper moves as the pad (or pads) on the outboard side pushes against the rotor and pulls the stationary pad (or pads) over to the rotor. Magura Gustav M, Amp, and RockShox brakes have this feature. It is almost impossible to eliminate brake rub with these brakes as the rotor is the only thing that pushes the brake back over. Another nonstandard feature is the "floating rotor" of the Pro Stop brake. The caliper is fixed, but the rotor slides laterally on plastic bushings. These also tend to rub.*

c. Installing the disc-brake caliper onto post mounts

Manitou forks have post mounts, as do many older (pre-2000) frames. But mounting post-mount brakes onto an adapter bracket for International Standard mounts—front or rear—follows the same procedure, once the bracket is bolted to the IS mounts. Hayes pioneered the post mount (Fig. 7.20), and Avid, Shimano two-piston, and some Magura brakes also bolt directly to post mounts. Mounting any International Standard brake to post mounts is possible with yet a different adapter.

The beauty of post mounts is that the brake can be moved laterally without needing to slip shims (thin washers) between the caliper and the mounts—as you must with IS mounts. This advantage applies even if you are mounting an IS brake via an adapter to a post-mount frame or fork, or vice versa.

1. If you are using an IS brake with an adapter on a post-mount frame or fork, tighten the adapter to the caliper first. Torque is usually 6–8 N·m.
2. Loosely bolt the post-mount caliper to the post mounts on the frame, fork (Fig. 7.20), or adapter (or, if you have an IS brake caliper, bolt it tightly onto its post-mount adapter, and loosely bolt its

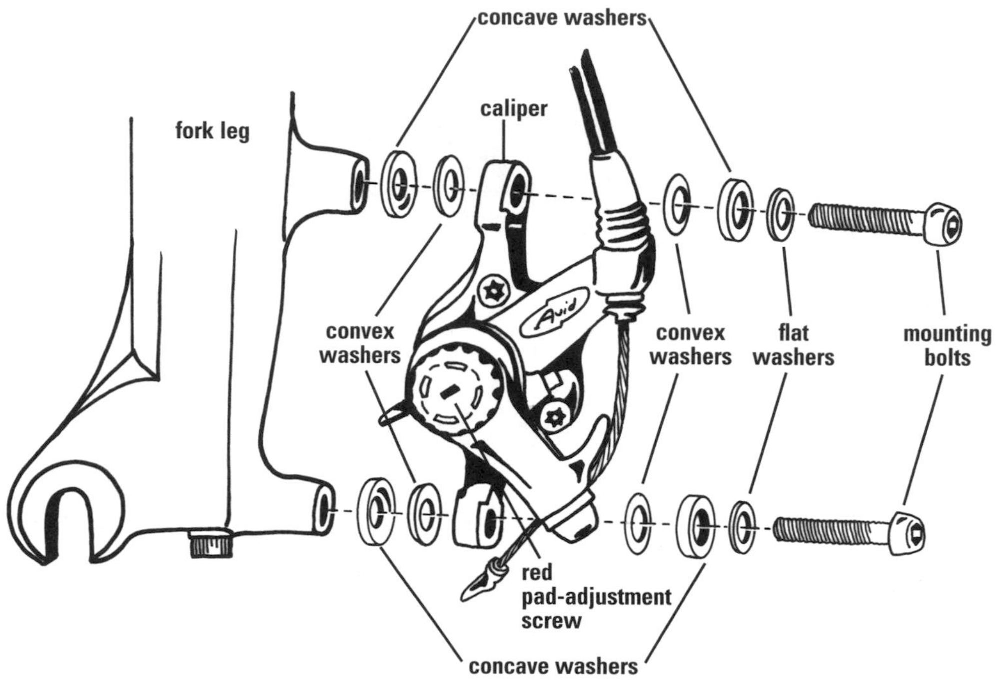

7.20 **Mounting a cable-activated Avid post-mount brake caliper on Manitou fork post mounts**

attached post-mount adapter onto the frame or fork post mounts). On Avid brakes, keep the concave and convex washers in the proper orientation and order.

NOTE: *If you are installing a caliper that is not connected to its lever, skip to section e to cut the hose to length; then skip to §vii-15a to fill it with fluid and bleed it; and then come back here and begin with step 3.*

3. Install the wheel. The caliper slot will be over the rotor, and the caliper will have some lateral freedom of movement.
4. Squeeze and hold the brake lever while tightening the mounting bolts.
5. Spin the wheel to check for brake rub. If you hear rub, peer through the gap between the rotor and the pads, and with a white background for contrast, note which pad (or worse, which side of the caliper slot) is rubbing. Loosen the bolts again, and slip a business card or two between the rubbing pad and the rotor.
6. Repeat steps 4 and 5 until the rotor spins without rub. If desperate, just loosen the bolts, eyeball the gap, push the caliper as you see fit, and tighten while holding the caliper; expect some frustration.
7. If the rotor is bent, you will have to straighten it. See §vii-18 on truing a rotor.

Shimano supplies little plastic clips to snap on over the bolts around the knurled part of their heads to prevent the bolts from unscrewing; it's a good idea to install these if you have them.

NOTE: *Some disc brakes that work by flexing the rotor toward a fixed pad are adjusted by first turning screws on the pads until they pinch the rotor. On Avid cable-actuated disc calipers, turn the large red screw on the wheel side until the fixed pad centers the rotor in the caliper slot. Then turn the red screw on the cable side*

(Fig. 7.20) until the rotor is pinched between the pads and centered in the slot. Loosen and then tighten the mounting bolts and back off the fixed-pad (wheel-side) screw until the rotor spins freely. Now tighten the cable (see §vii-14d, which follows), and back off on the red screws on either side a few clicks each to get the desired pad-to-rotor spacing. Note that Avids have convex and concave washers (Fig. 7.20) like those found on a V-brake pad to allow the brake to swing to compensate for misaligned mounts—make sure you retain the original order of these washers.

Similarly, the inboard (stationary) pad on hydraulic Magura Louise brakes, and on cable-actuated Hayes, SRAM, Grimeca, and Formula brakes, can be adjusted independently to get ideal pad rotor spacing. On Hayes mechanical brakes, turn the fixed pad adjuster counterclockwise until it stops (maximum pad spacing). Then turn it clockwise one-quarter of a turn (either with your fingers on the adjuster dial, or using a 4mm [old model] or 3mm hex key on the bolt, which on later models is concealed under a plastic cap). Squeeze the brake lever with the caliper loosely mounted over the rotor, shake the caliper into its favored position, and tighten the mounting bolts while still squeezing the lever. Then turn the fixed pad adjuster counterclockwise one-eighth turn to attain a pad-rotor spacing of 0.15–0.20 inches (0.38–0.50mm). The Magura Louise inboard pad is adjusted with a 5mm hex key until it just clears the rotor without rub. The entire caliper on SRAM, Grimeca, and Formula cable-actuated brakes can be moved laterally with a thumbscrew.

ANOTHER NOTE: *A bent rotor will rub or at least reduce pad adjustment range. Notice where it rubs on which pad, mark it with a felt-tipped pen, and carefully bend it into alignment with your fingers while it is still mounted on the hub.*

d. Hooking up cable-actuated disc brakes

Route the cable housing to the brake following the procedures in §vii-6 on cable installation. Tie it down with zip-ties where there are no cable stops. Push the cable through the housing stop on the caliper, and tighten it under the cable anchor bolt.

NOTE: *The above applies to cable-actuated mechanical disc brakes. There may still be a few cable-actuated hydraulic disc brakes around, with which the cable is routed similarly but connected differently. RockShox, Amp, and Hayes all had such systems, but these are now so rare that I do not devote space to them here. Problems such as overheating of the small volume of brake fluid inside caused the demise of these systems.*

e. Cutting hydraulic disc-brake hoses to length

When you route the hose to the brake, make it curve smoothly without kinks, and without large loops that can catch on things, and not so short that it is tight across spans where it is vulnerable. If your frame has snap-in disc-brake hose guides, use those. Otherwise, tie it down to the frame or fork with zip-ties, tape, little guides that hold the hose and that clip or screw into cable guides, or adhesive-backed hose guides.

Don't expect aftermarket brake hoses to be the right length for your bike; you will most likely need to cut them. If one end of the hose has a permanent crimped end on it, don't cut that end. Generally, on the end you can cut, there will be a brass, olive-shaped ring around the end of the hose crushed by a threaded hose-collar nut to seal against leaks (similar to Magura hydraulic rim brakes—see Fig. 7.47). This brass ring will need to be replaced after you cut the hose. Old Shimano hydraulic hoses sheathed in

7.21 **Shimano XT Dual Control master cylinder exploded**

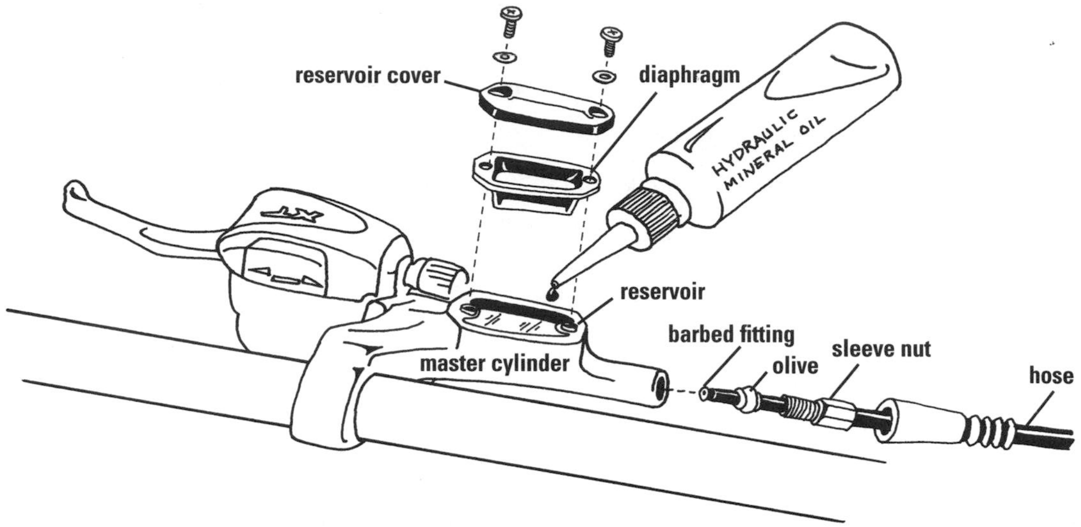

braided stainless steel wire cannot be cut; you have to buy them the right length.

1. Remove the wheel and the brake pads (§vii-16), so you don't accidentally get brake fluid on either the rotor or the pads.
2. If it's not already done, connect the hose to the caliper. The hose may attach straight into the caliper with a hose-collar nut in the same way that the hose attaches at the lever (Fig. 7.21). Alternatively, a screw with an oil port in it and passing through a "banjo" fitting may be used to attach the hose, as shown in Figure 7.25.
3. If the hose is not hooked up already to both the lever and caliper, skip to step 7. If the hose is already installed, at either the caliper or the lever, unscrew the hose-collar nut holding the hose on. The hose-collar nut is often covered by a plastic or rubber cover, which you slide up the hose first.
4. Try gently pulling the hose straight off, but be very careful, because on some brakes you can break a thin nipple that runs up into the tube—many brake fittings (Hayes HFX-Mag) have a thin barbed tube extending up inside the hose under the brass "olive" ring, and on some brakes, this barbed fitting is part of the lever. Because the olive has been compressed by the pressure of the hose-collar nut, the hose may be too tight to come off of the barbs. And if you bend the hose sideways at all while you pull on it, you can break off the barbed fitting. Break the barbed fitting on a Hayes HFX-Mag lever, and you will be replacing the complete lever guts.
5. If the hose did not pull off easily, carefully cut the brass olive open with a hacksaw and peel it away from the hose.
6. Now pull the hose off and slide the rubber nut cover and hose-collar nut up the hose beyond the place where you plan to make your cut.
7. Cut the hose to length with a sharp knife, making a clean, perpendicular cut. Many brakes come with a pair of little grooved plastic blocks with which you can clamp the hose in a vise while cutting. If the brake has a separate barbed fitting (as opposed to one sticking out of the master cylin-

der like that on a Hayes), then tap it into the hose while it is still held between the plastic grooved blocks (after first slipping the new brass olive over the end of the hose after the hose nut and rubber nut cover—Fig. 7.21). If the brake was already hooked up and you are careful to keep a "dome" of fluid on the end of the hose by tipping it up during the cutting process, it may be possible to avoid the entry of air into the hose and allow you to skip bleeding the brakes.

8. After installing the new brass olive and barbed fitting, tighten the hose-collar nut (maximum torque: 40 in-lbs). Slide the plastic or rubber nut cover back into place over the nut.
9. Generally, skip to §vii-15 (Hydraulic Disc Brake Bleeding), but if the brake was previously connected, and you think you might have prevented the entry of air into the system, then install the pads and wheel again, with the rotor between the pads.
10. Squeeze the lever. If the lever does not feel firm, and the brake does not stop well, or the lever can move all of the way to the handlebar, there is air in the line, and you must bleed it out (see §vii-15).

f. Lever reach, lever pull, and pad spacing

Most brake levers have a reach adjustment—usually a small setscrew under the lever blade. This may or may not be independent of any lever pull and pad spacing adjustments.

Lever pull and pad spacing are closely related, as the closer the pads are to the rotor, the less pull it takes to stop. But the pads will rub if too close. Adjustments exist on some brakes and not on others.

Lever pull with cable-actuated brakes can be adjusted by using the reach adjustment screw on the lever and the cable barrel adjuster (also on the lever and often on the caliper as well; see §vii-9 for details).

Pad spacing, and hence lever pull, on cable-actuated disc brakes can be adjusted with knobs at the caliper. Pad spacing on Magura Louise hydraulic brakes can also be adjusted with a screw on the caliper.

Some hydraulic brakes have an adjuster screw on the lever that pushes the master-cylinder piston, thereby changing the amount of lever travel required. Avid Juicy levers have knobs to adjust the pad contact point in the lever's travel while riding, so you can balance the left and right levers to engage at the same point. Hayes El Caminos have a knob to adjust leverage that actually moves the lever pivot in and out via a cam mechanism. Still others have an adjustment on the master-cylinder reservoir to alter pad position (Hope hydraulic brakes have a knob on top of the reservoir that you can turn while riding). Coda hydraulic brakes have a knob on the lever resembling a barrel adjuster that adjusts pad spacing.

Sometimes the pads in hydraulic disc brakes can rub because the pistons get pushed out too far, especially if the lever is applied without a rotor or spacer between the pads. You will have to push the pistons back in, usually by removing the pads (§vii-16) and pushing the pistons back with a plastic tire lever. On Hayes, the only thing pulling the pistons back in is the reversal of a twist the pistons apply to square-cross-section o-ring seals surrounding the waist of each piston, so the pistons tend to stay out too far once there. Pull out the pads (see Fig. 7.24), carefully push the pistons back in with the box end of a 10mm wrench (avoiding pressing on the pin sticking out of the piston, which hooks the wire catch on the back of the pad), and replace the pads.

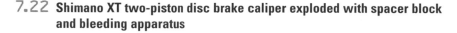

7.22 Shimano XT two-piston disc brake caliper exploded with spacer block and bleeding apparatus

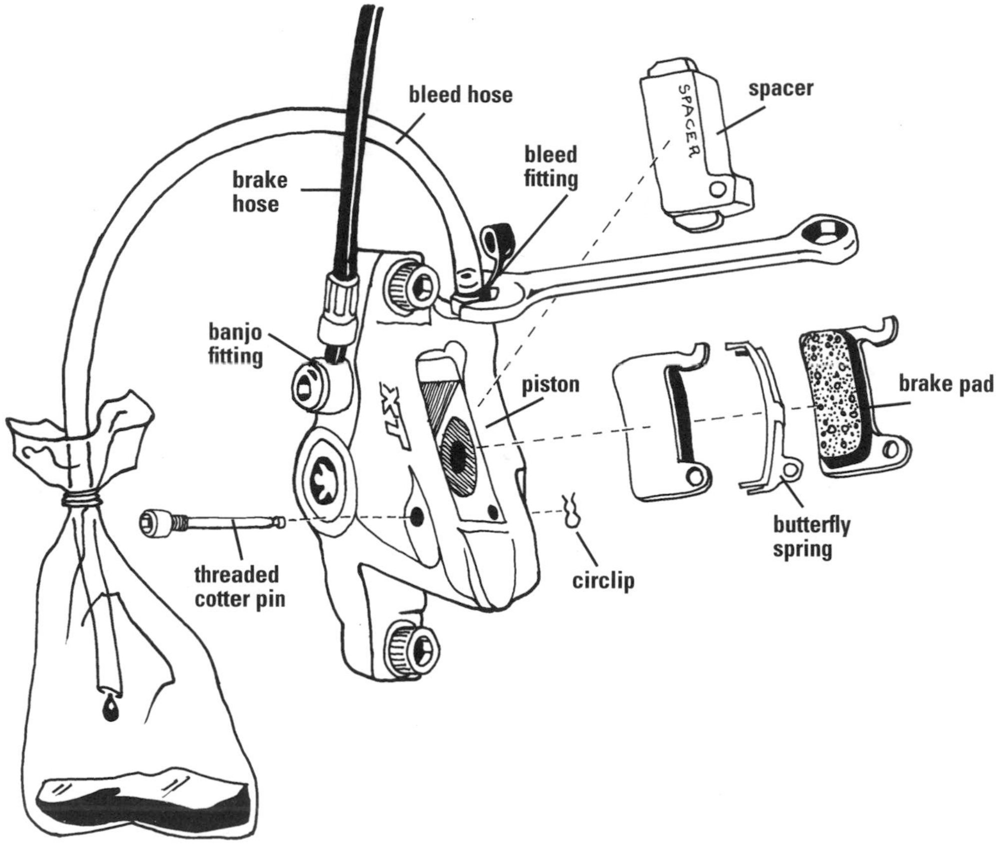

Shimano two-piston hydraulic calipers (Fig. 7.22) can have problems with fully retracting the pads so the pad spacing will be reduced to almost nothing and consequently rubbing and possibly even squealing noises will be the result. You can improve this situation by lubricating the pistons. Remove the pads (§vii-16). While holding one piston in place with a plastic tire lever or a broad screwdriver, carefully squeeze the lever to push the other piston out a bit more to expose more of it for lubrication. Using a rag on the end of a thin screwdriver, wipe off any grime from around the piston. Drip oil (chain oil is fine—just not dry chain lubes) so that it flows around the exposed flanks of the piston. This might loosen up some more dirt, so wipe it off again, and relubricate it. Carefully prying against the opposite side of the caliper, push the piston back into its bore with the plastic tire lever or the broad-tipped screwdriver. Repeat the procedure for the other side, and replace the pads and the butterfly spring. The butterfly spring is very weak and only intended to keep the pads against the pistons—it is not strong enough to push the pistons back. But it is worth bending the spring's legs outward a bit before replacing it so that it pushes against the pads more firmly and prevents them from rubbing the rotor on their own when the pistons aren't pushing them.

vii-15 HYDRAULIC DISC-BRAKE BLEEDING (OR FILLING)

The procedure for filling an empty brake system is the same as for bleeding one, with the exception that you can wait until fluid starts coming out of the fitting through the bleed tube before you have to close the bleed fitting with each squeeze of the lever.

IMPORTANT: *With all brakes, remove the wheel and remove the brake pads from the caliper (§vii-16) to avoid ruining the pads by getting fluid on them. Replace pads contaminated by brake fluid, and clean rotors contaminated by brake fluid with rubbing alcohol. Once the wheel and pads are removed, install a block between the pistons to keep them in place (Fig. 7.22); many brakes come with a bleed block (this step does not apply to Hayes brakes).*

IMPORTANT: *Use the recommended brake fluid for your brake. Some systems use mineral oil, and some use automotive brake fluid. If you put the wrong type of fluid in a brake, you will ruin the seals inside.*

a. Bleeding brakes that have a screw-on reservoir cover at the lever

When bleeding car brakes, you add extra fluid to the master cylinder (at the foot pedal) and squeeze it out through the wheel slave cylinders. Many bicycle disc brakes (Shimano and Magura, for instance) work the same way.

1. Turn the handlebar and the lever so the reservoir is level, and ensure that the hose is trending downward the entire way to the caliper.
2. Remove the screws securing the lever-reservoir cover, and pull off the cover and diaphragm (Fig. 7.21).

ATTENTION: *Make sure you remove the rubber diaphragm under the cover! You would not be the first one to think you were looking at the inside of the reservoir and not the top of the diaphragm, wondering why the fluid you keep adding does not disappear and why the brakes don't tighten up!*

3. Add fluid at the lever reservoir (Fig. 7.21).

IMPORTANT: *Shimano and Magura brake fluid is mineral oil—make sure you add no automotive brake fluid (DOT fluid)! And use mineral oil for your particular brakes, not from a pharmacy! Formula, Avid, and many other brake brands do use DOT 3 or DOT 4 fluid, however. Just use the stuff meant for your brakes.*

4. After removing the rubber cover completely from the fitting's nipple, put a hose on the caliper bleed fitting nipple (Figs. 7.19, 7.22) leading into a bottle or a plastic bag rubber-banded onto the piece of hose and unscrew the bleed fitting one-eighth turn with an open-end or box-end wrench. It is preferable to put a box-end wrench on the bleed fitting before pushing the hose onto the nipple—the wrench then stays in place as you open and the close the fitting.
5. Squeeze the lever repeatedly to push fluid in and air out until fluid flows out into the bleed tube attached to the caliper bleed fitting. Tighten the bleed fitting before releasing the lever each time, making sure you have a bleed block between the pistons (Fig. 7.22). You can make a bleed block out of a chunk of wood that just fits between the pistons. If you do not install a thick spacer like this between the pistons, you will have to leave the pads in and place either a spacer or a rotor between them for the following steps, but you risk contaminating the pads with brake fluid.
6. There are two possible techniques to be sure that you remove all the air:
   (a) You can push air bubbles down through the system by squeezing the lever with the bleed

nipple open, tighten the nipple, release the lever, open the bleed nipple, squeeze the lever, tighten the nipple, release the lever, and repeat, keeping the reservoir topped up, until no more bubbles appear in the bleed tube.

(b) Alternatively, you can repeatedly squeeze the brake lever with the bleed nipple closed, making sure that you keep the fluid level in the reservoir topped up. While you are squeezing, air bubbles should rise up through the port into the reservoir.

7. When bubbles stop, squeeze the lever fully.
   (a) If it feels stiff, as it should—meaning that it comes inward perhaps a third of the way toward the handlebar grip at most—then skip to step 8.
   (b) If it still does not feel stiff, with your bleed block in place, squeeze the lever and hold it while you shake the hose, move the caliper about, and tap on the hose and the caliper with the plastic head of a screwdriver to free any stuck air bubbles. When they have all been removed, squeezing the lever should feel firm, and the lever should not move all the way back to the grip. Continue with step 8.

HYDRAULIC DISC-BRAKE BLEEDING

8. With the brake lever depressed, open and close the bleed nipple in rapid succession for about half a second each time. This optional procedure can release trapped air bubbles from the caliper. Repeat two or three times, and finish by tightening the bleed nipple.
9. Refill the reservoir to the top (Fig. 7.21).
10. Put fluid on the diaphragm, flip it and the cover over and into place. Replace the cover screws (Fig. 7.21). Wipe any fluid off of the bike, particularly any DOT fluid that has gotten on painted parts.

7.23 Catching fluid bled from a Hayes HFX Mag brake

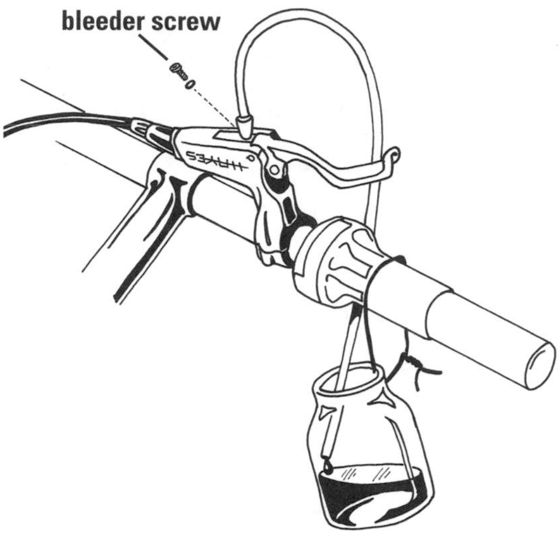

11. Install the pads and wheel and check the brake function.
12. Retighten the brake lever to the handlebar in its normal riding position.
13. Check for fluid leaks by zip-tying the lever around the handlebar overnight. If the zip-tie is still tight around the lever and the handlebar grip the next morning there are no leaks.

b. Bleeding Hayes hydraulic disc brakes

Hayes HFX and original hydraulic brakes have an expandable reservoir inside the lever, like the plastic sack in a baby bottle. Consequently, they are bled differently than brakes with a fixed-size reservoir, namely, from the bottom (the caliper) to the top (the lever). Hayes El Camino models have a different, yet still flexible, reservoir.

1. Mount the bike in a stand, turn the handlebar, and rotate the lever on the handlebar such that the lever is the highest point in the system. Turn the lever until the front of the lever on HFX

7.24 Changing Hayes brake pads (the caliper is shown apart only for the purpose of this illustration—the pads clip in and out without dismantling the caliper)

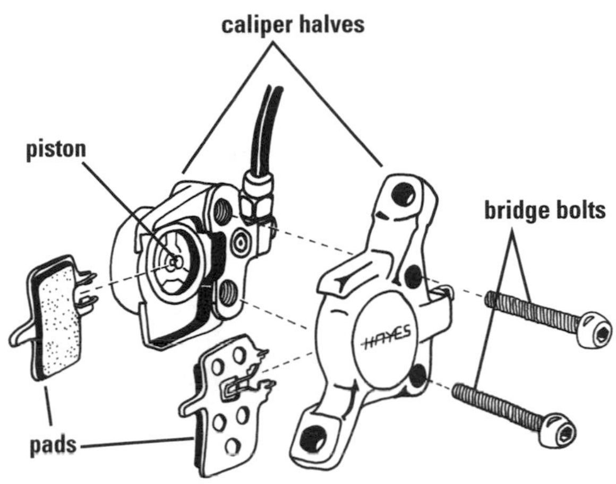

and original models points straight up (Fig. 7.23). El Caminos have two bleed screws—one at the base of the lever on each side. Make sure that one of them points straight up. Starting in 2003, Hayes introduced more economical hydraulic disc brakes with a "9" in the name, and these are distinct from the magnesium HFX and original versions both in looks and in bleeding technique. The HFX-9 models have more angular shaping to the lever body and a plastic plug over the lever bleed hole. HFX-Mag models (and original Hayes hydraulic brakes, basically the same even though they may not have carried the HFX-Mag name) have a smoother lever body and a small Phillips screw fills the lever bleed hole.

NOTE: *For an HFX-9, leave the bike level and the lever level, but for the HFX-Mag, tip the bike so that the rear wheel is lower than the front wheel and turn the handlebar so that the lever points up at a 45-degree angle. For the left lever, turn the handlebar all the way to the right, and vice versa.*

2. Push the pistons fully back into their cylinders by using the box end of a 10mm wrench, and avoid pressing on the pin sticking out of the piston that hooks the wire catch on the back of the pad (see Fig. 7.24).
3. If it hasn't already fallen off while riding, completely remove the rubber cover over the caliper bleed fitting. Stick a 2-inch section of clear tube onto the tip of the squeeze bottle (supplied with an aftermarket Hayes brake, or available by buying a bleed kit) of brake fluid (past the ridge on the tapered tip so it stays on!), and slip the other end over the bleed fitting (Fig. 7.25) on the caliper.

IMPORTANT: *Hayes uses DOT 4 or DOT 3 automotive brake fluid. Make sure you add no mineral oil! And watch out, because automotive brake fluid will remove paint.*

4. The brake or bleed kit should have come with a longer clear tube with a plastic fitting for you to press onto it for an HFX-Mag or with a thin aluminum fitting for you to press into it for an HFX-9. Stick the fitting into the bleed hole on the lever after removing the small screw covering it (HFX-Mag) or after pulling out the plastic plug covering it (HFX-9). Hang an old plastic bottle from the handlebar with wire or a twist-tie, and direct the other end of the tube into it (Fig. 7.23).
5. Before opening the bleed fitting at the caliper, squeeze the fluid bottle repeatedly until any air bubbles in the tube come back into the bottle. The bottle should be pointed straight down.
6. Loosen the bleed fitting on the caliper one-fourth turn, and squeeze new fluid in for a count of five. Let off for about three counts (until the squeeze bottle returns to its natural shape) to draw air out of the caliper and up into the tube and the squeeze

7.25 **Hayes caliper guts**

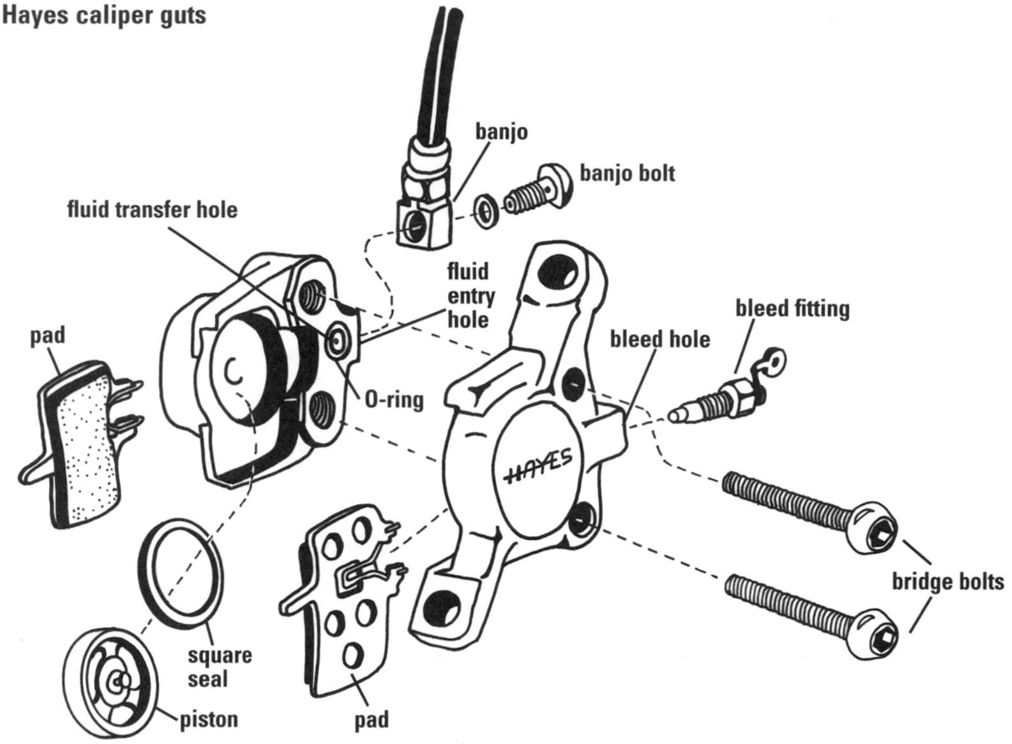

bottle. Squeeze for five, let off for three, etc., until no more bubbles come out of the caliper.

7. Squeeze firmly on the bottle until clean fluid without bubbles comes out of the tube at the lever. While still squeezing, quickly pull the lever until it contacts the grip and release, looking for air coming out of the bleed tube at the lever. Repeat until no more air emerges. While still squeezing, close the caliper bleed fitting (don't overtighten the fitting—it is small, and you only need to tighten it enough to create a seal, not to hold parts together!).
8. Remove the tubes from the caliper and the lever, and replace the lever bleed screw or plastic plug. Replace the little rubber cover on the caliper bleed fitting.
9. Install the pads (§vii-16) and wheel, and pump the lever. Squeezing the lever should feel firm, and it should not come back to the grip. Repeat bleed if it feels spongy.
10. With rubbing alcohol, clean the rotor and any paint on the frame that may have contacted brake fluid.
11. Check for fluid leaks by putting a zip-tie overnight around the lever. If the zip-tie is still tight around the lever and the handlebar grip the next day, your system is completely sealed.

vii-16 DISC-BRAKE PAD REPLACEMENT

Most disc brakes have pads that pop in and out easily. The wheel must be off. On cotterless types of pads, usually you grab a tab on the pad with your fingers or needle-nose pliers and pull it toward the center of the caliper slot and out (Fig. 7.24). The pads are constrained by the caliper body, and they may snap into the caliper or onto a nub on the piston with prongs, a wire catch (as on Hayes, Fig. 7.24), and/or magnetically. Some pads (hydraulic Shimano, SRAM, and some Grimeca) require that you remove a cotter pin or bolt before the pads will come out (Figs. 7.19, 7.22).

Check for pad wear, scoring, or glazing—anything that could damage the rotor or endanger braking effectiveness.

Replace the pads the way they came out, noting that the left and right pads may differ; it should be obvious if you try to put a pad in the wrong side. If you reverse the pads on a cotterless type (Fig.7.24), they will not snap back into place because the piston is usually offset from the center of the cutaway for the pad.

The pads on original Shimano hydraulic XT, Grimeca, and SRAM four-piston hydraulic disc brakes are more complicated to remove and install. All three of these have brake calipers that look like Figure 7.19. You have to remove the pin or bolt on top that holds the pads in; it unscrews on Shimano, whereas on Grimeca and SRAM you need to pry the circlip off of the end and pull it out. There is then a little butterfly-shaped spring-steel piece that pushes the pads apart; it must be pulled out with the pads and replaced between the new pads. Current two-piston Shimano hydraulic brakes (Fig. 7.22) have pads shaped differently from the four-piston type, which are nonetheless held in place with a cotter pin (you remove a circlip and unscrew it with a 3mm hex key) and separated by a butterfly spring.

vii-17 OVERHAULING DISC BRAKES

LEVEL 3

Eventually, the caliper will need to be overhauled. Obviously, the process is different with a mechanical brake than with a hydraulic one. (And again, for reasons mentioned under vii-14d, cable-actuated hydraulic disc brakes are not discussed here.)

On many brakes, an overhaul is relatively simple, but it normally does require an air compressor.

a. Overhauling hydraulic disc brakes

Regular bleeding cleans dirt out of the system and lengthens the time periods between overhauls. Buy a new set of seals for whichever part of your brake you are overhauling before you start. A speck of dirt or hair in a hydraulic disc brake can cause a leak, so work in a clean area with clean methods.

Caliper (a.k.a. slave cylinder)

1. Remove the caliper from the bike (see Figs. 7.19 and 7.20).
2. Disconnect the hose. If there is nothing wrong with the hose or its fittings, you want to save yourself the effort of replacing the brass "olive" ring seal on the hose (see §vii-14e and Fig. 7.21 or 7.47). Some brakes have a fitting screwed into the caliper with a hollow bolt to which the hose nut is attached. This is called a "banjo" fitting (Figs. 7.19 and 7.25) because the head of it looks like a . . . you guessed it. If yours has a banjo, unscrew the hollow banjo bolt holding it on, but don't disconnect the hose from the banjo.
3. Remove the bridge bolts (Fig. 7.25) holding the caliper clamshell halves together and pull the brake apart.
4. Remove the piston(s). This procedure often requires blowing compressed air into the fluid-transfer hole while plugging either the bleed hole or the fluid-entry hole with your finger (Fig. 7.25), depending on which piston you are removing. Be careful to not get hit with fluid or parts.

Wear safety glasses and cover the piston with your hand so that no springs or other parts fly away.

5. You will often find that there are relatively few parts inside of an object that might have seemed much more complicated—usually just a couple of pistons and a few seals (Fig. 7.25) and sometimes some return springs. Use a fingernail or a plastic or wooden implement to dig out the piston seals to avoid scratching the cylinder.
6. Clean all parts carefully with isopropyl alcohol, and wipe off the residue.
7. With compressed air, blow out the caliper-seal grooves, the bleeder hole, and the hole that transfers fluid from one side of the caliper to the other. Wear safety glasses. Check that the seal grooves are completely clean.
8. Lubricate the new seals with the brake fluid recommended for the brake, and put all of the parts back together in the way that you found them.
9. Bolt the caliper together to the recommended torque. Check Appendix D or your brake manual for torque specs.
10. Reinstall the hose.
11. Install and center the caliper (§vii-14b or §vii-14c).
12. Bleed the system (§vii-15).

Lever (a.k.a. "master cylinder")

Levers rarely need to be overhauled if you bleed your brakes regularly and don't break any fittings on the lever in the process. They are high above the dirt and grime, so any dirt getting into the piston has to travel up from the caliper, which ain't easy.

Generally, you need to remove the lever from the handlebar, disconnect the hose (Fig. 7.21), and remove the lever from the housing. Just keep unscrewing things until it comes apart, noting their order as you do. On some brakes (Hayes, for instance—Fig. 7.23), the cylinder is separate from the lever body, rather than being machined into it. You remove the cylinder assembly, and it is a cartridge that you replace as a unit; you do not take out the little piston and seals.

Clean up and inspect all of the parts, replace any worn ones, and put it back together. Install the lever, mount onto the handlebar, connect the hose, and bleed the system (§vii-15).

b. Overhauling mechanical disc brakes

Mechanical disc brakes (Fig. 7.20) usually push the pistons by means of a number of ball bearings rolling in a nautilus-shaped track. Methods to disassemble them vary, and the how-to is usually not in their accompanying instruction manual. But as long as you are careful, you keep the parts in order, and you don't lose any, it is not particularly complicated to take mechanical disc brakes apart and put them back together.

Remove the pads, after which the pistons will usually come out one at a time through the rotor slot. If you can do it this way, you can avoid taking the entire brake apart, which is fine, as the pistons are probably all you need to clean anyway. For example, on Avid, to get out either piston, you turn its red plastic screw (Fig. 7.20) clockwise until it pops out. The wheel-side piston is threaded on the outside and has a flat rectangular bar sticking out from its back to engage the plastic knurled disc. Once this piston is out, you can snap out the red knob—it just pops out with little prongs to hold it in when you replace it. After cleaning the inboard piston and its threaded receptacle, you grease the threads and put that piston and the red knob back (don't grease the knob).

The outboard piston has a rod sticking straight out from its back. A ring of spring steel around it holds it into a hole in the drive mechanism. Don't grease any part of this piston; it doesn't need it, and it will only attract dirt. The pistons are magnetic, so expect a bit of a hassle getting them lined up and back in, because one piston will be attracted by the other one. You can drive in the outboard piston with the inboard piston (turn the red knob). Installing the pads and a spacer in between may help.

If you want to get at the ball-bearing mechanism, you start by unbolting the arm. Simply clean and grease everything and put it back in the way you found it. Be careful, but don't be intimidated.

vii-18 TRUING DISC-BRAKE ROTORS

You may have gotten your calipers perfectly centered over your rotors, but they will squeal and howl if your rotor gets bent. The spacing between brake pads and rotor is so tight on a bicycle disc brake around 0.015 inch—that there is almost no room for any rotor wobble whatsoever. And unlike car brake discs, bicycle rotors are thin and relatively unprotected; they can be bent by rocks thrown up while riding, in a crash, when packing your wheel in a car or a bike bag, or from warping due to heat buildup on a long, steep descent on a hot day. Your rotors will get bent sometime, so you need to be able to straighten them.

If a rotor is really potato-chipped, you will first need to remove it from the hub and pound it as flat as you can with a hammer on an anvil. Then you can proceed with any of the methods below.

a. Eyeballing rotor in caliper

By eyeballing, you can often do an adequate enough job to at least minimize brake-pad rub, but be forewarned that this approach requires patience, because it can be hard to tell on which pad the rotor is rubbing as the gap is so small. Place a piece of white paper on the floor or the wall, below or level with the caliper, so that you can see the space between the rotor and the pads. Slowly turn the wheel, marking where the disc rubs on each pad with a felt-tipped pen. Carefully bend the disc into alignment with your fingers, rechecking it constantly by spinning it again through the brake. A rotor easily bends by hand.

b. Rigging up a pointer

A more accurate way that's almost as cheap as eyeballing, but requires as much patience, is to attach a pointer to your frame or fork in such a way that you can adjust it to graze the rotor similar to a feeler on a truing stand. This pointer may be made of wire bent around the caliper, perhaps, or by removing the caliper and screwing a piece of metal with a hole in it onto one of the caliper-mounting tabs. Then just bend the rotor away from the pointer where it touches. But unless you really spend some time mounting your pointer securely, you can make mistakes, thinking it is bent one way when it is actually bent the other.

c. Rotor truing with a Morningstar ROC tool

If you straighten rotors a lot, eyeballing the rotor or using a rigged up pointer will soon drive you mad. Happily, the Morningstar Rotors on Center (ROC) dial indicator tool (Fig. 7.26) shows the lateral position of the rotor within 0.001 inch, so you can get the rotor as straight as it was when it was brand new. The ROC indicator includes a base that clamps through the center of the hub in place of the skewer when it is on the bike or in a truing stand. The tool costs less than $90—a good deal if you align rotors frequently.

7.26 Truing a bent rotor with a Morningstar ROC dial indicator and Drumstix tools

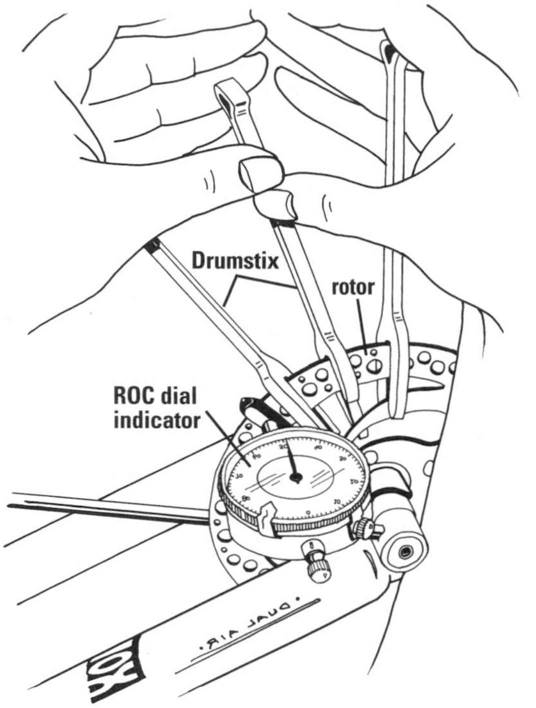

Tighten the ROC tool's long mounting screw through the axle and set the dial indicator foot against the rotor. Rotate the indicator face cover so that the needle is on zero, and where the needle indicates the greatest deflection in either direction, bend the rotor back, continually rechecking it with the dial indicator.

You can bend the rotor back with your thumbs, and I have aligned a lot of very badly bent rotors to near perfection this way. Better yet, Morningstar's "rotor tuning forks," dubbed "Drumstix" (Fig. 7.26), slip onto the rotor and provide leverage to precisely bend the rotor. Stabilize the rotor in position with the two symmetrical Drumstix, one on either side of the bent spot, and with the third Drumstix, which has an angled slot for the rotor, bend the rotor to eliminate the warped spot.

The Drumstix stabilizers, by isolating the bent spot, eliminate the need to account for the rotor's springback after bending. When bending it with your fingers, the entire rotor flexes and springs back, requiring guesswork to figure out how far to bend it so that it springs back to the position you want without going too far.

Cantilever Brakes

vii-19 INSTALLATION

1. Grease the brake bosses (Fig. 7.27). Avoid getting grease inside the brake boss or on the bolt threads; they are treated with thread-lock goop to prevent them from vibrating loose.
2. If you have the installation directions that came with your brakes, follow them. If not, follow the general installation instructions below.
3. Make sure you install the brakes with all of the parts in the order in which they were originally. In particular, the springs will often be of different colors not interchangeable from left to right.
4. If each brake has a separate inner sleeve bushing to fit over the cantilever boss, install that first. Slip the brake arm and return spring over it.
5. Determine what sort of return system your brakes use. If the brake arms have no spring-tension adjustment, or a setscrew on the side of one of the arms for adjusting spring tension, go to step 6. Such brakes use the hole in the cantilever boss to anchor the bottom end of the spring. If the brake arms have a large nut surrounding the mounting bolt for adjusting spring tension behind the brake arm or in front of it (Fig. 7.27), skip to step 8. These brakes do not use the hole in the cantilever boss as a spring anchor.

7.27 **Cantilever brake assembly**

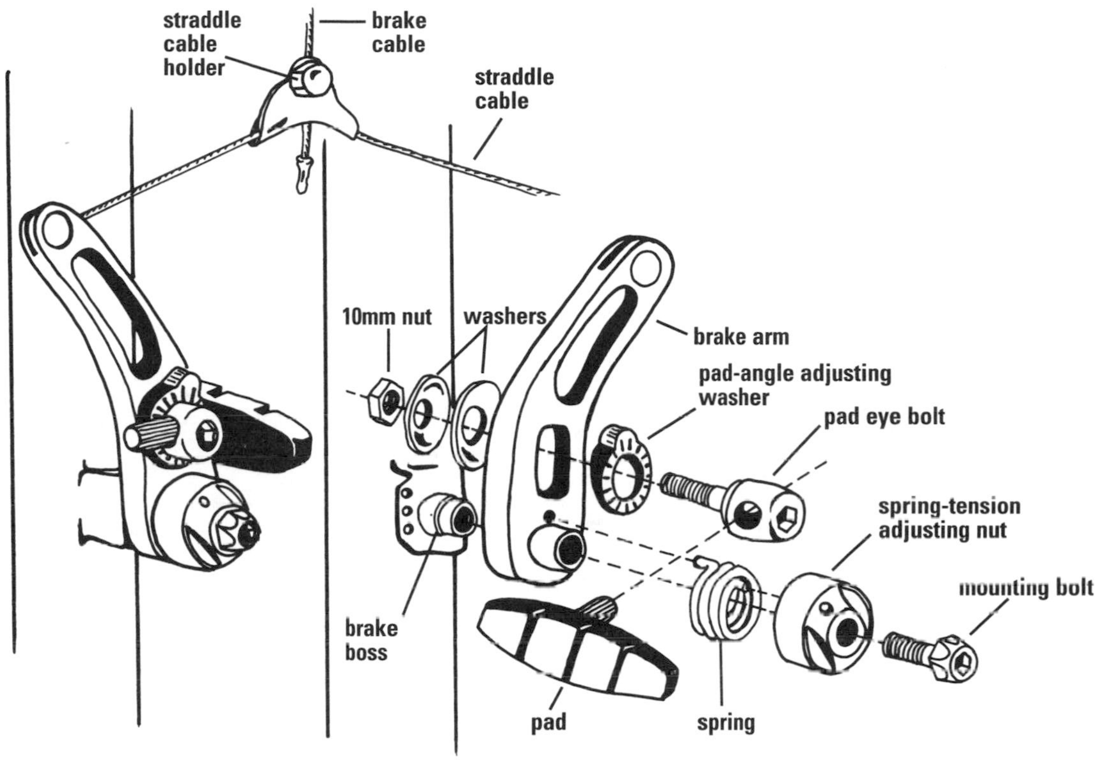

6. Slip the brake onto the boss, inserting the lower end of the spring into the hole in the cantilever boss (if the boss has three holes, try the center hole first; use a higher hole to make the brake snappier, a necessity with lower-quality or old brakes). You also want to make sure that the top end of the spring is inserted into its hole in the brake arm as well.
7. Install and tighten the mounting bolt into the cantilever boss. Skip the next three steps.
8. Slip the brake (with any included bushings) onto the cantilever boss.
9. Install the spring so that one end inserts into the hole in the brake arm and the other inserts into the hole in the adjusting nut.
10. Install and tighten the mounting bolt while holding the adjusting nut with the appropriate open-end wrench (usually 15mm) so that the pad is touching the rim. This step facilitates pad adjustment later.

vii-20 PAD REPLACEMENT AND INSTALLATION

1. Remove the old pad, if applicable.
2. Install the new pad. Most cantilevers rely on an eye bolt with an enlarged head and a hole through it to accept the pad post (Fig. 7.27). Some cantilevers (Avid and Onza, for example), have a slotted clamp with a hole for the pad post (Fig. 7.28). A few cantilevers use a threaded pad post that passes through a slot in the brake arm (Fig. 7.29) as on a V-brake.
3. If your brake spring can be adjusted so that it holds the pad against the rim, set it up that way

7.28 **Cylindrical clamp cantilever brake (Onza)**

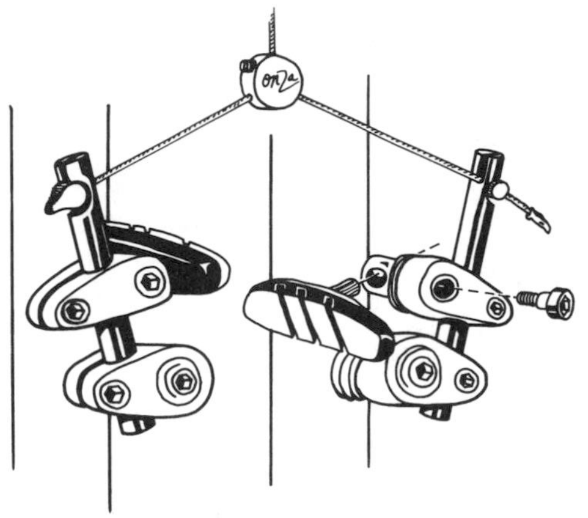

7.29 **Threaded-post cantilever brake**

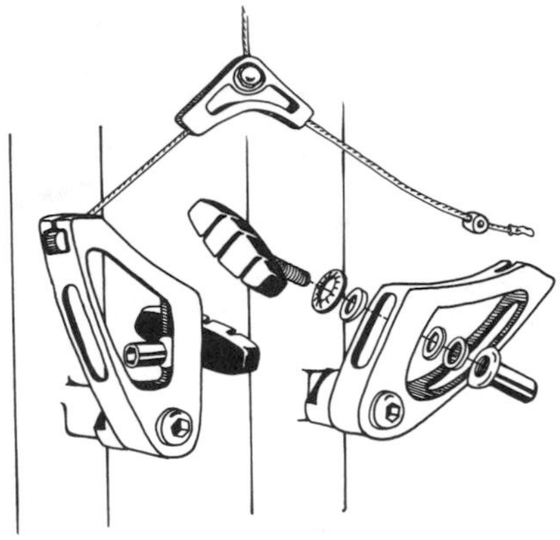

now. It will make the pad adjustments much easier. If not, you will have to push each arm toward the rim as you adjust the pad.

PAD ADJUSTMENT

vii-21 PAD ADJUSTMENT

There are five separate adjustments that must be made for each pad (labeled *a* through *e* in Figs. 7.30–7.32). These adjustments are quite easy with some brakes, and a real pain in the rear with others:

- **a.** offset distance of the pad from the brake arm (extension of the pad post) (*a*, Fig. 7.30);
- **b.** vertical pad height (*b*, Fig. 7.31);
- **c.** pad swing in the vertical plane for mating with the rim's sidewall angle (*c*, Fig. 7.30);
- **d.** pad twist to align the length of the pad with the rim's curvature (*d*, Fig. 7.31); and
- **e.** pad swing in the horizontal plane to set toe-in (*e*, Fig. 7.32).

Cantilevers that feature a cylindrical brake arm are by far the easiest to adjust (Fig. 7.28). Pad adjustment is simple because the pad is held to the cylinder with a clamp that offers almost full range of motion. Avid, Onza, Gravity Research Pipe Dreams, and Dia-Compe VC900 all rely on this type of system. Other cantilevers employ a single pad eye bolt to hold all five adjustments (the eye bolt and washers are exploded in Fig 7.27 and are seen from above in Fig. 7.32). It requires a bit of manual dexterity to hold all five adjustments simultaneously while tightening the bolt.

With all types of cantilevers:

1. Loosen the pad-clamping bolt, lubricate the pad anchor threads, and set the pad offset (*a*, Fig. 7.30) by sliding the post in or out of the clamping hole. The farther the pad is extended away from the brake arm, the greater the angle of the brake arm will be from the plane of the wheel. A benefit of this is that leverage is increased (see straddle-cable angle in Figs. 7.35 and 7.36). The drawbacks are that the brake feels less firm, because less force is required to pull the lever; and clearance between the rider's heel and the rear-brake arms is reduced, particularly for small frames. A good initial position is with the post clamped in the center of its length.

NOTE: *With threaded-post pads (Fig. 7.29), placing spacers between the brake arm and the pad sets the pad offset. Lube the pad threads.*

7.30 **Distance of pad to fixing bolt (a) and angle against rim (c)**

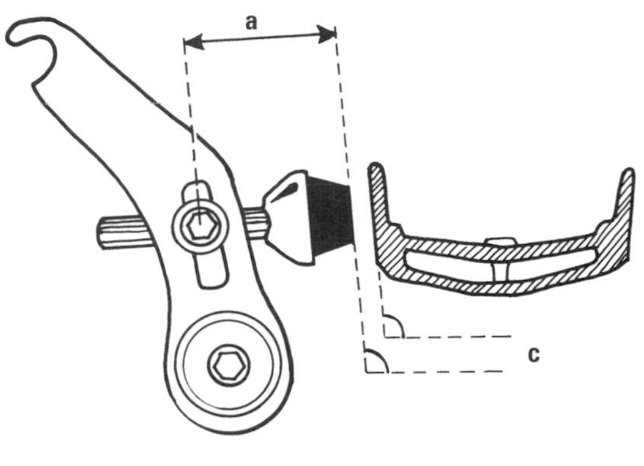

7.31 **Up and down (b) and twist (d)**

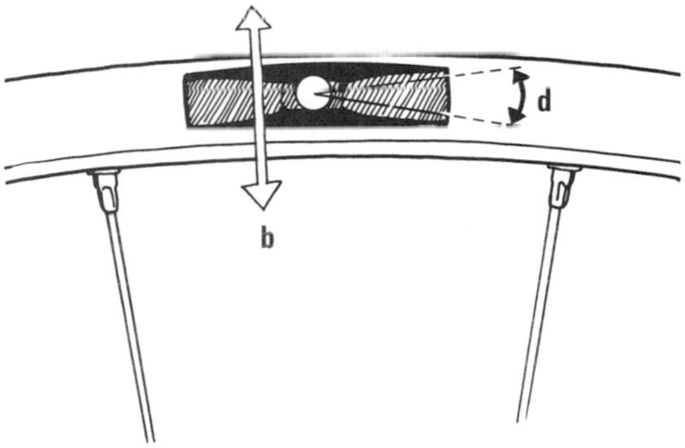

7.32 **Brake pad toe-in (e)**

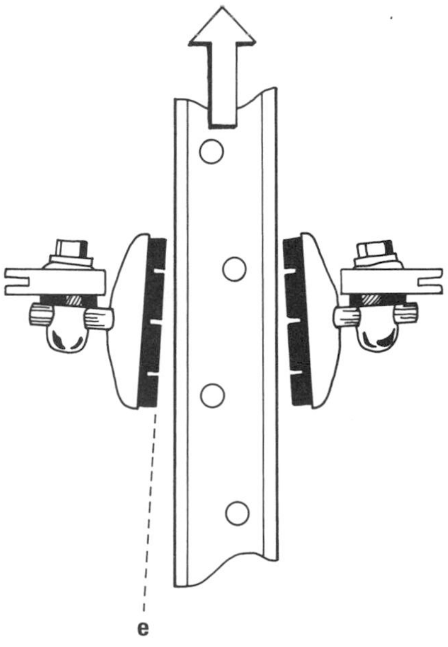

2. Roughly adjust the vertical pad height (*b*, Fig. 7.31), by sliding the pad clamping mechanism up and down in the brake-arm slot. With cylindrical-clamp brakes, loosen the bolt clamping the pad holder to the brake arm, and snug the bolt back up once the rough adjustment is reached. With all other types, leave the pad bolt just loose enough so that you can move the pad easily, and continue.
3. Adjust pad swing in the vertical plane (*c*, Fig. 7.30), so that the face of the pad meets the rim flat with its top edge 1–2mm below the top of the rim. Fine-tune this adjustment by simultaneously sliding the pad up or down while rotating it to meet the rim flat.
4. Adjust the pad twist (*d*, Fig. 7.31), so that the top edge of the pad is parallel to the top of the rim. Modern pads are quite long and require precision with this adjustment. With cylindrical-clamp brakes, the pad-securing bolt may now be tightened.
5. Finally, adjust the pad toe-in (*e*, Fig. 7.32). The pad should either be adjusted flat to the rim, or toed-in so that, when the forward end of the pad touches the rim, the rear end of it is 1mm to 2mm away from the rim.

If the pad is toed-out, the heel of it will catch and tend to chatter, making an obnoxious squealing noise. If the brake arms are not stiff, or they fit loosely on the cantilever boss, the same thing will happen when flat; toe-in is a must with flimsy brake arms and will have to be adjusted frequently as the pads wear to keep them quiet.

On cylindrical-arm brakes with two anchor bolts (Fig. 7.28), the toe-in is adjusted by again loosening the bolt that holds the vertical height adjustment of the pad. Because you have already

7.33 **Curved-face cantilever brake (Ritchey)**

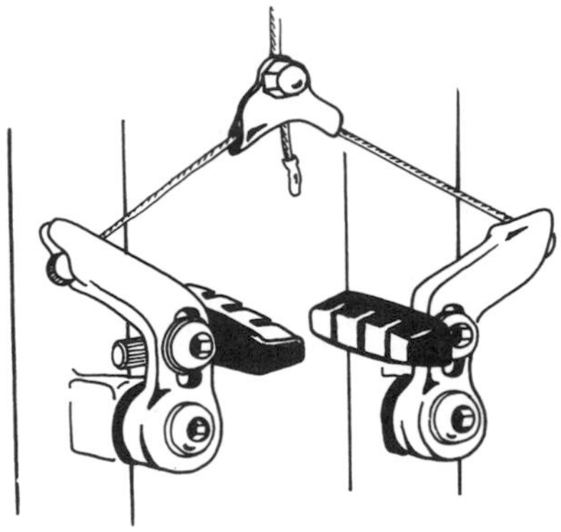

7.34 **Ball-joint cantilever brake (Campagnolo)**

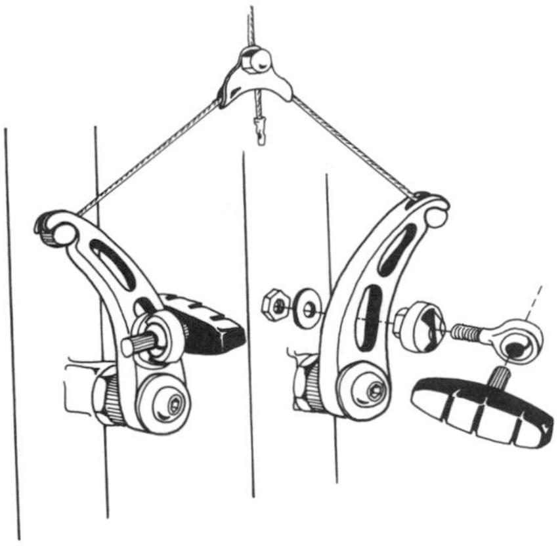

tightened the other bolt that holds the pad in place, you simply loosen this second bolt and swing the pad horizontally until you arrive at your preferred toe-in or flatness setting. Tighten the bolt again, and you are done with pad adjustment.

With any brake using a single bolt to hold the pad as well as control its rotation, you now have a tricky task of holding all of the adjustments you have made and simultaneously tightening the nut. Most eye-bolt systems are tightened with a 10mm wrench on the nut on the back of the brake while the front is held with a 5mm Allen wrench. Help from someone else to either hold or tighten is useful here. Probably the trickiest brake to adjust has a toothed or deeply notched washer between the head of the eye bolt and a flat brake arm (Fig. 7.27). The adjusting washer is thinner on one edge than the other, so rotating it (by means of the tooth or notch) toes the pad in or out. With this type, you must hold all of the pad adjustments as you turn this washer, and then keep it and the pad in place as you tighten the nut. It's not an easy job, and the adjustment changes as you tighten the bolt.

The other common type has a convex or concave shape to the slotted brake arm, and cupped washers separate the eye-bolt head and nut from the brake arm (Shimano, most Dia-Compe, Ritchey [Fig. 7.33], Paul, etc.). The concave against convex surfaces allow the pad to swivel, and tightening the bolt secures everything. Again, you may not get it on the first try. Threaded posts also employ such washers.

NOTE: *Some of these curved-face brakes do not hold their toe-in adjustment well; you may need to sand the brake-arm faces and washers to create more friction between them.*

Brakes with a cylindrical arm and a clamp secured only by the pad eye bolt (WTB, SRP, etc.) are adjusted functionally in the same way as the curved-face ones with cupped washers. A rare, but simple-to-adjust type (Campagnolo, Fig. 7.34) has a ball joint at each pad eye bolt.

STRADDLE CABLE ADJUSTMENT

vii-22 STRADDLE CABLE ADJUSTMENT

The straddle cable should be set so that it pulls on the brake arms in such a way as to provide optimal braking. This is not always the adjustment that produces the highest leverage, for sometimes brake feel (i.e., stiffness when pulling the lever) is improved when leverage is reduced, because you are doing

7.35 **Cable angle when open**

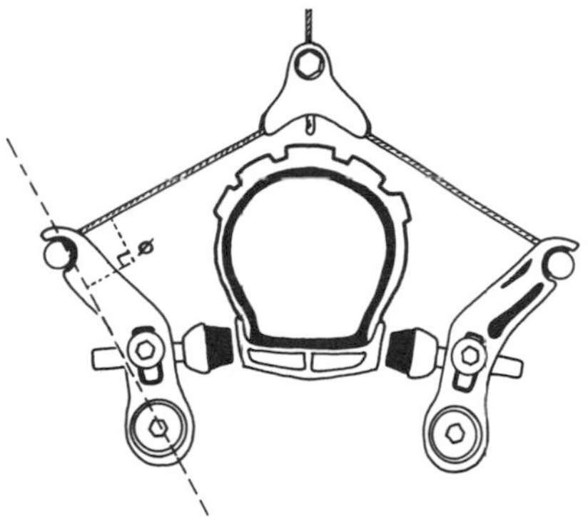

7.36 **Cable angle when closed**

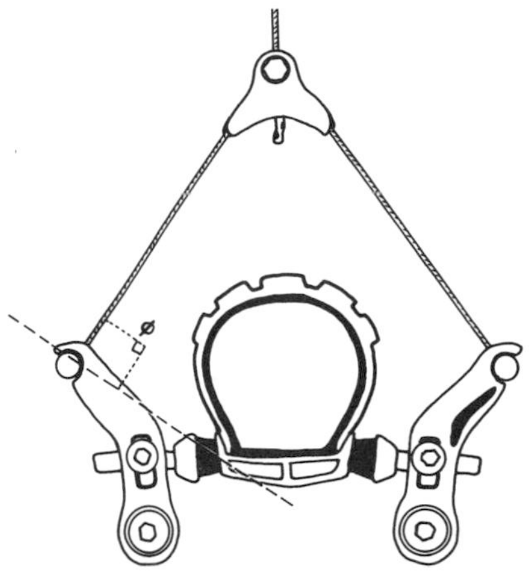

more of the work. In general, I recommend setting it for high leverage and reducing it from there to improve lever feel.

With any lever arm, the mechanical advantage is highest when the force is applied at right angles to the lever arm. For general purposes, set the straddle cable so that it pulls as close to 90 degrees to the brake arm as you can (Fig. 7.35). An esoteric and more precise argument is that once the pad hits the rim, the actual lever arm is the line from the face of the pad to the cable attachment point on top of the arm (because the pad, not the brake boss, now becomes the fulcrum). If you set the straddle cable at 90 degrees from this line, the leverage is maximized (Fig. 7.36).

With low-profile brake arms, a 90-degree straddle-cable angle results in a short straddle cable set very low and close to the tire. Make sure that you allow at least an inch of clearance over the tire to prevent mud, or a bulge in the tire, from engaging the brake.

The straddle cable usually has a metal blob on one end, and the other end is clamped to one brake arm by an anchor bolt (Figs. 7.37–7.39). The blob fits into the slotted brake arm and acts as a quick release for the brake.

7.37–7.39 **Straddle cables**

7.37 Standard

7.38 Two-end

7.39 Link-wire holder with pass-through housing

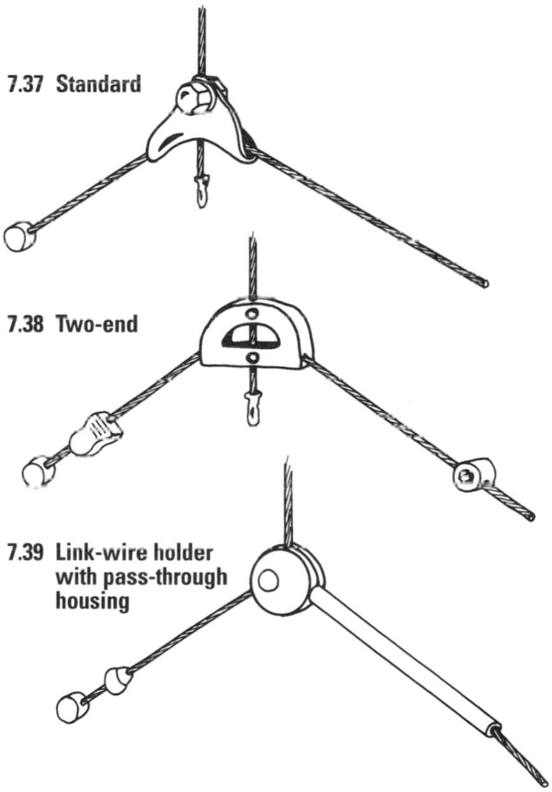

On Shimano cantilevers built since 1988, the brake cable connects directly to the cable clamp on one brake arm, and a link wire hooks to the other arm. On post-1993 Shimano cantilevers, the cable passes through a link-wire holder accommodating not only a

STRADDLE CABLE ADJUSTMENT

link wire but also a fixed length of cable housing (Fig. 7.39). The brake cable passes directly through the link-wire holder and housing segment to the cable clamp on the brake arm. The mechanic has no choice of straddle-cable settings; it is predetermined.

Between 1988 and 1993, Shimano brakes did not have the housing segment on the link-wire holder; instead the holder was clamped to the brake cable, and its position was set by a plastic gauge. If you have this type and no gauge, simply set the cable length from the link-wire holder to the brake arm the same on both sides.

Some brakes do not have a cable clamp on either brake arm; both arms are slotted to accept the blob on the end of a straddle cable or link wire. In this case, a small cylindrical clamp forms a second blob on the end of the straddle cable (Fig. 7.38), or a link-wire holder that holds two separate link wires is used.

With any straddle cable, after setting its length, the position of the straddle-cable holder is set by loosening the bolt or setscrews that hold it onto the end of the brake cable and sliding it up on the brake cable. Tighten it in place (Fig. 7.6; see Figs. 7.37–7.39 for other types). It is set properly when the brake engages quickly, and the lever cannot be pulled closer than a finger's width from the handlebar. Some cable slack can be taken up with the barrel adjuster on the brake lever (Fig. 7.1).

The lateral position of the straddle-cable holder can be changed with setscrews as well. The holder should generally be centered on the straddle cable, but, sometimes, the brake cable pulls asymmetrically as it comes around the seat tube. In these cases, the straddle-cable holder may need to be offset for the brakes to work (Fig. 7.40).

7.40 An offset straddle-cable stop requires an offset straddle hanger

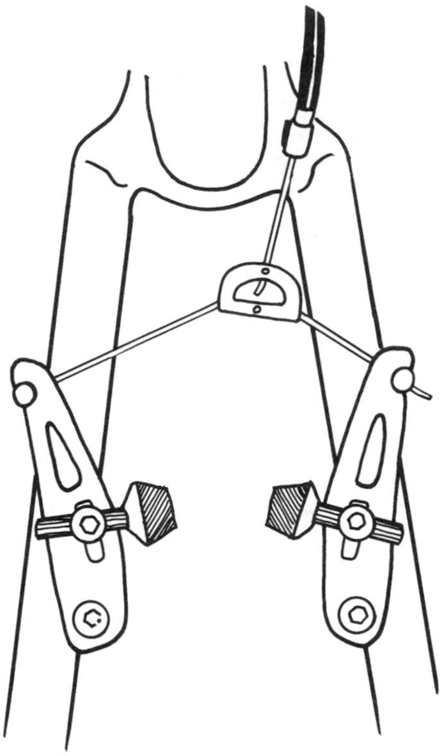

SPRING-TENSION ADJUSTMENT

vii-23 SPRING-TENSION ADJUSTMENT

The spring-tension adjustment centers the brake pads about the rim and also determines the return spring force. There is only one adjustment to make on brakes with a single setscrew on the side of one brake arm. Turn the screw until the brakes are centered and the pads hit the rim simultaneously when applied (Fig. 7.41). Higher spring tensions can be achieved by moving the spring to a higher hole in the brake boss.

Some brakes rely on large tensioning nuts surrounding the mounting bolt and do not use the holes in the brake bosses as anchors (Fig. 7.27). On these, the tensioning nuts may be turned on both arms to get the combination of return force and centering you prefer. You must loosen the mounting bolt while holding the tensioning nut with a wrench.

7.41 **Adjusting return-spring tension with a setscrew**

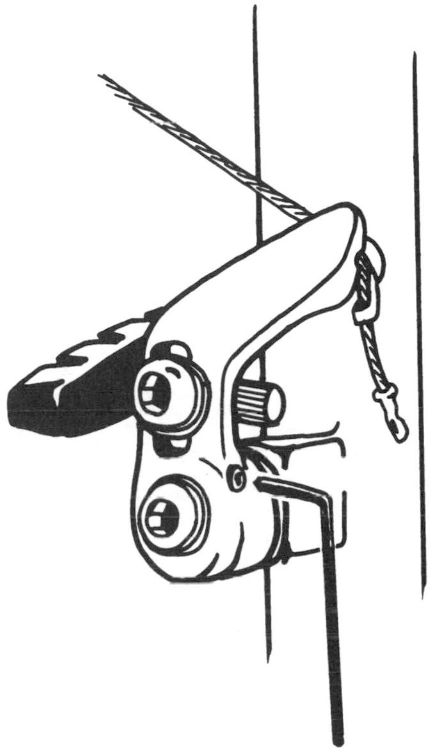

7.42 **Adjusting return-spring tension with tensioning nut**

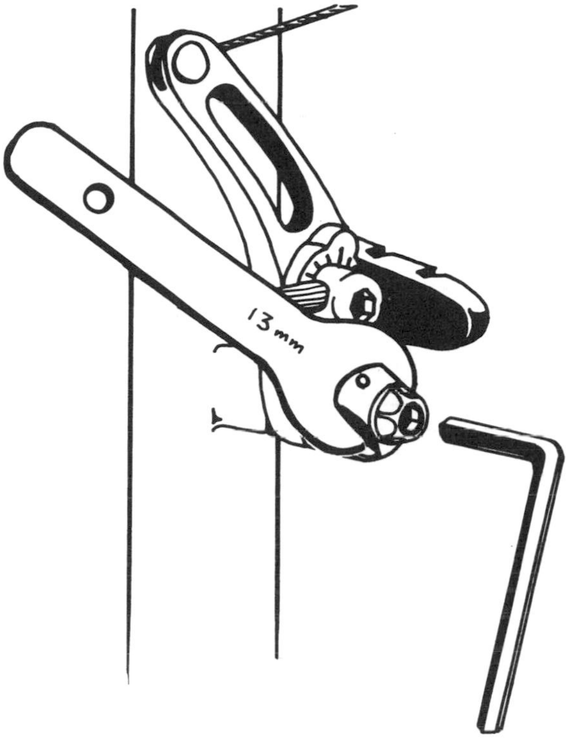

Turn the nut to the desired tension, and, while holding it in place with the wrench, tighten the mounting bolt again (Fig. 7.42).

On really old brakes without a tension adjustment, centering is accomplished by removing the brake arm and moving the spring to another hole on the boss. It is a rough adjustment at best, and some bosses do not have more than a single hole. When this adjustment fails, you can twist the arm on the boss to tighten or loosen the spring a bit. That, of course, is an even rougher adjustment.

NOTE: *If the brake arms do not rotate easily on the brake post, there is too much friction. Remove the brake and check that the post is not bent or split, in which case a new one needs to be screwed in or welded on. If not bent, the post is probably too fat to slide freely inside the brake arm, either owing to paint on it or bulging or mushrooming of the post because of overtightening of the brake mounting bolt. In this case, if it's the replaceable type, screw a new post into the frame or fork. Otherwise, file and sand the circumference of the post to reduce its diameter. File and sand uniformly, only a little at a time; avoid making it too thin.*

vii-24 CANTILEVER LUBRICATION AND SERVICE

The only lubrication necessary on cantilever brakes is on the cables, levers, and brake arms. This should be performed whenever braking feels sticky. Lever and cable lubrication is covered in §vii-5. Cantilevers can be lubricated by removing them, cleaning and greasing the pivots, and replacing them (§vii-19).

Hydraulic Rim Brakes

This term refers to brakes that are fully hydraulic and are mounted on the cantilever bosses. The most common type is Magura (Fig. 7.43), and these instructions, while possibly applicable to others, focus on Maguras.

The advantages to the Magura brake, in addition to its great stopping power, are that it is practically maintenance free and simple to adjust. The system is completely sealed from dirt, and there are no cables and housings to wear. Pads are replaced simply by pulling them out by hand and pushing new ones in. A screw on the lever adjusts pad-to-rim spacing as easily as turning a barrel adjuster on a cable-actuating lever.

NOTE: *As with a hydraulic disc brake, the "master cylinder" is the hydraulic cylinder inside the lever, and each "slave cylinder" (or "wheel cylinder") is the cylinder driving each brake pad (one cylinder for each pad).*

vii-25 MOUNTING MAGURA BRAKE LEVERS

Hydraulic levers are installed onto the handlebar with a 4mm or 5mm Allen wrench, as with cable-actuating levers.

vii-26 INSTALLATION AND ADJUSTMENT OF MAGURA BRAKE CALIPERS ONTO CANTILEVER BRAKE BOSSES

1. Snap a C-shaped plastic ring around each slave (wheel) cylinder.
2. Assemble the adapter brackets around the plastic ring on each wheel cylinder with the supplied 4mm bolts, installing the L-shaped elbow behind the top bracket hole (Fig. 7.45). Right and left wheel cylinders are normally determined by orienting the crossover hose connecting the cylinders toward the bike (Fig. 7.43), i.e., the hose from the lever and the bleed hole are away from the fork or seat stay.

7.43 Magura hydraulic brake

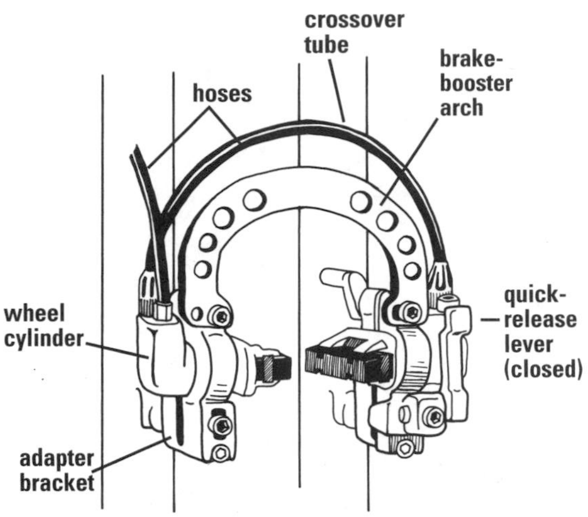

NOTE: *The adapter brackets (Fig. 7.43) are asymmetrical and can be reversed from left to right to move the slave cylinder closer to the rim or vice versa. Normal mounting is with the bracket imprinted with "Magura" on the right when facing the brake.*

3. Slide the included D-shaped washer onto the frame or fork cantilever boss with the flat side of the washer up. A thick washer with a setscrew must be used with some suspension forks to clear the fork brace.
4. Bolt the adapter bracket to the cantilever boss with a bolt and washer. If mounting a bracket with the quick-release feature, first screw the mounting bolt with the spool-shaped head a few turns into the brake boss. Slide the quick-release unit over the mounting slot on the adapter bracket (Fig. 7.44). Push the bracket onto the brake boss so the spool-shaped mounting bolt head comes through the hole in the quick-release unit. Flip the quick-release lever up to its closed

7.44 **Magura brake-pad installation and quick-release operation**

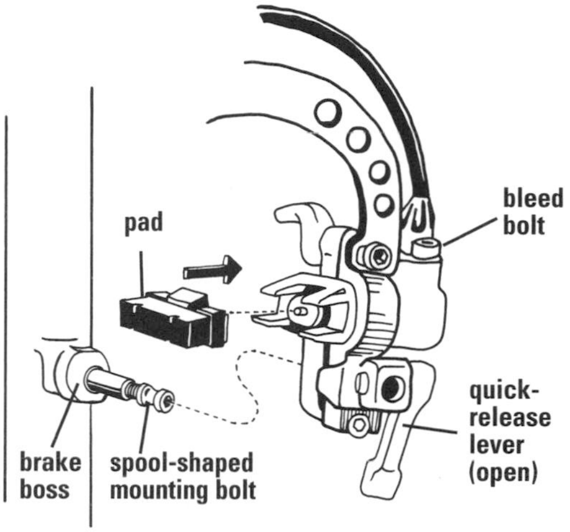

7.45 **Installing and/or adjusting elbow**

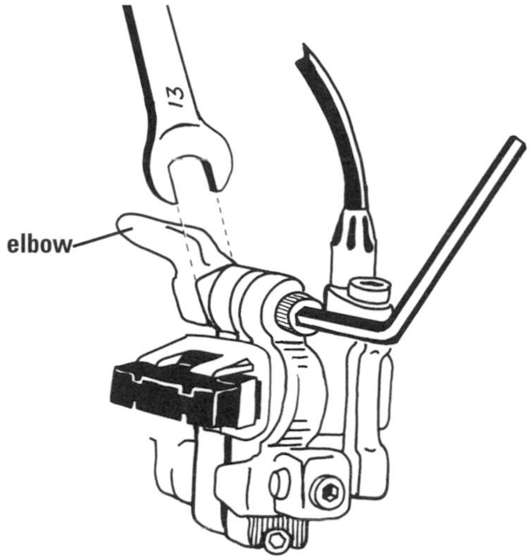

position. Tighten the mounting bolt with a 5mm Allen key. You can now remove this side of the brake by merely flipping the quick-release lever down and pulling the bracket straight off (Fig. 7.44). To install, push the bracket onto the boss so the bolt head sticks out through the hole in the quick-release unit, and flip the lever up.

NOTE: *The quick-release unit is installed properly when the quick-release lever's pivot pin is above the spool-shaped mounting bolt, not below it.*

5. Set the pad position: Sliding the adapter bracket up and down adjusts the height of the wheel cylinder. Loosening the mounting bolt and the other bolt (or bolts) holding the bracket together (Fig. 7.45) allows the cylinder to be slid in or out and rotated. By using these adjustments in tandem, set the pad-to-rim contact so that the pad hits the rim flat about 2mm below its upper edge. See to it that the pad holders do not drag on the tire. When retracted, the pads should sit 2–3mm away from the rim.
6. Once the brake is set to the proper position, the elbows need to be positioned (Fig. 7.45) to support the brake and simplify repositioning after removal. Loosen the bolt above the wheel cylinder. With a 13mm open end wrench, rotate the elbow until it contacts the inner side of the seat stay or fork leg, and tighten the bolt (Fig. 7.45). Aftermarket elbows are available to fit certain suspension forks better.
7. If you have the "brake booster" arch (Fig. 7.43), loosely bolt it onto the right bracket adapter through its oval mounting hole on the right side. Swing the arch over the wheel and slide it laterally until the booster's bottom left hole lines up with, and slips over, the bolt head on the left bracket. Tighten the top bolt on the right bracket to fix the booster in place. When releasing the brake, pull the left side of the booster off of the bolt head, and leave it attached to the right cylinder when pulling it off.
8. To fine-tune pad-to-rim spacing, especially as the pads wear, tighten the adjustment screw on the lever. Some systems take a 2mm Allen key; the screw is under the lever. Newer systems have a finger-operated knob on the front of the lever.

MAGURA HOSE ROUTING
—
MAGURA PAD REPLACEMENT
—
BLEEDING MAGURA RIM BRAKES

vii-27 MAGURA HOSE ROUTING

The hoses cannot go through the cable stops, so if the frame does not have hose guides, you secure them to the frame by means of plastic draw ties, stick-on hydraulic hose guides, or little plastic or aluminum clips that snap over the hose and press or bolt into the frame's cable guides. Make sure there are no kinks in the hoses and that they do not stick out from the bike far enough to hit your legs or hook on obstacles. Damaging hoses is to be avoided, as braking goes away if they become punctured.

Unless your frame is very small or very large, you may be able to get away with simply attaching the brakes to the frame as they come out of the box, already filled and bled, saving yourself the time and effort of bleeding the brakes. Skip to §vii-30 if you are adjusting the hose length.

vii-28 MAGURA PAD REPLACEMENT

Pad replacement is very simple.

1. Once the wheel is off, grab the pad and pull it straight out (Fig. 7.44).
2. Push the new pad in, paying attention to the rotation-indicator arrow on it. That's it!

vii-29 BLEEDING MAGURA RIM BRAKES

LEVEL 2

Sponginess of brakes indicates the need for bleeding air from the lines. Bleeding is a maintenance operation that also clears out dirt that has crept in and should be done every 500 miles or so. If the oil inside comes out clean, you will know you can wait longer next time. There is rarely a need to bleed due to air bubbles, because air does not get in unless the system is opened or gets damaged. That said, any air bubbles will rise toward the highest point in the system, so they should be up in the lever after any ride, meaning that it will not take much new fluid to drive them out.

1. Back up the 2mm microadjustment screw under the lever and the 2mm reach-adjustment screw on top of the lever; or, on newer models, back up the single knob on the front of the lever.
2. Keeping the bleed bolt at the lever closed, remove the bleed bolt (Fig. 7.44) on the right brake slave cylinder.

IMPORTANT: *Never squeeze the lever while the system is open; fluid will squirt out.*

3. The Magura syringe has a tube with a barbed fitting on the end (Fig. 7.46). Fill the syringe with Magura brake fluid or low-viscosity mineral oil meant for hydraulic brakes (never with automotive brake fluid), invert it, and push any air up and out with the plunger. Screw the fitting into the bleed hole on the wheel cylinder (Fig. 7.46). (In a pinch, a squirt bottle of fluid can be used instead of the syringe, but it is easy to allow air in

7.46 Bleeding and/or filling Magura brake hoses

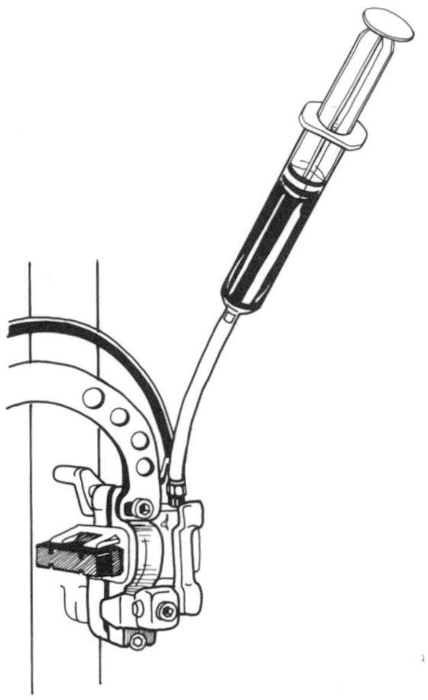

7.47 **Installing hydraulic brake hose**

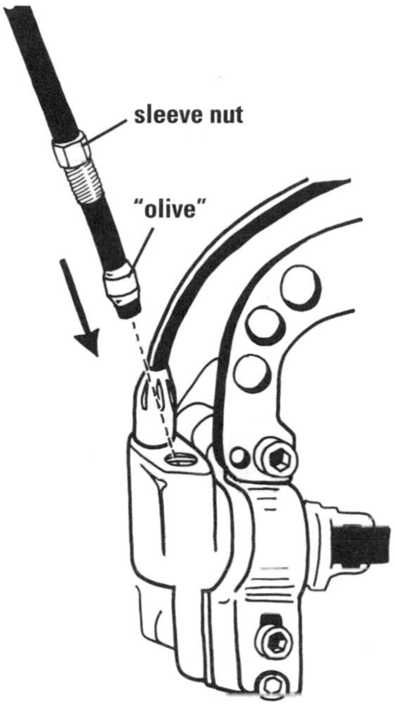

this way. You will need another person to hold the bottle tip tightly into the bleed hole and squeeze the bottle while you open and close the lever bleed bolt.)

4. Tip the bike or rotate the lever on the handlebar so the lever bleed bolt is at its highest point, and remove the bolt from the lever.
5. Push fluid into the wheel cylinder with the syringe (Fig. 7.46). Let it push fluid out of the lever.

NOTE: *A cleaner way to do this procedure is to screw in a piece of tubing with a barbed fitting into the lever bleed hole. Have the tube drain into a bottle of fluid hanging from the handlebar (Fig.7.23).*

6. While the fluid is still flowing, reinstall the bleed bolt at the lever and tighten it. Make sure the bolt and washer are free of grit.
7. Remove the syringe or bottle from the wheel cylinder, leaving a dome of fluid bulging from the hole. Put the bolt back in, and tighten it; again, the bolt and washer must be free of grit. If the bubbles have all been driven out, the brake will no longer feel spongy. Repeat until it is right. You may need to bleed it again after riding; the bubbles will have collected at the lever.
8. Adjust the pad spacing and lever reach as you wish with the two 2mm bolts or the single knob on the lever.

vii-30 CUTTING MAGURA HYDRAULIC BRAKE HOSES

1. Pull the plastic cover off of the crossover hose-sleeve nut and slide it up the hose to get it out of the way. Unscrew the main hose-sleeve nut with an 8mm wrench and pull the hose out (Fig. 7.47).

IMPORTANT: *Again, never squeeze the brake lever while the system is open.*

2. Cut the hose to length with a sharp blade, making sure it is a perpendicular cut. For every end you cut, you must have a brass "olive" fitting from Magura (Fig. 7.47); get them in advance.
3. Slide the 8mm sleeve nut up the hose.
4. Slide the brass olive on, with the step-cut end toward the sleeve nut.
5. Stick the hose into the brake-cylinder hole (Fig. 7.47), and screw in the sleeve nut by hand. Tighten the nut with an 8mm wrench. Push the plastic cover back onto the crossover hose-sleeve nut.
6. If shortening the hose, bleeding may not be necessary unless the brakes feel spongy. (If you cut the hose while holding it pointed up and drip a dome of oil into the hose hole on the wheel cylinder, you can reduce the chances of air getting in.)

7.48 Linkage brake

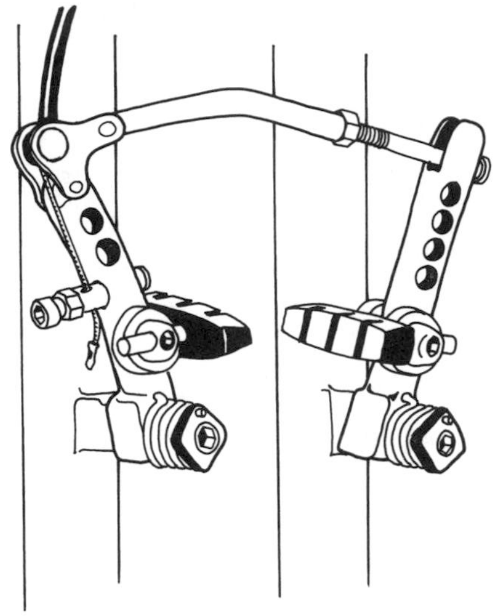

7.49 U-brake (usually under chainstays)

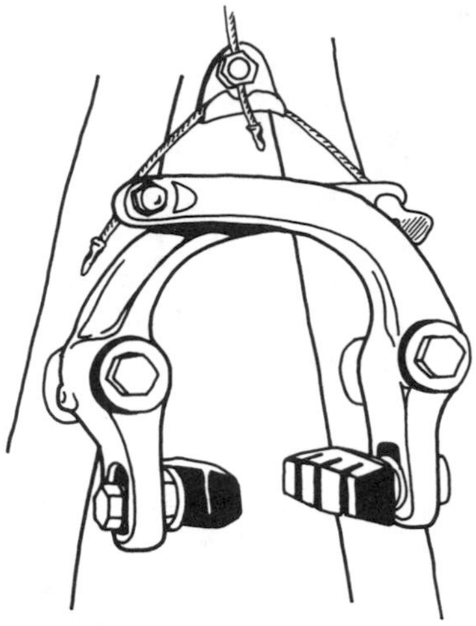

If installing new hose, make the connection at the brake lever the same way. Fill and bleed the line following the bleeding instructions in §vii-29.

Linkage Brakes

There are so many vastly different linkage brakes (Fig. 7.48) besides V-brakes floating around on older bikes that it would not be possible to include them all in detail here. Linkage brakes are often quite similar to cantilevers or V-brakes and are adjusted, centered, and mounted in much the same way. If in doubt, refer to specific instructions from the manufacturer.

U-Brakes

vii-31 U-BRAKE INSTALLATION

U-brakes (Fig. 7.49), once very popular under the chainstays of mountain bikes, mount on the same bosses that roller-cam brakes (Fig. 7.50) do, but at a greater distance from the hub than cantilever bosses. Like roller-cams, U-brakes cannot be mounted on cantilever bosses, as the pads would hit the tire rather than contact the rim.

1. Grease the pivots.
2. Slide the arms onto the pivots.
3. Screw in the mounting bolts.
4. Attach the straddle-cable yoke to the brake cable (Fig. 7.6).
5. Attach the straddle cable to the cable clamp on one arm.
6. An easy way to set the position of the straddle-cable yoke on a chainstay-mounted U-brake is to squeeze the lever to the grip after slipping the yoke up against the bottom-bracket cable guide. Then tighten it in place. This position is the highest it could be set on the cable and allows for the longest possible straddle cable.

vii-32 U-BRAKE ADJUSTMENT

1. Set the position of the rear straddle-cable yoke on the brake cable as outlined above. On a front brake, set it about 2 inches above the brake.
2. Tighten the straddle cable while pulling the brake cable tight with a pair of pliers (Fig. 7.6) and squeezing the pads against the rim with your

7.50 **Roller-cam brake**

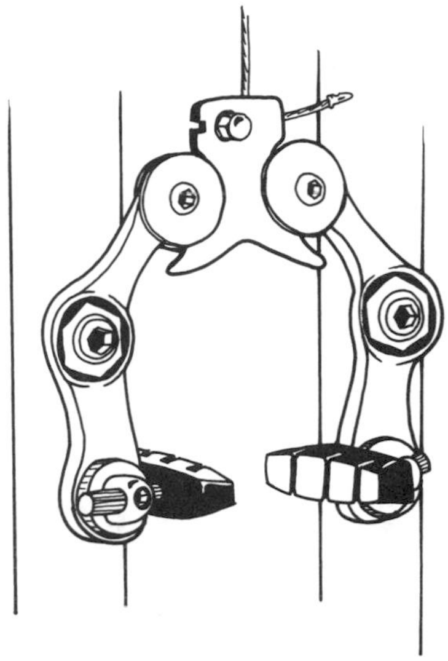

hand. Make sure you have tightened the anchor bolts enough that the cables do not slip.

3. Check that you cannot pull the lever closer than a finger's width from the grip. Tension the cable as needed with the straddle-cable yoke or the lever barrel adjuster (Fig. 7.1).
4. Set the spring tension by releasing the straddle cable, loosening the mounting bolt, and swinging the pad away from the rim; then tighten the mounting bolt. Center the brake by setting the spring tension on one arm first, followed by the other arm in the same fashion. If your brake has a small Allen setscrew on the side of one arm, use it to make fine spring-tension adjustments.

vii-33 REPLACEMENT AND POSITIONING OF U-BRAKE PADS

U-brakes rely on brake pads with threaded posts. Install them with the original spacers in their original orientation. The pads should hit the center of the braking surface and should have a small amount of toe-in. There is no adjustment for spacing from the brake arm. Hold the pad in place with your hand while tightening the nut with a wrench. As the pads wear, they tend to slide up on the rim and hit the tire, so check this adjustment frequently. You should also regularly clear hardened mud from inside of the brake arms; it can build up here on U-brakes and abrade the tire sidewalls.

Roller-Cam Brakes

vii-34 ROLLER-CAM REMOVAL AND INSTALLATION

Roller-cam brakes (Fig. 7.50) mount on U-brake bosses attached to the fork and either the chainstays or the seat stays. These are mounted farther from the hub than cantilever bosses, and, like U-brakes, they will not work on standard cantilever bosses.

Roller-cams are removed by first pulling the cam plate out from between the rollers on the ends of the arms. Remove the mounting bolt and pull the arms off of the bosses.

Installation is performed in reverse. Grease the bosses and the inside of the pivots as well as the edges of the cam plate and the mounting bolts.

vii-35 ROLLER-CAM ADJUSTMENT

1. Check that the pulleys spin freely, and loosen them with a 5mm Allen wrench on the front and an open-end wrench on the back. The pulleys should rest on the narrow part of the cam, which gives the greatest mechanical advantage when the brakes are applied. You change pad spacing by changing the location of the cam on the cable.
2. Use a 17mm wrench on the nut surrounding the mounting bolt to center the brake or to adjust spring tension. Loosen the mounting bolt, make

small adjustments to the 17mm nut, and tighten the mounting bolt down again.

3. Once the adjustments are set, tighten the cam onto the cable so it will not slip.

vii-36 REPLACEMENT AND POSITIONING OF ROLLER-CAM PADS

The pad eye bolt is held on the front with a 5mm Allen wrench. The bolt in the back is adjusted by using a 10mm open wrench. The pads should be toed in slightly. As the pads wear, they tend to slide up the rim and rub the tire, so check this adjustment periodically.

vii-37 BRAKE TROUBLESHOOTING

The first thing to check with any brake is that it stops the bike!

1. While the bike is stationary, pull each lever and see that it firmly engages the brake while the lever is still at least a finger's width away from the handlebar grip. If not, skip to §vii-2 to §vii-4 on cable tensioning, or to §vii-14 to §vii-15 for adjusting and bleeding hydraulic disc brakes or adjusting mechanical disc brakes, or to §vii-26 to §vii-29 for adjusting and bleeding hydraulic rim brakes, if those are what you have.
2. Move at 10 mph or so, and apply each brake one at a time. By itself, the rear brake should be able to lock up the rear wheel and skid the tire, and the front brake alone should come on hard enough that it will cause the bike to pitch forward. Careful. Don't overdo it and hurt yourself testing your brakes!

If you can't stop the bike quickly, you must make some adjustments and, perhaps, do a little cleaning. A brake works by forcing the brake pads into contact with the rim (or disc) to create friction. Anything that reduces the ability of these surfaces to generate friction against each other compromises braking. With this principle in mind, it should be obvious that these surfaces need to be clean and dry, that they should line up well with each other, and that the mechanism to pull them into contact should move freely and pull at an angle that offers high mechanical advantage.

That said, you can probably generate the following brake-inspection list to perform frequently:

1. **Cable length:** Check that the cable is short enough to pull the pads against the rims or discs without the levers contacting the handlebar grips, but long enough to allow the wheels to turn without dragging on the pads, once the pads are centered. See cable tensioning sections, vii-2 to vii-4, to adjust.
2. **Clean rims (or discs):** Check for and remove any grease or glaze buildup on rims and pads. Grease can be removed with rags or a solvent, and lightly buffing aluminum or steel (not ceramic!) rim surfaces with sandpaper will remove glaze. Solvent residues on pads, rims, and discs cause brake squeal. You can remove such residues with soap and water. Disc-brake rotors and pads are cleaned with alcohol. You can also clean disc-brake pads with a file or by rubbing them together.
3. **Pad wear:** Check that the pads are not excessively worn (Fig. 7.51); if they have crosswise wear-indicator grooves, make sure these are not worn off. Make sure the pads contact the rims effectively (Figs. 7.14 and 7.30–7.32). Dig out any rocks or pieces of aluminum that are embedded in the pads to prevent rim damage (Fig. 7.52). Beware of lip formation on the top edge of the

7.51 **Worn brake pad**

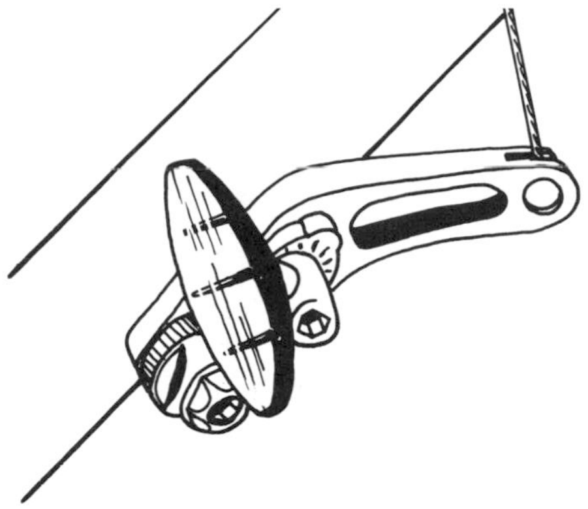

7.52 **Cleaning dirt from brake pad**

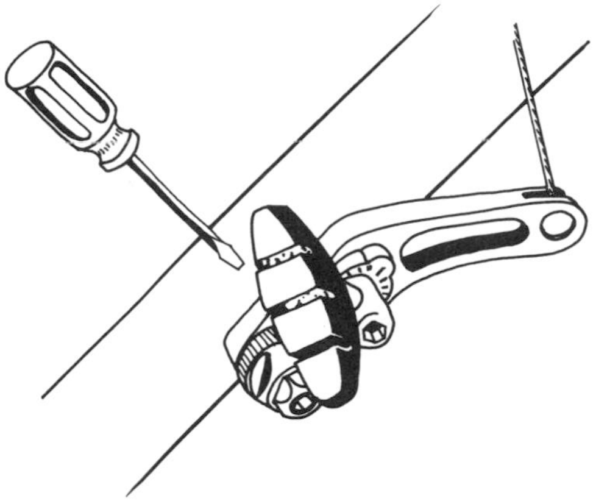

pad over the rim edge as the lower part of the pad wears away; this lip can prevent the pad from releasing from the rim. On disc brake pads, make sure the friction material is at least the thickness of a couple of business cards. Replace or adjust pads as needed, and adjust the brake (refer to the section that applies to your brake) to get the desired response. Get good pads; poor-quality pads can wear quickly and can require more than twice as much distance to stop as good ones!

4. **Cable wear:** Check the cables for fraying, wear, and free movement, and check that the angle at which the cable meets each cantilever brake arm is close to 90 degrees (pulling at right angles generates the most leverage [Figs. 7.35–7.36]). If replacing cables, see Cable Installation, §vii-6. Recognize that cables, housings, and pads are maintenance items; replace them frequently with good-quality ones. On hydraulic brakes, check the hoses for damage and wear.

5. **Centered brakes:** Check that the brakes are centered (the pads are spaced equally from either side of the rim or disc rotor) and that they apply and return easily. Readjust as needed (see adjustment section for your brake).

6. **Toe-in:** If rim brakes squeal, and the rims and pads are clean (steps 2 and 3 above), toe the pads in so that the forward corner of each pad touches the rim while the trailing corner is 1mm or so away from it (Fig. 7.32). See pad adjustment under your brake type. The flimsier the brake arms, or the looser they are on the brake bosses, the more toe-in is required.

7. **Brake-boss flex:** If the seat stays or the fork legs are too flexible, applying rim brakes will bow them outward and decrease braking pressure. This tendency can be counteracted by attaching a horseshoe-shaped "brake booster" connecting the brake mounting bolts and bridging over the tire. These boosters are available for V-brakes, cantilevers, hydraulic rim brakes (see Fig. 7.43), U-brakes, roller-cams, and other linkage brakes.

8. **Disc-brake howl or rub:** Clean the rotors with alcohol, check for hydraulic fluid leaks (step 11, §vii-15b), check rotor tightness (§vii-14a), check caliper centering (§vii-14b or §vii-14c), and check pad spacing (§vii-14f).

CHAPTER 8

CRANKS AND BOTTOM BRACKETS

If you don't have time to do it right the first time, you must have time to do it over again.
—Anonymous

TOOLS

5mm and 8mm Allen wrenches
pliers
file
crank puller
crank-bolt wrenches (Allen or socket)
chainring nut tool
splined bottom-bracket cup tool
integrated spindle, external-bearing bottom-bracket tool
⅜-inch drive socket
screwdriver
adjustable pin tool
lockring spanner
pin spanner

OPTIONAL TOOLS

shop-style fixed-cup installation tool

The crank and bottom bracket (a.k.a. BB) is the power center for you and your bike. It is through this system that your energy is converted into forward movement of the bike. The crankset consists of the crankarms, bottom bracket, chainrings, chainring bolts, and crank bolt (Fig. 8.1).

Any problem in the crankset can result in a large drop in available propulsion. The pedaling forces applied to it are so large that expensive damage can easily be done throughout the drivetrain if its parts are not set up correctly. All crankset parts need to be secured very tightly to oppose these large forces and prevent you from ruining expensive parts by using them when loose.

CRANKARMS AND CHAINRINGS

viii-1 CRANK REMOVAL AND INSTALLATION

To remove a traditional crankset, you will need either a thin-wall 14mm or 15mm socket wrench or a large, 8mm Allen wrench in order to remove the crank bolt. You may or may not need a crank puller (Fig. 1.2) to take off the crankarms. To remove integrated-spindle cranks (cranks in which one crankarm is permanently fixed to the spindle, and the bearings are external to the bottom bracket) you may only need a 5mm hex key. For Shimano, you also need a special splined tool for the left arm cap, and for FSA Mega Exo carbon, Race Face X-Type, and Truvativ Giga X Pipe (GXP) cranks, you need an 8mm hex key.

NOTE: *"Right," in this chapter and generally throughout this book, refers to the drive side of the bike, and "left" refers to the nondrive side.*

Most traditional mountain bike crank bolts take either an 8mm Allen wrench or a 14mm socket wrench. Older systems may take a 15mm socket or a 7mm Allen wrench, and you may still run across a few of those old French TA cranks with 16mm bolts.

8.1 Crankset exploded

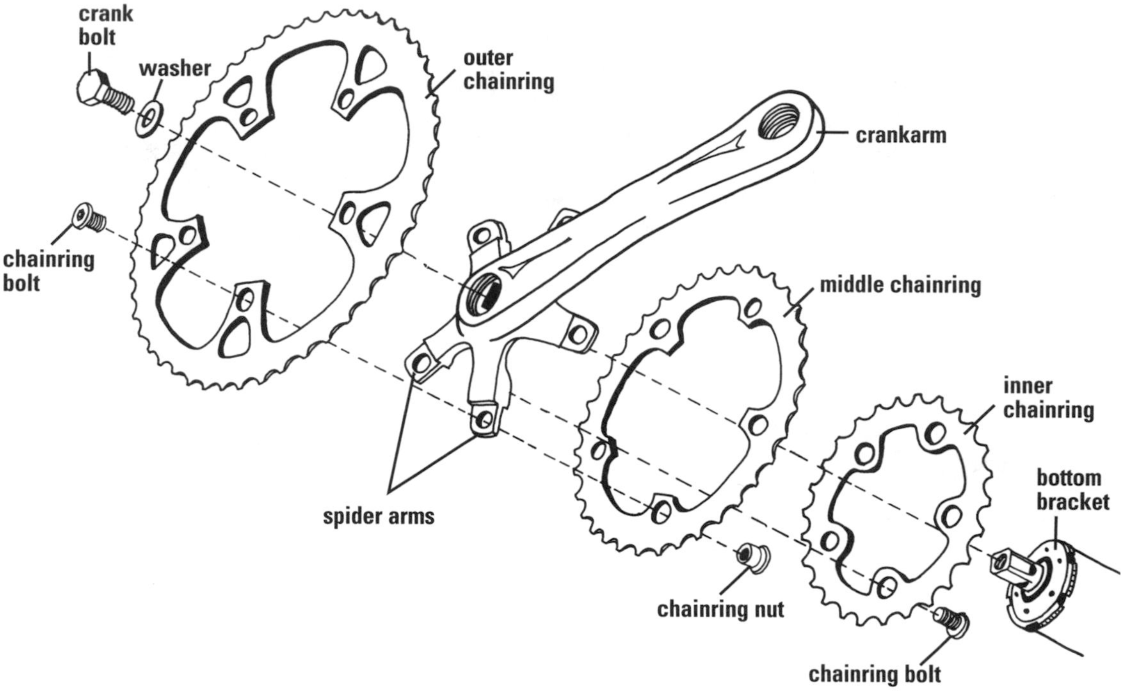

a. Removal

Traditional cranks

1. Older cranksets have a dust cap covering the crank bolt. If it's there, remove it with either a 5mm Allen wrench, a two-pin dust cap tool, or a screwdriver.
2. Remove the crank bolt with the appropriate wrench (Fig. 8.2). Make sure that you extract the washer with the bolt (Fig. 8.1), if there is a washer (if you leave it in, you will not be able to pull the crank off).

NOTE: *Some cranks, such as the Shimano Octalink 1996–2002 XTR pictured in Figures 8.8 and 8.13, are self-extracting and don't require a crank puller. The crank bolt has a lip held down by a retaining ring threaded into the crank; as the bolt is unscrewed, its lip pushes on the ring and pushes the crank off. Sometimes it doesn't work, and the retaining ring unscrews. In this case, you need to hold the ring with an adjustable pin tool while you unscrew the bolt with an 8mm Allen key. Self-extracting bolts are never to be used with ISIS spindles as doing so will void the warranty.*

ANOTHER NOTE: *"Square taper," "Octalink," and "ISIS" aer three different bottom-bracket and crankarm interface standards. Square taper bottom-bracket spindles are square on the end and fit into a square hole in the crankarm. The spindle ends are tapered (usually to a 2-degree angle) to tighten more into the crank the further the arm is pushed into the spindle. Octalink and ISIS are both oversized hollow spindles (a.k.a. "pipe spindles") with longitudinal splines on the ends. Octalink is a Shimano standard (there are actually two different Octalink standards), while ISIS is a standard mutually agreed upon by a number of Shimano's competitors (since Shimano prevents other manufacturers from infringing upon or licensing its Octalink standards).*

8.2 **Removing and installing a crank bolt**

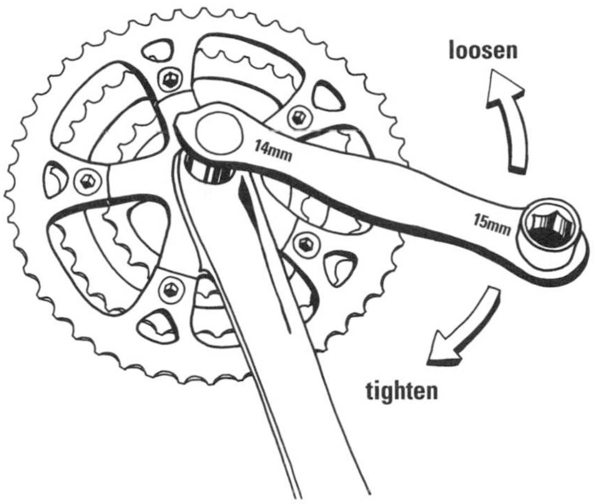

8.3 **Using a crank puller**

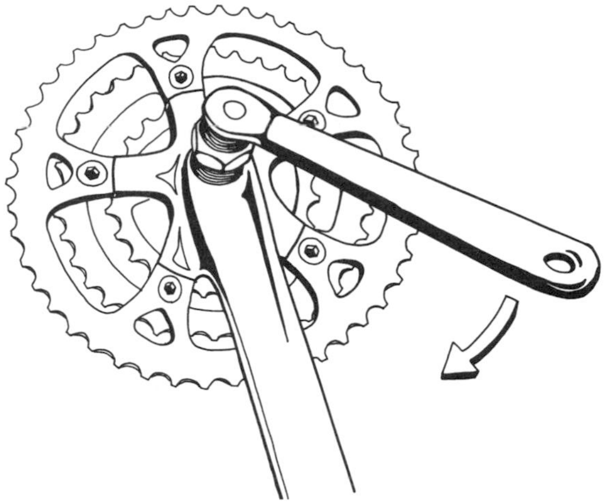

3. Holding the crank puller (Fig. 1.2) in your hand, unscrew its center push bolt so that the inner and outer threaded ends of the tool are flush. Make sure the flat end of the push bolt is the right size for your bottom bracket; the push bolt end is much smaller for a square-taper spindle than for an ISIS or Shimano Octalink splined spindle.
4. Thread the crank puller into the hole in the crankarm. Be sure that you thread it in (by hand) as far as it can go; otherwise, you will not engage sufficient crank threads when you tighten the push bolt, and you will damage the threads. Future crank removal depends on those threads being in good condition.
5. Tighten the push bolt clockwise (Fig. 8.3), either with the socket wrench or the included handle, until the crankarm pulls off of the spindle. Unscrew the puller from the crankarm.

Integrated-spindle, external bearing cranks

1. Removing the arms.
   (a) On Shimano and FSA aluminum cranks, unscrew and remove the cap on the end of the left arm (with the special splined tool for Shimano [Fig. 1.2]; with a hex key for FSA). With a 5mm hex key, loosen the two pinch bolts holding the arm onto the spindle, and pull off the left arm (Fig. 8.15).
   (b) On FSA Mega Exo carbon-fiber and Truvativ GXP cranks, unscrew the left arm with an 8mm hex key, the same as a nonintegrated self-extracting crank. The arm will come right off. The same holds for Race Face X-Type, except it is the right crankarm that is removable, not the left.
2. Pull the right arm straight outward by hand, which brings the spindle out of the cups with it. On some FSA cranks, you will have a rubber O-ring to pull off of each end of the spindle.

b. Installation

Traditional cranks (square-taper, ISIS, and Octalink)

1. Slide the crankarm onto the bottom-bracket spindle. With square-taper spindles, clean off all grease from both parts. Grease may allow the soft aluminum crank to slide too far onto the steel or

titanium spindle and could deform the square hole in the crank. Apply grease to an ISIS or Shimano Octalink splined spindle. With ISIS and Octalink cranks you must be careful to line up the crank splines with those on the spindle before tightening the crank bolt. You can wreck a crank if you don't, and no warranty covers improper installation.

2. Install the crank bolt. Apply grease to the threads, and tighten (Fig. 8.2). Apply titanium-specific antiseize compound for titanium spindles and for titanium crank bolts. If you have aluminum or titanium crank bolts, first tighten the cranks on with the greased steel bolt to the specified torque, then replace the steel bolt with the lightweight bolt, and tighten it to spec.

NOTE: *Here is where a torque wrench comes in handy; tighten the bolt to about 32–49 N·m (300–435 in-lbs) for regular bolts, and as high as 59 N·m for the steel oversized bolts used with splined (ISIS or Octalink) spindles (see the torque table, Appendix D). If you're not using a torque wrench, make sure the bolt is really tight, but don't muscle it until your veins pop.*

3. Replace the dust cover, if your crank has one.
4. Removing and reinstalling the right crankarm could affect chainring position and hence shifting, so check the front-derailleur adjustment. (See Chapter 5, §v-5.)
5. You're done. Go ride your bike. Recheck the torque after one ride as the crank may settle in and the bolt will need retightening. Periodically check the torque from then on.

CRANK REMOVAL & INSTALLATION

Integrated-spindle, external bearing cranks

1. Grease the end of the spindle, the face and bore of each bearing, and areas of the spindle that will contact the bearings. Push the bottom-bracket spindle (which is attached to the right crankarm) in through the cups (whose oversized bearings are external to the bottom-bracket shell) from the drive side (from the left for Race Face X-Type).
2. Slide the left arm onto the spindle protruding from the left cup (right arm and cup for Race Face), checking that the crank is at 180 degrees from the right arm (Shimano spindles have two wider splines to ensure this).
   (a) On Truvativ GXP cranks and FSA Mega Exo carbon-fiber cranks, tighten the left arm with an 8mm hex key, the same as a normal crank. Put on your pedals and go riding.
   (b) On Shimano and FSA Mega Exo aluminum cranks, tighten the left-side dust cap (Fig. 8.15), but not very tightly—0.4 to 0.7 N·m—just enough to pull the right and left cranks over against the bottom-bracket cups by using the special splined cap tool for Shimano or with a hex key for FSA. The Shimano tool is just a round disc meant to be turned by hand to prevent overtightening the dust cap (Fig. 1.2).
3. On Shimano and FSA aluminum arms, tighten the two opposing (greased) pinch bolts (Fig. 8.15) to 10–15 N·m by using a 5mm hex key, alternately tightening each bolt one-quarter turn at a time.
4. Recheck the torque after one ride as the crank may settle in and the bolts will need retightening. Periodically check the torque from then on.

NOTE: *All instructions for Truvativ GXP and FSA Mega Exo carbon cranks apply to Race Face X-Type cranks, except reversed, since the left Race Face crankarm is integrated with the spindle, and the right tightens and loosens onto the splined spindle end with a self-extracting bolt turned by an 8mm hex key.*

viii-2 CHAINRINGS

You should get into the habit of checking your chainrings regularly. They do wear out and need to be replaced. It's hard to say how often, so include chainrings as part of your regular maintenance checklist. Check your chainrings for wear when you replace your chain.

The chainring teeth should be checked periodically for wear; the chainring bolts should be checked periodically for tightness; the chainrings themselves should be checked for trueness by watching them as they spin past the front derailleur.

1. Wipe the chainring down and inspect each tooth. The teeth should be straight and uniform in size and shape. If the teeth are hook-shaped, the chainring needs to be replaced. The chain should be replaced as well (see Chapter 4, §iv-5), because this tooth shape effectively changes the spacing between the teeth and accelerates wear on the chain and because a worn chain causes hook-shaped teeth in the first place.

CAUTION: *Don't be deceived by the seemingly erratic tooth shapes designed to facilitate shifting; if such teeth repeat regularly that's probably what they are. Shifting ramps located on the inner side (Fig. 8.4) that are meant to speed chain movement between the rings often look like cracks on cheaper chainrings, since they are pressed into the ring rather than being a separate piece riveted on, as on better chainrings.*

NOTE: *Another wear evaluation method is to lift the chain from the top of the chainring; the greater the wear of either part, the farther the chain separates. If it lifts more than one tooth, at least the chain, and perhaps the chainring, needs to be replaced.*

2. Remove minor gouges and small burrs in the chainring teeth with a file.

8.4 **Chainring shifting ramps**

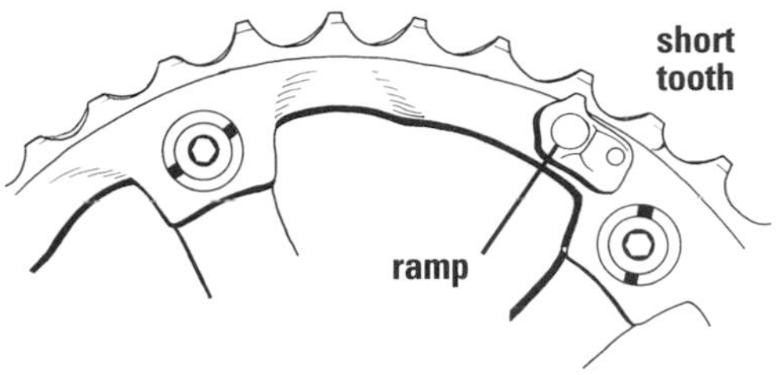

8.5 **Removing and installing chainring bolts**

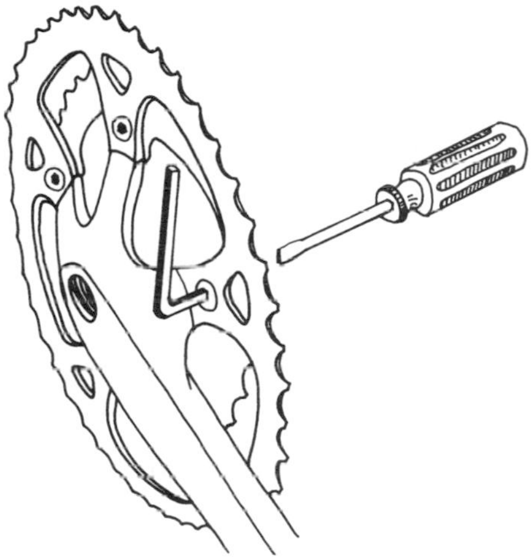

3. If an individual tooth is bent, try bending it back carefully with a pair of pliers or a crescent wrench. It will likely break off; take the message and buy a new chainring.
4. While slowly turning the crank, watch where the chain exits the bottom of the chainring. See if any of the teeth are reluctant to let go of the chain. That can cause chain suck. Locate any offending teeth and see if you can correct the problem. If the teeth are really chewed up or cannot be improved with pliers and a file, the chainring should be replaced.

viii-3 CHAINRING BOLTS

Check that the bolts are tight by turning them clockwise (usually with a 5mm Allen wrench—Fig. 8.5).

As you try to tighten the bolt, the nut on the backside may turn; if so, hold it with a two-pronged chainring-nut tool designed especially for this purpose (Fig. 1.2). If you don't have this tool, use a screwdriver—but do so with caution; it is difficult to grip the nut with a screwdriver (Fig. 8.5).

Some chainring bolts take a star-shaped TORX T30 tool instead of a 5mm hex key. Yet others take a 6mm hex key for the nut on the backside, rather than the pronged chainring-nut tool.

viii-4 WARPED CHAINRINGS

Looking down from above, turn the crank slowly and see whether the chainrings wobble back and forth relative to the plane of the front derailleur.

If they do, make sure there is no play in the bottom bracket by adjusting your bottom bracket (§viii-8, step 15). It is normal to have a small amount of chainring wobble and flex when you pedal hard, but excessive wobbling will compromise shifting. Small, localized bends can be straightened with an adjustable wrench (Fig. 8.7).

If the chainring is really bent, replace it.

viii-5 BENT CRANKARM SPIDERS

If you installed a new chainring and are still seeing serious back-and-forth wobble, chances are good that the spider arms (Fig. 8.1) on your crank are bent. If the crank is new, this is a warranty item, so return it to your bike shop.

viii-6 CHAINRING REPLACEMENT

a. Replacing either of the two largest chainrings (Fig. 8.6) is easy

1. Simply unscrew the five bolts holding the chainrings on the spider arms (Fig. 8.5), by using a 5mm Allen key, or for some bolts, a TORX T30 wrench. You may need to hold the nut on the backside with either a pronged chainring-nut tool or a thin screwdriver (or, for some nuts, a 6mm hex key).
2. Install the new rings, lubricate the bolts and the little recesses that accept them in the chainring faces, and tighten them (Fig. 8.5). The outer chainring has a protruding pin meant to keep the chain from falling down between it and the

8.6 Outer and middle chainrings

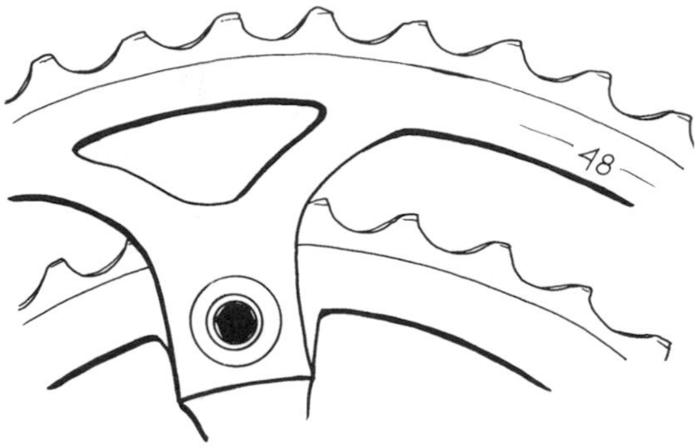

8.7 Straightening bent chainring

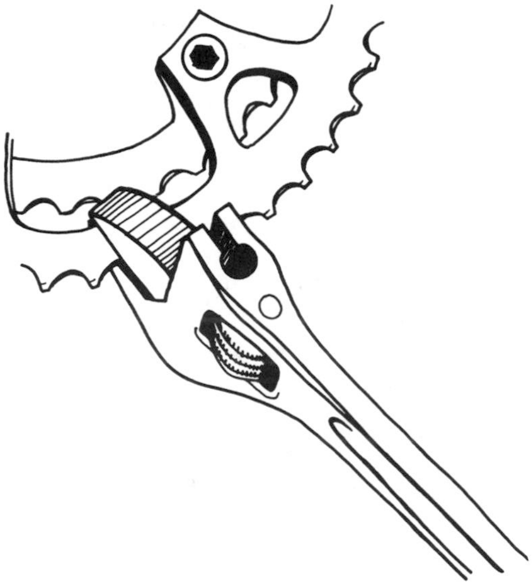

WARPED CHAINRINGS — BENT CRANKARM SPIDERS — CHAINRING REPLACEMENT

8.8 Removing and installing 1996–2002 Shimano XTR chainrings

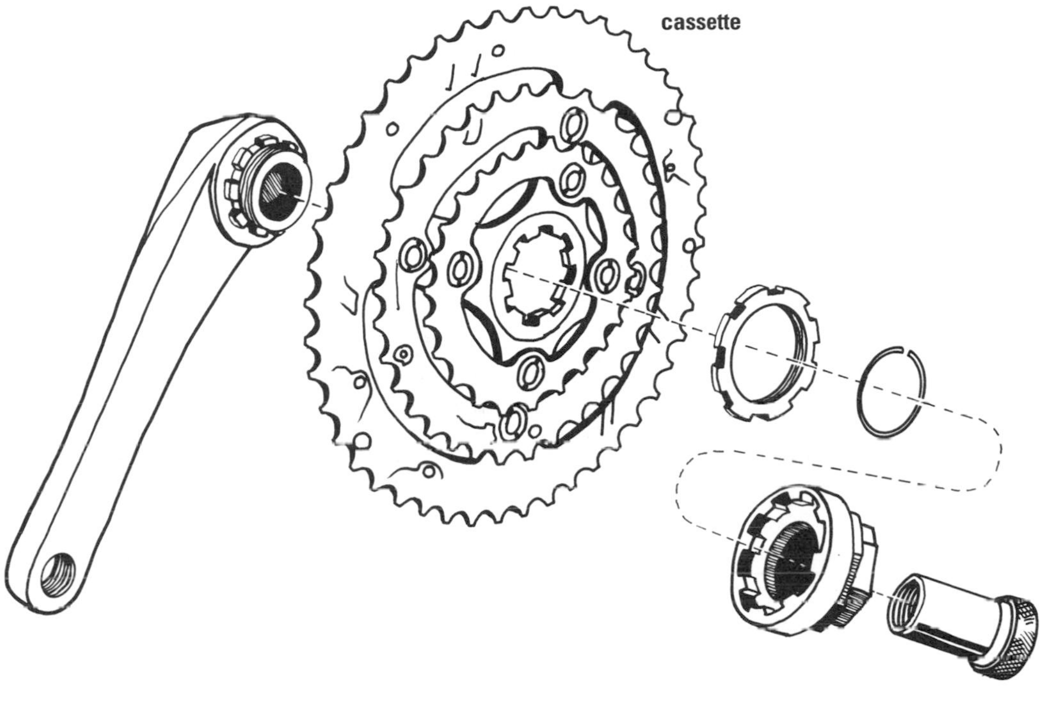

crankarm. Make sure this pin lines up under the crankarm and faces away from the bicycle. The middle and inner rings each have a little bump protruding radially inward that is also to line up under the crankarm. And all three chainrings will have recesses for the heads of the chainring bolts and nuts, so making sure that these recesses receive those parts and are not facing inward toward the spider at least ensures that the chainrings are properly facing outward. If the chainrings are rotated relative to the crank or inverted, the shift ramps will not work.

NOTE: *Any time you change the outer chainring size, you must reposition the front derailleur for proper chainring clearance, as described in Chapter 5, §v-5.*

b. To replace the inner chainring

1. Pull off the crankarm (§viii-1, Figs. 8.2 and 8.3).
2. With a 5mm Allen (or a TORX T30 key for FSA cranks), remove the bolts securing the chainring. These bolts are threaded directly into the crankarm (Fig. 8.1).
3. Install the new ring, and lube and tighten the bolts. The inner rings each have a little bump protruding radially inward that lines up under the crankarm. Make sure that the chainrings are oriented so that the recesses for the heads of the chainring bolts and nuts receive those parts and are not facing inward toward the spider.

NOTE: *Some chainrings do not accept separate chainrings; the chainrings come on and off as a set, or they are not removable. High-end, 1996–2002 Shimano XTR and 1997–2003 XT cranks rely on a slip-on spider system that allows you to spin off all three chainrings from the crankarm as a single unit (Fig. 8.8). After removing a circlip (by prying it off with a screwdriver), a special lockring tool loosens the chainring-spider–securing lockring; a female-threaded tool that goes on the crank bolt holds the lockring tool in place (Fig. 8.8). Once the spider is off, you can interchange chainrings within the set or simply pop on a whole new set.*

Economical cranks often have chainrings riveted to the crank or riveted to each other and bolted to the crank as a unit. In either case, if you want to replace a chainring, you must either replace the entire crank or the chainring set.

4. Replace the crankarm (§viii-1, Fig. 8.2). Now ride your bike.

BOTTOM BRACKETS

LEVEL 2

Most bottom brackets thread into the frame's bottom-bracket shell (Fig. 8.9). Simple enough, but it's important to remember that not all bottom-bracket shells are the same.

Almost all mountain bikes use English standard threads. That translates into a 1.370-inch diameter and a thread pitch of 24 threads per inch. These numbers are usually engraved on the bottom-bracket cups. If you are replacing a bottom bracket, make sure that the new cups have the same threads. It is important to remember that the threads on the drive side of an English standard bottom bracket are left-hand threads. In other words, you tighten the right-hand cup by turning it counterclockwise (Fig. 8.18). Meanwhile, the threads on the left cup are right-hand threads and are, therefore, tightened clockwise.

English-threaded mountain bike bottom brackets come in two bearing-spacing widths for two different standard bottom-bracket shell widths. One bottom-bracket shell width is 68mm, and most bottom brackets will have something like "68–114" stamped or printed on them, which means that the shell is 68mm wide, and the spindle is 114mm long. The other bottom-bracket shell width is 73mm, and this bottom bracket would have a demarcation like "73–118." Many bottom brackets are designed to work for both shell widths by means of spacers added between the bearing cups and the shell faces.

Other thread patterns you may run across are Italian (with a 36mm diameter), French, and Swiss (both of the latter come in 35mm diameter but use

8.9 Bottom-bracket assembly

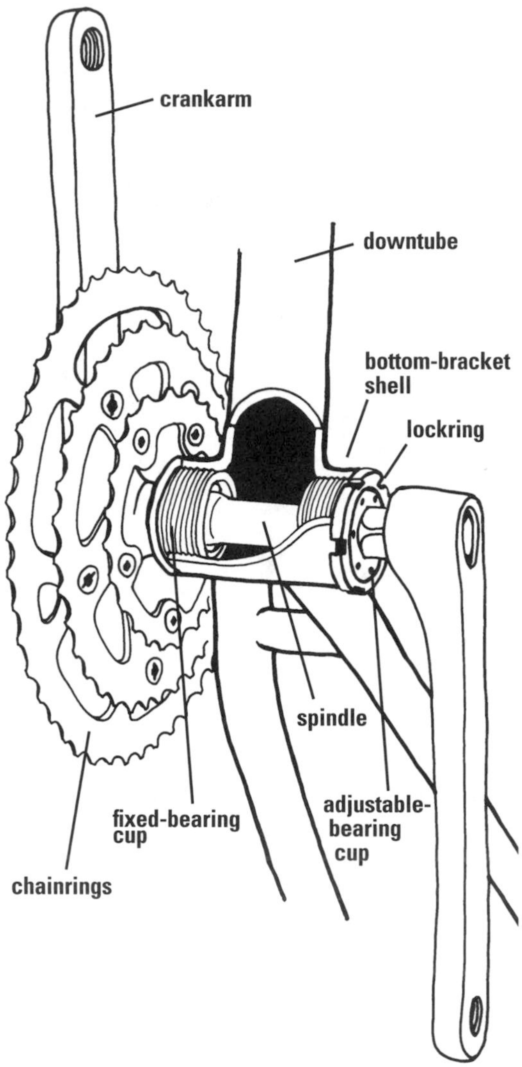

8.10–8.16 Types of bottom brackets

8.10 Shimano cartridge, square taper

8.11 Standard cup-and-cone, loose-ball bearing, square taper

8.12 Adjustable cartridge-bearing, square taper

8.13 Shimano XTR Octalink pipe-spindle type with loose bearings

8.14 ISIS cartridge bottom bracket

8.15 Shimano integrated-spindle, external-bearing crankset set up with spacers for a 68mm bottom-bracket shell

8.16 Mavic/Stronglight cartridge, square taper

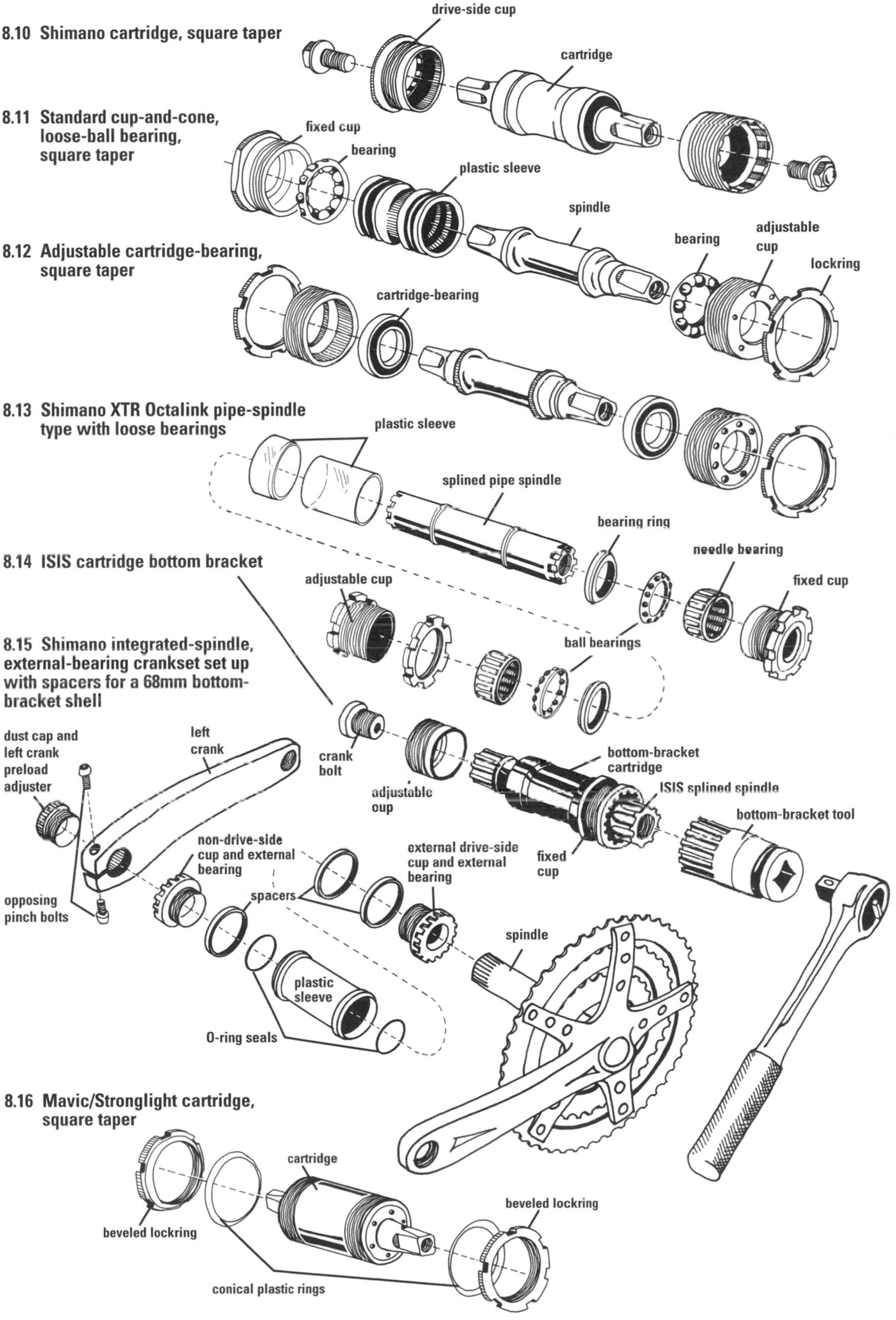

different thread directions). These thread patterns are very rare on mountain bikes.

The most common type of bottom bracket is probably the Shimano-style cartridge bottom bracket (Fig. 8.10); it has cups that accept a splined removal tool and is not adjustable. These bottom brackets can have a square-taper spindle (as illustrated in Fig. 8.10), a Shimano Octalink splined spindle, or a (non-Shimano) ISIS splined spindle.

NOTE: *Shimano has two Octalink standards: Octalink 1 and Octalink 2. Octalink 1 (pictured in Fig. 8.13) is found only on XTR and on Shimano road models. Each (of the eight—hence "Octa") spline valleys is 5mm long, and each spline ridge is 2.2mm wide. Octalink 2 works with Shimano XT, LX, and Deore cranks. The spline valleys are 9mm long, and the spline ridges are 2.8mm wide. Cranks are not interchangeable between these two Octalink spindle types.*

The most common mountain bike bottom bracket prior to the 1990s was the square-taper "cup-and-cone" style with loose ball bearings (Fig. 8.11). Another older type has cartridge bearings secured by an adjustable cup and lockring at either end (Fig. 8.12). From 1996 to 2002, Shimano's high-end bottom brackets were Octalink, featuring a large hollow "pipe" spindle with splined ends (Fig. 8.13), rather than square-taper ends. Most of these are still the cartridge type shown in Figure 8.10, but with a large splined axle. The first generation of splined-spindle Shimano XTR bottom brackets had four sets of loose, adjustable, and overhaulable bearings: two sets of tiny ball bearings and two sets of needle bearings (Fig. 8.13).

To counter Shimano's patented Octalink designs, which offer increased stiffness and lower weight than the square-taper designs, a number of manufacturers banded together in the late 1990s to create the ISIS standard (Fig. 8.14). Like Octalink, ISIS has a larger-diameter splined hollow "pipe" spindle, but it features longer and deeper splines.

In 2003, Shimano upped the high-end ante again with the integrated-spindle, external-bearing design (Fig. 8.15), in which the right arm is permanently joined to the spindle, and the bearing cups place the bearings external to the bottom-bracket shell, making a larger spindle and larger bearings possible. Other manufacturers have followed suit but offer different attachment systems for the left arm and different spindle diameters, so their bearings are not usually interchangeable with Shimano bearings, although Race Face X-Type are intended to work with Shimano XT, XTR, and Saint cranks.

Some bottom brackets do not thread into the bottom-bracket shell. One type utilizes cartridge bearings held into an unthreaded bottom-bracket shell by snaprings inserted into machined grooves. Another type is the Mavic (later by Stronglight) cartridge threaded on each end (Fig. 8.16); it slips into the bottom-bracket shell and is held in place by lockrings threaded onto the cartridge. The latter type is great for frames with damaged threads, as the bottom bracket secures on itself by compressing against the sides of the bottom-bracket shell and not on the frame's threads.

The most important item in bottom-bracket installation is to put the correct bottom bracket in. If a bike has the wrong length of bottom-bracket spindle, the chainrings will not line up well with the rear cogs (i.e., the center ring should be in line with the center of the cogset; this is called the chain line [see Fig. 5.43]). Some bikes come from the factory with the wrong length bottom bracket. No amount of fiddling with the derailleurs will get such a bike to shift properly. Get a bottom bracket specifically recommended for your crankset and with the proper thread and bottom-bracket shell width for your frame. Before installing a new bottom bracket of a different brand and model than your crank, see Figure 5.43, and read the chain-line section (§v-44) in Chapter 5.

With one-piece cartridge-style bottom brackets (Figs. 8.10 and 8.14), this warning is not as critical, but for integrated-spindle and loose-bearing bottom brackets (Figs. 8.11, 8.13, and 8.15) to work properly, the threads on both sides of the frame's bottom-bracket shell must be lined up with each other, and the end faces of the shell must be parallel. If you have any doubts about your frame and are installing an expensive bottom bracket, it is a good idea to have the bottom-bracket shell tapped (threaded) and faced (ends cut parallel) by a qualified shop possessing the proper tools. These tools are pictured in Fig. 1.4. This procedure will improve adjustment and freedom of movement with loose-bearing BBs and integrated-spindle BBs, and will reduce the likelihood of creaking with integrated-spindle cranksets.

viii-7 INSTALLATION OF SHIMANO-STYLE SEALED CARTRIDGE BOTTOM BRACKETS

As of this writing, most mountain bike bottom brackets are Shimano-style sealed cartridge units (Fig. 8.10) that are installed with a splined tool (Fig. 1.2). A Shimano-style cartridge bottom bracket can have either a square-taper axle (Fig. 8.10) or a large tubular axle with splined ends like the Octalink spindle in Figure 8.13 or the ISIS spindle in Figure 8.14. These instructions apply to cartridge bottom brackets like those shown in Figures 8.10 and 8.14, as well as to ones with this type of cartridge body and a Shimano Octalink splined spindle.

1. Thread the left cup (clockwise) in three to four turns by hand.
2. Slide the cartridge into the bottom-bracket shell, paying particular attention to the right and left markings on the cartridge. The cup with the raised lip and left-hand thread is the drive-side cup (the cup shown on the left in Fig. 8.10).
   - (a) If you have a 68mm-width bottom-bracket shell (yes, measure it!) and are using a bottom bracket designed for both 73mm and 68mm bottom-bracket shells, you will need to add at least one spacer on the drive side. Many ISIS and Octalink cartridge bottom brackets for mountain bikes are made to work in both 68mm and 73mm shells. If you were to install one in a 68mm shell without spacers, you would notice that the right crank would pass 5mm or so closer by its chainstay than would the left crank, and more than 5mm of the left cup's threads would remain exposed outside of the shell. (No spacers are used on the left side, because that cup has no lip and simply goes in as far as it needs to.)
   - (b) If you have a 68mm shell and a 68/73mm-compatible bottom bracket, place a 2.5mm spacer (usually included with the bottom bracket) between the lip of the right cup and the right face of the bottom-bracket shell. Alternatively, if you are using a Shimano "E-type" front derailleur, which features a bracket mount as shown in Figure 5.13, slip the derailleur bracket between the shell and the cup lip. Some bottom brackets—Race Face ISIS models come to mind—will only

INSTALLATION OF SHIMANO-STYLE SEALED CARTRIDGE BOTTOM-BRACKETS accept an E-type front derailleur with a 68mm shell, because there is only room for a single spacer with 68mm and no spacer room with a 73mm. Some Shimano bottom brackets are designed to accept an E-type front derailleur on either a 68mm or 73mm shell; with these, you install either two 2.5mm spacers or one spacer and the E-type bracket between the right cup and a 68mm shell. With a 73mm shell, you install either the E-type front-derailleur bracket or a single 2.5mm spacer against the shell.

(c) If you are using a chain guide (a chain retainer designed to keep the chain from jumping off of a single chainring and chain retainer meant for downhill or other gravity-driven riding), where you would insert a spacer between the bottom-bracket cup and the bottom-bracket shell, you can generally insert the bottom bracket cartridge through the flange hole of the chain guide instead.

3. Using the splined cup installation tool with either an open-end wrench or a ⅜-inch drive socket wrench on it, tighten the right (drive-side) cup until the lip seats against the face of the bottom-bracket shell (as shown in Fig. 8.17, except on the drive side). Recommended torque is high—see Appendix D.

INSTALLATION OF CUP-AND-CONE BOTTOM BRACKETS

NOTE: *Because almost all mountain bikes have English threads, this cup should tighten counterclockwise.*

4. With the same tool, turn the left (nondrive) cup clockwise until it tightens against the cartridge (Fig. 8.17). The torque required is usually the same as for the right cup (see Appendix D). There is no adjustment of the bearings to be done; you can put on the crank now (§viii-1b).

8.17 Tightening and loosening Shimano-style cartridge bottom bracket with socket wrench and splined bottom-bracket tool

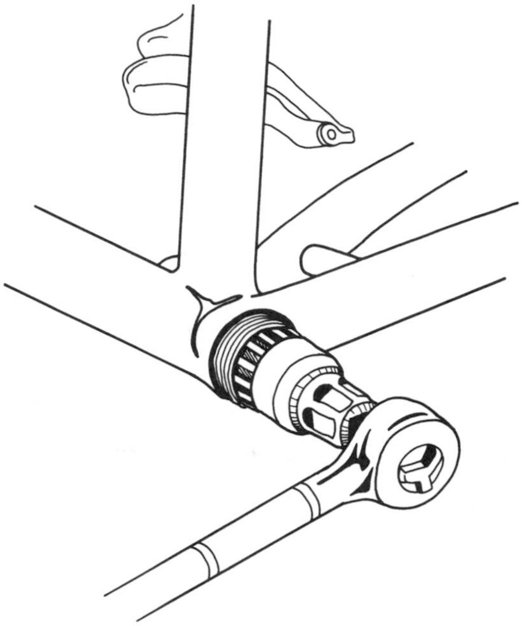

viii-8 INSTALLATION OF CUP-AND-CONE BOTTOM BRACKETS

Cup-and-cone (or "loose-ball") bottom brackets (Fig. 8.11) use ball bearings that ride between cone-shaped bearing surfaces on the spindle and cup-shaped races in the threaded cups. One cup, called the fixed cup (the left-hand cup in Fig. 8.11), has a lip on it and fits on the right (drive) side of the bike. The other, called the adjustable cup, has a lockring that threads onto the cup and against the face of the bottom-bracket shell. The individual ball bearings are usually held together by a retaining cage, which varies in shape depending on bottom bracket. Some folks prefer to do without the retainer; it works fine either way.

Again, it is a good idea to have the bottom-bracket shell tapped (threaded) and faced (ends cut parallel) by a qualified shop possessing the proper tools.

8.18 **Drive-side fixed cup**

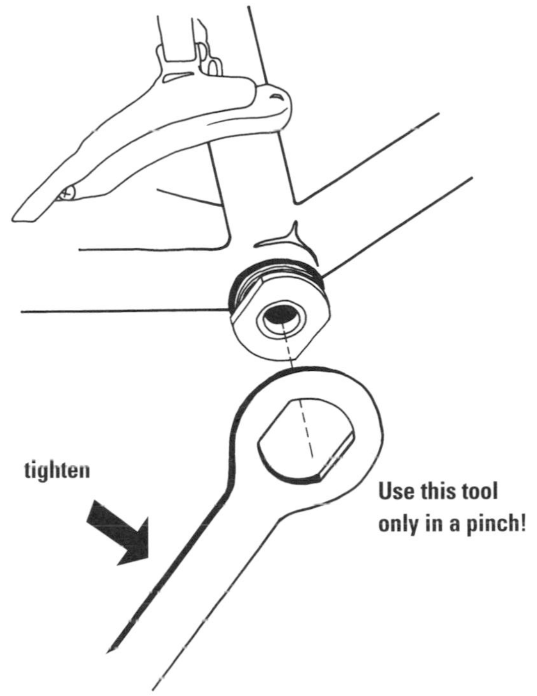

8.19 **Placing the axle in the bottom bracket shell**

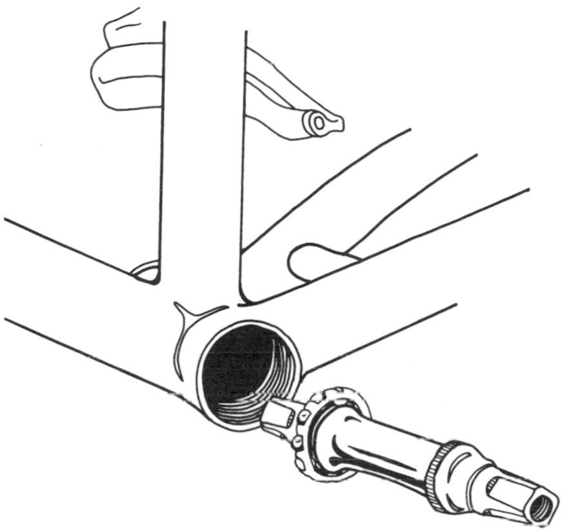

1. Unless you have a shop fixed-cup tool, have a shop install the fixed cup for you. The shop tool ensures that the cup goes in straight and very tightly. The tool pictured in Figure 8.18 can be used in a pinch, but it can let the cup go in crooked and will slip off before you get it really tight. The fixed cup must be very tight (see Appendix D for torque) so it does not vibrate loose. Remember that English-threaded fixed cups are tightened counterclockwise.
2. Wipe the inside surface of both cups with a clean rag, and put a thin layer of clean grease on the bearing surfaces. Put enough that the balls will be half-covered; any more is wasted and attracts dirt.
3. Wipe the axle with a clean rag.
4. Figure out which end of your bottom-bracket spindle (axle) is toward the drive side. The drive side may be marked with an "R," or you can simply choose the longer end (when measured from the bearing surface). If there is writing on the spindle, it will usually read right side up for a rider on the bike. If there is no marking and no length difference, the spindle orientation is irrelevant.
5. Slide one set of bearings, held in a retainer cage, onto the drive-side end of the axle (Fig. 8.19). Make sure you orient the retainer cage correctly. The balls, rather than the retainer cage, should rest against the axle-bearing surfaces. Because there are two types of retainer cages with opposite designs, you need to be careful to avoid binding, as well as smashing of the cages. If you're still confused, there is one easy test: If it's right, it will turn smoothly; if it's wrong, it won't. If, instead, you have loose ball bearings with no retainer cage, stick them into the greased cup. Most rely on nine balls; you can confirm that

you are using the correct number by inserting and removing the axle and checking to make sure that they are evenly distributed in the grease with no extra gap for more balls. The XTR loose-bearing BB (bottom bracket) in Figure 8.13 requires installing a bearing ring, a set of ball bearings, and a needle bearing set on the spindle.

6. Slide the axle into the bottom bracket so that it pushes the bearings into the fixed cup (Fig. 8.19). You can use your pinkie finger to stabilize the end of the axle from the fixed-cup end as you slide it in.
7. Insert the protective plastic sleeve (shown in Figs. 8.11 and 8.13) into the shell against the inside edge of the fixed cup. The sleeve keeps dirt and rust from falling from the frame tubes into the bearings, so if you don't have one, get one.
8. Now turn your attention to the other cup. Place the bearing set into the greased adjustable cup. If you are using a bearing retainer, make sure it is properly oriented. On an XTR loose-bearing BB (Fig. 8.13) install the bearing ring, ball bearings, and needle bearings on the spindle as you did on the other end.
9. Without the lockring, thread the adjustable cup (clockwise) by hand into the shell over the axle, assuring that it is going in straight. Screw the cup in as far as you can by hand, ideally all the way until the bearings seat between the axle and cup.
10. Locate the appropriate tool for tightening the adjustable cup. Most cups have two holes that accept the pins of an adjustable cup wrench called a "pin spanner" (Fig. 8.20) or a splined end like a cartridge bottom bracket that fits a tool as shown in Figure 8.17. The other common type of adjustable cup has two flats for a wrench; on this type, you may use an adjustable wrench.

INSTALLATION OF CUP-AND-CONE BOTTOM BRACKETS

8.20 Tightening lockring

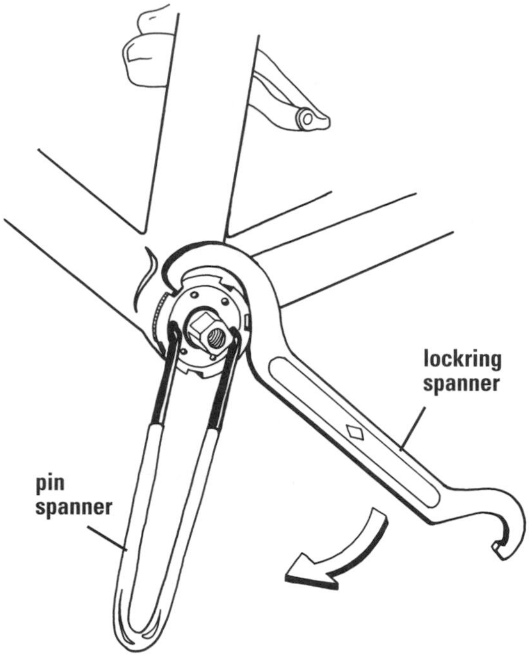

The XTR loose-bearing BB in Figure 8.13 requires a toothed lockring spanner or the tool shown in Figure 8.8.

11. Carefully tighten the adjustable cup against the bearings, taking great care not to overtighten. Turn the axle periodically with your fingers to ensure that it moves freely. If it binds up, you have gone too far; back it off a bit. The danger of overtightening is that the bearings can force dents into the bearing surfaces of the cups, and the bottom-bracket axle will never turn smoothly again.
12. Screw the lockring onto the adjustable cup, and select the proper tool for your lockring. Lockrings come in different shapes, and so do lockring spanners—make sure yours mate properly with each other.
13. Tighten the lockring against the face of the bottom-bracket shell with the lockring spanner,

while holding the adjustable cup in place (Fig. 8.20). If you turn the bicycle upside down, you can pull down harder on the wrenches.

14. As you snug the lockring up against the bottom-bracket shell, check the bottom-bracket spindle periodically, because the lockring pulls the cup out of the shell minutely, thereby loosening the adjustment. The spindle should turn smoothly without free play in the bearings. I recommend installing and tightening the drive-side crankarm onto the drive end of the spindle (Fig. 8.2) at this time so you can push the crank from side to side to check for free play.
15. Adjust the cup so that the axle play is just barely eliminated. While holding the cup in place, tighten the lockring as tightly as you can (Fig. 8.20) so the bottom bracket does not come out of adjustment while riding (recommended torque is in Appendix D; tightening it as tightly as you can is about right). You may have to repeat this step a time or two until you get the adjustment just right.

viii-9 INSTALLATION OF INTEGRATED-SPINDLE, EXTERNAL-BEARING BOTTOM BRACKETS

1. Add spacers as required.
   - (a) If you have a 68mm bottom-bracket shell, slip on the following supplied 2.5mm spacers over the threads of the left and right cup: On Shimano, FSA Mega Exo, and Race Face X-Type put two of the three spacers on the right, and the remaining one on the left (Fig. 8.15). On Truvativ GXP, put one spacer on the right and one on the left.
   - (b) If you have a 73mm shell, with Shimano and FSA, slip one spacer on the right cup and none on the left; use no spacers for Truvativ.
   - (c) In either case, instead of placing a spacer adjacent to the right cup's flange, insert the front-derailleur bracket if you are using an E-type front derailleur (Fig. 5.13).

NOTE: *There will be a removable plastic sleeve (Fig. 8.15) attached to the right cup to keep contamination from falling onto the spindle inside of the frame. Leave this on (or reinstall it if it is detached from the right cup) when installing the cup.*

2. After greasing their threads and starting them by hand first, tighten in the right (drive side) cup counterclockwise and the left cup clockwise by using the splined tool designed for the purpose, leaving the cup spacers in place. Torque is high (35–50 N·m), so yank on the tool pretty hard, because for this task you are not likely to have a splined tool that works with a torque wrench to measure it to spec.
3. Go back to §viii-1b to install the spindle (and cranks) of an integrated-spindle system.

viii-10 INSTALLATION OF OTHER TYPES OF BOTTOM BRACKETS

The three bottom-bracket types mentioned so far in this chapter probably represent more than 95 percent of the mountain bikes in circulation. There are, however, a few variations worth mentioning.

1. Cartridge-bearing bottom brackets with adjustable cups (Fig. 8.12) are reasonably easy to install. These come with a pair of adjustable cups for both ends. With this type, you simply install the drive-side cup and lockring, slide the cartridge bearing in (if it is not already pressed into the cup), slip the spindle in, and then install the other bearing, cup, and lockring. Tighten each lockring while holding the adjustable cup in

place with a pin spanner (Fig. 8.20) or a splined cup tool (Fig. 8.17). Adjust for free play as described in §viii-8, steps 11–15.

(a) The advantage of having two adjustable cups is that you can center the cartridge by moving it from side to side in the bottom-bracket shell. If the chainrings end up too close or too far away from the frame (see Fig. 5.43 and the chain-line discussion in the troubleshooting section in Chapter 5, §v-44), you can move one cup in and one out to shift the position of the entire cartridge.

(b) Sometimes cartridge-bearing bottom brackets bind up a bit during adjustment and installation. A light tap on each end of the axle usually frees them.

2. An unthreaded bottom-bracket shell with snapring grooves uses just a spindle and cartridge bearings without cups (not pictured); snaprings retain the bearings. This type was popular at the beginning of the 1980s and has virtually disappeared on new bikes. With a cupless bottom bracket, seat the cartridge bearings against the stops on either end of the spindle. Install one snapring with snapring pliers into the groove in one end of the shell. Push the entire assembly of axle and two bearings in from the other side of the bottom-bracket shell. Install the other snapring, and you're done.

3. Mavic or Stronglight cartridge-bearing bottom brackets (Fig. 8.16) require either end of the bottom-bracket shell to be chamfered at an angle to seat the angled lockrings. You need to go to a shop equipped with the Mavic tool for this. Once this is done, you simply slip the cartridge into the shell, slide on one of the angled plastic rings from either end (pictured in Fig. 8.16), and screw on a lockring, angled side inward, from either side. Holding the cartridge with a pin spanner, tighten the lockring on either side (Fig. 8.20). The beauty of these bottom brackets is that they work independently of the bottom-bracket shell threads, so they can be installed in shells with ruined threads or with nonstandard threads. Mavic stopped producing them in 1995, after which Stronglight took over the design.

4. Noncartridge XTR pipe-spindle bottom brackets (Fig. 8.13) are installed like cup-and-cone bottom brackets (§viii-8), with the exception that the ball bearings ride on bearing rings inboard of needle bearings within the cups. Two notched lockring spanners are required to adjust them.

OVERHAULING THE BOTTOM BRACKET

A bottom-bracket overhaul consists of cleaning or replacing the bearings, cleaning the axle and bearing surfaces, and regreasing them. With any type, both crankarms must be removed.

viii-11 OVERHAULING SHIMANO-STYLE CARTRIDGE BOTTOM BRACKETS

Standard Shimano-style cartridge bottom brackets (Fig. 8.10) are sealed units and cannot be overhauled. They must be replaced when they stop performing properly. Remove them by first removing the cranks as described in §viii-1, and then by unscrewing the cups with the splined cup tool (Fig. 8.17) after. Install a new bottom bracket as directed in §viii-7.

viii-12 OVERHAULING CUP-AND-CONE BOTTOM BRACKETS

Cup-and-cone bottom brackets (Figs. 8.11 and 8.13) can be overhauled entirely from the nondrive side, after you have removed the crankarms as described in §viii-1.

1. Remove the lockring with the lockring spanner (as shown in Fig. 8.20, with the lockring spanner and the rotation direction reversed).
2. Remove the adjustable cup with the tool that fits your cup (usually a pin spanner [Fig. 1.2], installed into the cup as shown in Fig. 8.20).
3. Leave the fixed cup in place, and check that it is tightened hard into the frame by putting a fixed cup wrench on it and turning it counterclockwise (Fig. 8.18).
4. Clean the cups and spindle with a rag. Use a solvent only if the parts are glazed.
5. Clean the bearings, without removing them from their retainer cages, with a citrus-based solvent. A simple way to do it is to shake the bearings about in a plastic bottle with solvent in it. A toothbrush may be required, and a solvent tank is certainly handy if you have access to one. If your bearings are not shiny and in perfect shape, go ahead and replace them. Balls with dull luster and/or rough spots or rust on them should be replaced.
6. Wash the bearings in soap and water to remove the solvent and any remaining grit. Towel them off thoroughly, and then let them dry completely. An air compressor is handy here.
7. Follow the installation procedure described in §viii-8.
8. Install the crankarms as described in §viii-1, Figure 8.2.

viii-13 OVERHAULING INTEGRATED-SPINDLE, EXTERNAL-BEARING BOTTOM BRACKETS

Following the method discussed in §viii-9, replace the cups and you are done! If you can get the bearings out of the cups, you could just replace the bearings, rather than the entire cups. If not, you may be able to pry off the outer cover of each bearing and clean it out (Fig. 6.26); it may be worth a try.

viii-14 OVERHAULING OTHER TYPES OF BOTTOM BRACKETS

If any cartridge-bearing bottom bracket becomes difficult to turn, the bearings must be replaced. If they are pressed into cups, and you can't remove them, then you may also have to buy new cups. Be doubly sure to get the correct size.

1. Reverse the installation procedure outlined in §viii-9 to remove your bottom bracket.
2. Replace the bearings.
3. Reinstall your bottom bracket (§viii-9) and crankarms (§viii-1).
4. You're done. Go ride your bike.

TROUBLESHOOTING CRANK AND BOTTOM-BRACKET NOISE

viii-15 CREAKING NOISES

Those mysterious creaking noises can be enough to drive you nuts. Just as you think you have your bike tuned to perfection, a little noise comes along to ruin your ride, and these annoying little creaks, pops, and groans can be a bear to locate. Pedaling-induced noises can originate from almost anything connected to your crankset, such as movement of the cleats on your shoes or of the crankarms on the bottom-bracket spindle, loose chainrings, or poorly adjusted bearings. Of course, they could also originate from seemingly unrelated components such as your seat, seatpost, frame, wheels, or handlebar. Creaking occurs when parts that are supposed to be fixed together instead move against each other. Insufficient tightening of fasteners or lack of grease between parts is often the cause.

Before spending hours overhauling your drivetrain, spend some time trying to isolate the source of the noise. Try different pedals and shoes and wheels. Pedal out of the saddle, and pedal without flexing the handlebar. If the source of the creak turns out to be the saddle, seatpost, wheels, or handlebar, turn to the appropriate chapter for directions on how to correct the problem.

If the creaking is in the crank area:

1. Check to make sure that the chainring bolts are tight, and tighten them if they are not (Fig. 8.5).
2. If that step does not solve the problem, make certain that the crankarm bolts are tight (Fig. 8.2). If they are not, the resulting movement between the crankarm and the bottom-bracket spindle is a likely source of noise. If your crank is of a different brand than your bottom bracket, check with the manufacturers or your local shop to make sure that they are recommended for use together. Incompatible cranks and spindles will never properly join and are a potential problem area.
3. Rust, and alternating wet and dry cycles, can break down the glue bond that holds the cup(s) onto the cartridge on a Shimano cartridge bottom bracket (Fig. 8.10). If the cartridge can move within the cup, it will creak. Fix it by removing the bottom bracket (§viii-7), and slathering grease inside the cup(s) and around the outside of the cartridge where the parts meet. Grease the cup threads too, because the cup can also make noise as it moves against the bottom-bracket shell. Tighten it back in (Fig. 8.17).
4. The bottom bracket itself can creak owing to improper adjustment, lack of grease, cracked bearings, worn parts, or loose cups. All of these things require adjustment or overhaul via the procedures outlined in §viii-11 through §viii-14 of this chapter. Many integrated-spindle designs are very sensitive to being out of parallel, and creaking can occur if the bottom-bracket shell is not perfectly tapped and faced. This is a job for a good bike shop.
5. Now for the bad news. If creaking persists, the problem could be rooted in your frame. Creaks can originate from cracks in and around the bottom-bracket shell, so be sure to check that area. The threads in your bottom-bracket shell could also be worn to the point that they allow the cups to move slightly. Neither of these is a good sign, unless, of course, you were hoping for an excuse to buy a new frame.

CLUNKING NOISE

viii-16 CLUNKING NOISES

1. Crankarm play: Grab the crankarm and push on it side to side.
   (a) If there is play, tighten the crankarm bolt (Fig. 8.2; torque spec is in Appendix D).
   (b) If there is still crankarm play and you have a cup-and-cone bottom bracket (Figs. 8.11 and 8.13) or a cartridge-bearing bottom bracket with a lockring on either side (Fig. 8.12), adjust the bottom-bracket spindle end play (§viii-8, see steps 11–15).
   (c) If bottom-bracket adjustment does not eliminate crankarm play, or you have a nonadjustable cartridge bottom bracket (Figs. 8.10,

8.14, or 8.16), the bottom bracket is loose in the frame threads, and you should tighten it up. With a cup-and-cone bottom bracket, you can go back to §viii-8, and start over, making sure that the fixed cup is very tight. A cheater bar (extension tube) may need to be used on the fixed-cup wrench to tighten it to high enough torque. Adjustable-cup lockrings need to be equally tight (Fig. 8.20) once the spindle end play is adjusted properly.

(d) The lockrings and fixed-cup flanges must be flush with the bottom-bracket shell all of the way around; if they are not, the bottom bracket must be removed, and the bottom-bracket shell must be faced (cut parallel) by a shop equipped with a facing cutter.

(e) If the crankarm play persists, or the bottom-bracket fixed cup or lockring will not tighten up completely or keeps coming loose, then either the bottom-bracket cups must be either stripped or undersized, or the frame's bottom-bracket shell threads are stripped or oversized. Either way, it's an expensive fix, especially the frame-replacement option! Get a second opinion if you reach this point. If you can find a Mavic-style bottom bracket (Fig. 8.16), you can still use the frame.

2. Pedal end play: Grab each pedal and wobble it to check for play. If either is loose, see Overhauling Pedals in Chapter 9 (page 210).

viii-17 HARD-TO-TURN CRANKS

If the cranks are hard to turn, you really ought to overhaul your bottom bracket (see §viii-11 through §viii-14)—unless you want to continue intensifying your workout or boosting the egos of your cycling companions. The bottom bracket may be shot and need to be replaced.

viii-18 INNER CHAINRING DRAGS ON CHAINSTAY

If you hear noise because the inner chainring is dragging on the chainstay, your bottom-bracket spindle is too short, the square hole in your crankarm is deformed so that the crank slides on too far, your frame is bent, or you have switched to a larger inner chainring. If the bottom-bracket spindle is too short, you need a new one of the correct length. If the square hole in the crank is badly deformed, you need a new crankarm; otherwise it will continue to loosen up and cause problems. If the frame may be bent, you can refer to Chapter 14, §xiv-6, to check on it and then decide what to do based on those instructions. If the chainring is too large, get a smaller one.

With an adjustable cartridge-bearing bottom bracket with a lockring on either end (Fig. 8.12), it is also possible that the entire bottom bracket is offset to the left. To move it to the right, screw the left cup in farther, back the right cup out some, adjust out the end play, and tighten the lockrings back down (Fig. 8.20).

NOTE: *See §v-44 in Chapter 5 (Fig. 5.43) on chain line to establish proper crank-to-frame spacing. The chainring might not be rubbing the frame, but the crank is still too far inboard if the derailleur cannot move inward far enough to shift to the granny gear. The mechanism on a Shimano "top-swing" front derailleur in particular can hit the seat tube and stop before the chain drops onto the inner ring. The problem is compounded with an oversized seat tube. And if your bottom bracket is too long, you can have the opposite problem—your front derailleur will not reach the large chainring.*

CHAPTER 9

PEDALS

To everything, turn, turn, turn . . .
—The Byrds

TOOLS

15mm pedal wrench

small and large adjustable wrenches

3mm, 4mm, 5mm, and 6mm Allen wrenches

screwdriver

pliers

knife

grease

oil (chain lubricant)

FOR OVERHAULING PEDALS

7mm, 8mm, 9mm, 10mm, 17mm, or 18mm open-end wrenches

Shimano splined pedal tool

- or -

Look splined pedal tool

- or -

snapring pliers for some Time pedals

13mm cone wrench

8mm socket wrench

bench vise

To best serve its purpose, a bicycle pedal needs only to be firmly attached to the crankarm and provide a stable platform for the shoe. A simple enough task, but you'd be amazed at the different approaches that have been taken to achieve this goal. Of the two basic types of mountain bike pedals, the standard cage-type pedal, with or without a toeclip and strap (Fig. 9.1), is the simplest and cheapest. The type found on most mid- to high-end cross-country mountain bikes, the "clip-in" pedal (Fig. 9.2), has a spring-loaded shoe-retention system, much like a ski binding. Clip-in pedals are also called "clipless" pedals because they have no toeclip.

Cage-type pedals are fairly common on lower-end bikes. They are relatively nonintimidating for the novice rider, and the frame (or "cage") that surrounds the pedal provides a large, stable platform (Fig. 9.1). For doing stunts and gravity-driven mountain biking, many riders prefer "flat" pedals to clip-in pedals, i.e., standard pedals with a broad platform and often little steel pins sticking up to provide more traction with the shoe sole. Without a toeclip, the top and bottom of a standard or flat pedal are the same, and you can use just about any type of shoe. Using a toeclip without a strap can keep your foot from sliding forward and still allow easy release in almost any direction. When you add a toe strap and use a stiff-soled mountain bike shoe with aggressive tread, the combination works well to keep your foot on the pedal while you are riding even the roughest of singletrack. When tightened, the strap allows you to pull up on the upward part of the pedal stroke—giving you more power and a more fluid pedal stroke. Of course, as you add clips and straps, the pedal becomes harder to enter and to exit, especially with boots or shoes with aggressive tread designs.

Clip-in models offer all of the efficiency advantages and then some of a good clip-and-strap combination, yet allow easier entry and exit from the pedal. These pedals are more expensive and require special shoes and accurate mounting of the cleats.

9.1 Cage-type pedal with toeclip and straps

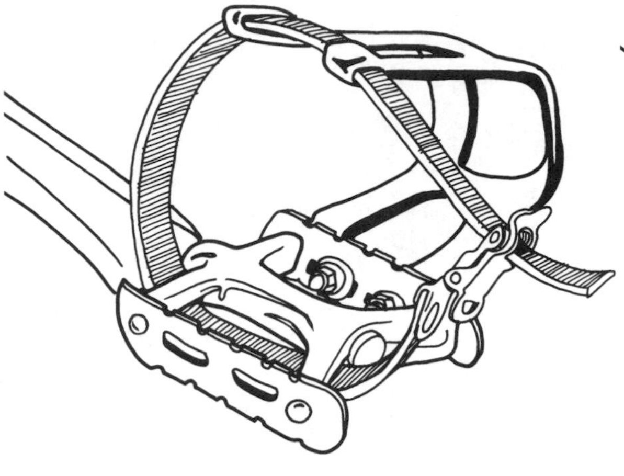

9.2 Clip-in pedal

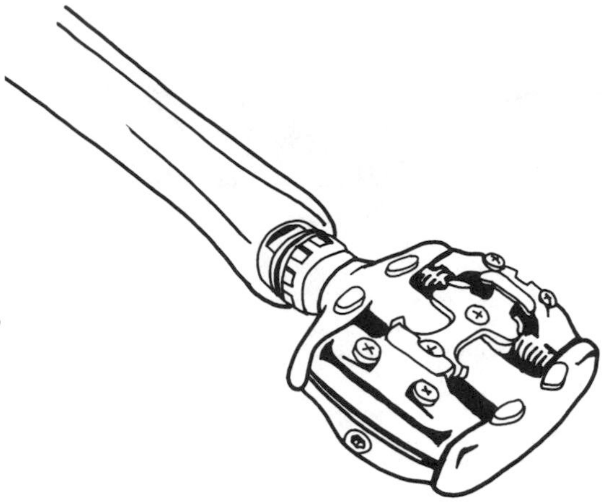

Your choice of shoes is limited to stiff-sole models that accept cleats for your particular pedal. Once you have them dialed in, you will find that clip-in pedals waste less energy through flex and slippage and allow you to transfer more power directly to the pedals. This greater efficiency combined with low weight explains their universal acceptance among cross-country mountain bike racers. Referring to the shoe sole, most clip-in mountain pedals are "SPD" compatible, where SPD stands for Shimano Pedaling Dynamics. Shimano produced the first successful clip-in mountain pedal in the mid-1980s (Fig. 9.2) and set the shoe standards. "SPD-compatibility" indicates that the cleat mounts with two side-by-side M5 screws, spaced 14mm apart, screwing into a movable, threaded cleat-mounting plate on a shoe with two longitudinal grooves in the sole (Fig. 9.6). However, SPD-compatibility does not necessarily mean that one company's cleat will work with the pedal of another company.

NOTE: *Some pedal cleats do work with other brands of pedals. Appendix E is a cleat compatibility chart that shows how well many common cleats do or do not work with particular pedals. Be careful. Some cleats and pedals do not mix and match, and you might find yourself unable to disengage at a most inopportune moment.*

This chapter explains how to remove and replace pedals, how to mount the cleats and adjust the release tension with clip-in pedals, how to troubleshoot pedal problems, and how to overhaul and replace spindles on almost all mountain bike pedals. Incidentally, I use the terms "axle" and "spindle" interchangeably.

PEDAL REMOVAL & INSTALLATION

ix-1 PEDAL REMOVAL AND INSTALLATION

Note that the right pedal axle is right-hand threaded, and the left is left-hand (reverse) threaded. Both unscrew from the crank in the pedaling direction.

a. Removal

1. Slide the 15mm pedal wrench onto the wrench flats of the pedal axle (Fig. 9.3). Or, if the pedal axle is designed to accept it, you can use a 6mm or 8mm Allen wrench from the backside of the crankarm (Fig. 9.4). This is particularly handy

9.3 **Removing or installing pedal with 15mm wrench**

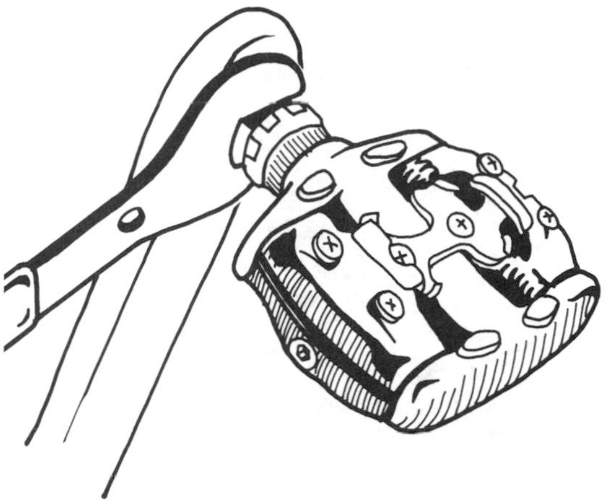

9.4 **Removing or installing pedal with a 6mm Allen wrench**

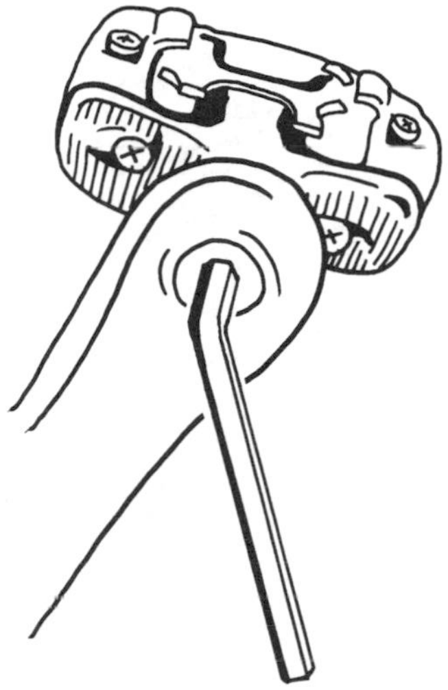

on the trail, because you probably won't be carrying a 15mm wrench anyway. But if you are at home and the pedal is on really tight, it will probably be easier to use the standard pedal wrench. Some pedals have no wrench flats and can only be removed with a 6mm or 8mm Allen wrench (Fig. 9.4), for example, the Time ATAC with plastic body (Fig. 9.14).

2. Unscrew the pedal in the appropriate direction. The right (or drive-side) pedal unscrews counterclockwise when viewed from that side. The left-side pedal is reverse threaded, so it unscrews in a clockwise direction when viewed from the left side of the bike. Once loosened, either pedal can be unscrewed quickly by turning the crank forward with the wrench engaged on the pedal spindle and the rear wheel positioned off of the ground so that it can turn.

b. Installation

1. Use a rag to wipe clean the threads on the pedal axle and inside the crankarm.
2. Grease the pedal threads.
3. Start screwing the pedal in with your fingers, clockwise for the right pedal, counterclockwise for the left one.
4. Tighten the pedal with the 15mm pedal wrench (Fig. 9.3) or a 6mm or 8mm Allen wrench (Fig. 9.4). This can be done quickly by turning the cranks backward with the wrench engaged on the pedal spindle.

SETTING UP CLIP-IN PEDALS

Setting up clip-in pedals involves installation and adjustment of the cleats on the shoes and adjusting the pedal-release tension.

ix-2 INSTALLING AND ADJUSTING PEDAL CLEATS ON THE SHOES

The cleat is important because its position determines the fore-and-aft, lateral (side-to-side), and rotational position of your foot. If your feet aren't properly oriented on the pedals, you could eventually develop hip, knee, or ankle problems.

9.5 Removing rubber cover concealing the cleat holes

9.6 Cleat setup on a SPD-compatible shoe

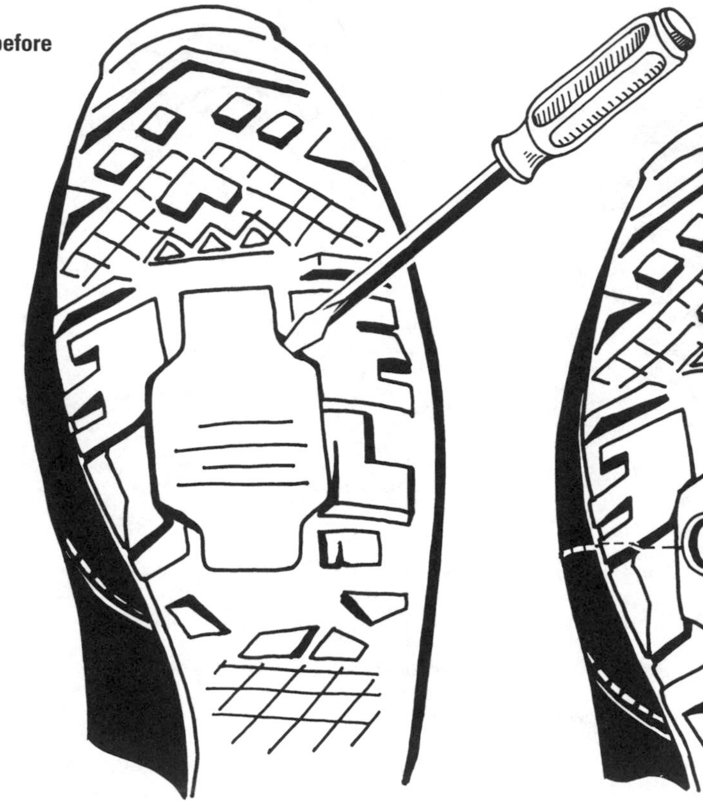

INSTALLING PEDAL CLEATS ON SHOES

1. If your shoe has a precut piece of rubber covering the cleat-mounting area, remove it. Cut around the cover's outline with a knife, pry an edge up with a screwdriver (Fig. 9.5), and yank it off with some pliers. Warming it up with a hair dryer beforehand softens the glue.
2. Put the shoe on, and mark the position of the ball of your foot (the big bump behind your big toe) on the outside of the shoe. This will help you position the cleat fore and aft. Take the shoe off, and continue drawing the line straight across the bottom of the shoe (Fig. 9.6).
3. If there are threaded holes in your shoe sole to accept the cleat screws, skip to step 4. If you do not have threaded shoe holes, you must install the backing plate and threaded cleat plate that came with your pedals. Remove the shoe's sock liner, put the rectangular backing plate inside the shoe over the two slots, and put the threaded plate on top of it with the threaded protuberances sticking out through the slots, rather than up at your foot.
4. Lube the cleat screw threads, and screw the cleat that came with your pedals to your shoe; this step usually requires a 4mm Allen wrench. Make sure you orient the cleat in the appropriate direction. Some cleats have an arrow indicating forward (Fig. 9.6); if yours do not, the instructions accompanying your pedals probably specify which direction the cleat should point. Also note if the right and left cleats are different (see Note under next step).

5. Position the cleat in the middle of its lateral- and rotational-adjustment range, and line up the mounting screws either over or (preferably) 1cm behind the mark you made in step 2 (Fig. 9.6). It is actually the position of the ball of the foot relative to the pedal spindle you are interested in, and with some systems, the centerline of the cleat screws is not actually at the center of the pedal. Adjust these cleats accordingly to establish your desired relationship between the pedal spindle and the ball of the foot (usually you want the spindle directly under or 1–2cm behind the ball of the foot).

NOTE: *Cleats for Time ATAC pedals (Figs. 9.14 and 9.22), Crank Brothers (Eggbeater, Candy, and Mallet), and Look 4×4 pedals have no lateral or rotational adjustment; just set the screws at your mark and tighten the cleat down, making sure the arrow on the Time cleat points forward; Crank Brothers and Look 4×4 cleats are symmetrical, so mount either end forward. Put the Time cleat with the imprinted stars (or the G/L imprint) onto the left shoe for less float range and earlier (13-degree) release angle; put it on the right shoe for more float and wider (17-degree) release angle. Conversely, put the Crank Brothers (or Look 4×4) cleat with the imprinted circles onto the right shoe for less float range and earlier (15-degree) release angle; put it on the left shoe for more float and wider (20-degree) release angle. You may now tighten the screws, skip the remaining steps, and go riding! (Incidentally, the older model Time TMT pedal, of which few were sold, also had only fore-and-aft cleat adjustment, but the only shoe you could use with it was Time's mountain shoe of the time. The ATAC pedals work with any SPD-compatible shoe.)*

As for the positioning of cleats for release angle, I recommend setting either system, especially Crank Brothers and Look 4×4 cleats, for the earlier release angle. That way, you are more likely to get out in a hurry when you need to. There is no spring retention adjustment on Crank Brothers, Look 4×4, or pre-2004 Time pedals (Time ATAC XS pedals, introduced in 2004, do have a spring-tension adjustment), so the only way to get more retention is to increase the release angle. If you find yourself blowing out before you want to, for instance when descending fast on rocky terrain, interchange the cleats to increase the release angle.

6. Snug the screws down enough that the cleat won't move when clipped in or out of the pedals, but don't tighten them down fully yet. Follow the same steps with your other shoe.
7. To set the lateral position, put the shoes on, sit on the bike, and clip into the pedals. Ride around a bit. Notice the position of your feet. Pedaling is more efficient the closer the feet are to the plane of the bike, but you don't want them in so far that they bump your cranks. Take the shoes off and adjust the cleats laterally, if necessary, to move the feet side to side. Get back on the bike and clip in again. Remember that Time, Crank Brothers, and Look 4×4 cleats have no lateral adjustability.)
8. To set the rotational position, ride around some more. Notice whether your feet feel twisted and uncomfortable. You may feel pressure on either side of your heel from the shoe. If necessary, remove your shoes and rotate the cleat slightly. Some pedals offer free-float, allowing the foot to rotate freely for a few degrees before releasing. Precise rotational cleat adjustment is less important if the pedal is free-floating. Again, Time, Crank Brothers, and Look 4×4 cleats have no rotational adjustability, only interchangeability from right to left to vary the amount of float until the release point is reached.

NOTE: *For Speedplay Frogs (Fig. 9.16), angle the cleat slightly toward the outside of the shoe, and tighten the mounting screws just enough that the cleat can still turn. Clip into the pedal and rotate the heel inward until it just touches the crankarm. Tighten the cleat in this position. Frogs have no inward release; this procedure sets the inward stop.*

9. Once your cleat position feels right, trace the cleats with a pen so that you can tell if the cleat stays put. While holding the cleat in place, tighten the bolts down firmly. Hold the Allen wrench close to the bend so that you do not exert too much leverage and strip the threads.
10. If the cleat holes are open to the inside of the shoe, place a waterproof sticker over the opening inside, and replace the sock liner.
11. When riding, take the 4mm Allen wrench along, because you may want to fine-tune the cleat adjustment over the course of a few rides.
12. Check cleat bolt tightness every few months with a torque wrench (4–5 N·m) so that you don't lose a screw (or a cleat) while riding.

ix-3 ADJUSTING RELEASE TENSION ON CLIP-IN PEDALS

If you find the factory release-adjustment setting to be too loose or too restrictive, you can adjust the release tension on most clip-in pedal brands; exceptions are Crank Brother and Look 4×4, Speedplay, and pre-2004 Time. The adjusting screws are usually located at the front and rear of the pedal (Fig. 9.7). The screws affect the tension of the nearest set of clips. The adjusters are usually operated with a small (usually 3mm) Allen wrench. Old Onza H.O. (Fig.

PRO TIP

Cleat and Clipping-In Problems

If your cleat will not engage the pedal, or not without excessive downward force, you may have to trim some of the rubber lugs on the bottom of the shoe. If the tread is too tall, it won't allow the cleat and pedal to engage without pushing down so hard that you squish the offending knobs. Even if you can clip in, the friction will be so high that the free-float will not work. Clip the shoe in and look where the pedal contacts the shoe knobs, and trim them in that area with a sharp knife. Alternatively, some cleats (Crank Brothers and Look 4×4) come with a shim to raise the cleat slightly off of the shoe sole to resolve tread interference.

If either the cleat screws or the threads in your cleat plate inside your shoe are stripped, you will need to change them. Some cleat plates have two sets of threaded holes, in which case you can move the cleat to the other set of holes. If yours does not, or if the other threads are also unusable, you can install a new threaded cleat plate. Many cleats come with spare backing plates and threaded plates. You interchange plates from inside the shoe—open the shoe wide, remove the shoe's sock liner and the cover concealing the screw slots, and pull out the old backing plate and threaded plate. Use new screws in the new threads or you could repeat the problem.

On pre-2004 Time ATACs with plastic bodies (Fig. 9.14), the yellow plastic covers surrounding the springs can break or fall off. These are easily replaced; just snap them into place.

9.8) and Look SL-3 (Fig. 9.15) pedals are adjusted differently; see §ix-4 below.

Before starting, clean your shoe cleats and the pedal clips. Lubricate the clip edges and cleat ends with dry lubricant (so you don't track it onto your carpet) and the pedal springs with wet chain lube (Fig. 9.23). Whenever you have trouble getting in or out, start with this step.

1. Locate the tension-adjustment screws. They are usually on either end of the pedal, fore and aft; you can see the screw in Figures 9.7 and 9.9–9.13. Time ATAC XS (2004 and later) spring adjustment screws are located on the outboard side at the front and back of the pedal.
2. To loosen the tension adjustment, turn the screw counterclockwise, and to tighten it, turn it clockwise (Fig. 9.7). It's the standard "lefty loosey, righty tighty" approach. There usually are click stops in the rotation of the screw. Tighten or loosen one click at a time (one-quarter to one-half turn), and go riding to test the adjustment. Many types include an indicator that moves with the screw to show relative adjustment. Make certain that you do not back the screw out so far that it comes out of the spring plate.

NOTE: *With early Ritchey, Scott, Girvin, Topo, Wellgo, and other dual-rear-clip–dual-rear-spring pedals, you will decrease the amount of free-float in the pedal as you increase the release tension.*

9.7 **Release tension adjustment**

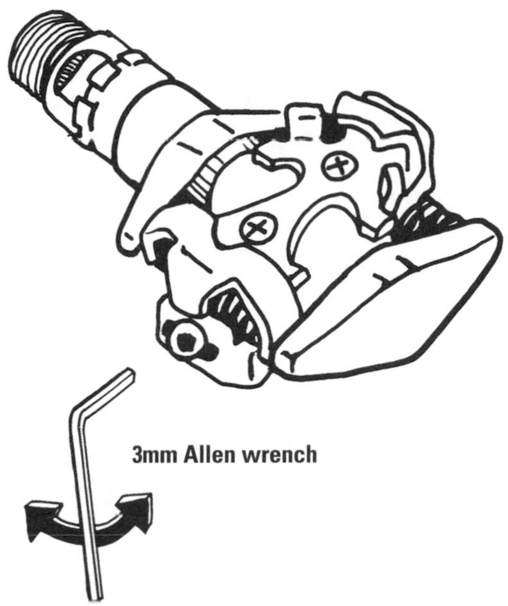

9.8 **Onza H.O. clip-in pedal, pre-1997**

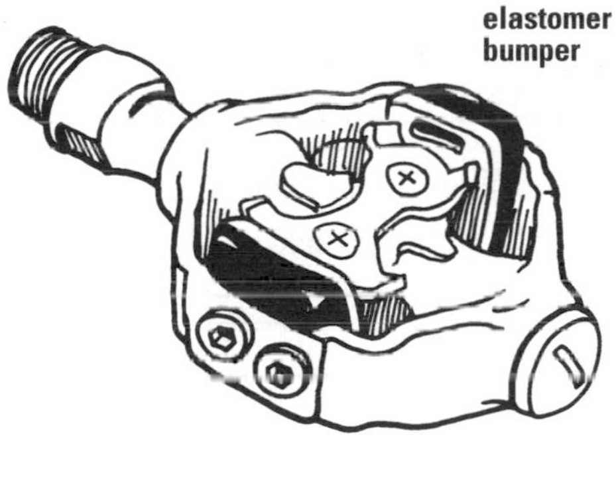

ix-4 ADJUSTING TENSION OF OTHER TYPES OF PEDALS

A. **Time (pre-2004, shown in Fig. 9.14), Crank Brothers, and Look 4×4 pedals** have no tension adjustment; they offer high retention and lots of float, yet they require low entry and release force and, therefore, require no adjustment. As mentioned in §ix-2 above, you can change retention by interchanging the right and left cleats to obtain a wider or narrower release angle.

B. **Old double-sided Look mountain pedals** have a single 5mm bolt that adjusts both sides. It has a large window (such as a ski binding) with a pointer to show the relative adjustment. The even older, one-sided Look models that resemble Look road pedals have a small slotted screw in the center to adjust the tension. More recently, Look SL-3 pedals (Fig. 9.15) have a 3mm adjustment screw with spring tension indicator on either side that is reached through a hole in the top of the rear clip. Current Look mountain pedals, dubbed 4×4, which are Crank Brothers Eggbeaters with Look axles and bearings, are adjusted like Crank Brothers Eggbeaters—you alter retention by interchanging the right and left cleats to obtain a wider or narrower release angle.

C. **Old Onza H.O. clip-in pedals** (Fig. 9.8) rely on elastomer bumpers to provide release tension. You adjust them by changing the elastomer. Bumpers of varying hardness are included with the pedals. Onza's black bumpers are the hardest, and the clear ones are the softest. There are several grades in between. The harder the bumper, the greater the release tension. To replace bumpers, unscrew the two Allen bolts holding each bumper on (Fig. 9.21). Pull the old bumper out and put in the new one. While you are at it, make sure that the Phillips screws that hold in the cleat guides are tight, because they have a tendency to loosen up and fall out. In fact, it wouldn't hurt to put a small dab of Loctite on the threads while you're checking them.

D. **Speedplay Frogs** (Fig. 9.16) have no tension adjustment; ease of release can be adjusted by rotating the cleat on the shoe sole to change the release angle.

OVERHAULING PEDALS

LEVEL 2

Just like a hub or bottom bracket, pedal bearings and bushings need to be cleaned and regreased regularly. Most pedals have a lip seal around the axle where it enters the pedal. Pedals without one get dirty inside very quickly.

First remove the pedal from the bike (Figs. 9.3 and 9.4) and inspect it to figure out which section of directions to follow for overhauling.

There is a wide variation in mountain bike pedal designs. This book is not big enough to go into great detail about the inner workings of every single model. Speaking in general terms, pedal guts fall into two broad categories: ones that have cartridge bearings and/or bushings (Figs. 9.13–9.16 and 9.21), and those that have loose ball bearings (Figs. 9.11, 9.12, and 9.18).

Many pedals are closed on the outboard end and have a nut surrounding the axle on the inboard end (Figs. 9.9–9.13). The axle assembly installs into the pedal as a unit and is accessed by this inboard nut. The axle assemblies on other pedal designs are accessed from the outboard end by removing a dust cap (Figs. 9.18, 9.21, and 9.22).

Before you start, figure out how the pedal is put together so you will know how to take it apart; the following paragraphs and the illustrations on subsequent pages should help. In a few cases, what the pedal guts are like may not be clear until you have completed step 1 in the overhaul process.

Shimano pedals usually have two sets of loose bearings and a bushing that comes out as a complete axle assembly (Figs. 9.11 and 9.12). You will see the tiny ball bearings at the small end of the axle (Fig. 9.17).

Many clip-in pedals use an inboard bushing and an outboard cartridge bearing (Figs. 9.13 and 9.21); Codas also have an additional needle bearing between the two. Brands include Crank Brothers, Wellgo, VP, Ritchey, Scott, Coda, Girvin, Topo,

9.9 **Removing the axle from a Shimano clip-in pedal**

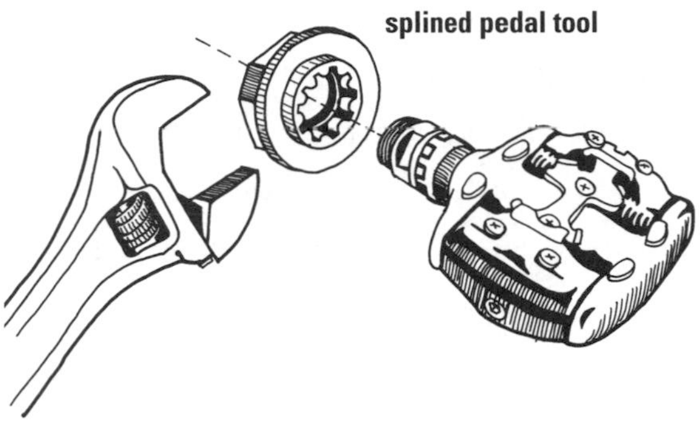

9.10 **Removing the axle from a Scott pedal**

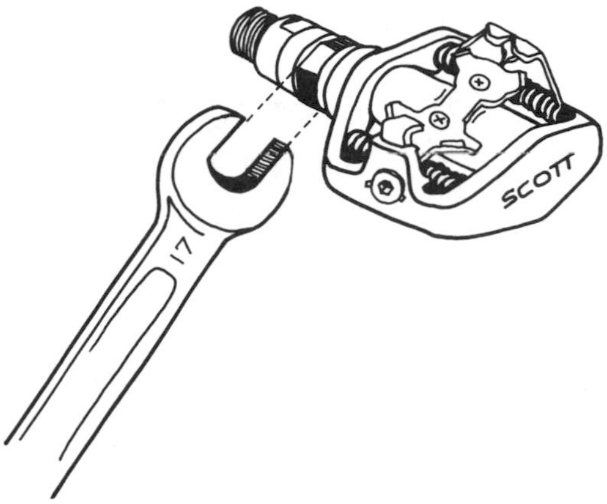

Nashbar, Onza, Exus, and Norco. Some of these are accessed from the crank side; others are accessed via an outboard dust cap. Speedplay pedals also have cartridge bearings and bushings; they differ in that they are opened like a clamshell (Fig. 9.16).

All pre-2002 Look, plastic-body Time ATAC, and Time TMT mountain pedals have an inboard cartridge bearing and an outboard needle bearing (Figs. 9.14 and 9.15). The axle assembly is accessed from the crank side.

Some pedals—even clip-in models (older Tioga comes to mind)—have no bearings at all. Instead, they just use bushings inside a plastic axle sleeve.

ix-5 OVERHAULING PEDALS CLOSED ON THE OUTBOARD SIDE

PEDALS CLOSED ON THE OUTBOARD SIDE

LEVEL 2

This includes Shimano, 2003 and earlier Time ATAC with plastic bodies, Time TMT, recent Ritchey, pre-2002 Look, Coda, Scott, Tioga, Exus, some VP, and Wellgo models.

1. With the tool designed for your pedal (Figs. 1.1A to 1.3), remove the axle assembly. On most varieties, this is accomplished by unscrewing the nut surrounding the axle where it enters the inboard side of the pedal (Figs. 9.9 and 9.10). See note below regarding thread direction. High-end pre-2004 Time ATACs with carbon-filled plastic bodies, later butterfly-shaped Ritcheys and current Ritchey V3 Pros, and old Time TMTs use a different approach. These pedals mostly rely on a snapring on the inboard end (Fig. 9.14) that must be removed with snapring pliers (Fig. 1.3). In place of the snapring, 2000–2003 Time ATACs with carbon-filled plastic bodies have an aluminum cup threaded onto the inboard end of the pedal.
   (a) Shimano (except M959), pre-2002 Look, and Exus take a plastic splined tool, but the Look tool is not compatible with the other two. Use a large adjustable wrench to turn the tool (Fig. 9.9). Most other closed-end pedals (including Shimano M959) take a 17mm or 18mm open-end wrench (Fig. 9.10).

NOTE: *The threads inside the pedal body are reversed from the crankarm threads on the axle; the internal threads on the drive-side pedal are left-hand threaded, and vice versa. That means the right axle assembly unscrews clockwise and the left axle assembly unscrews counterclockwise. It's confusing, but like bottom-bracket threads, pedal bodies are threaded so that pedaling forward works to unscrew the assembly.*

The nut is often plastic and can crack if you turn it the wrong way, so be careful. Hold the pedal body with your hand or a vise while you unscrew the assembly. The fine threads take many turns to unscrew.

(b) Look, Ritchey, and Time pedals: All pre-2002 Look, recent high-end Ritchey, and pre-2004 high-end Time mountain pedals have a large inboard cartridge bearing and an outboard needle-bearing cartridge. These bearings tend to stay very clean and seldom require overhaul.

(c) Axles in original Time plastic-body ATACs, recent high-end Ritchey, and old Time TMTs are removed via a snapring on the crank side (Fig. 9.14). Popping the snapring out requires inward-squeezing snapring pliers. Now skip to step 3 with any of these. On 2000–2003 Time ATACs with carbon-filled plastic bodies, unscrew the aluminum cup from the inboard end of the pedal body. You can try an adjustable pin tool on the small pinholes on its face, or you can carefully clamp it in a vise or grab it with pliers. Skip to step 3.

PEDALS CLOSED ON THE OUTBOARD SIDE

(d) There are four versions of Look clip-in mountain pedals. The oldest models, marketed under the Look and Campagnolo names, clip in only on one side and resemble Look road pedals in design and function. Later Look models resemble most double-sided mountain clip-in pedals and take a large steel cleat. Current Look 4×4 mountain pedals are Crank Brothers Eggbeaters on a Look axle assembly. Axle assemblies in the single-sided model are accessed with an 18mm open-end wrench, whereas double-sided Looks (Fig. 9.15) require a special splined tool that is purchased separately.

(e) Speedplay Frogs have a cartridge bearing and a needle bearing, which can be regreased without opening the pedal. Remove the Phillips screw from the outboard end of the pedal body and squirt grease in with a fine-tip bicycle grease gun (Fig. 1.2) until it squirts out the axle end. If you decide to open a Frog (reminds you of junior-high biology, doesn't it?), the pedal comes apart like a clamshell by unscrewing the single bolt on each side with a 2.5mm Allen wrench (Fig. 9.16). Before you put it back together, put a thin bead of automotive gasket sealer all of the way around the edge of one pedal half to seal water out.

2. Once you have removed the pedal body, take a look at the axle-bearing-bushing assembly. You will notice either one or two nuts on the thin end of the axle. These nuts serve to hold the bearings and/or bushings in place. Remove the nuts.

(a) If the axle has just a single nut on the end (Figs. 9.13 and 9.16), simply hold the axle's large end with the 15mm pedal wrench and unscrew the little nut with a 9mm wrench (or whatever size fits it). The nut may be very tight, because it has no locknut.

(b) If the axle has two nuts on the end, they are tightened against each other. To remove them, hold the inner nut with a wrench while you unscrew the outer nut with another wrench (Fig. 9.17). Shimano and older Tioga pedals use two nuts in this fashion; on Shimanos, the inner nut acts as a bearing cone—be careful not to lose the tiny ball bearings as you unscrew the cone!

3. Clean all of the parts.
   (a) If it is a loose-bearing pedal, use a rag to clean the ball bearings, the cone, the inner ring that the bearings ride on at the end of the plastic sleeve (it looks like a washer), the bearing surfaces on either end of the little steel cylinder, the axle, and the inside of the plastic axle sleeve (Figs. 9.11 and 9.12). To get the bearings really clean, wash them in the sink in soap and water with the sink drain plugged; the motion is the same as washing your hands, and it results in both the bearings and your hands being clean for a sterile reassembly. Blot dry.
   (b) If, on a pedal with a cartridge bearing (Figs. 9.13–9.16), the bearing is dirty or worn out, clean it if you can; otherwise replace it. These bearings often have steel bearing covers that cannot be pried off without damaging them, nor can the covers be replaced. If yours has plastic bearing covers, pry them off with a razor blade (Fig. 6.26), clean the bearing with solvent, let it dry, and repack it with grease.
   (c) Needle bearings (Time, pre-2002 Look, recent Ritchey, and Coda) can be cleaned with a solvent and a thin bottle brush slipped inside the pedal-body bore.
   (d) On a bushing-only pedal, such as older Tioga, just wipe down the axle and the inside of the bushings.
4. Lightly grease everything and reassemble the parts as they were, a simple process with bushings, cartridge bearings, and needle bearings—not so simple with loose bearings!
   (a) With a loose-bearing pedal, it is exacting work to place the bearings on their races and screw the cone on while keeping them in place. On a Shimano (Figs. 9.11 and 9.12), grease the bushing inside the plastic axle sleeve, and slide the axle into the sleeve. Slide the steel ring, on which the inner set of bearings rides, down onto the axle and against the end of the sleeve. Make sure that the concave bearing surface faces out, away from the sleeve. Coat the ring with grease, and stick half of the bearings onto the outer surface of the ring. Slip the steel cylinder onto the axle so that one end rides on the bearings. Make sure that all of the bearings are seated properly and none are stuck inside of the sleeve.
   (b) To prevent the bearings from piling up on each other and ending up inside the sleeve instead of on the races, grease the cone and start it on the axle a few threads. Place the remaining half of the bearings on the flanks of the cone. Being careful not to dislodge the bearings, screw the cone in until the bearings come close to the end of the cylinder but do not touch it. While holding the plastic sleeve, push the axle inward until the bearings seat against the end of the cylinder. Make sure that the first set of bearings is still in place. Screw the cone in without turning the axle or cylinder. Tighten it with your fingers only, and loosely screw on the locknut.
5. Adjust the axle assembly. Skip this step for Time, recent Ritchey, and Look.
   (a) Pedals with a small cartridge bearing and a single nut on the end of the axle, such as Exus,

PEDALS CLOSED ON THE OUTBOARD SIDE

9.11–9.16 Clip-in pedals without outboard dust caps

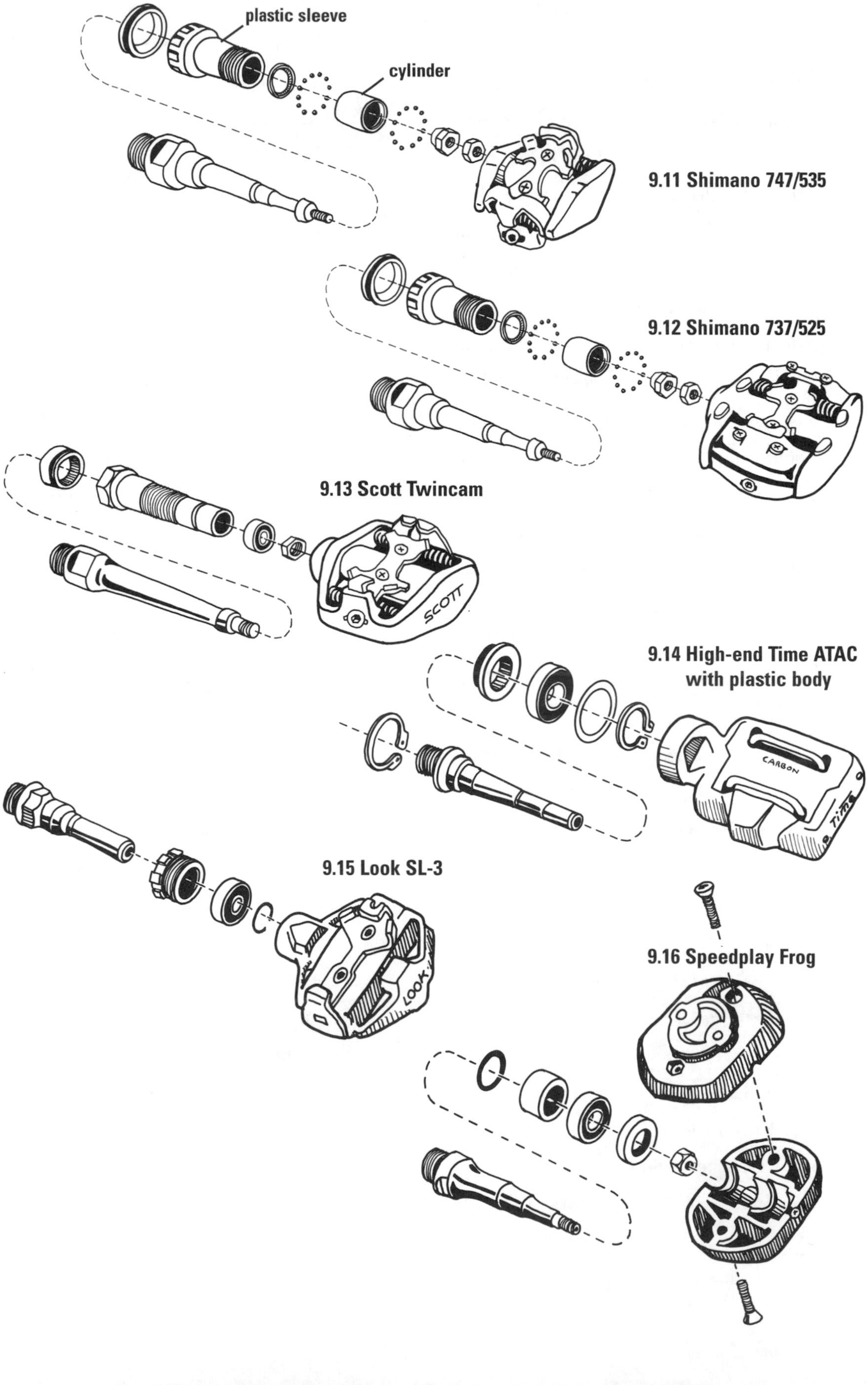

PEDALS CLOSED ON THE OUTBOARD SIDE

Coda, VP, Wellgo, Topo, Girvin, Speedplay, and Scott, simply require that you tighten the nut against the cartridge bearing while holding the other end of the axle with the 15mm pedal wrench. This approach secures the inner ring of the cartridge bearing against the shoulder on the axle, and proper adjustment is assured.

(b) On pedals with two nuts on the end of the axle, hold the cone or inner nut with a wrench and tighten the outer locknut down against it (Fig. 9.17). Check the adjustment for freedom of rotation, and be sure there is no play. Readjust as necessary by tightening or loosening the cone or inner nut and retightening the locknut.

6. Replace the axle assembly in the pedal body.

(a) Smear grease on the inside of the pedal hole; this will ease insertion and act as a barrier to dirt and water. Screw the sleeve back in place with the same wrench you used to remove it (Figs. 9.9 and 9.10).

9.17 Tightening a Shimano locknut

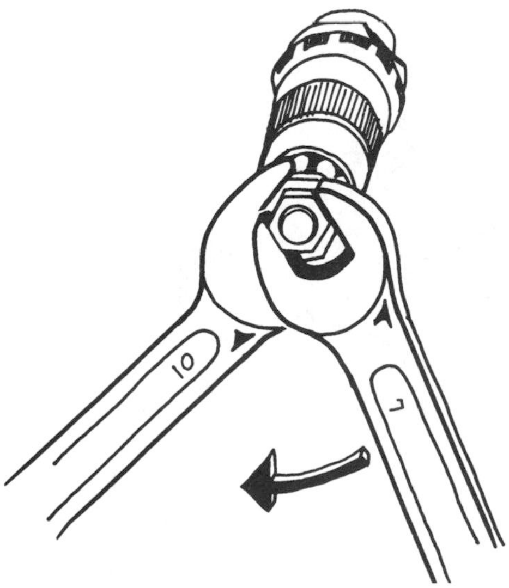

REMEMBER: *Pay attention to proper thread direction (see note in step 1). Tighten carefully; it is easy to overtighten and crack the plastic nut.*

(b) On original Time plastic-body ATACs, recent Ritcheys, and old Time TMTs, after replacing the axle assembly, pop the snapring back into its groove just inside the inboard lip of the pedal body. For 2000–2003 Time plastic-body ATACs, screw the aluminum retaining cup back onto the pedal body to hold the axle assembly in place.

7. Put the pedals back on your bike, and go ride.

ix-6 OVERHAULING LOOSE-BEARING PEDALS WITH OUTBOARD DUST CAP

NOTE: *Many non-clip-in pedals are not worth the effort to overhaul, and not all economical pedals are accessible to overhaul. Assess the value of your pedals and your time before continuing.*

1. Remove the dust cap with the appropriate tool. This could be a pair of pliers, a screwdriver, a coin, an Allen wrench, an adjustable pin tool, or a splined tool made especially for your pedals. Different dust cap styles are shown in Figures 9.18, 9.21, and 9.22 (although not all on loose-bearing pedals), and it should be pretty easy to figure out which tool is needed to remove the cap. If you see a cartridge bearing inside rather than loose balls, skip to §ix-7.
2. Hold the wrench flats on the inboard end of the axle with a pedal wrench, and unscrew the locknut with the appropriate size socket wrench (as shown in Fig. 9.20).
3. Holding the pedal over a rag to catch the bearings, unscrew the cone. Keep the bearings from

9.18 Loose-bearing pedal exploded

the two ends separate in case they differ in size or in number. Count them so you can put the right numbers back in when you reassemble the pedal. The guts should look like Figure 9.18.

4. With a rag, clean the bearings, cones, and bearing races. Clean the inside of the pedal body by pushing the rag through with a screwdriver. If there is a dust cover on the inboard end of the pedal body, you can either clean that in place or after popping it out with a screwdriver.
5. If you want to get the bearings really clean, wash them in a plugged sink with soap and water. The motion is the same as washing your hands, and it results in both the bearings and your hands being clean for a sterile reassembly. Blot dry.
6. If you removed it, press the inboard dust cover back into the pedal body. Smear a thin layer of grease in the inboard bearing cup and replace the bearings. Once all of the bearings are in place, there will be a gap equal to about half the size of one bearing.

9.19 Replacing the ball bearings

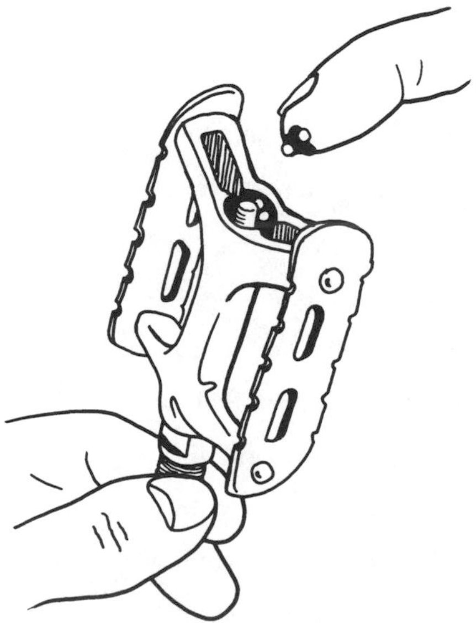

9.20 Removing the locknut from an Onza H.O. pedal

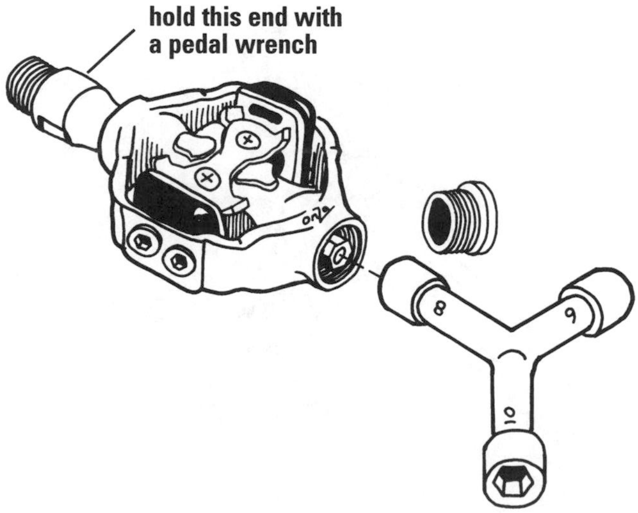

7. Drop the axle in and turn the pedal over so that the outboard end is up. Smear grease in that end, and replace the bearings (Fig. 9.19).
8. Screw the cone in until it almost contacts the bearings, then push the axle straight in to bring the cone and bearings together; this prevents the bearings from piling up and getting spit out as the cone turns down against them. Without turning the axle (which would knock the inboard bearings about), screw the cone in until it is finger-tight.
9. Slide on the washer and screw on the locknut. While holding the cone with a cone wrench, tighten the locknut (similar to Fig. 9.17, but you will be holding the cone with a 13mm or so cone wrench, not a 10mm standard open-end wrench).
10. Check that the pedal spins smoothly without play. Readjust as necessary by tightening or loosening the cone and retightening the locknut.
11. Replace the dust cap.
12. Put the pedals back on and go riding!

ix-7 OVERHAULING CARTRIDGE-BEARING PEDALS WITH OUTBOARD DUST CAP

Aluminum-body Time ATAC Alium, Alium HP (Fig. 9.22) and Z Control, and all 2004 (and later) carbon-composite-body ATACs (ATAC XS), Crank Brothers (Eggbeater, Candy, and Mallet), Look 4×4, older Ritchey, Onza H.O. (Figs. 9.8 and 9.20–9.21), some Wellgo, some VP, Nashbar, and Norco, among others, have an axle-end nut accessed from the outboard end by removing the dust cap. Inside is a sealed cartridge bearing on the outboard end and a brass or composite bushing on the crank side.

NOTE: *Crank Brothers pedals (Eggbeater, Candy, and Mallet models) have a lengthwise grease hole down the center of the axle. You can regrease the pedal without disassembly simply by removing the dust cap and screwing in the plastic knurled grease-adapter cap with a hole in the end (supplied with most aftermarket models and available from Crank Brothers). By using a fine-tip grease gun (Fig. 1.2), squirt grease into the hole. When done, replace the dust cap.*

9.21 **Onza H.O. clip-in pedal exploded**

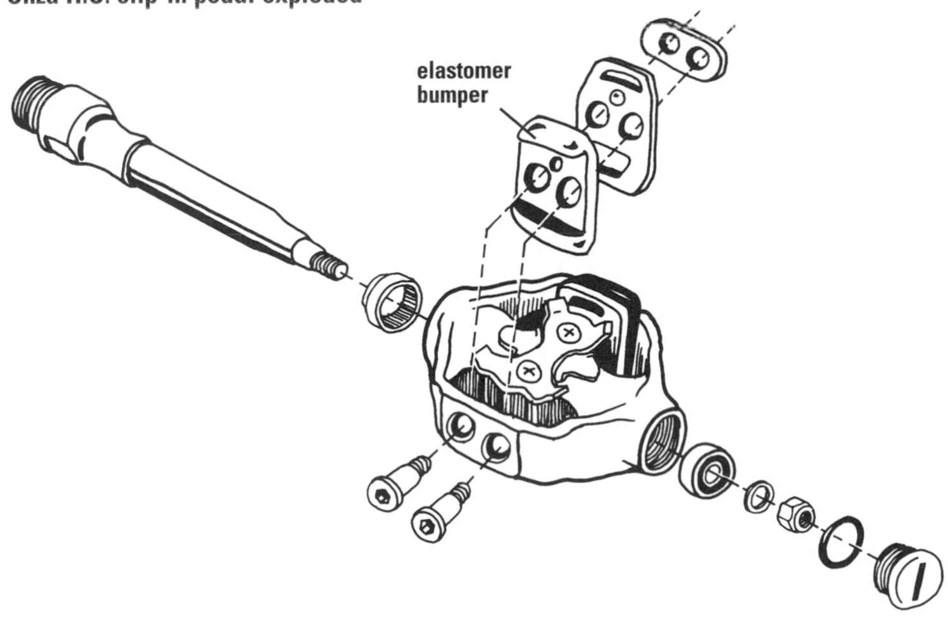

9.22 **Time ATAC Alium or Alium HP exploded**

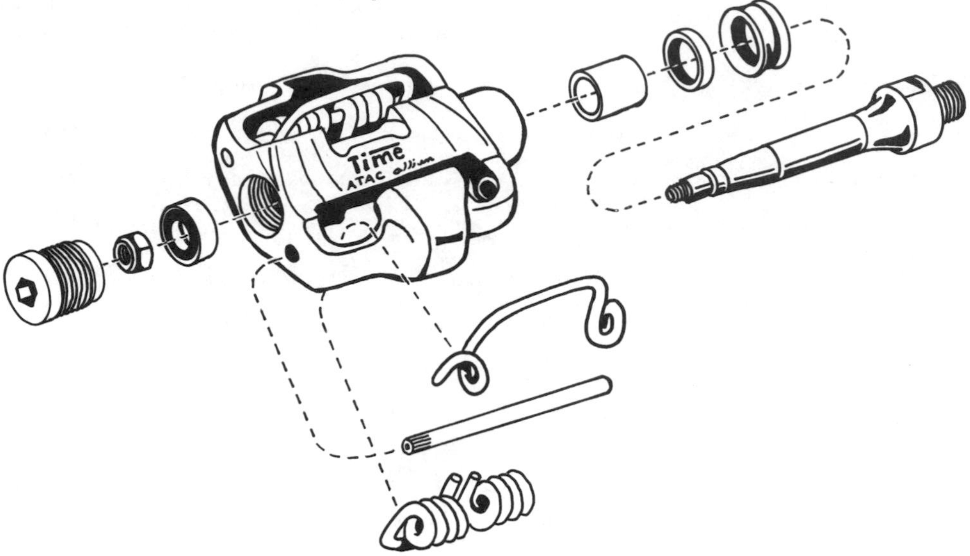

1. Take off the dust cap; some take a 5mm or 6mm Allen wrench, others take a coin or a screwdriver, Time ATAC XS takes an adjustable pin tool (Fig. 1.2, lower right-hand corner) with tiny pins (you can file your pins down to make them fit).
2. Hold the crank end of the axle with a 15mm pedal wrench, and unscrew the nut on the outboard end with a socket wrench (usually 8mm, 9mm, or 10mm [see Fig. 9.20]). The guts should look similar to Figures 9.21 and 9.22.
3. Push the axle out the inboard end, freeing the outboard cartridge bearing.
4. Clean and regrease the axle and the inside of the pedal body hole. Replace the cartridge bearing if necessary. On Ritcheys, Time Aliums, Alium HPs, and Z Controls, the brass bushings inside the pedal body are also replaceable, but you need a special (unavailable) tool so forget about replacing them.
5. Push the axle back into the pedal body, slip the cartridge bearing onto the outboard end of the axle, and thread on the end nut.
6. While holding the crank end of the axle with a 15mm pedal wrench, tighten the little nut down against the cartridge bearing.

NOTE: *Ritcheys will still have side play at this point; the dust cap is an integral part of the assembly. Once it is tightened down, the play goes away.*

7. Replace the dust cap.
8. Put the pedals back on your bike (Figs. 9.3 and 9.4), and you're done. Go ride.

AFTER-MARKET TITANIUM SPINDLES

ix-8 LIGHTEN YOUR BIKE WITH AN AFTER-MARKET TITANIUM SPINDLE

Some manufacturers offer aftermarket titanium axles for high-end pedals. Some offer only a titanium axle that is installed into the same sleeve, bushings, and bearings as the axle it replaces, and others sell a complete assembly, including the sleeve, bushings, and bearings.

If you are going to install a lightweight after-market axle or axle assembly into your pedals, make sure that you purchase one intended for your pedal brand and model. If all you are doing is replacing the axle, go ahead and follow the overhaul procedures outlined earlier in this chapter (§ix-5 and §ix-7). If you bought the entire assembly, just take out your old assembly. Again (I obviously feel the need to say this often), pay attention to the direction of the threads (see note in §ix-5, step 1). Following the procedures in §ix-5 or ix-7, install the new assembly.

Reinstall your pedals (Fig. 9.3 or 9.4). You'll be amazed how much lighter your bike feels . . . or is that your wallet?

9.23 **Lubing the release mechanism**

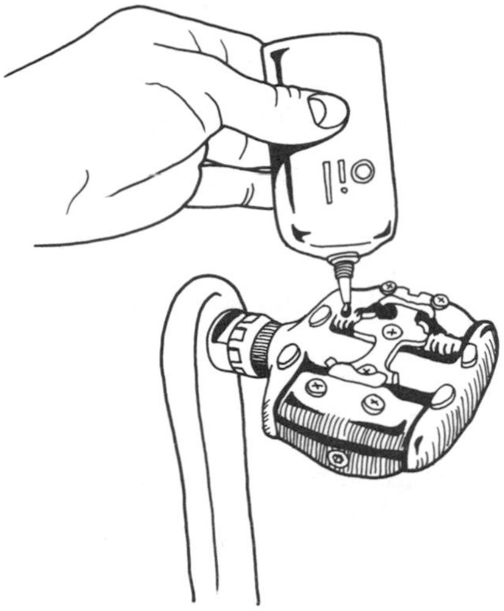

TROUBLESHOOTING PEDAL PROBLEMS

ix-9 CREAKING NOISE WHILE PEDALING

1. The shoe cleats are loose, or they are worn and need to be replaced (see §ix-2).
2. Pedal bearings need cleaning and lubrication (see Overhauling Pedals [page 210], §ix-5 to §ix-7).
3. The noise is originating from somewhere other than the pedals (see Chapter 8, Troubleshooting Crank and Bottom-Bracket Noise [page 199]).

ix-10 RELEASE OR ENTRY WITH CLIP-IN PEDALS IS TOO EASY OR TOO HARD

1. Release tension needs to be adjusted (see §ix-3).
2. Pedal-release mechanism needs to be cleaned and lubricated. Clean off the mud and dirt, and then drip chain lubricant onto the springs (Fig. 9.23) and dry lubricant onto the cleat contacts on the clips.
3. The cleats themselves need to be cleaned and lubricated. Clean off dirt and mud and put a dry chain lubricant or a dry grease (such as pure Teflon) on the contact ends of the cleats.
4. The cleats are worn out. Replace them (§ix-2).
5. The knobs on the shoe sole that contact the pedal might be so tall that they prevent the cleat from engaging. Locate where the pedal edges contact the sole, and trim some of the rubber with a knife. Alternatively, install a shim under the cleat.
6. The clips on the pedal are bent down. Straighten them if you can, or replace them. If you can't repair or replace the clips, you may have to replace the entire pedal.
7. If it is hard to clip into your pedals, check the metal cleat guide plate at the center of the pedal. It is held on with two Phillips screws, and they may be loose or may have fallen out.
8. Time ATAC spring clips can get bent and not hold the cleat as well. But they are replaceable by driving out the pin with a hammer and a punch (see Fig. 9.22).

ix-11 YOU EXPERIENCE KNEE AND JOINT PAIN WHILE PEDALING

1. Cleat misalignment often causes pain on the sides of the knees (see §ix-2).

2. You need more rotational float. Consider a pedal that offers more float; those offering the most are the Time ATAC and Speedplay Frog.
3. If your foot wants to roll inward (pronate), but your shoe and pedal force your foot to roll outward, then there is likely to be an increase in the tension on the iliotibial (I-T) band, the tendon connecting the hip and calf. This will eventually cause pain on the outside of the knee. You need to see a specialist, because you will probably need custom foot beds (insoles) to correct the problem.
4. Fatigue and improper seat height can also contribute to joint pain. Pain in the front of the knee right behind the kneecap can indicate that your saddle is too low. Pain in the back of the leg behind the knee suggests that your saddle is too high. (See Appendix C for seat-height guidelines.)

CAUTION: *If any of these problems result in chronic pain, consult a specialist. If you experience foot pain, a specialist can make custom foot beds to fit inside your shoes. Custom foot beds can also correct leg misalignments emanating from the foot.*

CHAPTER 10

SADDLES AND SEATPOSTS

Even if you're on the right track, you'll get run over if you just sit there.
—Will Rogers

TOOLS

4mm, 5mm, and 6mm Allen wrenches

open-end wrenches of various sizes

adjustable wrench

grease

After a few hours on the bike, I can pretty much guarantee that you will be most aware of one component on your bike: the saddle. It is the part of your bike with which you are most . . . uh . . . intimately connected. Nothing can ruin a good ride faster than a poorly positioned or badly designed saddle.

The seatpost connects the saddle to the frame. Some have shock-absorbing systems that cushion the ride. Some bikes, such as the Softride, employ a flexible beam attached to the front of the frame instead of a seatpost.

x-1 SADDLES

Most bike saddles are simply made up of a flexible plastic shell, some padding, a cover, and a pair of rails (Fig. 10.1). There are countless variations on (and a few notable exceptions to) this theme. Some have extra-thick foam or high-tech gel pads. Some have depressions, holes, or splits in the shell to reduce pressure in sensitive areas. Some have rails made of titanium, hollow chromoly steel, or even aluminum or carbon fiber. Others have synthetic leather covers, covers made from Kevlar, or covers made from the finest full-grain leather that money can buy. You can expect to spend anywhere from $20 to $200 for a decent saddle, and price may not be the best indicator of what makes a saddle really good—namely comfort.

You have a lot of choices when you decide to pick a saddle. My best advice is to ignore price, weight, fashion, and looks and instead choose a saddle that is comfortable. I could go on for pages about hi-tech gel padding, scientifically designed shells that flex in just the right places at just the right moment, and all sorts of factors that engineers consider when designing a saddle. None of it would count for squat if, after reading it, you ran out and bought a saddle that turned out to be a giant pain in the rear. Saddles are different because people are different. Try as many as you can before buying one.

The marketing war raging over saddles designed to prevent male impotency (Fig. 10.3) can blind a consumer's ability to select appropriately. If you buy a saddle out of fear, and it is uncomfortable, you have done yourself a disservice. Don't take it on faith or scientific studies that your saddle is protecting you. If it hurts, or you get numb while riding on it, it isn't working for you. What works for one person won't necessarily work for another.

Determine which saddle shape and design are the most comfortable for your body and then—and only then—start looking at things such as titanium rails, fancy covers, and all of the other things that improve a saddle. I know a lot of people who need 300g or 400g saddles with tons of thick padding to feel comfortable on even a short ride. I know others who can ride for hours on a skinny little sub-150g saddle. It's a matter of preference. Any decent bike shop worth its weight in titanium should let you try a saddle for a while before locking you into a sale.

Brooks and Idéale saddles have no plastic shell, foam padding, or cover. They are simply constructed from a single piece of thick leather attached to a steel frame with large brass rivets (Fig. 10.2). This was the main type of saddle up until the 1980s. Brooks still makes them and even offers them with titanium rails these days. This sort of saddle requires a long break-in period and frequent applications of a leather-softening compound that comes with the saddle or from a shoe store. Like a lot of old bike parts, you either love 'em or you hate 'em. If you're not familiar with them by now, go out and buy a modern saddle (Figs. 10.1 and 10.3).

A saddle with a plastic shell and foam padding requires little maintenance, except keeping it clean; check periodically that the rails are not bent or cracked (a good sign that you need to replace your saddle).

10.1 Modern lightweight saddle

10.2 Brooks leather saddle

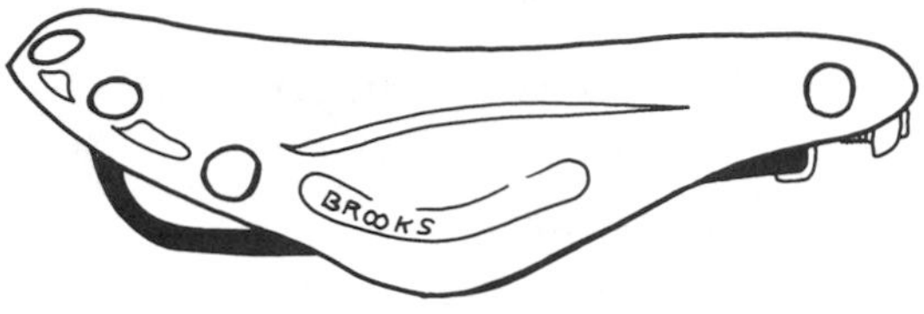

10.3 Saddle designed to not contact the perineum

X-2 SADDLE POSITION

Even if you have found the perfect saddle, it can still feel like some medieval torture device if it isn't properly positioned. Saddle placement is the most important part of finding a comfortable riding position. Not only does saddle position affect how you feel on the bike, but also with the saddle in the right place you suddenly become a much better rider. There are three basic elements to saddle position: tilt, fore-and-aft, and saddle height (Fig. 10.4).

10.4 **Saddle adjustments**

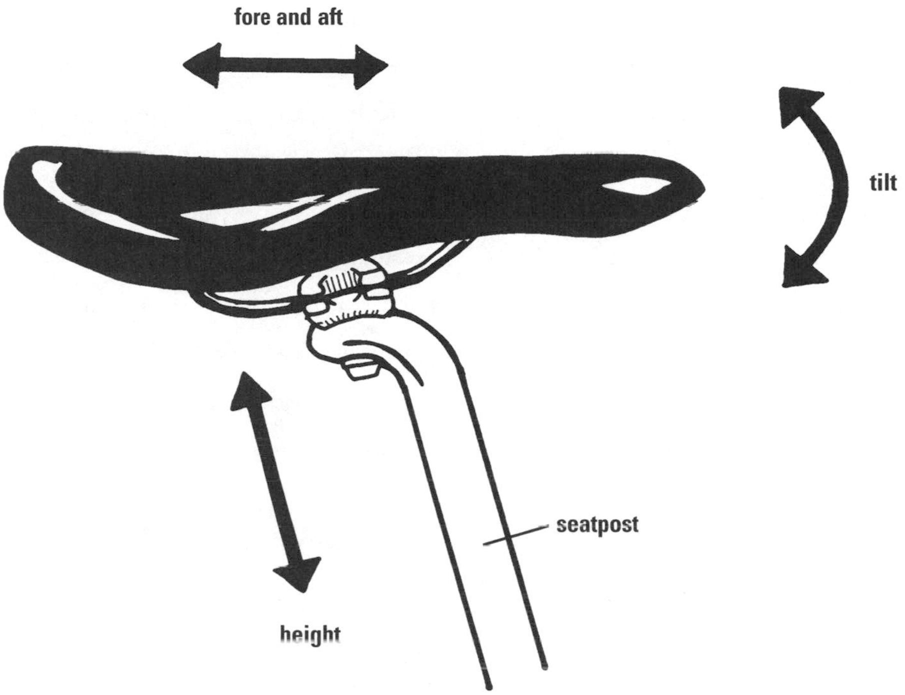

See Appendix C, §C-3, for a detailed explanation of setting saddle and handlebar position. The following are some short guidelines.

Proper saddle height (Fig. 10.4) is key to transferring good power to the pedals. The ideal road-bike saddle height places your leg in a 90–95 percent extension when you're riding; however, you may find this position to be too high for riding singletrack. Make sure your seatpost is inserted past the limit line, however. Again, consult Appendix C.

To improve your balance and center of gravity when riding a descent, you can bring the saddle height down—how far depends on you and the kind of riding you do. Pro downhill racers prefer very low saddle heights when compared to pro cross-country racers.

The most common cause of numb crotch and butt fatigue is an improperly tilted saddle (Fig. 10.4). The general rule of thumb is that you should keep the saddle level when you first install it, although it may take a slight downward tilt (maximum of 2 degrees) at the nose to accomplish this—the long seatpost extensions on many mountain bikes means that there may be enough flex in the seatpost and saddle that a saddle with a 2-degree downward slope becomes level when you sit on it. After a while, some people find that they prefer a slight upward or downward tilt to their saddles. Other than perhaps for downhill riders, I strongly recommend against making that tilt difference between nose and tail much more than one-quarter inch in height. Too much upward tilt and you place too much of your body weight on the nose of the saddle. Too much downward tilt will cause you to scoot down the saddle as you ride. That puts unnecessary pressure on your back, shoulders, and neck.

Fore-and-aft position (Fig. 10.4) determines where your butt sits on the saddle, the position of your knees relative to the pedals, and how much of your weight is transferred to your hands. Regardless of manufacturer,

SADDLE POSITION

all saddles are designed to have your butt centered over the widest part. If this is not where you sit, reposition the saddle. You want to position the saddle so that you have a comfortable amount of bend in your arms, without feeling too cramped or stretched out. If you find that your neck and shoulders feel tighter than usual and your hands are going numb, try redistributing your weight by moving the saddle back. Fore-and-aft saddle position also affects how your legs are positioned relative to the pedals. Ideally, your fore-and-aft position should be such that your knee pushes straight down on the forward pedal when your crankarms are in a perfectly horizontal position. If your saddle will not go back as far as you wish, and you have a short-length women's saddle, try replacing it with a standard-length men's model.

Butt pain is intimately connected to handlebar position, as are other aches and pains. The shorter the upper-body reach and higher the handlebar, the more weight will go on the butt. The longer the reach and lower the handlebar, the more the top of the pelvis rotates forward and moves the saddle pressure point from the sit bones to the soft tissue of the perineum and genital area. As a general rule, a novice rider will want a shorter reach and higher handlebar and perhaps a correspondingly wider saddle than will an experienced rider. Once again, consult Appendix C.

x-3 SEATPOST MAINTENANCE

A standard seatpost requires little maintenance other than removing it from the frame every few months. When you do that, wipe it down, regrease it, dry out and grease the inside of the frame's seat tube, and then reinstall it. This maintenance keeps it clean and moving freely for the purposes of adjustability. It also should prevent the seatpost from getting stuck in the frame (a very nasty and potentially serious problem), and it will prevent a steel seat tube from rusting out from the inside. I have outlined the procedures for installing a new seatpost and for removing a stuck seatpost in §x-11.

Suspension seatposts require periodic tune-ups—see §x-9. Regularly check any seatpost for cracks or bends so that you can replace it before it breaks with you on it.

x-4 INSTALLING A SADDLE

Most seatposts have either one (Fig. 10.5) or two bolts (Figs. 10.6 and 10.7) for clamping the saddle. Good single-bolt systems have a vertical bolt (Fig. 10.5) whereas cheap posts have a horizontal crosswise bolt.

Remember those heavy posts on your first bike as a kid? Those steel seatposts had the single horizontal bolt that pulled together a number of knurled washers with ears to hold the saddle rails. These weak seatpost clamps cannot hold up to adult use anymore; eschew them for posts with one or two vertical bolts holding aluminum clamshell clamp pieces together.

The two-bolt posts can rely on one of two systems. In one, the two bolts work together, pulling the saddle rails into the clamp (Fig. 10.7). On others, such as the American Classic post, a smaller second bolt works to offset the force of the main bolt (Fig. 10.6). No matter what type you have, it is reasonably easy to figure out how to remove, install, and adjust the saddle.

x-5 SADDLE INSTALLATION ON SEATPOST WITH A SINGLE VERTICAL CLAMP BOLT

Systems with a single vertical bolt (Fig. 10.5) usually have a two-piece clamp that fastens onto the saddle

10.5 **Single-bolt seatpost**

10.6 **Single-bolt seatpost with small adjusting bolt**

10.7 **Two-bolt seatpost**

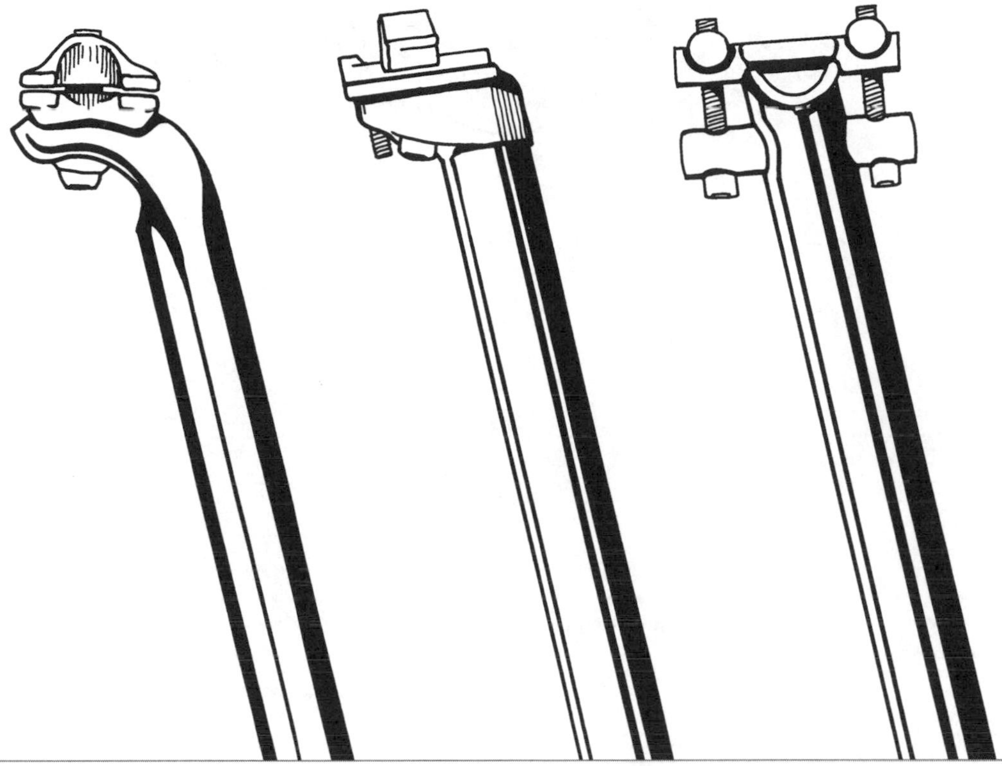

rails. On most single-bolt models, moving the clamp and saddle along a serrated curved platform controls saddle tilt. Before you tighten the clamp bolt, make sure there is not a second, much smaller bolt (or "set screw") that adjusts seat tilt. If you find a second bolt, skip to the next section (x-6).

1. Loosen the bolt until there are only a couple of threads still holding onto the upper clamp.
2. Turn the top half of the clamp 90 degrees and slide in the saddle rails. Do it from the back where the space between the rails is wider. You might need to remove the top of the clamp from the bolt completely if it is too large. If you do disassemble the clamp, pay attention to the orientation of the parts so you can put it back together the same way.
3. Set the seat rails into the grooves in the lower part of the clamp, and set the top clamp piece on top of the rails (Fig. 10.8). Slide the saddle to the desired fore-and-aft position.
4. Tighten the bolt and check the seat tilt. Readjust if necessary.

x-6 SADDLE INSTALLATION ON A SEATPOST WITH LARGE CLAMP BOLT AND SMALL SETSCREW

SEATPOSTS WITH LARGE CLAMP BOLT & SMALL SETSCREW

This type of post is illustrated in Figure 10.6.

1. Loosen the large bolt until the top part of the clamp can either be removed or moved out of the way so that you can slide the saddle rails into place.
2. Place the saddle rails between the top and bottom sets of grooves in the seat clamp. Slide the saddle to the desired fore-and-aft position. Tighten the large bolt.
3. To change the saddle tilt, loosen the large clamp bolt, adjust the saddle angle as needed by turning

10.8 **Saddle installation on single-bolt seatpost**

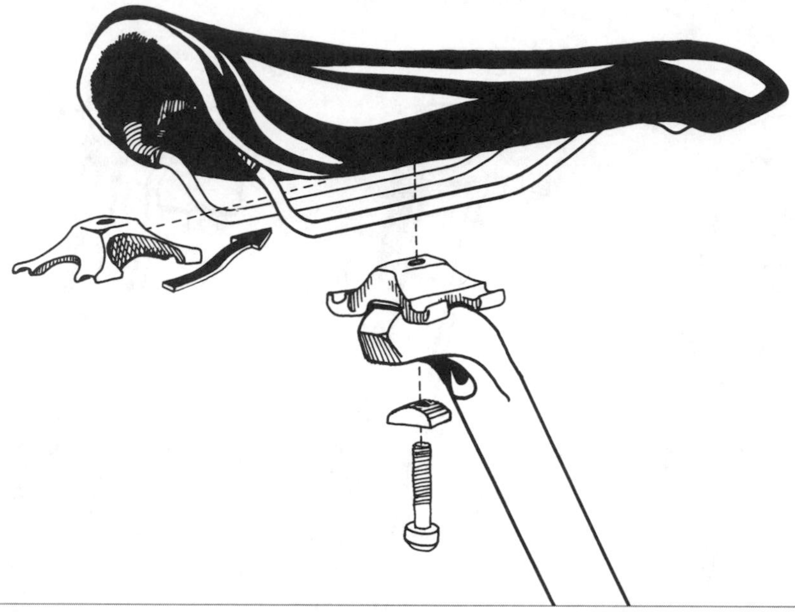

10.9 **Saddle installation on two-bolt seatpost**

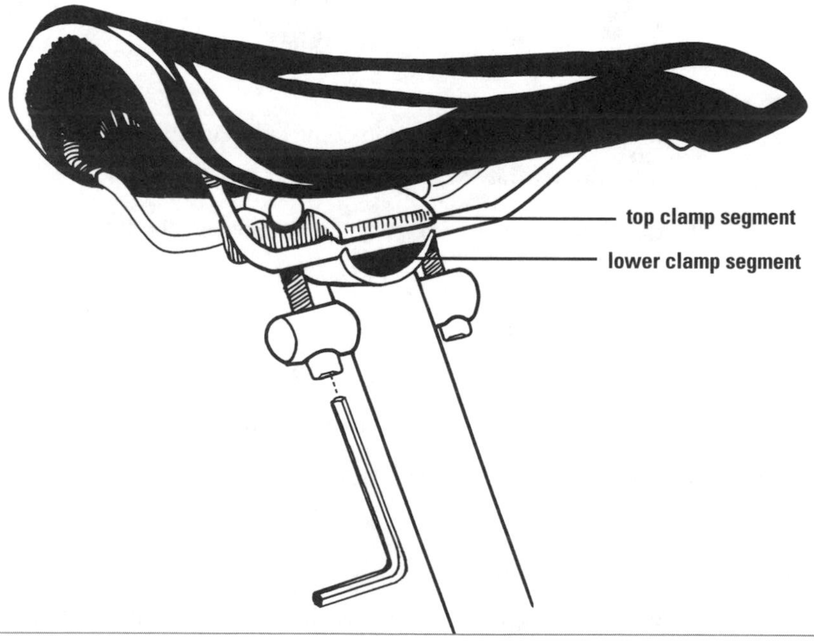

the setscrew, and retighten the clamp bolt. Repeat until the desired adjustment is reached.

NOTE: *On these types of seatposts, the setscrew may be either vertical or horizontal. On those with a vertical setscrew (Fig. 10.6), the screw is usually adjacent to the clamp bolt. A horizontal setscrew is usually placed at the top front of the seatpost, pushing back on the clamp. With such a setscrew, push down on the back of the saddle with the clamp bolt loose to make sure the clamp and setscrew are in contact.*

x-7 INSTALLING SADDLE ON A SEATPOST WITH TWO EQUAL-SIZED CLAMP BOLTS

This type of post is illustrated in Figure 10.7.

1. Loosen or remove one or both of the bolts to open the clamp enough that the saddle rails slide into their grooves between the two sides of the clamp. On some posts of this type, each piece that sits either on top of or under the rails is shaped like a cylinder that has been sliced longitudinally down the middle. Slide either the top or bottom piece out, set the saddle rails in their grooves in the remaining piece, and then slide the piece you removed back in from the side.
2. Slide the saddle to the desired fore-and-aft position. Tighten down one or both of the clamp bolts completely.
3. Loosen one clamp bolt and tighten the other to change the tilt of the saddle (Fig. 10.9). Repeat as necessary. Complete by tightening both bolts.

x-8 SEATPOST INSTALLATION INTO THE FRAME

1. Check for irregularities, burrs, and other problems inside the seat tube, visually and with your finger; if there are some, you may need to sand or otherwise clean out the inside of the seat tube. It may be necessary for a bike shop to ream the seat tube if a seat post of the correct size will not fit.
2. Grease the seatpost and the inside of the seat tube. Grease the seat-lug binder bolt. If you are using a sleeve or shim to adapt an undersized seatpost to fit your frame, grease it inside and out, and insert it.
3. Insert the seatpost (Fig. 10.10), and tighten the seat binder bolt. Some binder bolts are tightened with a wrench (usually a 5mm Allen), and some have a quick-release lever (Fig. 10.11). To tighten a quick release, flip the lever open so that it is directly in line with the body of the bolt—in other words, about halfway open. Finger-tighten the nut on the other end, and then close the lever. It should be fairly snug, about tight enough to

10.10 **Seatpost installation into the frame**

10.11 **Closing a quick-release seatpost binder**

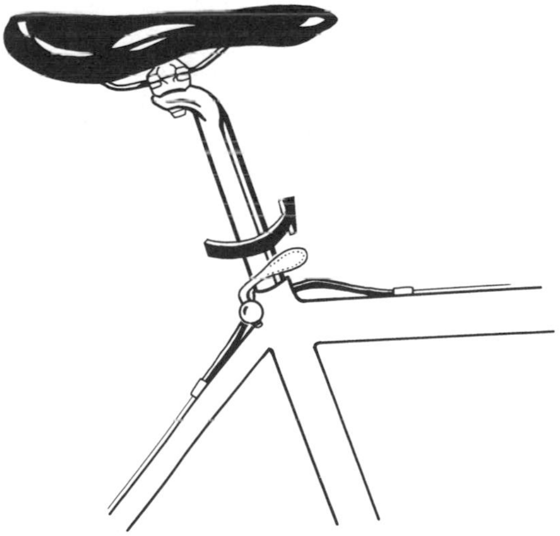

leave an impression in the heel of your hand for a few seconds. Open the lever, reposition the end nut, and close the lever again as necessary to get the right closing force.

4. After the saddle is attached, adjust the seat height to your desired position. It is a good idea to mark this height on the post with an indelible marker or a piece of tape. This way, if you remove the seatpost, you can just slide it right back into the proper place.

IMPORTANT: *Periodically remove the seatpost, invert the bike to drain water out of the seat tube, and let it dry out. The frequency depends on the conditions you are riding in. With a steel frame, spray oil (or better yet, "Frame Saver") into the seat tube to arrest the rusting process. regrease the post and the inside of the seat tube, and reinstall the post.*

x-9 SUSPENSION SEATPOSTS

SUSPENSION SEATPOSTS

Shock-absorbing seatposts come equipped with some sort of spring—either a steel coil, an elastic polymer ("elastomer"), or an air cushion. The telescoping, elastomer spring type (Fig. 10.12) is probably the most common, and air shocks are the rarest. Some seatposts have linkages that swing the saddle on an arc, rather than up and down.

To adjust the "boing" in most suspension seatposts, either you change the amount of preload on the elastomer spring, or you replace the elastomer(s). With telescoping seatposts (Fig. 10.12), and even with some parallelogram-linkage posts, you must first pull the seatpost out of the frame.

If you look up inside the post from the bottom, you will usually see a large slotted screw threaded into the walls of the post. If you tighten down clockwise on this screw, you will increase the preload on

10.12 Suspension seatpost

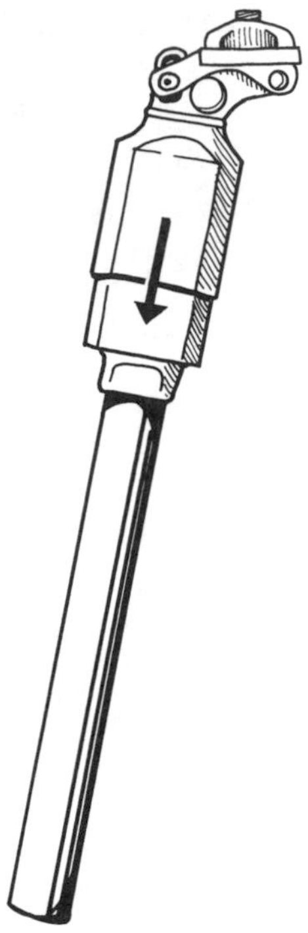

the spring and hence stiffen the seatpost. If you loosen this screw (counterclockwise), you reduce the preload and soften the ride.

To change springs, you remove the spring completely, make the switch (remember to grease the elastomers!), and replace the screw. You will find that as you change preload or elastomer combinations, the height of your saddle changes, so expect to slide the seatpost up and down in the frame to adjust for that.

Some parallelogram-linkage posts can be adjusted by turning a preload screw behind the saddle clamp and/or pushing the elastomer out from the side and replacing it (or interchanging small elastomer plugs into a larger elastomer).

There are other suspension-seatpost designs out there as well, and it is difficult to provide instructions that apply to all of them. Fortunately, most shock-absorbing seatposts are tuned as described above, and the others usually come with extensive instructions.

10.13 **Saddle on a Softride beam**

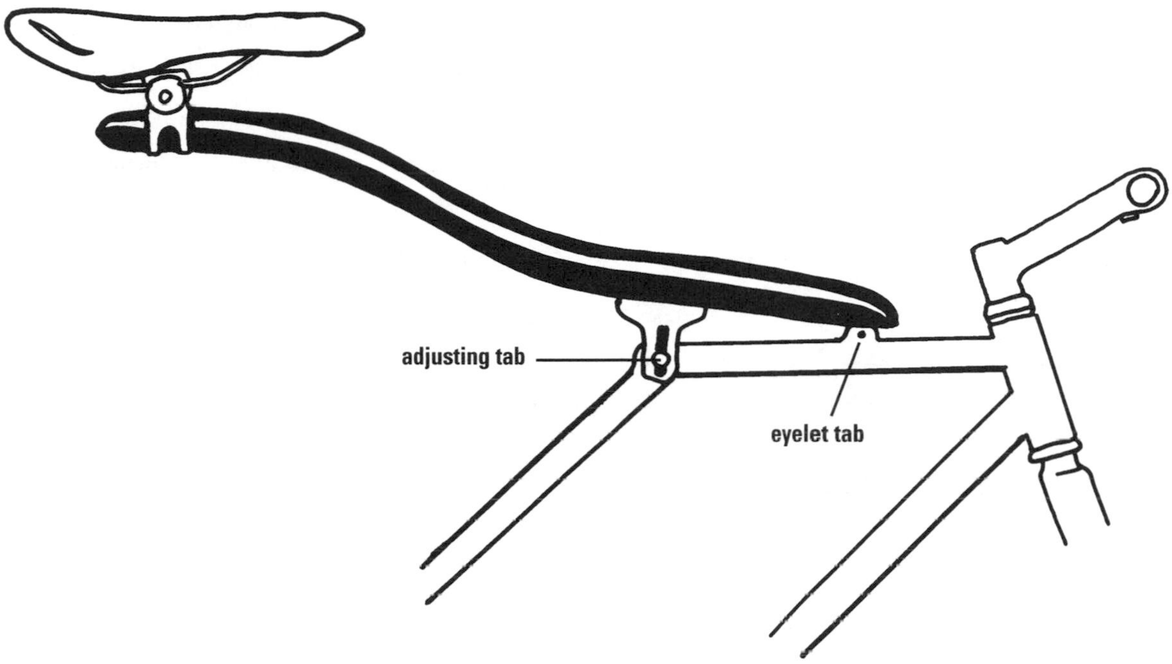

I recommend following the same regular maintenance schedule you would use for a standard seatpost (§x-3), in addition to maintenance of the suspension components.

IMPORTANT: *See the "important" note under §x-8 above.*

x-10 INSTALLING A SOFTRIDE SUSPENSION BEAM ONTO THE FRAME

LEVEL 2

The frame must be built to accept the beam, or you must purchase a retrofit kit from Softride to install it on a standard frame.

1. Attach the beam to the front frame-mounting bracket with a steel pin. The underside of the beam's nose has a small steel eyelet that fits between two tabs on the bracket, which is located on the top of the frame's top tube (Fig. 10.13). With a soft hammer, tap the included pin through the bracket, through the eyelet on the bottom of the beam, and out through the hole in the other side of the bracket.
2. Attach the beam to the rear frame-mounting bracket, located a few inches behind the front eyelet. The rear mount on the beam consists of two curved adjusting tabs separated by the width of the frame's mounting bracket that extend down. Long, curved slots in each adjusting tab (Fig. 10.13) are used to adjust the saddle height. Pass the bolt through one of the rectangular washers (with its knurled side pointing inward) and into the slot of one adjusting tab. Then pass it through the round end cap of the cylindrical frame mount, the frame mount itself, and out through the second end cap, the other oval tab hole, and the other rectangular washer. Screw on the nut after lining up the offset end-cap holes so that they fit into the mounting bracket with the bolt in place.

3. Swing the beam up to the desired height, with the anchor bolt loose. For starters, set it about an inch higher than what your normal seat height would be, to account for the beam's flex. If you reach the end of the adjustment in the bracket tab slots and the seat is still not as high as you need it to be, rotate the rear frame-mount end caps. The caps' offset holes offer two height positions for this very reason.
4. Tighten the anchor bolt. Readjust saddle height as needed.

x-11 REMOVING A STUCK SEATPOST

The hassle of a stuck seatpost happens when you do not follow the "important" note in §x-8. This is a level 3 job because of the risk involved. This may be a job best done by a shop, because if you make a mistake you run the risk of destroying your frame. If you're not 100 percent confident in your abilities, go to someone who is—or at least to someone who will be responsible if they screw it up.

1. Remove the seat binder bolt. Sounds easy enough.
2. Squirt penetrating oil around the seatpost and let it sit overnight. To get the most penetration, remove the bottom bracket (Chapter 8), turn the bike upside down, squirt the penetrating oil in from the bottom of the seat tube, and let it sit overnight.
3. The next day, stand over the bike and twist the saddle.
4. If step 3 does not free the seatpost, warm up the seat-lug area with a hair dryer to expand it. Discharge the entire cartridge of a CO_2 tire inflator at the joint of the seatpost and the seat collar to freeze it and shrink it. (Alternatively, ice the exposed seatpost with a plastic bag filled with crushed ice.) Now try twisting as in step 3.
5. If step 4 does not free the seatpost, you will need to move into the difficult and risky part of this procedure.
   (a) You will now sacrifice the seatpost. Remove the saddle and all of the clamps from the top of the seatpost. With the bike upside down, clamp the top of the seatpost into a large bench vise that is bolted to a very secure workbench.
   (b) Congratulations, you have just ruined your seatpost. Don't ever ride it again.
   (c) Perform the heat/ice or CO_2 trick from step 4. Grab the frame at both ends, and begin to carefully apply a twisting pressure. Be aware that you can easily apply enough force to bend or crack your frame, so be careful. If the seatpost finally releases, it often makes such a large "pop" that you will think that you have broken many things!
6. If that did not work, cut off the seatpost a few inches above the seat lug and clamp what's left of it in a vise. Warm up the seat-lug area with a hair dryer to expand it. Discharge the entire cartridge of a CO_2 tire inflator down inside the seatpost to freeze it and shrink it. Now try twisting as in step 5.
7. If step 6 does not work, you need to go to a machine shop and get the post reamed out of the seat tube.

If you still insist on getting it out yourself, you should really sit down and think about it for a while. Will the guy at the machine shop really charge you so much money that it is now worth the risk of completely trashing your frame? Have you thought about it for a while? And still you insist on doing this yourself? Okay, but don't say I didn't warn you.

8. Take a hacksaw and cut your seatpost off a little more than an inch above the seat lug on your frame. (Now you obviously have completely destroyed your seatpost, so I don't have to warn about riding it again.) Remove the blade from the saw and wrap a piece of tape around one end. Hold on to the taped end and slip the other end into the center of the post. Carefully (no, make that very carefully) make two outward radial cuts about 60 degrees apart. Your goal is to remove a wedge from the hunk of seatpost stuck in your frame. Be careful—this is where many people cut too far and go right through the seatpost into the frame. Of course, you wouldn't do that, now would you? Once you've made the cut, pry or pull this piece out with a large screwdriver or a pair of pliers. Be careful here, too. A lot of over-enthusiastic home mechanics have damaged their frames by prying too hard here. But you wouldn't do that, would you?
9. Once the wedge is out, work the remaining piece out by curling in the edges with the pliers to free more and more of it from the seatpost walls. It should eventually work its way out.

IMPORTANT: *Now, once your seatpost is out of the frame, remember to go back and reread §x-3 outlining the regular maintenance procedures required for a seatpost. In other words, take it out and apply grease every once in a while. You don't want to have to do this again, do you?*

x-12 TROUBLESHOOTING PROBLEMS IN THE SEAT AND SEATPOST

TROUBLE-SHOOTING THE SEAT & SEATPOST

1. **Loose saddle.** Check the bolts. They are probably loose. Re-establish your fore-aft saddle position (§x-2) and your saddle tilt, and tighten the bolts. Check for any damage to the clamping mechanism, and replace the post if necessary. If you need help, look up the instructions that apply to your seatpost.
2. **Stuck seatpost.** Having a stuck seatpost can be a serious problem. Follow the instructions in §x-11 carefully or you might damage your frame.
3. **Saddle squeaks with each pedal stroke.** The problem comes from the smooth leather or plastic moving against metal parts or from grit in the rail attachments.
   (a) On saddles that extend low on the sides, contact of the leather overlapping the saddle shell with the seatpost clamp or rails is likely the culprit. Greasing or powdering the contact area with talcum will eliminate the noise. Also, roughing up the leather at the point where it contacts metal will also quiet it down, because smooth leather sliding on metal can squeak.
   (b) Also try squirting chain lube into the three points where the rails are inserted into the plastic shell of the saddle, in case some grit working at the rails is making the noise.
4. **Creaking noises from the seatpost.** A seatpost can creak from movement of the clamp that holds the saddle or movement of the shaft against the sides of the seat tube while you ride. A dry seatpost can also cause creaks, so first try greasing it.
   (a) Some frames have an internal collar to adapt the seat tube to a certain seatpost diameter. Remember that the internal diameter of the seat tube is larger below the collar. I have seen bikes that creaked because the bottom of the seatpost rubbed against the sides of the seat tube below the extension of the collar. You can solve that problem by shortening the

seatpost a bit with a hacksaw. If you do saw off the seatpost, make sure that you still have at least 3 inches of seatpost inserted in the frame for security.

(b) Similarly, movement between the frame, sizing shims, and the post can cause creaking. Greasing all of these parts well should eliminate the noise.

(c) If the creaking originates from the seatpost head where the saddle is clamped, you should check the clamp bolts. Lubricate the bolt threads, and you will be able to tighten them a bit more.

(d) Shock-absorbing seatposts can squeak as they move up and down. Try greasing the sides of the inner shaft. Grease the elastomers inside, too.

5. **Seatpost slips down.**

(a) Tighten the frame binder bolt. If the seat-binder lug is pinched closed, and you still can't get it tight enough, you may be using a seatpost with an incorrect diameter, or the seat tube on your bike is oversized or has been stretched. Double-check the seat-tube diameter with a measuring caliper (Fig. 1.4). Your local shop may have one that you could use if you don't have one.

(b) Try putting a larger seatpost in the frame, and replace yours if you find one that fits better. If the next size up is too big, you may need to "shim" your existing post. Cut a 1-by-3-inch piece of aluminum from a pop can. Pull the seatpost out, grease it and the pop-can shim, and insert both back into your frame. Bend the top lip of the shim over to prevent it from disappearing inside the frame. You may need to experiment with various shim dimensions until you find a piece that will go in with the seatpost and will also prevent slippage. Go ahead, pop cans are cheap.

CHAPTER 11

HANDLEBARS, STEMS, AND HEADSETS

The great thing in this world is not so much where you stand, as in what direction you are moving.
—Oliver Wendell Holmes Jr.

TOOLS

- metric Allen wrenches
- headset wrenches sized for your particular headset
- grease
- rubbing alcohol
- scissors, tin snips, or knife
- mallet
- hacksaw
- round file
- flat file
- bike stand

OPTIONAL TOOLS

- bench vise
- headset-cup remover
- star-nut installation tool
- fork crown-race slide hammer
- Shimano or Chris King tool to protect fork-crown race when setting
- headset press
- Chris King headset press inserts to protect bearings during installation
- torque wrench

On a bike, you maintain or change your direction largely by applying force to your handlebar. If everything works properly, variations in that pressure will result in your front wheel changing direction. Pretty basic, right? Right. But there is a somewhat complicated series of parts between the handlebar and the wheel that makes that simple process possible. The parts of the steering system are illustrated in Figure 11.1. In this chapter, we'll cover most of that system by going over handlebars, stems, and headsets. The explanations in this chapter start at the outside of each end of the handlebar and move toward the middle.

BAR ENDS

xi-1 INSTALLATION OF BAR ENDS

Bar ends are meant to provide a powerful hand position while climbing, as well as an alternative stretched-out position while riding on smooth roads. They are not meant to be positioned vertically to provide a higher hand position. If you want your hands higher, get a taller, more vertical stem, and perhaps a riser handlebar that has a double bend to elevate the ends. This way you still have easy access to the brake levers.

1. Slide the shifters, brake levers, and grips inward to make room at the end of the handlebar for the bar end. See Grip Removal, §xi-3, for instructions on moving the grip, and Chapters 5 and 7 about shifters and brake levers.
2. Loosen the bolt on the bar-end clamp; this bolt usually accepts a 5mm Allen wrench. Slide the bar end onto the handlebar (Fig. 11.2).
3. Tighten the clamp bolt enough that it just holds the bar ends in place. Rotate the bar ends to the position you like (see Appendix C, §C-5e for position recommendations).
4. Tighten the clamp bolt. Make sure it is snug. (Recommended torque is in Appendix D.)

11.1 **Steering assembly (shown without brakes for clarity)**

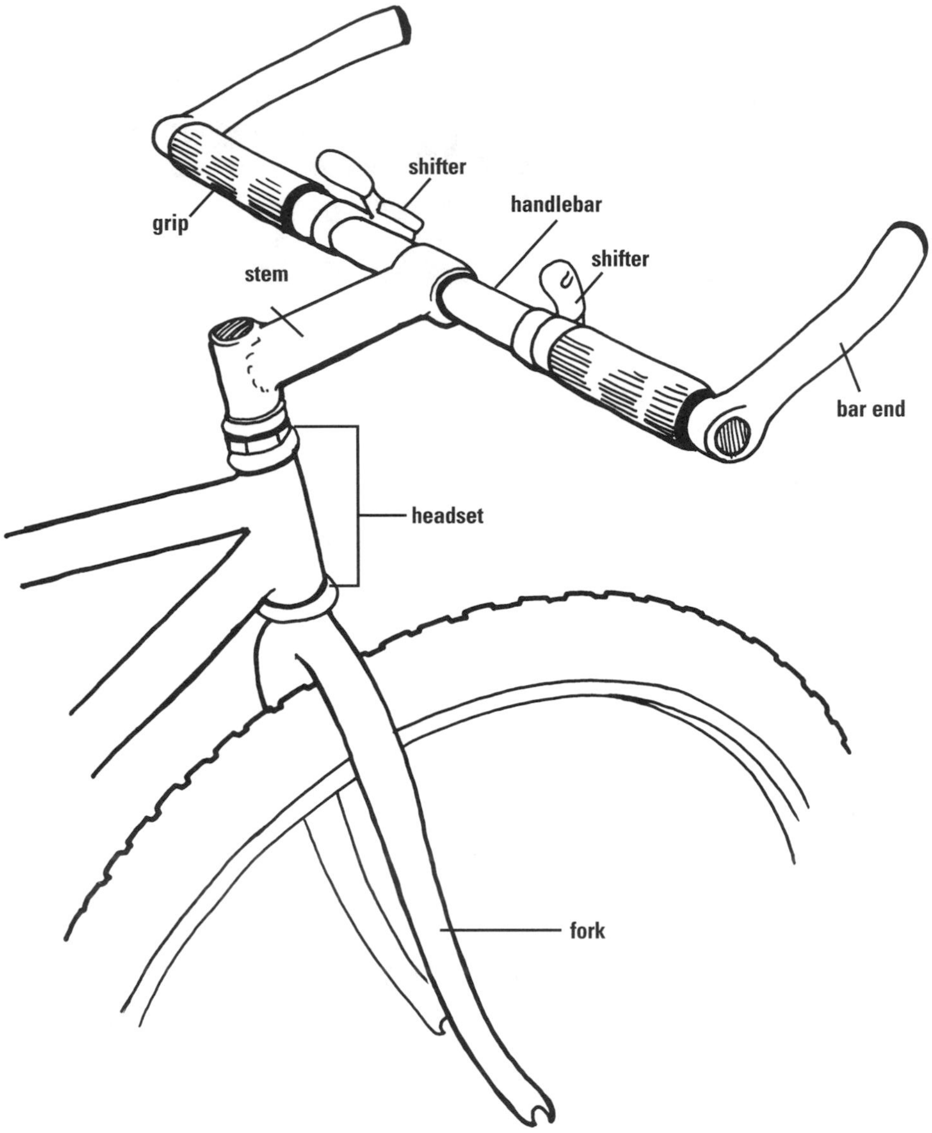

11.2 **Grip and bar-end assembly exploded**

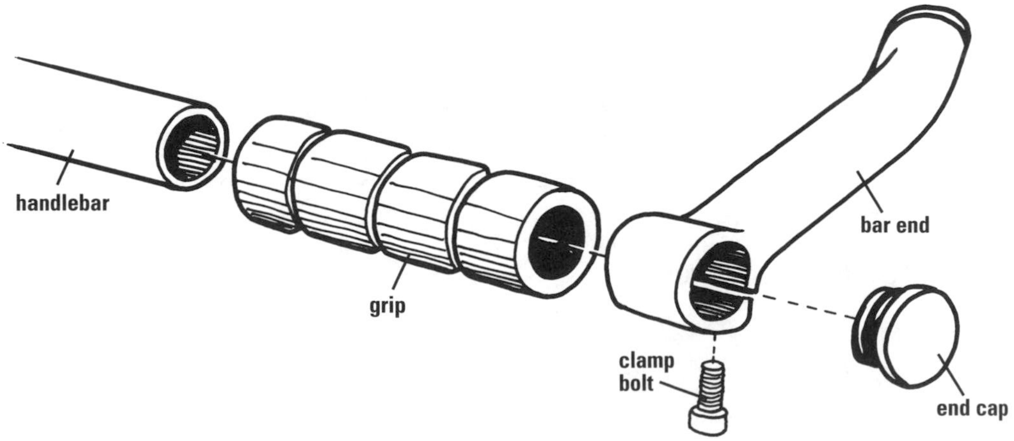

NOTE: *The ends of some superlight handlebars can be damaged by bar ends and, therefore, come equipped with small, cylindrical, aluminum inserts that provide support under the bar ends when inserted at the ends of the handlebar. Similarly, some composite handlebars have aluminum reinforcements at their ends to add support under the bar end. These types of handlebars cannot be shortened, as the bar ends will not have the support that they need.*

xi-2 REMOVAL OF BAR ENDS

1. Loosen the bolt on the bar-end clamp; this bolt usually accepts a 5mm Allen wrench.
2. Pull the bar end off (Fig. 11.2).

GRIPS

xi-3 GRIP REMOVAL

If the grip is shot, just cut it off with a knife. Otherwise:

1. Remove the bar ends and bar-end plugs (Fig. 11.2, §xi-2), if installed.
2. Roll back an edge of the grip on itself.
3. Squirt water or, better yet, rubbing alcohol on the handlebar and the exposed grip underside (Fig. 11.3). Flip the rolled-up edge back down, and repeat steps 2 and 3 on the other end of the grip.
4. Starting at the ends, twist the grip back and forth as you pull outward on it (Fig. 11.4). The wet sections will slip easily, and the dry middle section will start moving as the ends twist.

PRO TIP

A syringe can be used to inject rubbing alcohol under the grip. The needle can be slipped under the grip from the end, and it can even be pushed through the grip. With alcohol underneath, the grip will slide off in seconds.

xi-4 GRIP INSTALLATION

1. Squirt rubbing alcohol or water inside the grip. Rubbing alcohol lubricates well and dries quickly (immediately with a blast of compressed air!); water dries slowly, so the grip slips for a few days; hair spray and spray adhesives can be used to totally prevent grip slippage, but they are bad to breathe, and they set up permanently, thereby thwarting subsequent removal and repositioning.
2. Twist the grip onto the handlebar.

11.3 **Using water to remove grip**

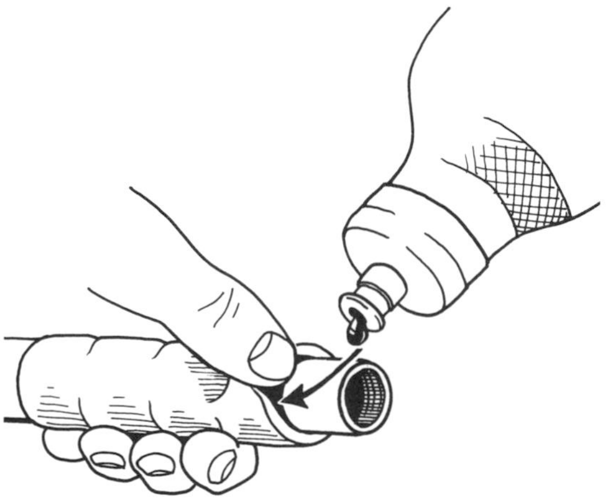

11.4 **Grip removal**

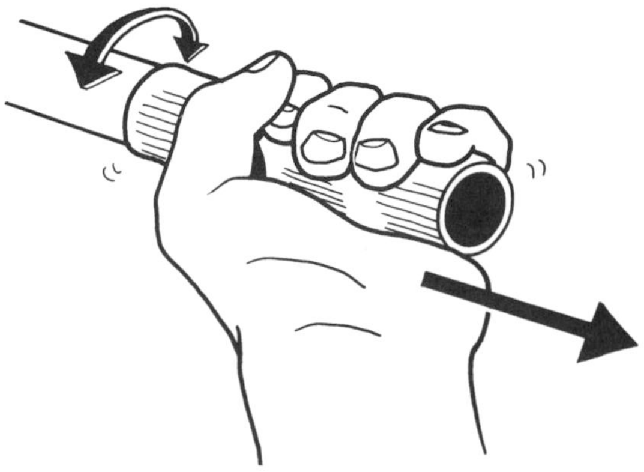

REMOVAL OF BAR ENDS
—
GRIPS
—
GRIP REMOVAL
—
GRIP INSTALLATION

11.5 **Trimming grip to accommodate bar end**

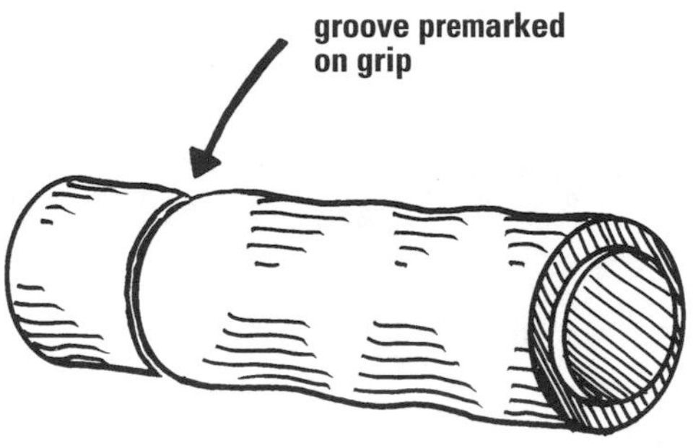

11.6 **Clamp-type stem for threadless headset**

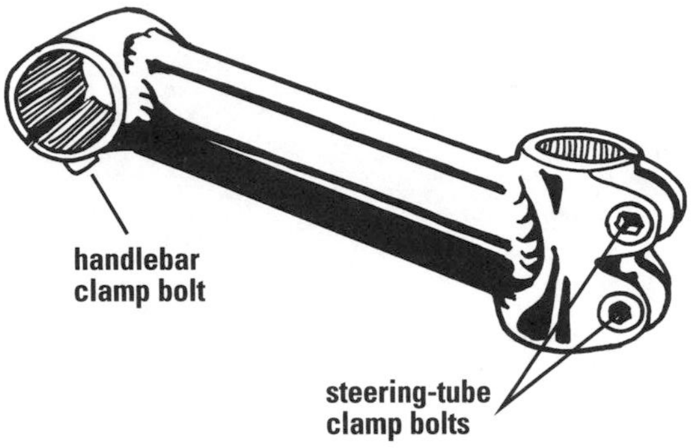

NOTE: *Some grips have a closed end. If you are going to use bar ends, you will need to cut off the closed end; you may also want to shorten the grip for your hand size or to adapt to a twist shifter. Some of these grips have a marked groove where they are meant to be cut with a pair of scissors (Fig. 11.5). Otherwise, you can cut them off anywhere you wish with scissors, tin snips, or a knife. If you have a thin, lightweight handlebar, you can easily cut off the end of the grip by hitting the end of the grip with a mallet or hammer after it is installed on the handlebar. The handlebar will cut a nice hole in the grip end like a cookie cutter!*

Grips used alongside Grip Shift and other twist shifters are shorter than standard grips, as part of the hand is sitting on the twist grip. Grips specifically designed for Grip Shift shifters are readily available in bike shops. If you can't find them, just cut yours down to the proper length.

HANDLEBARS

xi-5 HANDLEBAR REMOVAL

1. Unless you have a front-opening stem (Fig. 11.7) and you are going to replace the same handlebar, remove the bar ends and grips (Fig. 11.2), at least from one side. It is easier to remove grips when the handlebar is clamped into the stem than when it is sitting on a workbench; therefore, if you are moving the parts to another handlebar, remove them while the handlebar is still on the bike. For instructions for removing bar ends and grips, see §xi-2 and §xi-3.
2. Remove the brake levers and shifters unless you will be replacing the same handlebar, and have a front-opening stem (Fig. 11.7). (Turn to Chapter 7 for information on brake levers and Chapter 5 for shifters.)
3. With a single-bolt stem (Fig 11.6), loosen that bolt; it tightens the stem clamp that surrounds the handlebar. This bolt usually takes a 5mm Allen wrench. With a front-opening stem, completely remove the front cap by removing the two, three, or four bolts that hold it on, with a 4mm or 5mm hex key.
4. Pull the handlebar out (or let it drop off of the front if a front-opening stem).

xi-6 HANDLEBAR INSTALLATION

1. With a single-bolt stem, remove the stem-clamp bolts, grease the threads, and re-install the bolt. Grease the inside of the stem clamp, and grease

HANDLEBARS
—
HANDLEBAR REMOVAL
—
HANDLEBAR INSTALLATION

11.7 Threadless headset and stem (cutaway)

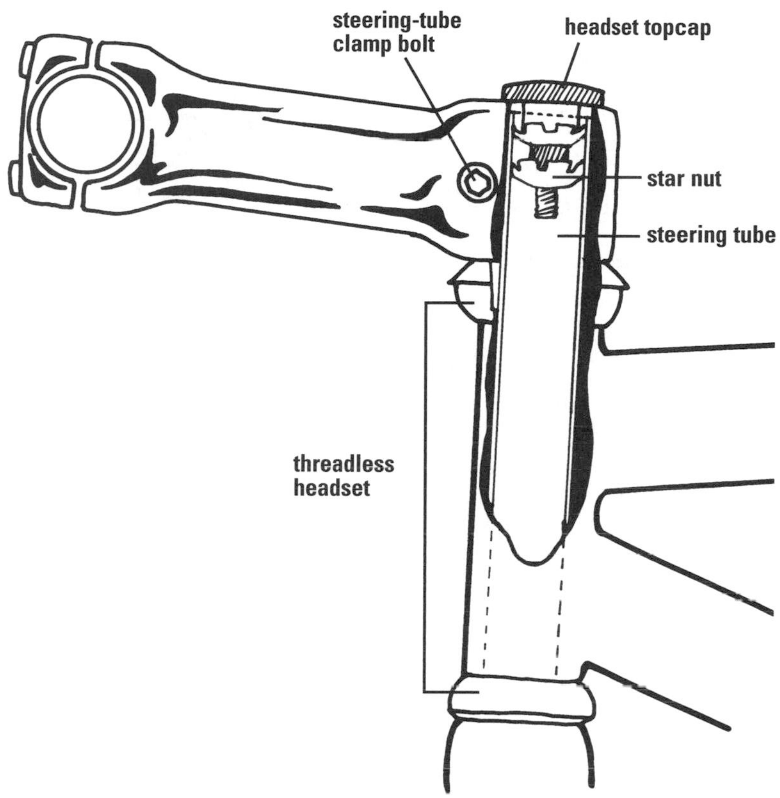

the clamping area in the center of the handlebar. With a front-opening stem, place the front cap over the handlebar and replace the bolts.

2. Twist the handlebar to the position that you find most comfortable. With a standard, single-bend handlebar, I prefer rotating the handlebar such that the ends point up and back, but the position is all a matter of personal preference.
3. Tighten the bolt or bolts that clamp the handlebar to the stem to the recommended torque—see the torque table in Appendix D. The torque applied is particularly important with expensive, lightweight stems and handlebars. You can pinch, and thereby weaken, a lightweight handlebar by overtightening, and the high-strength tubing will crack right by the stem. Light stems come with ever-smaller bolts with ever-finer threads, and overtightening can strip the threads inside the aluminum (or magnesium, etc.) stem. If you don't have a torque wrench, and you have a lightweight stem with small bolts (e.g., M5 or M6 bolts, which take 4mm and 5mm hex keys, respectively), use a short hex key so that you can't get much leverage. Proper torque is even more important with carbon-fiber handlebars.
4. Also, make sure that there is the same amount of space between the stem and either edge of the front plate on a front-opening stem. Any stem whose clamp gap(s) gets pinched close to touching when tightened around the handlebar needs to be replaced, along with the handlebar. This is because overtightening has stretched the stem cap, damaged the female threads in the stem, and deformed and weakened the handlebar.

xi-7 HANDLEBAR MAINTENANCE AND REPLACEMENT SCHEDULE

A bike cannot be controlled without a handlebar, so you never want one to break on you. Do not look at your handlebar as a permanent accessory on your bike. All aluminum handlebars will eventually fail. If titanium, steel, or carbon-fiber handlebars are repeatedly stressed above a certain level, they will eventually fail as well. What that level is depends on the particular handlebar. The trick is not to be riding when it fails.

Keep your handlebar clean. Regularly inspect it for cracks, crash-induced bends, corrosion, and stressed areas. If you find any sign of wear or cracking, replace it. Never straighten a bent handlebar—replace it! If you crash hard on your bike, consider replacing your handlebar even if it looks fine. If you have had a crash and can see no problems with the handlebar, remove the bar ends, and check whether it is bent at the bar-end edges. A carbon-fiber handlebar can be broken internally, and the damage may not be visible from the outside. If your handlebar has taken an extremely hard hit, it's a good idea to replace it rather than gamble on its integrity. This is especially true with lightweight handlebars; the high hardness of the materials used may prevent visible bending, but they may be so weakened that they will soon shear off.

The Italian stem and handlebar manufacturer 3T recommends replacing stems and handlebars every four years. If you rarely ride the bike, this time frame is overkill. If you ride hard and ride often, every four years may not be frequently enough. Do what is appropriate for you, and be aware of the risks.

STEMS

The approximately horizontal stem connects to the approximately vertical steering tube of the fork (which is either 1-, 1⅛-, or 1¼-inches in diameter) and clamps around the handlebar which has one of two diameters: 25.4mm or 31.8mm. Stems come in one of two basic types: for (1) threadless (Fig. 11.7) or (2) threaded (Fig. 11.9) steering tubes. Some stems have shock-absorbing mechanisms with pivots and springs to provide suspension (Fig. 11.10).

Stems for threadless steering tubes (Fig. 11.6) have a clamping collar for the fork steering tube. Because the steering tube has no threads, the top headset cup slides on and off. In this case, the stem plays a dual role: It clamps around the steering tube to connect the handlebar to the fork, and it also keeps the headset in proper adjustment by preventing the top headset cup from sliding up the steering tube (Figs. 11.7 and 11.11). If you have an old 1-inch diameter steering tube (the old standard) and a stem for a 1⅛-inch steering tube (the current standard), you can get a slotted aluminum reduction bushing (normally supplied with a new stem) to allow the stem to be used with the steering tube.

11.8 Quill-type stem

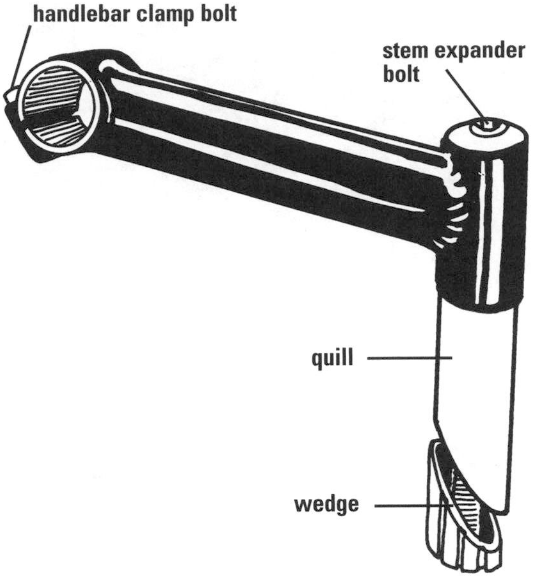

11.9 **Threaded headset and quill stem (cutaway)**

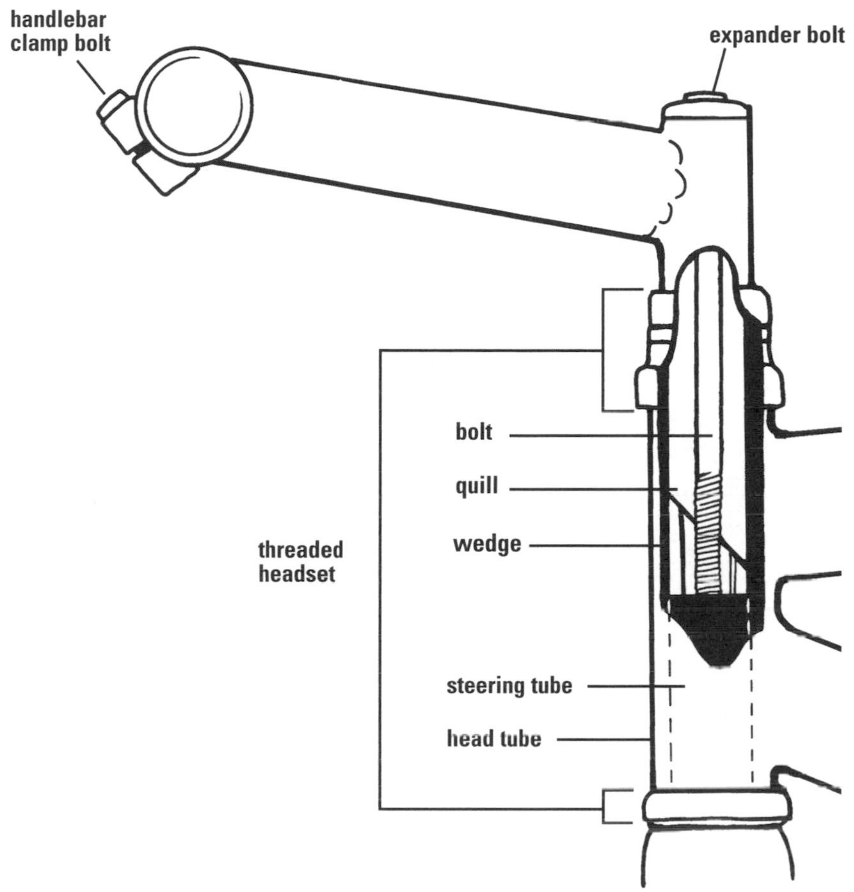

11.10 **Suspension stem**

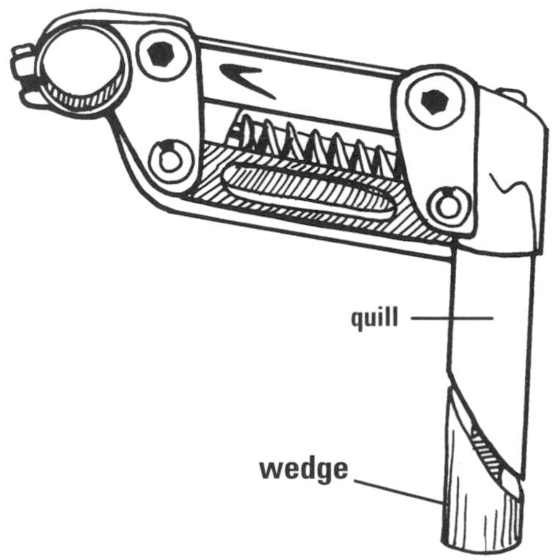

11.11 **Threadless headset upper cup held in place by the stem**

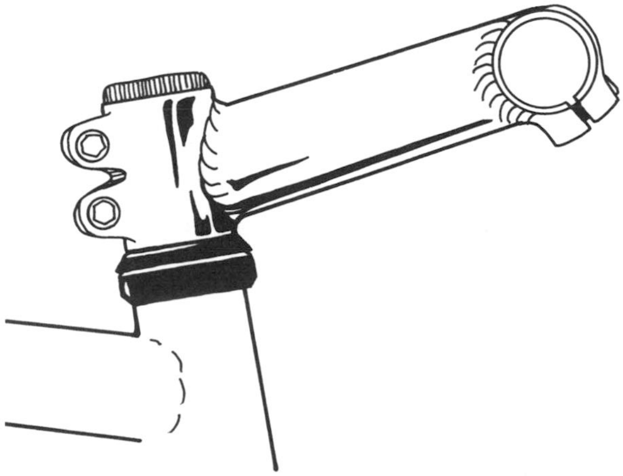

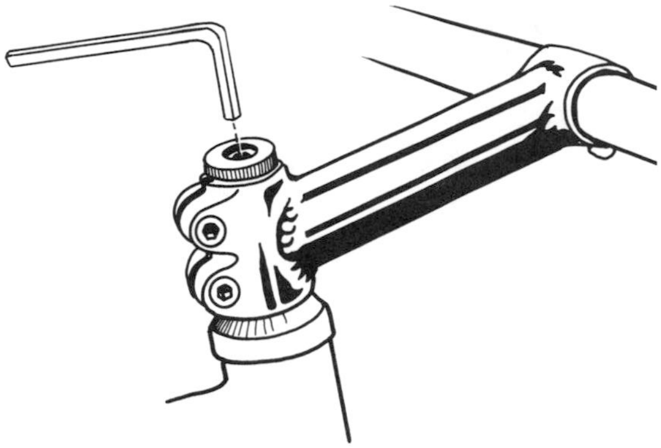

11.12 **Loosening and tightening a top-cap bolt on a threadless-style headset**

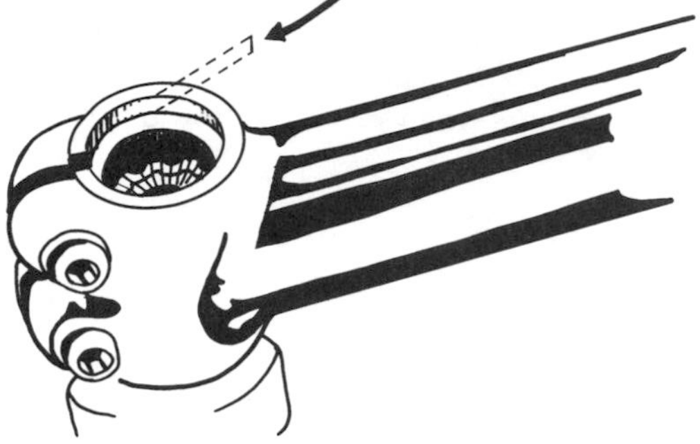

11.13 **Measuring the distance between the stem clamp and the top of the steering tube**

Stems for threaded steering tubes (Fig. 11.8) were the standard until the 1990s. They have a vertical "quill," which extends down into the steering tube of the fork and binds to the inside of the steering tube by means of a wedge-shaped plug pulled up by a long bolt that runs through the quill (Fig. 11.9).

Suspension stems used to be quite popular and were made for both threadless and threaded steering tubes. Some, such as Softride (Fig. 11.10), use a parallelogram system with four pivots to prevent the handlebar from twisting as it moves up and down. Others, such as Girvin, have a single pivot around which the handlebar swings in an arc. Both incorporate some sort of a spring for suspension, usually a steel coil or an elastic polymer ("elastomer"). Some suspension stems also come with a hydraulic damper to control the speed of movement.

xi-8 REMOVAL OF CLAMP-TYPE STEM FROM THREADLESS STEERING TUBE

1. Loosen the horizontal bolts clamping the stem around the steering tube. This should take about two or three turns.
2. With a 5mm Allen wrench, unscrew and remove the adjusting bolt in the top cap covering the top of the stem clamp and steering tube (Fig. 11.12). Removing this bolt will allow the fork to fall out, so hold the fork as you unscrew the bolt.
3. With the bike standing on the floor, or while holding the fork to keep it from falling out, pull the cap and the stem off of the steering tube. Leave the bike standing until you replace the stem, or slide the fork out of the frame, keeping track of all headset parts.
4. If the stem will not budge, see §xi-14a.

xi-9 INSTALLATION AND ADJUSTMENT OF HEIGHT OF STEM ON THREADLESS STEERING TUBE

LEVEL 2

Installing and adjusting the height of a stem on a threadless fork are much more complicated than installing and adjusting the height of a standard stem in a threaded fork. On a threadless fork, the stem is an integral part of the headset (Fig. 11.7), so any change to the stem position alters the headset adjustment. That's why this procedure carries a level 2 designation.

1. Stand the bike up on its wheels, so the fork does not fall out. Grease the top end of the steering tube if it is steel or aluminum, but leave it dry if it is carbon fiber. Loosen the stem-clamp bolts, and grease their threads. Slide the stem onto the steering tube.
2. Set the stem height to the desired level. If you want to place the stem in a position higher than directly on top of the headset, you must put some spacers between the bottom of the stem clamp and the top piece of the headset. No matter what, there must be contact—directly or through spacers (and including the top crown on a double-crown fork)—between the headset and the stem. Otherwise, the headset will be loose.
3. Check the steering tube length: To adjust the threadless headset, the top of the stem clamp (or spacers placed above it) should overlap the top of the steering tube by 3–6mm (⅛–¼ inch) (Fig. 11.13). If it does, skip ahead to step 6.

NOTE: *I recommend always having one spacer above the stem, especially with a carbon steering tube, and measuring the 3–6mm overlap from the top of the spacer not the stem. That way, the entire stem clamp is clamped onto the steering tube, and there is no chance for the upper part of the clamp to pinch the end of the steering tube.*

4. If the steering tube is too short:
   - (a) If the top spacer or the top of the stem clamp overlaps the top of the steering tube by more than 6mm (¼ inches), the steering tube is too short to set the stem height where you have it. If you have spacers below the stem, remove some until the top edge of the stem clamp overlaps the top of the steering tube by 3–6mm. If you cannot, or do not want to, lower the stem any further, you need a fork with a longer steering tube, a stem with a shorter clamp, or a stem that is angled upward more to attain your desired handlebar height. Stems for threadless steering tubes with different angles, or with clamps of differing lengths, are available. It is a lot cheaper and easier than replacing the fork.
   - (b) On many old suspension forks, you could simply replace the steering tube and fork crown assembly with a longer one and bolt your existing fork legs into it. But nowadays, to get a longer steering tube, you must replace the fork.
5. If the steering tube is too long:
   - (a) If the top of the steering tube is less than 3mm (⅛ inches) below the top spacer or the top edge of the stem clamp (or if the steering tube sticks up above the top of the stem clamp), you have a choice. If you want the option to raise the stem for a higher handlebar position, stack some headset spacers on top of the stem clamp until the spacers overlap the top edge of the steering tube by at least 3mm.
   - (b) If, however, you are sure you will never want the stem any higher, then go ahead and cut off the excess tube. First, mark the steering tube along the top edge of the spacer above the stem clamp or the stem clamp itself (if you are not heeding my advice to always have at least a single thin spacer above the stem). Remove the fork from the bike. Make another mark on the steering tube 3mm below the first mark. Place the steering tube into a

STEM HEIGHT ON THREADLESS STEERING TUBE

padded vise or bike-stand clamp. With the lower mark as a guide, cut the excess steering tube off by using a hacksaw or tube cutter.

(c) There is a star-shaped nut that is inserted inside the steering tube (Fig. 11.7). The bolt through the top cap screws into it to adjust the headset bearings. If the star nut is already inside of the steering tube, and it looks like the saw is going to hit it, you must move the star nut down—see step 6 for instructions on how to do it.

(d) Make your cut straight. Mark it straight by wrapping a piece of tape around the steering tube and cutting along the edge of the tape. If you are not sure your cut will be straight, start it a little higher and file it down flat to the tape edge. If you really want to be safe, use a tool specifically designed to help you make a straight cut. Park Tool's "threadless saw guide" will do the trick. Remember that you can always shorten the steering tube a little more, but you cannot make it longer! So apply the old adage of "measure twice, cut once." Use a round file on the inside of the tube and a flat file on the outside to remove any metal burrs left by the hacksaw or cutter.

STEM HEIGHT ON THREADLESS STEERING TUBE

(e) When you have completed cutting and deburring, put the fork back in, replacing all of the headset parts in the way that they were originally installed (Figs. 11.17 and 11.21–11.22). Return to step 1 above.

NOTE: *If you are cutting a carbon-fiber steering tube, cut three-quarters of the way through and then turn the steering tube over and cut from the other side to meet your prior cut. This will prevent cutting all of the way through and peeling layers of carbon back in the process.*

6. Check that the edges of the star-shaped nut are at least 12mm below the top edge of the steering tube. The nut must be far enough down that the bottom of the headset top cap does not hit it once the adjusting bolt is tightened. In the case of a steel or aluminum steering tube, if the nut is not in deeply enough, you need to drive it deeper into the steering tube after removing the stem. In the case of a carbon steering tube, you set the expander plug inside the steering tube under the stem clamp by tightening its bolt with a hex key. This procedure is a must in order to prevent crushing the carbon steering tube with the stem clamp.

(a) Driving the star nut deeper into a metal steering tube is best done with the star-nut installation tool (Fig. 1.3). The tool threads into the nut, and you hit it with a hammer until it stops; the star nut will now be set 15mm deep in the steering tube. If you do not have this tool, go to a bike shop and have the nut set for you. If you insist on doing it yourself, follow the steps to push the star nut in deeper as outlined below. Just remember that it is easy to mangle the star nut if you do not tap it in straight.

(b) To push the star nut in further without the proper tool, put the adjusting bolt through the top cap, and thread it six turns into the star nut. Next, if the star nut is not already inside the steering tube, set it over the end of the steering tube and tap the top of the bolt with a mallet. Use the top cap as guide to keep it going in straight. Finally, tap the bolt in until the star nut is 15mm below the top of the steering tube.

NOTE: *The wall thickness of steering tubes differs depending on whether they are made of steel or aluminum, what grade and heat-treating they have, and what the fork is designed for. Therefore, the stock headset star nut may not fit in, and it will just bend when you try to install it. Even pros sometimes ruin star nuts. This is not a big problem, because replacements can be purchased separately. If yours goes in crooked, take a long punch or rod, set it on top of the star nut, and drive it all of the way out of the bottom of the steering tube. Dispose of the star nut, and get another.*

If you have an aluminum steering tube, its internal diameter (I.D.) will be undersized. Standard I.D. is 22.2mm (⅞ inch) for a 1-inch steel steering tube, 25.4mm (1 inch) for a 1⅛-inch steel steering tube, and 28.6mm (1⅛ inches) for a 1¼-inch steel steering tube. If the stock star nut from the headset does not fit, get one that is the correct size. Fork manufacturers often supply one with each fork. In a pinch, you can make an oversized stock star nut fit by bending each pair of opposite leaves of the star nut toward each other with a pair of channel-lock pliers to reduce the nut's width. Now you can insert the nut; be aware that it may not grip as well as a properly sized one.

7. Install the headset top cap on the top of the stem clamp (or spacers you set above it). Grease the threads of the top-cap adjusting bolt, and thread it into the star nut inside the steering tube (Fig. 11.12).
8. Adjust the headset before tightening the stem bolts. The steps are outlined in §xi-16.

xi-10 REMOVING A STANDARD QUILL-TYPE STEM FROM A THREADED FORK

1. Unscrew the stem anchor bolt on the top of the stem. It should take three turns or so. Most stem bolts take a 6mm Allen wrench.
2. Tap the top of the bolt down with a mallet or hammer (Fig. 11.15) to disengage the wedge from the bottom of the quill. If the head of the bolt is recessed down in the stem so that a hammer cannot get at it, leave the Allen wrench in the bolt and tap the top of the Allen wrench until the wedge is free.
3. Pull the stem out of the steering tube. If the stem will not budge, see §xi-14b in this chapter.

xi-11 INSTALLATION AND ADJUSTMENT OF HEIGHT ON QUILL STEM IN A THREADED FORK

1. Grease the stem quill, the bolt threads, the outside of the wedge or conical plug (Fig. 11.8), and the inside of the steering tube.
2. Thread the bolt through the stem and into the wedge or plug until the bolt pulls the wedge or plug into place, but not so far as to prevent the stem from inserting into the steering tube.
3. Slip the stem quill into the steering tube (Fig. 11.9) to the depth you want. Make sure the stem is inserted beyond its height-limit line. Tighten the bolt until the stem is snug but can still be turned.
4. Set the stem to the desired height, line it up with the front wheel, and tighten the bolt. It needs to be tight, but don't overdo it. You can overtighten the stem bolt to the point that you bulge out the steering tube on your fork, so be careful. Recommended torque for this bolt is found in Appendix D.

xi-12 STEM MAINTENANCE AND REPLACEMENT SCHEDULE

A bike cannot be controlled if the stem breaks, so make sure yours doesn't break. Because aluminum has no fatigue limit, all aluminum parts will eventually fail. Steel and titanium parts that are repeatedly stressed more than about one-half of their tensile strength will eventually fail as well. Stems and handlebars are not permanent accessories on your bike. Replace them before they fail on you.

Always clean your stem regularly. Whenever you clean it, be sure to look for corrosion, cracks, bends, and stressed areas. If you find any, replace the stem immediately. If you crash hard on your bike, especially hard enough to bend the handlebar, replace your stem and possibly your fork. It makes sense to err on the side of caution. Lightweight, expensive stems, in particular, need to be replaced after a violent impact, even if you see no visible signs of stress. The hard, thin material is not likely to bend, but it may be so weakened that it will break soon.

Italian stem maker 3T recommends replacing stems and handlebars every four years. If you rarely ride the bike, this time frame is overkill. If you ride hard and ride often, every four years may not be frequently enough. Do what is appropriate for you, and be aware of the risks.

xi-13 SETTING STEM AND HANDLEBAR POSITIONS

Complete treatment of this subject is in Appendix C, §C-3. Here are some brief suggestions.

1. I recommend setting your handlebar twist so that the bends in the handlebar are pointed up and back. I also recommend setting your bar ends, if installed, so that they are horizontal or tipped up between 5 and 15 degrees from horizontal (Appendix C, §C-5e).
2. Setting handlebar height and reach is very personal. Much depends on your physique, your flexibility, your frame, your riding style, and a few other preferences. Again, this subject is covered in depth in Appendix C.
3. Because I do not know anything about you personally, I will leave you with a few simple guidelines:
   - (a) If you climb a lot, you will want your handlebar lower and farther forward to keep weight on the front wheel on steep uphill trails.
   - (b) If you descend technical trails a lot, you will want your handlebar higher and with less forward reach.
   - (c) If you ride a lot on pavement, a low, stretched-out position is better aerodynamically. A low position means that the handlebar grips are about 7–12cm lower than your saddle. A stretched-out position would place your elbow at least 2 inches in front of your knee at the top of the pedal stroke.

xi-14 REMOVING A STUCK STEM

A stem can get stuck onto, or into, the steering tube because of poor maintenance. Periodically regreasing the stem and steering tube will keep them sliding

11.14 Stick a coin in the crack to spread the stem clamp

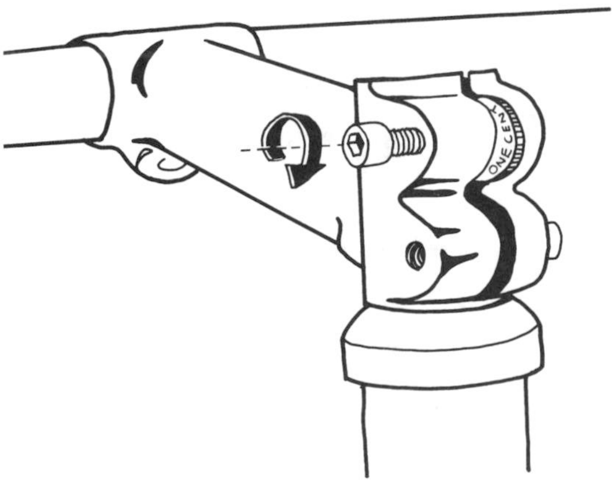

11.15 **Loosening the stem wedge**

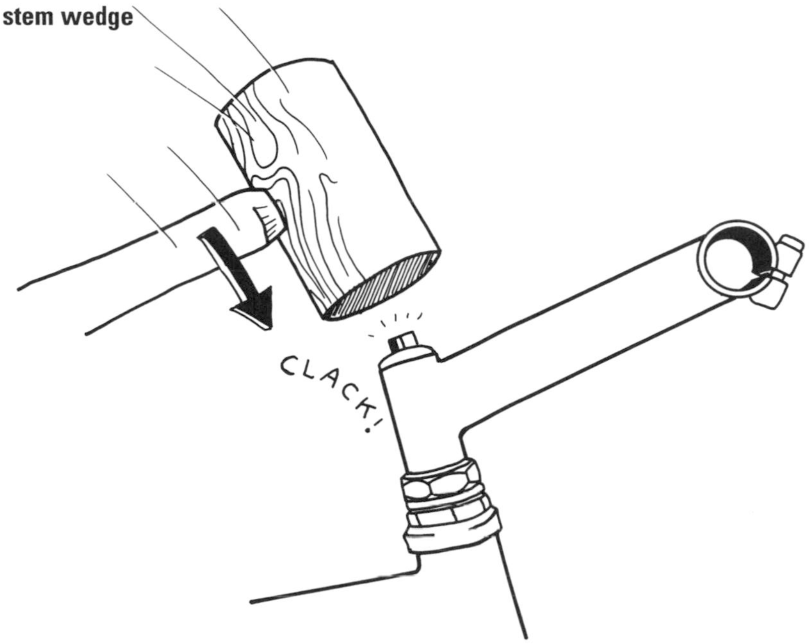

freely, and the grease will form a barrier against sweat and water getting in between the two. If your stem is really stuck, be careful; you can ruin your fork as well as your stem and headset while trying to get the stem out. In fact, you're better off having a shop work on removing the stem, unless you really know what you are doing and are willing to accept the risk of destroying a lot of expensive parts.

a. Removing a stuck stem from a threadless fork

1. Remove the top cap (Fig. 11.12) and the bolts clamping the stem to the steering tube.
2. Spread the stem clamp by inserting a coin into the slot between each bolt end and the opposing threadless half of the binder lug (Fig. 11.14). Turn the bolts around, install them from the opposite direction, and tighten each bolt against each coin so that the clamp slot opens wider. The stem should come right off of the steering tube now.

NOTE: *If your stem is the type that comes with a single bolt in the side of the stem shaft ahead of the steering tube (Fig. 11.7), loosen the bolt a few turns and tap it in with a hammer to free the wedge. It might still take some penetrating oil, and perhaps some heat to expand it, to free this type of stem from around the steering tube.*

3. If it still will not come free, try heating the stem clamp with a hair dryer and discharging a CO_2 cartridge tire inflator inside the steering tube. You may have to hold the crown in a vise, following instructions 6 and 7 in the next section (§xi-14b) on freeing a quill-type stem. Failing that, your last resort is to saw through the steering tube at the base of the stem clamp and then replace the stem, the fork (or at least the steering tube), and the headset.

b. Removing a stuck stem from a threaded fork

1. Unscrew the stem bolt on top of the stem three turns or more. Smack the bolt (or the Allen wrench in the bolt) with a mallet or hammer (Fig. 11.15) to completely disengage the wedge.

2. Grasping the front wheel between your knees, make one last attempt to free the stem by twisting back and forth on the handlebar. Don't use all of your strength, because you can ruin a fork and a front wheel this way.
3. If your stem didn't budge, squirt penetrating oil around the stem where it enters the headset. Let the bike sit for several hours and add more penetrating oil every hour or so.
4. Turn the bike over, and squirt penetrating oil into the bottom of the fork steering tube so that it runs down around the stem quill. Let the bike sit for several hours and add more penetrating oil every hour or so.
5. Now that it's totally soaked in penetrating oil, try step 2 again. Try heating the steering tube through the headset with a hair dryer to expand the steering tube (after removing the stem expander bolt), and discharging a CO_2 cartridge tire inflator inside the expander bolt hole to shrink the quill with cold.
6. If the stem doesn't come free, you have to go to your workbench and use that heavy-duty vise. Is it solidly mounted? You'll need it to be.
7. Remove the front wheel (Chapter 2) and the front brake (Chapter 7). Put pieces of wood on both sides of the vise. Clamp the fork crown into the vise (Fig. 11.16). To fit it into the vise, you will at least have to remove the brakes. If you have an old suspension fork with crown-clamp bolts, remove the inner fork legs from the crown by loosening the crown bolts and yanking the legs out.
8. Grab both ends of the handlebar and twist back and forth. Again, try heating the steering tube while removing the stem expander bolt and discharging a CO_2 cartridge tire inflator inside the expander bolt hole to shrink the quill with cold. If this doesn't work, you may have to saw off the stem just above the headset and have the bottom of the stem reamed out of the steering tube by a machine shop. I told you that you should have gone to a bike shop.

11.16 Clamping the fork crown in a vise

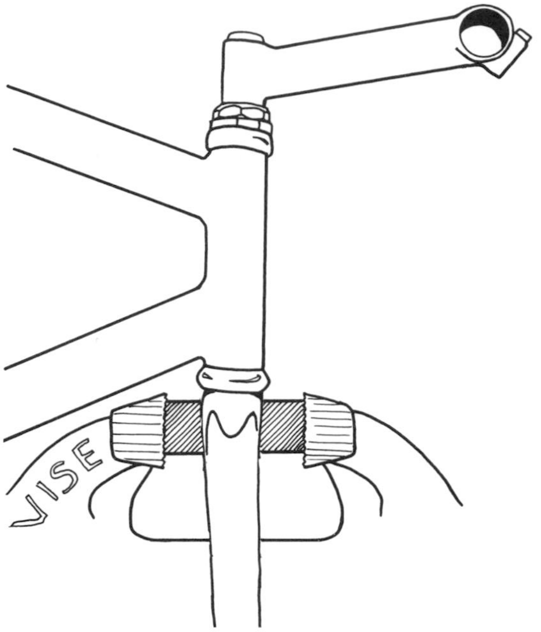

HEADSETS

HEADSETS

There are two basic types of headsets: threadless (Figs. 11.7, 11.17, and 11.19–11.22) and threaded (Figs. 11.9 and 11.18). They come in three sizes for mountain bikes: 1 inch, 1⅛ inches, 1¼ inches, and 1½ inches; 1⅛ inches is by far the most common nowadays.

The Dia-Compe (now Cane Creek) AheadSet was the first threadless headset (Fig. 11.17), a lighter system than a threaded one, because it eliminates the stem quill, bolt, and wedge. The connection between the handlebar and the stem is also more rigid than

11.17 **Threadless headset**

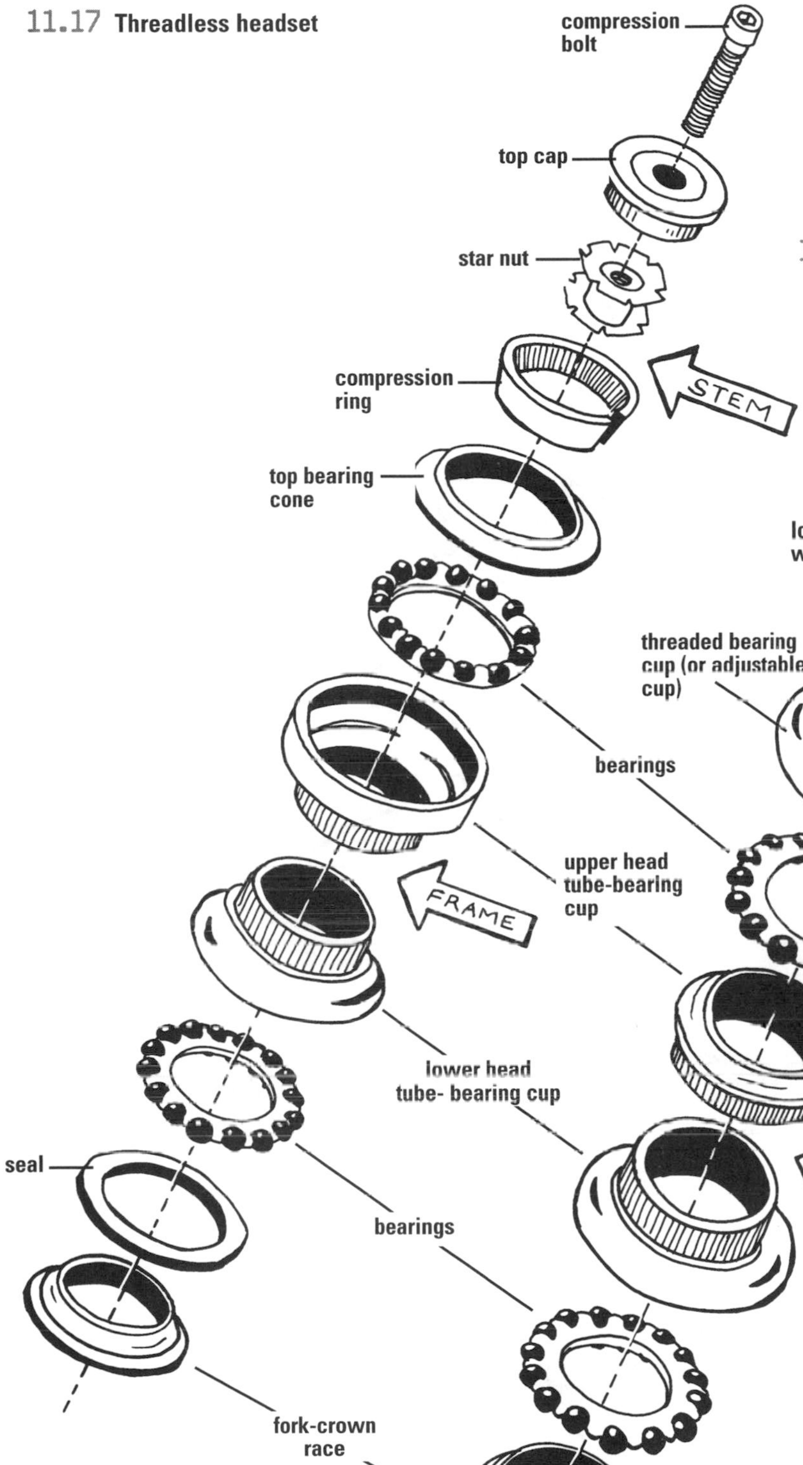

11.18 **Threaded headset**

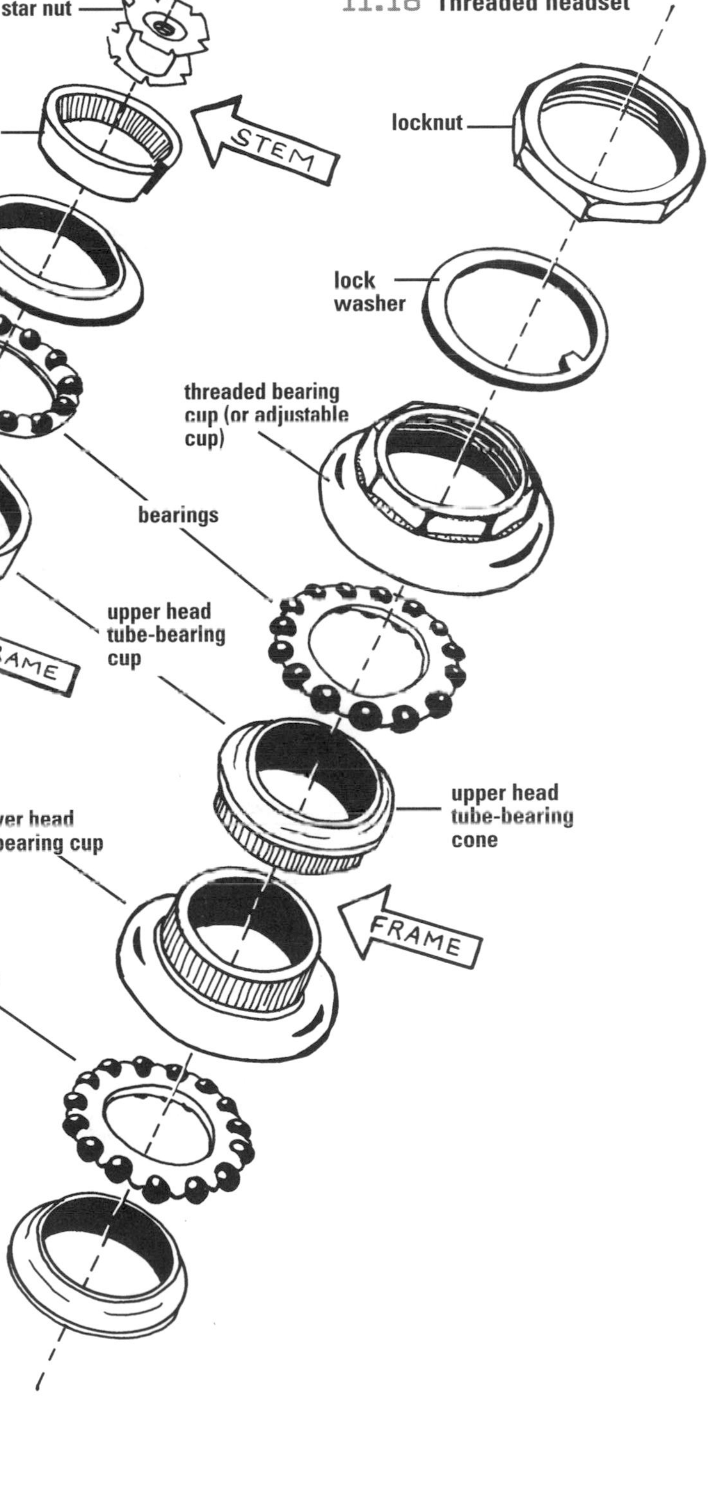

11.19 Internal headset system with press-in cups (cutaway)

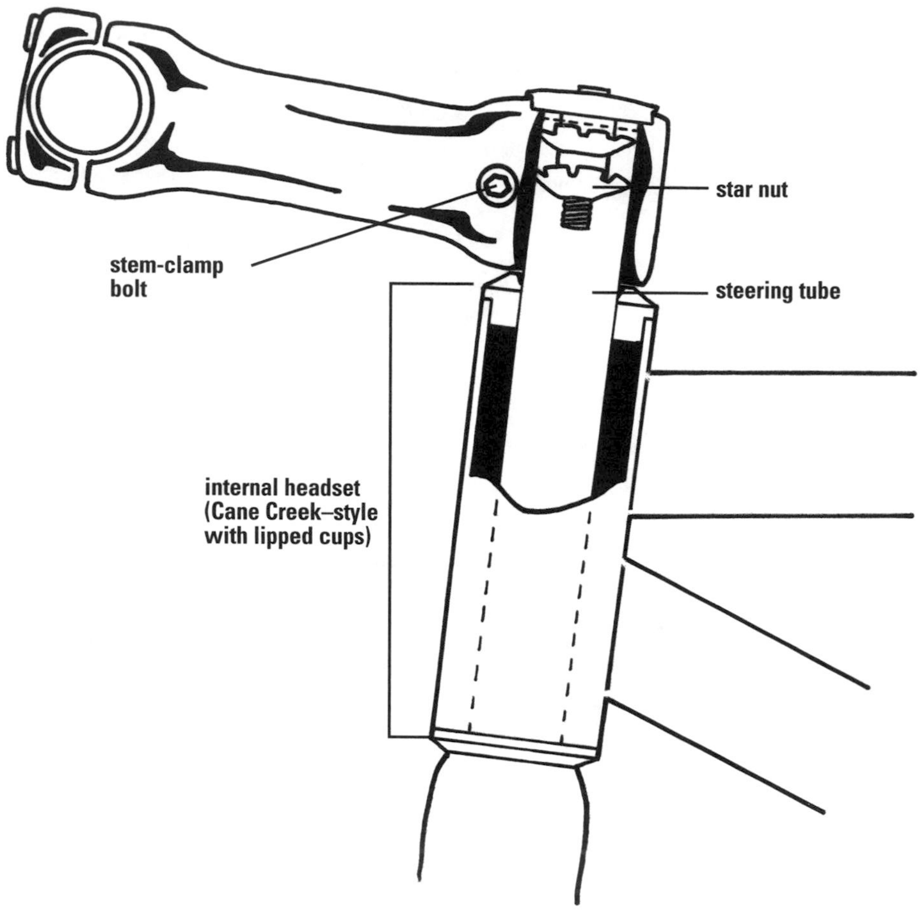

with an expanding stem wedge. Of course, fork manufacturers prefer threadless headsets because they do not have to thread their forks and/or they can offer various lengths of fork steering tubes; steering-tube diameter is now the only variable.

On a threadless headset, the top cup and a conical compression ring slide onto the steering tube (Figs. 11.17 and 11.21–11.22). The stem clamps around the top of the steering tube and above the compression ring. A star-shaped nut with two layers of spring-steel teeth sticking out from it fits into the steering tube and grabs the inner walls (Fig. 11.7).

A top cap sits atop the stem clamp and pushes it down by means of a long bolt threaded into the star nut to adjust the headset (Fig. 11.12). The stem clamped around the steering tube holds the headset in adjustment (Fig. 11.11).

The next generation of headsets are threadless internal ones, called "integrated headsets," concealed inside the frame's steering tube (Figs. 11.19 and 11.20). Where standard threaded and threadless headsets have bearing cups that are pressed into the head tube (Figs. 11.17 and 11.18), integrated headsets have bearings seated inside the head tube. The bearings either rest on a platform within the head tube itself (Figs. 11.20, 11.21) or have cups with thin flanges that extend out to the edges of the head tube (Figs. 11.19, 11.22). Otherwise, the headset is identi-

11.20 **Non-press-in integrated headset exploded (Campagnolo shown)**

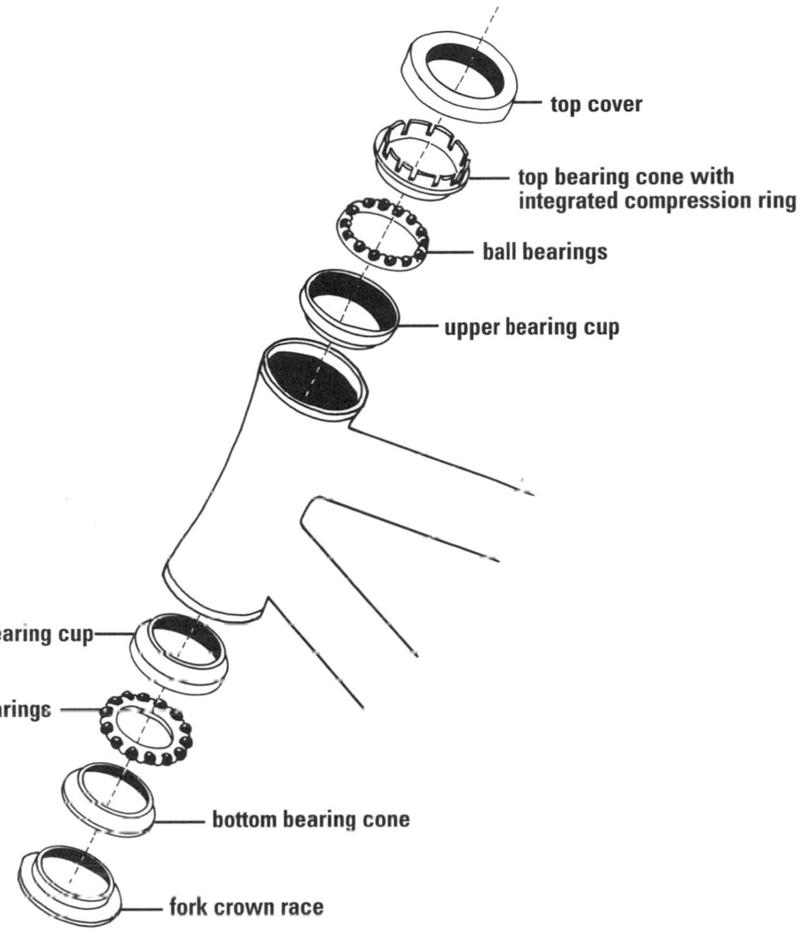

cal to, and is adjusted in the same way as, the standard threadless systems shown in Figure 11.17.

Prior to the 1990s, practically all headsets and steering tubes were threaded. The top bearing cup on a threaded headset has wrench flats, a toothed washer stacked on top of it, and a locknut that covers the top of the steering tube. That locknut tightens against the washer and top cup (Fig. 11.18). A brake-cable hanger (Fig. 7.4, Chapter 7) and extra spacers may be included under the locknut.

Most headsets, threaded or threadless, use loose ball bearings held in some type of steel or plastic retainer (or "cage") (Figs. 11.17 and 11.18) so that you are not chasing dozens of separate balls around when you work on the bike. A variation on this design (Stronglight, some Ritchey models) has needle bearings held in conical plastic retainers (Fig. 11.23) riding on conical steel bearing surfaces.

Cartridge-bearing headsets usually employ "angular-contact" bearings (Fig. 11.24), because normal cartridge bearings cannot take the side (axial) forces encountered by a headset. Each bearing is a separate, sealed, internally greased unit.

xi-15 CHECKING HEADSET ADJUSTMENT

If your headset is too tight, the fork will be difficult to turn, or at least will feel gritty when you do. If your headset is too loose, it will rattle or clunk while

11.21 **Exploded cupless (drop-in) internal headset**

11.22 **Exploded Cane Creek–style press-in internal headset with lipped cups**

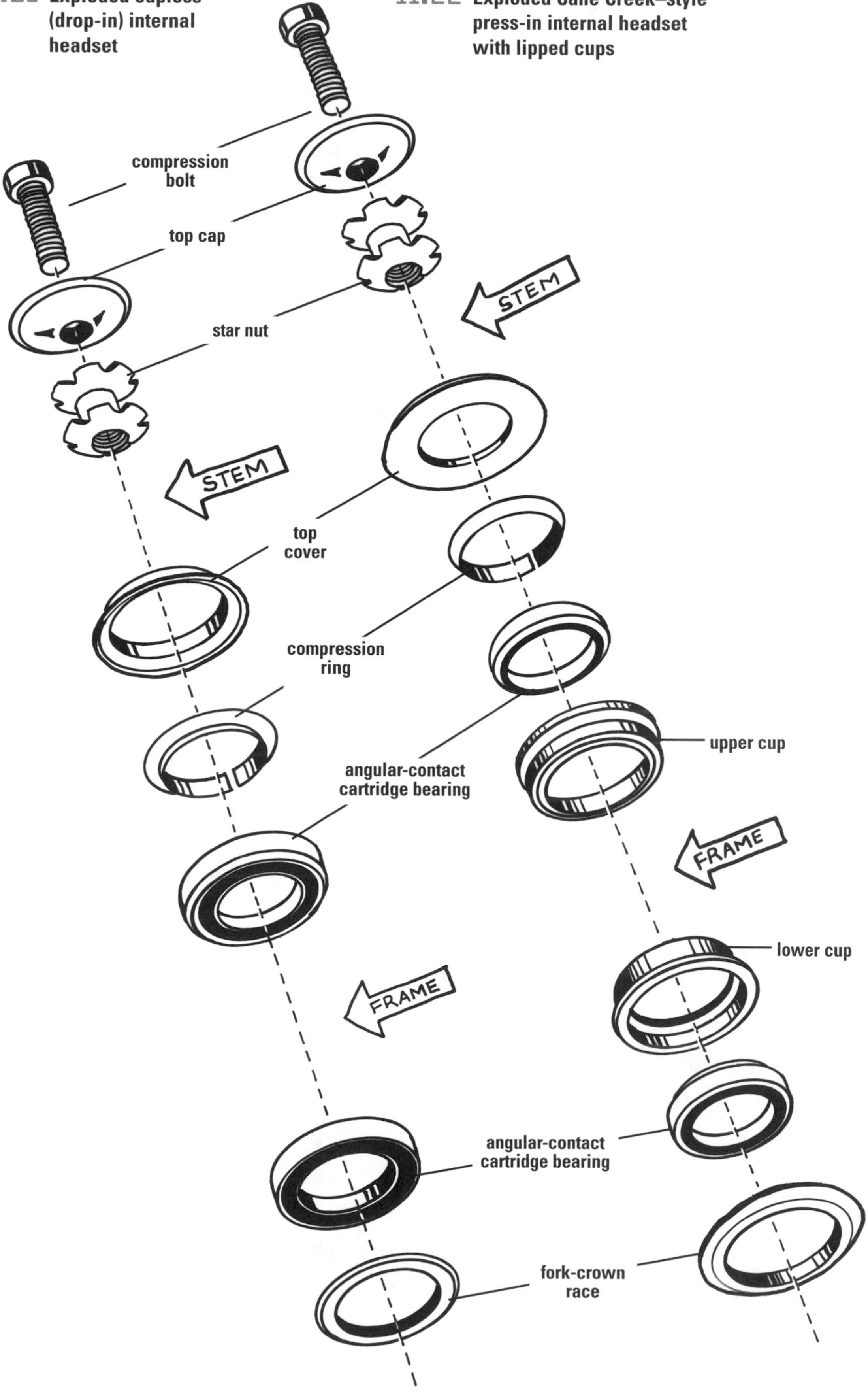

11.23 Needle bearings

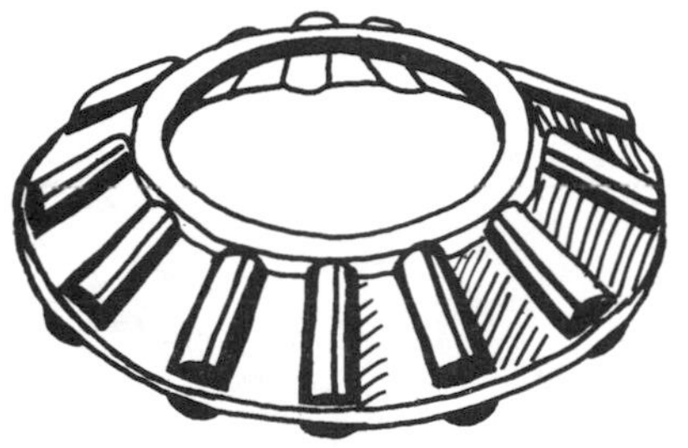

11.24 Lower parts of cartridge-bearing headset

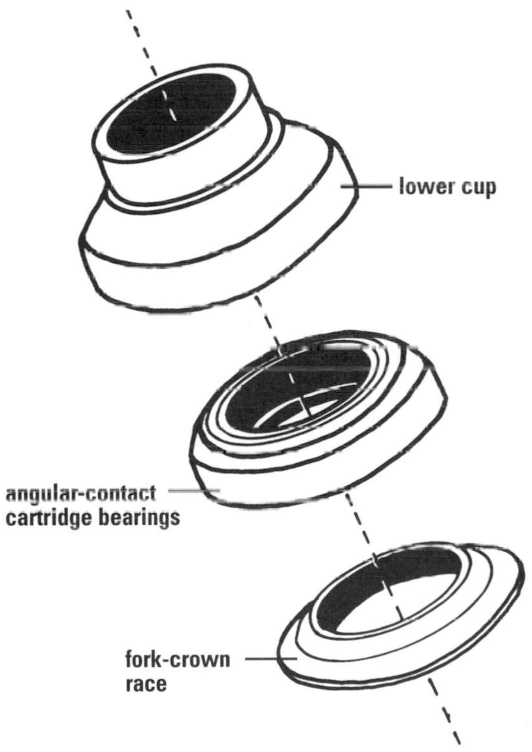

you ride. You might even notice some "play" in the fork as you apply the front brake.

1. Check for headset looseness by holding the front brake and rocking the bike forward and back. Try it with the front wheel pointed straight ahead and then with the wheel turned at 90 degrees to the bike. Feel for back-and-forth movement (or play) at the lower head cup with your other hand. If there is play, you need to adjust your headset because it is too loose.

NOTE: *This task is more complicated with a suspension fork and even with many rim-brake types. There is always some side-to-side play in any suspension fork, as well as in many brakes; this makes it hard to isolate whether the play you feel is from the headset, the fork, or the brakes. You have to feel each part as you rock the bike, and you may have to do some trial-and-error headset adjustment.*

If the headset is loose, skip to the appropriate adjustment section, xi-16 or xi-17.

2. Check for headset tightness by turning the handlebar back and forth. Feel for any binding or stiffness of movement. Also, check for the chunk-chunk-chunk movement to fixed positions characterizing a pitted headset (the pits are indentations made by the bearings' being overtightened); if you feel this, you need a new headset (skip to §xi-20). Lean the bike to one side and then the other; the front wheel should turn as the bike is leaned (be aware that cable housings can resist the turning of the front wheel). Lift the bike by the saddle so it is tipped down at an angle with both wheels off of the ground. Turn the handlebar one way and let go of it; then repeat the other way. See if it returns to center quickly and smoothly on its own. If the headset does not turn easily on any of the above steps, it is too tight, and you should skip to the appropriate adjustment section, xi-16 or xi-17.
3. If yours is a threaded headset, try to turn either the top nut or the threaded cup by hand. They should be so tight against each other that they can only be loosened with wrenches. If you can tighten

or loosen either part by hand, you need to adjust your headset; go to §xi-17.

xi-16 ADJUSTING A THREADLESS HEADSET

Adjusting a threadless headset, whether it is the new integrated type (Figs. 11.19–11.22) or the external type (Fig. 11.7), is much easier than adjusting the threaded style. It is a level 1 procedure and usually only takes a 5mm Allen wrench.

1. Check the headset adjustment (§xi-15 above). Determine whether the headset is too tight or too loose.
2. Loosen the bolt(s) that clamp the stem to the steering tube.
3. If the headset is too tight, loosen the bolt on the top cap about one-sixteenth of a turn with a 5mm Allen wrench (Fig. 11.25). Recheck, and repeat as necessary.
4. If the headset is too loose, tighten the bolt on the top cap about one-sixteenth of a turn with a 5mm Allen wrench (Fig. 11.25). Be careful not to overtighten it, thereby pitting the headset. If you're using a torque wrench, Dia-Compe recommends a tightening torque on this bolt of 22 in-lbs. Recheck the adjustment, and tighten or loosen further as necessary.
   - (a) If the cap does not move down and push the stem down, make sure the stem is not stuck to the steering tube. If it is, refer to §xi-14a earlier in this chapter.
   - (b) Another hindrance occurs if the conical compression ring (Figs. 11.17 and 11.21–11.22) is stuck to the steering tube, preventing adjustment via the top-cap bolt. With the stem off, gently tap the steering tube down with a mallet, and then push the fork back up to free the compression ring. Grease the ring and the steering tube, and reassemble.
   - (c) If neither the stem nor the compression ring are stuck, yet the cap still does not push the stem down, the steering tube may be so long that it is hitting the lip of the top cap and preventing the cap from pushing the stem down. The steering tube's top should be 3–6mm below the top of the top edge of the stem (Fig. 11.13) or of the spacers above the stem. If the steering tube is too long, add a spacer, or cut or file some off of the top (see §xi-9, step 5).
   - (d) Another thing that can thwart adjustment is if the star nut is not installed deeply enough and the cap bottoms out on the star nut. The highest point of the star nut should be 12–15mm below the top of the steering tube. With metal steering tubes, tap the nut deeper with a star-nut installation tool, or put the bolt through the top cap, thread it five turns into the star nut, and gently tap it in with a soft hammer while using the top cap to keep it going in straight (see §xi-9, step 6). With carbon steer-

11.25 Loosening and tightening the compression bolt on a threadless-style headset

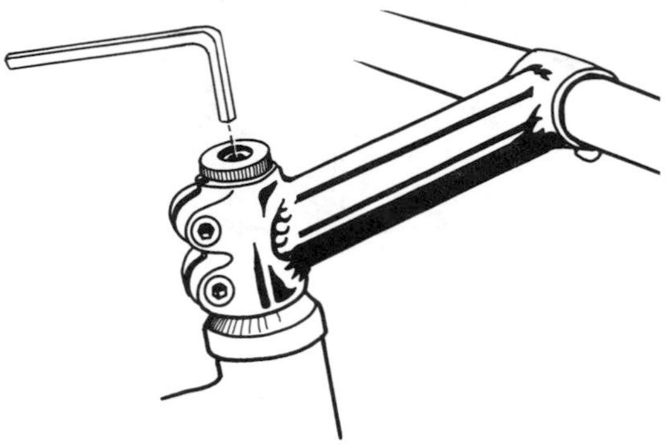

11.26 **Loosening a headset locknut**

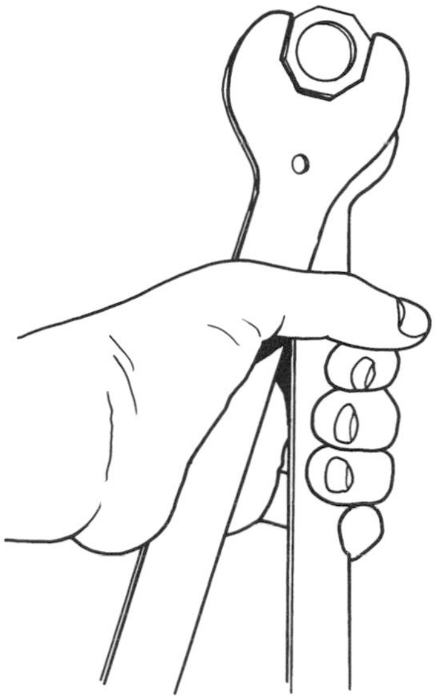

ing tubes, loosen the aluminum expander with a hex key, move it down, and retighten it.

(e) With a double crown fork (Fig. 13.13), you must loosen the clamp bolts on the upper crown. There are three of them—one clamps the steering tube, and the other two each clamp one upper fork tube (stanchion). If the headset is loose and these bolts are still clamped, tightening the headset compression bolt cannot push the stem and top crown down more. After the headset is adjusted properly, retighten the bolts to the torque specified by the fork maker.

(f) Once you have fixed the cause of the adjustment problem, return to step 1 above.

5. Tighten the stem-clamp bolts to the recommended torque, which is given in Appendix D.
6. Recheck the headset adjustment. Repeat steps 2–4 if necessary.

With some integrated headsets, you may need a shim under the top bearing cup (Fig. 11.20) so that the edges of the top cap do not drag and scrape on the top end of the head tube.

If the headset is adjusted properly, make sure that the stem is aligned straight with respect to the front wheel, and then go find something else to do, because you are done.

xi-17 ADJUSTING A THREADED HEADSET

The secret to good adjustment is simultaneously controlling the steering tube, the adjustable cup, and the locknut as you tighten the latter two together.

NOTE: *Perform the adjustment with the stem installed. Not only does it give you something to hold onto that keeps the fork from turning during the installation, but also there are slight differences in adjustment when the stem is in place as opposed to when it is not. Tightening the stem bolt can sometimes bulge the walls of the steering tube very slightly (Fig. 11.9), but just enough for it to shorten the steering tube slightly and throw your original headset adjustment off.*

1. Following the steps outlined in §xi-15, determine whether the headset is too loose or too tight.
2. Put a pair of headset wrenches that fit your headset on the headset's top nut (which I will also call the "locknut") and the top bearing cup (or "threaded cup" or "adjustable cup"). Headset nuts come in a wide variety of sizes, so make sure you have the proper sizes of wrenches. Place the wrenches so that the top one is slightly offset to the left of the bottom wrench. That way you can squeeze them together to free the nut (Fig. 11.26).

NOTE: *People with small hands or a weak grip will need to hold each wrench at the end in order to get enough leverage.*

3. Hold the lower wrench in place and turn the top wrench counterclockwise about one quarter of a

turn to loosen the locknut. It may take considerable force to break it loose, because it needs to be installed very tightly to keep the headset from loosening up.

4. Depending on whether the headset was too loose or too tight, do one of the following:
   (a) If the headset was too loose, turn the lower (or threaded) cup clockwise about one-sixteenth of a turn while holding the stem with your other hand. Be very careful when tightening the cup; overtightening it can ruin the headset by pressing the bearings into the bearing surfaces and making little indentations. The headset then stops at the indentations rather than turning smoothly, a condition known as a "pitted" headset.
   (b) If the headset was too tight, loosen the threaded cup counterclockwise one-sixteenth of a turn while holding the stem with your other hand. Loosen it until the bearings turn freely, but be sure not to loosen to the point that you allow any play to develop.
5. Holding the stem, tighten the locknut clockwise with a single wrench. Make sure that the threaded cup does not turn while you tighten the locknut. If it does turn, you either are missing the toothed lock washer separating the cup and locknut (Fig. 11.18), or the washer you have is missing its tooth. In this case, remove the locknut and replace the toothed washer. Put it on the steering tube so that the tooth engages the longitudinal groove in the steering tube. Tighten the locknut on again.

ADJUSTING A THREADED HEADSET

NOTE: *You can adjust a headset without a toothed washer by working both wrenches simultaneously, but it is trickier to adjust and often comes loose while riding. But if your steering tube is cut too short to accept a washer in the headset, you may have to do without one anyway!*

11.27 **Tightening a headset locknut**

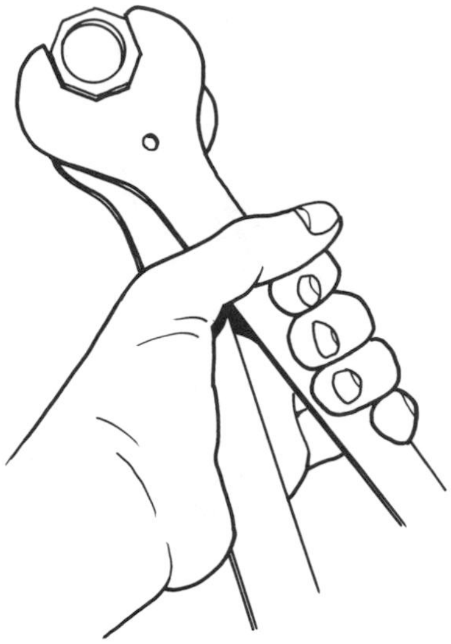

6. Check the headset adjustment again. Repeat steps 4 and 5 until the headset is properly adjusted.
7. Once it is properly adjusted, place one wrench on the locknut and the other on the threaded cup. Tighten the locknut (clockwise) firmly against the washer(s) and threaded cup to hold the headset adjustment in place (Fig. 11.27).
8. Check the headset adjustment again. If it is off, follow steps 2–7 again. If it is adjusted properly, make sure the stem is aligned with the front wheel, and go ride your bike.

NOTE: *If you constantly get what you think to be the proper adjustment, and then find it to be too loose after you tighten the locknut and threaded cup against each other, your steering tube may be too long, thereby causing the locknut to bottom out. Remove the stem and examine the inside of the steering tube. If the top end of the steering tube butts up against the top lip of the locknut, the steering tube is too long. Remove the locknut and add another spacer.*

11.28 Chris King–style pressed-in sealed bearing

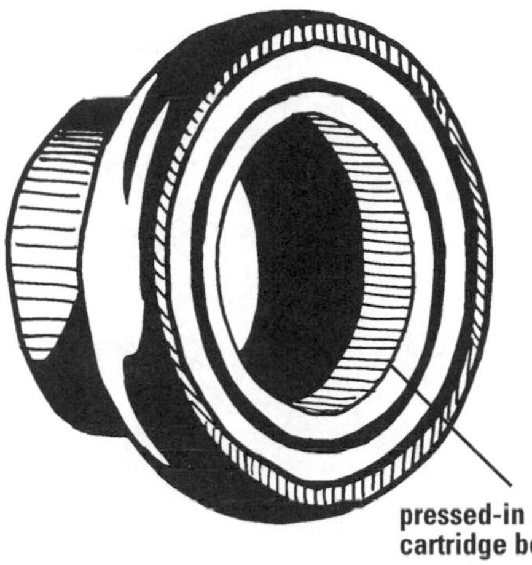

If you don't want to add another spacer, file off 1 or 2mm of the steering tube. Be sure to remove any burrs both inside and out. Avoid leaving filings in the bearings or steering-tube threads. Replace the locknut and return to step 5.

xi-18 OVERHAULING A THREADLESS HEADSET

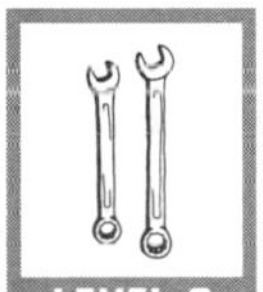
LEVEL 2

These instructions apply to both internal (Figs. 11.19–11.22) and external (Figs. 11.7 and 11.17) threadless headsets.

Just as any other bike part with bearings, headsets need periodic overhauls. If you use your bike regularly, you should probably overhaul your loose-bearing or needle-bearing (Fig. 11.23) headset once a year. Headsets with cartridge bearings (Fig. 11.24) need less frequent overhaul; some angular-contact bearings can be disassembled and cleaned, and some cannot. With those that cannot, if a bearing fails, you either replace the bearing, or, if it has press-in bearings (such as Chris King and Dia-Compe's "S" series, Fig. 11.28), you replace the entire cup (§xi-20).

Either place the bike upside down in the work stand or be ready to catch the fork when you remove the stem.

1. Disconnect or remove the front brake (Chapter 7), and unscrew the top-cap bolt (Fig. 11.25) and the stem-clamp bolts. Remove the top cap and the stem. If you have a double-crown fork Fig. 13.13), loosen the bolts on the top tube (i.e., stanchion), pull the top crown off.
2. Remove the top headset cup by sliding the top cup, conical compression ring, and any other spacers above it off of the steering tube (Figs. 11.17, 11.21, and 11.22). It may take a tap with a mallet on the end of the steering tube, followed by pushing the fork back up, to free the compression ring.
3. Pull the fork out of the frame. The lower bearing and seal may come with it.
4. Remove any bearing seals. Remember the position and orientation of each.
5. Remove any bearings remaining in the head tube or cups. Be careful not to lose any. Separate the top and bottom sets if they are of different sizes.
6. Clean or replace the bearings:
   (a) With either standard ball bearing (Fig. 11.17) or needle-bearing (Fig. 11.23) headsets, put the bearings (leave the balls or needles in their retainers) in a jar or old water bottle along with some citrus-based solvent. Shake. If the bearings from the top and bottom are of different sizes, keep them in separate containers to avoid confusion. Blot the bearings dry with a clean rag.
   (b) Some cartridge bearings (Fig. 11.24) can be pulled apart and cleaned. Hold the bearing over a container (to catch the balls) so that the beveled outer surface that fits into the

cup faces down, and push up on the bearing's inner ring. The bearing should come apart—the inner ring will pop up and out with the bearings stuck to its outer surface. It may take a little rocking of the inner ring as you push up. If the bearing does not come apart, first pry off the plastic seal covering the bearings with a knife or razor blade (as shown in Chapter 6, Fig. 6.26), and then try again. Wipe the bearings, bearing rings, and seals with a clean rag.

(c) If your bearings are the type that will not come apart, check to see if they turn smoothly. If they do not, buy new ones and skip to step 8.

7. Plug the sink, and wash the ball bearings in soap and water in your hands, just as if you were washing your palms by rubbing them together. Your hands will get clean for the assembly steps as well. Rinse bearings thoroughly and blot them dry. Air-dry completely.

8. Wipe all of the bearing surfaces with clean rags. Wipe the steering tube clean, and wipe the inside of the head tube clean with a rag over the end of a screwdriver.

9. Inspect all of the bearing surfaces of loose-ball headsets for wear and pitting. If you see pits (separate indentations made by bearings in the bearing surfaces), you need to replace the headset—skip to §xi-20.

10. Apply grease to all bearing surfaces. If you are using cartridge bearings, apply grease conservatively.

    For the angular-contact cartridge bearing that you have disassembled, smear grease around the outside of the inner bearing ring, and stick the balls into the grease in the channel around the ring. With the outer ring sitting beveled side down on the table, push the inner ring (that has the balls attached) down into it (the internal bevel on the inner ring should be facing up, opposite the bevel on the outer ring). Snap the bearing seals back into place.

11. Turn the bike upside down in the bike stand.

(a) Place a set of bearings into (or onto) the top cup and a set into the cup on the lower end of the head tube.

(b) With a cupless internal headset (Figs. 11.20 and 11.21), set a bearing into the seat in the bottom of the head tube itself.

(c) With loose-ball headsets, make sure you have the bearing retainer right side up so that only the bearings contact the bearing surfaces (note the different upper-cup styles and bearing orientations in Figs. 11.17 and 11.18). If you have installed the retainer upside down, it will come in contact with one of the bearing surfaces, and the headset will not turn well. This is a bad thing, because assembling and riding it that way will turn the retainer into jagged chunks of broken metal. To be safe, double- and triple-check the retainer placement by turning each cup pair and bearing in your hand before proceeding. Most loose-ball headsets have the bearings set up identically for both top and bottom (Fig. 11.18), where the top piece of each pair is a cup, the bottom piece is a cone, and the bearing retainer rides the same way in both sets. Many headsets, however, place both cups (and hence the bearing retainers) facing outward from the head tube (Fig. 11.17).

(d) If you have loose ball bearings with no bearing retainer, stick the balls into the grease in

11.29 **Setting the fork in the head tube to seat the bearings**

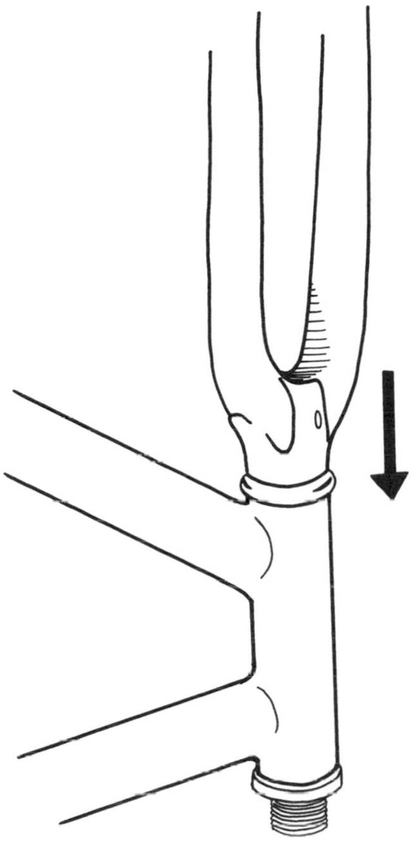

the cups one at a time, making sure that you replace the same number that you started out with in each cup.

(e) With angular-contact cartridge bearings, the beveled end faces into the cup (Fig. 11.24) or into the seat machined inside of the head tube (Fig. 11.21).

12. Reinstall any seals that you removed from the headset parts.

13. Slip the steering tube of the fork into the head tube so that the lower headset bearing seats properly (Fig. 11.29).

14. Slide the top cup, with the bearings in it (or on it), onto the steering tube. In the case of a cupless headset (Fig. 11.21), slide on the bearing alone. Keep the bike upside down at this point; it not only keeps the fork in place, it also prevents grit from falling into the bearings as you put the cup on.

15. Grease the compression ring and slide it onto the (greased) steering tube, followed by the top cover. Assure that the narrower end of the compression ring slides into the conical space in the top of the top cup (Figs. 11.17 and 11.22) or into the bearing of a cupless headset (Fig. 11.21). If you have a double-crown fork (Fig. 13.13), slide the top crown onto the steering tube and the upper fork tubes. Slide on any spacers you had under the stem. Slide the stem on, and tighten one stem-clamp bolt to hold it in place.

16. Turn the bike over. Check that the stem clamp, or spacer above it, extends 3–6mm above the top of the steering tube (Fig. 11.13). If it does, install the top cap on the top of the stem clamp and steering tube, and screw the bolt into the star nut set inside the steering tube (Fig. 11.25).

17. If the steering tube is too long, remove the stem. Add a spacer or file the steering tube shorter until the stem clamp, or spacer above it, overlaps it by 3–6mm. If the steering tube is too short, remove spacers from below the stem, if there are any. If there are no spacers to remove, try a new stem with a shorter clamp.

18. Adjust the headset (§xi-16). Go ride your bike.

xi-19 OVERHAULING A THREADED HEADSET

Just as any other bike part with bearings, headsets need periodic overhauls. If you use your bike regularly, you should probably overhaul your loose-bearing or needle-bearing (Fig. 11.23) headset once a year. Headsets with cartridge bearings (Fig. 11.24)

OVERHAULING A THREADED HEADSET

need less frequent overhaul; some angular-contact bearings can be disassembled and cleaned, and some cannot. With those that cannot, if a bearing fails, you either replace the bearing or, if it has press-in bearings (such as Chris King and Dia-Compe's "S" series, Fig. 11.28), you replace the entire cup (§xi-20).

A bike stand is highly recommended when overhauling a headset.

1. Disconnect the cable for the front brake (Chapter 7), and remove the stem by loosening the stem bolt three turns, tapping the bolt down with a hammer to free the wedge (Fig. 11.15), and pulling the stem out.
2. Either turn your bike upside down or be prepared to catch your fork as you remove the upper part of the headset. To remove the top headset cup, unscrew the locknut and threaded cup with headset wrenches. Place one on the locknut and one on the threaded cup. Loosen the locknut by turning it counterclockwise (Fig. 11.30). Unscrew the locknut and the cup from the steering tube. The headset washer or washers will slide off of the steering tube as you unscrew the threaded cup.
3. Pull the fork out of the frame.
4. Remove any seals that surround the edges of the cups. Make a point of remembering the position and orientation of each cup.
5. Remove the bearings from the cups. Be careful not to lose any. Separate the top and bottom sets of bearings if they are of different sizes.
6. Clean or replace the bearings:
   (a) With standard ball bearing (Fig. 11.17) or needle-bearing (Fig. 11.23) headsets, put the bearings in a jar or old water bottle along with some citrus-based solvent. Shake. If the bearings from the top and bottom are of different sizes, keep them in separate containers to avoid confusion. Blot the bearings dry with a clean rag.
   (b) Some cartridge bearings (Fig. 11.24) can be pulled apart and cleaned. Hold the bearing over a container (to catch the balls) so that the beveled outer surface that fits into the cup faces down, and push up on the bearing's inner ring. The bearing should come apart—the inner ring will pop up and out with the bearings stuck to its outer surface. It may take a little rocking of the inner ring as you push up. If the bearing does not come apart, first pry off the plastic seal covering the bearings with a knife or razor blade (as shown in Chapter 6, Fig. 6.26), and then try again. Wipe the bearings and bearing rings and seals with a clean rag.
   (c) If your bearings are the type that will not come apart, check to see if they turn smoothly. If they do not, buy new ones and skip to step 8.

11.30 Loosening a headset locknut

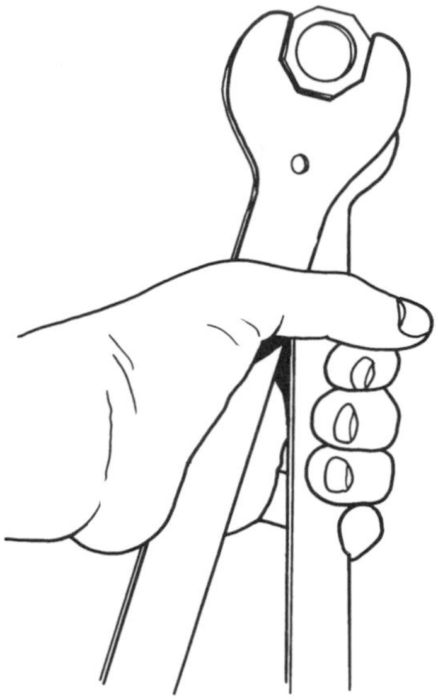

7. Plug the sink, and wash the ball bearings in soap and water in your hands, just as if you were washing your palms by rubbing them together. This helps keep your hands clean for the assembly steps as well. Rinse bearings thoroughly and blot them dry. Let them air-dry completely.
8. Wipe all of the bearing surfaces with clean rags. Wipe the steering tube clean, and wipe the inside of the head tube clean with a rag over the end of a screwdriver.
9. Inspect all of the bearing surfaces of loose-ball headsets for wear and pitting. If you see pits (separate indentations made by bearings in the bearing surfaces), you need to replace the headset. If that's the case, skip to §xi-20.
10. Apply grease to all bearing surfaces. A thin film will do, especially with cartridge bearings. For the angular-contact cartridge bearing that you have disassembled, smear grease around the outside of the inner bearing ring, and stick the balls into the grease in the channel around the ring. With the outer ring sitting beveled side down on the table, push the inner ring (that has the balls attached) down into it (the internal bevel on the inner ring should be facing up, opposite the bevel on the outer ring). Snap the bearing seals back into place.
11. Turn the bike upside down in the bike stand.
    (a) Place a set of bearings in the top cup and a set in the cup on the lower end of the head tube.
    (b) With loose-ball headsets, make sure you have the bearing retainer right side up so that only the bearings contact the bearing surfaces (note the different upper-cup styles and bearing orientations in Figs. 11.17 and 11.18). If you have installed the retainer upside down, it will come in contact with one of the bearing surfaces, and the headset will not turn well. This is a bad thing, because assembling and riding it that way will turn the retainer into jagged chunks of broken metal. To be safe, double- and triple-check the retainer placement by turning each cup pair in your hand with the bearing in between before proceeding. Most loose-ball headsets have the bearings set up identically for both top and bottom (Fig. 11.18), where the top piece of each pair is a cup, the bottom piece is a cone, and the bearing retainer rides the same way in both sets. Many headsets, however, place both cups (and hence the bearing retainers) facing outward from the head tube (Fig. 11.17). Also, watch for asymmetry in ball size; some Ritchey headsets have smaller balls on top than on the bottom.

NOTE: *Stronglight and Ritchey needle-bearing headsets come with two pairs of separate conical steel rings. These are the bearing surfaces that sit on either side of the needle bearings (Fig. 11.23). For each set of conical rings, you will find that one is smaller than the other. Place the smaller one on the lower surface of each pair: the fork-crown race and the cup on top of the head tube.*

    (c) If you have loose ball bearings with no bearing retainer, stick the balls into the grease in the cups one at a time, making sure that you replace the same number that you started out with in each cup.
    (d) With angular-contact cartridge bearings, the beveled end faces into the cup (Fig. 11.24).
12. Reinstall any seals that you removed from the headset parts.

11.31 **Inserting a cup-removal tool**

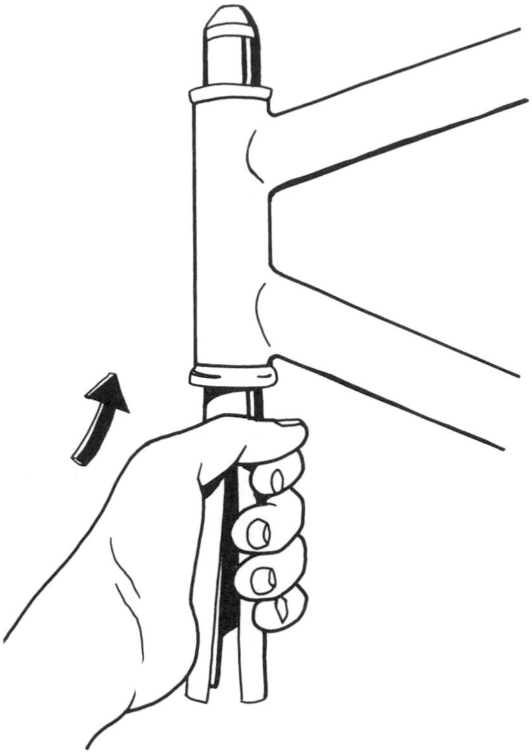

11.32 **Removing a lower headset cup**

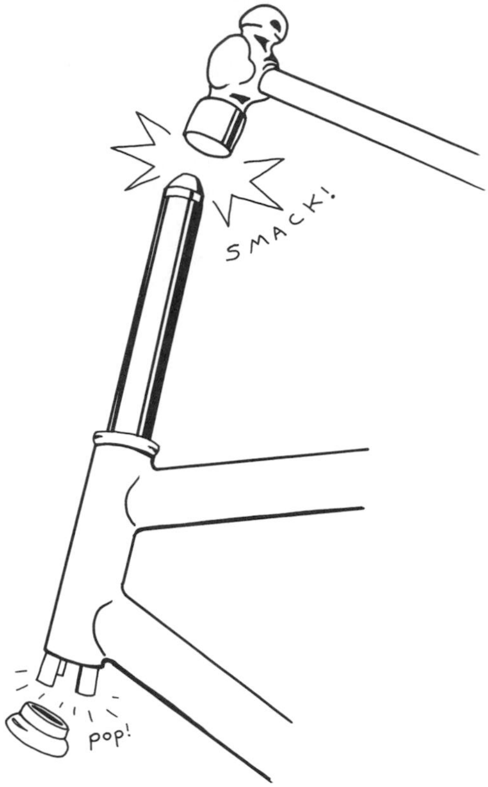

13. Slide the steering tube of the fork into the head tube so that the lower headset bearing seats properly (Fig. 11.29).
14. Screw on the top cup, with the bearings in it, onto the steering tube. Keeping the bike upside down at this point not only keeps the fork in place, it also prevents grit from falling into the bearings as you thread the cup on.
15. Slide on the toothed washer (Fig. 11.18). Align the tooth in the groove going down the length of the steering-tube threads. If you have one, install the brake-cable hanger (Fig. 7.4) the same way. Screw on the locknut with your hand.
16. Turn the bike over. Grease the stem quill and insert it into the steering tube (Fig. 11.9). Make certain that it is in deeper than the imprinted limit line. Line the stem up with the front wheel, and tighten the stem bolt—see Appendix D for recommended torque.
17. Adjust the headset as outlined in §xi-17.

HEADSET REMOVAL

xi-20 HEADSET REMOVAL

1. Open the headset and remove the fork and bearings by following steps 1–5 of §xi-18 or §xi-19, depending on headset type (i.e., threadless or threaded).
2. Remove the bearings.
   (a) If you have a cupless integrated headset with bearings seated on steps machined into the head tube itself (Figs. 11.20, 11.21), just pull the bearings out and skip to step 5.
   (b) If you have a headset with cups pressed into the head tube, first pull the bearings out (if they come out) of the cups, then slide the solid end of the headset-cup remover through

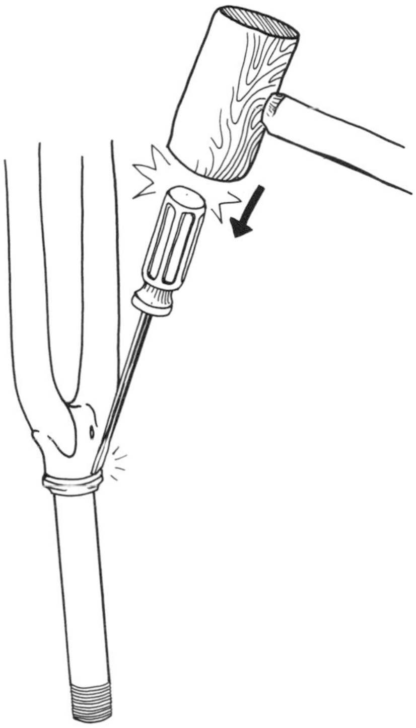

11.33 Removing a fork-crown race with a screwdriver

one end of the head tube (Fig. 11.31). As you pull the headset-cup remover through the head tube, the splayed-out tangs on the opposite end of the tool pull through the cup and spread out.

3. Strike the solid end of the cup remover with a hammer, and drive the cup out (Fig. 11.32).
4. Remove the other cup by placing the cup remover into the opposite end of the head tube and repeating steps 2 and 3 on the opposite end of the end tube.
5. Remove the fork-crown race.
   (a) If you have a suspension fork (or a rigid fork with a clamp-together crown), getting the fork-crown race off can be a bear. Clamp the steering tube into a vise or turn the fork upside down so that the top of the steering tube is sitting on the workbench. If you find a notch on the front and back of the fork crown under the fork-crown race, place the blade of a large screwdriver into the notch on one side of the crown so it butts against the bottom of the headset fork-crown race. Tap the handle of the screwdriver with a hammer to drive the race up the steering tube a bit (Fig. 11.33). Move the screwdriver to the groove on the other side, and tap it again to move that side of the race up a bit. Continue in this way, alternately tapping either side of the race up the steering tube, bit by bit, until it gets past the enlarged section of the steering tube and slides off.
   (b) If there is no notch, and there is not enough to the fork-crown race's edge protruding over the crown to get a screwdriver against it, get the race to start moving up by using a sharp chisel; tap the chisel with a hammer when its tip is between the race and the fork-crown edge. Once it has moved up a bit, start using a broad screwdriver as described above to "walk" the race up and off the steering tube's enlarged base.
   (c) If you are fortunate enough to have a Park Universal crown-race remover tool (Fig. 1.4), use it! Using the finger-tightened screws at the bottom, tighten the blades in under the fork-crown race until they stop. Then tighten the top screw to slide the race up the steering tube.
   (d) If you have a rigid fork, you can use a screwdriver or chisel to tap the fork-crown race off as outlined above (Fig. 11.33). You can also do it more elegantly with a crown-race remover or an appropriately sized bench vise.

HEADSET REMOVAL

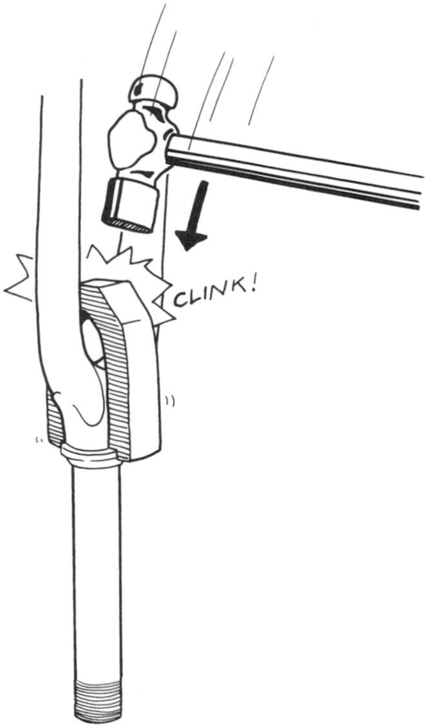

11.34 **Removing a fork-crown race with a u-shaped crown-race remover**

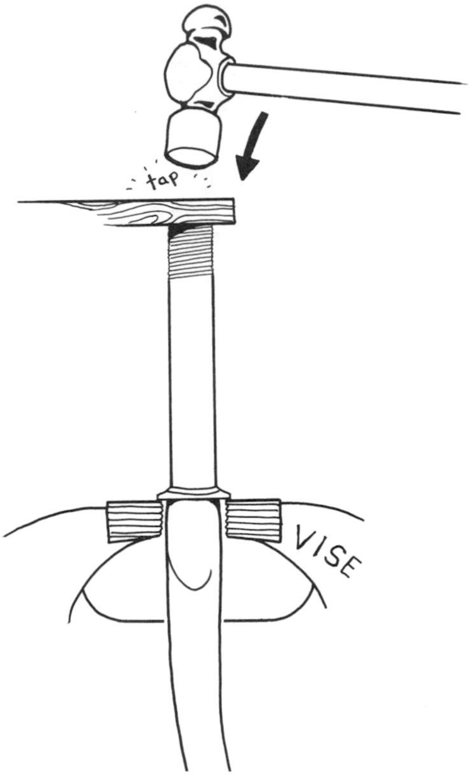

11.35 **Removing a fork-crown race with a vise**

Stand the fork upside down on the top of the steering tube. Place the U-shaped crown-race remover so it straddles the underside of the fork crown and its ledges engage the front and back edges of the fork-crown race. Smack the top of the crown-race remover with a hammer to knock the race off (Fig. 11.34).

(e) To do it with a bench vise, flip the brakes out of the way and slide the fork in, straddling the center shaft of the vise. Tighten the vise so its faces lightly contact the front and back of the fork crown with the lower side of the fork-crown race sitting on top of the vice faces. Put a block of wood on the top of the steering tube to pad it. Strike the block with a hammer to drive the fork down and knock the race off of it (Fig. 11.35).

FRAME & FORK PREPARATION PRIOR TO HEADSET INSTALLATION

xi-21 FRAME AND FORK PREPARATION PRIOR TO INSTALLATION OF HEADSET

When you get a new headset, you can install it yourself if you have the necessary tools. Otherwise, get a shop to do it. And the frame needs to be properly prepared for the headset prior to installation. If it is not, it requires tools only some shops possess.

If this is a frame for a non-press-in integrated headset (Fig. 11.20), you shouldn't need to do anything except drop the bearings in, beveled end toward the head-tube seat, and follow the steps in §xi-16. If those seats are so badly machined that the bearings are not parallel or the end of the tube is smashed, many bike shops now have a tool to recut the bearing seats so they are parallel.

With a headset with cups—be it an internal (Fig. 11.22) or standard (Figs. 11.17 and 11.18) headset—

on a new frame (or on one that has developed pitted headsets in the past), make sure that the head tube has been reamed and faced. If not, you will need a bike shop equipped with the proper tools to do it for you. Reaming makes the head-tube ends round inside and of the correct diameter for the headset cups to press in. Facing makes both ends of the head tube parallel so the bearings can turn smoothly and uniformly. A head-tube reaming-and-facing tool is shown in Figure 1.4 in Chapter 1.

The base of the steering tube also needs to be turned down to the correct diameter for the fork-crown race. The crown race seat on top of the fork crown must be faced in a way that places the race parallel to the head-tube cups. This is generally only a concern with rigid forks; suspension forks are usually shipped with the tube properly machined to accept the fork-crown race. But you do have to make sure that your fork-crown race is the right size for your fork; there are various standard internal crown-race diameters for each steering-tube diameter.

The fork steering tube (threaded or threadless) must also be cut to the proper length. Remember, you can always go back and cut more off. You can't go back and add any, so be careful! You can wait until the headset (and stem, in the case of a threadless headset) is installed. Or you can figure out the length first.

The safest way to make sure you don't cut the steering tube too short is to install the headset first (§xi-22). Once a threaded headset is installed, measure the excess length as shown in Figure 11.37, remove the top nut, and cut that much off the top. Determining the steering-tube length for an already-installed threadless headset is detailed in §xi-9.

If you choose to cut the steering tube before installing the headset, you can find the stack height of a headset in the headset owner's manual, or a bike shop can look it up in their copy of *Barnett's Manual.* Armed with this information about your threaded headset, measure the length of the head tube and add the headset stack height to this length. If you are adding extra spacers or a brake-cable hanger between the headset nuts, add their thickness in as well. This figure represents the length that the threaded steering tube must be from fork crown to top. If the steering tube is already more than 3–5mm shorter than this, you need to find another headset with a shorter stack height (or, if you have included spacers, remove some). If the threaded steering tube is longer than that sum (head-tube length + headset stack + spacers), then saw it down to length, and file off the burrs that the hacksaw left on the inside and outside edges of the steering tube end.

If you are using a threadless headset, add the headset stack-height to the length of the head tube, spacers, and stem clamp, and subtract 3mm from the total. This is the length the steering tube should be from fork crown to top. I recommend not cutting until the headset is assembled and the stem is installed so that you can see if you want some spacers under the stem to raise your handlebar higher.

xi-22 HEADSET INSTALLATION

HEADSET INSTALLATION

1. Slide the (greased inside) fork-crown race down on the fork steering tube until it hits the enlarged section at the bottom. Slide the crown-race slide punch up and down the steering tube, pounding the race down until it sits flat on top of its seat on the fork crown (Fig. 11.36). Some crown-race punches are longer and closed on the top and are meant to be hit with a hammer rather than to be slid up and down by hand. Check if installation

is complete by holding the fork up against the light to see whether there are any gaps between the fork-crown race and the crown. For a cupless, integrated headset (Fig. 11.20), you can skip the rest of this section and install and adjust the bearings (§xi-18 and §xi-16).

NOTE: *Extra-thin fork-crown races can be easily bent or broken by the crown-race punch. Chris King and Shimano both make support tools that sit over the race and distribute the impact from the punch.*

2. Put a thin layer of grease on the ends of the head-tube cups that will be pressed into the head tube, and inside the ends of the head tube itself.
3. By hand, place the headset cups into the ends of the head tube. Slide the headset-press shaft through the head tube. Press the button on the sliding end of the tool and slide it onto the shaft until it bumps into one of the cups (Fig. 11.38). This same method, and often the same press, can be used for internal (Fig. 11.22) and external (Figs. 11.17 and 11.18) headsets with cups. The press has separate inserts that may be appropriate to put into the cups before sliding the press into place. You must make sure that the press and any press inserts installed only make contact with the outer cup flange and not the bearing seat. Find the nearest notch on the tool's shaft and release the button to fix the detachable press end in place. Whatever you do, be certain that the parts that make contact with the cups are not touching the precision surfaces that the bearings roll in!

NOTE: *Dia-Compe "S" and Chris King headsets have bearings that are pressed into the cups and cannot be removed (Fig. 11.28). If you use a headset press that pushes on the center of the cups, you will ruin the bearings. You need a press that pushes the outer part of the*

HEADSET INSTALLATION

11.36 Setting a fork-crown race

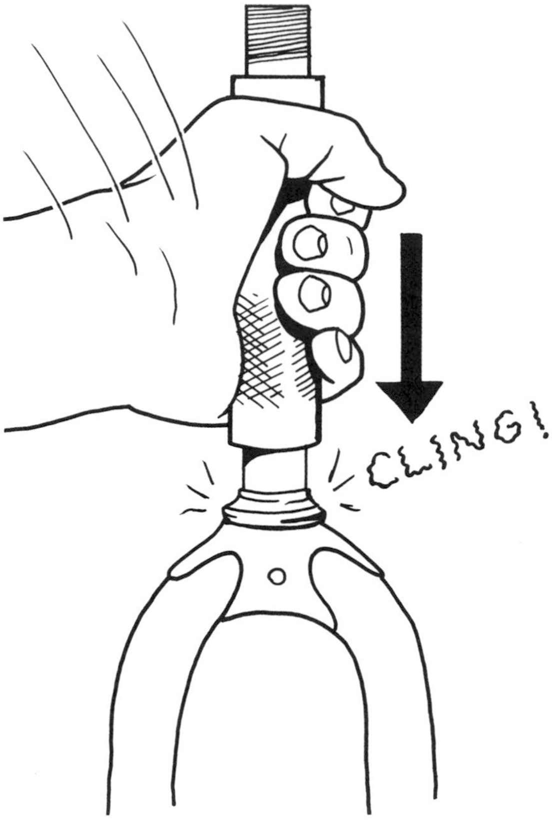

11.37 Measuring the amount of steering tube to cut

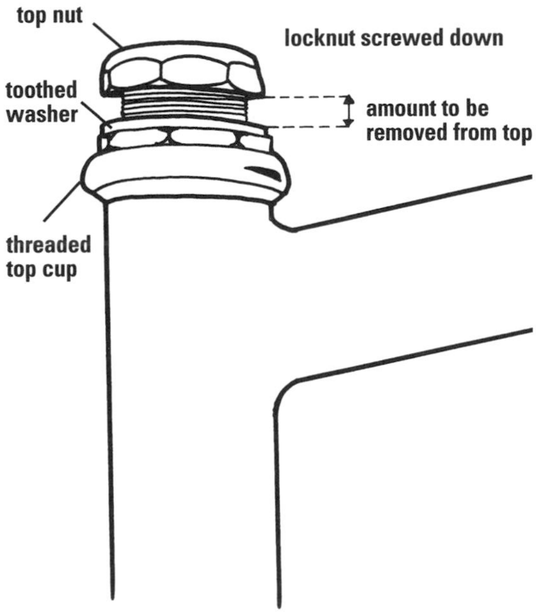

11.38 **Pressing in headset cups with a headset press**

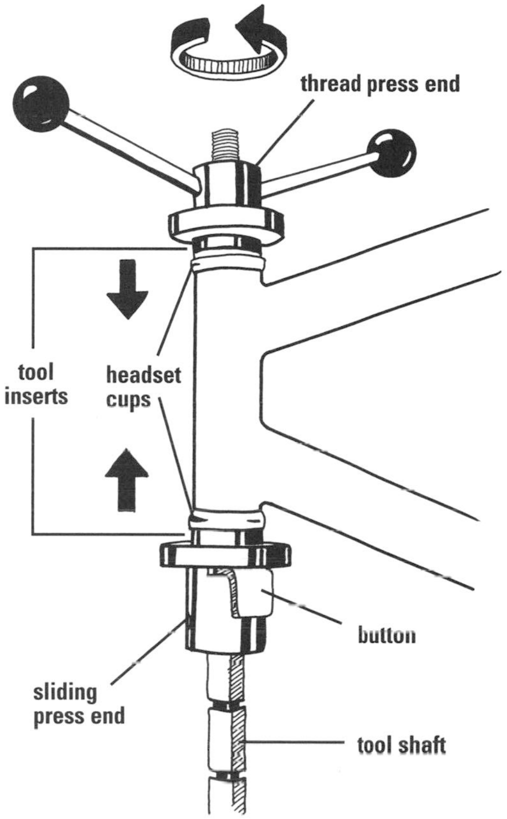

cup and does not touch the bearings. Chris King makes tool inserts that fit most headset presses, and Park has a headset press with large flat ends that also works.

4. Hold the lower end of the headset press shaft with a wrench. That will keep the tool from turning as you press in the cups. Tighten the press by turning the handle on the top clockwise (Fig. 11.38). Keep tightening down on the tool until the cups are fully pressed into the ends of the head tube. Examine them carefully to make sure that there are no gaps between the cups and the ends of the head tube.

NOTE: *You can easily crush thin headset cups with a flat-surface headset press when used without inserts, so be careful and stop when the cups reach the head tube.*

5. Liberally apply grease to all bearing surfaces. If you are using cartridge bearings (Fig. 11.24), a thin film will do.
6. Assemble and adjust the headset, following §xi-18 and §xi-16 for a threadless headset and §xi-19 and §xi-17 for a threaded one.

xi-23 TROUBLESHOOTING STEM, HANDLEBAR, AND HEADSET PROBLEMS

1. **Handlebar slips.** Tighten the pinch bolts on the stem that holds the handlebar, but not beyond the maximum allowable torque (see Appendix D). With a front-opening stem, make sure that there is the same amount of space between the stem and the front plate on both edges of the front plate. With any stem, if the clamp closes against itself without holding the handlebar securely, be sure to check that the handlebar is not deformed, and that the stem clamp is not cracked or stretched; replace any questionable parts (replace lightweight stems and bars if the clamp edges touch each other). You can slide a shim made out of a beer can between the stem and handlebar to hold it better if you have a heavy stem and handlebar, but don't try this with lightweight ones. Replacing parts is a safer option—there is always a reason why parts that are meant to fit together no longer do! With superlight stems and handlebars, you cannot just keep tightening the small clamp bolts as you can the larger bolts on heavy stems because you will strip threads and/or cause handlebar and stem failures.
2. **Handlebar makes creaking noise while riding.** Loosen the stem clamp, grease the area of handlebar that is clamped in the stem, slide the

handlebar back in place, and tighten the stem bolt. Also, sanding the hard anodized surface inside the stem clamp and on the clamping area of the handlebar can eliminate creaking.

3. **Bar end slips.** Tighten the bar-end clamp bolt. If you have to go beyond the specified torque, the handlebar or the bar end may be damaged and may need to be replaced.
4. **Stem is not pointed straight ahead.** Loosen the bolt(s) securing the stem to the fork steering tube, align the stem with the front wheel, and tighten the stem bolt(s) again. With a threaded headset, the bolt you are interested in is a single vertical bolt on top of the stem. Loosen it about two turns, and tap the top of the bolt with a hammer to disengage the wedge on the other end from the bottom of the stem (Fig. 11.15). With a threadless headset, there are one, two, or three horizontal bolts pinching the stem around the steering tube (Figs. 11.6 and 11.7) that need to be loosened to turn the stem on the steering tube. Do not loosen the bolt on the top of the stem cap (Fig. 11.12); you'll have to readjust your headset if you do.
5. **Fork and headset rattle or clunk when riding.** The headset is too loose. Adjust the headset (§xi-16 or §xi-17).
6. **Stem, bar, and fork assembly does not turn smoothly but instead stops in certain fixed positions.** The headset is pitted and needs to be replaced. See §xi-20 to §xi-22.
7. **Stem, bar, and fork assembly does not turn freely.** The headset is too tight. The front wheel should swing easily from side to side when leaning the bike or lifting the front end. Adjust the headset (§xi-16 or §xi-17, depending on type).
8. **Stem is stuck on or in fork steering tube.** See §xi-14.

CHAPTER 12

WHEEL BUILDING

A child of five could understand this. Fetch me a child of five.
—Groucho Marx

TOOLS

spoke wrench
truing stand
wheel-dishing tool
13mm, 14mm, and 15mm cone wrenches
17mm open-end wrench (or an adjustable wrench)
spoke prep

OPTIONAL TOOLS

linseed oil

Congratulations. You have arrived at the task most often used to gauge the talents of a bike mechanic. Next to building a frame or a fork, building a good set of wheels is the most critical, and creative, of a bike mechanic's tasks. Despite the air of mystery surrounding the art of wheel building, the construction of a good set of bicycle wheels is really a pretty straightforward task.

Clearly, wheels are the central component of a bike. For any bike to perform well, its wheels must be well made and properly tensioned. Once you learn how, it is quite rewarding to turn a pile of small parts into a set of strong and light wheels upon which you can bash around with confidence. You will be amazed at what they can withstand, and you will no longer go through life thinking that building wheels is something that just the "experts" do. With practice, you can build wheels at your house that are just as good as any custom-made set and far superior to those built by machine.

This is not meant to be an exhaustive description of how to build all types of wheel spoking patterns, but you will learn here how to build the three spoking patterns that are used in virtually all mountain bike wheels. (If you are interested in a more comprehensive treatment of the subject of wheel building, I recommend reading *Barnett's Manual* by John Barnett, *The Art of Wheelbuilding* by Gerd Schraner, or *The Bicycle Wheel* by Jobst Brandt.) In this chapter, you will learn how to build wheels in the classic "three-cross" spoking pattern in which each spoke crosses over three other spokes (Fig. 12.1) for either rim brakes or for disc brakes. Additionally, §xii-7 details how to build radially spoked wheels, and §xii-8 discusses heavier-duty wheels for big riders. Rear disc-brake wheels are covered in §xii-9. So let's get started.

xii-1 WHEEL BUILDING PARTS

Get together the parts you need: a rim, a hub (make sure that the hub you are using has the same number of holes as the rim does), properly sized spokes, and nipples to match. I suggest getting the spokes from your local bike shop. That way, a mechanic can help make sure you are getting the right spoke lengths

12.1 **The complete wheel with three-cross spoke pattern**

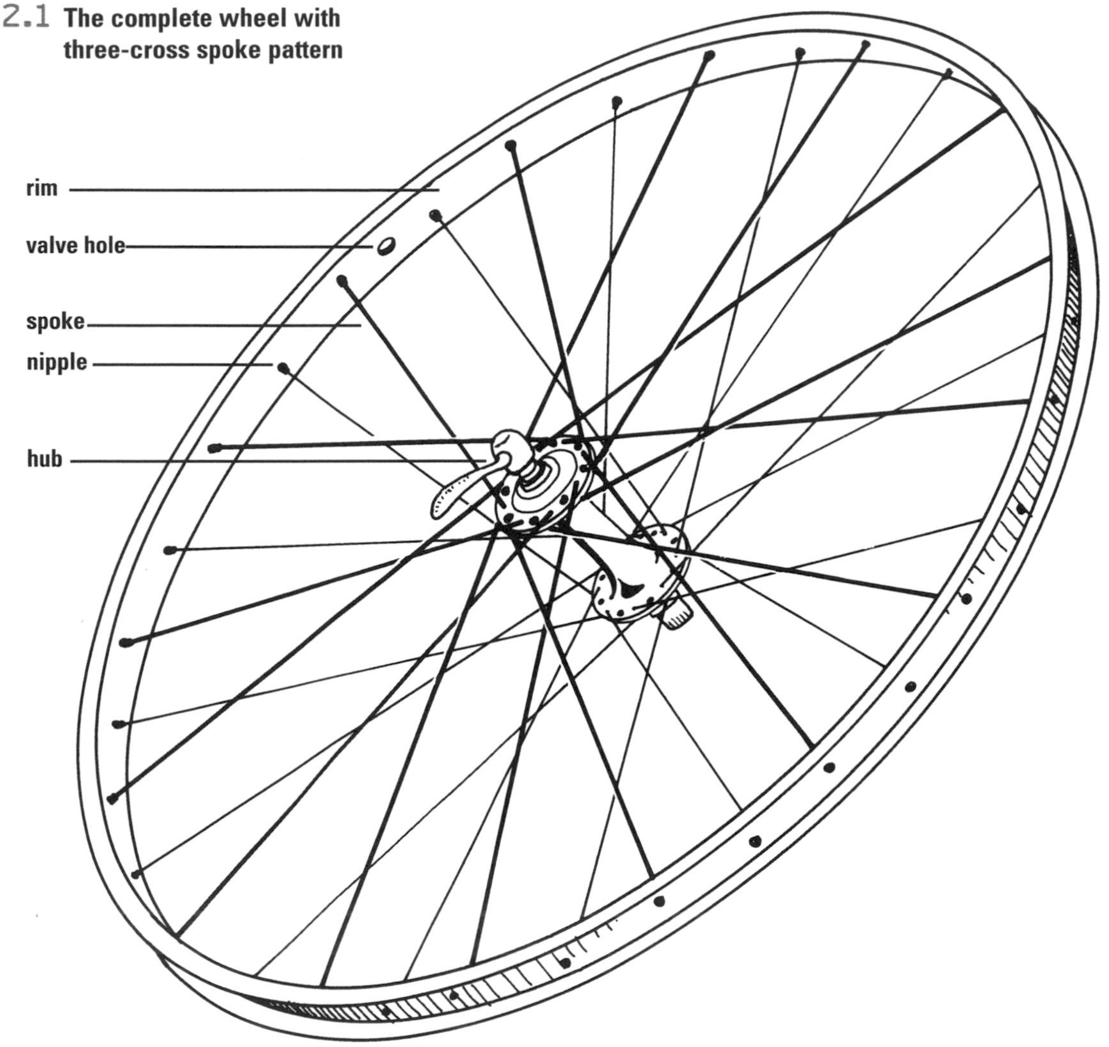

12.2 **spoke and nipple**

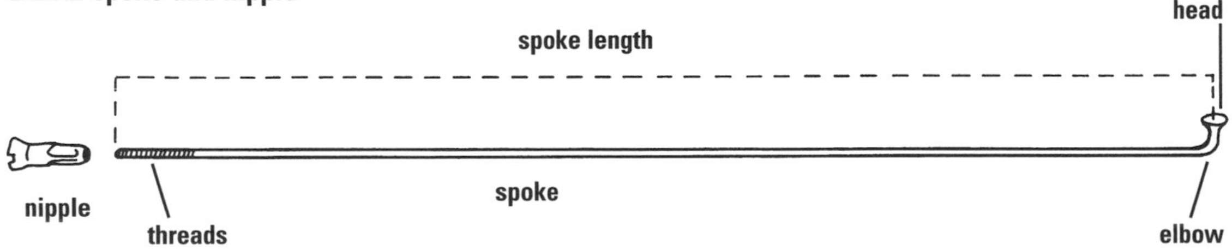

(Fig. 12.2) and can counsel you on what gauge (thickness) of spoke to buy, as well as what rim makes sense for your weight, budget, and the kind of riding you plan on doing. Remember: You must specify when purchasing spokes that you will be using a "three-cross" spoking pattern (unless you are building a radial wheel—see §xii-7). Make sure that you also have a spoke wrench that is the right size for the nipples you are using. And, if you are building up some UST tubeless rims from Mavic, the rim should come with threaded eyelets you screw into the rim to hold the nipple, as well as the tool needed to grasp their splined heads and screw them in. You also may want to consider longer spoke nipples to avoid losing any inside the rim, which has no access for you to get them out from the tire side.

NOTE: *If you are just replacing a rim on an old wheel, do not use the old spokes. You won't save all that much money reusing the old spokes, and the rounded-out nipples and weakened spokes will soon make you wish you had gone ahead and spent the extra money on a new set.*

ANOTHER NOTE: *If you are using thin (1.8mm = 15-gauge) or thinner spokes, there may be some play between the hub holes and the spokes. This will work the spokes over time and bring on premature spoke breakage. DT sells spoke washers to go between each spoke head and the hub flange to take up this slack.*

xii-2 LACING THE WHEEL

For the sake of brevity and clarity, I do not mention using spoke-prep compound with every instruction to thread a nipple onto a spoke. While spoke-prep compound is not mandatory, I think that the wheel is improved if it is used. It encourages the nipples to thread on more smoothly, it takes up some of the slop between the spoke and nipple threads, and its thread-locking ability discourages the nipples from vibrating loose. Better yet, use DT Pro Lock Nipples, which contain a two-component adhesive in the nipple thread to prevent the spoke-nipple connection from loosening under the effect of operating loads (loading and unloading of the wheel during riding), thereby ensuring constant spoke tension.

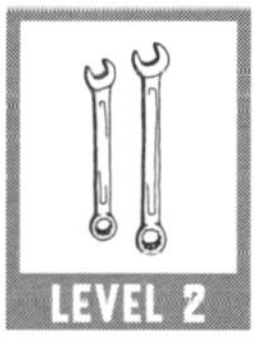

The spoke-prep compound is applied to the spoke threads before putting each nipple on. You do not want too much, as it will be hard to adjust the nipples months and years down the road; you want the spoke prep just in the dips of the threads. You can get the right amount if you dip the threads of a pair of spokes into the spoke-prep compound and then take two more dry spokes and roll the threads of all four spokes together with your fingers. With DT Pro Lock nipples, you don't have to do any of this, but you also want to complete the wheel in one sitting. Just as for epoxy glue, you will be bursting little beads of the two glue components inside the nipple. So if you get it done while the glue is viscous, the nipples will hold better than if you let the glue harden and then turn the nipples again in ensuing days.

In the absence of spoke-prep compound, at least dip the threads of each spoke in grease. Grease accomplishes everything spoke prep compound does, save for locking the threads.

1. Divide your spokes into four separate groups, two sets for each side of each hub flange, and rubber band each set together.

REMEMBER: *If you are building a rear wheel (or a front disc-brake wheel—Fig. 12.26), you should be working with two different spoke lengths, because spokes on the drive side (or brake-rotor side) are almost always shorter, due to different axle spacing and sometimes due to different hub flange diameters on the two sides. For a rear disc-brake wheel or a radial wheel, skip to §xii-9 or §xii-7.*

2. Hold the rim on your lap with the valve hole away from you. Notice that the holes alternate being offset upward or downward from the rim centerline. With an OCR rim (Fig. 12.3), have the spoke holes offset downward, toward your lap.

NOTE: *If you are building a rear wheel with an off-center drilled rim (e.g., Ritchey OCR, Bontrager ASYM), make sure as you are lacing that you orient the rim so that the spoke holes are offset to the left (nondrive) side*

12.3 **"OCR" (off-center rear) rim laced correctly**

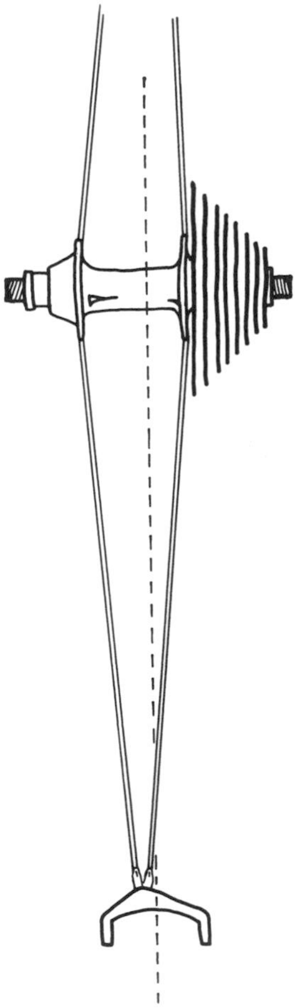

12.4 **First half of right-side spokes placed in hub**

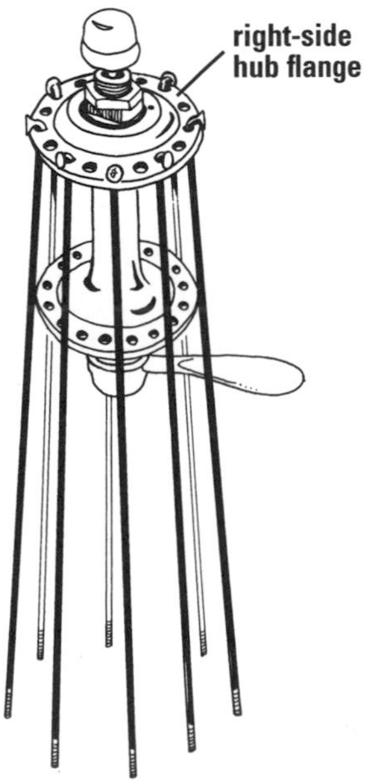

(see Fig. 12.3). If you are building a front disc-brake wheel with an off-center rim, make sure as you are lacing that you orient the rim so that the spoke holes are offset to the right (nonrotor) side. The rim is meant to reduce wheel dish by offsetting the nipples to reduce the otherwise very steep angle at which rear drive-side or front disc-side spokes normally hit the rim. The balanced left-to-right spoke tension should increase the lifetime of the wheel, and the lower spoke angle moves the rear drive-side spokes away from the rear derailleur. Also, when using the chain on the dished, titanium, ninth (largest) cog of Ritchey's "2×9" drivetrain, the derailleur does not snag the spokes because the rim offset moves them farther inboard.

3. Hold the hub in the center of the rim, with the right side of the hub pointing up. In the illustrations, the right side (or the rotor side of a disc-brake front hub—Fig. 12.26) is the one with the nut end of the quick release on it.

IMPORTANT: *On a rear hub, the right side is the drive side. Standard front hubs are symmetrical; pick a side to be the right side.* ***But if you are building a front disc-brake wheel (Fig. 12.26), I will ask you to call the left side the right side.*** *In other words, follow the lacing instructions to the letter, except substitute the rotor side of the hub (which is actually the left side) whenever the instructions refer to the right side. That way, the spokes on both sides that oppose the braking force on the rotor will come out of the outside of the hub flanges. The wheel will hence be stronger, because these "pulling" spokes come into the rim from a wider angle. If you are building a rear disc-brake wheel, read §xii-9 before continuing.*

a. First set of spokes

4. Drop a spoke down into every other hole in the

12.5 **First spoke, right side up**

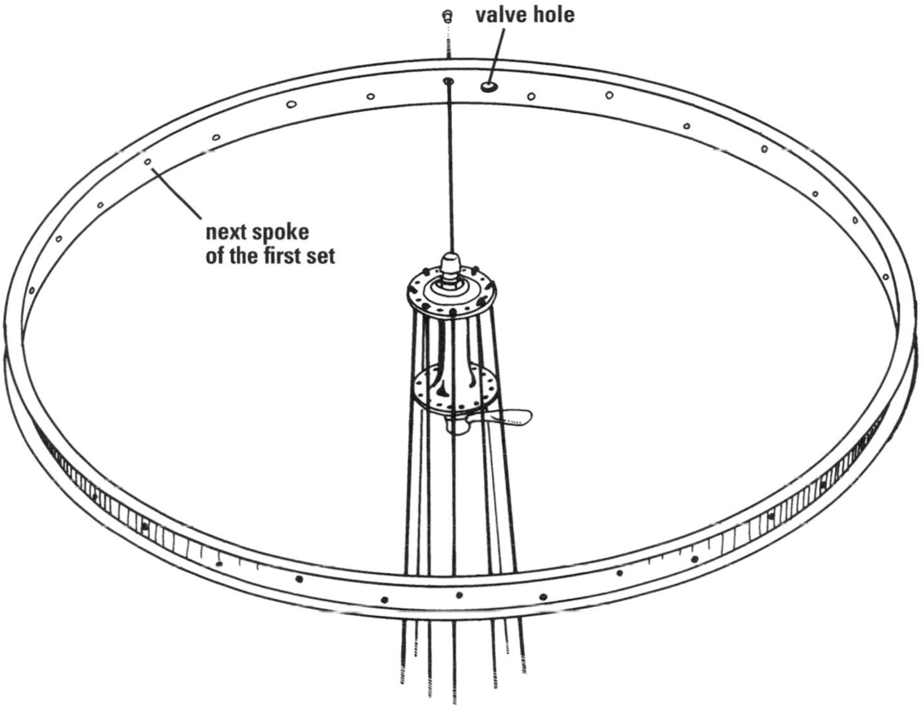

top (right-side) hub flange so that the spoke heads are facing up (Fig. 12.4). Make sure if it's a rear wheel or disc-brake front wheel that you put the shorter spokes on the right (drive) side. On some (older) hubs, half of the holes you are looking at will be countersunk deeper into the hub flange to provide a radius less stressful on the spoke elbow, so don't use those holes—use their neighbors. That said, most hubs anymore have the same countersinking on all holes to prepare for the possible eventuality of building a completely symmetrical, radially spoked wheel.

5. Bring a spoke from the hub into the first rim hole counterclockwise from the valve hole. Thread the nipple onto the spoke clockwise three turns to secure it yet not tighten the spoke (Fig. 12.5). Notice that this hole is offset upward (on an OCR rim, this means that the hole is offset upward from the centerline of the spoke holes, not the centerline of the rim). If the first hole that is counterclockwise from the valve hole isn't offset upward, you have a misdrilled rim, and you must offset all instructions one hole.

NOTE: *With Mavic UST tubeless rims, first slide the threaded eyelet onto the spoke, then thread the nipple onto the spoke clockwise three turns, and then tighten the threaded eyelet into the rim with the special splined tool. Putting some spoke threadlock on the eyelet threads, as well as on the spoke threads, is a good idea.*

6. Working counterclockwise, put the next spoke on the hub into the hole in the rim four holes away from the first spoke, and thread the nipple onto the spoke three turns. There should be three open rim holes between these spokes, and the hole you put the second spoke into should also be offset upward.
7. Continue counterclockwise around the wheel in the same manner. You should now have used half

12.6 **First set of spokes laced**

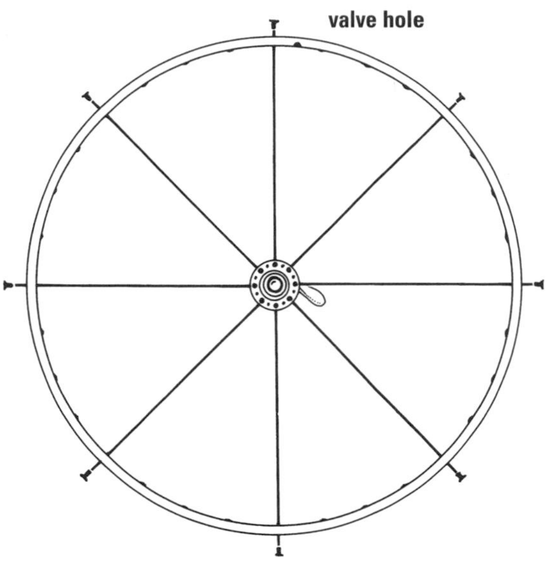

12.7 **Spoke-hole offset**

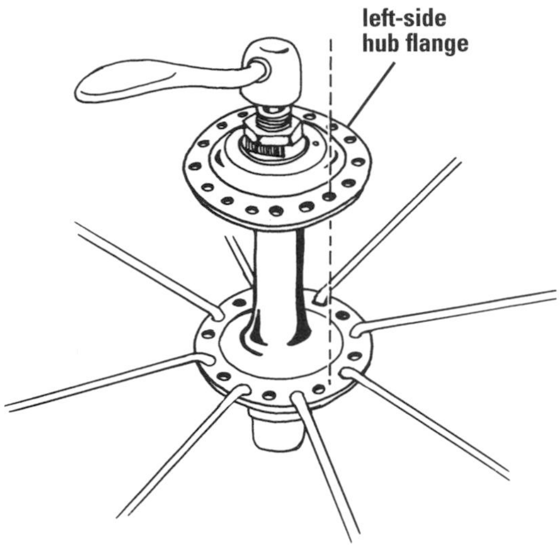

12.8 **Lacing second set**

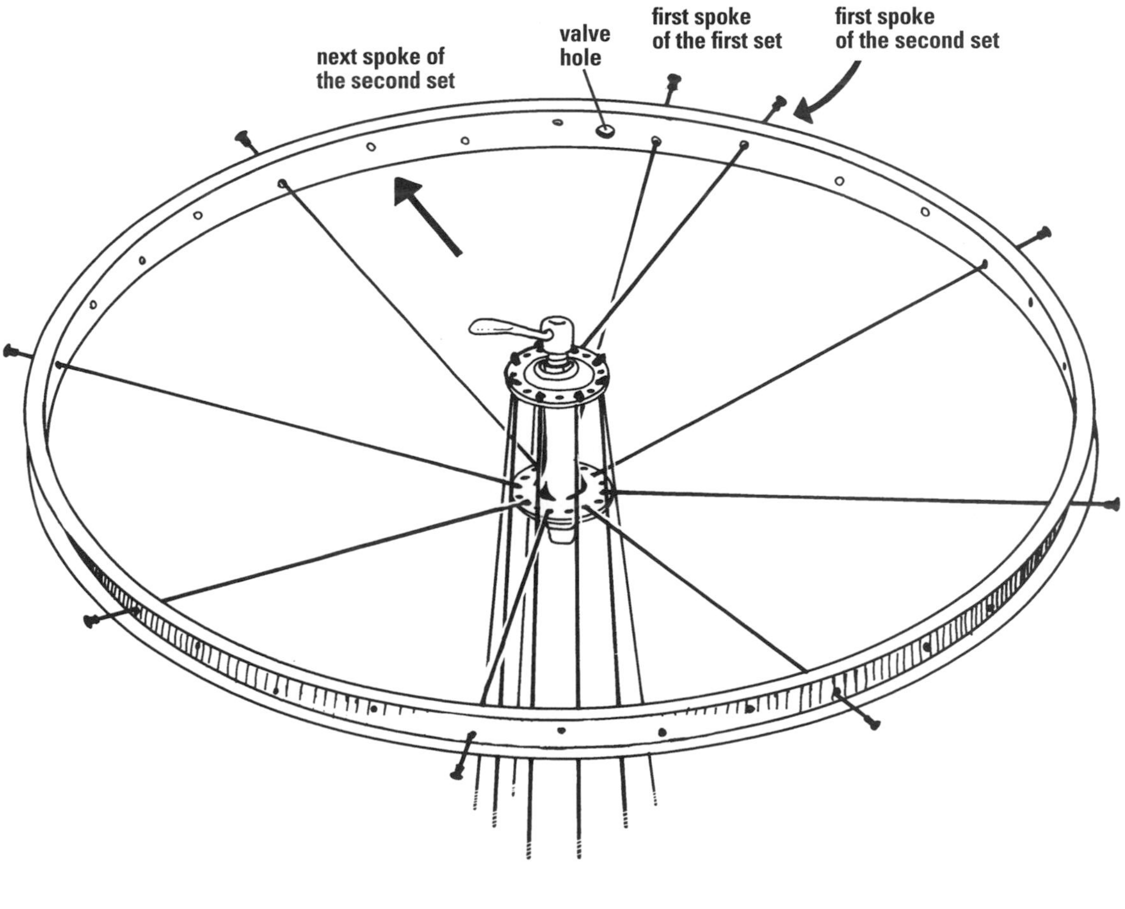

12.9 **Diverging parallel spokes**

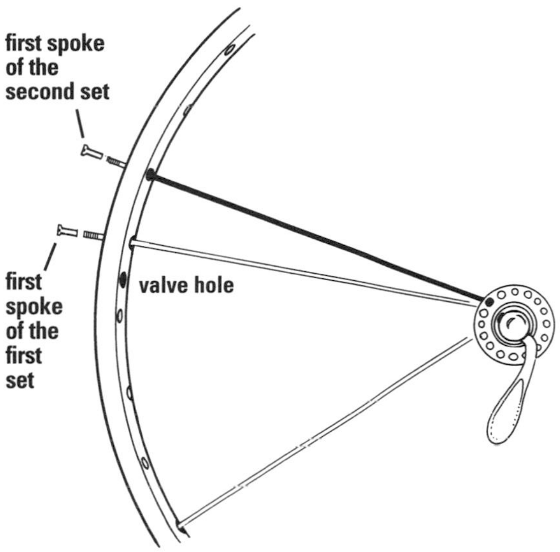

12.10 **Second set of spokes laced**

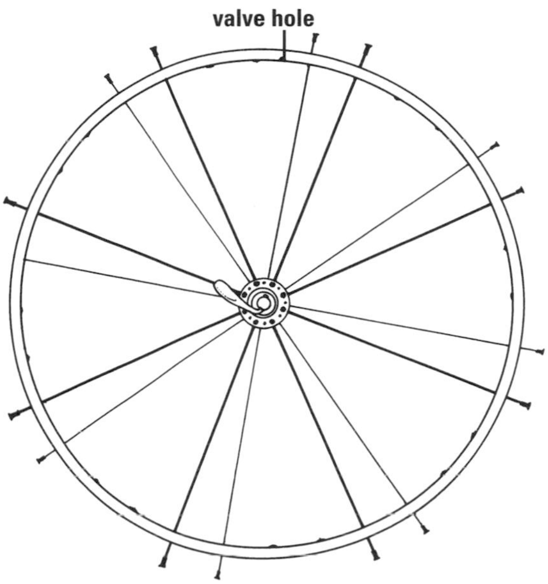

of the rim holes that are offset upward, and there should be three open holes between each spoke (Fig. 12.6).

8. Flip the wheel over.

b. Second set of spokes

9. Sight across the hub from one flange to the other flange. Notice that the holes in one flange do not line up with the holes in the other flange; each hole lines up in between two holes on the opposite flange (Fig. 12.7).
10. Drop a spoke down through the hole in the top flange that is immediately clockwise from the first spoke you installed (the spoke that is just clockwise from the valve hole). If this is a rear wheel or a front disc-brake wheel, you are now using the longer spokes.
11. Put this new spoke into the second hole clockwise from the valve hole, next to the first spoke you installed (Figs. 12.8 and 12.9). This hole will be offset upward from the rim centerline.
12. Thread the nipple clockwise onto the spoke three turns.
13. Double-check to make sure that the spoke you just installed starts at a hole in the hub's top (left-side) flange, which is one-half-a-hole space clockwise from the hole in the lower flange where the first spoke you installed started. These two spokes should be diverging but still nearly parallel (Fig. 12.9).
14. Drop a spoke down through the hole in the top (left-side) hub flange two holes away in either direction, and continue around until every other hole has a spoke hanging down through it (Fig. 12.8).
15. Working counterclockwise, take the next spoke from the hub and put it in the rim hole that is three holes counterclockwise from the valve hole. This hole should be offset upward and four holes counterclockwise from the spoke you just installed. Thread the nipple onto the spoke three turns.

12.11 **Placing third set of spokes in hub**

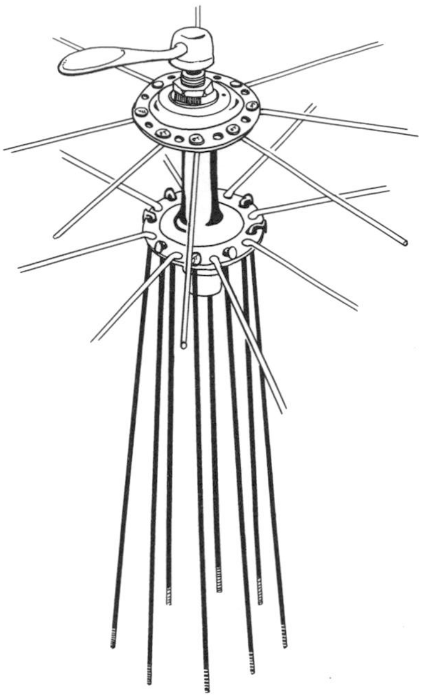

12.12 **Rotating hub counterclockwise**

12.13 **Lacing third set of spokes**

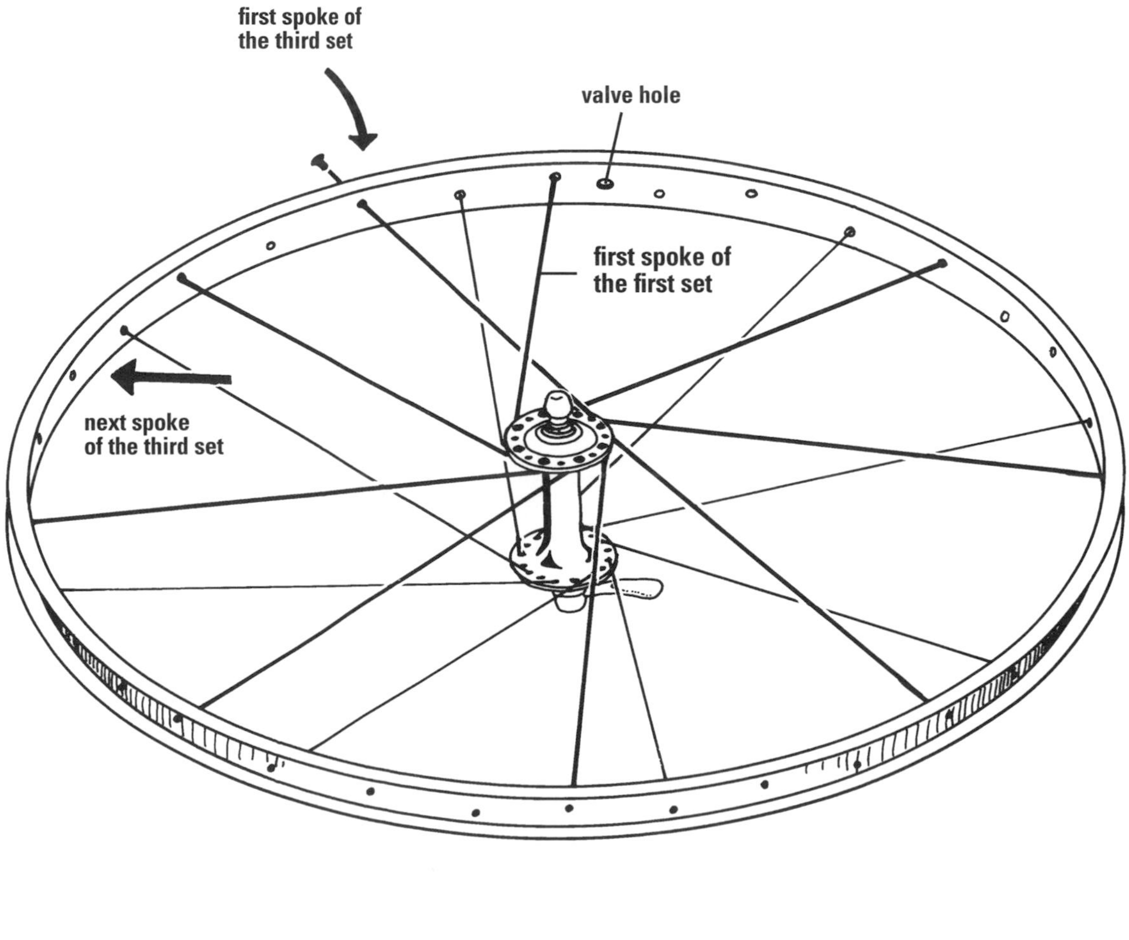

12.14 **Third set laced**

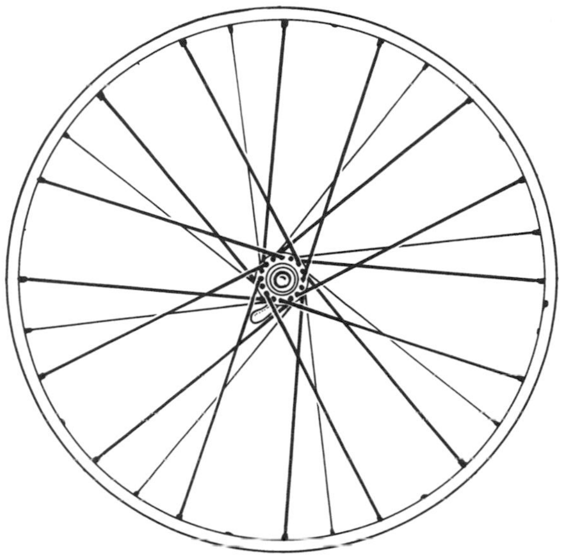

16. Follow this pattern counterclockwise around the wheel (Fig. 12.10). You should have now used half of the rim holes that are offset upward, as well as half of the total rim holes. The second set of spokes should all be in upwardly offset holes, one hole clockwise from each spoke of the first set.

c. Third set of spokes

17. Drop spokes through the remaining holes on the right side of the hub, from the inside of the hub out (Fig. 12.11). Remember: If it's a rear wheel or front disc-brake wheel, these should be the shorter spokes.

18. While grabbing the spokes you've just dropped through the hub (to keep them from falling out), flip the wheel over.

19. Fan the spokes out, so they cannot fall back down through the hub holes.

20. Grab the hub shell and rotate it counterclockwise as far as you can (Fig. 12.12).

21. Pick any spoke on the top (right-hand) hub flange that is already laced to the rim. Now find the spoke five hub holes away in a clockwise direction.

22. Take this new spoke, cross it under the spoke you counted from (the one five holes away), and stick it into the rim hole two holes counterclockwise from that spoke (Fig. 12.13). Thread the nipple onto the spoke three turns. Expect to bend the spokes some.

23. Continue around the wheel, doing the same thing (Fig. 12.14). You may find that some of the spokes don't quite reach far enough. If that's the case, push down on each one about 1 inch from the spoke elbow to help them reach.

24. Make sure that every spoke coming out of the upper side of the top flange (the spokes that come out toward you with their spoke heads hidden from view) crosses over two spokes and under a third. All three of these "crossing" spokes come from the underside of the same flange and have their spoke heads facing toward you. These crossing spokes begin one, three, and five hub holes counterclockwise from the spoke that you just inserted into the rim (Fig. 12.14). This is called a "three-cross" pattern because every spoke crosses three others on its way to the rim (over, over, under). Every upwardly offset hole should now be occupied on the rim.

d. Fourth (and final) set of spokes

25. Drop spokes down through the remaining hub holes in the bottom flange from the inside out (as shown in Fig. 12.11, but with the other side of the hub up). On a rear or front disc-brake hub, these are again the longer spokes.

26. While grabbing the spokes (to keep them from falling out), flip the wheel over.

12.15 **Lacing fourth set of spokes**

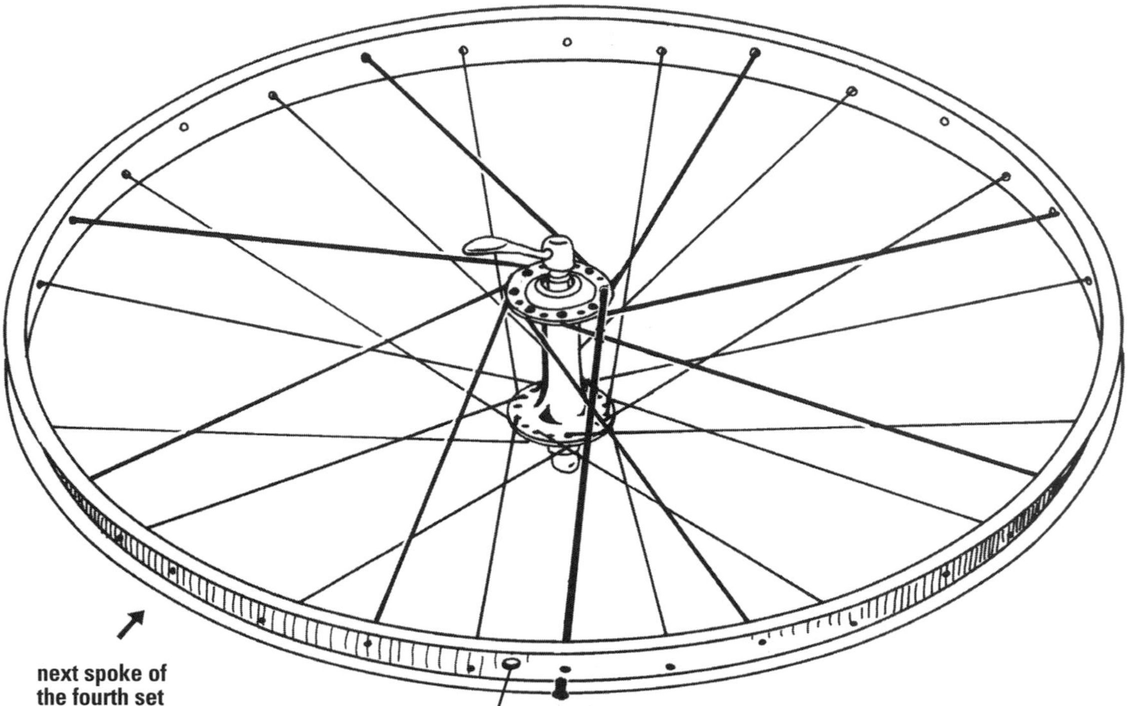

27. Fan the spokes out.

28. Pick any spoke on the top (left-hand) hub flange that is already laced to the rim. Now find the spoke five hub holes away in a counterclockwise direction.

29. Take that spoke, cross it over two spokes and under the spoke you counted from. Stick the spoke into the rim hole two holes clockwise from the spoke it crosses under (Fig. 12.15). Thread the nipple onto the spoke three turns.

30. Continue around the wheel, doing the same thing until the wheel is laced as shown in Figure 12.1. You may find that some of the spokes don't quite reach far enough. If that's the case, push down on each one about 1 inch from the spoke elbow to help them reach.

31. Make sure that every spoke coming out from the upper side of the top flange (the spokes that come out toward you with their spoke heads hidden from view) crosses over two spokes and under a third (Fig. 12.1). All three of these crossing spokes come from the underside of the same flange and have their spoke heads facing toward you. The crossing spokes begin one, three, and five hub holes clockwise from each spoke emerging from the top of the upper (left) hub flange (Fig. 12.1). Every hole should now be occupied on the rim. The valve hole should be between "converging parallel" spokes (Fig. 12.16) to make room for the pump head when inflating the tire.

IMPORTANT: *If it is a rear wheel, note that the spokes coming out of the outside of the hub flange on*

12.16 **Converging parallel spokes**

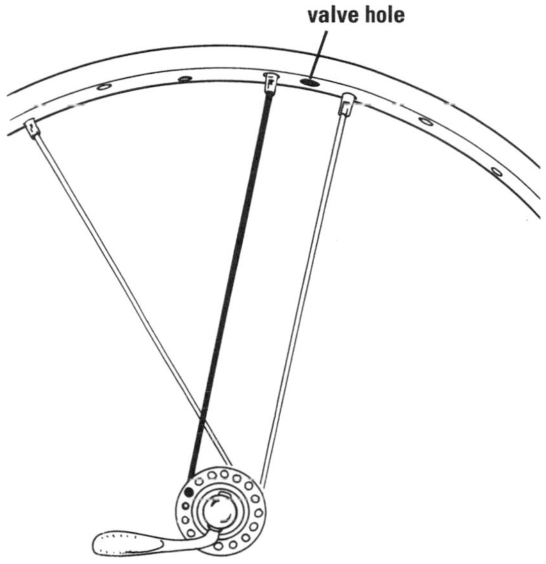

both sides oppose the clockwise twist the chain applies on the cogs. Similarly, if it is a front disc-brake wheel (Fig. 12.26), you will notice that the spokes coming out of the outside of both flanges oppose the twist the brake pads apply to the rotor. See §xii-6 for more on this.

xii-3 TENSIONING THE WHEEL

1. Put the wheel in the truing stand.
2. Tighten each nipple with a spoke wrench until only three threads are visible beyond the bottom of the nipple (see Figs. 12.17–12.20 for rotation direction).

NOTE: *From now on, every time you tighten or loosen a spoke nipple, turn it back the opposite direction by a one-eighth-turn afterward. This process unwinds the twist in the spoke that your tightening or loosening has just caused.*

3. Press the spokes coming outward from the outer side of the hub flanges down with your thumb at their elbow to straighten out their line to the rim. Spokes coming out of the inner side of the flange do not need this adjustment.
4. Go around the wheel, tightening each nipple a half-turn. Do this uniformly, so that the wheel is not thrown out of true.
5. Check to see whether the spokes are tight enough to give a tone when plucked. Squeeze pairs of spokes toward each other and compare their tension with that of a good wheel with spokes of the same gauge; your wheel should have considerably less tension at this point.
6. Repeat steps 4 and 5 until the spokes all make a tone but are under less tension than an existing, good wheel.

xii-4 TRUING THE WHEEL

a. Lateral true

The side-to-side trueness is the most obvious wheel parameter when you spin it.

1. Make sure the hub axle has no end play. If it does, adjust the hub (see Hub adjustment, Chapter 6, §vi-15d) to eliminate the end play.
2. Optional: Put a drop of linseed oil around the top of each nipple where it seats in the rim to lubricate the contact area between the nipple and the inside of the rim hole.
3. Set the truing-stand feelers so that one of them scrapes the side of the rim at the worst lateral wobble (Figs. 12.17 and 12.18).
4. Tighten the spokes coming from the opposite side of the hub from the scrape, and loosen the spokes coming from the same side of the hub (Figs. 12.17 and 12.18). Make these tightening and loosening adjustments on two or three spokes on either side of the spot where the rim scrapes. Start with one-quarter turn on nipples at the center of the

12.17 **Pull rim to the right**

12.18 **Pull rim to the left**

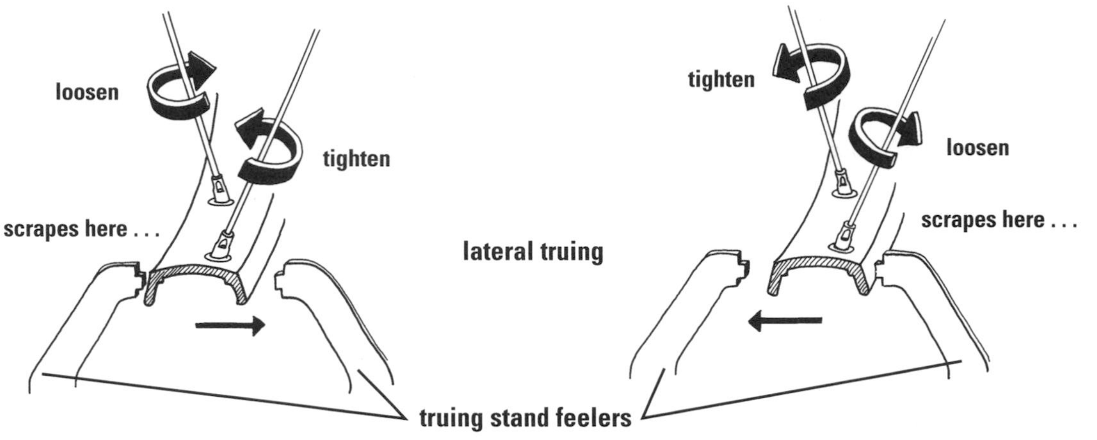

scraping area and decrease the amount you turn each nipple as you move away in either direction. This process pulls the rim away from the feeler. If your adjustments do the opposite, you are turning the nipples in the wrong direction.

REMEMBER: *You normally turn something to the right to tighten it and to the left to loosen it, but tightening and loosening spoke nipples at the bottom of the wheel is the opposite of what you would normally do (Figs. 12.17–12.20). This is because the nipple head is underneath your spoke wrench. This does not apply if you rotate the wheel so you are looking down on the nipple from the top. Try opening a jar that is upside down, and you will immediately understand the principle involved.*

5. Work around the wheel in this way, bringing the feelers in closer as the wheel gets truer.

NOTE: *On disc-brake rims, you may need to scrape decals off of the rim sides so that they won't hang up on the truing-stand feelers and make it hard to tell where the real wobbles are.*

b. Radial true

While not as obvious as side-to-side trueness, out-of-roundness is more important to the longevity of

12.19 **Pull rim in**

12.20 **Let rim out**

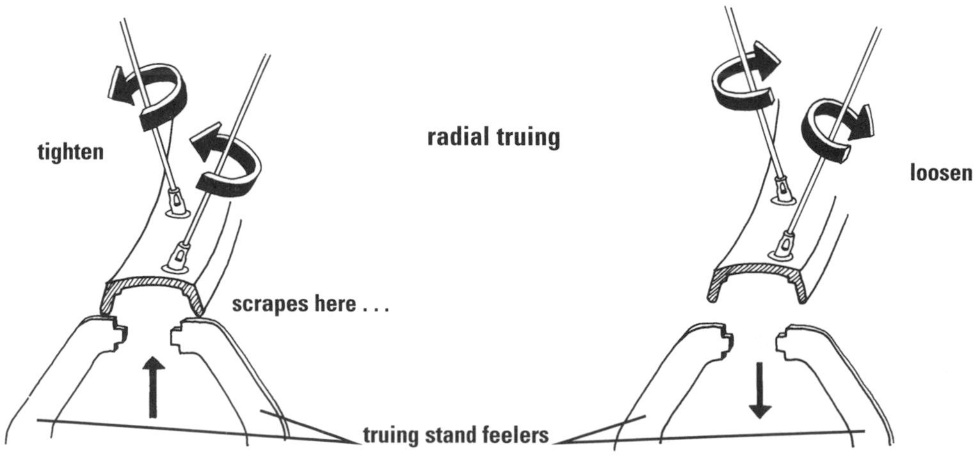

the wheel, because "uniformity of tension is the key to durability" (Portia Masterson, formerly of Self Propulsion bike shop in Golden, Colorado).

6. Set the truing-stand feelers so that they now contact the circumference of the rim, rather than the sides (Figs. 12.19–12.20).
7. Bring the feelers in until they scrape against the highest spot on the rim (Fig. 12.19).
8. Tighten the spokes one-quarter turn at the point where the rim scrapes. This will pull the rim inward. Decrease the amount of each turn (to an eighth-turn and less) as you move away from the center of the scraping area.
9. Work around the wheel this way, bringing the feelers up as the wheel becomes rounder. Loosen the spokes at a dip in the rim (Fig. 12.20). If the spokes are too tight at this point, they will be hard to turn and will creak and groan as you turn them. When the spokes become hard to turn (i.e., the nipples feel on the verge of rounding off), loosen all of the spokes in the wheel one-quarter turn before continuing. Compare the tension with a good wheel with the same gauge spokes; the tension should still be lower in the wheel you are building.

12.21 **Using the dishing tool to check the centering of the rim relative to the axle ends**

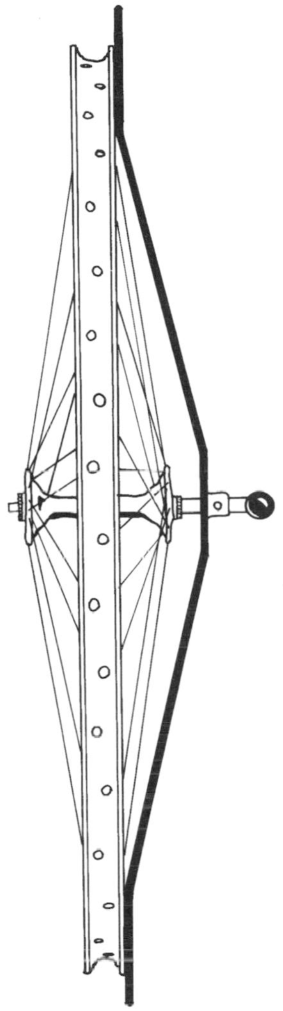

xii-5 CENTERING (OR DISHING) THE WHEEL

The rim on a good wheel must be centered in the frame or fork (between the brake pads, if you have rim brakes). On a rear hub or a disc-brake front hub, one hub flange is set back farther from the axle end (and hence from the frame or fork dropout) on that side than is the other flange. Although the wheel in Figure 12.21 (a front wheel for rim brakes) is symmetrical, an end view like this of either a rear wheel or a disc-brake front wheel would show the tighter spokes on the side with either the cogs or disc rotor (and hence farther inboard the hub flange) to be much flatter (i.e., less angle to the rim) than the (looser) spokes on the other side. Thus, the wheel will be dish-shaped when the rim is centered. This is what is meant by "wheel dish."

1. Place the dishing tool across the right side of the wheel, bisecting the center (Fig. 12.21).
2. Tighten or loosen the dishing gauge screw until the gauge contacts the outer face of the axle-end nut (Fig. 12.21).

12.22 Checking wheel dish on the other side of hub

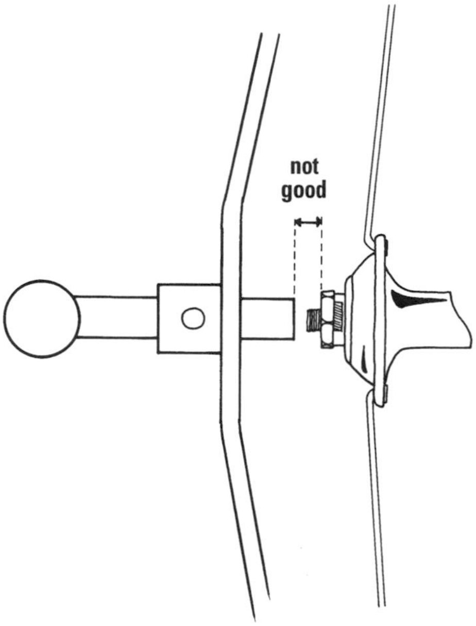

12.23 Relieving tension

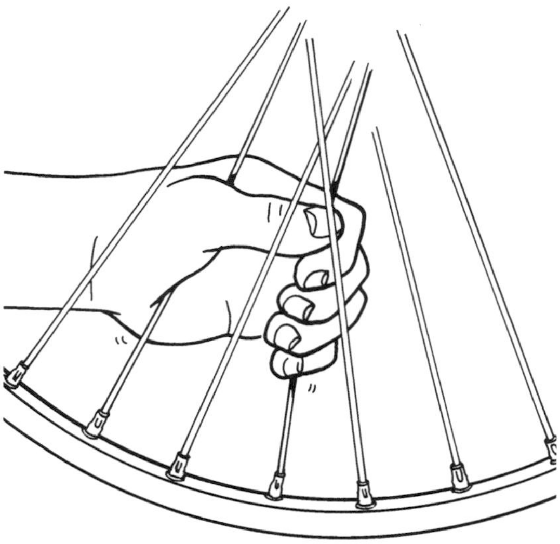

3. Flip the wheel over.
4. Place the dishing tool across the other side of the wheel.
5. Check the gap of the dishing gauge with this axle-end-nut face (Fig. 12.22). Any gap between the dishing gauge and the axle-end-nut face indicates the amount the rim is offset from the centerline of the wheel. If there is no gap, but an overlap instead, reset the dishing gauge on this side (the previously overlapped side). Then flip it over and check the other side (i.e., repeat steps 3, 4, and 5 on the opposite side).
6. Put the wheel back in the truing stand.
7. Pull the rim toward the center (reducing the gap between the dishing tool and the axle-end-nut face) by tightening the spokes on the opposite side of the wheel from the axle end that had the gap between the axle-end nut and the dishing gauge. Tighten a half-turn each. If the spokes start getting really tight (they will creak a lot when tightening, the nipples will start rounding off, and the spokes will feel much tighter than the spokes in a comparable wheel), then, instead, loosen the spokes on the opposite side of the wheel a half-turn each.
8. Recheck the wheel with the dishing gauge by repeating steps 1–5.
9. If the wheel is still off dish (there is still a gap between the dishing gauge and the end nut when you flip it over), repeat steps 6–8 until the gap is zero (i.e., the dish is correct).
10. Prestress the spokes by squeezing each pair of spokes together with your hands (Fig. 12.23). They will make a "ping" noise as they unwind.
    (a) Leaning on the wheel is a quicker way to prestress the wheel, but this method has the potential to wreck the wheel if you are not careful. To proceed, set the axle end on the workbench and carefully press down on the rim with your hands at the 9 o'clock and 3

o'clock positions. This procedure will affect an area of about three spokes on each side, so rotate the wheel three spokes, press down again, rotate three more spokes in the same direction, press down again, and so on. After you finish one side, flip the wheel over and do the other side. Do not press down with all of your might; although a well-built wheel's lateral strength is impressive, it is still easy to destroy your work with too much pressure.

(b) The amount of readjustment the spokes have to make will be reduced if you have been turning each nipple back an eighth-turn in the opposite direction after each rotational correction (as directed in §xii-3, step 2). If none of your spokes are twisted, there will be no pinging and readjustment during prestressing.

(c) If prestressing throws the wheel way out of true, the spokes are probably too tight. Loosen them all an eighth-turn. Some loss of wheel "trueness" is normal. If the loss is minor, you may overlook it.

11. Repeat "Truing the Wheel" (§xii-4), followed by "Centering (or Dishing) the Wheel" (§xii-5), prestressing the spokes frequently as you go. You keep improving the accuracy of the build this way.
12. Bring up the tension to that of a comparable wheel by making small tightening adjustments to every nipple, and adjusting dish and true after each time around, until the wheel is as you want it.
13. If the rim is oily, wipe it down with a citrus-based biodegradable solvent.
14. Congratulate yourself on building your wheel, and show it off to your friends.

xii-6 COMMENTS

Your wheel has some features that you won't find on machine-built wheels. Most significantly, on your rear wheel, the pulling spokes are to the outside. In plain speak, this means that you have a spoking pattern that best resists the twisting force on the hub produced by pedaling forces on the chain.

In the rear wheel you have just built, half of the spokes are called "pulling," or "dynamic," spokes, and the other half are called "static" spokes. The pulling spokes are the ones directed in such a way that a clockwise twist on the hub increases the tension in them. If you look at the wheel from the drive side, you will see what I am talking about.

You will also see that the static spokes do not oppose a clockwise twist on the hub. In fact, their tension decreases when you stomp on the pedals.

By placing all of the pulling spokes so that they come from the inside of the hub flanges out (i.e., the spoke heads are on the inward side of the flanges), we have attached the spokes doing the most work the farthest outward on the hub. This increases their angle to the rim, and hence their ability to oppose forces acting on the rim. Similarly, if you just built a front disc-brake wheel (Fig. 12.26), the pulling spokes opposing the braking force on the disc are to the outside of the hub flanges.

If you have chosen the appropriate parts for your weight and riding style, and have the proper spoke tension, then you should have a strong wheel that will last you a long time. Congratulations!

xii-7 RADIALLY SPOKED WHEELS

With the advent of stronger rim materials and stiffer rim cross sections, radially spoked wheels—in which the spokes emanate radially from the hub out to the rim, rather than crossing each other (Fig. 12.24)—are currently very popular. They are very simple to lace up, and radial spoking offers a number of advantages, but a completely radial wheel can only be used on the front. On the rear, you must still use a crossing pattern on one side (usually the drive side) to oppose the twist on the hub caused by the chain (Fig. 12.25). Similarly, you cannot use a radially spoked wheel with disc brakes, as the spokes cannot oppose the torque the brake applies to the brake rotor.

A radially spoked wheel is vertically stiffer than a crossed one because radial spokes allow little opportunity for spokes to absorb energy in the spoking pattern. The radial wheel can be laterally stiffer, too, because all of the spokes can come to the outside of the hub flange and increase the pulling angle to the rim.

A radial wheel is lighter because the spokes are shorter. Further weight can be removed with fewer spokes, and radial spoking allows any even spoke count to be used (with nonradial patterns, the spoke count must be a multiple of four). And radial spoking allows the use of flangeless direct-pull hubs and nail-head or double-threaded spokes (straight spokes without elbows), eliminating a potential weak spot in each spoke.

RADIALLY SPOKED WHEELS

Radially laced spokes line up behind each other and improve the aerodynamics of the wheel. Aero-shaped spokes can improve the aerodynamics further yet, but using aero-shaped spokes in a standard hub often requires you to slot the hub holes with a jeweler's file to get the spoke through. (If you slot the hub holes, make sure you only file radially inward from the hole. Slotting radially outward greatly weakens the hub and invites the spoke to rip the hub flange.) But aerodynamics is a very minor concern on a mountain bike (except perhaps a downhill bike, which can't use radial spokes anyway because of its disc brakes).

12.24 Radially spoked front wheel

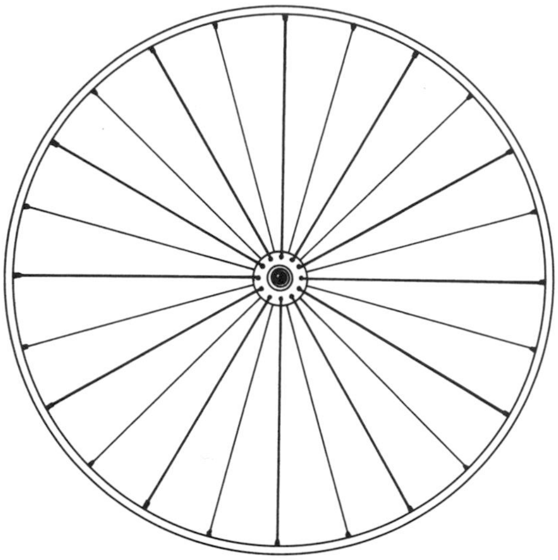

Speaking of torn hub flanges, the warranty of some hubs is voided when spoked radially. Shimano has this stipulation, for instance. The stress is greater on hub holes with radial spoking because there is less material to resist the tearing of the hub holes when the spoke is pulling straight outward than if it is pulling at an angle along the hub flange.

a. How to lace a radial front wheel

Simply drop all of the spokes from the inside of each flange outward and lace the spokes straight to the rim (Fig. 12.24).

b. How to lace a rear wheel with a radial left side and a three-cross drive side

First lace the drive side following the instructions in §xii-2a, steps 4–7, and §xii-2c, steps 17–24. Now lace the left-side spokes radially outward through the hub flange and straight to the rim (Fig 12.25).

12.25 **Radial/three-cross rear wheel**

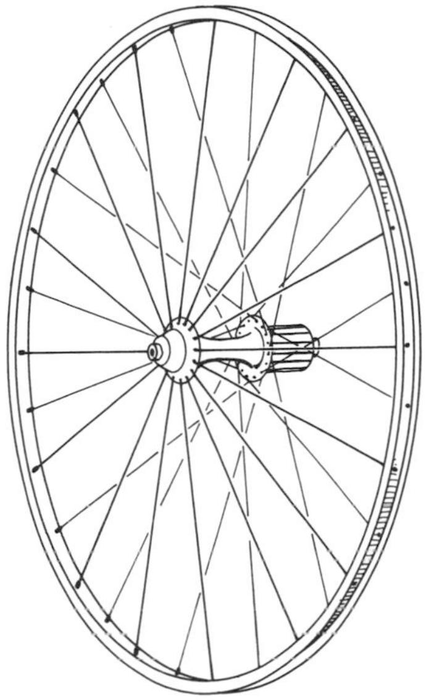

12.26 **Front disc-brake wheel**

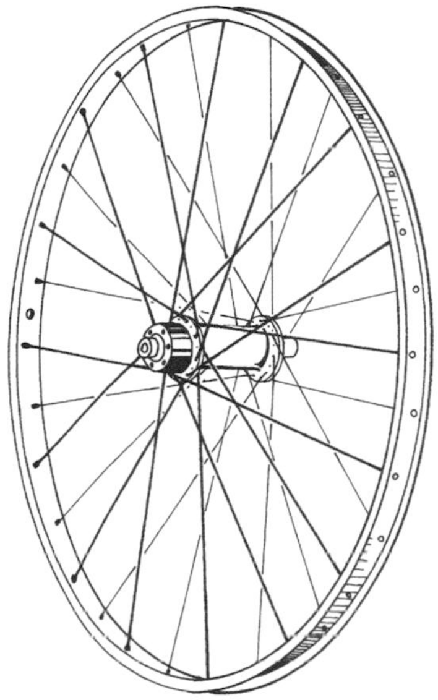

The tensioning and truing steps are the same for radial and radial–three-cross wheels as for standard three-cross wheels, but radial spoke tension should be higher to help prevent the spokes from vibrating loose. NOTE: *These instructions place the radial spokes to the outside of the hub flange so that their angle to the rim (and hence their ability to oppose lateral forces on it) is highest.*

xii-8 WHEELS FOR BIG RIDERS

Building wheels for heavy and tall riders requires greater lateral and vertical stiffness. The weight of the rider can more easily bend and laterally flex the rim, but it creates another problem as well. The heavier rider de-tensions the spokes at the bottom of the wheel more by making the rim more D-shaped at the bottom as it rolls. If the spokes are under less tension, or if the nipple flanges periodically lose contact with the bases of the rim holes, the nipples can unscrew, and the wheel will fall apart. To achieve the necessary higher strength, you can add the following characteristics.

a. Spoke count and thickness

First, the spoke count needs to be high: Thirty-six or more spokes is highly preferable for riders over 190 pounds. The spokes need to be heavier, as thicker spokes have less stretch as well as less breakage. Although 14/15-gauge (2.0mm or 14-gauge on each end, and 1.8 mm, or 15-gauge throughout the center section) double-butted spokes will probably have no more breakage than straight 14-gauge (2.0mm) spokes (because most breakage occurs at the nipple or the elbow, where butted spokes are thick), butted spokes will stretch more, allowing spoke loosening.

b. Rim section and drilling

The deeper the rim, the higher its hoop strength (vertical stiffness and strength). Very deep V-section rims work with low spoke counts because of this high hoop strength. The strongest wheel would be from a deep-section rim drilled for more spokes. Unfortunately for heavy riders, many deep V-section rims are also thinner to reduce weight and hence lose some strength.

c. Spoking pattern

With eight-speed and nine-speed rear wheels, dish is high (one side of the wheel is flatter than the other is), meaning that there is a great tension difference between spokes on the two sides. The loose spokes on the left can unscrew, especially under high pedaling forces, and the tight spokes on the right can break. As the chain twists the cogs clockwise, the spokes opposing the twist (the "pulling spokes") get tighter, while the "static spokes" are under reduced tension and can unscrew.

Using radial spokes on the left side (see §xii-7 above) can counteract the problem of grossly uneven tension. With a radial left side, the chain twisting the hub forward always tightens all of the left-side spokes, rather than loosening half of them as it would with a crossing pattern.

An off-center rim, such as a Ritchey OCR, can also help by reducing the wheel dish. The rim holes are offset to the left side (Fig. 12.3), so that the drive-side spokes come to the rim at a lower angle and can work with lower tension and more even tension between the two sides. The left-side spokes come to the rim at a higher angle and can be under higher tension without forcing the use of dangerously high tensions on the drive side. Before lacing an off-center rim, make sure you read the note in step 2 of §xii-2 above.

xii-9 LACING REAR THREE-CROSS DISC-BRAKE WHEELS

If you are building a rear disc-brake wheel (Fig. 12.28), you want the drive-side outer spokes opposing the chain force on the cogs, but you want the left-side outer spokes opposing the braking force on the rotor. This pattern makes for a stronger wheel, by having the wider-angle spokes doing more of the work.

The drive side will be laced in just the same way as described in the lacing instructions in §xii-2 above, but the nondrive side will be laced in the opposite way that the left side turns would be laced in §xii-2.

a. First set of spokes

1. Follow steps 1–9 from §xii-2.

b. Second set of spokes

2. Push a spoke up through the hole in the top flange that is immediately clockwise from the first spoke you installed (the spoke that is just clockwise from the valve hole).
3. Follow steps 11, 12, and 13 from §xii-2 and then step 4 below.
4. Drop one spoke down through each of the adjacent hub holes on either side of the newly laced spoke. Skip a hole, and continue around the hub flange dropping a spoke down into every other hole.
5. Rotate the hub shell clockwise as far as you can.
6. Find the spoke that is five hub holes counterclockwise from the single spoke coming up out of the flange that you installed in steps 2 and 3.
7. Take this new spoke, cross it over the spoke you counted from (the one five holes away), and stick it into the rim hole two holes clockwise from that spoke. Thread the nipple onto the spoke three turns.
8. Find the next spoke counterclockwise on the hub flange. Put it in the rim hole four holes counterclockwise from the spoke you just installed in step 7. Thread the nipple onto the spoke three turns.

12.27 **Rear disc-brake wheel: first two sets of spokes completed, first spoke of third set installed**

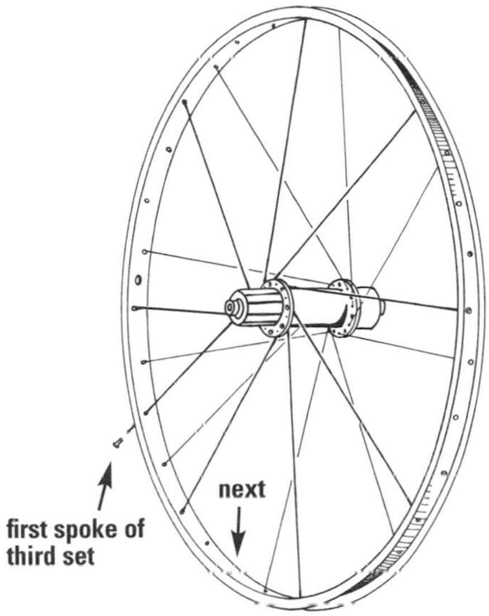

12.28 **Completed rear disc-brake wheel**

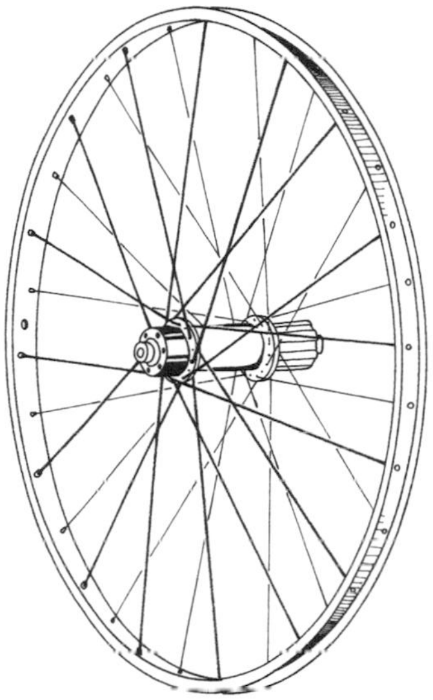

9. Continue counterclockwise around the top (brake-side) hub flange until all spokes whose heads stick out of the top flange are one rim hole counterclockwise from the first set of spokes installed in the rim.

c. Third set of spokes

10. Follow steps 17–27 in §xii-2. After you complete step 22, the wheel should look like the wheel shown in Figure 12.27 (except the other fanned-out unlaced spokes coming out of the top flange are not shown).

d. Fourth (and final) set of spokes

11. Pick any spoke on the top (rotor-side) flange whose head is facing up and is already laced to the rim. Now find the spoke five clockwise hub holes away.
12. Follow steps 22–24 in §xii-2.
13. Note that the drive-side outer spokes oppose the chain pull and the rotor-side outer spokes oppose the braking force on the rotor (Fig. 12.28). Your wheel is now laced. Give yourself a big pat on the back and then begin tensioning and truing your wheel, starting with §xii-3.

LACING REAR THREE-CROSS DISC-BRAKE WHEELS

CHAPTER 13

FORKS

If you come to a fork in the road, take it.
—Yogi Berra

TOOLS

metric Allen wrenches
metric open-end wrenches
adjustable wrench
needle-nose pliers
safety glasses
soft hammer
long screwdriver
nonlithium grease
citrus degreaser

OPTIONAL TOOLS

torque wrench
ruler or calipers
a pair of dropout-alignment tools
solid bench vise
snapring pliers
air pump for fork
metric socket wrenches
bike stand
medium-thread lock compound (like Loctite 242)
antiseize compound for titanium bolts
22mm, 24mm, and 26mm sockets

The fork serves a number of purposes. Most obviously, it connects the front wheel to the handlebar. Of course, the fork allows the bike to be steered, and it supports the front brake. The fork also offsets the front hub some distance forward of the steering axis. This offset distance (called the "fork rake"), combined with the steering axis (the "head angle") and the wheel size, determine how your bike is going to handle and steer.

All forks, suspended (Fig. 13.2) or rigid (Fig. 13.1), provide at least a minimum amount of suspension by allowing the front wheel to move up and down. The simple facts that the steering axis angles the fork forward from vertical and that the front hub is offset farther forward still make it possible for a "rigid" fork to flex along its length and absorb vertical shocks. Suspension forks add a much greater range of vertical wheel travel.

All mountain bike forks are made up of a steering tube, a fork crown, fork legs (sometimes called "blades"), brake bosses (usually cantilever or V-brake posts, and/or disc-brake mounts, but possibly roller-cam or U-brake posts), and fork ends (also called "dropouts" or "fork tips"). Figures 13.1 and 13.2 illustrate these parts on a rigid fork and a suspension fork, respectively. Mountain bike forks can be manufactured from steel, aluminum, magnesium, titanium, carbon fiber, and countless combinations of these materials.

These days virtually all mountain bikes come equipped with suspension forks (Fig. 13.2). Their most distinguishing feature is the spring inside. That spring can be made up of elastic polymer bumpers (elastomers), compressed air, steel or titanium coils, or a combination. A lot of suspension forks also include a damping system to control how fast the spring compresses and rebounds. It acts much in the same way as a shock absorber on a car or a door (you know—the thing that keeps your screen door from slamming).

13.1 **Rigid fork**

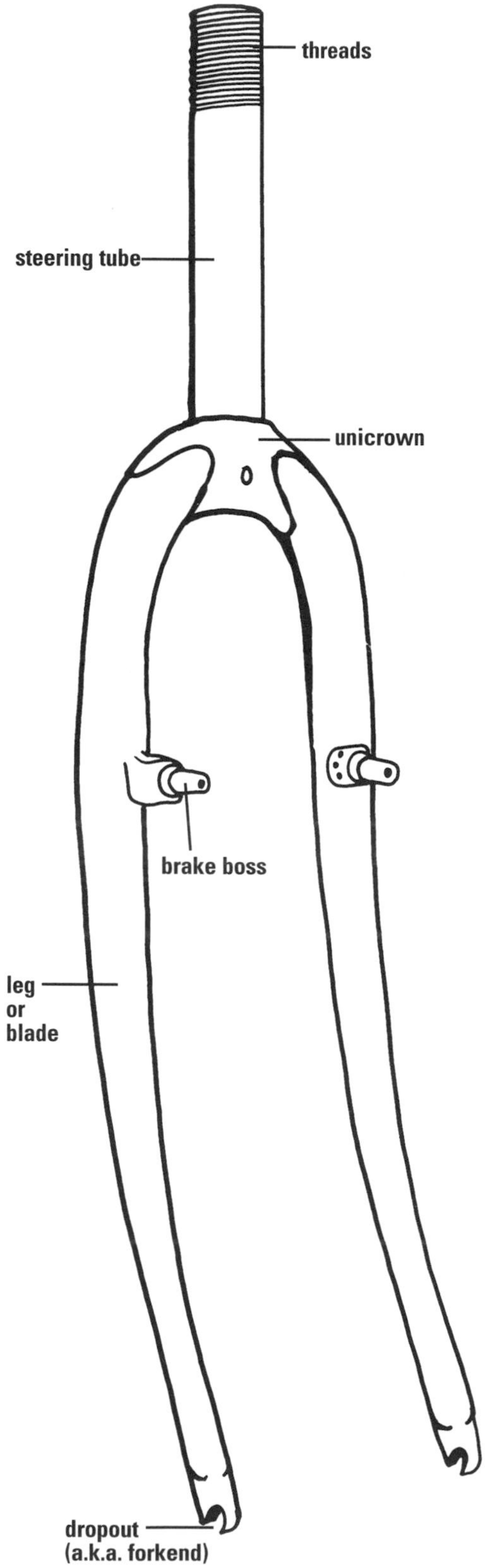

13.2 **Suspension fork**

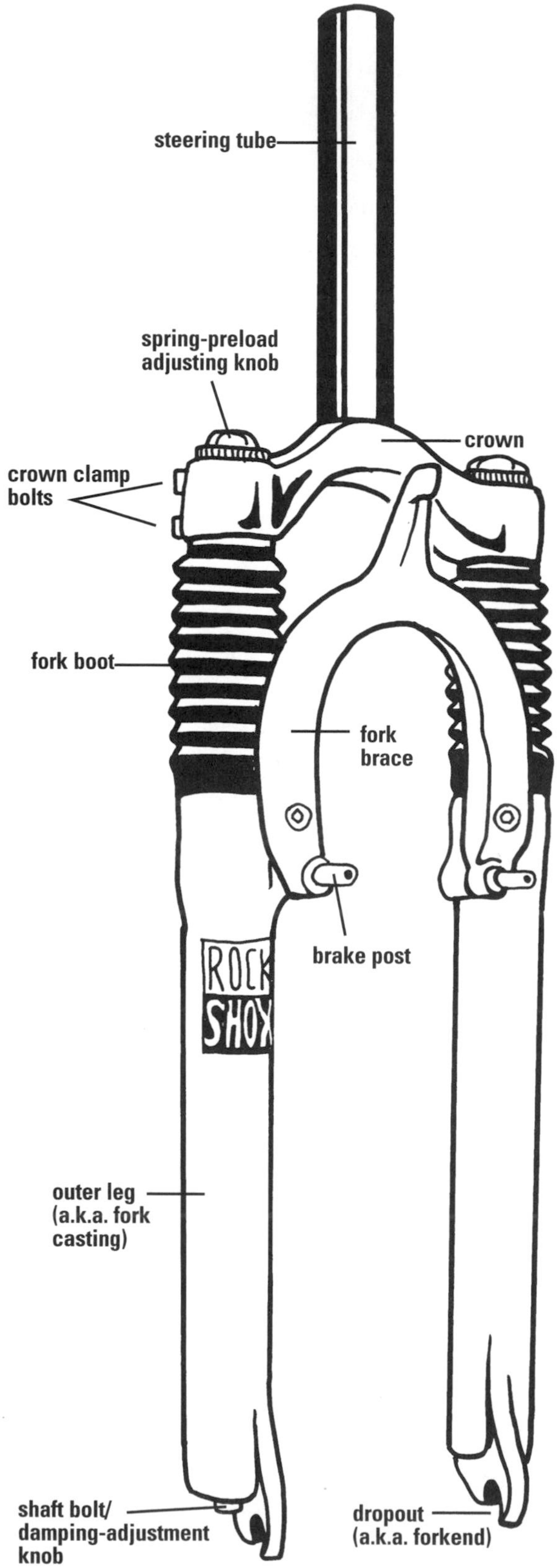

Hydraulic damping systems are the most common, relying on the controlled movement of oil from one chamber to another. That flow is usually regulated by a system of holes that act to slow the rate of flow. Some dampers operate on a similar principle with compressed air instead of oil.

The most commonly used suspension-fork design has "telescoping" fork legs that consist of two sections: inner legs attached to the fork crown and steering tube and outer legs attached to the front hub that slide up and down over the inner legs (Fig. 13.3). Although this description applies to the vast majority of suspension forks, there are a number of variations that vie for a small piece of the fork market. Cannondale's "HeadShok" design incorporates rigid fork legs attached to a single shock unit inside the head tube, and its "Lefty" fork has only a single, telescoping, left leg. "Upside down" telescoping forks have thinner lower legs sliding up and down inside fatter upper legs. There are also "linkage" suspension forks that use a system of pivots and movable arms attached to a spring.

13.3 How a suspension fork works

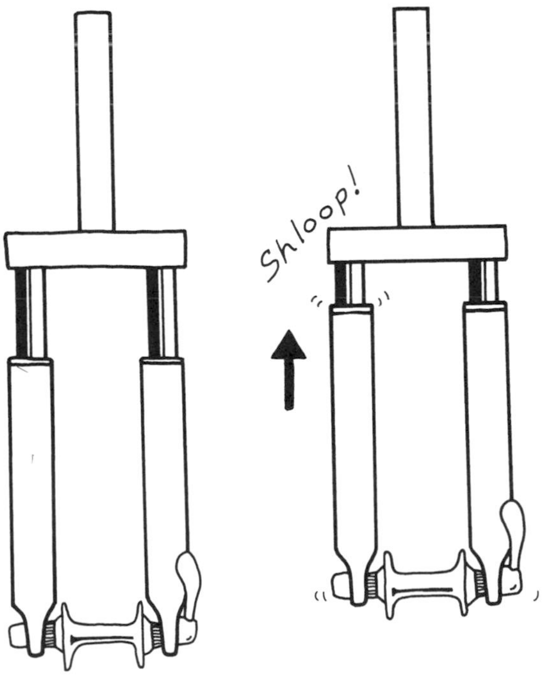

xiii-1 FORK INSPECTION

For the most part, forks are pretty durable, but they do break sometimes. A fork failure can ruin your day, because the means of control of the bike is eliminated. Such loss of control usually involves the rapid transfer of your body directly onto the ground, resulting in a substantial amount of pain.

Ever since I first opened my frame-building shop, people have regularly brought me an amazing collection of forks that had broken, sometimes with catastrophic consequences. Some had steering tubes broken either at the fork crown or in the threads. Others had fork crowns that broke or separated (releasing a fork leg or two), fork-crown bolts that broke or fell out, fork legs that folded, cantilever posts that snapped, fork braces supporting the brake cable that broke off, and front dropouts that broke off. Top caps can fly off of coil- or elastomer-sprung forks (and shoot up at your face!), and seals can blow on air-sprung forks, either one of which immediately bottoms out the fork. Pivots on linkage forks can break or fall apart. You can go a long way toward preventing problems such as these by regularly inspecting your fork.

With that in mind, get into the habit of checking your fork regularly for any warning signs of impending failure—bends, cracks, and stressed paint. If you have crashed your bike, give your fork a very thorough inspection. If you find any indication that your fork has been damaged, replace it. A new fork is cheaper than emergency room charges, brain surgery, or an electric wheelchair.

13.4 **One messed-up fork**

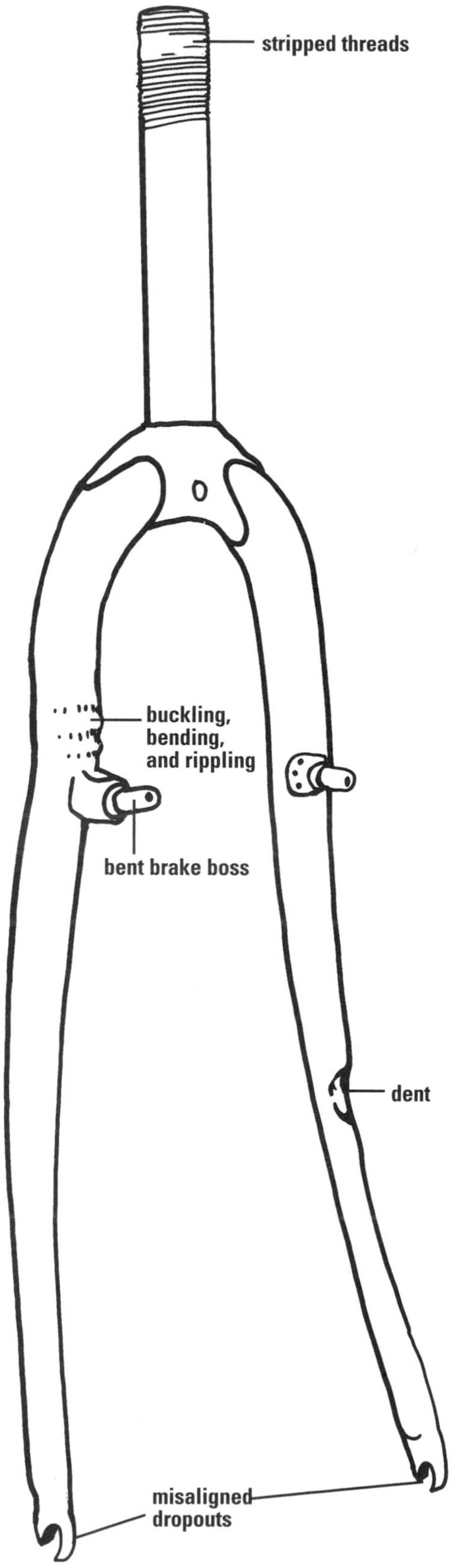

FORK INSPECTION

When you inspect a fork, remove the front wheel, clean the mud off, and look under the crown and between the fork legs. Carefully examine all of the outside areas. Look for any spots where the paint or finish looks cracked or stretched. Look for bent parts, from little ripples in fork legs to skewed cantilever posts and bent dropouts (Fig. 13.4).

Put your wheel back in and watch to see if the fork legs twist when you tighten the hub into the dropouts. Check to make sure that a true wheel centers under the fork crown. If it doesn't, turn the wheel around and put it back in the fork. That way you can confirm whether the misalignment is in your fork or your wheel. If the wheel lines up off to one side when it is put in one way and off the same amount to the other side when it is put in the other way, then the wheel is off true, and the fork is straight. If the wheel is skewed off to the same side in the fork no matter which direction you place the wheel, the fork is misaligned.

I recommend overhauling your headset annually (Chapter 11, §xi-18 and §xi-19), and when you do, carefully examine the steering tube for any signs of stress or damage. Check for bent, cracked, or stretched areas, stripped threads (Fig. 13.4), bulging where the stem expands inside (threaded steering tube), or crimping where the stem clamps around the top (threadless steering tube).

With a threaded fork, hold the stem up next to the steering tube to make sure that when your stem quill (Fig. 11.8) is inserted to the depth at which you have been using it, the bottom of the quill is always over an inch below the bottom of the steering-tube threads. If you expand your stem quill by tightening the expander bolt (Fig. 11.9), thereby pulling up the wedge when it is in the threaded region, you are asking for trouble; the threads cut the steering-tube wall thickness down by about 50 percent, and each thread offers a sharp breakage plane along which the tube can cleave.

On telescoping suspension forks, if your (old) fork has crown clamp bolts, check that they are tight (ideally, you would do this with a torque wrench to verify that they are tightened to the torque recommended by the fork manufacturer). If you have titanium clamp bolts on your fork crown and you do lots of fast and rough downhill riding, consider replacing them annually (or get a new fork without clamp bolts); the heads of titanium fork-crown bolts have been known to snap off. Nowadays, forks with crown bolts (Figs. 13.12 and 13.14) are rare, which is probably a good thing.

Check for oil leaks, either from around the top of the outer leg or around the bolt at the bottom of the outer leg. Check for torn, cracked, or missing seals around the top of the outer leg.

On linkage forks, there are a lot of bolts, pins, and pivots that need to be checked regularly. Make sure that all bolts are tight and all pins have their circlips or other retaining devices in place so they do not fall out. Check for cracks and bends around the pivot points.

If you have any doubts about anything on your fork, take it to the expert at your bike shop. When it comes to forks, err on the side of caution—replace them before they need it.

xiii-2 FORK DAMAGE

If your inspection has uncovered some damage that does not automatically require fork replacement, here are some guidelines to go by and some means of repair.

a. Dents

Not all fork dents threaten the integrity of the fork. On a rigid fork, particularly a steel one, a small dent usually poses little risk. A large dent (Fig. 13.4), of course, does. On a suspension fork, almost any dent can adversely affect the fork's operation, even if it does not pose a breakage threat. Many suspension-fork parts are replaceable.

b. Fork misalignment

Within limits, a rigid fork made of steel can be realigned if it is slightly off center. (See §xiii-5 in this chapter.) Rigid forks made out of any other material and suspension forks cannot be realigned. Don't try it!

c. Stripped steering-tube threads

If the threads on the steering tube are damaged (Fig. 13.4) so that the headset slips when you try to tighten it, you need to replace the steering tube. The steering tube and fork crown assembly can be replaced on some older suspension forks. You don't usually have that option when it comes to rigid forks, so you usually have to replace the whole thing.

d. Obvious bend, ripple, or crease in fork legs

Replace the fork if you feel, or see, ripples and bends in it (Fig. 13.4). The poor handling and potential breakage pose too great a threat to your safety to be worth saving a few bucks.

e. Bent or stripped cantilever bosses

On most suspension forks as well as some rigid forks, the cantilever studs can be unscrewed with an 8mm open-end wrench and replaced. It is a good idea to use a thread-locking compound such as Loctite 242 on the threads of the new mount.

13.5 **Measuring dropout spacing**

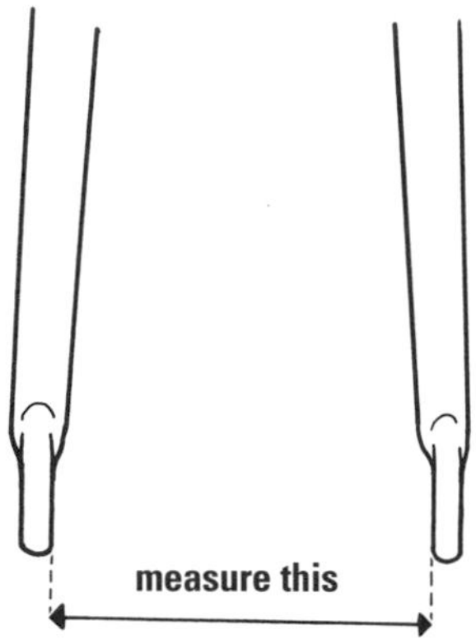

13.6 **Aligning dropout with dropout-alignment tool**

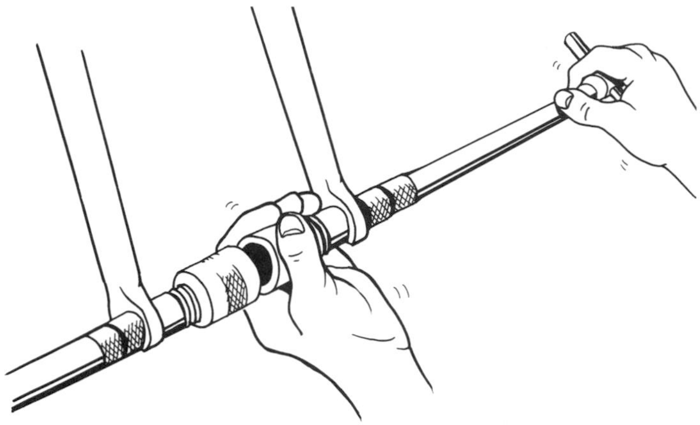

With few exceptions, bent or stripped cantilever bosses on a rigid fork (Fig. 13.4) usually mean that you have to buy a new fork. If you have a frame builder in your area, he or she may be able to weld or braze a new boss onto a steel fork. You will also need to repaint the fork.

xiii-3 MAINTAINING RIGID FORKS

Beyond touching up the paint on steel forks and performing regular inspections, the only maintenance procedure to do with a rigid fork is to check the alignment if your bike is handling badly. You can perform minor realignment on a steel fork if you find that it is off center; note that realigning is risky enough to qualify as a level 3 job. Do not try to realign titanium, carbon-fiber, aluminum, or suspension forks. (You've probably noticed that I am repeating myself here.)

xiii-4 CHECKING FORK ALIGNMENT

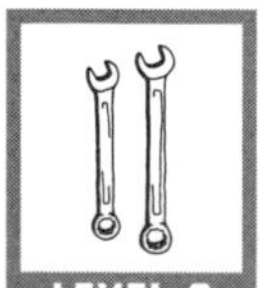
LEVEL 2

You will need a ruler, a true front wheel, and dropout-alignment tools (Fig. 1.4). With any type of fork other than a rigid steel one, this procedure is diagnostic only, because you should not try to realign any other type of fork. (Again, you might have noticed that I am repeating myself.) Checking the alignment may help explain bike-handling problems.

If you find the alignment to be off more than a couple of millimeters in any direction with any fork other than a steel, unsuspended one, you need a new fork. If your fork is new, misalignment should be covered as a warranty item.

If your steel fork is more than 8mm off in any direction, you ought to get a new fork. If the dropouts of a steel fork are slightly bent, you can realign them. You can also take a moderately bent (between 2mm and 8mm off) steel fork to a frame builder or a bike shop for realignment. Make sure that whomever you take it to is properly equipped with a fork jig or alignment table and is well versed in the art of "cold setting" (a fancy term for bending) steel forks.

1. Remove the fork from the bike (Chapter 11, §xi-18 and §xi-19).
2. With the front wheel out, measure the spacing between the faces of the dropouts (Fig. 13.5).

13.7 Correct dropout alignment

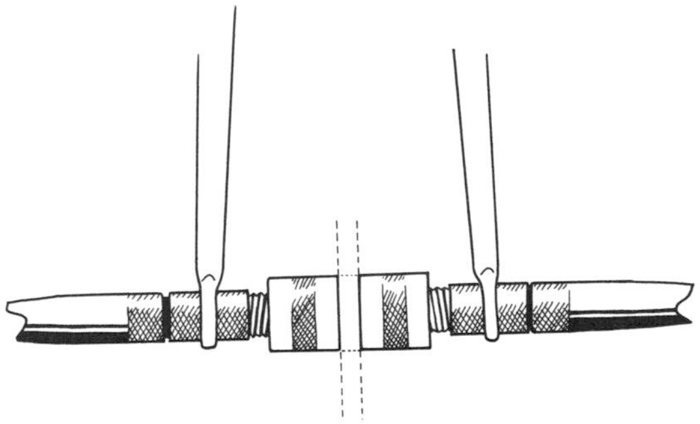

13.8 Incorrect dropout alignment (dropout is twisted or right fork leg is bent back)

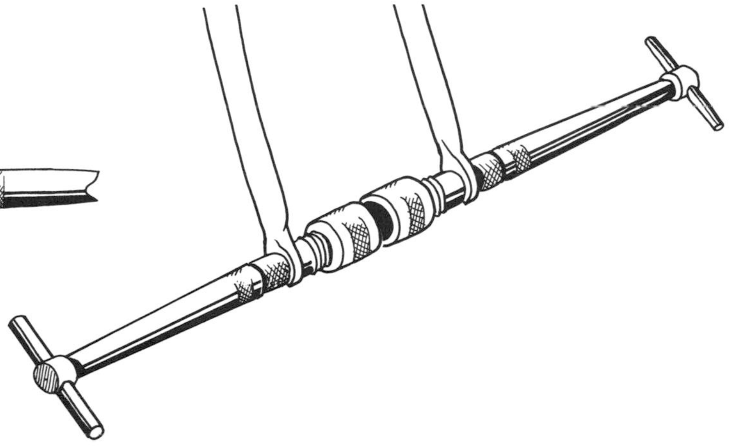

Adult and high-quality children's bikes should have a spacing of 100mm between the inner surfaces of the dropouts. (Some low-end kids' bikes have narrower spacing—about 90mm or so. If that's the type of bike you are working with, don't bother checking alignment; it isn't worth the trouble.) Remember that you are measuring the distance between the flat surfaces that meet the hub-axle faces, not between wheel-retaining bumps. Dropout spacing up to 102mm and down to 99mm is acceptable. Beyond that in either direction means a trip to the bike shop for a new fork. If you have a rigid fork made of steel, you can go to a bike shop or frame builder for realignment.

3. Clamp the steering tube of the fork in a bike stand or a padded vise. Install the dropout-alignment tools (Fig. 13.6). The tools are made to be used on either the fork or the rear triangle of the bike, so they have two axle diameters and spacers for use in the (wider-spaced) rear dropouts. Move all of the spacers to the outside of the fork ends so that only the cups of the tools are placed inside of the dropouts. Install the tool so that the shaft is seated up against the top of the dropout slot. Tighten the handles down.
4. Ideally, the ends of the cups on the dropout-aligning tools should be parallel and lined up with each other (Fig. 13.7). The cups of Campagnolo dropout-alignment tools are non-adjustable and are nominally 50mm in length; the ideal space between their ends is 0.1–0.5mm. The cups on Park dropout-aligning tools (illustrated in Figs. 13.6–13.8) can be threaded in and out so that you can bring the faces up close to each other no matter what the dropout spacing. If they are lined up with each other (Fig. 13.8), and the dropouts are spaced between 99mm and 102mm apart, continue on to step 5. If the dropouts on your rigid fork made of steel are not lined up straight across with each other and the dropouts are within the 99–102mm spacing range, skip to §xiii-5 to align them.

NOTE: *It is crucial that the fork dropout faces be parallel before continuing with step 5, or the rest of the alignment procedures will be a waste of time. Clamping the hub into misaligned dropouts will force*

CHECKING FORK ALIGNMENT

the fork legs to twist. If your dropouts are misaligned, any measurement of the side-to-side and fore-and-aft alignment of the fork legs will not be accurate.

5. Remove the tire from a front wheel. Make sure the wheel is true and properly dished (Chapter 12, §xii-4 and §xii-5).
6. Install the wheel in the fork. Make sure the axle is seated against the top of the dropout slot on either side and that the quick-release skewer is tight. Lightly push the rim from side to side to be certain that there is no play in the front hub. If there is play, you first must adjust the hub (Chapter 6, §vi-15d).
7. Test the alignment visually.
   (a) Look down the steering tube and through the rim's valve hole to the bottom side of the rim (Fig. 13.9). The steering tube should be lined up with this line of sight through the wheel (Fig. 13.10). When you are sighting through the steering tube and the valve hole, you should see the same amount of space between either side of the rim and the sides of the steering tube while you see the seam side of the rim centered through the valve hole.
   (b) Turn the wheel around and install it again so that what was the right end of the hub is now the left, and vice versa. Sight through the steering tube and the wheel valve hole again. Placing the wheel in the fork both ways corrects for deformation in the axle or any wobble in the wheel. If the wheel is true and properly dished and the axle is in good shape, the wheel should line up exactly as it did before. If it does not line up, but the wheel is off by the same amount to one side as it is to the opposite side when the wheel is turned around, the wheel is off and the fork is fine side to side.
   (c) If this test indicates that the fork is up to 2–3mm off to the side, that is close enough; continue on, please. If it is off by more than 3mm, get a new fork or have it aligned by a frame builder (if it is steel, because, by now you know that you should not try to realign suspension, titanium, carbon-fiber, or aluminum forks).

CHECKING FORK ALIGNMENT

13.9 Sighting through steering tube to check fork alignment

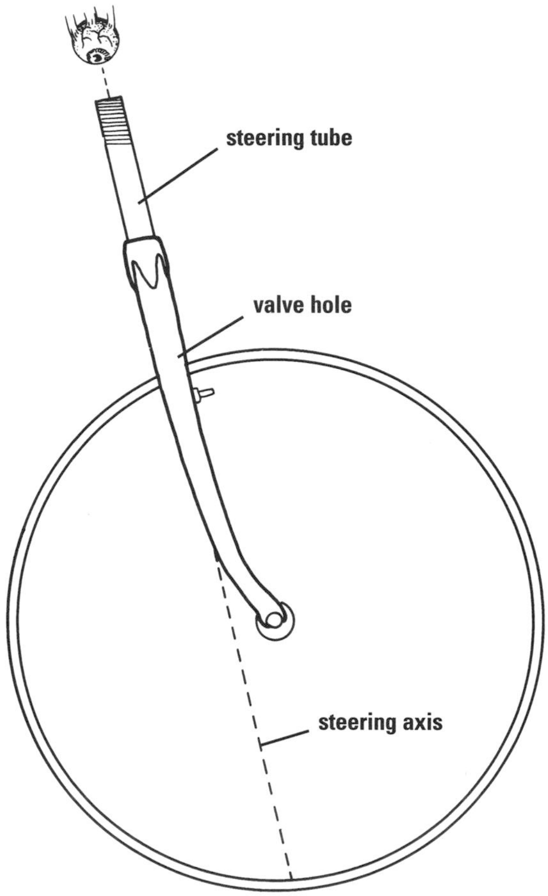

NOTE: *If you are sighting through the wheel in this way, and you cannot see the bottom side of the rim through the valve hole because the hub is in the way,*

13.10 Correct alignment of valve hole in a straight fork

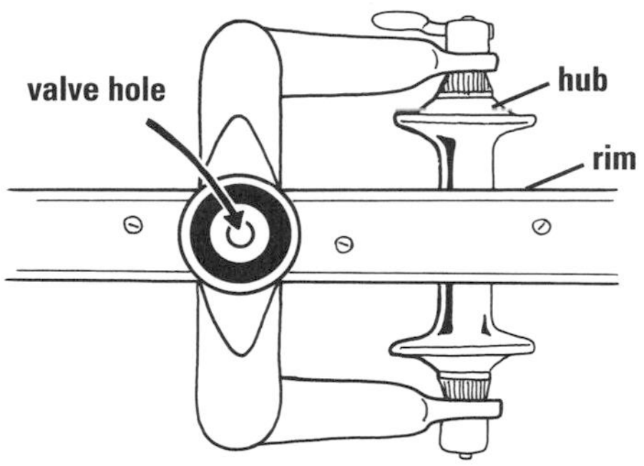

13.11 Checking fork alignment with a ruler

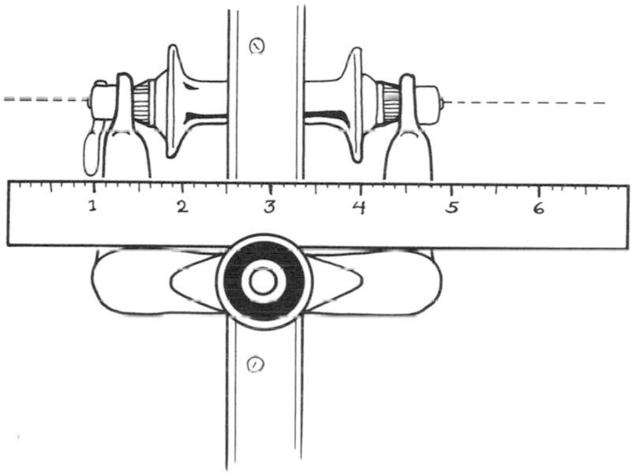

your fork has big problems. For the bike to handle properly, the front hub must have some forward offset from the steering axis (Fig. 13.9). This offset, or "rake," is usually around 4cm on a mountain bike. If you sight through the steering tube and see the front hub, the fork is bent backward so much that it has little or no offset! If this is the case, you need a new fork.

8. With the wheel in the fork, place a ruler on edge across the fork legs just below the fork crown (Fig. 13.11). Make sure the ruler is perpendicular to the steering tube.
9. Holding the ruler in place, lift the fork toward a light source so that you are sighting across the ruler and the front hub toward the light. The ruler's edge should line up parallel with the axle ends sticking out of either end of the hub (Fig. 13.11). This test will tell you if one fork leg is bent back relative to the other one. If the axle lines up parallel to the ruler, or very close to that, your fork alignment has checked out completely, and you can put it back in the bike. If one fork leg is considerably behind the other, you need to get a new fork or have this one aligned (if it is steel).

xiii-5 ALIGNING DROPOUTS ON A RIGID FORK MADE OF STEEL

You can only do this with a steel, nonsuspension fork!

Dropouts are easy to tweak out of alignment; simply pulling the bike off of a roof rack and failing to lift it high enough to clear the rack skewer will do it. Your forks may also have come with misaligned dropouts when new.

If the dropout is bent more than 7 degrees or so, or if the paint is cracked at the dropout where it is bent, it is too dangerous to bend it back. Replace the fork.

1. Install dropout-alignment tools and check the alignment as in steps 3 and 4 described in "Check Fork Alignment," §xiii-4.
2. If they are not lined up with each other, and the fork spacing is between 99 and 102mm, you can align the dropouts. If the fork spacing is wider than 102mm or less than 99mm, there is no point in aligning the dropout faces, because you must bend the fork legs as well to correct the spacing. Without an alignment table or fork jig, you cannot do this accurately. You should get a new fork or have a qualified mechanic or frame builder align your fork.

If your fork spacing is between 99mm and 102mm apart, clamp the crown or unicrown (Fig. 13.1) of the fork very tightly between two wood blocks in a well-anchored vise (Fig 11.35).

3. Grab the end of the dropout-alignment tool handle with one hand and the cup of the tool with the other. Bend each dropout until the open faces of the dropout-alignment tools are parallel, and the edges line straight up with each other (Fig. 13.7).
4. Remove the tools, and continue with §xiii-4, step 5.

xiii-6 MAINTAINING SUSPENSION FORKS

Suspension forks (Fig. 13.2) are now the standard on mountain bikes. They offer a significant performance advantage and increase the versatility of the bike. Rapid improvements in the science of bicycle suspension have resulted in a proliferation of numerous types of forks. Of course, with this rush of technology, older models quickly become obsolete. Because of that, you should remember that the details outlined here are applicable to forks commonly used in 2004 and prior years. As of this writing, the market is dominated by telescoping forks with coil springs, elastomer springs, air springs, or a combination of these inside. Many are also equipped with hydraulic damping systems. These forks share so many similarities that they lend themselves to common basic service steps.

You will be on your own if you have linkage-style forks or aftermarket upgrades retrofitted to forks; read your owner's manual carefully. Linkage-style forks rely on several pivot points, so there are plenty of places for things to go wrong. Be especially vigilant about inspecting these forks regularly.

The reality is that one of the most important things you can do in the way of suspension-fork maintenance is to check periodically with your bike shop to make sure that your fork has not been recalled by the manufacturer. If it has, make sure you get it to your shop or the manufacturer before riding it any more.

xiii-7 REMOVE FORK LEGS FROM THE FORK CROWN

This only applies to single-crown forks from prior to 1998 as well as to double-crown (a.k.a. "triple-clamp") forks—forks with a crown above and below the head tube (Fig. 13.13). The inner legs in most of the later single-crown models are pressed into the crown and cannot be removed. If you have a slotted crown, pulling the inner legs out of the crown is a more convenient way to add or replace dust boots than by pulling the outer legs off of the inner legs (§xiii-14).

When pulling the inner legs out of the crown, you can leave the fork brace and brakes on, and leave the fork steering tube and crown in the bike as you do it. Removing the fork legs from the crown is not necessary to change coil springs or elastomers or to pump (add air to) an air-oil fork.

1. Disconnect the brake cable by removing the cable end from the brake lever (Chapter 7, the reverse of §vii-6, steps 8–10).
2. Loosen the crown bolts (shown in Figs. 13.12–13.14 and 13.21). If there are two bolts on each side of your fork crown, do not completely undo one bolt while leaving the other fully tightened. Doing that places a great deal of clamping force on the remaining tight bolt, and you can strip the head while you are trying to loosen it. Instead, unscrew one bolt about one-quarter turn and then do the same to the other. Then go back to the first bolt and loosen it by another

13.12 **1995 RockShox Judy fork exploded (the inner leg is shortened for clarity)**

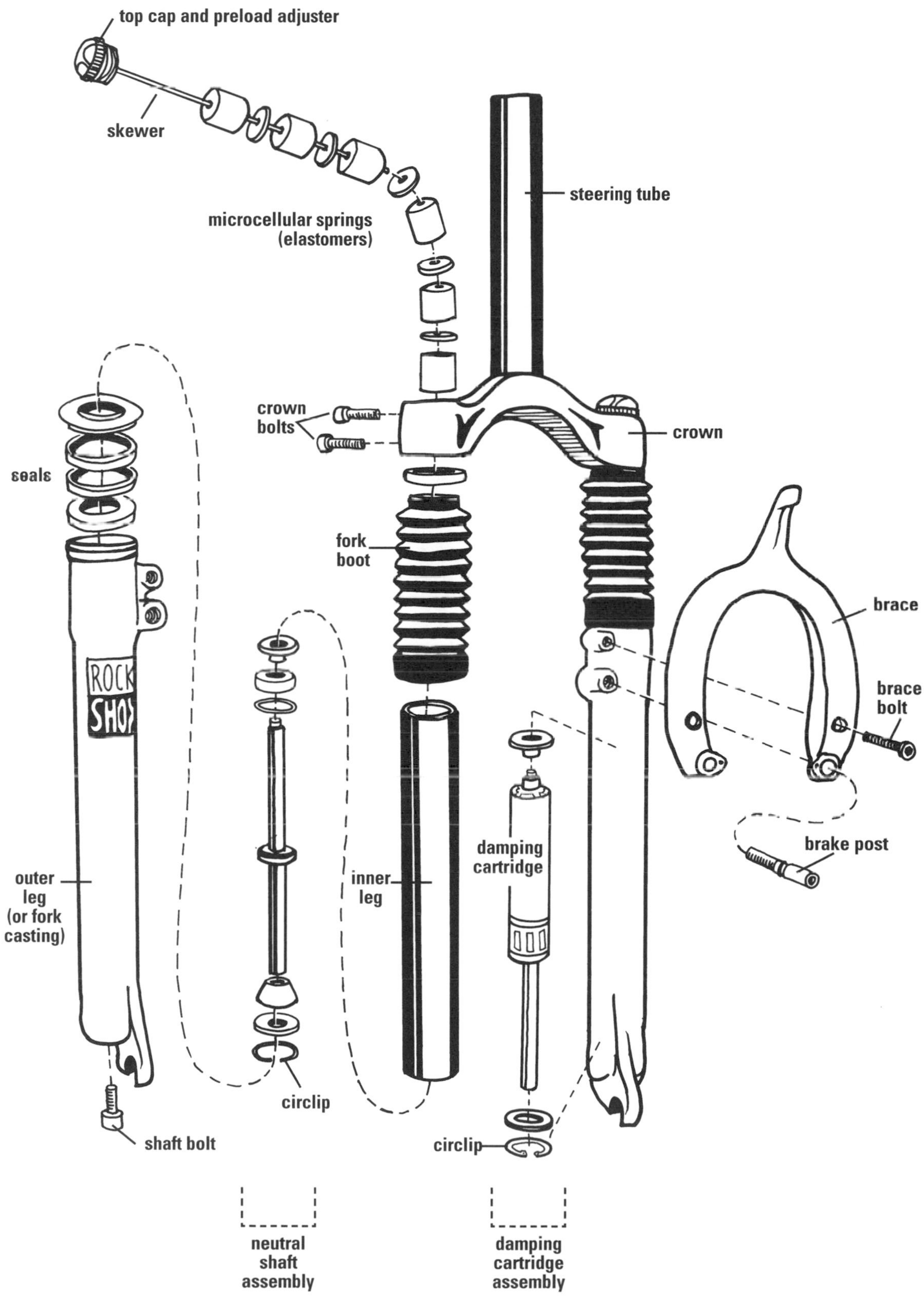

13.13 Upper crown height and orientation for head tubes of different lengths with triple-clamp forks (example shown is for RockShox)

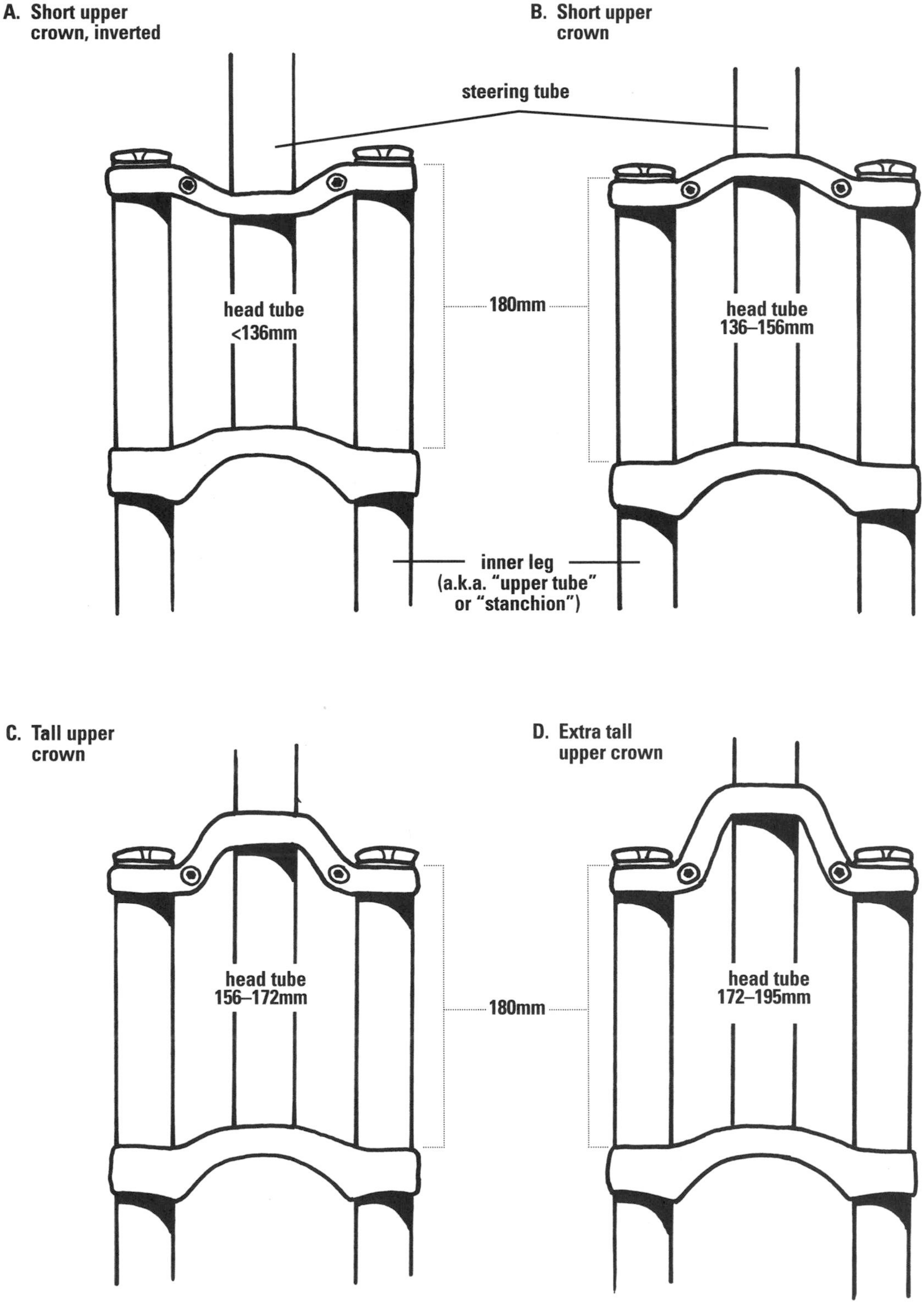

quarter-turn. Repeat until the crown is loose enough to free the leg.

3. Pull both fork legs out of the crown(s) by using a gentle rocking motion.

xiii-8 REMOVAL AND INSTALLATION OF FORK BOOTS

Any telescoping forks will stay cleaner inside with fork boots on the inner legs (shown in Figs. 13.12 and 13.21) to keep dirt off of them and the seals at the top of the outer legs. But since the 2000 model year, this is less of a big deal, thanks to effective multiple sealing systems from manufacturers. Conversely, to check your fork's travel (§xiii-10), you will need to remove the boots, if installed.

1. With a pre 1998 fork, or a double crown model, remove the fork legs from the crown (see §xiii-7 above). Pressed-in legs require you to pull off the outer legs—see §xiii-14, steps 1–4.
2. Pull the fork boots off.
3. To install boots, slide them on to the inner legs, with the large end down toward the outer legs. Make sure that you are using boots designed for your fork.
4. Pull the lip of each fork boot into the groove in the top of the outer leg. You may need to stretch the boot with a pair of needle-nose pliers to get it to slide over the outer leg behind the fork brace.
5. Replace the inner legs in the fork crown (see §xiii-9 below) or in the lower legs (§xiii-14, steps 5–9).

xiii-9 INSTALLING INNER LEGS IN A FORK CROWN

Again, this procedure only applies to single-crown forks from prior to 1998 as well as to double-crown, or triple-clamp, forks (forks with a crown above and below the head tube) (Fig. 13.13).

1. Wipe the inner legs clean, and make sure that the fork-crown bolts are loose. Install the fork boots (§xiii-8 above).
2. Insert the inner legs (a.k.a. "upper tubes") into the fork crown.

   Single-crown forks. Some Manitou forks have a lip against which the inner leg is supposed to rest. Slide the inner leg up into the crown until it hits the lip. Otherwise, on single-crown forks, push the inner leg through the crown until the top of the leg sticks up no more than 2mm above the top of the crown (Fig. 13.14).

13.14 **Using zip-tie to measure travel**

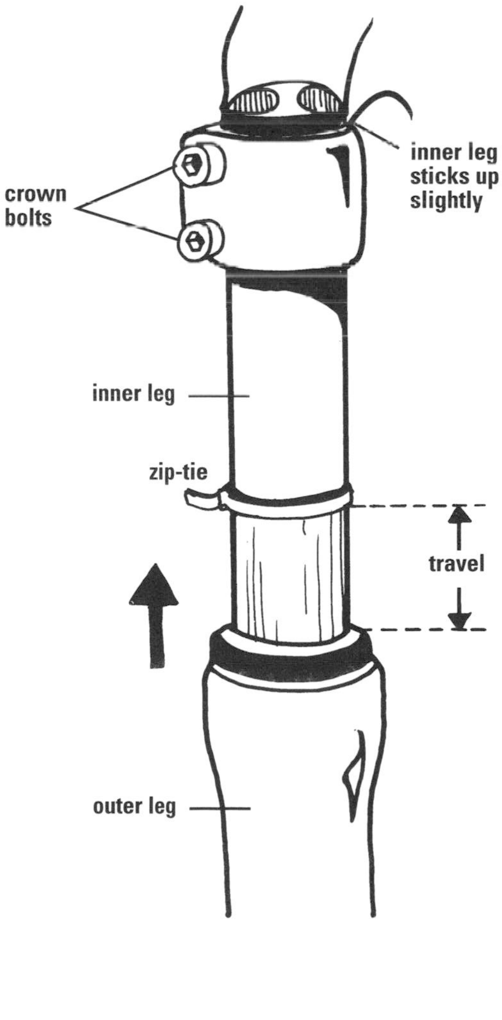

(b) **Triple-clamp forks.** Slide the inner legs up through both crowns. Make sure that the upper crown is the right shape and orientation to work with your head-tube length (Fig. 13.13). For instance, most RockShox triple-clamp forks specify that the lower crown must be located so that there are 180mm of exposed upper tubes above the lower crown. Upper crowns come in different heights (i.e., short, tall, extra tall) for different frame sizes. They can be installed either right-side up or inverted so that the crowns clamp the upper tubes just below the top while ensuring that the specified length of upper tube extends above the lower crown (Fig. 13.13).

IMPORTANT CAUTION ON DOUBLE-CROWN FORKS: *If more than the manufacturer's specified length of upper tubes is above the lower crown, then the lower crown will be too close to the tire and could hit it during large impacts, which can stop you and the bike dead, and leave you that way. Furthermore, some triple-clamp forks have shims to be inserted into the lower crown's clamping slots; other triple-clamp forks have reinforcements around the upper tubes under the lower crown. To avoid fork failure, make sure you include whatever the manufacturer intended.*

MEASURING FORK TRAVEL

3. Tighten the crown bolts to the manufacturer's specified torque. If you have paired bolts on the crown (Fig. 13.14), alternately tighten each of the two bolts on each side.

(a) Older, pre-1997, Manitou single-crown forks had a single M6 crown bolt (tightened with a 5mm hex key) on each side. The 1997 Manitou forks use a small pair of M5 bolts (tightened with a 4mm hex key) on each side (Fig. 13.21), like RockShox (Figs. 13.12 and 13.14) or RST, tightened to approximately the same torque. In 1999 and 2000, some RockShox forks utilized a small shim in their bolt-on single and double (Fig. 13.13) crowns, and their bolts require considerably higher torque.

IMPORTANT: *Fork-crown bolts are critical bolts—make sure you tighten them to the required torque specified in Appendix D!*

(b) Using an antiseize compound on titanium bolts and a medium-strength threadlock compound on steel bolts is generally recommended.

xiii-10 MEASURING FORK TRAVEL

a. Measure sag

"Sag, " also called "ride height," is the amount of fork compression that occurs when the rider sits on the bike without moving. It is a critical measurement you will need in order to properly tune a fork (§xiii-12, §xiii-13, §xiii-19, and §xiii-20). You'll need a friend to help you. Have your friend measure the distance from the top of the outer leg to the bottom of the fork crown when you are on the bike and when you are off of the bike. The difference between the two measurements is the sag. The sag can also be measured by using the trusty zip-tie method (Fig. 13.14):

1. After removing the fork boot (if installed; §xiii-8 for old forks, and xiii-14 for the rest), tighten a plastic zip-tie around one inner leg, and slide it down against the lower leg seal.
2. Gently get on the bike in your riding stance and leaning against a wall for balance.
3. Gently get off of the bike.
4. When you are off of the bike, measure the distance from the top of the outer leg to the zip-tie

(Fig. 13.14). The tuning sections (xiii-12, xiii-13, xiii-19, and xiii-20) explain what to do with the sag measurement you just obtained.

NOTE: *To measure the amount of travel you normally use while riding, go ride with the zip-tie on. Hit bumps and check the travel after you stop.*

5. Sag measurement is different with "intelligent" forks that distinguish between bumps and pedaling forces.
   (a) Because a Fox TerraLogic F80X or F100X fork is essentially locked out until the tire hits a bump, you might have the impression that it does not sag. Actually, it does; it just takes a little while to sag, because there is only a small bleed port in the TerraLogic damper that allows oil to pass by the piston so that the bike can settle to ride height. So, the only difference with measuring sag on a TerraLogic fork is that you must wait 30 seconds in step 2 above for the fork to settle to ride height before dismounting.
   (b) You can measure sag in the traditional manner on a Manitou fork with SPV (Manitou's inertial valve technology meant to distinguish between bumps and rider inputs) because first it will sink into its sag point and then provide its "platform" against pedaling forces from there.
   (c) To measure sag on a RockShox fork with Motion Control, you need to turn the compression knob to open or hit the release button on the PopLoc handlebar lever. This will give you an accurate sag reading for the fork in the open state. In the lock mode, you will get some sag as a result of the spring tube's compressing, but not as much as in the open state.

b. Measure maximum possible travel

Your fork manual should say how much travel the fork has, but its full travel can also be measured by removing the spring and then compressing the fork.

When riding with zip-ties on the inner legs, check to see if you are using up the total travel when you hit big bumps. This helps you determine the proper spring rate, preload, and damping to use. If the fork is adjusted properly for the course you are riding, it will bottom out (i.e., use the full travel) at least once on the course; otherwise, you are not using the fork's full potential. The tuning sections (xiii-12, xiii-13, xiii-19, and xiii-20) go into more detail on this subject.

1. Sit on the wheel and push up on the handlebar to extend the fork to its maximum length (some forks have negative springs pulling them down, so you have to manually extend them to find the full length); measure the distance from the crown to the top of the lower leg.
2. Remove the springs from one or both fork legs. With a coil-spring and/or elastomer fork, remove the top cap (Fig. 13.15) from either both sides of the fork crown or from just one side, depending on whether it has springs in both or in only one leg. Some forks have plastic knurled nuts (Figs. 13.12 and 13.15), whereas other forks need to be removed with a wrench (usually 22mm). On older forks that have crown bolts and a split crown, loosening the crown bolts makes it easier to unscrew the cap.
   (b) With an air-oil fork, release the air from one or both legs, depending on whether both have compressed air chambers, usually by simply depressing the pin on the Schrader valve atop the crown under the valve cap. On older

MEASURING FORK TRAVEL

13.15 **Removing spring stack from Manitou SX**

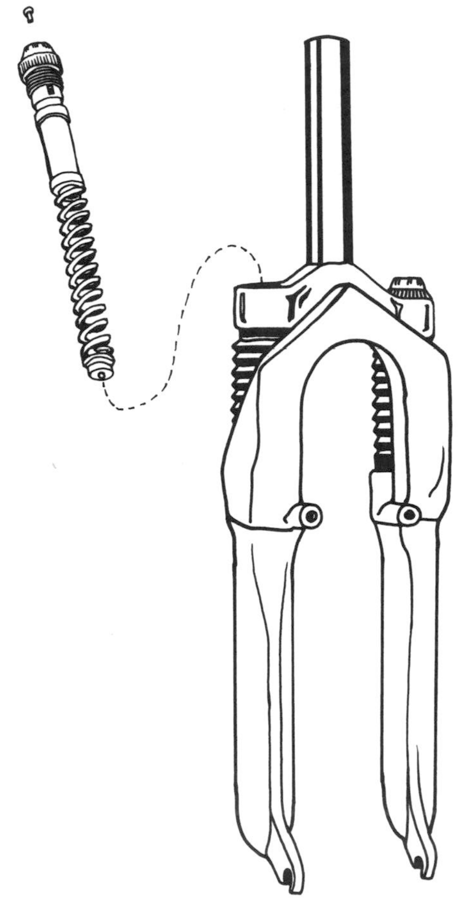

RockShox Mag-series forks, remove either the Phillips screw (Fig. 13.17) or the plastic snap-on cap covering the air hole, turn the compression-damping adjustment to the highest setting, moisten the needle of a ball-pumping adapter, and stick it down into the hole to release the air. On RockShox SIDs, original models require a moistened ball needle, whereas subsequent models (up until 2001) have an inset Schrader valve and require a special pump adapter that is screwed into the valve for inflation. Current air forks from most manufacturers have standard Schrader valves. Also, some air forks have multiple valves—either two on the top of the leg or on both ends of the leg, the second one being a negative spring, which you need not let out to fully compress the fork.

3. Push down on the handlebar and measure the distance from the bottom of the crown to the top of the outer leg when the fork is fully compressed. The difference between the fully extended and fully compressed measurements is the total available travel you have. Note that negative springs and top-out and bottom-out cushions make this a bit less simple. Pulling the fork up to full extension before removing the springs and leaning on it with your full weight after removing them gets you the most accurate numbers.

CAUTION: *To make sure that your tire cannot hit the fork crown, measure the distance from the top of your tire to the bottom of the fork crown. Compare this measurement to your total fork travel, or remove the springs and push the fork down as hard as you can toward the tire. If the crown can hit your tire on full compression, it can stop you dead (literally!). Use a smaller tire if necessary to ensure that the tire cannot hit the crown. Many fork manuals specify the largest tire you can safely use with a specific fork.*

xiii-11 MINOR MAINTENANCE OF TELESCOPING SUSPENSION FORKS

On old fork models, if you do minor maintenance frequently and keep the inner legs covered with fork boots, you can greatly increase the life of the seals as well as the time between fork overhauls. A dry or dirty dust seal rubbing on a dry or dirty inner leg usually causes stickiness in suspension forks.

1. With the fork boots removed or slid up, wipe off the outside of the seal on top of each outer leg

and the length of the inner leg between the outer leg and crown.

2. Put a thin coat of Teflon-fortified lubricant on the outside of the seals and inner legs (the area under the zip-tie in Fig. 13.14).
3. Pull the fork boots back into position. You may need to stretch the bottom of each fork boot with needle-nose pliers to get it in the groove around the top of the outer leg and behind the fork brace.

xiii-12 TUNING COIL-SPRING AND ELASTOMER FORKS

Telescoping elastomer and coil-spring suspension forks (Figs. 13.12, 13.15, and 13.21) are quite simple in principle and are generally straightforward to adjust and maintain. After you understand the why and the how of adjusting your coil-spring or elastomer fork from reading this section, you can use §xiii-19 and §xiii-20 as guides for refining the adjustments.

a. Setting spring preload

Spring preload, the amount of compression of the spring at rest, can be adjusted on most mid- to high-end coil-spring or elastomer forks, but it should be done only after you have installed the correct spring for you. On most mid- to high-end coil-spring or elastomer forks, you can adjust the preload simply by turning the adjuster knobs on the top of the fork crown (Fig. 13.16)—even while riding, as you encounter terrain variations. On forks that have springs in only one leg (usually the left leg), you have only one preload adjuster. (Note that the "U-Turn" knob on some RockShox models adjusts travel, not preload.)

Rotating the adjuster knobs clockwise gives a firmer ride by tightening down on (and thus shortening) the spring stack. Rotating the adjuster knobs counterclockwise softens the ride. Make sure the top cap surrounding the knob does not unscrew from the fork crown; you may need to hold it tight with one hand (or a wrench) when you loosen the adjuster knob. Check the top cap occasionally to make sure it is not unscrewed or being forced out because of stripped threads. If its threads seem to be stripped, before you ride any more, get a new top cap right away; if the top cap pops off, the spring can shoot up into your face at high velocity.

13.16 Adjusting spring preload

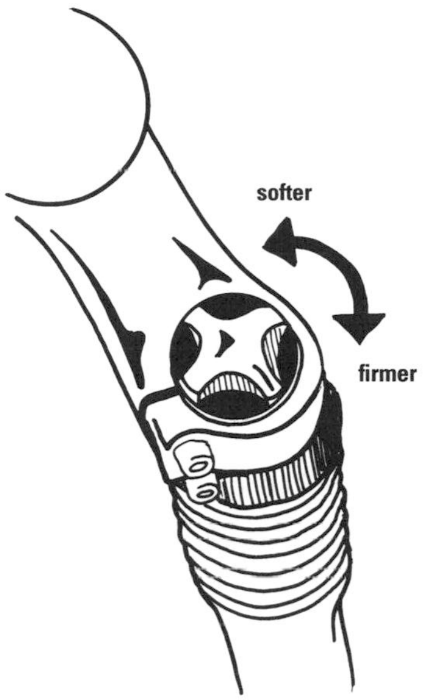

Preloading the springs does not limit the full travel for large bumps; it determines the force required for a bump to initially compress the fork, and it uses up some of the spring's length and therefore makes it stiffen up faster as the fork moves. Varying the preload also changes the fork's sag, and it shortens the life of the springs, as they are being compressed even while your bike is hanging in the garage. It is better to change the spring stack (see xiii-12b, which follows) to get the ride you want and minimize preload; use the preload adjustment only as a way to change the fork quickly during a particular ride.

b. Replacing elastomers and coil springs

To make major changes in the fork's spring rate, you must change the springs inside of the fork (Fig. 13.15). Manufacturers usually color-code the elastomers—and often coil springs as well—for stiffness, although you can tell the difference between stiff and soft elastomer bumpers by squeezing them between your fingers. (Some manufacturers refer to the elastomers as "MCUs" for "micro-cellular urethane," referring to small air voids trapped inside the urethane spring.) Extra springs usually come with the fork, or you can buy them from a dealer.

The fork needs stiffer springs (or, as a poor second choice, more spring preload) if it sags excessively when you sit on it. Set your sag at about 20 percent of your fork's total travel, and perhaps closer to 10 percent for cross-country racing. The fork needs softer springs (or less compression damping—see the following section) if hard impacts with large bumps do not use the fork's full travel.

TUNING COIL-SPRING & ELASTOMER FORKS

1. Unscrew the top cap (or caps, if you have springs in both legs) counterclockwise. On its old, pre-1998 forks, RockShox recommends that you first loosen the crown bolts to relieve inward pressure on the fork legs before unscrewing the caps. On some forks, the top caps can be unscrewed with your fingers, whereas others require a wrench (22mm is common) to unscrew the top cap. Again, on Manitou TPC (Twin Piston Cartridge) or RockShox "Pure" damping systems, you only have springs in one leg.
2. Pull the spring(s) out of the fork (Fig. 13.15). Oftentimes, they will come out attached to the top cap(s), and several springs may be snapped together to each other with plastic connectors. On many older (pre-1996 or so) forks, the top cap is connected to a rod (the "skewer" in Fig. 13.12) that runs through each of the elastomer bumpers. If the springs do not come out with the top caps, turn the bike upside down or compress the fork to get them out.
3. Clean any old grease off of the coil springs, elastomers, skewers, plastic connectors, and whatever else you found in the fork.
4. Choose the coil springs and/or elastomers that you intend to use.
   (a) Again, when choosing the springs, don't be afraid to bottom the fork (as long as you do not use a tire bigger than recommended by the manufacturer so it can't hit the crown). If you do not bottom it once on the course, you are not getting the full potential out of the fork.
   (b) If any of the elastomers are misshapen or look squished or worn in any way, replace them. Some manufacturers provide a nominal and replacement length for coil springs and elastomers. Measure your springs and check them!
5. Apply a new coating of grease to the new parts and everything you just cleaned. Make sure you grease the outside of the coil springs to reduce the noise of the springs rubbing inside the legs. However, in forks with open-bath dampers, hydraulic oil sloshes all around in the spring chamber, so there is no need to grease the springs. Make sure you don't let any dirt fall down into the leg.
6. Put the spring stack in the fork legs (Fig. 13.15), and screw the caps down. Be sure to retighten the crown bolts to the required torque, if you loosened them.

c. Fine-tuning damping

High-end elastomer- and coil-spring forks have a hydraulic damping cartridge or cylinder (Figs. 13.12 and 13.21) inside one or both lower legs. Some elastomer forks do not have these. (If there is no bolt at the bottom of the fork leg—as in Figs. 13.18 and 13.19—it does not have a damper.) Of those with damping cartridges, not all are adjustable. You can be sure that almost any high-end fork (other than superlight race-only models) has adjustable damping—look for adjuster knobs on the top and bottom of the legs.

Compression damping

Compression damping controls the speed at which the spring compresses during the fork's downstroke. Speed of movement is controlled by oil (or compressed air, in the case of the Englund TotalAir system) as it moves through or around a piston that is being forced through the oil chamber. Varying the size of the hole or the thickness of the oil varies how easily the piston can move through the oil. Excessive compression damping will give you a harsh ride over repeated rocks, but it will feel good when you hit something big. Too little compression damping will lead to harsh bottoming out on big hits, and the bike will bob noticeably when you are climbing, but will feel smooth as you ride fast over small, closely spaced bumps.

Some forks have a "lockout," which closes off the orifice in the compression-damping piston, thus preventing the fork from compressing rapidly. If you really slam into something with most lockout systems, you can still blow off the emergency shim stack covering the oil hole through the piston, and the fork will compress. The lockout knob is generally on top of the fork leg, but on a Cannondale single-sided Lefty fork with E.L.O. (electronic lockout), the lockout button is on the handlebar, and many manufacturers offer handlebar-mounted lockout-lever options.

You can crank down your compression damping (or use the lockout, if you have it) to stiffen your fork for riding on smooth surfaces.

Some modern forks have an automatic "inertial valve" overriding the compression damping adjustment that distinguishes between pedaling forces and bump forces. The fork will be highly damped until a bump of a certain threshold magnitude of impact is encountered, at which point the inertial valve opens and the fork moves freely (within the constraints of the compression damping adjustments you have set). This threshold impact magnitude to open the inertial valve is also adjustable on some forks. An inertial valve system is often called "pedal platform," and, depending on manufacturer, carries an acronym like Terra Logic (Fox), SPV (Maritou), Motion Control (Rock Shox), TST (Marzocchi), Spul (Spinner), etc.

Rebound damping

Rebound damping controls the speed at which the fork returns to its original position after it has been compressed and released. As with compression damping, speed of movement is controlled by oil (or compressed air, in the case of Englund TotalAir) moving through or around a piston as it is being drawn back through the oil chamber. Varying the size of the hole or the thickness of the oil varies how easily the piston can move through the oil. The damper can have two pistons, one for compression damping and one for rebound damping, or the same piston can control both compression and rebound.

Rebound damping is too high when you get a harsh ride over repetitive bumps because the fork packs up (i.e., it keeps getting shorter with each bump, because it cannot return fully before the next impact). Too little rebound damping will let the fork snap back too fast (called "the pogo effect"). It is usually best to start with minimal rebound damping so the fork is very active and then increase the damping to limit the pogo effect.

Damping adjustments

On most high-end fork models, compression damping is adjusted by turning the knob on the top of the right-hand fork leg (except for early Manitou TPCs, which had the damping chamber in the left leg). This knob controls orifices in the upper piston. On forks with a lockout lever, the compression-damping adjuster is eliminated in favor of providing lockout, but some lockout levers are multiposition for compression-damping adjustment, rather than just on or off. (You can still adjust compression damping on a fork with just an on/off lockout lever, but you have to do it internally. On older Manitou TPCs, you pull out the upper piston [§xiii-16, Fig. 13.28] and turn a setscrew on the side of the shaft with a hex key.) On most forks with a damper only in one leg, a knob on the bottom of the same leg controls rebound damping by regulating orifices in the lower (or only) piston. For both the compression and rebound knobs, turning the knob clockwise increases damping and turning it counterclockwise decreases damping.

Some high-end RockShox forks (2000-model SID SL) have a damping adjuster on the bottom of the leg that you push in (its normal position) and turn to adjust rebound. If you pull the knob outward until it clicks and then turn it, you adjust compression damping.

On pre-TPC (pre-1998) Manitou Mach 5, SX, SX-Ti, or EFC, the rebound damping is adjustable by turning a knob at the bottom of the left leg. Turning the adjuster knob (Fig. 13.18) clockwise increases rebound damping (and slows the return stroke) and turning counterclockwise decreases rebound damping. You can only change compression damping in these Manitou forks by varying the shim stack inside the damping unit.

On all pre-1997 adjustable RockShox Judy models, the compression damping is adjusted by inserting a 2mm hex key through the center of the hollow shaft bolt at the bottom of the left leg (the bolt is pictured in Fig. 13.19). Clockwise rotation increases compression damping. Later models, including Judy, SID, and Psylo, have a removable knob attached to a 2.5mm or 3mm hex key inserted through the bolt similar to that on the Manitou (Fig. 13.18).

Early (1997–1998) Judy DH and DHO forks include an additional adjustable cartridge in the right leg to control rebound damping. It can also be adjusted with a 2mm hex key on a DH through the center of the hollow shaft bolt on the bottom of the right fork leg, and with a 3mm hex key, or an operational knob, on the DHO. Clockwise rotation increases rebound damping (slows the return stroke). It is very important that you do not turn this adjuster any more than two full turns counterclockwise!

Marzocchi Bombers and Fox models also generally have adjustable rebound damping knobs at the bottom of the leg.

If you have no damping adjustment knobs, you can also adjust damping by changing to a different viscosity of hydraulic oil—see §xiii-15 and §xiii-16 for instructions on how to do it. If the fork is moving too fast, go up 2.5 points in viscosity. To speed it up, or adjust for wintertime cold, lighten the oil by 2.5 points in viscosity.

The inertial valve on some forks is adjustable either with a knob or lever, or with an air valve which prevents the inertial valve from opening until a threshold impact is encountered. Adjust it (by turning the knob or lever by adjusting the air pressure behind the inertial valve) so the fork stays as damped as you want against pedaling and moves in response to the bump size you wish.

xiii-13 TUNING AIR-SPRUNG FORKS

The lightest forks use compressed air as a spring. It would, after all, be hard to come up with a spring lighter than one made of air!

After you understand the why and the how of adjusting your air-sprung fork from reading this section, you can use §xiii-19 and §xiii-20 as guides for refining the adjustment.

a. Adjusting positive air pressure

Greater air pressure in the positive spring chamber means a stiffer fork, and vice versa. It is a good idea to check your air pressure every couple of weeks, for all forks lose pressure over time.

Do not use a tire pump on the fork; the large stroke volume is poor for adjusting low volumes of air at high pressure. The gauge won't tell you how much air is left in the fork, and unless your fork takes a ball-inflation needle, you will lose most of the pressure when removing the pump head. You need a shock pump with a no-leak fitting, as the Schrader valves on air forks can lose air when removing the pump. RockShox Mag-series forks, early SIDs, and the air assist on post-2002 Judys use valves that require a ball-inflation needle (the kind you use for a soccer ball). SID forks from 1999 to 2000, and all Marzocchi air forks, require a special adapter that fits down in the recessed Schrader valve and prevents air from escaping as the adapter is removed. Newer shock pumps have a no-leak fitting built into the head that prevents leakage from any standard Schrader valve.

Pump to the desired pressure—something that varies widely with manufacturer; you will have to consult your fork manual and/or experiment. Early air forks such as RockShox Mags run low pressure—around 40 psi—but many air forks use considerably higher pressure than that. Experiment with different pressures to find what you like best.

IMPORTANT: *If your fork has an air negative spring as well as an air positive spring, always pump the positive spring chamber first. If you pump the negative spring first, it can pull the fork down (i.e., shorten it) and increase the volume of the negative spring chamber.*

13.17 Inflating a RockShox Mag or early SID air-oil fork

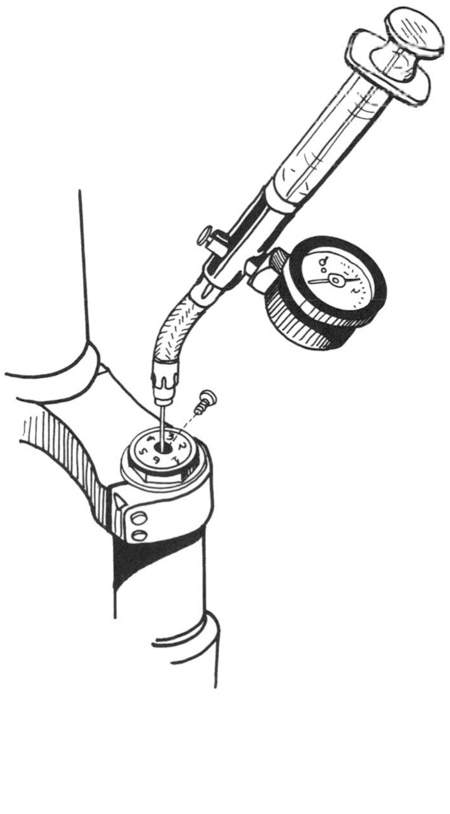

Then, if you pump the positive spring, it will drive the pressure in both chambers, reaching incredibly high-pressure levels and still not bringing the fork up to full length.

For RockShox Mag 10, 20, 21, 21 SLTi, RockShox's pump is just a plastic syringe with a dial gauge on it (Fig 1.1A). The air valve on each leg is located beneath either a Phillips screw or a plastic pry-off cap on top of the compression-damping adjustment knob (Fig. 13.17). Tighten down the adjustment knob before inserting the pump needle to avoid pinching the rubber valve on the top of the adjuster rod inside, causing it to leak. Moisten the needle, and insert it into the valve hole (Fig. 13.17).

The fork needs higher air pressure if it sags excessively when you sit on it. Set your sag at about 20 percent of your fork's total travel—and perhaps as little as 10 percent for cross-country racing. The fork needs softer springs (or less compression damping—see §xiii-12c) if hard impacts with large bumps do not use the fork's full travel. Remember that the main spring will be partially balanced by the negative spring, if you have one—see the next section (§xiii-13b).

TUNING AIR-SPRUNG FORKS

b. Adjusting the negative spring

The negative spring in an air fork works against the main air spring to actually compress the fork. This action makes the fork more compliant over small bumps and causes it to behave more like a coil spring (which has a linear, rather than a progressive [see the following paragraph for explanation] increase in spring force as it is shortened) through its initial stage of travel. Early air forks did not have negative springs, and the rider suffered on stutter bumps owing to the high initial force it took to get the spring moving.

Air springs have a "progressive spring rate," meaning that as the spring is compressed, the force it takes to move the next increment of travel goes up exponentially, rather than linearly. You will feel this exponential increase in the force required if you try to pump up a bike tire without first opening the tire's Presta valve. Your tire pump will have just become a big air spring! A coil spring, on the other hand, has a "linear spring rate" through much of its stroke—it takes the same increase in force to move 1mm farther in the travel, whether you are at the beginning or middle of the spring's compression. Also, the tight air seals in an air fork usually mean it has more "stiction" (coefficient of static friction—the force it takes to make it move initially) than a coil-spring fork. So it takes more force to get the air fork to move initially on a little bump, and the force it takes to keep moving farther into the stroke on bigger bumps ramps up. A negative spring, by pulling the fork down, can help the fork react quickly to small bumps. An air-type negative spring will also start in its fully compressed (hence fully ramped-up point), so as it moves through the stroke, its force ramps down rapidly while the main spring's force is ramping up rapidly, so the net spring rate of the fork is fairly linear.

Newer high-end air forks usually have an air-type negative spring, with a second Schrader valve either at the bottom or the top of the left leg. It is simple with these forks to play with the balance between the pressure in your main air spring(s) and in the negative spring to find the ride you like.

Again, be sure to pump the positive spring before pumping the negative spring. Some air forks (such as some RockShox Hydra-Air Dukes and SIDs, Manitou MARS, and Black) have a coil-type negative spring, and many of these are not adjustable. Early (1998) SID forks have a coil-type negative spring on top of the cartridge shaft under the right-hand piston that is adjustable. There is a circlip constraining the top end of the spring, and you can clip it into any of six grooves to vary the compression of the negative spring. You have to take the fork apart and remove the cartridge to do it, though (§viii-14 and §viii-15).

c. Adjusting damping

See §xiii-12c on how and why to adjust damping on most air forks, as it is the same as on coil-spring or elastomer forks. Even early air forks such as old RockShox Mag-series forks can be adjusted by turning the knobs on top of the fork crown (Fig. 13.17); turning the knob clockwise increases the compression damping. Be aware that not all forks have adjustable damping without disassembling and reconfiguring the damper.

d. Other adjustments

Changing air volume in an air-sprung fork is similar to varying preload in a coil-spring or elastomer fork. Reducing air volume makes the fork stiffen up faster as it moves (i.e., the spring rate ramps up faster), and vice versa. For example, if you find an air pressure that works well, but you bottom the fork too often, you can decrease the air volume to stiffen the fork sooner with the same air pressure. On virtually any air fork, you can decrease the volume in an air cylinder by removing the valve and pouring some oil into the chamber. On the 1998 RockShox SID, you can change the air volume by changing the piston height: increase the volume by tightening the piston deeper into the fork and decrease it by unscrewing the piston. You get at the piston by releasing the air with a ball needle and unscrewing the top nut with an adjustable wrench. Screw the piston in or out with an 8mm hex key.

If you have the fork apart (§xiii-14), you can change oil viscosity (§xiii-15 and §xiii-16) or the size of compression- or rebound-damping bleed holes to change the speed of the fork (see §xiii-12c) on compression or rebound. You can also change travel on some models (see §xiii-17).

xiii-14 OVERHAULING FORKS WITH BOLTS AT THE BOTTOM OF THE OUTER LEGS

Frequent fork overhaul is not generally as necessary with modern (say, post-2000 or so) forks as it is with rear shocks or with old forks. This is true because of the far larger amount of oil in a fork than in a rear shock, as well as the far better seals, oil baths, and other lubrication systems that most forks in the 1990s lacked. Nonetheless, it is an important maintenance procedure to keep your bike performing optimally. Your fork needs overhauling if, as you gradually lean harder on your handlebar, it is hard to get started moving downward, and, when the fork finally does compress, it goes down chunk, chunk, chunk like going down a set of stairs.

This section deals with standard telescoping suspension forks whose lower legs slide up over the inner legs and in which the damper shafts and spring-side shafts are bolted through the bottom of the lower leg (Fig. 13.2). Really early forks, and cheap forks, often lack this external bolt securing the lower leg to the internal shaft. I make no attempt to explain their service, because there are very few of the old ones left around, and the cheap ones aren't worth the time spent working on them, because performance will still be terrible despite the effort.

On the other hand, the current number of suspension-fork brands, and particularly the proliferation of fork models, makes a detailed description of the service of all of them in this book unrealistic. This book does a good job with the old forks that were the top models in 2001 and earlier, which often shared many characteristics and had fewer features than current high-end forks. The seals and lubrication systems on those forks tended to be wanting, and as they are getting long in the tooth now, frequent service is a necessity. Simpler, lower-end modern forks can often also be overhauled by following the instructions in this section.

However, the high-end forks of today (particularly the ones with sophisticated damping systems that can distinguish between impacts and pedal forces) are so complicated (and vary so much from model to model and manufacturer to manufacturer) that if you want to do anything more than change the oil in one, the only realistic thing to do is to refer you to their Web sites to download your fork manual. Printed manuals that come with forks often do not have detailed service information because most consumers will not use it, and if printed in six or so languages would be too big a tome to include in the box. But manufacturer Web sites, which hardly existed when the first edition of this book came out in 1996, now offer a wealth of easily accessible information. Go to www.sram.com for RockShox, www.answerproducts.com for Manitou, www.marzocchi.com for Marzocchi, and www.foxracingshox.com for Fox. There are others of course, but you get the idea.

On 1999 (and later) Manitou forks with the "Microlube" grease fitting on the back of the leg, you do not need to take the fork apart. Just inject the proper Manitou Microlube grease (it is thinner than most bicycle grease) with a fine-tipped grease gun into the grease fitting. A few squirts in each leg, and your fork will feel smooth again. It only takes a bit; if you try to fill it with grease, you will lock up the

13.18 Damping adjuster knob on Manitou SX fork

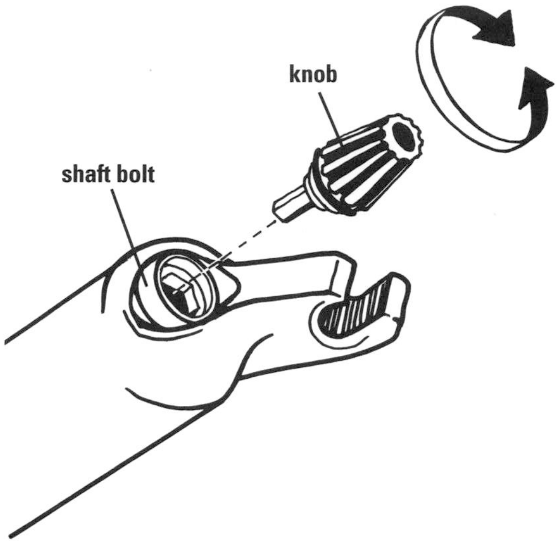

fork! However, you can still take it apart as described below if you want to.

These instructions apply to most mid- to high-end forks later than 1995 or so. The fork must have bolts on the bottoms of the outer legs to be disassembled in this way—see Figures 13.18 and 13.19. (Forks without bottom bolts are usually either very old or low end. You can usually get these forks apart, too. You either need snapring pliers to remove the snapring at the top of each outer leg or a long hex key to get at the head of the compression bolt way down inside after removing the springs. Keep track of everything and put it all back together the same way after cleaning and lubricating.)

Now, back to overhauling:

1. Disconnect the cable for the front brake (Chapter 7) and remove the front wheel (Chapter 2, §ii-2). It is easier if you remove the fork from the bike as well (Chapter 11, §xi-18 and §xi-19).
2. Unscrew the bolts on the bottoms of the fork legs (Figs. 13.18 and 13.19), leaving a few

13.19 **Adjusting damping on early RockShox Judy fork**

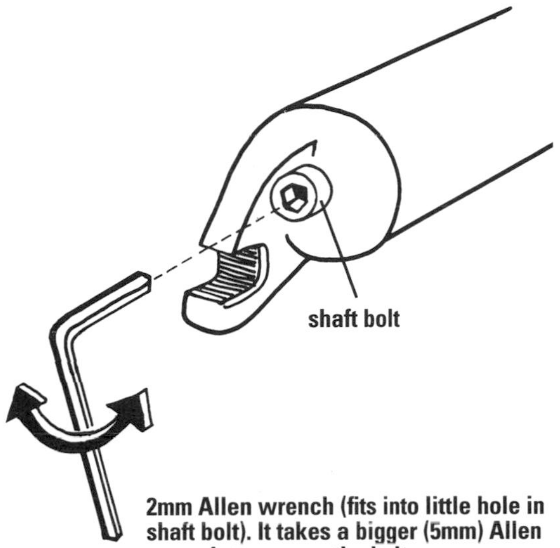
shaft bolt
2mm Allen wrench (fits into little hole in shaft bolt). It takes a bigger (5mm) Allen wrench to remove the bolt.

13.20 **Freeing an inner leg from the lower bushings**

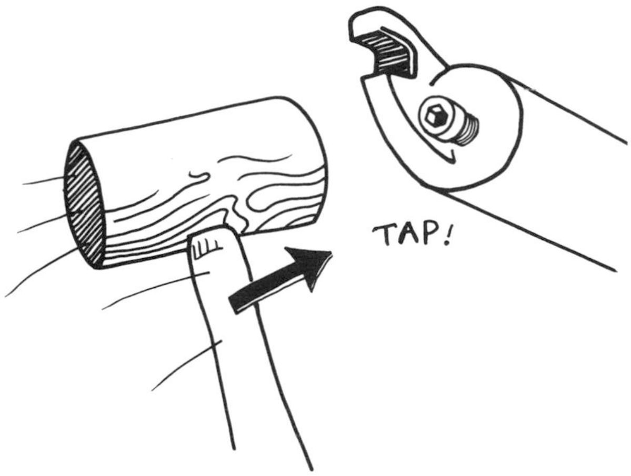
TAP!

threads left engaged. If the bolts are not backing out, you are turning the shafts inside the fork along with them, and you may need to tighten down on the preload adjuster on a coil-spring or elastomer fork (Fig. 13.16) or add air to an air fork (Fig. 13.17).

NOTE: *The hex key size usually needed for these bolts varies from 4mm to 8mm, and the bolt is sometimes hidden under a damping adjustment knob that you must first yank out (Fig. 13.18). Some forks (2000-year SID SL) have a damping adjuster knob that you remove with a Phillips screwdriver, and then you use an open-end wrench on the bolt. Some air forks (SID Race and SL, Duke Race) have an air valve at the bottom of one leg for the air-type negative spring. After deflating this valve, you unscrew the bolt the valve emerges from with an open-end wrench.*

WARNING: *Do not unscrew the 5mm bolt in the center of an old Manitou's 8mm aluminum bolt. This is the damping adjuster, and if you unscrew it a bunch of turns, you will break it. This will create an oil spill all over your work area, and you will have to buy a new damping unit. Use an 8mm hex key on the large bolt itself (Fig. 13.18) to unscrew it. The same goes for an old RockShox Judy (Fig. 13.19)—use a 5mm hex key on the bolt, not the 2mm hex key that reaches through it to the damper adjuster.*

3. Before unscrewing the bolts completely (while they are still threaded in a few turns), tap the bolts with a mallet (Fig. 13.20) until the inner legs are free from the lower bushings. Remove the bolts. Do this over a bucket, in case your fork has an oil bath inside (or has a blown cartridge that has leaked oil inside the leg). Pull the entire assembly—including both lower legs and the fork brace—off of the inner legs.

NOTE: *On a fork with a removable fork brace (Fig. 13.12), there is no need to remove the brace. If you do remove it, be very careful not to overtighten the brace bolt or the brake post, as it is not hard to strip the threads in the aluminum or magnesium outer legs. Use Loctite on the threads.*

13.21 **1997 Manitou SX partially exploded**

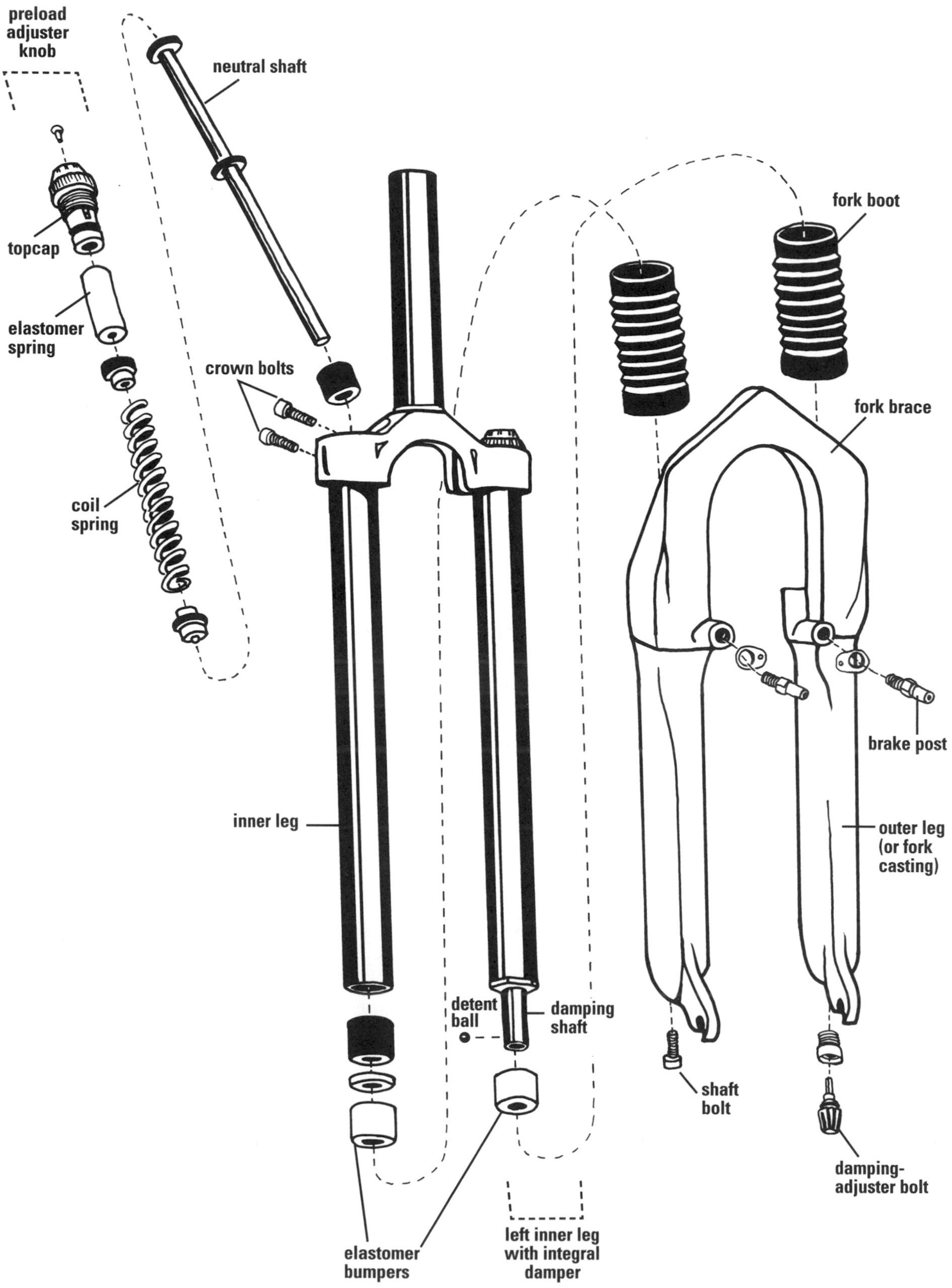

13.22 **Cleaning lower bushing**

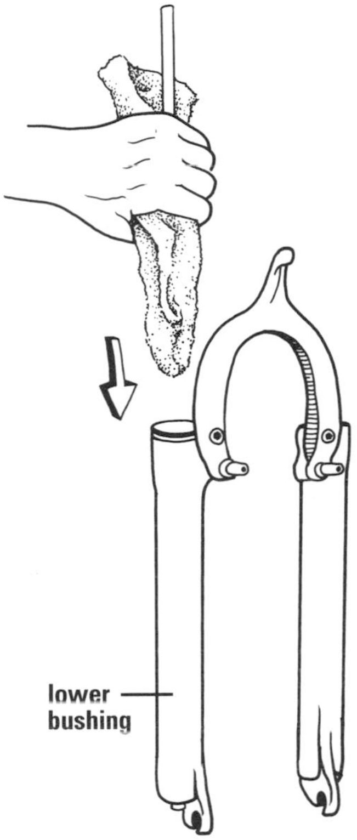

13.23 **Greasing lower bushing**

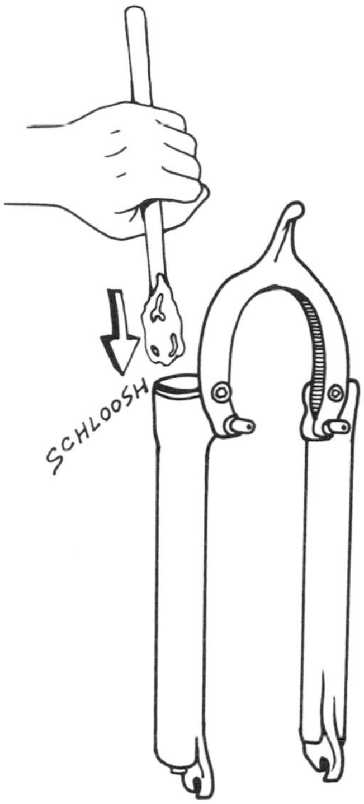

13.24 **Greasing inner leg**

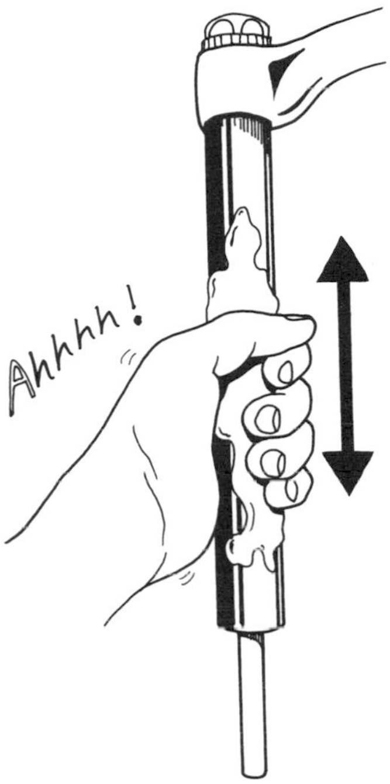

4. With a clean, lint-free rag, clean the inner legs and the shafts sticking out of them. Check the damper shaft (Figs. 13.12 and 13.21) for surface abrasion or bending and for oil leaking from the damper. If you want to work on the damper, skip to the next sections (xiii-15 and xiii-16).

NOTE: *On many older Manitous, there is an elastomer around the damper shaft that extends from the inner leg (Fig. 13.21). It is a good idea to clean and grease it, but if you remove it, be ready to catch the steel ball that will fall out. This is the "detent" ball for the damper that puts the clicks in the damper adjustment!*

5. Clean the wiper seals and bushings inside of the outer legs. There are two bushings in each outer leg: one at the top and one halfway down. You need to reach the bottom one with the rag wrapped around a long rod (Fig. 13.22). The top seals can be pried out and cleaned or replaced if need be. If there is a foam ring between two wiper seals, you may want to at least pull that out and clean it well with solvent so that it can do its job properly. Be sure to relube the foam ring with shock oil prior to reinstallation. If the bushings are shot (there would be movement of the inner leg wobbling inside the bushings), they can be replaced—but the job generally takes tools that only a well-equipped bike shop or service center would have.
6. Apply a thin layer of nonlithium grease (such as RockShox Judy Butter or Buzzy's Slick Honey lube) to the bushings and wipers in the outer legs. To grease the lower bushings, use a long rod (make sure it is clean), slather grease on the end of it, and reach down to the lower bushings with it (Fig. 13.23). It is counterproductive to grease

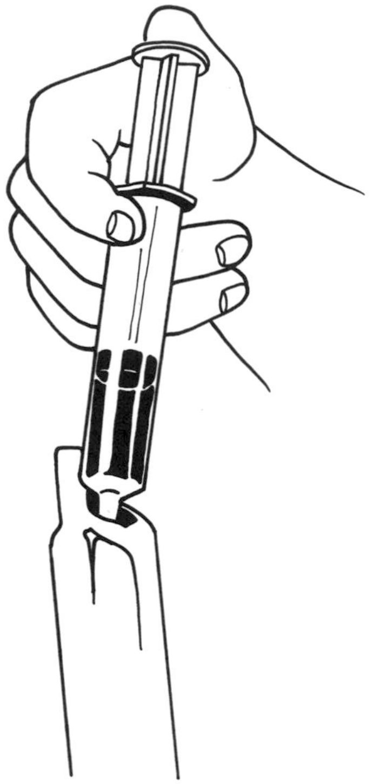

13.25 **Making an oil bath**

PRO TIP

OLD FORKS

If your fork does not have an oil bath or the Manitou Microlube system, you can keep it lubricated longer by putting an oil bath in. Squirt 15cc or so of automatic transmission fluid in through the bottom bolt holes before replacing the bolts (Fig. 13.25). It keeps lubricant sloshing around up to the upper bushings as you ride. Use a brass washer under your bottom bolt (Fig. 13.19) to reduce leakage. Don't put an oil bath in forks with internal shaft bolts you reach from the top (hint: there is no bolt on the bottom of the outer leg), as you can crack the legs by tightening the bolts down onto trapped oil.

between the upper and lower bushings, so don't do it. With your (clean) hand, smear a thin layer of the same grease on the inner legs (Fig. 13.24).

7. Slide the outer legs gently over the inner legs (after the fork boots, if you have them). Take care not to damage the upper dust seals or the lower bushings. Push the outer legs on completely. It may help if you spread the outer tube and fork brace assembly slightly while you rock it side to side to engage the bushings on the inner legs.
8. Replace the oil bath (Fig. 13.25) if your fork has a closed cartridge and a bath inside the outer legs. For example, in the bottom of a SID XC right leg, pour 100cc of 15-weight fork oil (or automatic transmission fluid); in both legs of a SID SL and the left leg of a SID XC, pour 10cc of RedRum (RockShox thick red oil).
9. Put the shaft bolts (Figs. 13.18–13.19) back in the bottom of the outer legs, engaging the threads in the damper and neutral shaft. Push in the inner legs farther, if the bolt threads do not engage.
10. Tighten the bolts. RockShox recommends 60 in-lbs of torque. Manitou recommends 110–130 in-lbs. See Appendix D for other torques.
11. Turn the fork upright.
12. Replace the oil bath in open-oil-bath systems. On SIDs and Dukes, pour 2ml of RedRum on top of the air piston, and replace the top caps. On Judys, drop the springs in both legs, and pour 120cc of 5-weight fork oil in with each spring.
13. Replace the springs (on coil-spring or elastomer forks).
14. Replace the top caps. On air forks, inflate the main spring(s) and the negative spring (if included).

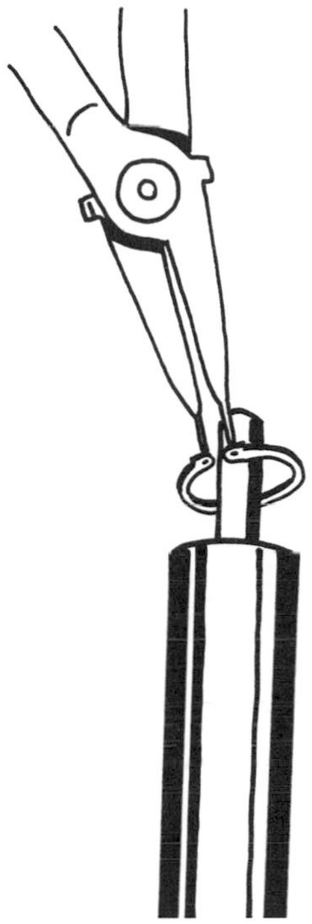

13.26 **Removing cartridge-retaining circlip from RockShox inner leg**

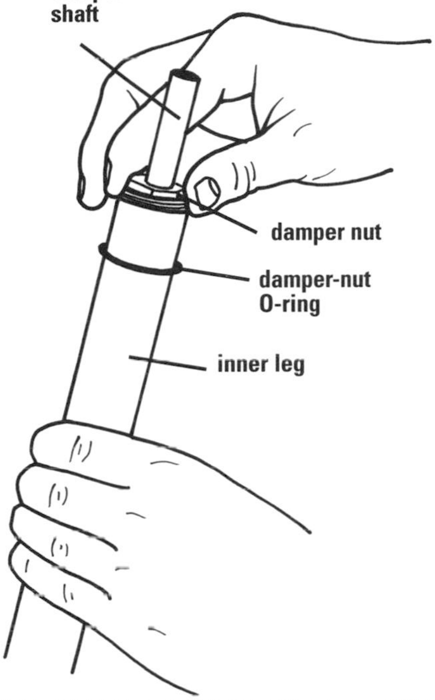

13.27 **Hand tighten old-style (pre-TPC) Manitou damper nut with O-ring slipped down around inner leg**

xiii-15 DAMPER OIL CHANGE ON PRE-1998 MANITOUS AND REPLACING ROCKSHOX CARTRIDGES

LEVEL 3

This section focuses primarily on Manitou pre-TPC dampers because they are easily worked on and built right into the inner leg; skip to §xiii-16 for Manitou TPC and RockShox "Pure" damping systems.

RockShox HydraCoil and Marzocchi open-bath dampers get an oil change whether you want it or not when you pull the fork apart as described above in §xiii-14. For removing and replacing a closed RockShox cartridge, follow these instructions as well:

1. Start by taking the fork apart through step 4 in §xiii-14 above.
2. Remove the coil-spring or elastomer fork springs (§xiii-12b) or deflate the air spring(s). If you don't, the shaft or cartridge on some forks will shoot out at you when you remove its retainer. The temptation to push the damper shaft up and down will be great, but be very careful. The shaft is meant to be supported in the fork and move straight up and down, and if you put a side load on it, you can allow oil to leak out around the seal.
3. On most RockShox, if you want to remove and inspect (or replace) the cartridge and/or neutral shaft (Fig. 13.12), remove the circlip at the bottom of the inner leg with inward-squeezing snapring pliers (Fig. 13.26). When you replace the cartridge (or neutral shaft), orient the snapring so that its sharp edge faces away from the springs.

(a) Starting in the 1999 model year, some air-spring models require a special tool for removing the negative spring and the cartridge that is essentially a hollow 15mm hex key. Be careful when you unscrew the cartridge retainer with this tool—it is left-hand threaded!

(b) For an older, non-TPC Manitou (Fig. 13.21), unscrew the damper seal nut at the bottom of the leg (Fig. 13.27). Do this with the fork upside down so oil won't pour out.

4. Pour out the old oil (we're back to talking specifically about Manitou now).
5. Add a little new oil of the weight you want. Automatic transmission fluid (ATF) is 15 weight and works fine for non-TPC Manitou forks if you don't have fork hydraulic oil. Slosh it around inside to rinse the damper clean, and pour it back out.
6. With an older, non-TPC Manitou damper, fill with new fork oil or ATF to the top of the inverted inner leg. Stroke the shaft a few times to get the air bubbles out and top off with oil again. Slide the nut back down onto the shaft and start it in the threads. Roll the rubber O-ring down off of the nut so it surrounds the fork inner leg (Fig. 13.27). Tighten the end nut down by hand. Air and excess oil are vented out through a hole under the nut's lip when the O-ring is not covering it. Replace the O-ring when its groove is about to go inside the tube, and tighten the nut with a wrench.
7. Continue with reassembly of the fork (§xiii-14, step 5).

CHANGING OIL

xiii-16 CHANGING OIL IN MANITOU TPC OR ROCKSHOX PURE DAMPER

Manitou TPC (Twin Piston Cartridge) dampers rarely need oil changes because of the high oil volume keeping them cool and the absence of springs in the oil to grind aluminum into it. But they are easy to service when needed. The RockShox "Pure" damping system, as found in post-2001 SID SL and high-end Psylo forks, is very similar to Manitou TPC, and almost the same instructions apply. If the information is not printed on the outer leg, hints that your Manitou is TPC, or your high-end RockShox is Pure, are springs (air, coil, or elastomer) in only one leg. (Many post-1999 low-end RockShox forks have a single-sided spring with single-piston cartridge in the other leg, but these are not Pure.)

1. The springs should be installed (or inflated) in the other leg so that the fork is at its full length. Keeping the fork right side up, unscrew the adjuster-knob cap on the top of the damper leg (usually on the right side, but early TPC dampers were in the left leg). (You may need to remove the lockout or adjustment lever first.) The upper (compression-damping) piston is attached to the cap—jiggle it as you pull the piston up and through the threads (Fig. 13.28).
2. Pour out the old oil.
3. Add a little new 5-weight fork oil (both TPC and Pure always use 5 weight). Slosh it around inside to rinse the damper clean, and pour it back out.
4. Keeping the fork straight up and down, pour in new 5-weight oil up to the level below the top of the crown specified in your fork owner's manual. You will need to fashion a dipstick out of a dowel rod or wire.
5. Slip the piston back in (Fig. 13.28) and tighten the cap back on. That's it for Manitou. Easy, huh?
6. For RockShox Pure, there is an extra bleeding step required to squeeze the air out, because the Pure damper, unlike the TPC, has no air in it. You stick

13.28 **Getting the Manitou TPC's top piston in and out**

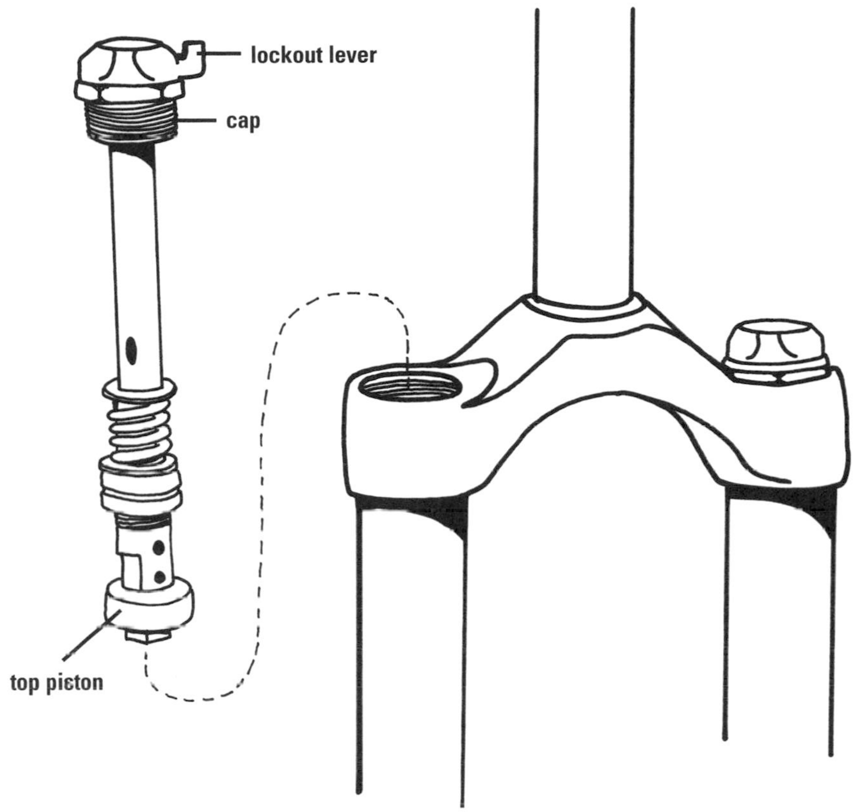

a small plastic syringe (without a plunger in it) half full of 5-weight fork oil into the hole in the top cap. Remove the springs from or deflate the other leg. Stroke the fork up and down slowly to push air bubbles up into the syringe and pull oil down out of it. When no more air comes up, replace the springs or inflate the other leg to make the fork full length. Remove the syringe and screw the adjuster lever back on (remember to put the little detent ball—it makes the lever click—back onto its spring in the cap). Piece o' cake, huh?

xiii-17 CHANGING FORK TRAVEL

Many new forks have a simple lever or knob to change travel.

On the other extreme, changing travel on old forks requires a different damping cartridge, neutral shaft, and spring stack (these parts are shown in Figs. 13.12 and 13.21). If you are persistent, you can probably find parts from at least an aftermarket supplier for many older high-end forks. You then take apart the fork as in §xiii-14 and §xiii-15, put in the new pieces, reassemble it, and you are set. Just make sure that you check your total travel as in §xiii-10b and that there is no way your fork crown can hit your tire when the fork is compressed fully. Although changing travel does not make the crown come down farther, the temptation may be to use a bigger tire with the longer travel.

Manitou categorically recommended against changing travel for safety reasons until the 2002 Black fork, which has a travel-adjustment lever at the bottom of the left leg. You flip the lever to one of the two positions and push down once on the handlebar to engage the spring in its new position.

RockShox has made travel change easier and easier since the 2000 model year. Changing travel on RockShox forks from 2000 and later is as easy as finding your travel-adjuster type below.

a. U-Turn

On 2002 Psylo SL, XC, and C and on post-2003 Boxxer, Pike Judy, and Duke forks, you just turn the large "U-Turn" knob on top of the left leg to increase or decrease travel. The big coil spring itself screws down or up along large threads around the outside of a big plastic plunger to shorten or lengthen the fork. You can shorten it while riding by turning the U-Turn knob clockwise. You have to stop and take your weight off the spring to turn it counterclockwise and lengthen the fork. There is also a U-Turn Air option on all Reba fork models and it is adjusted the same way as the U-Turn on coil springs.

b. Vari-Travel

The next easiest travel change is in 2001 Psylo SL and Psylo XC forks. The "Vari-Travel" system simply requires removing the left top cap and removing the coil spring. Reach down inside with a long screwdriver and turn the screw on the top of the plunger. Each turn changes the travel by 1mm, and the length is infinitely variable from 80mm to 125mm (3 inches to 5 inches).

c. All Travel

The Reba, Pike, SID SL, and Psylo Race have one "All Travel" system, the SID XC has another, and Judys have yet another.

Judy All Travel

Judy Race, SL, and XC forks have two plastic All Travel spacers installed inside each leg (Fig. 13.29). Each spacer is tubular with lips at one end to snap into a spring or insert into another spacer.

Note in Figure 13.29 that if both spacers are on top of the plunger, the shaft can stick out to full length, and the fork has 100mm of travel; placing both spacers under the plunger limits travel to 63mm, and one spacer above and one below gives you 80mm of travel. Having spacers below the plunger limits travel by reducing the length of the shaft that can extend out of the bottom of the inner leg.

1. Pull the fork apart as in §xiii-14 (steps 1–4) and remove the springs.
2. Using inward-closing snapring pliers, remove the snapring from the bottom of each inner leg (Fig. 13.26).
3. Carefully pry out the plastic ring, and pull out any washers and plastic rings you find in there.
4. Remove the shaft assembly.
5. If you want 63mm of travel, remove the spacers from the main spring, and slide them up onto the shaft, snapping the lips of the upper spacer into the bottom of the small spring that sits below the plunger (Fig. 13.29). For 100mm of travel (note that the 2001 Judy Race only goes up to 80mm), snap both spacers into the bottom of the main spring. For 80mm, snap one in the big spring and one in the small spring. Set both legs up the same.
6. Reinstall the plunger assembly and snapring (Fig. 13.26). On Judys, replace the springs and top caps (Fig. 13.29). Inflate SIDs.
7. Reassemble the fork as in §xiii-14 (steps 5–14).

13.29 **Changing travel on post-2000 RockShox Judy**

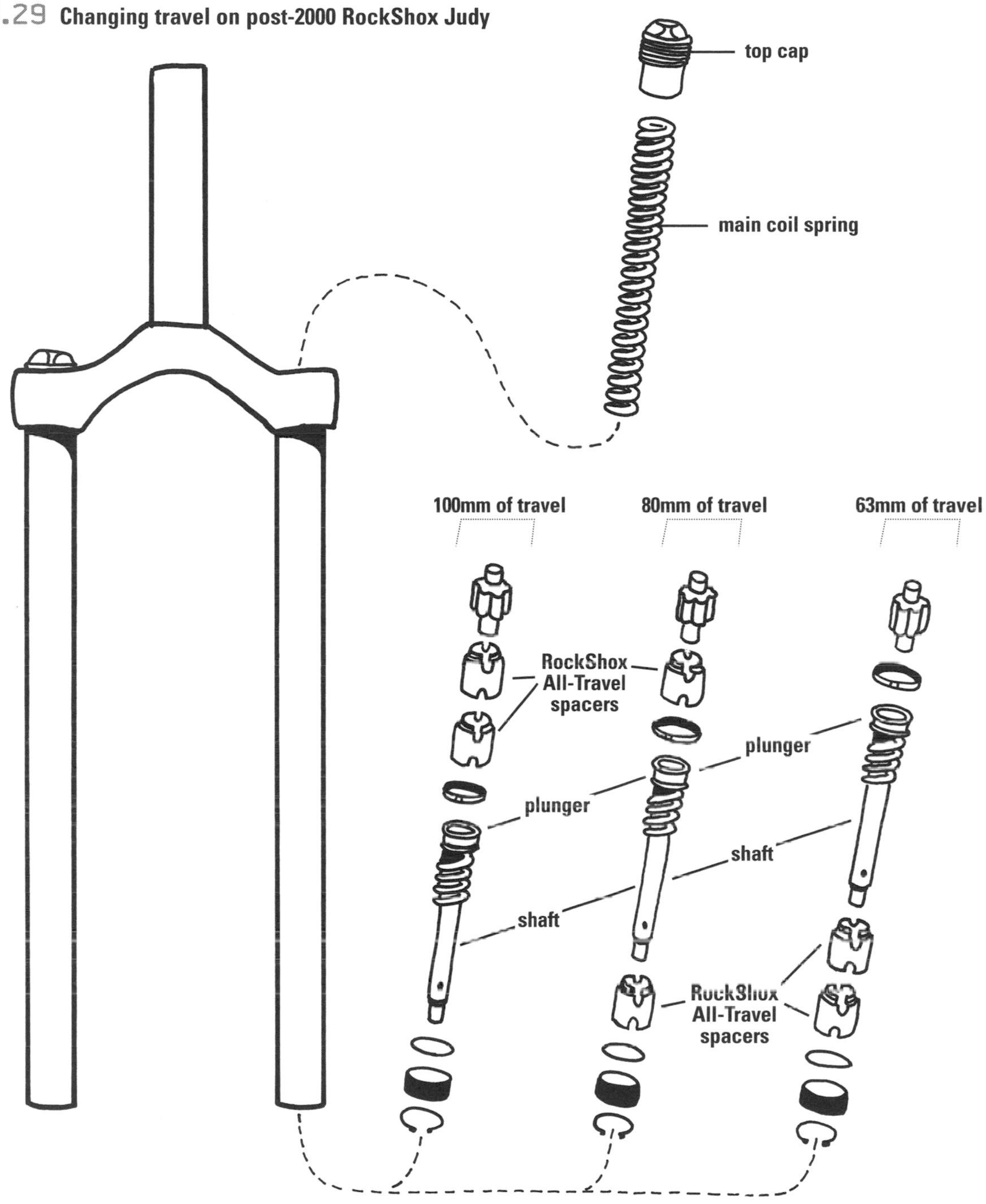

Reba, Pike, SID SL, Psylo Race All Travel

This system is simpler.

1. Pull the fork apart as in §xiii-14 (steps 1–4) and release the air from the valves.
2. Remove the negative-spring shaft from the left inner leg. On the Psylo Race, remove the standard circlip with snapring pliers (Fig. 13.26). On the SID, use the special SID cartridge-removal tool, a hollow 15mm hex key that fits over the shaft and engages the threaded cap at the bottom of the inner leg. Put a 15mm socket or box wrench on the other end of the tool and unscrew it clockwise.

IMPORTANT: *This SID cap is left-hand threaded!*

3. The fork comes with a couple of hard, cylindrical spacers split open on one side to snap onto the shaft between the piston and the glide ring below. Pop one in to reduce the travel by the length of the spacer.
4. Reinstall the plunger assembly and inflate the fork.
5. Reassemble the fork as in §xiii-14 (steps 5–14).

SID XC All Travel

The SID XC system is the most interesting. Its packaging includes a single All Travel spacer identical to those on the Judy (Fig 13.29).

1. Pull the fork apart as in §xiii-14 (steps 1–4) and release the air from the valves.
2. Remove both shafts from the inner legs with a small blade screwdriver to pry out the snapring. The cool feature of this fork is the reversibility of the negative-spring neutral shaft. If you want 80mm of travel, leave the All Travel spacer out of the fork, and set up the neutral shaft so that the end with a circumscribed line around it points down, and the piston is screwed into the opposite end. The scribed end is longer from the glide ring to the end, so having it down allows more shaft to extend out of the inner leg and—voilà!—more travel. The negative spring goes on the longer end, below the glide ring. Once you get it apart you'll see what I mean.
3. If you want a 63mm fork, you slide the All Travel spacer up onto the damper shaft (the shaft from the right leg), and snap it into the spring below the piston. Remove and save the thin spring guide that had been snapped into the spring.
4. The neutral shaft (from the left leg) must now be reversed. Unscrew the piston from the short end (without the circumscribed mark), and pull the negative spring off of the long end.
5. Screw the piston into the longer, scribed end, and put the negative spring onto the shorter, unscribed end. The negative spring has a tight-fitting plastic spring guide snapped into the piston end, so it does not slide easily. I find it simpler to snap the spring off of the guide and move them separately. With the short end of the neutral shaft down and the All Travel spacer limiting the downward extension of the damper shaft, travel is shortened.
6. Reassemble the fork as in §xiii-14 (steps 5–14).

xiii-18 OTHER SUSPENSION SYSTEMS AND UPGRADES

There are a number of variations on suspension forks. If you have something other than those described in this chapter, you should consult the owner's manual for service requirements and procedures.

There are also a number of retrofit units designed to improve the performance of the forks covered above. So you need not feel that you are stuck with a certain low level of performance from your fork. You can significantly upgrade an old fork's performance without replacing it. Modern upgrades involve a lot more than just a few lightweight titanium fork bolts. Englund compressed-air (TotalAir) units, for example, were made to replace the elastomer spring and the hydraulic damper in a high-end coil- or elastomer-sprung, fluid-damped fork. These units are air sprung, and the damping is controlled by airflow through small orifices rather than by oil.

Many of the evolutionary improvements on newer RockShox and Manitou models will retrofit into the older models if you can get the parts (for example, you can turn a Manitou Mach 5 into a Manitou SX-Ti).

xiii-19 SUSPENSION-FORK ADJUSTMENT GUIDE

It is a good idea to have a short test course with a hill and some sharp turns in it. Make one change at a time and ride the bike again so you can isolate what each change does. Immediately after every ride, keep track of your observations in a notebook that you keep by your bike, rather than waiting until you have time to work on your bike and have forgotten what it was that you wanted to change. Much of the text below was taken (with permission) from a Manitou fork-tuning manual.

Before adjusting your fork, there are two important things to keep in mind:

1. A bottoming sensation (even if the fork is not bottoming) may actually be caused by the inability of the bike and rider to overcome an overly stiff spring or excessive damping.
2. A harsh sensation (even if the bike has soft springs) may actually be caused by a spring rate too soft for the bike and rider, causing the suspension to ride with much of the travel compressed (i.e., the fork is packed up).

Aspects of your fork that can be adjusted are listed below, generally in the order in which the adjustments should be made.

a. Spring rate

1. If the spring rate is too soft, you will experience bottoming of the fork, a high preload needed, and a front end that is too low on downhill stretches.
2. If the spring rate is too hard, the fork rarely or never bottoms (e.g., the fork does not use the full travel possible).

b. Spring preload (coil-spring or elastomer forks)

Adjust the spring rate before you adjust the preload.

1. If the spring preload is too low, the bike will exhibit excessive static sag, the front end will be too low entering turns, and oversteering will occur.
2. If the spring preload is too high, the bike will exhibit too little static sag, the fork will feel stiff and/or harsh, and understeering and poor low-speed, tight-turning will be characteristic.

c. Rebound damping

1. If rebound damping is set too high, the fork extends too quickly and the wheel springs up from the ground after landing from a jump, you will have difficulty in maintaining a straight path through rocks, the front end attempts to climb the berm or groove while cornering, the ride height is too high, and understeering is characteristic.
2. If rebound damping is set too low, you will experience a harsh feeling (especially through successive rapid hits), bottoming after several successive large hits, failure to rebound after landing from a jump, low ride height, oversteering, and bottoming even though compression damping and spring rate are correct.

d. Compression damping

1. If compression damping is set too high, the symptoms include bottoming, fork dives while braking, oversteering, and an unstable fork.
2. If compression damping is set too low, you will experience a harsh feeling, the fork rarely or never bottoms, the ride height is high despite a soft spring and/or little preload, and understeering is typical.

e. Inertial valve

1. If the inertial valve adjustment is set too high, the fork will not respond to small bumps.
2. If the inertial value is set too low, the fork will bob when pedaling on smooth surfaces.

xiii-20 SOME COMMON RIDE SYMPTOMS AND SOME FIXES

a. Fork too hard

1. Decrease compression damping.
2. Decrease rebound damping.
3. Decrease spring rate.
4. Decrease oil viscosity.
5. Increase spring rate.
6. Decrease inertial valve adjustment.

NOTE: *While you of course normally need softer springs if the fork is too hard, if you are running a spring rate that is too soft for your weight and ability, you can be misled into thinking that the spring rate is too stiff. This is because you are using up the fork travel before you begin to ride. Furthermore, the fork is working in a stiffer spring-rate range on smaller hits, giving the impression of the fork being harsh and stiff. This is where the ride-height (sag) adjustment (§xiii-12b and §xiii-13a) is important.*

b. Fork too soft

1. Increase spring rate.
2. Increase compression damping.
3. Increase oil viscosity.
4. Replace worn-out oil in damper.
5. Put oil in (empty) cartridge.

c. Front end searching or "nervous" on descending

1. Increase rebound damping.
2. Increase spring preload.
3. Increase spring rate.
4. Decrease compression damping.

d. Front end "knifes" or oversteers

1. Decrease rebound damping.
2. Increase spring preload.
3. Increase spring rate.
4. Increase compression damping.

e. Front end pushes or washes out in turns

1. Increase rebound damping.
2. Decrease spring preload.
3. Decrease spring rate.
4. Decrease compression damping.

f. No response to small bumps

1. Decrease compression damping.
2. Decrease spring preload.
3. Decrease spring rate.
4. Increase negative spring rate.
5. Decrease rebound damping.
6. Overhaul dirty fork.
7. Decrease inertial valve adjustment.

CHAPTER 14

FRAMES

Come to kindly terms with your Ass for it bears you.
—John Muir, *How to Keep Your Volkswagen Alive*

TOOLS

- ruler or caliper
- string
- bike stand
- metric wrenches and hex keys

OPTIONAL TOOLS

- dropout-alignment tools
- derailleur-hanger alignment tool
- metric taps
- English-thread bottom-bracket tap set
- thread-cutting oil
- drill and drill bits
- 16mm cone wrench

Your Volkswagen is not a donkey . . . and your mountain bike is not a Volkswagen. Still, you'd be well served to follow the sage advice given above and stay on good terms with your bike. In doing so, pay close attention to the frame, because it is the most important part of your bike. It is the one part of your bike that is nearly impossible to fix on the trail, and when it fails, the consequences can be serious. Therefore, get to know your frame. Come to kindly terms with it . . . for it bears your ass . . . or something like that.

xiv-1 FRAME DESIGN

The traditional "diamond," or "double-diamond," mountain bike frame design evolved from a combination of postwar cruiser bikes and road-racing bikes. The rigid design of a road bike relies on a "front triangle" and a "rear triangle" (Fig. 14.1); never mind that the front triangle is not actually a triangle—or much of a diamond, for that matter. Although the basic concept is similar, there are some notable differences between road and mountain bike geometries. Mountain bike frames feature a higher bottom bracket for more ground clearance; a longer and wider rear triangle for more tire clearance; a shorter seat tube (and correspondingly lower top tube) for more stand-over clearance; brake bosses; and larger-diameter tubing. Another rigid-frame variation is the "elevated chainstay" design, in which the chainstays attach to the seat tube rather than to the bottom-bracket shell. This design enjoyed great popularity for a few years. Its primary benefit is the elimination of "chain suck," the jamming of the chain between the chainring and the chainstay—and its primary drawback is added weight. When the chainstay-mounted U-brake and roller-cam brake (Figs. 7.49 and 7.50) went out of fashion, many chain suck problems evaporated, as well as sales of elevated-chainstay rigid frames.

These and other modifications—sloping top tubes, large-diameter head tubes, the use of materials other than steel, and, of course, rear suspension—are

14.1 **Rigid frame**

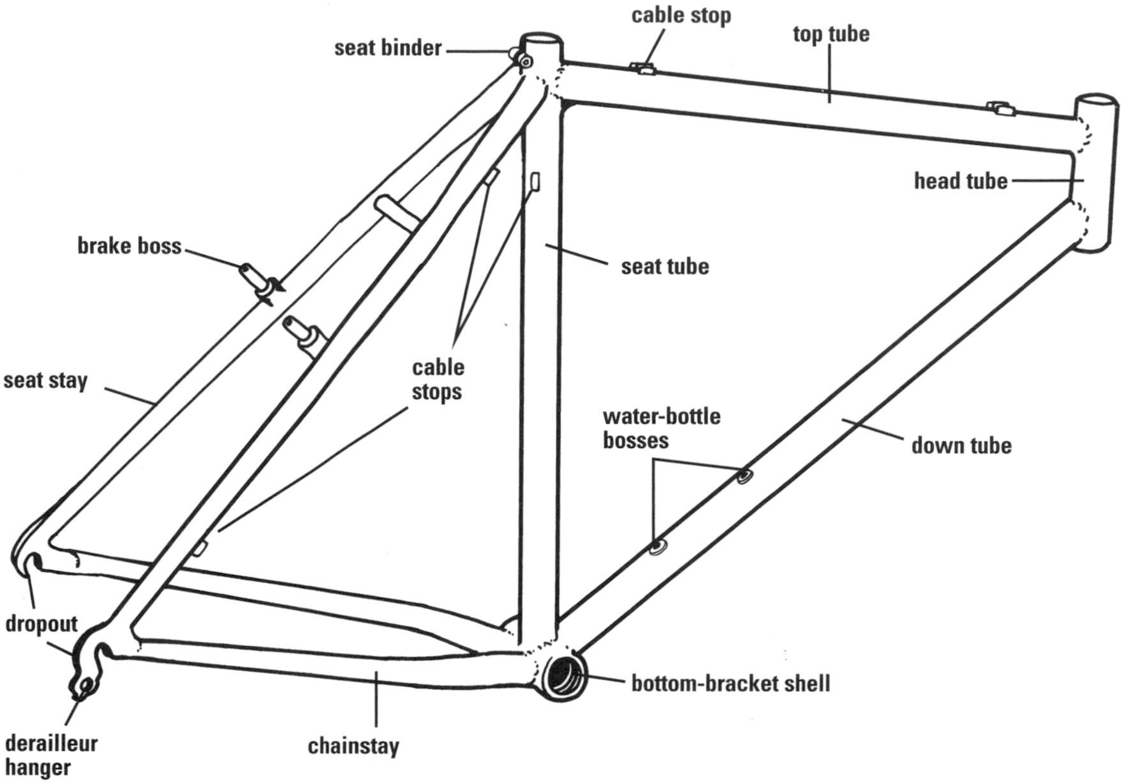

generally aimed at bringing a bike closer to the Holy Grail of bicycle design: low frame weight and price coupled with high frame strength, durability, and performance.

FRAME DESIGN — SUSPENSION-FRAME DESIGN

As a result of this pursuit, mountain bike frame design has changed radically in the short time since the inception of the sport. Take a look at a modern mountain bike and compare it to the Marin County Repack–style bikes of the late 1970s or the Crested Butte off-road "cruisers" that popped onto the scene around the same time. The difference is amazing, even if you are just comparing modern design without suspension (Fig. i.3) to one of the early models made from or patterned after circa 1940 Schwinn-style cruisers. Start looking at full-suspension models (Figs. i.4 and 14.2), and you have a whole new breed of animal. And full suspension has now become so common that you even find it on cheap department-store bikes.

xiv-2 SUSPENSION-FRAME DESIGN

Rear suspension (also called "full suspension" because it is usually combined with a suspension fork) involves a design totally different than the traditional double diamond. Most suspension frames have a front triangle and a "rear swingarm" (Fig. 14.2).

There are almost as many rear-suspension designs (and names for them) as there are suspension-frame designers. Over the past few years, the changes have been fast and furious, and I'll wager that within another few years there will be a whole new crop of popular designs with a whole new crop

14.2 **Rear-suspension frame**

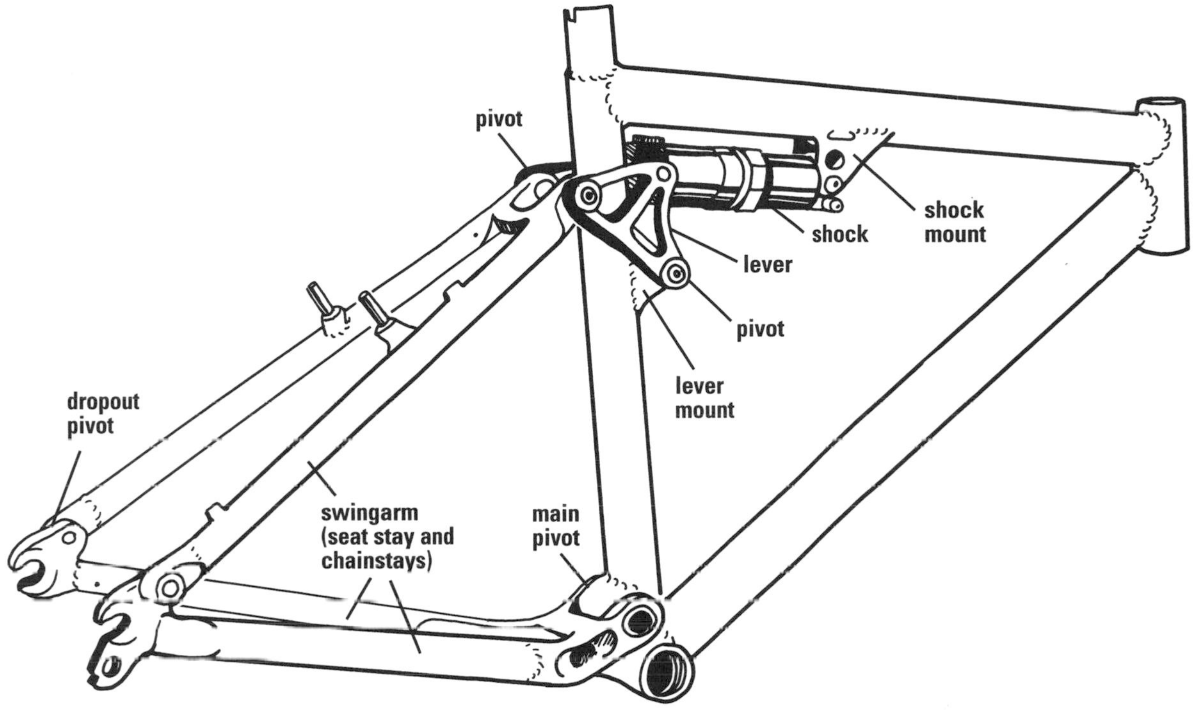

of catchy names. Although it would be pointless to go on at length about specifics of current designs, this chapter will divide suspension frames into broad categories and give general maintenance guidelines for them.

xiv-3 FRAME MATERIALS

The revolution in bicycle-frame materials has been going on since the birth of the bicycle. Wood was the material of choice for the first bicycles, but that was soon replaced by steel, aluminum, and even bamboo. Aluminum and steel are still the materials most commonly used to build mountain bike frames, but with the end of the Cold War, titanium, carbon composites, and metal matrix composites now account for a significant share, too. Because the materials used in mountain bike frames come in a variety of grades with varying costs and physical properties, assume that I am talking about the highest grades for the materials used in bicycles. For example, the aluminum used in window frames is a lot different than the heat-treated 6000- and 7000-series aluminum used in high-end bicycle frames.

Steel has the highest modulus of elasticity (a principal determiner of stiffness) as well as the highest density and tensile strength of any of the metals commonly used in frames. The modulus of elasticity, the density, and the tensile strength of aluminum is much lower than those values for steel; and titanium has values between the two. Metal tubing characteristics are maximized for bicycles by (1) butting (i.e., placing thickness where it is needed and not where it adds useless weight), (2) increasing diameter to add stiffness, and (3) heat-treating and alloying to boost certain of the metal's physical properties. With intelligent use of materials, long-lasting frames of comparable stiffness-to-weight and/or strength-to-weight ratios can be built out of any of these metals.

Carbon fiber and similar composite frame materials consist of fibers embedded in a resin (plastic) matrix. These materials can be extremely light, strong, and stiff. Bikes can be built by gluing carbon-fiber tubes into lugs (usually made of carbon fiber or aluminum), or they can be molded in a single piece ("monocoque" construction). A big advantage of composites is that they can be molded to be thicker where extra strength is needed. The tricky part is holding them together in a frame that does not come apart.

Metal-matrix composite frame materials contain hard, nonmetallic materials included in the metal to increase its mechanical properties (usually its tensile strength). These added materials are not alloying materials (i.e., they are not melted together with the metal), as that would usually contaminate the metal. Rather, pieces of sand-like materials (aluminum oxide, silicon oxide, etc.) are worked into the metal without melting them. The trick with these materials is making them weldable without weakening the frame at the joints.

Frame builders have and will continue to experiment with all sorts of exotic materials and designs. My recommendation regarding them is just not to be one of the first ones riding on a new material or suspension design. Let the engineers discover, and correct, the shortcomings with other guinea pigs before you jump on.

xiv-4 FRAME INSPECTION

You can avoid potentially dangerous or at least ride-shortening frame failures by inspecting your frame frequently. If you find damage, and you are not sure how dangerous the bike is to ride, take it to a bike shop for advice.

1. Clean your frame every few rides so that you can spot problems early.
2. Inspect all tubes for cracks, bends, buckles, dents, and paint stretching or cracking, especially near the joints where stress is at its highest. If in doubt, take it to an expert for advice.
3. Inspect the rear dropouts and the welds around the brake bosses and cable stops for cracks (see Fig. 14.1 for names and locations of frame parts). Check to be sure that the dropouts, brake bosses, and cable stops are not bent. Some dropouts and brake bosses bolt on and are replaceable. Otherwise, badly bent or broken dropouts, brake bosses, disc-brake mounts, and cable stops require having a new one welded, riveted, or brazed on; a frame builder in your area may be able to do it.
4. Look for deeply rusted areas on steel frames. Remove the seatpost every few months and invert the bike to see if water pours out of the seat tube. Look and feel for deep rusted areas inside or for rust falling out. I recommend squirting a rust protective spray designed for bicycle frames (Frame Saver), WD-40, or oil inside your tubes periodically (after letting the frame dry out upside-down with the seatpost removed). Remember to grease both the seatpost and inside of the seat tube when you reinsert the seatpost. After sanding off the rust from any external areas where the paint has come off, touch them up with touch-up paint or nail polish (hey, it's avail-

able in lots of cool colors, but be advised that it is not as durable as good paint and requires periodic retouching).

5. On suspension frames, disconnect the shock. Move the swingarm up and down, and flex it laterally, feeling for play or binding in the pivots. Check the shock for leaking oil, cracks, a bent shaft, or other damage.
6. Check that a true and properly dished wheel sits straight in the frame, centered between the chainstays and seat stays and lined up in the same plane as the front triangle. Tightening the hub skewer should not result in bowing or twisting of the chainstays or seat stays.

xiv-5 CHECK AND STRAIGHTEN THE REAR-DERAILLEUR HANGER

LEVEL 3

1. If you have a derailleur hanger alignment tool (Fig. 1.4), thread it into the derailleur hanger on the right dropout (Fig. 14.3).
2. Install a true rear wheel without a tire on it.
3. Swing the tool around, measuring the spacing between its arm and the rim all of the way around. The arm of the tool should be the same distance from the rim at all points. Some tools, such as the one in Figure 14.3, have an extension rod extending at right angles from the arm and held by a hand-turned setscrew that you can adjust to check the spacing; others require you to measure it with a ruler or caliper.
4. If your tool has play in it, keep it pushed inward lightly as you perform all of the measurements, or you will get inconsistent data.
5. If the spacing between the tool arm and the rim is not consistent (within 1mm or 2mm all of the way around), carefully bend the hanger by pulling outward on the arm of the tool lightly where it is closest to the rim.
6. If the derailleur hanger is really bent, you may not be able to align it without breaking it (you may even have trouble threading the tool in because the threaded hole has become oval shaped). If you have a replaceable bolt-on dropout, replace it.
7. If the threads or the hanger itself are really screwed up, and you do not have a replaceable dropout, see Fixing Damaged Threads, §xiv-8 below, for other derailleur hanger options.

14.3 Checking derailleur-hanger alignment

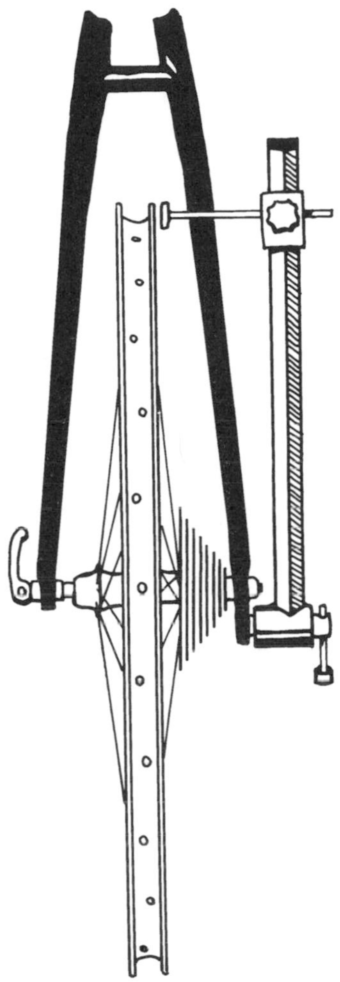

xiv-6 CHECKING FRAME ALIGNMENT AND ADJUSTING DROPOUT ALIGNMENT

LEVEL 2

These are inexact methods for determining frame alignment. If your alignment is way off, these methods will tell you. If you find alignment problems, other than perhaps moderately bent dropouts or derailleur hangers, do not attempt to correct them. Adjusting frame alignment is a difficult and delicate task; if it can be done at all, only someone who is practiced at aligning frames should perform this task with an accurate frame-alignment fixture.

1. With the frame clamped in a bike stand, tie the end of a string to one rear dropout. Stretch it tightly around the head tube, and tie it symmetrically to the other dropout (Fig. 14.4).
2. Measure from the string to the seat tube on either side (Fig. 14.4). The measurement should be at least within 1mm of being the same on both sides.
3. Put a true and properly dished rear wheel in the frame, and check that it lines up in the same plane as the front triangle. Make certain that the wheel is centered between the seat stays and chainstays (or swingarms). The hub should slide in easily without requiring you to pull outward or push inward on the dropouts. Tightening the hub quick release should not result in bowing or twisting of frame members.
4. Remove the wheel, and measure the spacing between the dropouts (Fig. 14.5). On most mountain bikes made since 1990, this spacing should be 135mm. Mountain bikes made between 1984 and 1990 or so should have a rear spacing of 130mm. Mountain bikes made prior to 1984 are likely to have a rear spacing of

FRAME & DROPOUT ALIGNMENT

14.4 Checking frame alignment with a string

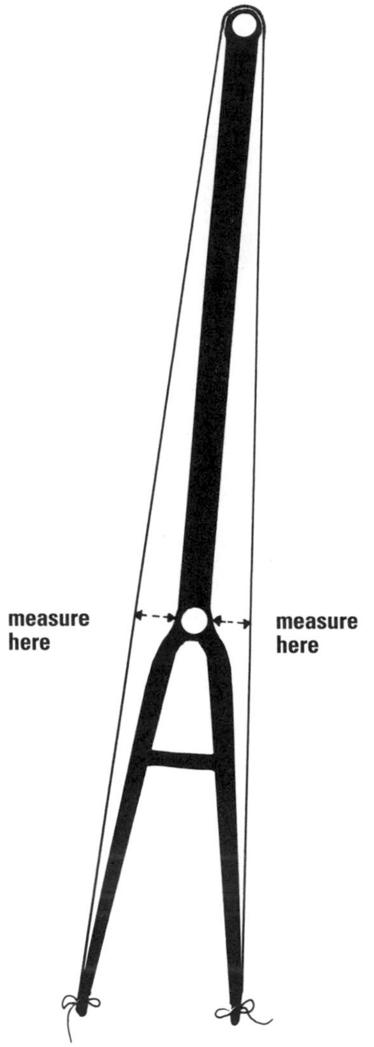

14.5 Measuring dropout width (or axle overlock dimension)

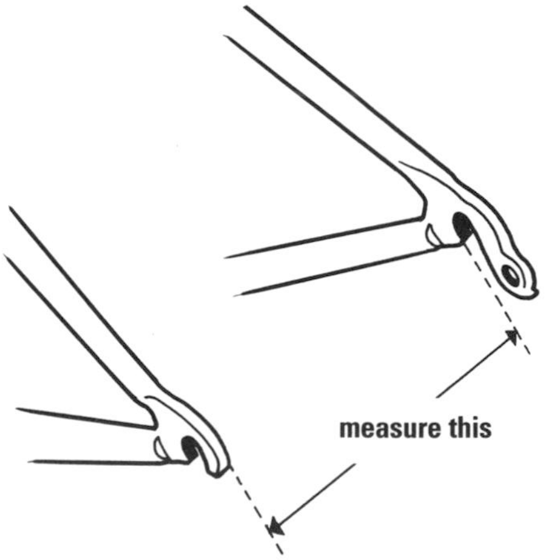

14.6 Using dropout alignment tools on rear dropouts

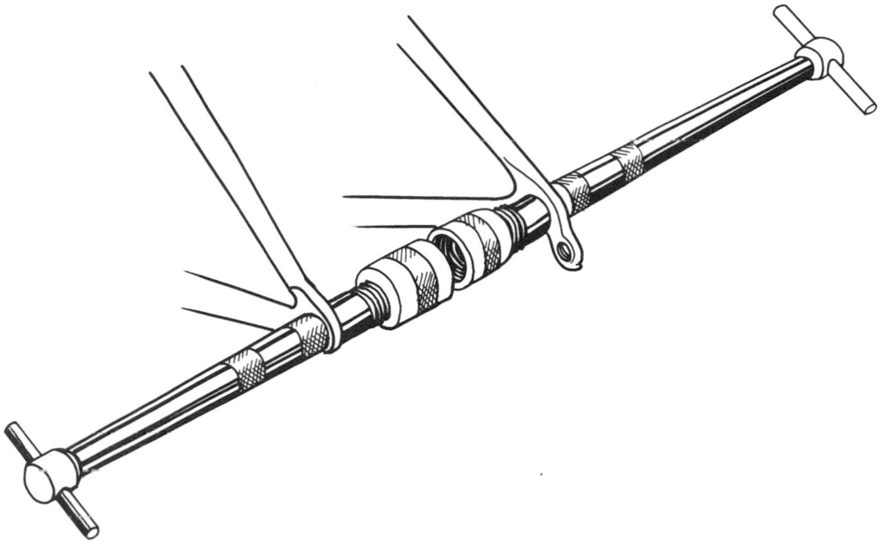

125mm. Some high end cross country mountain bikes (older Manitous, for instance) and downhill bikes have custom rear hubs with wider spacing (such as 150mm) to decrease the wheel dish. Measure the width of the rear hub with a caliper to see what the rear-end spacing of the frame should be. No matter what the nominal measurement for your frame should be, if it is between 1mm less or 1.5mm more than the nominal, it is acceptable. For instance, if you have a frame whose rear spacing should be 135mm, acceptable spacing is 134–136.5mm.

5. If you have dropout-alignment tools, put them in the dropouts so their shafts are fully seated into the dropouts (Fig. 14.6). Arrange the tool spacers (and the cups, if they are adjustable) so that the faces of the cups are within 1mm of each other. Tighten the handles on the tools. The tool cups should line up straight across with each other, with their faces parallel. If the tools do not line up with each other, one or both dropouts are bent. If you have replaceable bolt-on dropouts, go ahead and replace them. If you have a composite or bonded rear triangle of any kind, there is nothing you can do about it if your bike is not equipped with replaceable dropouts. If you have a steel rear triangle, you can align the dropouts by bending them carefully with the dropout-alignment tools. Hold the cup of the tool with one hand and push or pull on the handle with the other. Aluminum or titanium rear dropouts can sometimes be aligned, but it is something you should have a shop do. Titanium is hard to bend because it keeps springing back, and you run a great risk of breaking aluminum by bending it.

6. Suspension frames have one other alignment feature not shared with rigid frames. To ensure proper swingarm movement, every separate link in the swingarm puzzle must be in perfect alignment with the next link so that there are no side forces applied to the pivots. If, for example, the rear shock has to be forced into position between the two pivot points it connects, then

there is unnecessary strain on the frame. These stresses will accelerate the rate of wear of the parts and compromise the linkage's ability to move smoothly.

xiv-7 CORRECTING FRAME DAMAGE

Other than the alignment items described above, the only frame problems you can correct are damaged threads, chipped paint, and small dents. Broken braze-on bosses and bent, broken, or deeply dented tubes require a frame builder to replace them, or else a new frame is called for.

xiv-8 FIXING DAMAGED THREADS

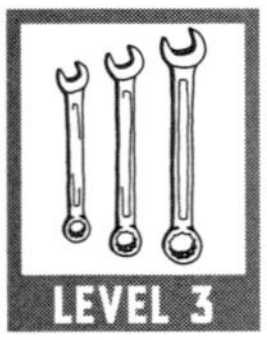

A mountain bike frame has threads in the bottom-bracket shell, cantilever brake bosses, some disc-brake bosses, the water-bottle bosses, and the rear-derailleur hanger (Fig. 14.1). Some bikes have a threaded seat binder, and some also have a small threaded hole in the bottom of the bottom-bracket shell onto which a plastic derailleur-cable guide is bolted. Some frames also have a threaded front-derailleur mount.

1. Whenever you have to retap any threads, first brush them clean and then use oil on the tap (use canola oil with titanium threads). Specific thread-cutting oil is not necessary on old threads because they are already cut.
2. If any threads on the frame are stripped or are cross-threaded, try chasing through (retapping) the threads with the appropriately sized thread tap.
3. Except in the case of the left-hand-threaded drive side bottom bracket threads, turn the tap forward (clockwise) a bit, then turn it back, then forward (two steps forward and one back), etc., to prevent the tap from binding and possibly breaking. Be aware that taps are made of very hard and brittle steel. If you put any side or twisting forces on small taps, they can easily break off. Be careful. If it breaks, you'll have a real mess, because the broken tap in the hole is harder than the frame, so it's impossible to drill the broken tap out. If you break off a tap in your frame, do not try to get it out yourself. Take it to a bike shop, a machine shop, or a frame builder before you break off what little is left sticking out. Unless you put the tap in crooked, breaking one should not be a problem when retapping damaged frame threads, as these threads will be so worn; getting the tap to find any metal to bite into will probably be your biggest problem.

IMPORTANT: *Tapping a bottom-bracket shell takes a good amount of expertise. You really need expert supervision if you have never done it before and still want to do it yourself. In addition to making sure that you place the correct tap in the correct end of the shell, you must also be certain that the taps go in straight. Most bottom-bracket taps have a shaft between the two taps to keep them parallel to each other (Fig. 1.4). They must both be started at the same time from both ends. If you mess it up, you can ruin your frame. So, if in doubt, ask an expert.*

The following tap sizes are commonly found on mountain bikes:

Water-bottle bosses	M5 (5mm × 0.8)
Bottom-bracket shell hole for shift-cable guide	M5 (5mm × 0.8)
Seat binders and brake bosses	M6 (6mm × 1)
Hayes disc-brake post mounts	M6 (6mm × 1)
Derailleur hanger	M10 (10mm × 1)
Bottom-bracket shells	1.37 inches × 24 t.p.i.

NOTE: *Remember, the chain-side bottom-bracket threads are left-hand threaded; the other side is right-hand threaded.*

4. Replace the old bolt with a new one, except in the case of a bottom-bracket or rear derailleur.
5. If tapping the threads and using a new bolt does not work, some specific remedies follow.
   (a) **Brake bosses.** Some brake posts are replaceable. Replaceable posts have wrench flats (usually 8mm) at the base, and they thread into a boss welded to the frame. If yours are not like this, you must take it to a frame builder to get a new boss welded on. Threaded disc-brake mounts (i.e., Hayes-style post mounts) are usually part of the dropout. If the threads are stripped, then the entire dropout may need to be replaced.
   (b) **Water-bottle bosses and threaded front-derailleur braze-on bosses.** Some bike shops have a tool that rivets bottle bosses into the frame. Check for this possibility first, because you can avoid a new paint job that way, although such riveted bosses tend to loosen up over time. Otherwise, take it to a frame builder to get a new boss welded or brazed on.
   (c) **Derailleur-hanger threads.** Some bikes have replaceable rear dropouts that bolt onto the frame. Another option is to use a "Dropout Saver" derailleur-hanger backing nut (Fig. 14.7) made by Wheels Manufacturing and available at bike shops. A Dropout Saver is simply a sleeve threaded the same as your dropout was, with 16mm wrench flats on one end. You drill out the hole in your damaged derailleur hanger with a 15/32-inch drill bit, push the Dropout Saver in from the back side, and screw in your derailleur. Dropout Savers come in two lengths, depending on the thickness of the dropout. Another option is to saw off the derailleur hanger with a hacksaw and use a separate derailleur hanger from a really cheap bike that fits flat against the outside of the dropout and is held in by the hub axle bolts or quick release. The final options are to have the dropout replaced by a frame builder, or you could always get a new frame.
   (d) **Seat binders.** These can be drilled out and used with a quick release or a bolt and nut. Seat-binder threads rarely get stripped, however; it is usually the bolt that is the problem.
   (e) **Bottom-bracket shell threads.** You can use a Mavic or Stronglight cartridge bottom bracket (Chapter 8, §viii-10, Fig. 8.16), if you can still find one, as it does not depend on the threads in the shell to anchor it. You must have a shop bevel the ends of your bottom-bracket

14.7 Inserting dropout saver

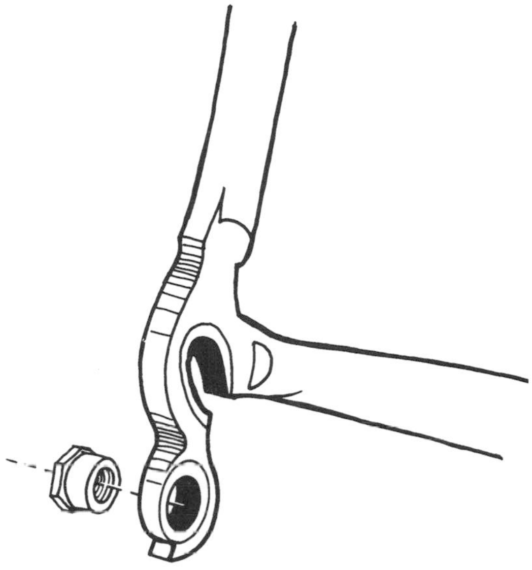

shell with a special cutting tool, and the shop will have the tools to install the bottom bracket as well.

(f) **Bottom-bracket cable-guide bolt-hole threads.** A new hole in the bottom of the bottom bracket can be drilled and tapped, or the stripped hole can be tapped out with larger threads for a larger screw. Make sure the screw you use is short enough that it does not protrude into the inside of the bottom-bracket shell.

xiv-9 REPAIRING CHIPPED PAINT AND SMALL DENTS

Fixing paint chips is simply a matter of cleaning the area and touching it up. Sand any chipped paint or rust completely away before touching up the spot. Use touch-up paint for your bike, model paint, or fingernail polish.

Small dents can be filled with automotive body putty, but there is little point to filling them if you are only doing a touch-up, because the area probably won't look that great anyway.

There are plenty of frame painters around the country who can fill dents, repaint frames, and even match original decals. Many of them advertise in bike magazines and online.

xiv-10 SUSPENSION-FRAME MAINTENANCE

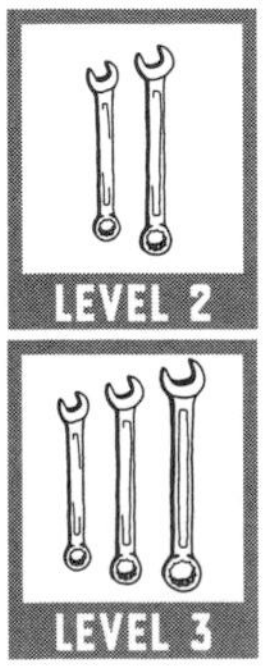

The complexity of suspension frames is variable; hence the ambiguity in the maintenance level. The maintenance to be performed, besides the regular inspections described early in this chapter, is on the shock and the pivots.

a. Evaluate the condition of your suspension

You can tell if your suspension needs some lubrication while the bike is standing still. Stand next to the bike, pull the rear brake, and push down lightly on the saddle. Gradually increase the pressure. Notice how much pressure it takes before the bike finally compresses. If the suspension does not compress as you push harder and harder, and then it finally goes down chunk, chunk, chunk, like going down a set of stairs, you've got a dry system. You need to clean and lubricate the pivots and the shock. There is no point in tuning the suspension until you have it moving smoothly.

If the swingarm begins compressing smoothly under a relatively gentle push, then you have a pretty clean, well-lubricated system.

Also, remove the rear wheel and the shock and lift the swingarm and let it drop. If the swingarm falls under its own weight, your pivots are not sticky. If you have to forcefully move it through its travel, you had better get to work on those pivots! New frames usually take a little force to move until the pivot bushings and bearings work in; if your frame is like this and there is no noticeable lateral wiggle to the swingarm, your pivots are in decent shape.

b. Pivot maintenance

The pivots on any suspension frame require periodic attention. Pivots usually rely on cartridge bearings or bushings (usually steel or brass, but some are made of ceramic or plastic). They are held together by through bolts, by clamps with pinch bolts surrounding the pivot shaft, or by pins secured with cotters or snaprings. Crummy bushing material just wears thinner and gets loose. High-quality bushings often let you know they are wearing by getting sticky

14.8 **Removing bearing seal**

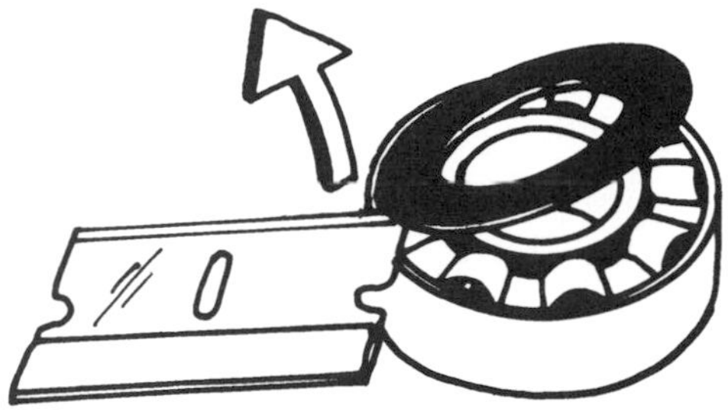

before they get loose. Bearings fail if the seal fails and they get dirty or lose their lubricant, or they get overloaded. Side loads, in particular on a bearing not designed to take forces from the side (as opposed to radial), can wreck a bearing. This is more likely to happen on installation or removal than on usage on the bike, however, unless some suspension members are way out of alignment.

The shock also pivots at its "eyelets" at either end (Fig. 14.9) on brass bushings or on bearings.

Figure on cleaning and greasing pivot bushings after at least every 40 hours of riding. Inspect them for wear frequently. Again, check for wear by feeling for lateral play and binding with the shock deflated or disconnected. If the rear end is loose from side to side, or it is so sticky that you can hardly move it, go through the system by taking the linkage apart one piece at a time (this usually just requires removing screws and bolts). Test each joint for wiggle and bind once you have isolated it from the other joints. Check the bushings for scoring and deformation into an oval shape, and lubricate any squeaky ones. Be careful about using solvents on plastic bushings, as some materials can swell. Bearings should wear longer than bushings as long as they are kept greased. If not yet ruined, they can be opened and repacked with grease as is done for other cartridge bearings (Fig. 14.8). When they are worn out, they can be replaced, and unlike most bushings found in bike frames, pivot bearings are often stock sizes that you can find at an automotive bearing store.

If you have grease fittings on any of your pivots, by all means put a grease gun on them frequently and pump some grease in (you can spoon bicycle suspension grease into your grease gun). For suspension grease, Buzzy's Slick Honey is one that seems to work well.

To replace worn bushings and bearings, you will need to push them out of the holes in the ends of the linkage arms in which they are seated. This requires some socket wrenches and perhaps box-end wrenches, and maybe even a hammer and a punch.

1. Push the old bushing or bearing out.
   (a) If the linkage member has a through hole the same size on both sides (i.e., the bushing or bearing can go in from either side), then you can push it out with a vise and a socket. Select a socket just slightly smaller than the outer diameter of the bushing or bearing, and set it against the bushing or bearing between the jaws of your vise (Fig. 14.10). You never want to apply pressure to the inner bore or against the seals of a cartridge bearing (at least one you want to keep—the old trashed one you can do what you want with), so the socket should be against the outer ring of the bearing. Against the opposite jaw of the vise, place the box end of a wrench just bigger than the bushing or bearing so it surrounds it up against the face of the linkage member (you can also instead employ a second socket, open

end toward the bushing or bearing, whose inner diameter (I.D.) is just larger than the bushing or bearing). Tighten the vise until it pushes the bushing or bearing out (into the box wrench or larger socket).

(b) You must employ a different technique if the bushing or bearing is up against a seat in the linkage arm. In other words, the hole is not the same diameter on both sides as the bushing or bearing, but instead is bored in from one side such that the bushing or bearing has a pocket—it seats against the flat bottom of the hole. On the other side there is only a small hole for the pivot bolt to pass through. In this case, get the bushing or bearing out by placing a punch, screwdriver, or bolt against its inside diameter from the side of the link arm with the small hole. Support the link arm adjacent the bushing or bearing somehow (perhaps on a socket just bigger than the bushing or bearing) and tap the bushing or bearing out with a hammer.

2. Grease the hole the new bushing or bearing will go into, and press it in.

(a) On link arms that have parallel faces at the bushing or bearing hole, just place the bushing or bearing against the hole in the link arm and press it in with the flat jaws of the vise; put aluminum plates against the vise jaws if they do not have smooth faces. Place the old bushing or bearing against the new one, if it needs to be pressed in farther than flush with the link in the arm's face.

(b) You must press in the bushing or bearing by using an appropriately sized socket on link arms that do not have parallel faces at the bushing or bearing hole. Link arms like this will usually have a seat (or pocket) for the bushing or bearing in the eyelet at the end of the arm. The walls of the bearing pocket will not be parallel, because the eyelet will be welded to a tube larger than the thickness of the bearing on one side, and the eyelet's edges will be tapered down on the other sides to approach the thickness of the bearing at the tip (Fig. 14.11). Obviously, a flat vise cannot push a bearing into a configuration like this without using something, such as a socket, behind the bearing that can enter the pocket and still be pulled back out. (You could perhaps use the old bearing to push the new one in, but then you might have a problem getting the old bearing out of the pocket.) Select a socket the size of or slightly less than the outer diameter of the bearing. Squeeze the bushing or bearing with one (smooth) jaw of the vise against the back of the link-arm eyelet pocket and the other jaw against the socket (Fig. 14.11).

SHOCK MAINTENANCE

xiv-11 SHOCK MAINTENANCE

a. Daily maintenance

Keep the shock shaft, shaft seals, and bottom-out bumper clean. Clean them after every ride (you know—when you wipe down and lube your chain), but do not use high-pressure water on them. The high pressure can blow the seals inward and contaminate the shock. Lightly lubricate the shaft or shock body (the part that slides in and out).

Keep the bushings in the "eyelets" (mounting holes on either end of the shock—Fig. 14.9) clean and greased.

14.9 Rear-shock parts and adjustments

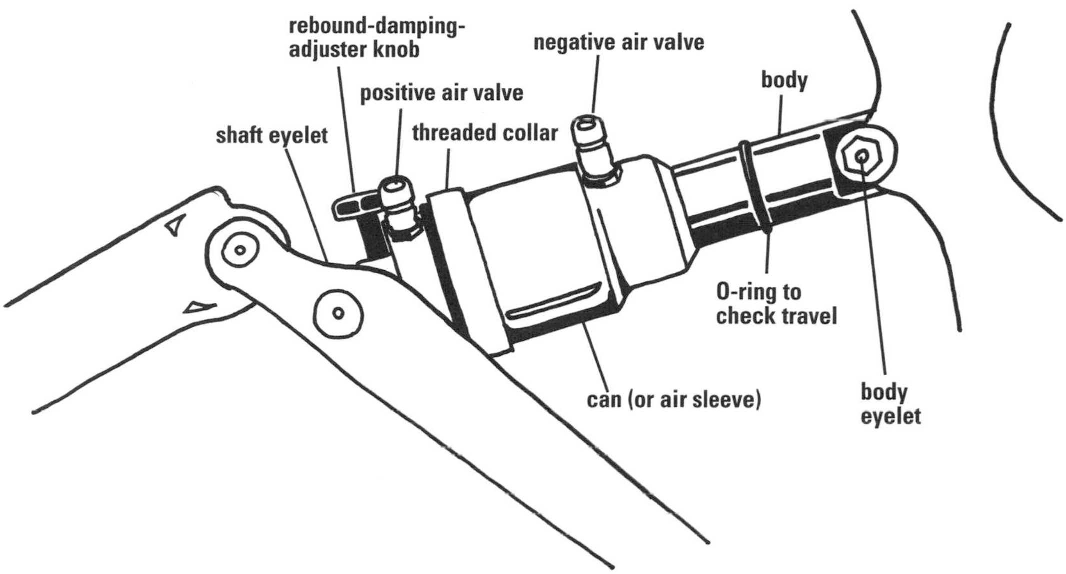

b. Every 40 hours maintenance: air sleeve service

At a minimum, you need to take off the air sleeve (or "can"—see Fig. 14.9) on an air shock after every 40 hours of riding unless you are riding in very clean conditions.

This may seem like a ridiculously frequent schedule of maintenance, but if you think about it for a second you will see that it makes sense. You don't think twice (or I hope you don't) about changing the oil in your car's engine every 3,000 miles, do you? Well, 3,000 miles is 50 hours of driving at 60 mph, and your engine has a lot of oil volume and an oil filter to keep pulling contaminants out of the oil every time it circulates.

Now consider your bicycle shock. Its piston is constantly going up and down as you ride, it has less

14.10 Pushing bearing out (or in) with a vise, using a socket

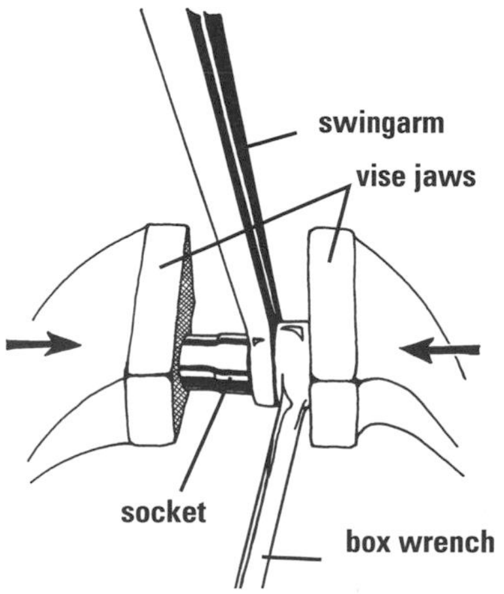

14.11 Pushing a bearing into a tapered swingarm eyelet with a socket

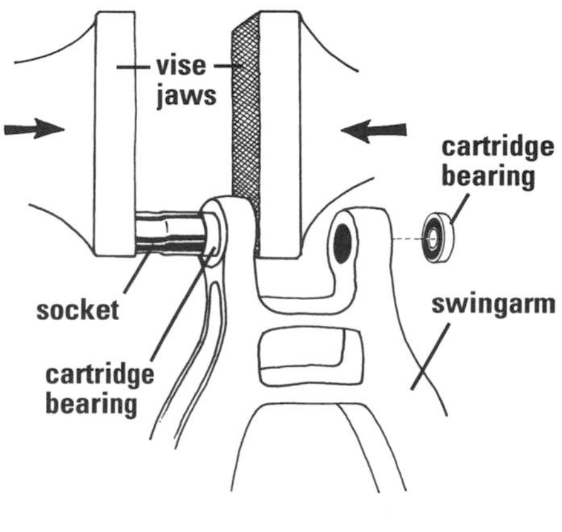

than a teaspoon of lubricant in it, and it has no room for an oil filter. Forty hours does not seem so extreme in that context, does it?

Of course, the time you spend with the shock locked out while riding on the road need not count toward the 40 hours, because the shock is not moving. And if you don't do the air-sleeve service yourself every 40 hours, have a qualified mechanic do it for you.

You also need to regrease the eyelet bushings once a month and/or after every 40 hours of riding, but you will of course do this anyway while you are reinstalling the shock after doing the air-sleeve service after every 40 hours on the trail.

Air-sleeve overhaul

1. Deflate the shock while the bike is weighted, and remove it from the bike.
2. Clamp the faces of the "shaft eyelet" (the eyelet at the big end of the shock—see Fig. 14.9) between the soft jaws of a vise (Fig 14.12). In the absence of soft jaws, use pieces of wood against the jaw faces. You may need to first remove the aluminum sleeves (if installed) from the eyelet by hand or perhaps with an "easy out" (a cone-shaped reverse-threaded tool to remove broken bolts) if you see that they will be damaged by the vise.
3. Grasp the air sleeve with your hands and unscrew it counterclockwise. If you cannot get enough of a grip on it to twist it, wrap an inner tube around it first.

WARNING: *If the air sleeve is hard to unscrew, there might still be pressure inside the shock, in which case you have a bomb in your hands. The can (air sleeve) will come shooting out straight at you if you manage to unscrew it with pressure inside. Some shocks have two positive air chambers inside—the main one below the piston and a secondary one above it. When you deflate the piston when it is at full length, you will only empty the top chamber and the bigger, lower chamber will still be pressurized. With such shocks, you must put the shock back on the bike and then sit on the saddle to compress the shock while depressing the valve pin so that it will deflate. As a result, the piston moves to the end once the first chamber is exhausted and allows the air from the lower chamber to go out of the valve as well.*

4. Slide the sleeve off (Fig. 14.12).
5. Clean the seals around the piston and the O-ring at the top of the threads (that the can screws up against; visible in Fig. 14.12) with a clean, lint-free rag and perhaps some biodegradable cleaning solvent. Wipe down the piston shaft and the shock body as well. Clean the seals at the narrow end of the can and clean the inside of the can thoroughly.
6. Inspect the seals. If any are damaged, or you have had significant air or oil leakage, buy a seal kit for your shock (usually available for less than five bucks) and install those seals. You remove O-rings, rubber square-cross-section seals (sometimes called "quad seals"), glide rings, seal-backing rings, etc., with a sharpened pick of some sort. A couple of long nails you sharpened by spinning them in a drill up against a belt sander will do fine. Leave one straight and bend the other one near the tip so you have some options for digging the seals out of their grooves. Rather than going in under the edge of each seal with your tool, which could scratch the shock's anodized coating and create an air leak, stab each rubber seal and Teflon backing ring with your sharp pick and stretch it up over the lip of its groove and pull it out. Press the

14.12 DT air shock disassembled in vise for air sleeve service

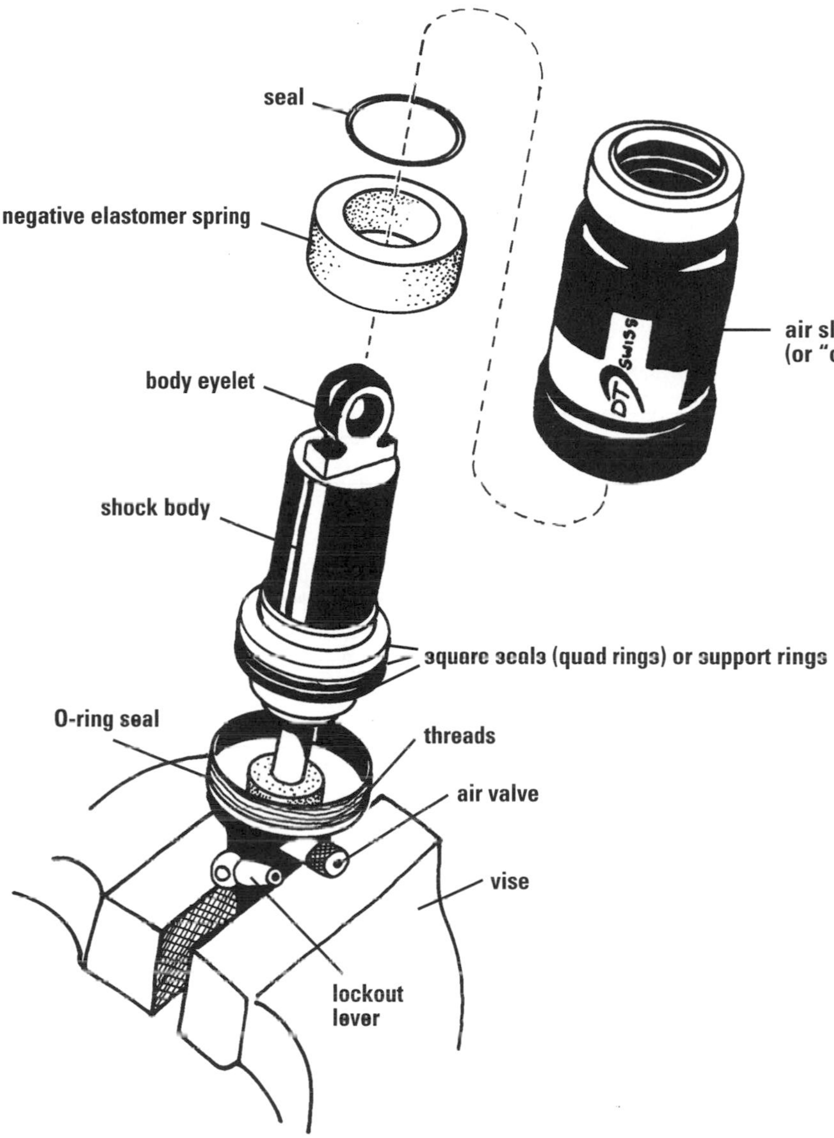

new O-rings, rubber square seals, glide rings, seal-backing rings, etc., back in place where the old ones were.

7. Wipe some Slick Honey grease on all of the seals.
8. Slip the air sleeve back onto the shock body, and if you can, up against the threads. If you can, screw it on (clockwise) hand tight, and then you're done. If you can't get it screwed on, go to step 9.
9. Install the shock in the bike (grease the eyelets and reinstall the aluminum sleeves if you removed them) and sit on the saddle before screwing the sleeve back on (or even sliding it up against the threads). You build negative-spring pressure as soon as the seals engage on the shock body, and it is often too hard to even push it to the threads, much less screw it on. Instead, use the leverage of the bike to push it together.

You're ready to ride another 40 hours!

c. Annual maintenance

Do a shock oil change at least once a year. The oil inside degrades over time, and damping is reduced. If you notice a damping loss, you need an oil change.

d. Tips on tearing apart a shock

Many good mechanics are leery of hydraulic items such as shocks, but hydraulics are often a simpler means of accomplishing something that would require much more complexity and more parts if done with a mechanical system. As with a hydraulic disc brake, you may be amazed at how few parts there are inside. Just make sure you use your shock's manual and keep track of all of those parts!

Shim stacks on shock pistons, just as in fork dampers, can be changed to alter damping. Replacement oil and springs can be obtained at many bike shops. So can knowledgeable shock service. Because special tools are recommended for many shock services, such as replacing air valves, glide rings, shaft bushings, shaft seals, and pivot eyelet bushings, it may not make sense for you to own these tools, in which case a good relationship with a shock-literate shop is in order.

xiv-12 PIVOTLESS FRAME MAINTENANCE

LEVEL 2

Suspension frames without moving pivots fall into two categories: beam bikes and bikes with a shock that depends on the flex of the chainstay, rather than on pivots.

The principal beam suspension used on mountain bikes is the Softride beam (Fig. 10.13), and Softride, Breeze, Otis Guy, and Ritchey are some of the frame brands that have used it. Installation and replacement of the beam are covered in Chapter 10, §x-10. Inspect the beam-mounting points on the frame periodically for fatigue indications (stretched, bulged, or cracking metal or paint). There is not much else to say about Softride beams; they are fairly maintenance-free.

One of the simplest and lightest rear-suspension designs out there relies on a small shock behind the seat tube and flexing chainstays. Beyond checking the chainstays for indications of fatigue (stretched, bulged, or cracking metal or paint), all you really need to do with these is to keep the shock serviced as described above and tuned to your weight and riding style as described below.

xiv-13 REAR-SUSPENSION TUNING

LEVEL 2

There are three main variables to take into account when setting up the rear-suspension system: sag, compression damping, and rebound damping.

The four main types of shocks are air-oil (Fig. 14.9), air-air, coil spring (or "coil over"), and elastomer (or "elastomer over"). In both air-oil and air-air shocks, compressed air acts as the spring. Air-oil shocks rely on the flow of oil through a small opening separating two chambers to slow the suspension movement. Air-air shocks operate on the same basic principle but rely on the movement of compressed air to damp the suspension. Coil-over and elastomer-over shocks use either a coil spring or an elastomer spring surrounding an oil chamber or gas plus oil chamber. The oil provides the damping, and the pressurized gas provides an additional spring. Nitrogen is commonly used as the gas, as it is less likely to emulsify with the oil. This type of shock is not to be inflated by the consumer.

Air-oil and air-air shocks are tuned for the spring rate by varying the air pressure. You must have a shock pump with a no-leak head to pump air into these or to check the air pressure, because the air volume is so small and the air pressure is so high. Start with the pressure recommended by the bike manufacturer for your weight, and experiment from there. Because the location of the shock and pressure requirements vary from bike to bike, the recommendations will come from the bike manufacturer and not from the shock manufacturer.

You can change the spring rate of most coil-over and elastomer-over shocks by turning a threaded preload collar around the shock body, or by replacing the spring.

On rear shocks with hydraulic damping systems, damping is adjusted by varying the size of the orifices through which the oil (or compressed air) flows or by changing the viscosity of the oil. On many models, the damping orifices are adjusted with knobs (Fig. 14.9), and many shocks have a lockout lever as well (Fig. 14.12), but the technique varies from shock to shock, so be sure to read the owner's manual that came with yours.

Please review Chapter 13, §xiii-12 and §xiii-13, on front suspension for an explanation of suspension spring rates, preload, compression damping, rebound damping, and other considerations—it is the same for rear suspension. The same recommendations for setting up forks found in §xiii-19 and §xiii-20 apply to rear suspension, too.

The general recommendations below apply to cross-country, full-suspension bikes as well as to downhill versions, although more specific downhill considerations are found in §xiv-14.

a. Setting sag

Sag, or ride height, is the amount the bike compresses when you just sit on it. Ride height is not dependent on damping because there is no movement involved; it is only dependent on the spring rate and preload.

Sag is affected by changing your springs and/or your spring preload adjustment. A good rule of thumb is to set your springs so that sag uses up one quarter of the bike's travel.

Measure the shock shaft length or the eye-to-eye length of the entire shock when you are off the bike. Have someone else measure it again when you are sitting on the bike. On a coil or elastomer shock, if less than 75 percent of the shaft length is still showing, increase the spring rate or preload, and if more than 75 percent of the shaft length is showing, decrease the spring rate or preload. On an air shock, measure the travel and sag either by looking at the movement of the shock with an O-ring or zip tie wrapped around the shock body (Fig. 14.9). Find the shock's full travel length by setting the O-ring position against the end of the air sleeve, and/or measuring the eye-to-eye shock length with the shock inflated and unweighted. Find the O-ring position and/or eye-to-eye length at full compression with the shock deflated and a rider sitting on the saddle.

Adjust the sag by adjusting the air pressure in an air shock.

If you have an air negative spring, make sure you pump the positive spring first (see §xiii-13). Adjust the sag on either a coil-over shock or an elastomer shock by adjusting the spring preload, and/or by changing the spring. In both of these systems, the preload is usually set by turning a threaded collar surrounding the shock body that compresses the coil spring or the elastomers. Depending on the shock and the spring used, if you have used more than two to six preload turns of the spring collar to reach 25 percent travel usage in ride height, you need a stiffer spring.

WARNING: *Excessive preload on a soft shock can cause the shock to fail. "Coil bind" ruins coil-over shocks; if you have to preload the shock more than two full turns to set the sag, you are in danger of coil bind and need a stiffer spring. Coil bind means that there is no space between coils—each loop of the coil is stacked up against the next one. Consider, for instance, if the bottom-out of your rear suspension occurs at 2 inches of shock travel and the shock has 2⅜ (2.375) inches of total travel. If you tighten the preload collar down more than 0.375 inches, the coil will bind and stop the shock before the swingarm bottoms out. Coil bind puts tremendous stress on the shock and breaks important parts that you would like to keep. It is more of an issue and occurs at fewer preload-collar turns, especially with stiffer springs, because the thicker wire used to make the spring leaves less space between coils to begin with.*

If the preload is zero and you get 25 percent sag, you've got the adjustment you are seeking. Get on the bike carefully while supporting yourself against the wall when measuring sag. On steep downhill courses, more of your weight will be shifted to the front of the bike, so more sag in the rear is a good idea.

REAR-SUSPENSION TUNING

b. Compression damping

If adjustable, set the compression damping as light as possible without bottoming out the shock more than once or twice on your course. Some shocks have an adjustment knob.

c. Rebound damping

If adjustable, set the rebound damping as low as you can get without causing the bike to "pogo" (bouncing repeatedly after a bump). Do the "curb test," starting with the rebound knob fully counterclockwise. Ride off the curb and note how many times the shock bounces. You want only one bounce. Turn the rebound knob clockwise one-quarter turn and ride off the curb again, repeating until you get only one bounce. Record the number of turns in of the knob it took.

If you can adjust your rebound on the fly and you have no lockout lever, turn the rebound damping up when you climb. It does not need to throw you up as much when you hit things, as you are going much slower, anyway. You will climb faster this way. If you have one, use the lockout lever on smooth climbs. Remember to reduce the rebound damping or open the lockout when you head back down.

d. Front and rear compatibility (balance)

You will want to have the front and rear suspension balanced so that everything works together like a beautiful symphony in motion. You can check the front-rear balance by standing next to the bike on level ground, lightly applying the front brake, and stepping straight down on the pedal closest to you while the crankarm is at bottom dead center. If the top tube doesn't tip forward or back as the suspension is compressed, the spring rates are well balanced. Next, sit on the bike in riding position. If one end drops noticeably more than the other, you need to increase the spring preload and/or the spring rate on the end that dropped farther (or soften the spring on the end that dropped less).

e. Inertial valve setting

Some modern shocks have an "inertial valve" on the compression damping system designed to distinguish between bump forces and pedaling forces. Such a system is often said to provide a "pedal platform" for the rider to push against while pedaling without bobbing up and down. Depending on manufacturer, acronyms for these pedal platform systems include ProPedal (Fox), SPV (Manitou), Brain (Specialized/Fox), Motion Control (RockShox), HVR (DT), TST (Marzocchi), and CV/t (5th Element). The threshold bump force magnitude required to open the inertial valve and make the shock fully active is adjustable on some shocks, either with a lever you can flip on the fly like a lockout lever, or with a knob, or by changing the air pressure in an air chamber behind the valve. If adjustable, set it as low as possible (so it blows open most easily when hitting a bump) yet high enough that when you pedal aggressively on a smooth surface the read suspension does not move.

f. Shock mounts

Some shocks have adjustable attachment positions. Usually, these have a number of different mounting holes for one eye of the shock, but some frames (Cannondale Jekyll, for one) mount the body end of the shock via a threaded collar that can be turned to vary the position of the shock. Varying the shock position varies the head angle, bottom-bracket height, and ride height of the bike, and it may also change the rear travel length as well.

Some frames also have adjustable head angles to accomplish similar things. A shallower head angle makes the bike more stable at high speed and gets the front wheel farther out ahead for steep drops.

g. Riding it

Again, see Chapter 13 (§xiii-19 and §xiii-20) and follow the guidelines about picking a test course and taking notes. You want to bottom out a couple of times on the front and rear on a course. If the suspension is never bottoming out, the spring is too stiff or the compression damping is too high.

Change settings in small increments. It is easy to overadjust. Make only one adjustment at a time. Also, once you have balanced your front and rear ends, any adjustment you make to the front, you should also make to the rear, and vice versa. Read your frame manual as well as your shock manual for adjustment methods and recommendations.

Suspension tuning is affected by (1) rider weight, (2) rider ability, (3) riding speeds, (4) course conditions, (5) rider style, and (6) rider's position on the bike. If any or all of these things change, so should the tuning.

Use the softest springs you can with little preload: You want to bottom out occasionally, but not frequently. If you are bottoming out too much, you need to change your compression damping or your spring rate. If the compression is slow, yet you are still bottoming out, your spring is too soft. You will feel beaten up on the intermediate hits, or, when bottoming out on a big hit, it will be harsh through the entire stroke. Stiffen the spring rate and lighten the compression damping. The ride height (again, you want to use up 25 percent of the stroke when you sit on the bike) dictates some of your spring rate.

Preload makes the spring rate ramp up faster. If you can use a stiffer spring and back off on preload, you will be a lot happier for it.

Set the compression damping to blow off quickly: Your plush spring won't bottom out harshly, anyway! The compression damping should be set high enough that on big hits you use up all of your travel, but the saddle doesn't smack you in the butt when you hit bottom. Tighten up compression damping if you blow through the stroke and get bounced too hard.

Decrease the rebound damping to return quickly without the pogo effect: You want a lively rebound, because a sluggish return will allow the suspension to pack up (as you go over stutter bumps, water bars, or closely spaced rocks, the bike will ride lower and lower).

Again, if you have no damping adjuster, change your oil viscosity.

Tighten up the rebound damping if the bike springs back too fast: The rebound should not be so quick that you are getting bounced (remember the curb test—§xiv-13c). Tighten it up for climbs if you have a quick adjuster or lockout lever.

Damping is speed-sensitive. Don't worry about settings that feel good at low speeds being too light for high speeds; the shock will get stiffer as you hit things faster. At all speeds, you want the shock to pop back as quickly as possible without kicking back.

If you have an adjustable pedal platform (i.e., inertial valve), set it as low as possible to get the amount of firmness you want when pedaling aggressively on smooth surfaces (a high setting gives the firmest, locked-out feel). The low threshold setting will allow the shock's compression-damping system to open up and move freely on smaller bumps.

Damping is temperature sensitive. Oil is thick and sluggish in the cold, but when it gets hot, your shock gets really lively. You will need to adjust accordingly in summer, with stiffer springs and firmer damping adjustments. You can lighten up your springs and damping adjustments even more in the cold of winter. Your overall speeds are slower, the grease and oil in the shock is thicker, and elastomer-over and coil-over springs will be stiffer. Lighter oil in the shock will help.

If you have no damping adjuster, you can vary the oil viscosity. Find out what oil weight you have from your manual, the shock manufacturer, or a shop. Rely on manufacturer recommendations to help you decide on your new oil weight. Heavier oil slows the shock; lighter oil speeds it up. Changing the oil in your shock is a good idea, even if you like its performance. Replacing the oil is necessary periodically, because it breaks down with use, and there are little worn bits of your shock floating in it, sometimes even on a new shock. Using lighter oil in winter and heavier in summer is also a good policy.

xiv-14 ADJUSTMENT RECOMMENDATIONS FOR RIDING DOWNHILL COURSES

Everything I said above in §xiv-13 applies, with a few additions. Again, you are looking for a setup in which your front and rear shocks bottom out on the biggest bump on the course, but make sure it is at race speed.

On rougher courses, increasing the spring rate (or preload) will keep you from bottoming out so much. Compensate for small bumps by reducing rebound damping to keep the shock from packing in on successive hits. If the bike is bucking, increase damping a bit.

NOTE: *Too much damping, and not just too little, can sometimes cause bucking. Heavily damped shocks will respond so slowly that they will pack in over repeated bumps, giving you a rigid bike and low ride height (i.e., the suspension will be fully compressed and won't return).*

On smoother courses, try decreasing the spring rate (or preload) and increasing damping. Negotiating turns will usually be the major challenge, and the lower ride height (sag) provided by the softer springs will keep you closer to the ground. The greater sag will also increase the amount of negative fork travel (the amount the wheel can go down) available, which will help maintain tire traction in turns and when braking. Higher compression damping, while making the shock absorption slower, will still be fast enough to deal with isolated bumps and will eliminate the harshest bottoming out. Higher rebound damping will reduce the bouncing of the bike after the isolated bumps.

Where there is no general rough or smooth characterization of the course, set up your suspension to perform best on the sections in which you have the most trouble for the most elapsed time. In other words, don't set it up ideally for a tricky section you get through in a couple seconds; set it up for a challenging section on which you will spend half a minute.

CHAPTER 15

CYCLING COMPUTERS

For a list of all the ways technology has failed to improve the quality of life, please press three.
—Alice Kahn

TOOLS

electrical tape

flat and Phillips screwdrivers

A cycling computer (Fig. 15.1) can be a useful tool if it is set up correctly, and if you want the information it provides. However, it can give you incorrect information if not set up properly, and it can also give you information you might be better off not having.

xv-1 WHY HAVE A CYCLING COMPUTER?

Most likely, you ride your mountain bike because you love it. Or at least that is why you started. If having a computer on your handlebar adds to your pleasure, then by all means use one.

You may love watching yourself eat up the miles on a long ride. Or you may get a thrill from seeing how fast you went on a gnarly downhill. Timing yourself periodically on a favorite loop may bring satisfaction as your times drop with improving fitness. You may like watching your cadence or working on keeping your pedaling rate in a certain range. An altimeter feature may be fun to watch in the mountains. An "electronic road book" feature is cool for mapping trails.

You may have a specific workout schedule with which a heart monitor or even a power meter can assist you in realizing your goals more rapidly. Effectiveness of interval training can be enhanced with proper use of a power meter or at least a computer with a heart monitor. Duration, speed, and intensity of the intervals (and, at least as important, the intensity of the rest periods between intervals, and the intensity of recovery rides between interval days) can be monitored and even stored for later playback.

On the other hand, if you start using your computer to tell you whether you have ridden "far enough" or "hard enough" or "correctly" today, or this week, or this year, then you may want to reconsider using one. We all are probably compulsive enough in our work that we don't need to be compulsive in our play as well. My intention in writing this book is to add to your enjoyment of cycling, and

15.1 **Shimano Flight Deck mounted above the stem**

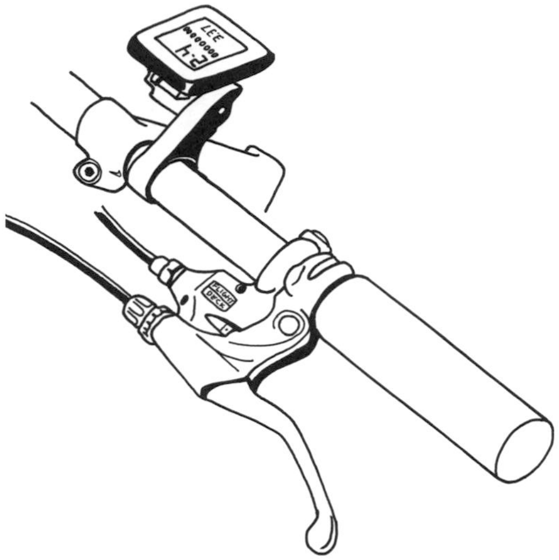

I am not interested in your judging yourself harshly about what you have or have not done on your bike. It can be an insidious feature of a cycling computer—what starts as a fun way to monitor yourself can become a way in which you beat yourself up. And it can creep up on you. Bike riding devolves slowly from fun to drudgery without your noticing, until riding a certain way becomes another thing that you have to do. Yank the computer off your bike if you see this happen. Remember, even if you're a pro, you got into this for the fun of it!

XV-2 SETTING UP A CYCLING COMPUTER

Computers vary from brand to brand. Without having this book become an unmanageably large, dry tome, I can't go into the exact details of which buttons to push when for which computer. But I can give you some general guidelines that work for setting up any computer, and you can get the specifics about which buttons to push from the owner's manual, or from a friendly guy at the bike shop.

a. Measure the circumference of the wheel and tire

1. Inflate the tire mounted on the wheel that will carry the magnet—generally this will be the front wheel. Wrap a piece of tape around the rim and tire in one spot on the wheel.
2. Put a piece of tape crosswise on a hard floor or driveway, and set the wheel on it so that the tape around the tire is lined up over it (Fig. 15.2).
3. Holding the ends of the axle, roll the wheel forward one revolution until the piece of tape is at the bottom again. If you ride your tires at low pressure (25–35 psi), you will get more accuracy if you inflate them only to say, 15 psi, and push down on the handlebar as you roll the bike forward.
4. Put another piece of tape on the floor lined up with the tape on the tire (Fig. 15.2).
5. With a tape measure, find the distance from the leading edge of one piece of tape on the floor to the other. This is the circumference of the inflated tire. Your computer needs this information to properly measure speed and distance, as it is counting revolutions of the wheel and must know distance covered with each revolution.
6. In the computer owner's manual, you will find either a way to enter the circumference, or you will find a table of code numbers corresponding to ranges of circumference and instructions on how to enter the proper code number. I know that everyone loses those instruction booklets, making it tough to reprogram when you change a battery or otherwise "zero out" your computer. File the instructions away. You will need them. But if you do lose them, go to the Internet. Many manufacturers post their instructions and those codes on their Web sites.

15.2 **Rolling out the front wheel to measure its circumference**

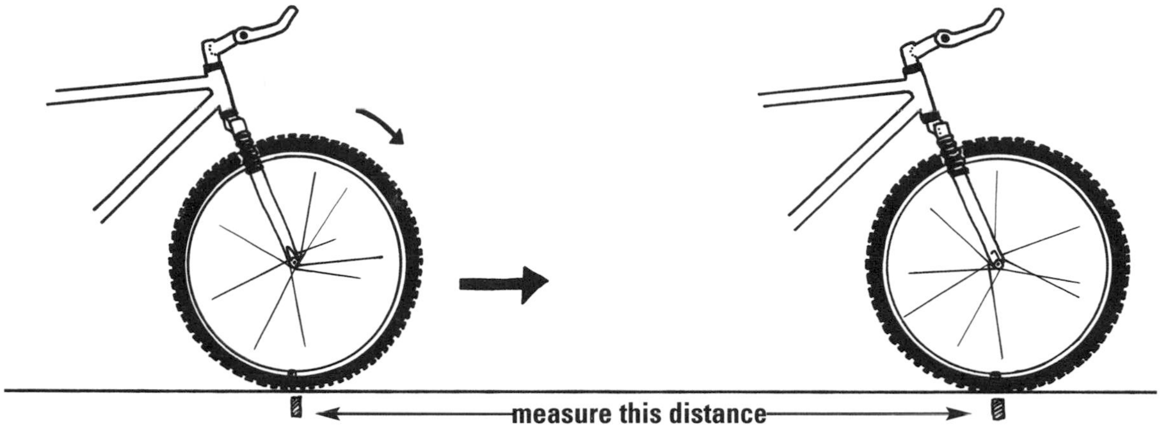

b. Install the computer and sensor

1. Snap the handlebar bracket mount around the handlebar next to the stem (Fig. 15.1). If it fits too loosely onto the handlebar, wrap the handlebar at that spot with one of the rubber pieces that come with the computer or with layers of electrical tape.
2. Tighten the screw to secure the mount, and snap the computer onto the mount.
3. If the computer has a wire to the sensor, wrap the wire around the cable for the front brake to take up slack, and strap the sensor (Fig. 15.7) around the fork leg. With a wireless computer, you need only strap the sensor to the fork leg.
   (a) The sensor usually mounts to the inside of the fork leg about midway down, but the position may need to be changed later for

15.3 **Attaching a Shimano Flight Deck shifting sensor to a Rapidfire shift lever**

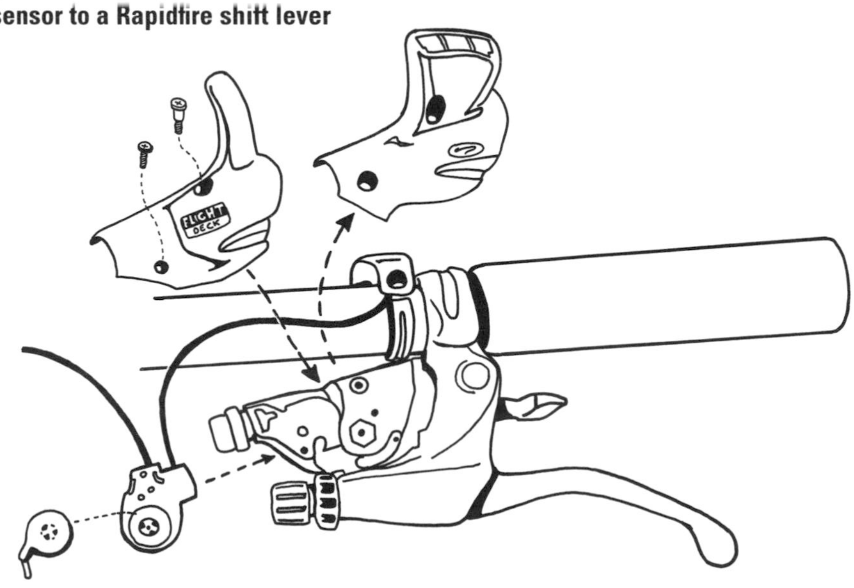

SETTING UP A CYCLING COMPUTER

15.4 **Slotted wheel magnet**

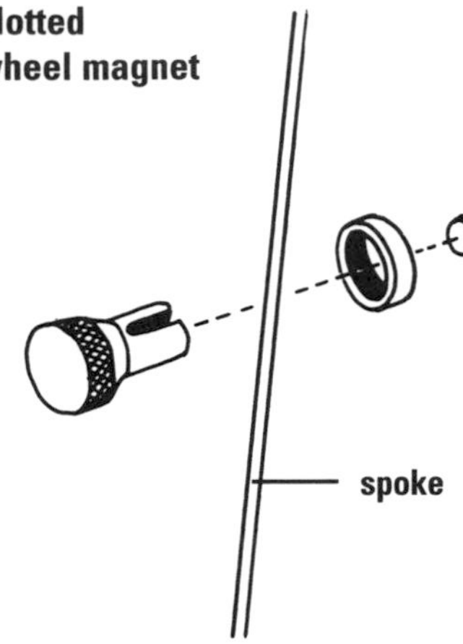

15.5 **Plastic wheel-magnet holder that folds around two spokes**

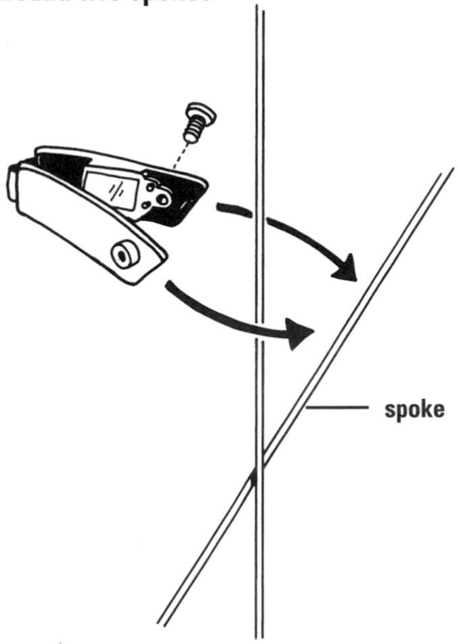

15.6 **Snap-on wheel magnet**

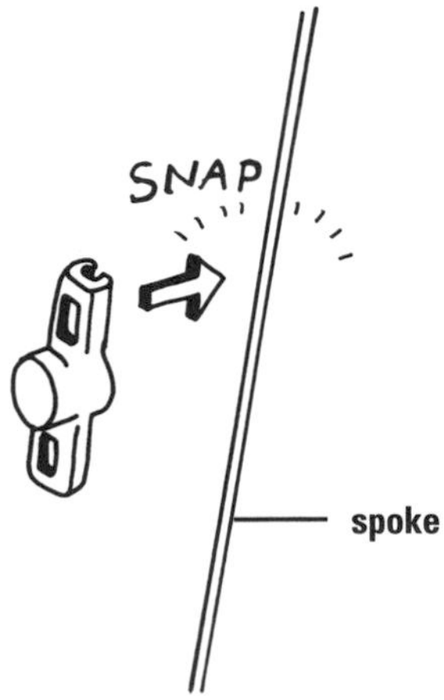

optimal clearance with the wheel magnet. With a wireless computer, the sensor must be fairly close to the computer head, so mount it high on the fork, near the top of the outer leg on a suspension fork. There is usually a built-in zip-tie on the sensor, or separate zip-ties are used to hold the sensor.

(b) Secure the wire to the fork leg with tape or zip-ties.

(c) Shimano cycling computers also have a wire and sensor that must be connected to each Rapidfire shift lever in order to sense when you shift (Fig. 15.3). If your shifter has a gear indicator, you will have to remove it to attach the computer sensor. You won't be putting the indicator back on; chuck it out or throw it in a drawer. To hook up the shifting sensor, you will be installing a plastic insert into the hole the gear indicator came out of—three of them come with the computer, and you will need to look in the manual to find out which one to use for your shifter. The same goes for figuring out which plastic screw-on cover will fit your lever to cover the shifting sensor.

4. Attach the wheel magnet (Figs. 15.4–15.6) to the spokes. Ideally, you want the magnet to sit fairly close to the hub, but clearance with the sensor will largely dictate the position.

(a) Some magnets have a slot in the holder and hold the spoke into the slot with a collar and a screw tightened against the spoke (Fig. 15.4). Other magnets sit in a plastic housing that wraps around two spokes and is retained by a screw (Fig. 15.5). Some recent magnets come in a plastic housing that snaps onto the spoke (Fig. 15.6).

15.7 **Position the magnet close to the sensor and align with one of the scribed lines**

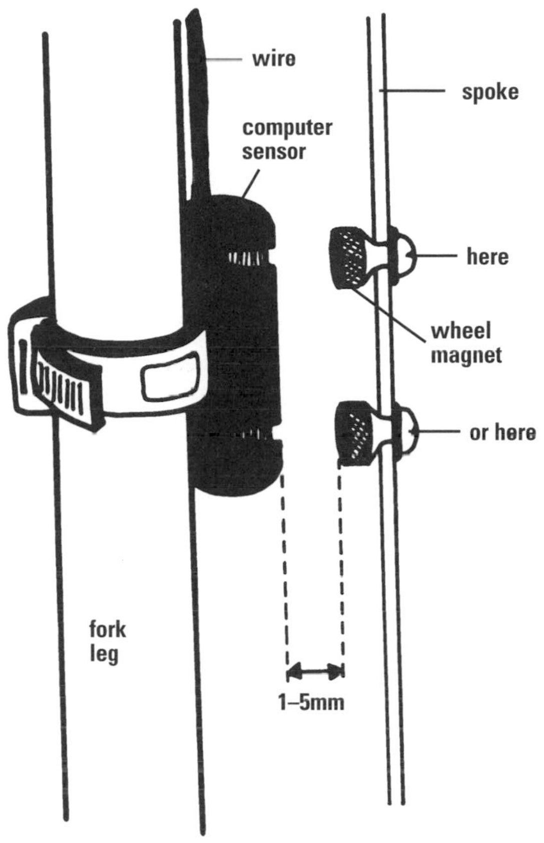

(b) To fit a slotted wheel magnet like the one shown in Figure 15.4 on flat spokes, file the slot in the magnet holder wider, or use a plastic clip-on type as shown in Figures 15.5 or 15.6.

(c) Make sure the wheel magnet passes close to the sensor. If the computer does not indicate a speed when you spin the wheel, the positions of the sensor and/or the magnet need to be changed. Many sensors have a scribed line indicating where the magnet should pass (some sensors have lines at either end, giving you a couple of options). Make sure the magnet passes by the line and that it is close to the sensor (1mm to 5mm away), but it doesn't touch (Fig. 15.7). You may need to slide the sensor and the magnet up or down the fork leg and spoke to get them the right distance apart.

5. If the computer has a separate cadence sensor and magnet, the magnet usually goes on the crankarm, and the sensor mounts to the chainstay. Shimano computers calculate cadence from wheel speed and gear size.
6. On a Shimano Flight Deck computer, you will also need to enter the number of teeth on each of your chainrings and each of your cogs so it can give accurate gear-size and cadence information.
7. Write down all of the settings you inputted into the computer so you can save time and trouble when you have to replace the battery, since you will have to reenter all of the settings.

XV-3 POWER METERS AND HEART MONITORS

SRM power meters have strain gauges built into the spider arms on the right crank. Sensors near the bottom bracket pick up the torque on the crank wirelessly. PowerTap power meters require a special rear hub. Polar power meters only require sensors on the chainstays. Ergomo power meters require a special bottom bracket.

Heart monitors require no additional hookups on the bike, just a strap around your chest.

XV-4 DIAGNOSING COMPUTER PROBLEMS

a. No display

The battery probably needs to be replaced. Some computers have a battery not only in the computer (Fig. 15.8) but also in the sensor, so check both places. Some computers have two batteries in the computer itself. A bike shop (or a camera store)

15.8 Replacing the computer battery

should have a battery to match. You may have to reenter the wheel circumference and other data after changing the battery.

If the battery is not the problem, check for broken wires.

b. Computer is on, but speed does not register

The wheel magnet may be missing, or it may be too far from the sensor as it passes by. Adjust the positions of the sensor and the magnet so that the magnet passes close by the scribed line on the sensor but does not touch it (Fig. 15.7).

c. Cadence reading does not display

Check that your computer does have a cadence feature. If so, check that the sensor and magnet on the crank and frame pass closely by each other (except with a Shimano Flight Deck, which calculates cadence from speed and gear size).

e. Computer reads wrong speed and distance

The wrong wheel size may have been entered. Follow the owner's manual for the button-pushing sequence to find the number programmed into the computer for wheel size. See §xv-2a for instructions on measuring wheel circumference.

f. Can't find computer owner's manual

Here are a number of options:

1. Check the computer maker's Web site for an online owner's manual or ordering instructions for getting a new one.
2. Check with a bike shop for a new manual.
3. Get the contact information for the manufacturer or distributor from the bike shop, and contact the company directly.
4. Find a friend or shop employee who knows how to work your computer, and learn from them. Take notes.

APPENDIX A

TROUBLESHOOTING INDEX

This index is intended to assist you in finding and fixing problems. If you already know wherein the problem lies, consult the Table of Contents for the chapter covering that part of the bike. If, however, you are not sure which part of the bike is affected, this troubleshooting index can be of assistance. It is organized alphabetically, but because people's descriptions of the same problem vary, you may need to look through the entire list to find your symptom.

This index can assist you with a diagnosis and can recommend a course of action. Following each recommended action is a list of chapter numbers to which you can refer for the repair procedure to fix the problem.

SYMPTOM	LIKELY CAUSES	ACTION	CHAPTER
bent wheel	misadjusted spokes	true wheel	6
	broken spoke	replace spoke	6
	bent rim	replace rim	12
bike pulls to one side	wheels not true	true wheels	6
	tight headset	adjust headset	11
	pitted headset	replace headset	11
	bent frame	replace or straighten	14
	bent fork	replace or straighten	13
	loose hub bearings	adjust hubs	6
	tire pressure really low	inflate tires	2, 6
bike shimmies	frame cracked	replace frame	14
at high speed	frame bent	replace or straighten	14

SYMPTOM	LIKELY CAUSES	ACTION	CHAPTER
bike shimmies (cont.)	wheels are way out of true	true wheels	6
	loose hub bearings	adjust hubs	6
	wheels too flexible	tighten spokes or stiffen wheels	6, 12
	headset too loose	tighten headset	11
	flexible frame/heavy rider	replace frame	14
	poor frame design	replace frame	14
bike vibrates when braking *see* "chattering and vibration when braking" under "Strange Noises"			
brake doesn't stop bike	misadjusted brake	adjust brake	7
	worn brake pads	replace pads	7
	wet rims	keep braking	7
	greasy rims	clean rims	7
	sticky brake cable	lube or replace cable	7
	steel rims in wet weather	use aluminum rims	12
	brake damaged	replace brake	7
	sticky or bent brake lever	lube or replace lever	7
	air in hydraulic brake	bleed brake	7
	worn disc-brake pads	replace pads	7
	brake pads missing	install pads	7
brake rubs on rim (*see also* "bent wheel")	brake misaligned	adjust brake	7
chain falls off in front	misadjusted front derailleur	adjust front derailleur	5
	chain line off	adjust chain line	8
	chainring bent or loose	replace or tighten	8
chain jams in front between chainring and chainstay ("chain suck")	dirty chain	clean chain	4
	bent chainring teeth	replace chainring	8
	chain too narrow	replace chain	4
	chain line off	adjust chain line	8

SYMPTOM	LIKELY CAUSES	ACTION	CHAPTER
chain jams in front (cont.)	stiff links in chain	free links, lube chain	4
	thick inner chainring teeth	use thinner chainring	8
chain jams in rear	misadjusted rear derailleur	adjust derailleur	5
	chain too wide	replace chain	4
	small cog not on spline	reseat cogs	6
	poor frame clearance	return to dealer	14
chain skips	tight chain link	loosen tight link	4
	worn out chain	replace chain	4
	misadjusted derailleur	adjust derailleur	5
	worn rear cogs	replace cogs and chain	6, 4
	dirty or rusted chain	clean or replace chain	4
	bent rear derailleur	replace derailleur	5
	bent derailleur hanger	straighten hanger	14
	loose derailleur jockey wheels	tighten jockey wheels	5
	bent chain link	replace chain	4
	sticky rear shift cable	replace shift cable	5
chain slaps chainstay	chain too long	shorten chain	4
	weak rear-derailleur spring	replace spring or derailleur	5
	terrain very bumpy	ignore noise	n/a
derailleur hits spokes	misadjusted rear derailleur	adjust derailleur	5
	broken spoke	replace spoke	6
	bent rear derailleur	replace derailleur	5
	bent derailleur hanger	straighten or replace	14
knee pain	poor shoe cleat position	reposition cleat	9
	saddle too low or high	adjust saddle	10
	clip-in pedal has no float	get floating pedal	9
	foot rolled in or out	replace shoes or get orthotics	n/a

SYMPTOM	LIKELY CAUSES	ACTION	CHAPTER
pain or fatigue when	incorrect seat position	adjust seat position	10
riding, particularly in	too much riding	build up miles gradually	n/a
the back, neçk, and arms	incorrect stem length	replace stem	11
	poor frame fit	replace frame	14
	incorrect handlebar height	adjust stem height or get	
		stem with different angle	11
pedal moves laterally,	loose crankarm	tighten crank bolt	8
clunks, or twists	pedal loose in crankarm	tighten pedal to crank	9
while pedaling	bent pedal axle	replace pedal or axle	9
	loose bottom bracket	adjust bottom bracket	8
	bent bottom-bracket axle	replace bottom bracket or axle	8
	bent crankarm	replace crankarm	8
	loose pedal bearings	adjust pedal bearings	9
pedal entry difficult	mud in cleat or pedal	clean cleat and pedal	9
(with clip-in pedals)	spring tension set high	reduce spring tension	9
	shoe sole knobs too tall	trim knobs	9
	loose cleat	tighten cleat	9
	dry cleat and pedal	lubricate cleat and pedal clips	9
	cleat guide loose or gone	tighten or replace	9
pedal release difficult	spring tension set high	reduce spring tension	9
(with clip-in pedals)	loose cleat on shoe	tighten cleat	9
	dry pedal spring pivots	oil spring pivots	9
	dirty pedals	clean and lube pedals	9
	bent pedal clips	replace pedals or clips	9
	dirty cleats	clean, lube cleats	9
	worn cleat	replace cleat	9
pedal release too easy	release tension set too low	increase release tension	9
(with clip-in pedals)	cleats worn out	replace cleats	9

SYMPTOM	LIKELY CAUSES	ACTION	CHAPTER
rear shifting working poorly	misadjusted derailleur	adjust derailleur	5
(*see also* "chain jams in	sticky or damaged cable	replace cable	5
rear" *and* "chain skips")	loose rear cogs	seat and tighten cogs	6
	worn rear cogs	replace cogs	6
	worn/damaged chain	replace chain	4
resistance while	tire rubs frame or fork	adjust axle and/or true wheel	2, 6
coasting or pedaling	brake drags on rim	adjust brake	7
	tire pressure really low	inflate tire	2, 6
	hub bearings too tight	adjust hubs	6
	hub bearings dirty/worn	overhaul hubs	6
	mud packed around tires	clean bike	2
resistance while	bottom bracket too tight	adjust bottom bracket	8
pedaling only	bottom bracket dirty/worn	overhaul bottom bracket	8
	chain dry/dirty/rusted	clean/lube or replace	4
	pedal bearings too tight	adjust pedal bearings	9
	pedal bearings dirty/worn	overhaul pedals	9
	bent chainring rubs frame	straighten or replace	8
	chainring rubs frame	adjust chain line	8
stiff steering	tight headset	adjust headset	11
suspension problems	fork needs tuning	tune fork	13
front or rear	fork needs overhaul	overhaul fork	13
	rear suspension misadjusted	tune rear shock	14
	rear shock dirty	overhaul rear shock	14
	suspension pivots worn/dirty	overhaul pivots	14
tire loses air or is flat	deflated tire	pump tire	6
	hole in tube	patch or replace tube	6
	bad valve	replace tube or valve	6
	hole in tubeless tire	patch or replace tire	6
	leaky seal around tubeless tire	seal, replace, or Slime	6

STRANGE NOISES: Weird noises can be hard to locate; use this list to assist in locating them.

SYMPTOM	LIKELY CAUSES	ACTION	CHAPTER
creaking noise (*see also* "squeaking noise")	dry handlebar/stem joint	grease handlebar and inside stem clamp	11
	hard-anodizing of stem and handlebar	sand inside stem clamp	11
	dry stem/steering-tube joint	grease steering tube and inside stem clamp	11
	cartridge BB moves inside cup	grease inside cup	8
	loose seatpost	tighten seatpost	10
	loose shoe cleats	tighten cleats	9
	loose crankarm	tighten crankarm bolt	8
	cracked frame	replace frame	14
	dry, rusty seatpost	grease seatpost	10
clicking noise	cracked shoe cleats	replace cleats	9
	cracked shoe sole	replace shoes	9
	loose bottom bracket	tighten BB	8
	loose crankarm	tighten crankarm	8
	loose pedal	tighten pedal	9
chattering and vibration when braking	bent or dented rim	replace rim	12
	loose headset	adjust headset	11
	brake pads toed out	adjust brake pads	7
	wheel way out of round	true wheel	6
	greasy sections of rim	clean rim	6
	loose brake pivot bolts	tighten brake bolts	7
	rim worn out and ready to collapse	replace rim ASAP!	12
	oily disc-brake rotor	clean rotor and pads	7
clunking from fork	headset loose	adjust headset	11
	suspension-fork bushings worn	replace bushings	13

SYMPTOM	LIKELY CAUSES	ACTION	CHAPTER
rubbing or scraping noise when pedaling	crossed chain	avoid extreme gears	5
	front derailleur rubbing	adjust front derailleur	5
	chainring rubs frame	longer bottom bracket or move bottom bracket over	8
rubbing, squealing, or scraping noise when coasting or pedaling	tire dragging on frame	straighten wheel	2, 6
	tire dragging on fork	straighten wheel	2, 6
	brake dragging on rim	adjust brake	7
	mud packed around tires	clean bike	2
	dry, dirty hub dust seals	clean dust seals	6
squeaking noise	dry hub or BB bearings	overhaul hubs or BB	6, 8
	dry pedal bushings	overhaul pedals	9
	squeaky saddle	grease leather-rail contact and oil rail attachments	10
	dry suspension pivots	overhaul suspension	13, 14
	rusted or dry chain	lube or replace chain	4
	dry suspension fork	overhaul fork	13
	dry suspension seatpost	overhaul seatpost	10
squealing noise when braking	brake pads toed out	adjust brake pads	7
	greasy rims	clean rims and pads	7
	loose brake arms	tighten brake arms	7
	flexible seatstays	use brake booster plate	7
	oily disc-brake rotor	clean rotor and pads	7
computer display is blank	battery dead	replace battery	15
inaccurate mileage reading	incorrect wheel circumference in computer	measure wheel circumference	15

APPENDIX B

GEAR DEVELOPMENT

The gear table on the following page is based on a 26-inch (66cm) tire diameter. Your gear-development numbers may be slightly different if the diameter of your rear tire—at inflation, with your weight on it—is not 26 inches. Unless your bike has 24-inch wheels or some other non-standard size, these numbers will be very close.

If you want to have totally accurate gear-development numbers for the tire you happen to have on your bike at the time, at a certain inflation pressure, then you can measure the tire diameter very precisely with the procedure below. You can come up with your own gear chart by plugging your tire diameter into the gear-development formula below the chart on the following page, or by multiplying each number in this chart by the ratio of your tire diameter divided by 26 inches (the tire diameter we used).

Here are the steps to measure the diameter of your tire:

1. Sit on the bike with your tire pumped to your desired pressure.
2. Mark the spot on the *rear* rim that is at the bottom, and mark the floor adjacent to that spot.
3. Roll forward one wheel revolution, and mark the floor again where the mark on the rim is again at the bottom (Fig. 15.2).
4. Measure the distance between the marks on the floor; this is the tire circumference at pressure with your weight on it.
5. Divide this number by π (pi; $\pi = 3.14159$) to get the diameter.

NOTE: *This roll-out procedure is also the method to measure the wheel size with which to calibrate your bike computer, except you do it on the front wheel with most computers.*

CHAINRING GEAR TEETH

REAR HUB COGS	**20**	**22**	**24**	**26**	**28**	**30**	**32**	**34**	**36**	**38**	**39**	**40**	**41**
11	47	52	57	61	66	71	76	80	85	90	92	95	97
12	43	48	52	56	61	65	69	74	78	82	84	87	89
13	40	44	48	52	56	60	64	68	72	76	78	80	82
14	37	41	45	48	52	56	60	63	67	70	72	74	76
15	35	38	42	45	49	52	55	59	62	66	68	69	71
16	33	36	39	42	45	49	52	55	58	61	63	65	67
17	31	34	37	40	43	46	49	52	55	58	60	61	63
18	29	32	35	38	40	43	46	49	52	55	56	58	59
19	27	30	33	36	38	41	44	47	49	52	53	55	56
20	26	29	31	34	36	39	42	44	47	49	51	52	53
21	25	27	30	32	35	37	40	42	45	47	48	50	51
22	24	26	28	31	33	35	38	40	43	45	46	47	48
23	23	25	27	29	32	34	36	38	41	43	44	45	46
24	22	24	26	28	30	32	35	37	39	41	42	43	44
25	21	23	25	27	29	31	33	35	37	39	41	42	43
26	20	22	24	26	28	30	32	34	36	38	39	40	41
27	19	21	23	25	27	29	31	33	35	37	38	39	39
28	18	20	22	24	26	28	30	32	33	35	36	37	38
30	17	19	21	23	24	26	28	29	31	33	34	35	36
32	16	18	20	21	23	24	26	28	29	31	32	33	33
34	15	17	18	20	21	23	24	26	28	29	30	31	31
38	14	16	16	18	19	21	22	23	25	26	27	27	28
	20	**22**	**24**	**26**	**28**	**30**	**32**	**34**	**36**	**38**	**39**	**40**	**41**

CHAINRING GEAR TEETH

THE FORMULA IS:

Gear development = (number of teeth on chainring) × (wheel diameter) ÷ (number of teeth on rear cog)

To find out how far you get with each pedal stroke in a given gear, multiply the gear development by 3.14159265 (π).

CHAINRING GEAR TEETH

42	43	44	45	46	47	48	49	50	51	52	53	REAR HUB COGS
99	102	104	106	109	111	113	116	118	121	123	125	**11**
91	93	95	97	100	102	104	106	108	111	113	115	**12**
84	86	88	90	92	94	96	98	100	102	104	106	**13**
78	80	82	84	85	87	89	91	93	95	97	98	**14**
73	75	76	78	80	81	83	85	87	88	90	92	**15**
68	70	72	73	75	76	78	80	81	83	85	86	**16**
64	66	67	69	70	72	73	75	76	78	80	81	**17**
61	62	64	65	66	68	69	71	72	74	75	77	**18**
57	59	60	62	63	64	66	67	68	70	71	73	**19**
55	56	57	59	60	61	62	64	65	66	68	69	**20**
52	53	54	56	57	58	59	61	62	63	64	66	**21**
50	51	52	53	54	56	57	58	59	60	61	63	**22**
47	49	50	51	52	53	54	55	57	58	59	60	**23**
45	47	48	49	50	51	52	53	54	55	56	57	**24**
44	45	46	47	48	49	50	51	52	53	54	55	**25**
42	43	44	45	46	47	48	49	50	51	52	53	**26**
40	41	42	43	44	45	46	47	48	49	50	51	**27**
39	40	41	42	43	44	45	46	46	47	48	49	**28**
36	37	38	39	40	41	42	42	43	44	45	46	**30**
34	35	35	37	37	38	39	40	41	41	42	43	**32**
32	33	33	34	35	36	37	37	38	39	40	41	**34**
29	29	30	31	31	32	32	33	34	35	36	36	**38**
42	**43**	**44**	**45**	**46**	**47**	**48**	**49**	**50**	**51**	**52**	**53**	

CHAINRING GEAR TEETH

APPENDIX C

MOUNTAIN BIKE FITTING

If you are getting a new bike, you might as well get one that fits you properly. Fit should be the primary consideration when selecting a bike; you can adapt to heavier bikes and bikes not painted your favorite color, but your body will soon protest on one that doesn't fit. The simple need to protect your more sensitive parts should keep you away from a bike without sufficient stand-over clearance (Fig. C.1), but there are a lot of other factors to consider as well. You need to make certain that your bike has enough reach to ensure that you don't bang your knees on the handlebar. You also need to check that your weight is properly distributed over the wheels so that you don't end up going over the handlebar on downhill stretches or unweighting the front end on steep climbs. An improperly sized bike is both inefficient and terribly uncomfortable. Therefore, take some time, and find out how you can pick the properly sized bike.

I've outlined two methods for finding your frame size. The first is a simple method of checking your fit on bikes at your local bike shop. The second is a bit more elaborate, as it involves taking body measurements. This more detailed approach will allow you to calculate the proper frame dimensions whether the bike is assembled or not.

C-1 SELECTING THE SIZE OF A BUILT-UP BIKE

a. Stand-over height

Stand over the bike's top tube and lift the bike straight up until the top tube hits your crotch. The wheels should be at least 2 inches off of the ground to ensure that you can jump off of the bike safely without hitting your crotch. There is no maximum dimension here. Though it may seem like a lot, 5 inches or more of stand-over height is fine, as long as the top tube is long enough for you and the handlebar height can be set properly for you.

NOTE: *If you have 2 inches of stand-over clearance on one bike, do not assume that another bike with the same listed frame size will also offer you the same stand-over clearance. Manufacturers often measure frame size*

C.1 **Bike height**

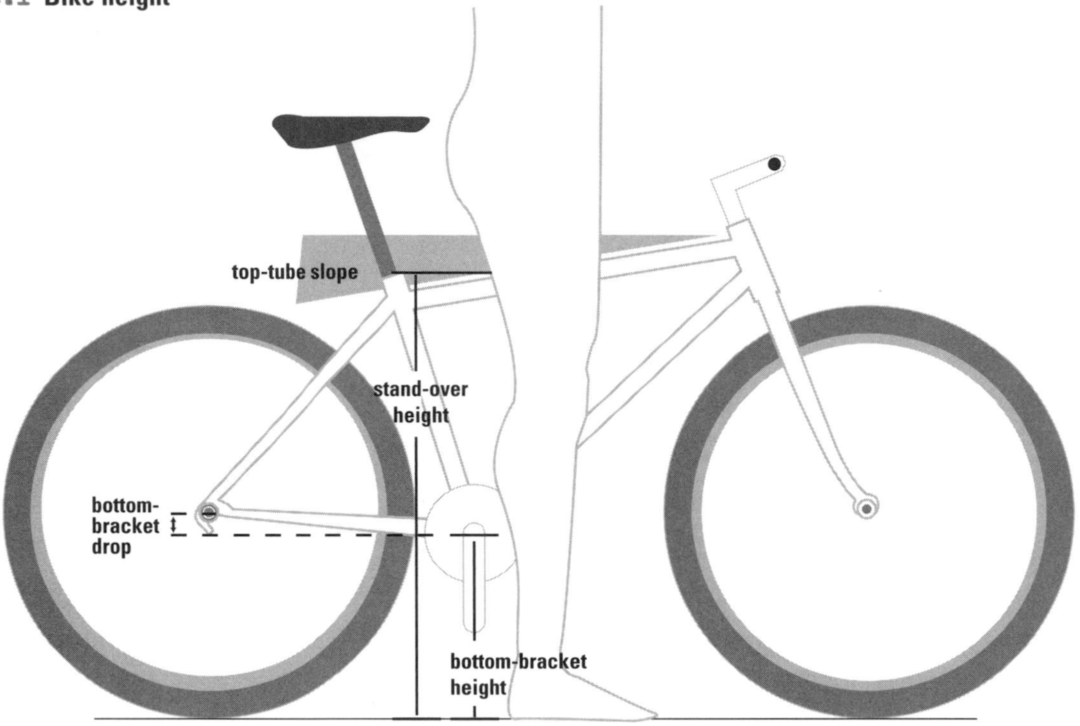

differently. They also slope their top tubes differently and use different bottom-bracket heights (Figs. C.1 and C.2), all of which affect the final stand-over height.

All manufacturers measure the frame size up the seat tube from the center of the bottom bracket, but the top end of the measurement varies. Some measure to the center of the top tube ("center-to-center" measurement), some measure to the top of the top tube ("center-to-top" measurement), and others measure to the top of the seat tube (also called "center-to-top" measurement), even though there is wide variation in the length of the seatpost collar above the top tube. Obviously, each of these methods will give you a different frame size for the same frame.

No matter how the frame size is measured, the stand-over height of a bike depends on the slope of the top tube (Fig. C.1). Top tubes that slant up to the front are common, so stand-over clearance is obviously a function of where you are standing. With an up-angled top tube, stand over it 1 or 2 inches forward of the nose of the saddle, and then lift the bike up into your crotch to measure stand-over clearance.

A bike with a 125mm-travel suspension fork will have a higher front end than a bike with an 80mm- or 100mm-travel fork, or one with a rigid fork would, because the longer the travel length suspension fork. This makes it difficult even to compare listed frame sizes from the same manufacturer to determine stand-over height.

Stand-over height is also a function of bottom-bracket height above the ground. There is substantial variation here, especially with bikes with rear suspension whose bottom brackets are often very high so that ground clearance is still sufficient when the suspension is fully compressed.

Unless the manufacturer lists the stand-over height in its brochure and you know your inseam length, you need to actually stand over the bike.

C.2 **Knee and toe clearance**

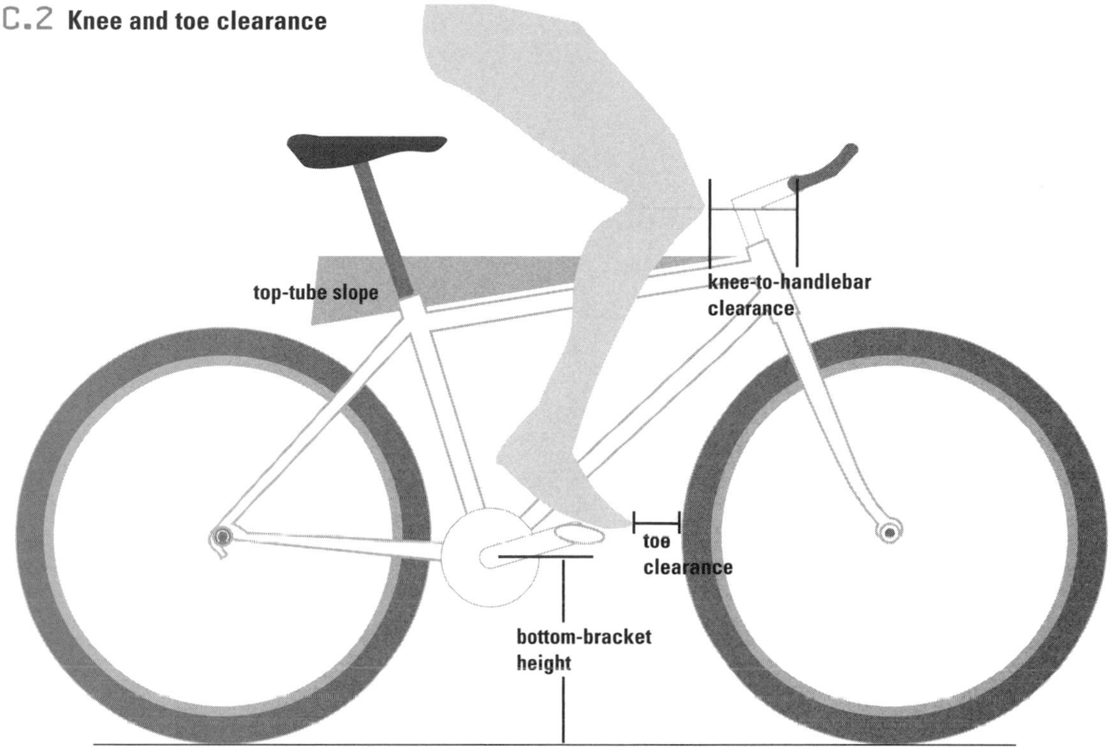

ANOTHER NOTE: *If you are short and cannot find a frame size small enough for you to get at least 2 inches of stand-over clearance, consider a bike with 24-inch wheels instead of 26-inch wheels.*

b. Knee-to-handlebar clearance

Make sure your knee cannot hit the handlebar (Fig. C.2). Do this standing out of the saddle as well as seated and with the front wheel turned slightly. Be certain that your knees will not hit when you are in the most awkward pedaling position you might use.

c. Handlebar reach and drop

Ride the bike. See if the reach feels comfortable to you when holding the handlebar grips or the bar ends. Make sure you can grab the brake levers easily and that your knees do not hit your elbows as you pedal. Check to see that the stem can be raised or lowered enough to achieve a comfortable handlebar height for you.

NOTE: *Threadless headsets (the standard on all bikes today) allow very limited adjustment of stem height. Large changes in height require a change in stems.*

d. Pedal overlap

"Pedal overlap" is a misnomer, because you are actually interested in whether your toe, not the pedal, can hit the front tire when turning sharply at low speeds. Sitting on the bike with the crankarms horizontal and your foot on the pedal, turn the handlebar and check that your toe does not hit the front tire (Fig. C.2). Toe overlap is to be avoided for any kind of slow-speed, technical riding, as pedaling up rocky terrain slowly can often result in the front wheel turning sharply back and forth as the feet pass by. Toe overlap is not an issue for most riding, because at higher speeds, turning the bike does not require turning the front wheel at enough of an angle to hit the foot.

C-2 CHOOSING FRAME SIZE FROM YOUR BODY MEASUREMENTS

You will need a second person to assist you.

By taking the three easy measurements shown in Figure C.3, most people can get a very good frame fit. When designing a custom frame, I go through a more complex procedure than this, involving more measurements. For picking an off-the-shelf bike, this method works well. To avoid the trouble of making these calculations yourself, you can go to the free FIT page at www.zinncycles.com (http://www.zinncycles.com/FitIntro.aspx), and it will automatically calculate your frame size from these measurements.

a. Measure your inseam

Spread your stocking feet about 2 inches apart, and measure up from the floor to a broomstick held level and lifted firmly up into your crotch. You can also use a large book and slide it up a wall to keep the top edge horizontal—as you pull it up as hard as you can—into your crotch. You can mark the top of the book on the wall and measure up from the floor to the mark. With the book method, it is harder to pull up enough to compress the soft tissue up against the bottom edge of the pelvis—so pull up hard.

b. Measure your inseam-plus-torso length

Hold a pencil horizontally in your sternal notch, the U-shaped bone depression just below your Adam's apple. Standing up straight in front of a wall, mark the wall with the horizontal pencil. Measure up from the floor to the mark.

c. Measure your arm length

Hold your arm out from your side at a 45-degree angle with your elbow straight as shown in Figure C.3.

C.3 Body measurements

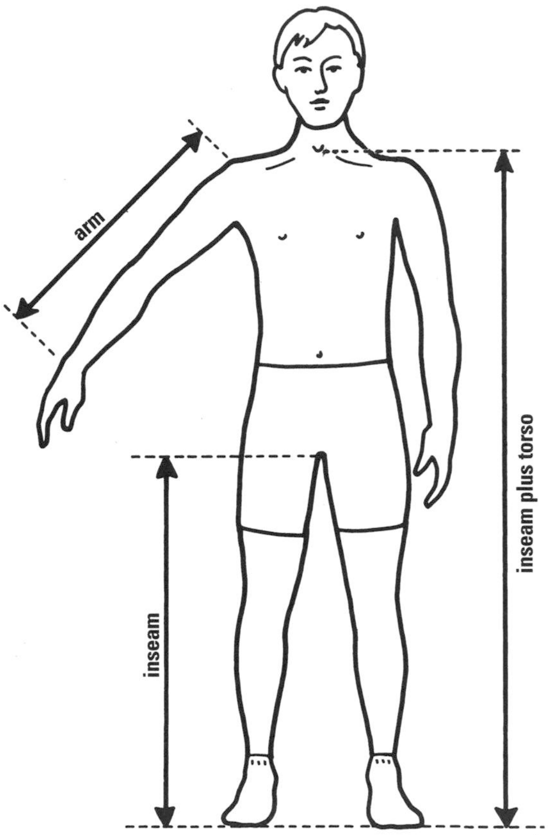

Measure from the sharp bone point directly behind and above your shoulder joint (the lateral tip of the acromion) to the wrist bone on your little finger side.

d. Find your frame size

Subtract 36cm to 42cm (13.5 inches to 16.5 inches) from your inseam length. This length is your frame size measured from the center of the bottom bracket to the top of a horizontal top tube. If the frame you are interested in has a sloping top tube (most mountain bikes do), you may need a bike with an even shorter seat-tube length. With a sloping-top-tube bike, project a horizontal line back to the seat tube (or seatpost) from the top of the top tube at the center of its length (Fig. C.4). Mark the seat tube or seatpost at this line. Measure from the center of the

C.4 **Bike dimensions**

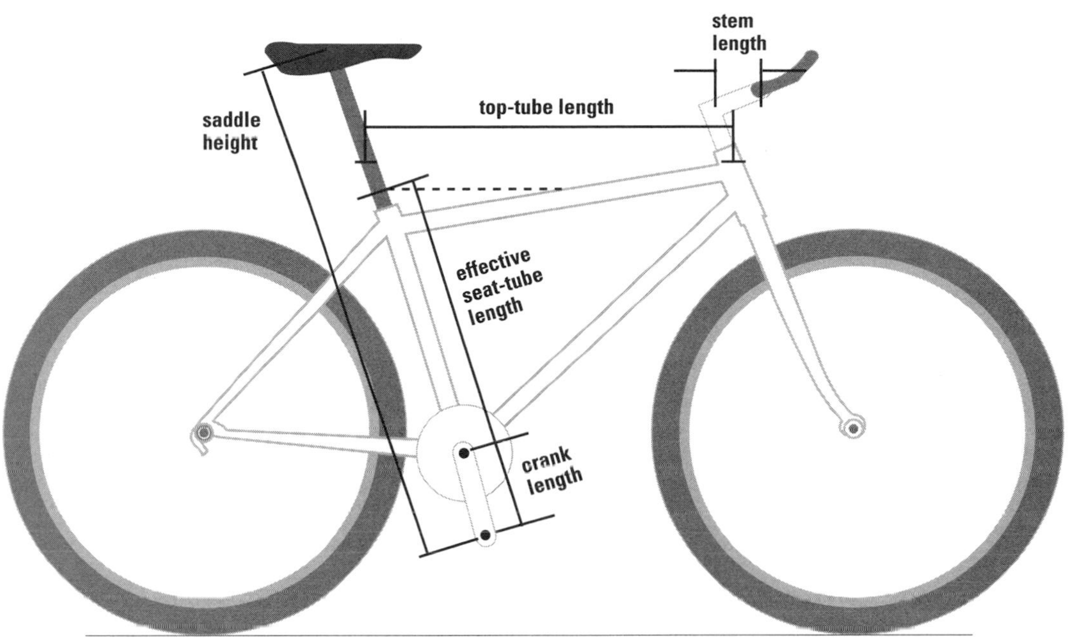

bottom bracket to this mark; this length should be 36–42cm less than your inseam measurement. Also, if the bike has a bottom bracket higher than 29cm (11½ inches), subtract the additional bottom-bracket height from the seat-tube length as well.

Generally, smaller riders will want to subtract closer to 36cm from their inseam, while taller riders will subtract closer to 42cm. However, full suspension frames generally have higher bottom brackets, which reduces stand-over height, so the more suspension travel you have, the shorter the seat-tube length you will want. There is considerable range here. The top-tube length (next step) is more important than a specific frame size, and, if you have short torso and arms, you can use a small frame to get the right top-tube length, as long as you can raise your bars as high as you need them. Be aware that interrupted-seat-tube configurations of some full-suspension frames make measuring frame size challenging.

You really want to be sure that you have plenty of stand-over clearance, so do not subtract less than 36cm from your inseam for your seat-tube length; this should ensure at least 2 inches (5cm) of stand-over clearance. If you are short and cannot find a bike small enough for you to get at least 2 inches of stand-over clearance, consider one with 24-inch wheels instead of 26-inch wheels.

NOTE: *A step-through frame (i.e., "women's frame," "mixte frame," or "girl's bike") having a steeply up-angled top tube meeting near the bottom-bracket shell makes seat-tube length for stand-over clearance nearly irrelevant. With a step-through bike, the only considerations will be horizontal reach and vertical drop to the bars.*

e. Find your top-tube length

To find your torso length, subtract your inseam measurement (found in step 1) from your inseam-plus-torso measurement (found in step 2). Add this torso length to your arm-length measurement (found in step 3). To find the top-tube length, multiply this arm-plus-torso measurement by a factor in the range between 0.47 and 0.5. If you are a casual rider, use 0.47; if you are a very aggressive rider, use 0.5; and, if you are in between, use a factor in between.

The top-tube length is measured horizontally from the center of the seat tube (or seatpost) to the center of the head tube (Fig. C.4). Obviously, the horizontal top-tube length is greater than the length found by measuring along the top tube on a sloping-top-tube bike, so don't just measure along your sloping top tube. Your body position is dictated by the horizontal distance your hands reach forward from your butt—measuring along a sloping line does not give you useful information.

NOTE: *Full-suspension bikes with an interrupted seat tube often have a seatpost clamp that angles the seatpost back sharply along a line that would not intersect the bottom bracket. If you are tall and would have your seat high, your seat would end up far back of where it normally would on a bike of that size, and vice versa. You need to account for this shallow seatpost angle by estimating where the center of your virtual seat tube would be by extrapolating a line from the center of your saddle to the center of the bottom bracket. Measure from this imaginary line horizontally forward to the center of the head tube to find your top-tube length.*

f. Find your stem length

Multiply the arm-plus-torso length you found in step 5 by 0.085 up to 0.115 to find the stem length. Again, a casual rider will multiply by 0.085 or so, while an aggressive rider will multiply by closer to 0.115. This is a starting stem length. Finalize the stem length once you are sitting on the bike and see what feels best.

If you will have to accept a top-tube length different from one that is ideal for you, you will need to make a corresponding adjustment of your stem length.

g. Determine crankarm length

Most mountain bikes come with 175mm cranks (measured hole to hole—see Fig. C.4), and it is rare to find another crank length on a bike, or even available in a shop. But tall riders will often be better off with 180mm crankarms (or even longer custom cranks—see http://www.zinncycles.com/cranks.aspx), and short riders with 165mm or 170mm (or even shorter custom cranks—again, see http://www.zinncycles.com/cranks.aspx).

C-3 POSITIONING OF YOUR SADDLE AND HANDLEBAR

The frame fit is only part of the equation. Except for the stand-over clearance, a good frame fit is relatively meaningless if the seat setback, seat height, handlebar height, and handlebar reach are not set correctly for you.

a. Saddle height

When your foot is at the bottom of the pedal stroke, lock your knee without rocking your hips. Do this sitting on your bike on a trainer with someone else observing. Your foot should be level, or the heel should be slightly higher than the ball of the foot. Another way to determine seat height is using your inseam measurement (Fig. C.3), found in step a under §C-2, Choosing Frame Size from Your Body Measurements. Multiply your inseam length by 1.09; this is the length from the center of the pedal spindle (when the pedal is down) to one of the points on the top of the saddle where it contacts your butt bones

C.5 **Saddle and stem position**

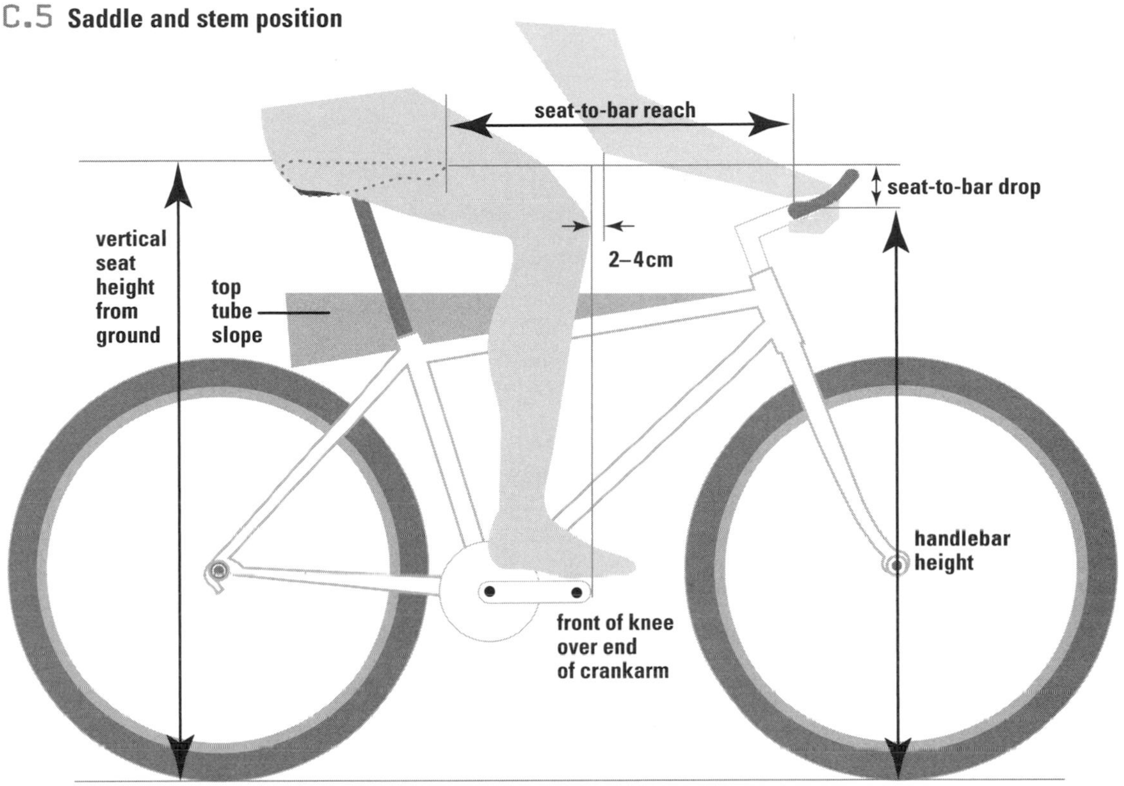

(ischial tuberosities) (Fig. C.4). Adjust the seat height (Chapter 10) until you get it the proper height.

NOTE: *These two methods yield similar results, although the measurement-multiplying method is dependent on shoe sole and pedal thicknesses. Both methods yield a biomechanically efficient pedaling position, but if you do a lot of technical riding and descending, you may wish to have a lower saddle for better bike-handling control, or you may at least want to install a quick-release seat binder and drop your saddle down when you are about to negotiate a technically challenging descent.*

b. Saddle setback

Sit on your bike on a stationary trainer with your crankarms horizontal and your foot positioned at a natural angle (as if you were pedaling). Have a friend drop a plumb line from the front of your kneecap. You can use a heavy ring, washer, etc., tied to a string for the plumb line. The plumb line should touch the end of the crankarm (thus placing the center of rotation of the knee over the center of rotation of the pedal) or fall 2cm behind it (Fig. C.5); you will need to lean the knee out to get the string to hang freely. A saddle positioned fore-and-aft in this manner encourages smooth pedaling at high revolutions per minute, while a position 2cm farther back will encourage powerful seated climbing. You may also wish to experiment with a more forward saddle position; this can keep the front wheel on the ground on steep climbs.

You also will want to make sure that your cleat position (§ix-2 in Chapter 9) is set properly. Generally, you will want your foot deep enough into the pedal that the ball of the foot is right over the pedal spindle or up to 2cm ahead of it; riders with big feet will want their cleats farther back, and vice versa.

Slide the saddle back and forth on the seatpost (Chapter 10) until you achieve the desired fore-and-aft saddle position. Set the saddle level or very slightly tipped down at the nose (downhill racers and big-air freeriders sometimes tip their saddles up steeply at the nose, but their saddles are set very low, and you cannot pedal in an efficient, high seat position this way). Recheck the seat height in step 1 above, as fore-and-aft saddle movements affect seat-to-pedal distance, too.

c. Handlebar height

Measure the handlebar height relative to the saddle height by measuring the vertical distance of the saddle and handlebar up from the floor (Fig. C.5). How much higher the saddle is than your handlebar (or vice versa) depends on your flexibility, riding style, overall size, and the type of riding you prefer.

Aggressive and/or tall cross-country riders will prefer to have their saddle at least 10cm higher than their bar. Shorter riders will want proportionately less drop, as will less aggressive riders. Riders doing lots of downhill stretches will want their bars higher; handlebars on downhill and dual-slalom bikes are commonly considerably higher than the saddle. Generally, people beginning mountain bike riding will like their bars high and can lower them as they become more comfortable with the bike, with going fast, and with riding more technical terrain.

If in doubt, start with 4cm of drop for general cross-country riding and vary it from there. The higher the bar, the greater the tendency is for the front wheel to pull up off of the ground when climbing, and the more wind resistance you can expect, while the more comfort and control you will have going down technical terrain with drop-offs. Change the handlebar height by raising or lowering the stem (Chapter 11), or by switching stems and/or bars.

Again, threadless headsets allow only limited stem-height adjustment without substitution of a differently-angled stem.

d. Setting handlebar reach

The ideal reach from the saddle to the handlebar is also very dependent on personal preference. More aggressive riders will want a more stretched-out position than will casual riders. This length is subjective, and I find that I need to look at the rider on the bike and get a feel for how they would be comfortable and efficient before suggesting a length for handlebar reach.

A useful starting place is to drop a plumb line from the back of your elbow with your arms bent in a comfortable riding position. This plane determined by your elbows and the plumb line should be 2–4cm horizontally ahead of each knee at the point in the pedal stroke when the crankarm is horizontal forward (Fig. C.5). The idea is to select a position you find comfortable and efficient; pay attention to what your body wants.

Vary the saddle–handlebar distance by changing stem length (Chapter 11), not by changing the seat fore-and-aft position, which is based on pedaling efficiency (step b above) and not on reach.

NOTE: *There is no single formula for determining handlebar reach and height. I can tell you that using the all-too-common method of placing your elbow against the saddle and seeing if your fingertips reach the handlebar is close to useless. Similarly, the oft-suggested method of seeing if the handlebar obscures your*

C.6 **Bar-end angle for performance riders**

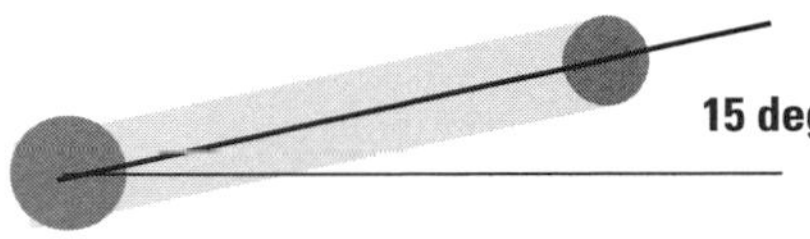

C.7 **Bar-end angle for casual riders**

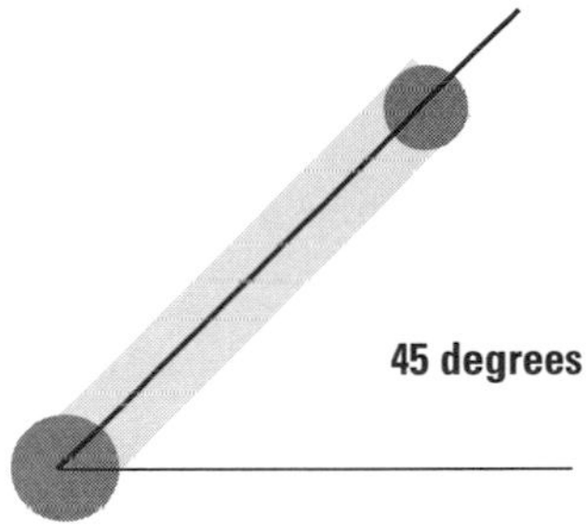

vision of the front hub is not worth the brief time it takes to look, as it largely depends on elbow bend, the inclination of your neck, and the front-end geometry of the bike. Another method involving dropping a plumb bob from the rider's nose is dependent on both the handlebar height and elbow bend and thus does not lend itself to a prescribed relationship for all riders.

e. Bar-end position

Bar ends are an optional item and generally only appear on cross-country bikes. Performance riders should position the bar ends in the range between horizontal and 15 degrees up from horizontal (Fig. C.6). Bar-end angles in this range allow powerful pulling on the bar ends when climbing out of the saddle, because the bar ends are perpendicular to the forearms when standing. This bar-end angle also makes for a lower, more extended position when seated, especially when grabbing the hooks of the bar ends. Use the bar-end position you find comfortable for pulling against when climbing standing or seated and for pedaling on extended paved stretches while seated.

Casual riders often prefer a higher angle (Fig. C.7) in order to pull with a straight wrist and closed fist while seated. Leave the bar-end mounting bolts a bit loose, sit on the bike, and grab the bar ends comfortably. Tighten them down in that position.

NOTE: *Do not use the bar ends to raise your hand position by pointing them vertically up. If you want a higher hand position, get a taller or more up-angled stem, and/or a higher-rise handlebar. Bar ends are not meant to be positioned straight up and held on to for cruising along sitting up high; you cannot reach the brakes when you need them.*

CAUTION: *Some handlebars are not to be used with bar ends for durability reasons. Some superlight carbon, aluminum, and titanium bars either prohibit the clamping of bar ends or come with inserts you must first install to support the clamping area under the bar end.*

APPENDIX D

TORQUE TABLE

One of the single biggest sources of mechanical problems (and breakage risk) is overtightening or undertightening of fasteners, particularly on lightweight equipment. It is great to have the feel for what is tight enough, but many people do not have this, and feel really should only supplement torque measurement. With some parts, particularly today's superlight stems and handlebar, it is important to tighten them to exact torque specifications or you could have a stem or handlebar break while you are riding, which results in an immediate and terrifying loss of control of the bicycle. Even "old guard" mechanics, with their "feel" from years of practice, often overtighten the small, light bolts on lightweight stems.

That said, I also recommend that you develop a feel for bolt tightness. On small bolts, even if you are using a torque wrench (except with a beam-type torque wrench), choke up on the wrench so you can feel with your fingers how hard you are twisting it. *Torque* = *Force* × *Radius*, and because you are reducing the radius at which you apply the force, you have to apply more force to get the same torque on the bolt, so you are aware of the effort it takes. You don't get this sensation when tightening a small bolt by pulling from the end of a long lever where it takes little force to apply a lot of torque. Don't worry about throwing off the torque reading by choking up, as long as you are pulling smoothly. Most torque wrenches have a spring inside to balance the torque on the square bit drive, and this spring action is independent of hand position (the spring pulls from the end of the wrench, and it is the tension on this spring that determines the reading measured by the wrench, irrespective of where you grab the wrench as long as you don't grab its head).

There is also danger to undertightening fasteners. The handlebar in an undertightened stem clamp can come loose and twist, or an undertightened brake cable can pull free when you really yank hard on the brakes. Also, an undertightened bolt suffers more fatigue during use than one that is preloaded.

The standard method of calculating torque specifications is to load the fastener to 80 percent of its yield strength. When you have a rigid joint, this method works. High bolt preload assures that the fastener is always in tension to prevent metal fatigue in the fastener. However, many bike parts are not rigid, and high torques can overcompress or crush components. This is especially important when you are using parts of different brands, eras, or materials together. For instance, a stem manufacturer's torque specification for a handlebar clamp may not have anticipated that a carbon handlebar would be used, and what would work for an aluminum handlebar could crush the carbon one. There is no springback in a rigid joint, but if parts flex under tightening (a handlebar is a good example), that flex may provide the preload that the bolt needs at a considerably lower torque setting than if it were bolted through solid steel parts.

Flex-head torque wrenches usually have a twist knob at the base of the handle to pull tension on the internal spring. You read the torque setting on a vernier scale or against a line on an indicator window on the side of the handle. When the set torque is reached, the head of the wrench snaps over to the side to alert you. Alternatively, a beam-type torque wrench has a needle arm parallel to the wrench shaft that moves across a scale.

You actually need two torque wrenches for working on bikes. The big one cannot measure torques accurately for small bolts. The little one cannot tighten a bottom bracket or crank bolt enough because it does not have a long enough handle, and its scale does not go up high enough.

Using a torque wrench is not a guarantee against a screwup; it simply reduces the chances of one. First, you must make sure that the torque setting you are going for is the one recommended for the bolt you are tightening. The torque table in this appendix includes a lot of bolts, but it obviously cannot include all bolts from all manufacturers, so if you can consult your owner's manual, do it.

Second, lubrication of the bolt, temperature, and a wide variety of other variables will affect torque readings as well. Bicycle bolts generally assume lubrication or threadlock (which provides lubrication before it dries) on the threads, but often not under the bolt head. Lubricating under the bolt head allows the bolt to turn farther at the same torque setting than the same bolt would turn without lubrication under the head, and it thus increases the tension on the bolt.

Third, the torque reading will depend on whether the bolt is turning or you are starting a stationary bolt into motion, because its coefficient of static friction will be higher than its coefficient of dynamic (sliding) friction. If you try to determine the torque of a bolt by checking what torque setting is required on the handle to unscrew the bolt, you will have estimated a higher torque than the actual one, particularly if the bolt has been in place for some time and has corrosion or dirt around it.

Fourth, the reading on the torque wrench assumes that the head is centered over the bolt; the torque reading will be low if you have a radius multiplying the torque. For instance, measuring tightening torque on a pedal axle (if not using a 6mm or 8mm hex key in the hex hole in the axle end) requires a "crow's foot" 15mm open-end wrench attachment on a torque wrench. The crow's foot creates an offset between the axle centerline and the tool head centerline, which, if lined up straight with the torque wrench, multiplies the torque setting displayed on the wrench handle (i.e., it will make the wrench—the radius in the torque equation—

effectively longer). The decimal by which you must multiply the torque reading on the wrench to determine the actual torque applied to the bolt will usually be imprinted on the crow's foot.

Finally, torque wrenches are not 100 percent accurate, and their accuracy changes over time with wear on the internal spring. Most torque wrenches can be calibrated; there will be a bolt attached to the spring that can be screwed in or out to adjust the reading on the wrench to match a known torque. Ultimately, your feel and common sense are also necessary to ensure safety.

It will be worth your while to review §ii-17 in Chapter 2 to help you develop a feel for bolt tightness. Whether or not you have "the touch," a torque wrench is a wonderful thing, as long as you know how tight the bolt is supposed to be.

Listed below are tightening torque recommendations of many bike component manufacturers. Where there is only one number listed and not a range, that is the maximum torque allowable. You can figure around 80–90 percent of that number for the minimum torque.

Most torques are for steel bolts; where possible, aluminum and titanium bolts are described as such in the table. Note that it is particularly important to use a copper-filled lubricant such as Finish Line "Ti-Prep" on titanium bolts to prevent them from binding and galling.

CONVERSION BETWEEN UNITS

The following table is in inch-pounds (in-lbs) and in newton-meters (N·m) (the latter being the one which I find to be easier to use, because the numbers tend to be nice, round one- or two-digit numbers). Divide in-lb settings by 12 to convert to foot-pounds (ft-lbs). Multiply in-lb settings by 0.113 to convert to newton-meters (N·m).

BOLT SIZES

M5 bolts are 5mm in diameter and take a 3mm or 4mm hex key (except on derailleurs, where they often take a 5mm hex key or an 8mm box wrench).

M6 bolts are 6mm in diameter and generally take a 5mm hex key.

M7 bolts are 7mm in diameter and generally take a 6mm hex key.

M8 bolts are 8mm in diameter and generally take a 6mm hex key (or 8mm for crank bolts).

M10 bolts are 10mm in diameter and on bikes will likely take a 5mm or 6mm hex key (rear-derailleur mounting bolt).

The designation M in front of the bolt size number means millimeters and refers to the bolt shaft size, not to the hex key that turns it; an M5 bolt is 5mm in diameter, an M6 is 6mm, and so on, but it may not have any relation to the wrench size. For instance, an M5 bolt usually takes a 4mm hex key (or in the case of a hex-head style, an 8mm box-end or socket wrench), but M5 bolts on bicycles often accept nonstandard wrench sizes. M5 bolts attach bottle cages to the frame, and although some accept the normal 4mm hex key, many have a rounded "cap" head and take a 3mm hex key or sometimes a 5mm hex key. The M5 bolts that clamp a front derailleur around the seat tube, or that anchor the cable on a front or rear derailleur, also take a nonstandard hex key size, namely a 5mm. And M5 disc-brake-rotor bolts often take a TORX T25 key. Conversely, the big single-pinch bolts found on old stems usually take only a 6mm hex key, but they may be M6, M7, and even M8.

Generally, tightness can be classified in three levels:

1. Snug (10–30 in-lbs, or 1–3 N·m): small setscrews (such as Grip Shift mounting screw), bearing-preload bolts (such as on threadless-headset top caps), and screws going into plastic parts need to be snug.
2. Firmly tightened (30–80 in-lbs, or 3–9 N·m): this refers to small M5 bolts, such as shoe-cleat bolts, brake and derailleur cable anchor bolts, derailleur band clamp bolts, small stem faceplate or steering-tube clamp bolts, and brake-rotor mounting bolts. It also refers to many bigger, M6 bolts, especially when threaded into aluminum or magnesium, such as brake- and shift-lever clamp bolts and some disc-brake-caliper mounting bolts. M6 brake-arm mounting bolts and some M5 and M6 seatpost clamp bolts need to be firmly tightened.
3. Tight (80–240 in-lbs, or 9–27 N·m): wheel-axle nuts, old-style single-bolt stem bolts (M6, M7, or M8), some M6 disc-brake-caliper mounting bolts, seatpost binder bolts, and seatpost saddle-clamp bolts need to be tight.
4. Really tight (280–600 in-lbs, or 31–68 N·m): crankarm bolts, pedal axles, cassette-lockring bolts, and bottom-bracket cups are large parts that need to be really tight.

MOUNTAIN BIKE FASTENER TORQUE TABLE

(unit conversion factors are at bottom below)

	inch-lbs		N·m	
BOTTOM BRACKETS AND CRANKS	min	max	min	max
Shimano M8 steel crank bolt	285	435	32	49
FSA M8 steel crank bolt	304	347	34	39
FSA M12 steel crank bolt	434	521	49	59
FSA M14 steel crank bolt	434	521	49	59
FSA M14 aluminum crank bolt	391	434	44	49
FSA M15 steel crank bolt	434	521	49	59
FSA M15 aluminum crank bolt	434	521	49	59
Shimano steel chainring bolt	60	100	7	11
Shimano aluminum chainring bolt		44		5
FSA chromoly Allen chainring bolt		122		12
FSA aluminum Allen chainring bolt		87		10
FSA aluminum TORX chainring bolt		104		11
FSA aluminum bottom-bracket cups	347	434	39	49
loose-ball-bearing bottom-bracket fixed cup	609	695	69	79
loose-ball-bearing bottom-bracket lockring	609	695	69	79
Shimano integrated-spindle bearing cups	305	435	35	50
Shimano cartridge bottom-bracket cups	435	610	49	69

	inch-lbs		N·m	
BOTTOM BRACKETS AND CRANKS, CONT.	min	max	min	max
Race Face X-Type crank bolt	363	602	41	68
Truvativ M8 crank bolts		372		42
Truvativ M12 crank bolts, ISIS		425		48
Truvativ M15 crank bolts, ISIS		425		48
Truvativ M15 crank bolts, Giga X-Pipe		478		54
Truvativ Giga X-Pipe left crank bolt	363	416	41	47
Truvativ self extractor ring–16mm hex key required	106	133	12	15
Truvativ English BB cup, 1.37"	363		41	
Truvativ Giga X-Pipe BB cup	301	363	34	41
Truvativ ISIS Overdrive M48 BB cup	602		68	

BRAKES

Rim Brakes: Cantilevers and V-brakes

brake-lever clamp bolt, M6	50	70	6	8
brake-lever clamp—slotted screw	22	26	2.5	2.9
brake arm–mounting bolt, M6	40	60	5	7
Avid split-clamp lever-mounting bolts	28	36	3.2	4.1
brake-cable anchor bolt, M5	50	70	6	8
V-brake pad nut	50	70	6	8
cantilever brake pad bolt	70	78	8	9
straddle-cable yoke nut	35	43	4	5
Shimano V-brake leverage-adjuster bolt	9	13	1.0	1.5
Avid Arch Supreme arch-mounting bolt	35	40	4	5
Magura hydraulic rim brake:				
M6 center bolt		52		6
M5 housing clamp bolt		35		4
bleed screws		35		4
brake-line sleeve nuts		35		4

Disc Brakes

Avid disc brake:				
rotor-mounting bolts, M5, TORX		55		6
front caliper adapter–mounting bolts, M6	80	90	9	10
rear caliper adapter–mounting bolts, M6	40	60	5	7

	inch-lbs		N·m	
BRAKES, CONT.	min	max	min	max
caliper-mounting bolts to adapter, M6	70	90	8	10
banjo bolt	50	55	5	6
single-lever clamp bolt	30	40	4	5
cable-fixing bolt	40	60	5	7
Coda disc brake:				
rotor-mounting bolts, M5	40	50	5	6
caliper-mounting bolts, M6	69	78	8	9
lever clamp bolt	72	108	8	12
hose sleeve	69	78	8	9
DiaTech disc brake:				
mounting pins	62	80	7	
Formula disc brake:				
rotor-mounting bolts, M5	42	47	5	5
caliper-mounting bolts, M6	76	84	9	9
valve couplers	101	111	11	13
Hayes disc brake:				
rotor-mounting bolts, M5	45	55	5	6
caliper-mounting bolts, M6	100	120	11	14
master-cylinder jam nut	45	55	5	6
caliper bleeder	Torque to seal			
caliper-bridge bolts	100	120	11	14
master-cylinder (brake-lever) clamp bolts:				
98/99, DH Purple (1-pc clamp)	15	20	1.7	2.3
Mag, Mag plus, EC, HFX-9 (2-pc clamp)	15	20	1.7	2.3
HFX-9, Sole (1-pc clamp)	30	35	3.4	4.0
hose connections:				
MC (HFX-9, Sole, El Camino)	55	65	6.2	7.3
MC (HFX-Mag, Mag Plus)	40+1 turn		4.5 + 1 turn	
Caliper—G1	40+1 turn		4.5 + 1 turn	
Caliper—G2	55	65	6.2	7.3
banjo bolt	50	60	5.7	6.8
Hope disc brake:				
rotor-mounting lockring		310		35

	inch-lbs		N·m	
BRAKES, CONT.	min	max	min	max
RockShox disc brake:				
rotor-mounting bolts, M5		50		6
caliper-mounting bolts, M6		50		6
cable-guide hardware		50		6
Magura disc brake:				
rotor-mounting bolts, M5		34		4
master-cylinder (brake-lever) clamp bolts		34		4
master-cylinder hose fitting		34		4
master-cylinder reservoir cover screws		5		0.6
caliper-mounting bolts, M6		51		6
caliper hose fitting, 0-degree		51		6
caliper hose fitting, 90-degree (banjo bolt)		51		6
Shimano hydraulic disc brake, old 4-piston XT type:				
rotor-mounting bolts, M5	18	35	2	4
caliper-mounting bolts, M6		55		6
lever clamp bolt		70		8
caliper bleed nipple	27	44	3	5
reservoir screws	2.5	4.5	0.3	0.5
pad axle bolt	20	35	2.3	4
banjo bolt	44	60	5	7
Shimano hydraulic disc brake, 2-piston LX/XT/XTR type:				
lever hose-sleeve nut	44	60	5	7
rotor-mounting splined lockring	350		40	
caliper-mounting bolts, M6	53	69	6	8
lever clamp bolt	53	69	6	8
caliper bleed nipple	35	53	4	6
reservoir screws	2.7	4.4	0.3	0.5
banjo bolt	44	60	5	7

CHAIN GUIDES				
Truvativ M4, Box Guide		40		4.5
Truvativ M5, Box Guide		40		4.5
Truvativ M6, Box Guide		71		8
Truvativ M6, Box Guide		97		11

	inch-lbs		N·m	
DERAILLEURS AND SHIFTERS	**min**	**max**	**min**	**max**
Shimano front-derailleur cable anchor bolt, M5	44	60	5	7
Shimano front-derailleur clamp bolt, M5	44	60	5	7
Shimano rear-derailleur cable anchor bolt, M5	44	60	5	7
Shimano rear-derailleur mounting bolt, M10	70	90	8	10
Shimano rear-derailleur pulley center bolts, M5	27	34	3.1	4
Shimano Rapidfire shifter clamp bolt, M6	53	69	5.9	8
Shimano thumb-shifter clamp bolt, Allen, M6	53	69	6	8
Shimano thumb-shifter clamp bolt, slotted screw	22	26	2.5	2.9
Shimano thumb-shifter parts anchor screw	22	24	2.5	2.7
Shimano XT/XTR lever cable-access screw cover	3	4	0.3	0.5
SRAM front-derailleur cable anchor bolt, M5		44		5
SRAM 3.0 front-derailleur clamp bolt, M5		70		8
SRAM X-Gen front-derailleur clamp bolt, M5	44	62	5	7
SRAM rear-derailleur cable anchor bolt, M5	35	45	4	5
SRAM rear-derailleur mounting bolt, M10	70	85	8	10
SRAM rear-derailleur pulley center bolts, M5		22		2.5
SRAM rear-derailleur cage-stop screw		13		1.5
SRAM Grip Shift lever-mounting screw		17		1.9
SRAM trigger lever-mounting bolt		44		5
HUBS, CASSETTES, QUICK RELEASES				
Shimano hub quick-release lever closing	43	65	5	7
bolt-on steel skewer		65		7
bolt-on titanium skewer		85		10
nutted front hub		180		20
nutted rear hub		300		34
quick-release axle locknut	87	217	10	25
Shimano freehub cassette body–mounting bolt	305	434	35	50
Shimano cassette cog lockring	261	434	30	50
Mavic cassette cog lockring		354		40
Cannondale Lefty front-axle bolt		133		15
MISCELLANEOUS				
AheadSet bearing preload, M6		22		2.5

	inch-lbs		N·m	
MISCELLANEOUS, CONT.	min	max	min	max
fender to frame bolts, M5	50	60	6	7
water-bottle cage bolts, M5	25	35	2.8	4
PEDALS AND SHOES				
Crank Brothers pedal axle to crankarm	301	363	34	41
Shimano pedal axle to crankarm	304	355	34	40
Time pedal axle to crankarm		310		35
pedal spindle into Truvativ crankarm	186	301	21	34
Crank Brothers shoe-fixing cleat bolt, M5	35	44	4	5
Shimano shoe-fixing cleat bolt, M5	41	52	5	6
shoe spike, M5		34		4
toeclips to pedals, M5	25	45	2.8	5
Speedplay Frog spindle nut	35	40	4	5
SEATPOSTS AND SEAT BINDERS				
seatpost saddle rail–clamp bolt, M8	175	345	20	39
cheap steel seatpost band–clamp bolt	175	345	20	39
Campagnolo seatpost saddle-rail clamp bolt, M8		194		22
Easton seatpost saddle-rail clamp bolts	95	105	11	12
ITM K-Sword M6 (for GWS system)	88	97	10	11
ITM K-Sword Special Bolts (saddle clamp bolt)	88	97	10	11
ITM Forged Lite, all series (aluminum, aluminum-carbon, carbon) M7	62	71	7	8
Oval Concepts M6 saddle-rail clamp bolts		133		15
Ritchey saddle-rail clamp bolt: Comp, Old Pro, M8		400		45
Ritchey saddle-rail clamp bolt: WCS, New Pro, M6		165		19
Selcof saddle-rail clamp bolt, M6		71		8
Selcof saddle-rail clamp bolt, M8		177		20
Thomson saddle-rail clamp bolt, M6		60		7
Truvativ M6 two-bolt		62		7
Truvativ M8 single bolt		80		9
two-piece seat binder bolt, M6	35	60	4	7
seat-tube clamp binder bolt, M6	105	140	12	16

	inch-lbs		N·m	
STEMS AND BAR ENDS	**min**	**max**	**min**	**max**
single stem handlebar clamping bolt, M8	145	220	16	25
wedge expander bolt for quill stems, M8	140	175	16	20
bar end M6 bolt	120	140	14	16
3T M5 bolts (front clamp, steering-tube clamp)	80		9	
3T M6 bolts (single steering-tube clamp)		130		15
3T M6 bolts (two-bolt front-clamp plate)		130		15
3T Bono M6 bolts (two-bolt front-clamp plate)		120		14
3T M8 bolts (single steering-tube clamp; expander)		175		20
3T M8 bolts (single handlebar clamp)		220		25
Bontrager M8 steering-tube clamp bolts		200		23
Deda M5 steel bolts (bar clamp, steering-tube clamp)		90		10
Deda M5 titanium bolts (bar clamp, steering-tube clamp)		70		8
Deda M6 bolts (bar clamp, steering-tube clamp)		160		18
Deda M6 old-model hidden steering-tube clamp bolt		130		15
Deda M8 bolts (quill expander)		160		18
Dimension two-bolt face-plate bar clamp, M6	80	90	9	10
Dimension two-bolt steering-tube clamp, M6	80	90	9	10
Dimension one-bolt handlebar clamp, M8 bolt	205	240	23	27
Easton EA50, 70 bar and steering-tube clamp bolts	60	70	7	8
Easton MG60, EM90 bar clamp bolts	50	60	6	7
Easton MG60 (two M6) steering-tube clamp bolts	50	60	6	7
Easton EM90 (single M8) steering-tube clamp bolt	70	80	8	9
FSA M5 titanium bolts—use Ti prep		68		8
FSA M5 chromoly bolts		78		9
FSA M6 chromoly bolts		104		12
FSA M8 chromoly bolts		156		18
ITM M8 bolts (single-bolt clamp or expander)	150	160	17	18
ITM M7 bolts (single-bolt front clamp)	106	120	12	14
ITM M6 bolts (fork collar)	88	105	10	12
ITM M5 bolts (bar clamp, steering-tube clamp)				
2 front bolts	62	70	7	8

	inch-lbs		N·m	
STEMS AND BAR ENDS, CONT.	min	max	min	max
ITM M5 bolts (bar clamp) 4 front bolts	35	44	4	5
ITM aluminum M6 bolts in magnesium stem	44	53	5	6
Oval Concepts titanium M5 faceplate bolts for alloy bars		84		9.5
Oval Concepts titanium M5 faceplate bolts for carbon bars		49		5.5
Oval Concepts M6 faceplate bolts for alloy bars		93		10.5
Oval Concepts M6 faceplate bolts for carbon bars		58		6.5
Oval Concepts titanium M6 clamp bolts for alloy steering tubes	84		9.5	
Oval Concepts titanium M6 clamp bolts for carbon steering tubes	53		6.0	
Oval Concepts M6 clamp bolts for alloy steering tubes		93		10.5
Oval Concepts M6 clamp bolts for carbon steering tubes		58		6.5
Ritchey WCS M5 faceplate bolts for alloy bars	26	52	3	6
Ritchey WCS M5 faceplate bolts for carbon bars		35		4
Ritchey WCS M6 clamp bolts for alloy steering tubes	52	86	6	10
Ritchey WCS M6 clamp bolts for carbon steering tubes		78		9
Salsa SUL two-bolt face-plate bar clamp, M6	120	130	14	15
Salsa one-bolt handlebar clamp, M6 bolt		140		16
Salsa one-bolt steering-tube clamp, M6 bolt	100	110	11	12
Thomson Elite, X2, X4 steering-tube clamp bolts, M5		48		5
Thomson Elite handlebar clamp bolts, M5		48		5
Thomson X4 handlebar clamp bolts, M5		35		4
Truvativ M5 bolts		50		6
Truvativ M6 bolts—bar		60		7
Truvativ M6 bolts—steering-tube		80		9
Truvativ M7 bolts		120		14

	inch-lbs		N·m	
SUSPENSION	**min**	**max**	**min**	**max**
Rear shocks				
Manitou:				
air canister	13	21	1.5	2.4
Schrader valve stem	4	9	0.5	1.0
RockShox:				
Schrader valve core	8	12	0.9	1.4
Schrader valve housing	25	35	2.8	4.0
Shaft-eyelet assembly	100	110	11	12
Air-can lockring	55	75	6	8
U-Turn air-can assembly	60	70	7	8
Suspension Forks				
Fox fork torque specs:				
32, 36, 40 top caps (Damper, Preload, Air, TALAS)	160	170	18	19
Air tank valve	40	50	5	6
Schrader valve core	3	5	0.3	0.6
All 32, 36, and 40 bottom nuts	45	55	5	6
brake post	75	85	8	10
Vanilla preload topcap knob screw (inside top cap)	10	12	1.1	1.4
All 32, 36 and 40 rebound knob screws	10	12	1.1	1.4
Lockout threshold knob set screw (RLT & RLC)	10	12	1.1	1.4
Low- & high-speed compression knob setscrew (36, 40)	10	12	1.1	1.4
Top cap to old chrome damper shaft upper insert	70	80	8	9
Top cap to LW aluminum damper shaft assembly (all F80-F100X & 05 R-RL-RLC dampers)	70	80	8	9
LW aluminum damper shaft to rebound piston insert & upper insert (all F80-F100X & 05 R-RL-RLC dampers)	50	60	6	7
LW Al vanilla plunger shaft to upper & lower inserts (Loctite 262)	65	75	7	8
LW Al float air shaft to lower inserts (Loctite 262)	65	75	7	8
Rebound adjuster screw to rebound rod	3.7	5.7	0.4	0.6
All rebound piston bolts	50	60	6	7
Base valve bolt R & RL-RLC	50	60	6	7
Base valve assembly to cartridge tube	50	60	6	7

	inch-lbs		N·m	
SUSPENSION, CONT.	min	max	min	max
Cartridge Tube to seal head	50	60	6	7
Slim cartridge tube to slim sealhead	40	50	5	6
F80X IV shaft	115	125	13	14
F80X IV shaft extension	115	125	13	14
F80X compression cylinder	105	115	12	13
F80X IV comp. piston bolt 8-32 × .250"	50	60	6	7
IV body to slim cartridge tube	40	50	5	6
TALAS T-port end cap (Loctite 242, 1 drop)	4	6	0.5	0.7
TALAS hex fitting (Loctite 242)	17	19	1.9	2.1
TALAS ball screw fitting to top cap (Loctite 242)	50	60	6	7
TALAS IFP shaft bolt to IFP shaft (Loctite 242)	50	60	6	7
TALAS base stud (Loctite 242, 1 drop)	50	60	6	7
TALAS lower piston bolt (Loctite 242, 1 drop)	50	60	6	7
TALAS tank valve (Loctite 262, 360 degrees)	35	45	4	5
TALAS M2 screw tank valve to hex adapter (Loctite 242)	3.7	5.7	0.4	0.6
TALAS top cap to IFP shaft (Loctite 242, 1 drop)	50	60	6	7
Crown pinch-bolts on 40 upper and lower crowns		30	0	3
DH axle to lower leg on 36 and 40 forx	14	24	1.6	2.7
Axle pinch-bolts on 36 and 40 lower leg	14	24	1.6	2.7
Manitou fork torque specs:				
EFC/Mach 5/SX cartridge bolt	10	30	1.1	3.4
neutral shaft bolt	10	30	1.1	3.4
brake post	90	110	10	12
EFC/Mach 5/SX cartridge cap	30	50	3.4	6
M8 (6mm key) crown clamp bolt	110	130	12	15
M6 (5mm key) crown clamp bolt		60		7
fork-brace bolt	90	110	10	12
leg caps	25	35	2.8	4
comp rod screw	13	53	1.5	6
damper screw	13	20	1.5	2.3
adjuster caps and top caps	35	50	4	6
Marzocchi fork torque specs:				
26mm top caps	80		9	11
Cartridge foot nut and pump rod	80		9	11

	inch-lbs		N·m	
SUSPENSION, CONT.	min	max	min	max
Monster cartridge foot nut			23	26
Upper and lower crown bolts			5	7
Upper and lower crown bolts–Monster, Shiver	80		9	11
brake post	71		8	10
RockShox fork torque specs:				
Top cap aluminum, all	55	75	6	8
Top cap, plastic, all	55	75	6	8
Bottom bolt, 8mm, solid	45	70	5	8
Bottom bolt, 8mm, hollow	45	75	5	8
Bottom bolt, 8mm, Boxxer	45	75	5	8
Bottom bolt, 8mm, dual air	35	55	4	6
Brake post	65	95	7	11
Crown bolt, Boxxer	50	80	6	9
Knob screw, 4mm, U-turn/Pure Climb-It knob	10	14	1.1	1.6
Axle pinch bolt, Boxxer	20	30	2.3	3.4
Air valve core, Schrader type	8	12	0.9	1.4
Axle bolt, Boxxer	40	60	4.5	7
SID upper-tube threaded retainer	45	75	5	8
Air-valve assembly, Schrader type	20	40	2.3	5
Topcap, U-turn air	115	145	13	16
Pure compression piston bolt	30	50	3.4	6
Pure rebound piston bolt	30	50	3.4	6
PopLoc clamp bolt	18	22	2.0	2.5
BlackBox Lever clamp bolt	6	10	0.7	1.1
Pure remote knob cable set-screw	6	10	0.7	1.1
Pure remote cable-set clamp screw	6	10	0.7	1.1
RST fork torque specs:				
Mozo brake arch bolt	70	80	8	9
Mozo fork crown clamp bolt	70	80	8	9

CONVERSION BETWEEN UNITS:

Divide in-lb settings by 12 to convert to foot-pounds (ft-lbs). Multiply in-lb settings by 0.113 to convert to newton-meters (N·m).

APPENDIX E

PEDAL AND CLEAT COMPATIBILITY

Since the introduction of the SPD (Shimano Pedaling Dynamics) mountain bike pedal, there has been a flood of very successful competitors in a market once dominated by the Japanese component giant. Numerous manufacturers produce "SPD-compatible" pedals. But anyone who has tried more than one brand can attest to the fact that the word "compatibility" means different things to different people.

It is safe to assume that the cleats of any SPD-compatible system will mount on standard mountain bike shoes that have two lengthwise slots in the sole. What compatibility doesn't guarantee is whether those cleats will work in other pedals. Indeed, no manufacturer I have found will even mention whether its cleats work in other pedals, and vice versa. I will, because pedal and cleat compatibility is an issue on the dirt. Riders want to try different equipment, so mountain bikes get traded around a lot.

Included, in addition to current models, are old standbys, many of which are no longer made, namely, Shimano 858, 747, 737, 636 (and 525—similar to 636; and A515—similar to 737), Onza HO, and 1996 Scott pedals (which are representative of a slew of other concurrent Wellgo-made pedals under various brands). Note that Onzas produced since 1998 are completely different than the old HO and resemble 1997 Wellgo/Coda/Scott models in function. Note also that Wellgo cleats (with a WP number on them) come with many different brands of pedals. The same goes for VP, another Taiwanese pedal maker.

I first made this chart in 1997. When revising it in 2001 and 2004, some of these pedals were no longer available, so I did not test the latest cleats on all of them, or vice versa—hence, the dash line in some boxes. Numbers such as "96," "97," and "99" refer to the model year (1996, 1997, or 1999).

The listed pedals, along with private-label models virtually identical to some of these, represent the vast majority of the clip-in mountain bike pedals out there. All pedals were tested at midrange spring tension. Pedals are graded according to how easy they are to enter and release, how well they retain the foot when pulling up hard or bouncing over rough terrain, and how much they allow the foot to float rotationally.

Float is a must: It makes cleat setup much easier, can save your knees the agony of maladjusted cleats, and prevents premature release when wending one's way through twisty singletrack or bouncing down a bumpy descent on the verge of losing control. High retention is also a must, as it can be very disconcerting, if not dangerous, to come out of the pedal when not expecting it. Ease of entry and intentional exit is also a must for convenient and safe use. As you can see, some pedals perform these functions better with another brand of cleat than with their own.

Two pedals not on the chart are Speedplay and Bebop. Both are free-floating, and neither is compatible with any other cleats.

PEDAL AND CLEAT COMPATIBILITY

	PEDAL									
	Shimano PD-					Time ATAC	Crank Bros.	Ritchey		Wellgo
CLEAT	959	858	747	737	636	all	all	'96	'99	#800
SM-SH52	A	A	A	-	-	F	F	-	A	-
SM-SH51	A+	A	A	A	A	F	F	D	A	C
SM-SH50	A	A	A	A	A	F	F	D	-	C
TIME ATAC	F	F	F	F	F	A+	F	F	F	F
Crank Bros.	F	F	F	F	F	F	A+	F	F	F
Ritchey '99	-	A	A	-	-	F	F	-	A	-
Ritchey '96	-	-	B	B	B	F	F	A	-	C
WP-98A	-	-	A	A	B	F	F	B-	-	C
WP-97A	-	A	A	A	B	F	F	A	A	C
LOOK SL3	F	F	F	F	F	F	F	F	F	F
Onza HO	F	F	F	F	F	F	F	F	F	F
VP E-C01	-	-	A	B	B	F	F	D+	-	C
Tioga	F	F	F	F	F	F	F	F	F	F

THE GRADING SCALE

A+ very easy entry and release, abundant float, and very high retention

A good entry, good release, good retention, good float

A- good entry, good release, good retention, small float range

B+ good entry, retention, and float; hard or intermittent release (or break-in required)

B good entry, retention, and release; no float

B- same as **B** with hard or intermittent release (or requiring break-in)

C good entry, release, and float; poor retention (foot can be pulled straight up and out)

C- same as **C,** and pedal is fixed (no float)

D+ can clip in, but foot can only be released by twisting inward

D can clip but cannot release

F cleat will not clip in

Note: Combinations graded D+, D, or F are unsafe to ride with.

PEDAL

Scott	**Scott**	**Coda**	**Look**	**VP**	**VP**	**Exus**	**Tioga**	**Onza**		
'97	'96	'97	SL3	103	104	EM2	Clip	'93	'98	CLEAT
-	-	-	F	-	-	-	F	F	-	SM-SH52
C	B-	C	F	B	C	B+	F	F	C	SM-SH51
C	B-	C	F	B	C	B+	F	F	C	SM-SH50
F	F	F	F	F	F	F	F	F	F	TIME ATAC
F	F	F	F	F	F	F	F	F	F	Crank Bros.
-	-	-	F	-	-	-	F	F	-	Ritchey '99
A	A-	A	F	D	-	-	F	F	-	Ritchey '96
C	B	C	F	B	C	B+	F	F	C	WP-98A
C	C	C	F	B	C	B+	F	F	C	WP-97A
F	F	F	A	F	F	F	F	F	F	LOOK SL3
F	F	F	F	F	F	F	F	B+	F	Onza HO
C	C	C	F	B	C	B+	F	F	C	VP E-C01
F	F	F	F	F	F	F	B+	F	F	Tioga

GLOSSARY

adjustable cup: the nondrive-side cup in the bottom bracket (Fig. 8.9). This cup is removed for maintenance of the bottom-bracket spindle and bearings, and it adjusts the bearings. The term is sometimes applied to the top cup of the headset as well (Figs. 11.17, 11.18).

AheadSet: a style of headset that allows the use of a fork with a threadless steering tube (Fig. 11.7). The name is a trademark of Dia-Compe and Cane Creek.

Allen key (Allen wrench, hex key): a hexagonal wrench that fits inside a hexagonal hole in the head of a bolt (Fig. 1.1A).

all-terrain bike (ATB): another term for mountain bike.

anchor bolt (cable anchor, cable anchor bolt): a bolt securing a cable to a component.

Answer Products: American bicycle- and motorcycle-component company, and parent company of Manitou.

Avid: a brake manufacturer. Subsidiary of SRAM.

axle: the shaft about which a part turns, usually on bearings or bushings.

axle overlock dimension: the length of a hub axle from dropout to dropout, referring to the distance from locknut face to locknut face (Fig. 14.5).

ball bearing: a set of balls, generally made out of steel, rolling in a track to allow a shaft to spin inside a cylindrical part. May also refer to one of the individual balls.

bar end: a short handlebar extension clamped onto the end of the handlebar and extending approximately perpendicular to it (Fig. 11.1).

barrel adjuster: a threaded cable stop that allows for fine adjustment of cable tension. Barrel adjusters are commonly found on rear derailleurs, shifters, and brake levers (Figs. 5.3, 5.26, 5.27, 7.1).

BB (*see* "bottom bracket").

bearing (*see* "ball bearing").

bearing cone: a conical part with a bearing race around its circumference. The cone presses the ball bearings against the bearing race inside the bearing cup (Fig. 6.19).

bearing cup: a polished dish-shaped surface inside of which ball bearings roll. The bearings roll on the outside of a bearing cone that presses them into their track inside the bearing cup (Figs. 6.19, 8.9, 11.17).

bearing race: the track or surface the bearings roll on. It can be inside a cup, on the outside of a cone, or inside a cartridge bearing.

binder bolt: a bolt clamping a seatpost in a frame, a bar end to a handlebar, a handlebar inside a stem, or a threadless steering tube inside a stem clamp.

bonk: (1) *v.* to run out of fuel for the (human) body so that the ability to continue further strenuous activity is impaired. (2) *n.* the state of having such low blood sugar from insufficient intake of calories that the ability to perform vigorous activity is impaired.

bottom bracket (BB): the assembly that allows the crank to rotate. Generally the bottom-bracket assembly includes bearings, an axle, a fixed cup, an adjustable cup, and a lockring.

bottom-bracket drop: the vertical distance between the center of the bottom bracket and a horizontal line passing through the wheel-hub centers. Drop is equal to the wheel radius minus the bottom-bracket height (Appendix C, Fig. C.1).

bottom-bracket shell: the cylindrical housing at the bottom of a bicycle frame through which the bottom-bracket axle passes (Fig. 8.9).

bottom-bracket height: the height of the center of the bottom-bracket spindle above the ground (Appendix C, Fig. C.1).

brake: the mechanical device that decelerates or stops the motion of the wheel (and hence of the bicycle and rider) through friction.

brake block: (*see* "brake pad").

brake booster: an arch-shaped part bolted to the ends of the brake bosses to reduce the flex of the bosses and seat stays when the cantilever brakes or V-brakes are applied (Fig. 7.43).

brake boss (*or* brake post *or* pivot; cantilever boss, post, *or* pivot): a fork- or frame-mounted pivot for a brake arm (Figs. 13.1, 13.2, 14.1).

brake caliper: brake part fixed to the frame or fork containing moving parts attached to brake pads that stop or decelerate a wheel (Figs. 7.12, 7.13, 7.19, 7.20, 7.28, 7.29, 7.33, 7.34, 7.43, 7.48, 7.49, 7.50).

brake pad (*or* brake block): a block of rubber or similar material used to slow the bike by creating friction on the rim, hub-mounted disc, or other braking surface (Figs. 7.16, 7.24).

brake post (*see* "brake boss").

brake shoe: the metal pad holder that holds the brake pad to the brake arm (Fig. 7.15).

braze-on boss: a generic term for most metal frame attachments, even those welded or glued on.

brazing: a method commonly used to construct steel bicycle frames. Brazing involves the use of brass or silver solder to connect frame tubes and attach various "braze-on" items including brake bosses, cable guides, and rack mounts to the frame. Although rarely done, it is also possible to braze aluminum and titanium.

bushing: a metal or plastic sleeve that acts as a simple bearing on pedals, suspension forks, suspension swing arms, and jockey wheels.

butted tubing: a common type of frame tubing with varying wall thicknesses. Butted tubing is designed to accommodate high-stress points at the ends of the tube by being thicker there.

cable (inner wire): wound or braided wire strands used to operate brakes and derailleurs.

cable anchor (*see* "anchor bolt").

cable anchor bolt: an anchor bolt that attaches cables to brakes or derailleurs.

cable boss (*see* "cable stop").

cable hanger: cable stop on a stem, headset washer, fork, or seat-stay arch used to stop the brake-cable housing for a cantilever or U-brake (Figs. 7.3–7.5).

cable housing: a metal-reinforced exterior sheath through which a cable passes (Fig. 5.18).

cable stop: a fitting on the frame, fork, or stem at which a cable-housing segment terminates (Fig. 14.1).

cable-end cap: a cap on the end of a cable to keep it from fraying (Fig. 5.18).

cable-housing stop (*see* "cable stop").

cage: two guiding plates through which the chain travels. Both the front and rear derailleurs have cages. The cage on the rear also holds the jockey pulleys. Also, a water-bottle holder.

caliper (*see* "brake caliper" *and* "measuring caliper").

Campagnolo: Italian bicycle-component company.

Cane Creek: American bicycle-component company and originator of the threadless headset. Originally known as Dia-Compe USA.

cantilever boss (*see* "brake boss").

cantilever brake: a cable-operated rim brake consisting of two opposing arms pivoting on frame- or fork-mounted posts. Pads mounted to each brake arm are pressed against the braking surface of the rim via cable tension from the lever (Figs. 7.27–7.29).

cantilever pivot (*see* "brake boss").

cantilever post (*see* "brake boss").

cartridge bearing: ball bearings encased in a cartridge consisting of steel inner and outer rings, ball retainers, and, sometimes, bearing covers (Figs. 6.18, 6.26, 6.27, 11.24).

cassette: the group of cogs that mounts on a freehub (Fig. 6.27). Also the group of chainrings that mounts on a spiderless crankarm (Fig. 8.8).

cassette hub (*see* "freehub").

casting (*see* "fork casting").

chain: a series of metal links held together by pins and used to transmit energy from the crank to the rear wheel (Fig. 4.1).

chain line: the imaginary line connecting the center of the middle chainring with the middle of the cogset. This line should, in theory, be straight and parallel with the vertical plane passing through the center of the bicycle. The chain line is measured as the distance from the center of the seat tube to the center of the middle chainring (Chapter 5, §v-44, Fig. 5.43).

chain link: a single unit of bicycle chain consisting of four plates with a roller on each end and in the center (Fig. 4.5).

chainring: a multiple-tooth sprocket attached to the right crankarm (Fig. 8.1).

chainring-nut tool: a tool used to secure the chainring nuts while tightening the chainring bolts (Fig. 1.2).

chainstay: a frame tube on a bicycle connecting the bottom-bracket shell to the rear dropout (and hence to the rear-hub axle; *see* Figs. 14.1, 14.2).

chain suck: the dragging of the chain by the chainring past the release point at the bottom of the chainring. The chain can be dragged upward until it is jammed between the chainring and the chainstay (Fig. 4.15).

chain whip (*or* chain wrench): a flat piece of steel, usually attached to two lengths of chain (Fig. 1.2). This tool is used to remove the rear cogs on a freehub or freewheel.

chase, wild goose (*see* "goose chase").

circlip (*or* snapring *or* Jesus clip): a C-shaped snapring that fits in a groove to hold parts together.

clip-in pedal (*or* clipless pedal): a pedal that relies on spring-loaded clips to grip a cleat attached to the bottom of the rider's shoe, without the use of toeclips and straps (Fig. 9.2).

clipless pedal (*see* "clip-in pedal").

cog: a sprocket located on the drive side of the rear hub (Fig. 6.27).

compression damping: diminishing the speed of compression of a spring on impact by hydraulic or mechanical means.

cone: a threaded conical nut that serves to hold a set of bearings in place and also provides a smooth surface upon which those bearings can roll (Fig. 6.19). Can refer to the conical (or male) member of any cup-and-cone ball-bearing system (*see also* "bearing cone").

crankarm: the lever attached at the bottom-bracket spindle and to the pedal used to transmit a rider's energy to the chain (Fig. 8.1).

crankarm anchor bolt (*or* "crank bolt"): the bolt attaching the crank to the bottom-bracket spindle on a cotterless drive train (Fig. 8.1).

crank bolt (*see* "crankarm anchor bolt").

crank length: the distance between the centerline of the bottom-bracket spindle and the centerline of the pedal axle (Appendix C, Fig. C.4).

crankset: the assembly that includes a bottom bracket, two crankarms, chainring set, and accompanying nuts and bolts (Fig. 8.1).

cross-three: (see three-cross)

cup: a cup-shaped bearing surface that surrounds the bearings in a bottom bracket (Fig. 8.9), headset (Fig. 11.17), or hub (Fig. 6.19) (*see also* "bearing cup").

damper (*or* "damping cartridge"): a mechanism in a suspension fork or shock that reduces the speed of the spring's oscillation (Fig. 13.12).

damping: the reduction in speed of the oscillation of a spring, as in a suspension fork or shock.

damping cartridge: (*see* "damper").

derailleur: a gear-changing device that allows a rider to move the chain from one cog or chainring to another while the bicycle is in motion (Figs. 5.3, 5.12).

derailleur hanger: a metal extension of the right rear dropout through which the rear derailleur is mounted to the frame (Fig. 14.1).

diamond frame: the traditional bicycle frame shape (Fig. 14.1).

disc brake: a brake that stops the bike by squeezing brake pads attached to a caliper mounted to the frame or fork against a circular disc attached to the wheel (Figs. 7.17–7. 20).

dish: a difference in spoke tension on the two sides of the rear wheel (Figs. 12.3, 12.21).

dishing: centering the rim in the frame or fork by adjusting spoke tension in a wheel.

dishing tool: a tool to check the centering of a wheel rim relative to the axle ends.

double: a two-chainring drivetrain setup (as opposed to a three-chainring, or " triple," one).

down tube: the frame tube that connects the head tube and bottom-bracket shell together (Fig.14.1).

drivetrain: the crankarms, chainrings, bottom bracket, front derailleur, chain, rear derailleur, and freewheel (or cassette).

drop: (1) the difference in height between two parts (*see also* "bottom-bracket drop"). (2) a terrain discontinuity you may or may not want to ride off of. (3) something not to do with your tools.

dropouts: the slots in the fork and rear triangle where the wheel axles attach (Figs. 13.1, 14.1).

DT (a.k.a. DT Swiss): manufacturer of spokes, other bicycle components, and tools.

dust cap: a protective cap keeping dirt out of a part.

elastomer: a urethane spring sometimes used in suspension forks and rear shocks (Fig. 13.12). Also called an "MCU."

endo: a (usually unintentional) rotation of the bike and rider forward over the front wheel.

expander bolt: a bolt that, when tightened, pulls a wedge up inside or alongside the part into which the bolt is anchored to provide outward pressure and secure said part inside a hollow surface. Expander bolts are found inside quill stems (Figs. 11.8–11.10) and some handlebar-end plugs and handlebar-end shifters.

expander wedge: a part threaded onto an expander bolt and usually used to secure a quill stem inside the fork steering tube or handlebar-end plugs or handlebar-end shifter inside a handlebar. An expander wedge is threaded down its center axis to accept the expander bolt and is either cylindrical in shape and truncated along an inclined plane (Figs. 11.8–11.10) or conical in shape and truncated parallel to its base.

ferrule: a cap for the end of cable housing (Fig. 5.18).

fixed cup: the nonadjustable cup of the bottom bracket located on the drive side of the bottom bracket (Fig. 8.9).

flange: the largest diameter of the hub where the spoke heads are anchored (Fig. 12.4).

fork: the part that attaches the front wheel to the frame (Figs. 13.1, 13.2).

fork casting: the outer legs of a suspension fork, so named because it is generally cast out of molten magnesium (Figs. 13.2, 13.12, 13.21).

fork crown: the cross piece connecting the fork legs to the steering tube (Figs. 13.1, 13.2).

fork ends (*see* "dropouts").

fork rake (rake or wheel offset or offset): the perpendicular offset distance of the front axle from an imaginary extension of the steering-tube centerline (*see also* "steering axis").

fork steerer (*see* "steering tube").

fork tips (*see* "dropouts").

fork trail: the distance measured on the ground between the vertical line passing through the center of the front-hub axle (i.e., the center of the wheel contact patch) and the extension of the centerline of the head tube.

frame: the central structure of a bicycle to which all of the parts are attached (Figs. 14.1, 14.2).

freehub: a rear hub that has a built-in freewheel mechanism to which the rear cogs are attached (Fig. 6.27).

freewheel: the mechanism through which the rear cogs are attached to the rear wheel on a derailleur bicycle (Figs. 6.27, 6.28). The freewheel is locked to the hub when turned in the forward direction, but it is free to spin backward independently of the hub's movement, thus allowing the rider to stop pedaling and coast as the bicycle is moving forward (*see also* "freehub").

friction shifter: a traditional (nonindexed) shifter attached to the frame or handlebar. Cable tension is maintained by a combination of friction washers and bolts.

front triangle (*or* main triangle): the head tube, top tube, down tube, and seat tube of a bike frame (Fig. 14.1).

FSA: a bicycle-component manufacturer. Stands for "Full Speed Ahead."

girl's bike (*see* "step-through frame").

goose chase, wild (*see* "wild goose chase").

granny gear: the lowest gear on the bike. In the granny gear the chain is on the inner (of three) front chainring and the largest rear cog.

Grip Shift: a twist shifter of the SRAM Corporation that is integrated with the handlebar grip of a mountain bike (Figs. 5.26, 5.33). The rider shifts gears by twisting the grip (*see also* "twist shifter").

handlebar: the curved tube, connected to the fork through the stem, that the rider grips in order to turn the fork and thus steer the bicycle. The brake levers and shift levers are attached to it (Fig. 11.1).

head angle: the acute angle formed by the centerline of the head tube and the horizontal.

headset: the bearing system consisting of a number of separate cylindrical parts installed into the head tube and onto the steering tube that secure the fork and allow it to spin and swivel in the frame (Figs. 11.17, 11.18, 11.21, 11.22).

headset cup (*see* "bearing cup").

headset topcap (*see* "topcap").

head tube: the front tube of the frame through which the steering tube of the fork passes (Fig. 14.1). The head tube is attached to the top tube and down tube and contains the headset.

hex key (*see* "Allen key").

hub: the central part of a wheel to which the spokes are anchored and through which the wheel axle passes (Fig. 6.18).

hub brake: a disc, drum, or coaster brake that stops the wheel with friction applied to a braking surface attached to the hub.

Hurricane Components: a bicycle-component company.

Hutchinson: French tire company.

hydraulic brake: a type of brake that uses oil pressure to move the brake pads against the braking surface (Figs. 7.19, 7.43).

index shifter: a shifter that clicks into fixed positions as it moves the derailleur from gear to gear.

inner leg: on a telescoping suspension fork, a tube, usually clamped into the fork crown (except in the case of an "upside-down fork"), that slides in and out of the larger-diameter outer leg as the fork compresses and rebounds (Fig. 13.21). On a standard (non-upside-down) fork, it is also called an "upper tube," "inner," or "stanchion."

inner wire (*see* "cable").

integrated headset: a headset in which the bearing seats are integrated into the head tube (rather than requiring separate headset cups) and the bearings are completely concealed inside of the head tube (Fig. 11.20).

Jesus clip (*see* "circlip").

jockey wheel (*or* "jockey pulley"): a circular, cog-shaped pulley attached to the rear derailleur that is used to guide, apply tension to, and laterally move the chain from rear cog to rear cog (Fig. 5.40).

knobby tire: an all-terrain tire used on mountain bikes (Fig. 6.1).

lawyer tabs (*see* "wheel-retention devices").

link: a pivoting steel hook on a V-brake arm that the cable-guide "noodle" hooks into (Fig. 7.14) (*see also* "chain link").

locknut: a nut that serves to hold the bearing adjustment in a headset, hub, or pedal.

lockring: a large circular locknut. On a bottom bracket, the outer ring that tightens the adjustable cup against the face of the bottom-bracket shell (Fig. 8.9). On a rear shock, the threaded ring that tightens the coil spring on a coil-over shock or is used to secure the fore-aft position of the shock body on some air shocks. On a freehub, the lockring holds the cogs on (Fig. 6.27). On a Center-Lock disc-brake–compatible hub, a lockring secures the rotor to the hub shell (Fig. 7.18).

lock washer: a notched or toothed washer that serves to hold surrounding nuts and washers in position.

Low Normal: a style of rear derailleur (originally called Rapid Rise) pioneered by Shimano in which the return spring is connected to the opposite vertices of the rear derailleur's parallelogram linkage elements compared to the setup for a standard rear derailleur. This arrangement results in the derailleur's moving to the low-gear position (the largest, most inboard rear cog) when the cable tension is removed, rather than to the high-gear position (the smallest, most outboard cog), as on a standard rear derailleur.

main triangle: (*see* "front triangle").

Manitou: American suspension-fork and component company. Subsidiary of Answer Products.

Marzocchi: Italian suspension-fork and component company.

master cylinder: the piston chamber at the lever end of a hydraulic brake system (Figs. 7.21, 7.23).

master link: a detachable link that holds the chain together. The master link can be opened by hand without a chain tool (Figs. 4.12–4.14).

Mavic: French bicycle-component company. Subsidiary of Salomon, which is a subsidiary of Adidas.

MCU (*see* "elastomer").

measuring caliper: tool for measuring the outside dimensions of an object or inside dimensions of a hole by means of movable jaws (Fig. 1.4).

Michelin: French tire company.

mixte frame (*see* "step-through frame").

mounting bolt: a bolt that mounts a part to a frame, fork, or component (*see also* "pivot bolt").

needle bearing: steel cylindrical cartridge with rod-shaped rollers arranged coaxially around the inside walls (Fig. 8.13).

nipple: (1) a thin nut designed to receive the end of a spoke and seat it in the holes of a rim (Figs. 12.1, 12.2). (2) the flared tip of a hydraulic caliper bleed fitting onto which a bleed hose can be attached (Fig. 7.22).

noodle: curved cable-guide pipe on a V-brake arm that stops the cable housing and directs the cable to the cable anchor bolt on the opposite arm (Fig. 7.12).

NoTubes (*or* NoTubes.com) (*see* "Stan's NoTubes").

offset (*see* "fork rake").

outer leg: in a telescoping suspension fork, a tube, usually cast out of magnesium and attached to the front-wheel axle (except in the case of an "upside-down fork"), that slides up and down over the smaller-diameter inner leg as the fork compresses and rebounds (Fig. 13.2). On a standard (non upside down) fork, it is also called the "casting," "fork casting," "slider," or "outer."

outer wire (*see* "cable housing").

outer wire stop (*see* "cable stop").

pedal: platform the foot pushes on to propel the bicycle (Figs. 9.1, 9.2).

pedal overlap: the overlapping of the toe with the front wheel while pedaling (Appendix C, Fig. C.2).

pin spanner: a V-shaped wrench with two tip-end pins. Often used for tightening the adjustable cup of the bottom bracket or other lockrings (Fig. 1.2).

pivot: a pin about which a part rotates through a bearing or bushing. Found on brakes, derailleurs, and rear-suspension systems.

pivot bolt: a bolt on which a brake or derailleur part pivots.

preload (*see* "spring preload").

Presta valve: thin, metal tire valve that uses a locking nut to prevent air from escaping out of the inner tube or tire (Fig. 1.1B).

quick release: (1) the tightening lever and shaft used to attach a wheel to the fork or rear dropouts without using axle nuts (Fig. 6.18). (2) a quick-opening lever and shaft pinching the seatpost inside the seat tube, in lieu of a wrench-operated bolt. (3) a quick cable release on a brake. (4) a fixing mechanism that can be quickly opened and closed, as on a brake cable or wheel axle. (5) any anchor bolt that can be quickly opened and closed by a lever.

quill: the vertical tube of a stem for a threaded headset system that inserts into the fork steering tube. It has an expander wedge and bolt inside to secure the stem to the steering tube (Fig. 11.8).

quill stem: a stem with a quill to insert inside a threaded fork steering tube (Fig. 11.8).

race: a circular track on which bearings roll freely (*see also* "bearing race").

Race Face: Canadian bicycle-component company.

rake (*see* "fork rake").

Rapidfire shifter: an indexing shifter manufactured by Shimano for use on mountain bikes with two separate levers operating each shift cable (Figs. 5.22, 5.24).

Rapid Rise (*see* "Low Normal").

rear triangle: the rear part of the bicycle frame, including the seat stays, the chainstays, and the seat tube (Fig. 14.1).

rebound damping: the diminishing of speed of return of a spring by hydraulic or mechanical means.

rim: the outer hoop of a wheel to which the tire is attached (Fig. 12.1).

riser bar: a handlebar with a double bend on each side of the stem clamp so that the grips are higher than the stem.

Ritchey: American bicycle and bicycle-component company.

RockShox: American suspension-fork and component company. Subsidiary of SRAM.

roller-cam brakes: a brake system using pulleys and a cam to force the brake pads against the rim surface (Fig. 7.50).

saddle (*or* seat): a platform made of leather and/or plastic upon which the rider sits (Fig. 10.1).

Schrader valve: a high-pressure air valve with a spring-loaded air-release pin inside (Fig. 1.1B). Schrader valves are found on some bicycle inner tubes and tubeless tires and air-sprung suspension forks and rear shocks as well as on automobile tires and tubes.

sealed bearing: a bearing enclosed in an attempt to keep contaminants out (Fig. 6.26) (*see also* "cartridge bearing").

seat (*see* "saddle").

seat angle: the acute angle formed by the centerline of the seat tube and the horizontal.

seat cluster: the intersection of the seat tube, top tube, and seat stays.

seat stay: a frame tube on a bicycle connecting the seat tube or the rear shock to the rear dropout (and hence to the rear-hub axle; *see* Figs. 14.1, 14.2).

seatpost: the element supporting and securing the saddle (Fig. 10.4).

seat tube: the frame tube to which the seatpost (and, usually, the cranks) are attached (Fig. 14.1).

shim: a thin element inserted between two parts to ensure that they are the proper distance apart. On bicycles, a shim is usually a thin washer and can be used to space a disc-brake caliper away from the frame or fork or to space a bottom-bracket cup away from the frame's bottom-bracket shell. Shims can also be found inside suspension forks and rear shocks to control suspension movement by permitting or hindering passage of hydraulic fluid through an orifice.

Shimano: Japanese bicycle-component company and maker of XTR, XT, Saint, LX, and STX component lines as well as Rapidfire (shifters), SPD (pedals), and STI (shifting systems).

sidepull cantilever brake (*see* "V-brake").

singletrack: a trail with a single furrow made for feet or a two-wheeled vehicle, as opposed to a road or "doubletrack," which has a track for each set of wheels on a four-wheeled vehicle.

skewer: (1) a long rod. (2) a hub quick release (Fig. 6.18). (3) a shaft passing through a stack of elastomer bumpers in a suspension fork (Fig. 13.12).

slave cylinder: piston chamber in the caliper of a hydraulic brake.

slider (*see* "outer leg").

Slime: tire sealant consisting of chopped fibers in a liquid medium injected inside a tire or inner tube to flow to and fill small air leaks (Fig. 6.14).

snapring (*see* "circlip").

socket: a cylindrical tool with a square hole in one end to mount onto a socket-wrench handle and with hexagonal walls inside the opposing end to grip a bolt head or nut to turn it (Fig. 1.2).

socket wrench: a cylindrical wrench handle with a ratcheting square head extending at right angles to the handle onto which sockets or other wrench bits for turning bolts or nuts are installed (Fig. 1.2). Also called "socket-wrench handle" or simply "wrench handle."

spacer: on a bicycle, generally a thick washer cylindrical in shape intended to space two parts farther apart. Spacers can be found between the headset and the stem and between the stem and the topcap on a threadless steering tube, or between the upper bearing cup and the top nut on a threaded steering tube. Spacers may also be used to space a bottom-bracket cup away from the frame's bottom-bracket shell.

spanner: a wrench in primarily British parlance.

spider: a star-shaped piece of metal that connects the right crankarm to the chainrings (Fig. 8.1).

spline: one of a set of longitudinal grooves and ridges designed to interlock two mechanical parts together (Figs. 6.31, 7.18).

spokes: metal rods that connect the hub to the rim of a wheel (Figs. 12.1, 12.2).

spring: an elastic contrivance that, when compressed, returns to its original shape by virtue of its elasticity. In bicycle suspension applications, the spring used is normally either an elastic polymer cylinder, a coil of steel or titanium wire, or compressed air.

spring preload: the initial loading of a spring so part of its compression range is taken up prior to impact.

sprocket: a circular, multiple-toothed piece of metal that engages a chain (*see also* "cog" *and* "chain ring").

SRAM: American bicycle-component company and maker of Grip Shift, Half Pipes, and ESP (derailleurs). Owner of Sachs, RockShox, Avid, and Truvativ bicycle-component companies.

Stan's NoTubes ("NoTubes"): a brand of tire upgrade system named after inventor Stan Koziatek that includes a latex-based tire sealant to convert a standard tire to a tubeless tire.

stanchion (*see* "inner leg").

stand-over height (*or* stand-over clearance): the distance between the top tube of the bike and the rider's crotch when standing over the bicycle (Appendix C, Fig. C.1).

star nut (star-fangled nut): a pronged nut that is forced down into the steering tube and anchors the headset top-cap bolt to adjust a threadless headset (Figs. 11.7, 11.17).

steerer (*see* "steering tube").

steering axis: the imaginary line about which the fork rotates (Fig. 13.9).

steering tube: the vertical tube on a fork that is attached to the fork crown and fits inside the head tube and swivels within it by means of the headset bearings (Figs. 13.1, 13.2). A steering tube can be threaded or threadless, meaning that the top headset cup can either screw onto the steering tube or slide onto it, and the stem can either (1) insert inside the steering tube and clamp with an expander wedge (threaded) or (2) clamp around the steering tube (threadless). Also called "steerer" or "forksteerer."

stem: connection element between the fork steering tube and the handlebar (Fig. 11.1). An archaic word for stem is also "gooseneck."

stem length: the distance between the center of the steering tube and the center of the handlebar measured along the top of the stem (Appendix C, Fig. C.4).

step-through frame (*or* women's frame, girl's bike, mixte frame): a bicycle frame with a steeply up-angled top tube connecting the bottom of the seat tube to the top of the head tube. The frame design is intended to provide ease of stepping over the frame and ample stand-over clearance.

straddle cable: short segment of cable connecting two brake arms together (Figs. 7.37–7.39).

straddle-cable holder (*see* "yoke").

swingarm: the movable rear end of a rear-suspension frame (Fig. 14.2).

threaded headset: a headset whose top bearing cup and top nut above it screw onto a threaded steering tube (Fig. 11.18).

threadless headset (*see* "AheadSet").

three-cross: a pattern used by wheel builders that calls for each spoke to cross three others in its path from the hub to the rim (Fig. 12.1).

thumb shifter: a thumb-operated shift lever attached on top of the handlebars (Fig. 5.21).

tire bead: the edge of the tire that seats down inside of the rim (Fig. 6.7). The bead's diameter is held fixed to established standards by means of a strong, stretch- and tear-resistant material—usually either steel or Kevlar. These strands alone are also referred to as the "bead."

tire lever: a tool to pry a tire off of the rim (Figs. 6.4, 6.5).

tire sealant (*see* "Slime").

toe overlap (*or* toeclip overlap) (*see* "pedal overlap").

topcap: the round top part of a headset that has a bolt passing through it that screws into the star nut to apply downward pressure on the stem to properly load and adjust the headset bearings on a threadless steering tube (Fig. 11.17).

torque: the rotational analogue of force. Torque is a vector quantity whose magnitude is the length of the radius from the center of rotation out to the point at which the force is applied, multiplied by the magnitude of the force directed perpendicular to the radius. On bicycles, we are primarily interested in (1) the tightening torque applied to a fastener (this value can be measured with a torque wrench—*see* Appendix D) and (2) the torque applied by the rider on the pedals to propel the rear wheel and hence the bicycle.

top tube: the frame tube that connects the seat tube to the head tube (Fig. 14.1).

torque wrench: a socket-wrench handle with a graduated scale and an indicator to show how much torque is being applied as a bolt is being tightened (Figs. 1.3, 2.12; *see also* Appendix D).

TORX wrench: a tool with a star-shaped end that fits in the star-shaped hole in the head of a TORX bolt (Figs. 1.3, 1.5).

trail: (1) where to ride your mountain bike. (2) (*see* "fork trail").

triple: a term used to describe the three-chainring combination (Fig. 8.2) attached to the right crankarm.

Truvativ: a bicycle-component manufacturer. Subsidiary of SRAM.

twist shifter: a cable-pulling derailleur control handle surrounding the handlebar adjacent to the hand grip; it is twisted forward or back to cause the derailleur to shift (Figs. 5.25, 5.33). (*see also* "Grip Shift").

U-brake: a mountain-bike brake consisting of two arms shaped like inverted Ls affixed to posts on the frame or fork (Fig. 7.49).

unicrown: a manufacturing method of nonsuspended (i.e., rigid) forks in which the fork legs curve toward each other and are welded directly to the steering tube (Fig. 13.1).

upper tube (*see* "inner leg").

upside-down fork: a suspension fork whose lower legs (attached to the wheel axle) are the inner legs of the forks and move up and down within the upper, outer legs of the fork. Motorcycle forks are generally built this way.

UST: tubeless-tire system originated by Mavic, Michelin, and Hutchinson in which the tire seals over a " hump" on the ledge inside a rim free of spoke holes on its outer circumference (Fig. 6.7).

V-brake (*or* sidepull cantilever brake): a cable-operated cantilever rim brake consisting of two vertical brake arms pivoting on frame- or fork-mounted pivots pulled together by a horizontal cable. A brake pad is affixed to each arm, and there is a cable link and cable-guide pipe on one arm and a cable anchor on the opposite arm (Figs. 7.12–7.14).

wedge (*see* "expander wedge").

wheel base: the horizontal distance between the two wheel axles.

wheel dish (*or* wheel dishing) (*see* "dish" or "dishing").

wheel-dishing tool (*see* "dishing tool").

wheel-retention devices (*or* wheel-retention tabs *or* lawyer tabs): cast-in or separate fixtures at the fork ends designed to prevent the front wheel from falling out if the hub quick-release lever or axle and nuts are loose.

wild goose chase (*see* "chase").

women's frame (*see* "step-through frame").

wrench: a tool having jaws, a shaped insert, or a socket to grip the head of a bolt or a nut to turn it. In British parlance, also called a "spanner."

yoke: the part on a cantilever or U-brake attaching the brake cable to the straddle cable (Fig. 7.6).

Zinn: author of this book. Not to be confused with Zen. ☺

BIBLIOGRAPHY

Barnett, John. *Barnett's Manual: Analysis and Procedures for Bicycle Mechanics, 4th ed.* Boulder, CO: VeloPress, 2000.

Brandt, Jobst. *The Bicycle Wheel.* Menlo Park, CA: Avocet, 1988.

Dushan, Allan. *Surviving the Trail.* Tumbleweed Films, 1993.

Langley, Jim. *Bicycling Magazine's Complete Guide to Bicycle Maintenance and Repair.* Emmaus, PA: Rodale Press, 1994.

Leslie, David. *The Mountain Bike Book.* London: Ward Lock, 1996.

Lindorf, W. *Mountain Bike Repair and Maintenance.* London: Ward Lock, 1995.

Muir, John, and Tosh Gregg. *How to Keep Your Volkswagen Alive: A Manual of Step by Step Procedures for the Compleat Idiot.* Santa Fe, NM: John Muir Publications, 1969.

Pirsig, Robert. *Zen and the Art of Motorcycle Maintenance.* New York: William Morrow & Co., 1974.

Schraner, Gerd. *The Art of Wheelbuilding: A Bench Reference for Neophytes, Pros & Wheelaholics.* Denver, CO: Buonpane Publications, 1999.

Stevenson, John, and Brant Richards. *Mountain Bikes: Maintenance and Repair.* Mill Valley, CA: Bicycle Books, 1994.

Taylor, Garrett. *Bicycle Wheelbuilding 101: A Video Lesson in the Art of Wheelbuilding.* Westwood, MA: Rexadog, 1994.

Van der Plas, Robert. *The Bicycle Repair Book.* Mill Valley, CA: Bicycle Books, 1993.

———. *Mountain Bike Maintenance.* San Francisco: Bicycle Books, 1994.

Zinn, Lennard. *Mountain Bike Performance Handbook.* Osceola, WI: MBI, 1998.

———. *Zinn and the Art of Road Bike Maintenance.* Boulder, CO: VeloPress, 2000.

ILLUSTRATION INDEX

Adjuster knob, damping, 310
Air chuck, 19
Air compressor, 19
Aliup HP clip-in pedal, exploded, 218
Avid brakes, mounting, 154
Axle nuts, loosening, 26
Axles:
- installing, 121, 122
- removing, 211
- in shells, 195

Axle spline tool, 211

Ball bearings, 117, 126.
See also Cartridge bearings
- in pedals, 216

Band-clamp adapters, 77
Bar ends, 7, 234
- angles of, casual/performance rider, 326
- assembly, exploded, 234
- grips and, 236

Barrel adjusters, 70, 72, 137
Batteries, replacing, 350
Bearing seals, 124, 333, 335
Bike stands, 14, 17.
See also Truing stands
Bits, 19
Blowguns, 19
Body measurements, 366
Bolts:
- cable-fixing, 70
- chainring, 187
- crank, 184
- fixing, 169
- pivot, 76
- shaft, 310, 311

Bottom brackets:
- adjustable cartridge, 191
- assembly, 190
- installing, 195, 196
- Mavic/Stronglight cartridge, 191
- Shimano, 191, 194
- standard bearing, 191

Bottom-bracket shells, 324
- placing axles in, 195

Bottom-bracket tools, 15, 18, 35
Brake bosses, 288, 324
- bent, 290

Brake cables:
- cantilever, 140
- changing tension on, 137
- housing for, 81
- installing, at brake levers, 83, 138
- tightening, 140

Brake levers, 7
- adjusting, 43, 143
- installing, 141
- Rapidfire, 143
- Shimano, 143

Brake lines:
- bleeding/filling, 176
- Magura, 176

Brake pads:
- adjusting rims to, 145, 169
- changing, 161
- cleaning, 181
- fixing bolts and, 169
- holder assembly for, 146
- installing, 175
- Magura, 174, 175
- replacing, 148
- toeing-in, 169
- worn, 181

Brake posts, 288, 297, 312
Brake reach, adjusting, 143
Brakes:
- adjusting, 143
- cantilever, 25, 145, 167, 168, 170, 171
- front, 7
- Hayes, 160, 162
- hydraulic, 152, 156, 174, 175
- linkage, 178
- Magura, 174, 175
- rear, 6
- roller-cam, 179
- Shimano, 152, 156, 158
- U-, 178
- V-, 24, 143, 145, 146, 148

Bushings:
- cleaning, 313
- freeing inner legs from, 311
- greasing, 313
- sleeves, 97

Cable bosses, 6, 324
Cable caps, 81
Cable cutters, Shimano, 15
Cable ends, crimping, 90
Cable hangers, 140
Cables, 17
- Gore-Tex, 81

Cages:
- derailleur, opening, 45
- water bottle, 7

Cantilever brakes:
- ball joint, 167
- cable angle for, open/closed, 171
- Campagnolo, 170
- curved-face, 170
- cylindrical clamp, 168

Cantilever brakes, continued
exploded, 167
releasing, 25
Ritchey, 170
threaded post, 168
Cartridge bearings, 97, 125, 252
front hub, 117
press-in angular, 255
rear shock, 335
tapping out, 123
Cartridge bottom-bracket tools, 15, 35
Chain-elongation indicators, 17, 57
Chain line, measuring, 101
Chain links, 20, 57
loosening, 59, 63
stiff, 59, 63
Chainring nut tools, 15
Chainrings, 6
outer/middle, 188
removing/installing, 189
Shimano, 189
straightening bent, 188
Chainring shifting ramps, 187
Chain rivets, removing, 57
Chains, 6
assembling, 58, 59
broken, fixing, 41
checking wear on, 57
cleaning, 31, 33, 54, 55
determining length of, 58
jammed, freeing, 40
lubing, 54
master links for, 60, 61
Chainstays, 6, 324
Chain suck, 62
Chain tension, 96
Chain tools, 12, 20
Chain whips, 15, 16
Circlips, removing, 315
Clearance, knee/toe, 365
Cleats, installing, 206
CO_2 cartridges, 20
Cog lockring tools, 15, 35
Cogs:
cassette, 125
cleaning, 32, 127
rear, 6
Cog-wear indicator, 19
Crank pullers, 15, 185
Cranks, 7
Cranksets, exploded, 184
Crown-race removers, 260

Damper nuts, tightening, 315
Damping, adjusting, 310, 311

Derailleur cables:
attaching, 88
broken, 49
routing, 89
Derailleur-hanger alignment tools, 19
Derailleur hangers, 324
checking alignment of, 327
Derailleurs, 6, 80
adjusting, 70, 75
damaged, bypassing, 46
exploded, 68
large-caged, 96
pivots, 98
proper cage alignment/ clearance for, 78, 79
SRAM, adjusting, 75
XTR bottom-bracket-mount, 77
Dishing tools, 16, 279
Down tubes, 7, 324
Drills, 19
Driveside fixed cup, 195
Drive-train parts, extra, 17
Dropout alignment tools, 18, 293, 329
Dropouts, 288, 324
aligning, 292
measuring spacing for, 292
measuring width of, 328, 329
misaligned, 290, 293
right rear, 69
Dropout savers, inserting, 331
Duct tape, 21
Dustcaps, removing, 119, 131

Elastomer bumpers, 209, 217

Feeler gauges, 19
Ferrules, 81
Files, round/flat, 15
Fork boots, 288, 312
Fork braces, 312
Fork crown race punches, 17
Fork-crown races
removing, 261, 262
setting, 264
Fork mounts, IS, 152
Forks, 234
aligning, 294, 295
clamping, 246
Manitou, 302, 310, 312, 317
messed-up, 290
rigid, 288
RockShox, 297, 307, 311, 319
setting in head tubes, 257
SID air-oil, 307
straight, 295
suspension, 7, 140, 288, 289, 297, 298, 299, 302, 307, 312, 319
triple-clamp, 298
Frames:
checking alignment of, 328
rear-suspension, 325
rigid, 324
Freehub Buddy, 17, 131
Freehubs:
with cartridge bearings/ cassette cogsets, 125
Shimano, 131
Freewheel removers, 17
Freewheels, 126

Gear cables:
changing, 85, 86
housing for, 81
Grease, 12, 15, 21.
See also Lubricants; Oil
Grease guns, 15
Grips, 234
assembly, exploded, 234
bar ends and, 236
removing, 235
trimming, 236
Grip Shift shifters, 87, 91, 141

Hacksaws, 15
Hammers:
ball-peen, 14, 16, 260, 262
soft, 16, 245, 260, 311
Handlebars, 234
Hayes brakes:
bleeding fluid from, 160
caliper guts, 162
changing pads on, 161
Headset cup removers, 17, 260
Headset cups:
pressing in, 265
removing, 260
threadless, 239
Headset locknuts, loosening/ tightening, 253, 254, 258
Headset/pedal tools, compact, 21
Headset presses, 17, 265
Headsets, 7, 140, 234
Cane Creek-style press-internal, 250
cartridge-bearing, 252
cupless internal, 250
cupless integrated, 249
cutaway view of, 248
loosening/tightening, 240, 252

threaded, 239, 247
threadless, 237, 240, 247, 252
Head tube reaming and facing tools, 19
Head tubes, 7, 324
setting fork in, 257
upper crown height/ orientation for, 298
Hex keys, 17, 75, 76
High gear, 71
Hollow-crank chainring cassette tools, Shimano, 15
Hoses, 17
hydraulic brake, 178
Housings, 17, 81, 82
Hubs, 7
bolting rotors onto, 150
with cartridge bearings, 117
lacing spokes in, 270–76
with standard ball bearings, 117, 126

Inner legs:
freeing, 311
greasing, 313
RockShox, 315
Inner tubes, 12, 20, 21.
See also Tires
checking for punctures in, 107
removing, 107
seating, 111
International-Standard fork mounts, mounting brakes onto, 152

Jockey cages, 76
Jockey wheels, 6, 97
cleaning, 32
J-tools, 17, 131

Knives, 15

Level 1 repairs, tool kits for, 12–13
Level 2 repairs, tool kits for, 14–15
Level 3 repairs, tool kits for, 16–17
Locknuts:
loosening/tightening, 119, 122
removing, 216
Shimano, 215
Lockrings, removing, 127
Low gear, 71
Lubricants.
See also Grease; Oil
chain, 12, 21

Magnets, 348
aligning, 349
Magura hydraulic brakes, 174
adjusting, 175
bleeding/filling lines of, 176
Manitou fork post mounts, mounting brakes onto, 154
Manitou forks:
damping adjuster knob on, 310
exploded, 312
removing spring stack from, 302
TPC top piston, getting in/out, 317
Master links, 60, 61
Matches, 21
Mountain bikes:
basic, 6–7
dimensions of, 367
exploded, 6–7
fully suspended, 5
height of, 364
hybrid, 9
rigid, 4

Needle bearings, 252
Nipples, 268
Noodles, releasing, 24

Oil:
See also Grease; Lubricants
hydraulic, 17
Oil baths, making, 314
Onza H.O. clip-in pedals, 209
exploded, 217
removing locknuts from, 216
O-rings, 315

Parts washers, 16
Patches, applying, 108
Patch kits, 12, 20
Pedals:
adjusting tension on, 209
Aliup, 218
ATAC, 218
clip-in, 7, 204, 209, 211, 214, 217, 218, 219
dropping bearings in, 216
Look, 214
loose-bearing, 216
lubing, 219
Onza, 209, 217
removing axle from, 211
removing/installing, 205
Scott, 211, 214
Shimano, 211, 214
Speedplay Frog, 214
Time, 214
toeclip and strap, 204
Pivots, upper/lower, 98
P-knuckles, 70, 75
Pliers, 21
channel-lock, 14
needle-nose, 13
snapping, 17
Power Link, 60
P-springs, 76
Pumps, 20
with gauges, 13
RockShox fork, 13, 21
shock, 12, 21
Punctures, checking for, 107

Quick-release skewers, 175
opening, 25
tightening, 27
Quill stems, 238

Rapidfire Shifters, 82, 91, 143, 347
Release mechanism, lubing, 219
Release tension, adjusting, 173, 209
Rims, 7
adjusting brake pads to, 145, 160
bent, 44
lacing spokes in, 270–76
RockShox forks:
adjusting damping on, 311
changing travel on, 319
exploded, 297
inflating, 307
Rotors, bolting on, 150
Rubber donuts, 90
Rubbing alcohol, 13
Rulers, 295

Saddles, 6
adjusting, 223
Brooks, 222
installing, 226, 226
modern lightweight, 222
perineum-protecting, 223
positioning, 369
on Softride beams, 229
Scott pedals, removing axles from, 211
Screwdrivers, 20
Screws:
bleeder, 160
B-, 69
derailleur, 45, 48
limit, 70, 80
set, 173
stopper, 76
Sealant, for tubeless tires, 111

Sealed bearings, Chris King–style
pressed-in, 255
Seat bags, 20
Seatpost binders, 6, 227, 324
Seatposts, 6
installing, 227
single-bolt, 225
single-post, 226
suspension, 228
two-bolt, 225, 226
Seat stays, 6, 324
Seat tubes, 6, 324
Shifters, 72, 234
Grip Shift, 87, 91, 141
installing, 141
Rapidfire, 82, 91, 143, 347
replacing cable in, 83, 85
SRAM Half Pipe, 86, 93, 94
thumb, 82, 91, 96, 141
XTR, 85
Shimano Flight Deck, 346, 347
Shocks:
adjusting, 335
air sleeve service, 337
cartridge bearings, 335
parts of, 325, 335, 337
Shoes, cleat setups on, 206
Shop aprons, 15
Skewers:
bolt-on, 26
opening, 25
quick release, 25, 27, 175
tightening, 27
Softride beams, 229
Solvent-bath chain cleaners, 33, 55
Spanners:
lockring, 15, 35, 196
pin, 15, 16, 35, 196
Spare tubes. *See* Inner tubes
Splined pedal spindle removal tools, 14
Splines, 128
Spoke-hole offset, 272
Spokes, 7, 268.
See also Truing
broken, wrapping, 42
converging parallel, 277
diverging parallel, 273
Kevlar, 21
lacing, 270–76
loose, 42
relieving tension in, 280
spare, 21
tightening/loosening, 278
weaving in, 116
Spoking:
disc-brake wheel, 283, 285
front wheel, 283
radial, 282, 283
rear wheel, 283, 285
three-cross, 283
Spring reload, adjusting, 303
Spring stacks, removing, 302
Spring tension, 96
SRAM Half Pipe shifters:
changing cables on, 86
disassembled, 94
releasing retaining washer on, 93
springs on, 94
Star-nut installation tools, 17
Steering assembly, 234
Steering tubes, 288, 297
fork alignment and, 294
measuring/cutting, 264
and stem clamps, 240
Stem clamps, 140
spreading, 244
and steering tubes, 240
Stems, 7, 234, 239
clamp-type, 236
cutaway view of, 248
positioning, 369
quill-type, 238
suspension, 239
threadless, 239
Stem wedges, loosening, 245
Straddle cables, types of, 171
Straddle hangers, offset, 172
Straps, 204
Subpins, snapping ends off, 60
Super Link, 60
Syringes, 16

Taillight/flasher, 20
Taps, 16
Tensioning nuts, 173
Third Eye Chain Watcher, 102
Thumb shifters, 82, 91, 96, 141
Time ATAC Alium clip-in pedals,
exploded, 218
Tire casings, temporary fix for, 39
Tire levers, 12, 20, 106
Tires, 7.
See also Inner tubes; Wheels
extra, 17
installing, 110
removing, 106
UST tubeless, 107, 111
Toeclips, 204
Tool kits:
Level 1, 12–13
Level 2, 14–15
Level 3, 16–17
take-along, 20, 21
Top tubes, 7, 324
TORX T25, 17, 20
Truing.
See also Spokes
lateral, 115, 278
radial, 278
Truing stands, 16. *See also* Bike stands
Tubes. *See* Inner tubes

U-brakes, 30, 178–79, 324
Upper crowns, short/tall, 298

Valve holes, fork alignment and, 295
Valves:
Presta, 12, 105
Schrader, 12, 105
types of, 12
V-brakes:
adjusting, 143
pad holder assembly, 146
releasing, 24
replacing pads on, 148
Shimano parallel-push, 145
simple, 145
Vises, 15, 17
clamping forks in, 246
removing fork-crown races with, 262

Wheels.
See also Tires
complete, 268
dish, checking, 280
measuring circumference of, 347
rear, 30, 104
removing/installing, 30
Wrenches:
adjustable, 13
Allen, 13, 20, 35, 205, 209, 311
combination, 20
headset, 15, 35
metric open end/box end, 13, 20, 35
pedal, 12, 216
socket, 15, 35
splined spoke, 17
spoke, 13, 20, 21
torque, 17, 35
TORX, 17, 20

Zip-ties, 299

INDEX

Adjusting, test riding and, 36, 321
Adjustment knobs, 303–4, 306, 308, 309, 311
AheadSet, 246
Air chucks, 19
Air compressors, 19, 111, 142, 163, 199. *See also* Compressed air
Air pressure, 103, 110, 111
- adjusting, 307–9
- in shocks, 336, 341

Alcohol. *See* Rubbing alcohol
Alignment:
- disc-brake rotors, 18
- frame, 328–30

All Travel spacers, 318–20
Answer Products, 337
Anti-chain suck devices, 63
Anti-seize compounds, 18, 287
Arm length, measuring, 366
Art of Wheelbuilding, The (Schraner), 267
Automatic transmission fluid, 314, 316
Avid, 377–78
- brake pads, 148–49
- brake levers, 143, 157
- brakes, 145, 147, 148, 150–55, 159, 164, 167, 168

Axle nuts, 118, 279
- detaching wheels with, 24, 26
- tightening, 23, 28

Axle overlock dimension, 101
Axles, 118, 119, 195, 204, 212, 218. *See also* Spindles
- large splined, 192
- through-axles, 28–29, 118

Backcountry riding, preparing for, 37
Balance, front-rear, 339, 340
Ball bearings, 117, 192. *See also* Cartridge bearings
- angular contact, 249, 255
- cleaning, 120, 199, 210, 213, 216, 255, 256, 258, 259
- loose, 195–96, 210, 212–13, 249
- replacing, 120–22

Ball-pumping adapters, 302, 307, 309
Band clamps, 77–78
Banjo fitting, 156, 163
Bar ends:
- grips and, 236
- handlebars and, 235
- installing, 91–92, 233–35
- positioning, 233, 244, 371
- removing, 92, 235, 236, 238
- slippage, 266
- tightening torques, 382–83

Barnett, John, 267
Barnett's Manual (Barnett), 263, 267
Barrel adjusters, 68, 74, 81, 83
- increasing/reducing tension with, 72–73, 137–38, 139, 141

Bearing races, 117, 121, 194, 195, 216
Bearing rings, 196, 256, 258, 259
Bearings. *See* Ball bearings
Bebop pedals, 388
Berra, Yogi, 287
Bicycle Wheel, The (Brandt), 267
Bike stands, 14, 16, 31, 233, 258, 287, 323, 328
- for derailleur work, 69
- for truing. *See also* Truing stands

Blades. *See* Fork legs
Bleeding brakes, 159–69, 176–77
Blowguns, 19, 142
Bluto, 53
Bolts:
- anchor, 88, 141, 147
- binder, 245
- bottom, 309, 310
- chainring, 183, 187–88, 200
- clamp, 224–27, 233, 291
- crank, 183, 184, 185
- derailleur, 65, 99
- fork-crown, 246, 289, 291, 296, 300, 304
- mounting, 65, 142, 172
- rotor, 150–52
- self-extracting, 184, 186
- sizes, 36, 300, 375–76
- stem. *See* Stem clamps
- stock, 99
- titanium, 375
- tightness, 237, 300, 373–86

Book of Mormon, quote from, 11
Bottom brackets, 183, 190–99
- adjusting, 193, 200–201
- bearing spacing widths, 190
- cartridge-bearing, 192, 193–94, 197–98, 199
- cup-and-cone, 192, 194–97, 199
- FSA, 197
- installing, 192–98
- loose-ball, 194
- Mavic/Stronglight, 192, 201
- overhauling, 198–99
- quality of, 102
- Race Face, 192, 193, 197

Bottom brackets, continued
Shimano, 184, 192, 193–94, 197, 198, 200
splined pipe-spindle, 192
thread retapping, 330–31, 332
tightening torques, 376–77
troubleshooting, 199–201
Bottom bracket shells, 19, 190, 192–94, 197
retapping, 330, 331–32
thread damage, 330
twisted, 201
Bottom bracket tap sets, 19, 323
Bottom bracket tools, 15–16
Brake arms, 23, 24, 168, 169
Brake boosters, 175, 181
Brake bosses, 136, 323
broken, 148, 326, 330, 291–92
flexing by, 181
Magura brake calipers on, 174–75
replacing, 331
retapping, 331
roller-cam brakes on, 179
thread damage on, 330
U-, 179
Brake cables, 136–41
broken, 49
disconnecting, 296, 310
installing/replacing, 138–41
length, 180
straddle, 139, 170–72, 179
tension, 137–38, 141
wear on, 137, 181
Brake fluid, 155, 159, 161
Brake-hose cutters, 19
Brake levers, 23, 135, 142, 233, 365
Avid, 143, 157
checking, 141
dual-lever, 142
installing, 142, 174
integrated, 92
leverage adjustments, 142–44, 157–58
lubricating, 141
Magura, 174
overhauling, 164
Rapidfire, 83, 84–85, 91, 92, 143, 144
reach adjustments, 142–44, 157–58
Shimano, 83–84, 85, 91, 99, 137, 143, 144
SRAM, 83, 143, 144
trigger, 83
V-brake, 143
Brake pads, 43
Avid, 148–49
adjusting, 138, 145–47, 168–70
checking, 23
cleaning, 180
disc, 162–63
installing, 167–68
Magura, 157, 174, 176
offset, 146
replacing, 148–49, 159, 167–68, 176, 156, 181
roller-cam, 180
spacing, 157–58
toeing-in, 147, 169–70, 181
V-brakes, 144–45, 148–49
wear on, 137, 180–81
Brakes, 135–81
Amp, 153, 155
Avid, 145, 147, 148, 150–55, 159, 164, 167, 168
cantilever. *See* Cantilever brakes
centered, 181
center-pull, 135, 136
checking, 24, 29
closing, 29
Coda, 157, 378
Dia-Compe, 25, 145–46, 147, 168, 170
disc. *See* Disc brakes
Formula, 150, 155, 159
Grimeca, 150, 163
Hayes, 149–50, 155, 156, 159, 160–62
hydraulic. *See* Hydraulic brakes
IS, 152–54
linkage, 136, 178
Magura. *See* Magura brakes
Onza, 167, 168
Paul, 170
Pro Stop, 153
releasing, 24–25, 136
rim, 135–36, 181, 267, 377
Ritchey, 170
RockShox, 153, 155
roller-cam, 25, 136, 179–80, 323
Shimano. *See* Shimano brakes
sidepull cantilever, 25, 29, 135. *See also* V-brakes
SRAM, 152, 155, 163
for tandems, 135
testing, 180
tightening torques, 153, 377–79
troubleshooting, 180–81
types of, 135–36
U-. *See* U-brakes
V-. *See* V-brakes
Brake hoses, cutting, 177–78
Brandt, Jobst, 267
Braze-ons, 292, 330, 331
Breakdowns, fixing, 4, 5
Breeze beam suspension, 338
Bump forces, 340, 341
Bungee cords, 22
Bushings, 238, 313
cleaning, 210, 333
eyelet, 333, 334, 336, 338
greasing, 333
pedal, 210, 211, 218
pivots and, 332–34
replacing, 333–34
Butt fatigue, 223, 224
Buzzy's Slick Honey, 313, 333, 337
Byrds, The, 203

Cable clamps, 89, 139, 141
Cable crimp caps, 81, 89, 141
Cable cutters, 14, 67, 82, 135, 139
Cable ends, 81, 89
Cable hangers, 140, 249, 263
Cable housings. *See* Housings
Cables. *See also* Brake cables; Shift cables
die-drawn, 90, 138
friction, 90, 137
Gore-Tex, 81, 89–90, 138–39, 147
lubricating, 90, 138
maintaining, 138
Cable stops, 82, 90, 138, 139, 140, 176
broken, 326
Cages, 40, 96, 99, 195
Calipers, 144–49
disc brake, 149–59
floating, 153
Magura, 174–75
measuring, 19, 100, 287, 329
overhauling, 163–64
Campagnolo, 170, 212, 293
Cane Creek, 246
Cannondale:
HeadShok design, 289
Jekyll frames, 341
Lefty forks, 24, 26, 103, 107, 289, 305
Cantilever brakes, 29, 135, 166–73. *See also* V-brakes
installing, 141, 166–67
lubricating, 173
releasing, 25, 136
spring tension adjustment, 147, 172–73
tightening torque, 377

Cartridge bearings, 192, 197–98, 264–65
angular-contact, 249, 255–59
cleaning, 255–56, 258
greasing, 195, 256, 259, 333
headsets, 249, 254
overhauling, 123–24
pedal, 212–13, 217–18
pivots and, 332–34
press-in, 255, 258, 264–65
Cassette hubs. *See* Freehubs
Cassette lockring removers, 103
Cassettes, 125
changing, 126–29
tightening torques, 380
Chain-cleaning tools, 54–55
Chain elongation gauges, 18, 53, 56, 64, 65
Chain gap, 74–75
Chain guides, 194, 379
Chain hangers, 31
Chain lines, 100, 192
measuring, 100–102
Chain links. *See also* Master links
spare, 21, 40
stiff, 63
Chain pull, 284
Chainring-cassette removal tools, 15
Chainring-nut tools, 15, 188
Chainrings, 61, 68, 100–101, 183, 187–90
alignment, 192
chain jams and, 40
chainstay drag, 201
changing size of, 189
checking, 187, 200
front derailleurs and, 189, 201
replacing, 63, 188–90
warped, 188
Chain rollers, 65, 96
Chains, 53–65
broken, 40–41, 55
checking, 24, 56–57
cleaning, 31, 33–34, 54–56
connecting, 59–60
derailleurs and, 40, 64
disassembling, 55
elongation, 53, 56–57, 64
installing, 58–59
KMC, 55, 57
jammed, 40
length of, 58, 64
lubricating, 1, 33, 53–54, 63, 64, 70
maximizing life of, 53–54
removing, 55–56, 57–58
Sachs, 20, 21, 55, 57
Shimano, 20, 21, 55, 57–58, 59, 60
skipping, 63–65, 99
squeaking, 63
SRAM, 20, 21, 55, 57, 60–61
Taya, 55, 57, 61–62
tension, 67
troubleshooting, 62–65
wear, measuring, 56–57
wheel removal and, 29–30
Wippermann, 21, 55, 57, 61, 64, 65
worn-out, 56, 64
Chainstays, 193, 201, 327
chain jams and, 40, 62
elevated, 323
motion, 332
Chain suck, 100, 187
fixing, 62–63, 323
Chain tools, 12, 53, 57
carrying, 21, 40, 48
Chain whips, 16, 126–27
Cheater bars, 201
Chris King:
crown race tools, 233, 264
headset presses, 233, 265
headsets, 255, 258, 264
Circlips, 98, 118, 163, 189, 291, 309
Circumferences, measuring, 346–47, 350
Cleaning, 4, 31–34
Cleats, 8, 203–4
installing/adjusting, 205–8
lateral/rotational-adjustment range of, 207
lubricating, 209
maladjusted, 219, 388
pedal compatibility, 204, 207, 387–89
problems with, 208
Wellgo, 387
Clip-in pedals, 8, 203–4
bearings for, 210–11
release tension adjustments, 208–9
setting up, 205–8
Clips, 208, 209, 219
CO_2 cartridges, 20, 40, 230, 245, 246
Coda:
brakes, 157, 378
pedals, 210, 211, 213, 215, 389
Cog lockring tools, 16
Cogs, 67–68
bolt-together, 128
cleaning, 32, 33, 126–27
compatibility among, 74, 128–29
11-tooth, 128
replacing, 64, 126–28
Shimano, 128
titanium, 270
worn, 64
Cogsets, 74, 128, 192
Cog-wear indicators, 19, 53, 127
Coil bind, 340
Coil springs, 287, 296, 303–7, 308
Cold setting, 292
Compatibility, front-rear, 340
Compressed air, 235, 289, 305, 307, 320. *See also* Air compressors
Compression rings, 252, 255, 257
Computers, 345–50
batteries, 349–50
magnets for, 346, 348–49, 350
setup/installation, 346–49
troubleshooting, 349–50
Cones, 117
ConneX Link, 61, 64, 65
Crankarms, 183–90, 198, 203, 224, 340
bent, 188
length, 368
play in, 200–201
Crank Brothers pedals, 207, 208, 210, 212, 217
Crank pullers, 14, 183–85
Cranks/cranksets, 184
FSA, 183, 185, 186
installing, 185–86, 194
Race Face, 183, 185, 186
removing, 183–85
Shimano, 183–86, 192
spider arms, 188
TA, 183
tightening torques for, 376–77
troubleshooting, 199–201
Truvativ, 183, 185, 186
Crested Butte off-road "cruisers," 324
Crown race. *See* Fork-crown races
Cups:
adjustable, 197–98, 253, 329
bearing, 117, 190, 192–98, 200, 253
drive-side, 190, 193, 194
fixed, 183, 195
headset, 238, 248, 253, 255, 256, 258–61, 264
removing, 198
threaded, 253, 254
tightening, 194, 196–97, 376–77

Dampers, 313, 315
detent ball for, 313
hydraulic, 240
open-bath, 315
Damping, 287, 289, 301, 305
adjusting, 306–7, 309, 311, 339, 341
cartridges, 314, 315–17

Damping, continued
compression, 305, 306, 308–9, 321, 322, 339, 340, 343
decreasing, 321, 322, 338
environmental sensitivities, 342
excessive, 321
fine-tuning, 305–7
hydraulic, 269, 305, 339
increasing, 321, 322, 342–43
rebound, 305–6, 321, 322, 339, 342, 343
shocks, 338, 339
Deda Elementi Dog Fang, 102
Delta patches, 108
Dents, 291, 330, 332
Derailleur hanger alignment tools, 19, 65, 323, 327
Derailleur hangers, 67
bent, 65, 99, 327, 328
checking/straightening, 327
retapping, 331
thread damage on, 330
Derailleur mounts, 65, 100, 330
Derailleurs, 30
adjusting, 64–65, 67, 69–77, 79–81
attaching cable to, 88–89
bottom-bracket mounted, 77, 78–79, 193–94, 197
cables, broken, 47–49
chainrings and, 189
chains and, 40, 64
cleaning, 32–33
damaged, 45–47, 65
differential plate, 80
ESP, 74, 99
front, 77–81, 101–2
installing, 69, 78
maintaining, 96–100
Mavic, 99
misadjusted, 64
overhauling, 87–99
rear, 67–77, 99–100
Sachs, 73, 79, 82
Shimano. *See* Shimano derailleurs
SRAM, 73, 74–75, 82, 96, 99
SunTour, 73, 79
tightening torques, 380
troubleshooting, 99–102
Dia-Compe:
brakes, 25, 145–46, 147, 168, 170
headsets, 246, 255, 258, 264
torque recommendations, 252
Disc brakes, 135–36, 149–66
adjusting, 149–58, 181
bleeding, 159–62
cable-actuated, 140, 155
calipers, 149, 152–55
hydraulic. *See* Hydraulic brakes
installing, 149–58
mechanical, 153, 164–65
mounts, 149–50, 152–53, 287, 326
overhauling, 163–64
pad replacement, 162–63
releasing, 24–25, 136
rotor alignment, 18, 165–66
tightening torque, 377–79
wheels for, 267, 269, 270, 284–85
Discs, cleaning, 180
Dishing, 279–81, 294
Dishing tools, 18, 103, 267, 279, 280
Downhill adjustments, 96, 339, 342–43
Drills/drill bits, 19, 323
Drivetrains, 56, 183, 270
cleaning, 32–33
downhill-specific, 96
Dropout alignment tools, 19, 287, 292–93, 295, 296, 323, 329
Dropout hangers, alignment of, 65
Dropouts, 26, 30, 67, 287
aligning, 292–94, 295–96, 328–30
bent, 290, 296, 328
bolt-on, 326, 327, 329
broken, 326
inspecting, 326
spacing of, 292–93, 328–29
Dropout Saver, 331
Drumstix rotor alignment tool, 18, 166
DT-Hügi freehubs, 130, 132–33
DT Pro Lock Nipples, 269
DT spoke washers, 269
Duct tape, 22
Dust boot, 147, 296
Dust caps, 123, 131, 132
cranks, 184, 186
pedals, 210, 215–18
Dust cap tools, 184

Easy out, 336
Einstein, Albert, 23
Elastomers, 228, 240, 287, 289, 313
greasing, 228, 232
pedal bumpers, 210
replacing, 304
shocks, 338, 339
suspension forks, 296, 301, 303–7, 315
Electronic lockout (E.L.O.), 305
Emergencies and emergency gear, 22, 37
Englund TotalAir, 305, 320
Enjoyment of ride, 4, 5, 23
Extension tubes, 201
Exus pedals, 211, 213, 389
Eyelets, 333, 334, 336, 338
spoke, 271

Feeler gauges, 19
Ferrules, 81–82, 83, 139
Fields, W. C., 37
Files, 14, 187, 233, 242
Finish Line products, 34, 35, 73, 87, 375
Fitting/sizing your bike, 363–71
Fixed-cup tools, 183, 195
Flat tires, 37–38. *See also* Inner tubes
fixing, 38–40, 103–14
pinch, 39, 110, 111, 113
Fluids, 18
Ford, Henry, 67
Fork boots, 299, 302–3
Fork brace, 311
Fork-crown race punches, 17, 263–65
Fork-crown race remover, 18–19, 261, 262
Fork-crown races, 233, 261–62, 263
Fork-crowns, 296, 302
inner leg installation, 299–300, 313
removing fork legs from, 296, 298–99
Fork ends. *See* Dropouts
Fork legs, 287, 290
removing, 296, 298–99
telescoping, 289
Fork rake, 287, 295
Forks, 287–322.
See also Steering tubes
alignment, 291, 292–96
Cannondale Lefty, 24, 26, 103, 107, 289, 305
damage to, 244, 291–92
failure of, 49, 300
headset installing and, 262–63
inspecting, 289–91
linkage, 289, 291, 296
misaligned, 290, 291
noisy, 266
overhauling, 291–92
play in, 251
purposes of, 287
rigid. *See* Rigid forks
single-leg, 24, 26, 103, 107, 205
suspension. *See* Suspension forks
threaded, 240, 243, 245–46, 290–91
threadless, 240–41, 245, 248
upgrading, 320–21
Fork tips. *See* Dropouts

Fork travel:
- changing, 317–20
- measuring, 299, 300–302

Formula, 150, 155, 378
Fox forks, 301, 305, 310
Frame builders, 292, 326, 330, 331
Frame mounts, 229–30
Frame painters, 332
Frames, 323–43.
    See also Suspension frames
- damage, 230, 288, 330
- design, 323–25
- diamond, 323
- disc-brake, 150–51
- double-diamond, 323, 324
- grades, 325
- headset installing and, 262–63
- inspecting, 326–27
- materials, 323, 325–26
- rigid, 10
- size, 363–68
- step-through, 367

Frame Saver, 228, 326
Freehub Buddy, 17, 130–32
Freehubs, 125
- DT-Hügi, 130, 132–33
- frozen, 50
- lubricating, 18, 129–33
- Mavic, 130, 132
- Shimano, 130–32

Freehub Soup, 130, 131
Freewheel removers, 17
Freewheels, 103, 125–26
- changing, 129
- frozen, 50
- lubricating, 133

Gauges:
- chain-elongation, 18, 56, 64, 65
- cog-wear indicator, 19
- feeler, 19
- spoke-tension, 19

Gear charts, 8, 359–61
Gear development, 359–61
Gears, checking, 24
Geax tires, 113
Girvin:
- pedals, 209, 210, 215
- suspension system, 240

Glide rings, 320, 336, 337
Gravity Research Pipe Dreams brakes, 168
Grease, 18, 22, 121, 203, 221, 233, 269.
    See also Lubricants; Oil
- cables, 90, 138
- Freehub Soup, 130, 131
- Jonnisnot, 87, 93
- lithium-based, 138
- Microlube, 130, 310, 314
- molybdenum sulfide, 138
- nonlithium, 16, 94, 287, 313
- silicone-based, 16, 94
- Slick Honey, 313, 333, 337
- tube/jar, 12

Grease guns, fine-tipped, 16, 217, 310, 333
Grease injection systems, 125, 130
Grimeca brakes/pads, 150, 155, 163
Grips, 142
- bar ends and, 233, 236
- installing, 91, 235–36
- removing, 91, 235

Grip Shift, 16, 90, 99
- grips for, 236
- maintaining, 93–95
- replacing, 92
- replacing cable in, 85–88

Grub, 90, 139, 147
Guide pipes. *See* Noodles

Hacksaws, 14, 231, 233, 242, 263
Half Pipe shifters,85, 86, 93–95
Hammers, 261
- ball-peen, 16
- slide, 233
- soft, 18, 123, 229, 287

Handlebars, 144, 233, 240
- bar ends and, 234
- broken, 49–50, 238, 244
- carbon-fiber, 142, 237
- checking, 24
- composite, 235
- height, 233, 241, 244, 370
- installing, 236–37
- maintaining, 238
- noisy, 265–66
- positioning, 224, 237, 244, 368, 370–71
- reach/drop, 365, 370–71
- removing, 236
- replacing, 238, 244
- troubleshooting, 265–66
- twist, 240, 244

Hayes:
- brakes, 149–50, 155, 156, 159, 160–62
- lever fittings, 156, 157
- post mounts, 149–50, 153
- torque recommendations, 378

Head angles, 287, 341
Headlights, 22
Headset cup removers, 17, 233, 260–61
Headset presses, 17, 264–65
Headsets, 233, 240, 246–65
- adjusting, 240–41, 249–55, 257, 260
- cartridge-bearing, 248, 249, 255–58
- with cups, 238, 248, 253, 255, 256, 258–61, 264
- installing, 263–65
- integrated, 248–49, 260, 264
- internal, 248, 256, 262
- loose-bearing, 255, 256–57, 259
- needle-bearing, 249, 255, 257, 258, 259
- overhauling, 255–60, 290
- pitted, 251, 252, 254, 256, 259, 266
- removing, 260–62
- stack height, 263
- threaded, 246, 249, 253–55, 257–60
- threadless, 246–49, 252–53, 255–57, 263
- troubleshooting, 24, 251, 266

Head tube reaming and facing tools, 19, 263
Head tubes, 248, 253, 255, 256, 259, 260, 323
- headset installation and, 263, 264
- length of, 263

Heart monitors, 349
Hex keys, 12, 18, 35, 36, 50.
    See also Wrenches
Holmes, Oliver Wendell, Jr., 233
Hoses, disc-brake, 155–57, 176, 177–78
Housings, 81, 138–41, 330
- cutting, 82–83

How to Keep Your Volkswagen Alive, 323
Hub flanges, 282, 283
Hubs, 270, 328–29. *See also* Freehubs
- with adapters, 152
- adjusting, 122, 277, 294
- assembling, 120–22
- cartridge-bearing, 117–18, 123–24
- cassette, 120
- cleaning, 120
- cup-and-cone, 117
- direct-pull, 282
- disassembling, 118–19
- disc brake, 150–52
- front, 270, 273, 275, 294

Hubs, continued
grease guard, 125, 130
lubricating, 120–21
Mavic, 18, 123, 124, 152
overhauling, 118–22, 123–24
radial spoking and, 271, 282
Sanshin, 124
sealed-bearing, 117
Shimano, 118, 129, 282
Specialized, 124
SRAM, 152
SunTour, 124, 125
tightening torques, 380
Hub shells, 117, 275
Hutchinson, 106, 110
Hydraulic brakes, 136, 174–78
bleeding/filling, 159–62
cutters, 19
Hope, 157
Magura. *See* Magura brakes
overhauling, 163–64
pads for, 162–63
releasing, 25–26, 136
rim brakes, 174–78
Hydraulic cylinders, 174, 174, 305
Hydraulics, 18, 338

Injuries, dealing with, 50–52
Inner tubes, 12, 38, 113.
See also Flat tires
anti-pinch-flat, 110
carrying, 20, 22, 38
finding leaks in, 107–8
installing, 109–110
latex/urethane, 107
patching, 108–9
repairing/replacing, 103–114
sealant-filled, 113–14
with tubeless tires, 108
Inseam, 366
Inspection, preride, 23–24
International Mountain Bike Association (IMBA) rules, 51
International Standard (IS):
brakes, 152–54
mounts, 149, 152–53

Jockey wheels, 30, 67
cartridge-bearing, 97
damaged/lost, 46, 47
loose, 64–65
maintaining, 32, 96–97
Jonnisnot, 87, 93
Judy. *See* RockShox forks
Jump Stop, 102

Kahn, Alice, 345
Knee/joint pain, 219–20
Knee-to-handlebar clearance, 365
Knives, 14, 135, 203, 233
Knuckle springs, 47, 67, 68

Lawyer tabs, 29
Leather-softening compounds, 222
Leg alignment, 219–20, 224
Lennon, John, 103
Level 1 tasks, 5
tool kits for, 11, 12–14
Level 2 tasks, 5
tool kits for, 11, 14–16
Level 3 tasks, 5
tool kits for, 11, 16–18
Lever pull, 157–58
Lickton Cycle Super Link, 55, 57, 60–61
Link rivets/pins, 34, 57–60
Linseed oil, 103, 267
Locknuts, 249, 253, 254
loosening, 118
tightening, 121–22
Lockouts, 301, 305, 306, 339, 340, 342
Lockrings, 127, 196–97
bottom brackets, 197–98, 201
Loctite, 34, 65, 73, 124, 287, 291, 311
Look pedals, 207, 208, 210, 211–14, 217, 389
Lubricants, 18, 32, 36, 130.
See also Grease; Oil
chain, 12, 22, 32, 53–54, 55, 138, 203, 231
Teflon-fortified, 303
wet-condition, 54

Magnets (computer), 346, 348–49, 350
Magura brakes, 150, 153, 377
bleeding, 159, 176–77
calipers, installing/adjusting, 174–75
hoses for, 155, 177–78
lever mounting, 174
pads, 157, 174, 176
releasing, 136
tightening torque, 379
Maintenance, 1, 4–5, 10
classification of, 11
complicated, 5
Manitou, 291, 310, 384
Manitou forks, 149, 153, 299, 301, 304–6, 308, 311–17, 385
changing oil in damper, 315–17
greasing, 310
overhauling, 310–11, 313
retrofitting, 320–21
through-axles, 28–29
Marin County Repack-style bikes, 324
Marx, Groucho, 267
Marzocchi forks, 29, 305–7, 310, 341, 385–86
Master cylinders, 157, 159, 174
overhauling, 164
Master links, 21, 34, 55, 57
connecting/disconnecting, 60–62, 65
Masterson, Portia, 279
Mavic:
cartridges, 198, 331
derailleurs, 99
freehubs, 130, 132
hubs, 18, 123, 124, 152
rims, 106, 110–13, 268, 271
tools, 130, 198
tubeless tires, 106
MCUs. *See* Elastomers
Measurements:
body, 366–68
center-to-top, 364
Mechanical work, 5, 10, 34–36
Mechanics, 1, 4
Michelin, 106
Micro-cellular urethane (MCU).
See Elastomers
Microlube, 130, 310, 314
Mineral oil, 132, 159, 161
Mixte frames, 367
Morningstar Tooling, 130
Drumstix, 166
Freehub Buddy, 17, 130–32
J-tool, 18, 131
ROC-Tech alignment tool, 18, 135, 165–66
Muir, John, 323
Multi-tools, 20

Nashbar pedals, 211, 217
Needle bearings, 192, 198, 210, 211, 213
headsets, 249, 255, 257, 258, 259
Negative springs, 301, 302, 320
adjusting, 308–9, 322
air, 307–8
coil, 308
Nipples, 268, 269, 270, 271, 276, 277, 281
Nokon housings, 138
Noises, 356–57
Noodles, 24, 139–40, 144, 146
threading cable through, 147

Norco pedals, 211, 217
Nylon brushes, cleaning with, 31, 33

Oil, 18, 203, 314, 326. *See also* Grease; Lubricants
damper, 305, 315–17
hydraulic, 289, 306, 316
linseed, 103, 267
lightweight, 132
mineral, 132, 159, 161
outboard-motor, 18, 131
penetrating, 230, 245, 246
replacing, 322, 338, 342
shocks, 338, 339
thread-cutting, 323, 330
viscosity of, 305, 306–7, 309, 322, 339, 341
Oil baths, 309, 311, 314
Olive fittings, 155–57, 177
Onza pedals, 208–9, 210, 387, 389
bearings for, 211
overhauling, 217–18
O-rings, 131, 132, 147, 157, 316, 339
Otis Guy, 338
Outer wires. *See* Housings

Paint, 160, 161, 162, 332
touch-ups, 326–27, 330, 332
Parallel-push linkages, 144, 145, 147, 148
Park Tool, 265
cable-housing cutters, 82
dropout alignment tools, 293
fork-crown race remover, 18–19, 261
threadless saw guide, 242
Parts specifications, 4
Parts washing tanks, 16
Patches, 38–40, 107, 108–9
Patch kits, 12, 108–9
taking along, 21, 38–40
Pedal overlap, 365
Pedal platform systems, 305, 340–41, 342
Pedal-release mechanism problems, 219
Pedals, 203–20
cage-type, 203
cartridge bearing, 210, 213, 217–18
cleat compatibility, 204, 387–89
clip-in. *See* Clip-in pedals
Coda, 210, 211, 213, 215, 389
Crank Brothers, 207, 208, 210, 212, 217
Exus, 211, 213, 389
float, 207, 209, 220, 388
Girvin, 209, 210, 215
installing, 205
knee/joint pain with, 205, 219–20, 388
Look, 207, 208, 210, 211–14, 217, 389
loose-bearing, 210, 213, 215–17
Nashbar, 211, 217
Norco, 211, 217

Onza. *See* Onza pedals
outboard closed, 211–15
overhauling, 210–18
play in, 201
removing, 204–5
Ritchey, 209, 210, 211–15, 217, 218
Scott, 209, 210, 211, 215, 389
Shimano, 210, 211, 212, 213, 387
Speedplay, 208, 210, 211–15, 387
tightening torques, 381
Time. *See* Time pedals
Tioga, 211, 212, 213, 389
toeclip and strap, 203
Topo, 209, 210, 215
troubleshooting, 219–20
VP, 210, 211, 215, 217, 389
Wellgo, 209, 210, 211, 215, 217, 387
Pedal springs, 209
Pedal tools, splined, 16, 203, 211, 212
Pin tools, 124, 183, 218
Pirsig, Robert M., 1, 135
Pivots, 289, 332–34
derailleur, 65, 97–98, 100
Pliers, 22
channel-lock, 16
needle-nose, 12, 287, 299, 303
regular, 12
snapring, 18, 203, 211, 212, 287, 310
Post mounts, 149–50, 153, 224
Power Link, 57, 60–61
Power meters, 349
Preload. *See* Spring preload
P-springs, adjusting, 75–77
Pulley wheels. *See* Jockey wheels
Pumps, 12, 307
air, 20, 111, 287, 302, 307–9
floor, 111
shock, 14, 22, 307, 339

Quick releases, 118, 122, 328, 369
brakes, 174–75
checking, 23
closing, 26–27
detaching wheels with, 25–26
seatpost, 227
tightening, 26–27, 380
Quills, 243, 260, 290

Race Face cranks, 183, 185, 186
Races:
bearing, 117, 121, 194, 195, 216
fork-crown, 233, 261–62, 263
Radial spoking, 267, 268, 271, 281–83
Rags, 13
Rapidfire:
brake levers, 83, 84–85, 91, 92, 143, 144
shifters, 95, 348
Rear suspension. *See* Suspension
RedRum, 314
Release tension, adjusting, 204, 208–10
Rema patches, 108, 109
Repairs, 10, 11
Ride height, 300–301, 339–40
Rigid forks, 10, 251, 263, 287
alignment of steel, 291, 292, 295–96
maintaining, 292
Rims, 103, 2, 267–69.
See also Spokes; Wheels
bent, 44–45, 114
Bontrager, 129, 269
brake pads and, 24, 145–47
cleaning, 180
deep-section, 104
disc-brake, 277
drilling, 283
Hed, 104
OCR, 129, 269, 271
off-center, 269, 271, 284
Ritchey, 129, 269, 284
Spinergy, 104, 105
truing, 114–16
UST, 106, 110–13, 268, 271
Zipp, 104
Rim strips, 38, 112
Rim tape, 109
Ritchey, 338
brakes, 170
cassette cogs, 128–29
drivetrain, 270
headsets, 249, 259
pedals, 209, 210, 211–15, 217, 218
rims, 129, 269, 284
RockShox, 310
brakes, 153, 155
cartridge removal tools, 316, 319
damping system, changing oil in, 315–17
Judy Butter, 313
oil (RedRum), 314
torque recommendations, 314, 379, 384, 386

RockShox forks, 300, 301–9, 311
adjusting travel on, 317–20
retrofitting, 320–21
through-axles, 28, 29
Rogers, Will, 221
Rohloff, 53, 56, 64, 127
Rolling resistance, 110, 111
Roll-out procedure, 359
Roof racks, 29
Rotors, 150–52. *See also* Disc brakes
aligning/truing, 18, 153, 165–66
cleaning, 181
floating, 153
RST, 386
Rubbing alcohol, 13, 159, 162, 233
for grip installation/removal, 142, 235

Sachs:
chains, 20, 21, 55, 57
derailleurs, 73, 79, 82
Power Link and, 57, 60–61
shifters, 85–86
Saddles, 191–227
Brooks, 222
comfort, 221–22, 224
height, 220, 222, 223, 228, 368–69
Ideale, 222
installing, 224–27
maintaining, 222, 231
positioning, 222–24, 224–27, 368–70
setback, 369–70
troubleshooting, 231–32
Safety, 23, 50–52, 289
Safety glasses, 14, 287
Sag, 300–301, 304, 308, 338, 339–40, 343
Schraner, Gerd, 267
Scott pedals, 209, 210, 211, 215, 389
Screwdrivers, 45, 103, 183, 188
carrying, 21
flat, 135, 345
long, 287
Phillips, 12, 135, 345
standard, 12
Screws:
b-, 68, 69, 74–75
dishing gauge, 279
limit, 67, 68, 70–72, 80
reach-adjustment, 142
set, 75–76, 98, 118, 225–26
tension-adjustment, 208–9
tensioning, 68
tightening torques for, 237, 376
Sealants, 37, 38, 111, 113–14. *See also* Slime
Stan's No Tubes system, 112–13
Seat binders, 230, 232, 330
retapping, 331
tightening torques, 381
Seatposts, 221
American Classic, 224
broken, 49
clamps, 49, 77, 224
inspecting, 326
installing, 227–28, 229–30
maintaining, 224, 229, 232, 326
parallelogram-linkage, 228
shock-absorbing, 228–30
single-bolt, 224–25
stuck, 230–31
suspension, 221, 224, 228–30
telescoping, 228
tightening torques, 381
troubleshooting, 231–32
two-bolt, 224, 227
Seats. *See* Saddles
Seat tubes, 232, 328, 323, 366–67
inspecting, 326
Shell facers, 19
Shift cables, 64, 81–90, 99
attaching to derailleurs, 88–89
buying, 81–82
friction reduction, 90
housings, 81–83
lubricating, 90, 99
replacing, 81, 83–88
tension, 67, 72–74, 80–81
Shifters, 91–93, 349. *See also* Grip Shift
adjusting, 71–77
compatibility with other parts, 99
dual-lever, 142
friction, 81, 91, 95
indexed, 24, 72–74, 81, 95
maintaining, 93–96
nonindexed rear, 74
replacing, 91–93
thumb, 83, 91, 92–93, 95, 142
tightening torques, 380
troubleshooting, 99–102
twist, 92, 142, 236
Shifting, 90
trouble with, 69–74, 81, 99–102
Shimano:
bottom brackets, 184, 192, 193–94, 197, 198, 200
brake levers, 83–84, 85, 91, 99, 137, 143, 144
cable-housing cutters, 82
chain line, 101
chains, 20, 21, 55, 57–58, 59, 60
cogs, 128
computers, 348, 349
cranks, 183–86, 192
crown race tools, 233, 264
freehubs, 130–32
hubs, 118, 129, 282
pedals, 210, 211, 212, 213, 387
shifters, 73, 83–85, 144
splined bottom-bracket tools, 183
splined cap tool, 186
splined cassette lockring tool, 152
splined pedal tool, 203
Shimano brakes, 147, 150, 152, 153, 159, 170
cantilevers, 171–72
pads, 158, 163
parallel-push, 144, 148
torque recommendations, 379
V-brakes, 144, 145, 147, 148
Shimano derailleurs, 75, 77, 90, 98, 99
E-type (front), 77, 78–79, 193–94
Low Normal, 48–49, 67–68, 70, 72, 73
Rapid Rise, 48, 49, 67, 70, 72, 73
Saint, 69
XTR, 79
Shimano Pedaling Dynamics (SPD), 204, 387
Shock pumps, 14, 22, 307, 339
Shocks, 384
air, 335–37, 338, 339
coil-over, 338, 339, 340
elastomer-over, 338, 339
maintaining, 327, 334–38
mounts, 341
oil, 338, 339
testing, 341–42
Shoes, 203–4, 205–8, 381. *See also* Cleats
Shops, stocking and organization, 14, 20
Shortie shifters, 93–95
Sidewalls, patching, 38–39, 113, 114
Skewers, 304
bolt-on, 25–26, 27
hub, 327
quick-release, 25–27, 122
Skill, 1, 4, 10
Slave cylinders, 159, 163–64, 174. *See also* Calipers
Slime, 37, 108, 111, 113–14. *See also* Sealants

Softride suspension system, 221, 229–30, 240, 338
Solvents, 16, 333
  citrus-based, 33, 55, 56, 97, 124, 281, 287
  cleaning with, 31, 33–34, 120
  petroleum-based, 55
Spanners:
  lockring, 35–36, 183, 196, 198
  pin, 18, 36, 183, 195
Spare tubes. *See* Inner tubes
SPD. *See* Shimano Pedaling Dynamics
Speedplay Frogs pedals, 208, 210, 211–15, 387
Spindles. *See also* Axles
  axles, 195, 204, 218–19
  bottom bracket, 192, 193, 195, 197, 201
  foot alignment and, 207
  titanium, 218–19
Spinner, 305
Spin Skins, 38
Splined bottom-bracket tools, 183, 193
Splined cassette lockring tools, 127, 152
Splined cup tools, 192, 194
Spokes, 103, 268. *See also* Wheels
  aero-shaped, 282
  broken, 42–43, 116
  converging parallel, 276
  crossing, 275, 275–76
  double-butted, 283
  double-threaded, 282
  loose, 41–42
  nail-head, 282
  outer, 283, 284
  prestressing, 280–81
  pulling, 270, 281, 282
  readjusting, 281
  rear drive-side, 269–70
  replacing, 42–44, 269
  size, 116, 269
  spare, 21–22, 42
  tension and tensioning, 114, 115, 269, 277, 279, 281, 284
  thickness, 268, 269, 283
  truing, 44, 114–16, 281
  wider-angle, 284
Spoke-tension gauge, 19
Spoke washers, 269
Spoking, 267
  nonradial, 282
  radial, 267, 268, 271, 281–83
  three-cross pattern, 267, 268, 269–77, 284–85
Spring plates, 209
Spring preload, 228, 301, 321, 322, 339, 340
  adjusting, 303–4, 309
Spring rates, 301, 321, 338–39, 341
  decreasing, 321, 339, 342–43
  increasing, 321, 322, 339, 340, 342
  linear/progressive, 308
Springs, 287, 340.
  See also Suspension forks
  adjusting, 147–48, 172–73, 179
  air, 287, 289, 296, 338
  butterfly, 158, 163
  coil, 287, 296, 303–7, 308
  coil-over, 338
  knuckle, 47, 67, 68
  negative, 301, 302, 308–9, 320, 322
  p-, 75–77
  pedal, 209
  replacing, 303, 304, 339
  return (vertical), 145, 147
SRAM:
  brake levers, 83, 143, 144
  brakes, 152, 155, 163
  chains, 20, 21, 55, 57, 60–61
  derailleurs, 73, 74–75, 82, 96, 99
  Power Link, 57, 60–61
  shifters, 85–88, 90, 93–95
Standover height, 323, 363–65
Stan's No Tubes systems, 112
Star nut installation tools, 17, 233, 242, 252
Star nuts, 242–43, 248, 257
  installing, 252, 252–53
Steering axis, 287
Steering tubes, 252, 253, 255–58, 260
  fork alignment and, 294, 295
  length, 241–42, 248, 254–55, 257, 263
  stems and, 238–43, 244, 245, 266
  thickness, 242–43, 248
  threaded, 238–240, 249, 290, 291
  threadless, 238–43, 290
Stem clamps, 240, 241, 242, 245, 248, 253, 255
Stems, 233, 238–46
  front-opening, 236
  height adjustments, 240–43
  length, 368
  maintaining, 24, 243–44
  quill-type, 240, 243
  removing, 240, 243, 244–46, 266
  setting position, 244
  steering tubes and, 238–43
  suspension (shock-absorbing), 238, 240
  tightening torques, 382–83
  troubleshooting, 266
Straddle cables, 139, 170–72, 179
Stronglight, 198, 249, 259, 331
SunTour:
  derailleurs, 73, 79
  hubs, 124, 125
Super Link, 55, 57, 60–61
Suspension, 238, 240, 287, 320–21
  balance (front/rear), 339, 340
  evaluating condition of, 332
  full, 100, 324, 339
  rear, 50, 323, 338–42
  tires and, 103
  tuning, 341–42
Suspension forks, 251, 261, 287, 296–322
  adjusting, 321–22
  air, 302, 307–9
  air-oil, 301
  coil-spring, 301, 303–7, 308
  dents, 291
  double-crown, 241, 253, 255, 257, 299, 300
  elastomer, 296, 301, 303–7, 315
  flat, 49
  high-end, 309–10
  hydraulic, 305
  Lefty (Cannondale), 24, 26, 103, 107, 289, 305
  linkage, 289, 291, 296
  lubricating, 16, 313–14
  maintaining, 292, 296, 302–3
  Manitou. *See* Manitou forks
  manuals, 310
  Marzocchi, 29, 305–7, 310, 341, 385–86
  overhauling, 309–14, 321–22
  RockShox. *See* RockShox forks
  single-crown, 296, 299
  spring rate. *See* Spring rates
  telescoping, 289, 291, 296, 299, 302–3, 309
  tightening torques, 384–86
  too hard/too soft, 322
  triple-clamp, 296, 299, 300
  upside-down, 28, 289
Suspension frames:
  aligning, 328–30
  beam, 338
  design, 324–25
  inspecting, 326–27
  maintaining, 332–34, 338
Swingarm. *See* Chainstays
Syringes, 18, 176–77, 235, 317

Taillights, 21
Talcum powder, 12, 109, 231
Taps, 18, 323, 330–31
Taya chains, 55, 57, 61–62
Telander, Todd, 5
Tension:
  arms, 96
  cable, 72–74, 137–38
  release, 204, 209–10
  spokes, 269, 281
  spring, 147–48, 172–73, 179
  wheel, 267, 277, 279
Third Eye Chain Watcher, 102
Threaded parts, prepping, 34–35
Threadless saw guide, 242
Threadlock fluids/compounds, 18, 287
Thread-prepping compounds, 34–35
Threads, 34–35, 190, 194
  anti-seize, 35
  fixing, 73, 327, 330–32
  locked, 34–35, 269, 291
  pedals, 204, 205, 211–12
  retapping, 330–32
Three-cross spoking, 267, 268, 275
  lacing, 269–77, 282–83, 284–85
3T, 238, 244
Thumb shifters, 83, 91, 92–93, 95, 142
Time pedals:
  adjusting, 209
  bearings, 211
  cleats for, 207
  overhauling, 211–15, 217–18
  problems with, 219
  removing, 205
Tioga pedals, 211, 212, 213, 389
Tire bead, 105–6, 110
Tire casings, temporary fixes for, 38–39, 113
Tire levers, 12, 105–6, 110
  take-along, 21
Tire liners, 38
Tire pumps, 12, 20
Tires, 24, 103. *See also* Flat tires; Inner tubes
  diameter, 359
  direction of, 109, 111, 112
  installing, 109–10, 112–13
  leaks, finding, 107–8
  pressure, 24, 111, 112
  removing, 105–6
  repairing, 103–14
  replacing, 1, 109
  sizes/shapes of, 10
  standard installed as tubeless, 112–13
Tires, tubeless, 38, 103
  installing, 110–111
  patching, 107–9
  removing, 106–7
  sealants in, 38, 113
Titanium, 35
Toeing-in, 147, 169–70, 181
Tools and tool kits:
  Level 1, 11, 12–14
  Level 2, 11, 14–16
  Level 3, 11, 16–18
  saddlebag, 5
  take-along, 11, 20–22, 37
Toothbrushes, 33, 124
Top caps, 255, 257, 289, 301, 303, 304, 314
Topo pedals, 209, 210, 215
Top tubes, 363
  length, 367–68
Torque recommendations, 36, 151, 197, 314, 373–86
Transmission, 67–102. *See also* Derailleurs; Shifters
Triangles (frame), 323, 324, 327
  front, 328
  rear, 329
Troubleshooting, 8, 351–57
Truing, 114–16, 277–79, 284, 285
  lateral, 277–78
  radial, 278–79
  side-to-side, 277–78
Truing stands, 18, 115, 267, 277, 280. *See also* Bike stands
Truvativ, 183, 185, 186
Tube cutters, 19, 242, 242
Tubing, 323, 325–26, 330, 392
Twist shifters, 92, 142, 236

U-brakes, 25, 29, 136, 178–79, 323
  adjusting, 178–79
  chainstay-mounted, 323
  installing, 178
  replacing/positioning pads, 179
Unified-rear-triangle bikes, 46
UST, 106, 110–13, 268, 271
U-Turn knobs, 303, 318

Valve holes, 269, 271, 273
  fork alignment and, 294
Valves:
  extenders for, 104–5
  inertial, 305, 307, 322, 340–41, 342
  Presta, 12, 20, 103–5, 106–7, 109, 114, 308
  Schrader, 12, 14, 103, 106–7, 113, 301, 307, 308
  UST, 106
Vari-Travel system, 318
Vent holes, 32
V-brakes, 25, 26, 135, 144–49
  adjusting/installing, 135, 139–40, 145–48
  calipers, 144–45
  centering/spring tension adjustment, 147–48
  closing, 29
  leverage maximization, 144
  levers, 143, 145
  pad adjustment, 145–47
  pad replacement, 148–49
  parallel-push, 144, 145, 147, 148
  releasing, 24, 136
  Shimano, 144, 145, 147, 148
  tightening torque, 377
Vises, 16, 203, 233, 246, 261, 262, 287
VP pedals, 210, 211, 215, 217, 389

Water-bottle bosses, 47, 330, 331
WD-40, 326
Welds, inspecting, 326
Wellgo pedals, 209, 210, 211, 215, 217, 387
Wheels, 103. *See also* Rims; Spokes
  bent, 41, 44–45
  for big/heavy/tall riders, 267, 283–84
  building, 267–85
  checking, 23–24
  circumference, 346
  for disc brakes, 267, 269, 270, 284–85
  dishing, 116, 279–81, 294
  installing, 26, 28–29, 30–31
  lacing. *See* Spoking
  lateral/vertical stiffness in, 282, 283
  locking up, 180
  machine-built, 267, 281
  parts for, 267–69
  radial, 268, 281–83
  removing, 24–26, 29–30
  tensioning, 267, 277, 279
  truing, 115–16, 277–79, 281, 290
Wheelsmith Spoke-Prep, 35
Wilderness Trail Bikes, 125
Willerton, Paul, 51
Wippermann chains, 21, 55, 57, 61, 64, 65
Wrench Force cable-housing cutters, 82
Wrenches, 35–36
  adjustable, 12, 103, 135, 203
  Allen, 12, 21, 35, 43, 45–46, 64, 204–5
  box-end, 35

cone, 16, 103, 118, 203, 217, 267, 323
crank bolt, 183
headset, 16, 233, 253
open-end, 12, 21, 35, 135, 203
pedal, 12, 22, 203, 204
socket, 14, 35, 183, 203
splined, 18, 35
spoke, 12, 18, 21, 42, 43–44, 115, 268
torque, 18, 186, 233, 287, 291, 373, 374–75
TORX, 18, 21, 35, 135, 188

Yokes, 179

Zen and the Art of Motorcycle Maintenance (Pirsig), 1, 135

ABOUT THE AUTHOR

Lennard Zinn is a bike racer, frame builder, and technical writer. He grew up cycling, skiing, running rivers, and tinkering with mechanical devices in Los Alamos, New Mexico. After receiving a physics degree from Colorado College, he became a member of the U.S. Olympic Development (road) Cycling Team. He went on to work in Tom Ritchey's frame-building shop and has been producing custom road and mountain frames at Zinn Cycles since 1982.

Zinn has been writing for *VeloNews* since 1989 and is currently the senior technical writer for *VeloNews* and *Inside Triathlon* magazines. Other books by Zinn are: *Zinn's Cycling Primer* (VeloPress, 2004), *Zinn & the Art of Road Bike Maintenance* (VeloPress, 2000), *Mountain Bike Performance Handbook* (MBI, 1998), and *Mountain Bike Owner's Manual* (VeloPress, 1998).

ABOUT THE ILLUSTRATOR

A former mechanic and bike racer, Todd Telander devotes most of his time now to artistic endeavors. In addition to drawing mountain bike parts, he paints and draws wildlife for publishers, museums, design companies, and individuals. Birds are his favorite subject, so he has included a little house sparrow.